Give Your CPA Exam Score a Boost
with these Essential Study Tools

Cram Course

Boost your score by 8-10 points!

- Get a final review with this condensed CPA Exam Review supplement – the perfect complement to your full review course

- Reinforce your understanding of the most heavily tested topics on the CPA Exam

- Take the Cram Course leading up to Exam Day to refresh your mind on important topics

Audio Lectures

Maximize every minute leading up to the exam!

- Easy MP3 download – ideal for Apple or Android devices

- Turn any moment into a study opportunity! Listen to lectures on your commute, at the gym, or even as you nod off to sleep

- Immerse yourself in the most important CPA Exam topics

CPA Exam Flashcards

Make studying portable, accessible, and fun!

- Harness overarching CPA Exam concepts

- Create important connections to actual CPA Exam usage and application

- Make studying more exciting by involving family & friends – pull out your flashcards for a quick & interactive study method.

Share Your CPA Story

Would you like to inspire other CPA Candidates to reach their goals like you are? If so, we invite you to create a video to share your story—your successes, your painpoints, and lessons learned.

Email your video to CustomerExperience@rogercpareview.com, and you could be featured on our social channels.

As always, connect with us @RogerCPAreview

ROGER
CPA Review

AUD

Auditing and Attestation

Written By:

Roger Philipp, CPA, CGMA

Roger CPA Review
2261 Market St. #333
San Francisco, California 94114
www.RogerCPAreview.com
(877) 764-4272
(415) 346-4272

Permissions_____

The following items are utilized in this volume, and are copyright property of the American Institute of Certified Public Accountants, Inc. (AICPA), all rights reserved:

- Uniform CPA Examination and Questions and Unofficial Answers, Copyright © 1991, 1992, 1993, 1994, 1995, 1996, 1997, 1998, 1999, 2000, 2001, 2002, 2003, 2004, 2005, 2006, 2007, 2008, 2009, 2010, 2011, 2012, 2013, 2014, 2015, 2016 and 2017
- Audit and Accounting Guides, Auditing Procedure Studies, Risk Alerts, Statements of Position, and code of Professional Conduct
- Statements on Auditing Standards, Statements on Standards for Consulting Services, Statements on Responsibilities in Personal Financial Planning Practice, Statements on Standards for Accounting and Review Services, Statements on Quality Control Standards, Statements on Standards for Attestation Engagements, and Statements on Responsibilities in Tax Practice
- Accounting Research Bulletins, APB Opinions, Audit and Accounting Guides, Auditing Procedure Studies, Risk Alerts, Statements of Position, and Code of Professional Conduct
- Uniform CPA Examination Blueprints
- Independent Standard Board (ISB) Standards

Portions of various FASB and GASB documents, copyright property of the Financial Accounting Foundation, 401 Merritt 7, PO Box 5116, Norwalk, CT 06856-5116, are utilized with permission. Complete copies of these documents are available from the Financial Accounting Foundation. These selections include the following:

Financial Accounting Standards Board (FASB)
- *The FASB Accounting Standards Codification* ™ and Statements of Financial Accounting Concepts
- FASB Statements, Interpretations, Technical Bulletins, and Statements of Financial Accounting Concepts

Governmental Accounting Standards Board (GASB)
- GASB Codification of Governmental Accounting and Financial Reporting Standards, GASB Statements, GASB Concepts Statements, and GASB Interpretations
- GASB Statements, Interpretations, and Technical Bulletins

The following items are utilized in this volume, and are copyright property of the International Financial Reporting Standards (IFRS) Foundation and the International Accounting Standards Board (IASB), all rights reserved:
- IASB International Reporting Standards (IFRS), International Accounting Standards (IAS) and Interpretations

Acknowledgement_____

This book includes contributions by members of the Roger CPA Review Editorial Team.

ABOUT THE AUTHOR

Roger S. Philipp, CPA, CGMA
CEO, Founder, and Instructor, Roger CPA Review

Roger Philipp, CPA, CGMA is one of the most celebrated motivators and instructors in the accounting profession. Known as the dynamic and engaging instructor that makes learning accounting concepts enjoyable, Roger has been helping aspiring accountants across the globe reach career success for almost 30 years.

Roger launched the company in 2001 with the goal to create a CPA review course that would alter the landscape of accounting education. His unique approach to teaching has fueled the company's growth and resulted in the signature teaching methodology, The Roger Method™. Using this approach, Roger breaks down and simplifies complex topics, with support from ingenious memory aids and mnemonic devices to help students retain information. Faculty across the country have been inspired to adopt aspects of The Roger Method™ in their classrooms, which has helped increase students' knowledge of and interest in the CPA designation.

Roger's career began in public accounting working for Deloitte & Touche before transitioning to educational instruction. He was a lead instructor at Mark Dauberman CPA Review before branching off to launch Roger CPA Review. Since then, he's remained committed to guiding and motivating generations of accountants throughout their careers, starting as early as their undergraduate years. In 2014, Roger was featured as one of Accounting Today's Top 100 Most Influential People in Public Accounting.

Roger received a B.A. in accounting from California State University-Northridge. Today, he is a member of the AICPA, CalCPA, and is on the Board of Directors for the American Professional Accounting Certification Providers Association (APACPA). He resides in San Francisco with his wife and co-founder of the company, Louisa, and their three children. He enjoys traveling with his family and the challenges that come with being an entrepreneur.

ABOUT THE EDITOR

Mark E. Dauberman, CPA, EMBA
Senior Editor, Roger CPA Review

Mark Dauberman, CPA, EMBA is known as an expert in helping students take technical knowledge from an academic understanding to a practical understanding. This skillset has proven invaluable to his role at Roger CPA Review in which he ensures educational materials are current and effective with a high level of academic excellence.

Mark has over 50 years of experience in the accounting profession, with a particularly strong background in accounting education, having taught at numerous universities including UCLA, Loyola Marymount University, and California State University-Northridge. In 1975 he launched Mark Dauberman CPA Review, which at one point held the position of the largest CPA Exam preparation course in Southern California.

Throughout his career, Mark has spent several years in both public and private accounting, including serving as a partner and director of the audit practice at NSBN. He has taught continuing professional education (CPE) courses for the AICPA and the CalCPA Education Foundation while also providing staff training for CPA firms and private industry employers. He has furthermore authored several publications, including CPE Course materials, and CCH's "Knowledge Based Preparation, Compilation, and Review Engagements."

Mark earned his Executive MBA in management from Claremont Graduate University. He currently lives in Upland, CA and enjoys an active life of ziplining, skydiving, traveling, and time with his children, grandchildren and great grandchildren.

AUD

Table of Contents

Introduction

Table of Contents

Section - Introduction

Corresponding Lectures

Watch the following course lectures with this section:

Lecture 0.01 – Course Introduction
Lecture 0.02 – AUD Introduction

Welcome to your Roger CPA Review Course!

Greetings Student,

As you begin your journey with Roger CPA Review, you will quickly learn why our students experience an 88% pass rate. Your motivating and engaging instructor, Roger Philipp, CPA, CGMA, focuses you on the information you need to know to pass the CPA Exam. Our course is structured for a variety of student types. Each topic is broken down from the beginning and taught as if the student has little to no prior knowledge of the particular topic at hand.   Whether you are a first-time review student who has never attempted an exam part, or a seasoned professional returning to the exam after an earlier attempt, you will be prepared. Using the proven *Roger Method*™, you will learn and retain the necessary information rather than simply memorizing terms. Furthermore, all of your course materials and online study tools are part of a fully integrated system to help you reach your goal with as little pain as possible.

Ultimately, you control your destiny. As Roger always says, "The CPA Exam is not an IQ test. It is a test of discipline. If you study, you will pass!" With 300-400 hours of minimum preparation time recommended by the AICPA, the ability to manage your studies is essential. For this reason, your course includes Study Planners and adaptive course diagnostic tools to help you keep your eye on the ball throughout the process. To get the most out of your course, please **read through this Introduction** to understand more about the exam, course content, and study strategies. This book serves as a guide to course lectures; everything covered in the lectures is covered in the book. Within you will find our recommended approach to using your course and its support features, including these following overarching key steps of the *Roger Method*™:

- **Plan** your studies
- **Learn** with your course lectures and textbooks
- **Practice** your skills and understanding
- **Review** for exam day

This course is designed to prepare you to PASS the CPA Exam. The lectures and materials are comprehensive and focus on the most frequently tested topics, saving you time and effort by streamlining your study process. You will learn the topics tested on the exam without wasting time delving into topics not historically emphasized on the exam. All exam question types are taken apart piece-by-piece and presented from scratch to demonstrate the logical progression. Task-Based Simulations (TBSs, including Document Review Simulations or DRSs) and multiple choice questions are also covered during the lecture and reinforced with the Interactive Practice Questions (IPQ) software provided within your course.

Best,

Roger CPA Review Team

FOLLOW ROGER CPA REVIEW ON TWITTER **FOR CPA EXAM TIPS AND TRICKS** AT **@ROGERCPAREVIEW** AND SUBSCRIBE TO OUR BLOG TO GET THE MOST UP-TO-DATE EXAM INFO AS WELL AS PLENTY OF ADVICE ON CAREERS, EDUCATION AND THE CPA EXAM AT **ROGERCPAREVIEW.COM/BLOG**.

USING THE COURSE
A step-by-step guide to successfully studying with your Roger CPA Review course

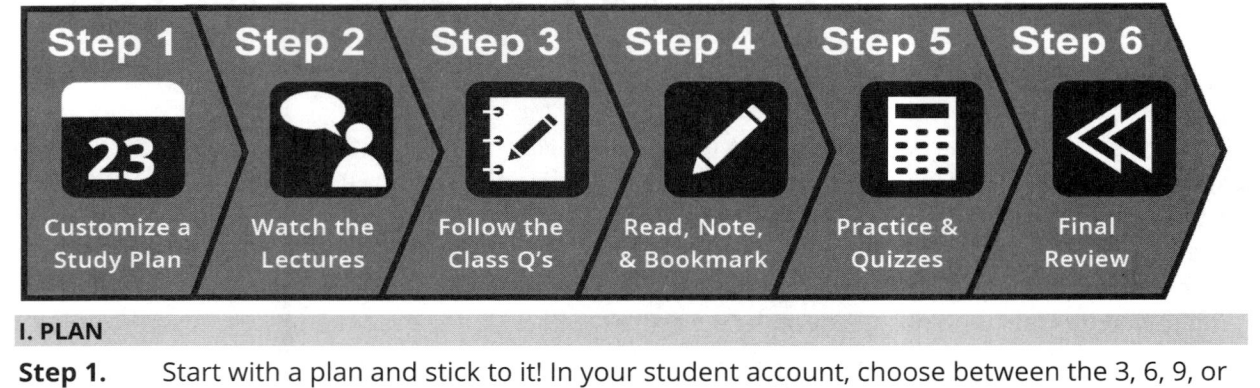

I. PLAN

Step 1.   Start with a plan and stick to it! In your student account, choose between the 3, 6, 9, or 12-month "Study Planner," whichever best suits your projected timeline for exam completion. Then, customize your planner to help build a personalized agenda that meets your individual study needs.

II. LEARN

Courses are broken into sections and topics. Work sequentially through the course and start with the first section. Cover all topics within the first section before moving on to the second section.

Step 2:   Watch one lecture at a time in full, without frequent stops, and simultaneously follow along in your course textbook.

Step 3:   As you proceed through all topics in a section, also watch the *Class Question* lectures and follow along with the Class Questions covered at the end of each section of your course textbook. Make sure to read the solution descriptions in order to understand why each answer option is correct or incorrect.

Step 4:   After watching the lectures for the section, go back to your course textbook and thoroughly read all corresponding pages, making notes as needed. Helpful Note-taking and Video Bookmark functions are available in your course online. You can also follow along, highlight, and take notes in the physical textbooks if you prefer.

III. PRACTICE

Step 5:   Use your Interactive Practice Questions (IPQ) software to reinforce and practice applying the concepts in each section of your course. As you complete every 2-3 sections in your textbooks and lectures, log into the IPQ to quiz yourself on what you've learned. Carefully work through each question, and read answer explanations to understand why you've answered each question correctly or incorrectly. Make sure to flag difficult questions for later review. Keep in mind that repeated exposure to the same questions will help you fully understand the concepts taught.

IV. REVIEW

Step 6:   Revisit any lectures and rework any questions that you have bookmarked or noted for final review. This is also a great time to take a Roger CPA Review Cram Course, which will focus you only on the most heavily tested topics.

Step 7:   To prepare for exam day, take full-length practice exams using the CPA Exam Simulator tool in your IPQ. This will help you hone your test taking strategy, time management and self-discipline under exam-like conditions, while continuing to expose you to the material.

Need help as you study? *Not sure why a question solution is either correct or incorrect, even after double checking in your course textbook and watching the lecture video? Visit the Homework Help Center in your student account for expert support.*

Application, Scheduling & Taking the Exam

** All information regarding AICPA, NASBA and Prometric rules and regulations in this introduction are up to date as of September 2017. Please see aicpa.org and nasba.org for the most current information.

To ensure that the Uniform CPA Examination keeps pace with the evolution of the accounting and business worlds, the examination is a computer-based test (CBT). The computerized exam:
- Enables testing of higher-level cognitive skills.
- Permits integration of real-world entry-level requirements.
- Provides flexibility and convenience to candidates.
- Offers greater consistency in evaluation.
- Helps save time in administration, grading, and reporting.
- Provides added exam security.

A tutorial that reviews the examination's format and navigation functions is available at aicpa.org. Choose the "Become a CPA" tab and then pick "CPA Exam" from the options in the list. From there, candidates can find the tutorial and sample tests. All exam candidates are encouraged to review this prior to sitting. The tutorial is intended to familiarize candidates with the functionality and types of questions and responses used in the examination format. The tutorial does not focus on examination content and is not intended as a replacement for study materials.

EXAM APPLICATION

State boards strongly urge candidates to apply online as the processing time is reduced. The applications for the CPA Exam are available online, and the link for the individual states can be found on our website at RogerCPAreview.com. Qualified candidates who have met all of the educational requirements may apply at any time. See individual state boards or NASBA.org for their specific application process. It is the candidate's responsibility to understand their jurisdiction's requirements to sit for the CPA exam and applicants are encouraged to familiarize themselves with licensure requirements prior to applying for the CPA exam.

Depending on the jurisdiction, candidates will apply directly through either their state board of accountancy or CPAES (CPA Examination Services, a division of NASBA). Some states have specific rules regarding coursework, applications and transcripts so candidates should contact their board if they are unsure on or unclear about any requirements. If candidates do not follow instructions and forget to submit required information with their application (fingerprint cards, photographs, etc.), the candidate will be rejected to sit in their state, forfeit application fee(s) and must re-apply.

Candidates in the following states must apply through **NASBA's CPA Examination Services** and may call **800-CPA-EXAM** for further information on application requirements and procedures:

Alaska, Colorado, Connecticut, Delaware, Florida, Georgia, Hawaii, Indiana, Iowa, Kansas, Louisiana, Maine, Massachusetts, Michigan, Minnesota, Missouri, Montana, Nebraska, New Hampshire, New Jersey, New Mexico, New York, Ohio, Pennsylvania, Puerto Rico, Rhode Island, South Carolina, Tennessee, Utah, Vermont, Washington, or Wisconsin.

Candidates in the following states must apply with their **Board of Accountancy**. See a full list of boards of accountancy and contact information at the end of this Introduction.

Alabama, Arizona, Arkansas, California, District of Columbia, Guam, Idaho, Illinois, Kentucky, Maryland, Mississippi, Nevada, North Carolina, North Dakota, Oklahoma, Oregon, South Dakota, Texas, U.S. Virgin Islands, Virginia, West Virginia, or Wyoming.

Application Steps

STATE BOARD OF ACCOUNTANCY

1. Meet requirements and submit educational documents to Board
2. Create client account and obtain password from Board
3. Complete application using client account (print Application Remittance Form)
4. Submit signed Application Remittance Form and fee
5. Receive Board approval and select exam section(s)

NASBA

6. Receive Payment Coupon from NASBA
   - If you do not receive the Payment Coupon within 10 business days after section selection, visit NASBA's Web site at *nasba.org* to pay online.
7. Pay NASBA Exam Section Fee(s)
   - NASBA's Online Credit Card Payment Form: Answer only the required fields when paying online. In accordance with the Board's Privacy Policy, NASBA does not collect or require exam applicants to fill in the Mother's Maiden Name field on NASBA's form. Please enter the word UNKNOWN in the Mother's Maiden Name field. This will allow you to continue processing your online payment. For additional payment information, telephone 1-866-696-2722.
8. Receive Notice to Schedule (NTS) from NASBA
   - If you do not receive the NTS within 10 business days after you pay the section fee(s), notify the Board or NASBA. Your NTS is valid in most states for 6 months, in others it can be good for 3, 6, 9, or 12 months.

PROMETRIC

9. Schedule with Prometric
10. Take CPA Exam at a Prometric Testing Center
    - You MUST bring your NTS with you to the testing center. You will be denied entry to the CPA Exam if you do not present the NTS.

BOARD

11. Receive Score Report from Board

Additional Information

For additional information on how to get answers to common questions, consult this table.

For questions about:	Contact:
• Eligibility to take the examination • Special testing accommodations • Completing application forms • Name and/or address changes • Examination scores • Your Board of Accountancy's fees	Write, call or send an e-mail to the appropriate Board of Accountancy. A complete list of Boards of Accountancy may be found at end of this Introduction.
• Receiving your Notice to Schedule (NTS) • Replacing a lost NTS • Payments to NASBA • General comments about the test center where you took your examination	Call NASBA at 1-800-CPA-EXAM (1-800-272-3926) or send an e-mail to cbtcpa@nasba.org
For questions about:	**Contact:**
• Scheduling, rescheduling or canceling your examination appointment • Directions to your test center	All information and instant scheduling is available at prometric.com/cpa Additionally, candidates may contact the Prometric Candidate Services Call Center at 1-800-580-9648
• Content of the examination • Specific multiple-choice questions and/or task-based simulations on the examination • Questions about rescore requests	Visit the AICPA's CPA Page: aicpa.org/BecomeACPA/CPAExam Or send an e-mail to cpaexam@aicpa.org

Test Centers

Test centers move, new ones are opened, and some close from time-to-time. The most current list of test centers may be found on the Prometric website at prometric.com/cpa.

Testing Windows

The Uniform CPA Examination is offered the first two months plus 10 days of each calendar quarter. These months of testing are known as the "testing windows." The examination is given in these testing windows to allow for systems and database maintenance. The exam is not available during the following times: March 11-March 31, June 11-June 30, September 11-September 31, and December 11-December 31. It is important to plan accordingly; it is the candidate's responsibility to schedule the remaining un-passed sections of the examination or the candidate may risk losing credit for previously passed sections. Candidates will be able to take any or all sections of the examination during any testing window and in any order but will not be allowed to take the same section more than once during any testing window. If a section is failed, the candidate must wait for the next available testing window and submit a re-application to receive a new NTS.

Testing is Available	Testing is NOT Available
January, February, March 1-10	March 11 to end of month
April, May, June 1-10	June 11 to end of month
July, August, September 1-10	September 11 to end of month
October, November, December 1-10	December 11 to end of month

EXAM SCHEDULING

Eligibility to Test

In order to make appointments at test centers, candidates must have a valid Notice to Schedule (NTS). Candidates receive an NTS after they apply to take an examination and are deemed eligible by their state boards of accountancy. An NTS is provided for every section a candidate has been approved to take. The NTS is valid only for a specified period of time and cannot be used once it expires. Therefore, **it is important that candidates schedule their test appointments as soon as they receive the NTS.** The NTS is good for **6 months** in most jurisdictions except the following:

- Texas   90 days from date of application
- California   9 months from date NTS is issued
- Hawaii   9 months from date NTS is issued
- Louisiana   9 months from date NTS is issued
- Utah   9 months from date NTS is issued
- North Dakota   12 months from date NTS is issued
- South Dakota   12 months from date NTS is issued
- Virginia   12 months from date NTS is issued

Testing Centers

Prometric will administer the exam at authorized CPA Exam testing sites throughout the United States, Guam, Puerto Rico, the Virgin Islands, and the District of Columbia, as well as at international sites in Japan, Bahrain, Kuwait, Lebanon, the United Arab Emirates, and Brazil. Other international locations are on the horizon. Special citizenship requirements and fees apply to testing internationally.

Candidates are not required to take the CPA Exam at a Prometric site located in the state where they applied and may schedule their exams at any authorized Prometric site regardless of location.

After submitting an application, receiving approval by the State Board of Accountancy (Board), and submitting the required fees to NASBA, the candidate will be authorized to contact Prometric to schedule a specific testing date and time. The test sites are normally open six days each week. Candidates are encouraged to check Prometric's Web site at _prometric.com_ to locate a testing site near them.

Schedule Early

Scheduling is available throughout the year, but candidates should schedule examination appointments as soon as possible after receiving their NTS. Being proactive about scheduling will help to secure the candidate's first choice of date and location of test centers. Tests are scheduled on a first come, first served basis. To ensure that candidates are able to take their examination section(s) on the first desired date and time, candidates should make their appointment(s) at least 65 days before the date they want to take the examination. **The earlier candidates schedule**

appointments, the better their chances are of obtaining the location, date, and time of their choice. Test appointments **cannot** be scheduled fewer than five days in advance of the desired test date. Walk-in testing is **not** allowed. The last two weeks of an exam window tend to fill up early, so candidates should plan ahead and schedule as early as possible.

Candidates may schedule examination sessions at _prometric.com/CPA_ or by calling Prometric's Call Center at 1-800-580-9648. Candidates must have their Notice to Schedule available when making test appointments. Examination section(s) must be taken within the time period for which an NTS is valid (3-12 months depending on jurisdiction) and may not be rescheduled after the NTS has expired. Boards of Accountancy, NASBA and Prometric are not responsible if a candidate cannot schedule an appointment before deadlines in your jurisdiction; it is imperative to plan ahead.

Candidates have three scheduling options:

1. Visit prometric.com/cpa on the Internet

Candidates will find that the easiest and quickest way to schedule an examination appointment (as well as reschedule and cancel an appointment if necessary) is on the Internet. Using the Internet provides 24-hour access to scheduling and avoids any "on hold" waiting time. Because of this, candidates have the quickest and most direct access to preferred dates and test center locations. Additionally, they will quickly receive a detailed confirmation of exam appointments (on screen and via e-mail). Before making any appointments, candidates must have received a valid NTS and should have this available before beginning the scheduling process. Additionally, candidates must be ready to identify the dates, times and locations where they want to take each section. It is not necessary to make all appointments at one time and candidates may schedule one exam at a time even if they have paid for more than one on any particular NTS. During the scheduling process, candidates will be required to provide various pieces of information from the NTS. Online scheduling is done by completing the following easy steps:

1. Go to prometric.com/cpa. Select SCHEDULE APPOINTMENT.
2. Select CPA Exam and Country/State.
3. Read all the information on the Information Review screen, and click NEXT.
4. After viewing welcome screen, click NEXT, read all of the policy information and click "I Agree" to proceed.
5. On the Program Identifier Screen, enter your examination section identification number from your NTS (you have one identification number for each section of the examination—be sure to use the correct examination identification number for the section you are scheduling). Click "Next."
6. Confirm proper section and click NEXT.
7. Follow on-screen instructions to select the date and location you would like to schedule your section.
8. Select COMPLETE REGISTRATION to finalize your scheduling. Print the confirmation number for your appointment and keep it for your records.

2. Call 1-800-580-9648 (Candidate Services Call Center)

Prometric's Candidate Services Call Center is open Monday through Friday from 8:00 a.m. to 8:00 p.m. Eastern time. (Hearing-impaired candidates using teletypewriter (TTY) may call 1-800-529-3590 to schedule appointments.) Candidates must schedule a separate appointment for each section of the examination that they are planning to take. If calling to schedule two or more sections, candidates should be prepared to identify the dates, times and locations they want to take each section. It is not necessary to make all appointments in one call and candidates may make one appointment at a time. Before calling, the candidate must have an NTS and should have access to it during the call as they will be required to provide the customer service representative with various pieces of information from the NTS.

Candidates will NOT receive written confirmation of their appointment so must write down the date, time, location, and confirmation number for each appointment. Candidates may also visit prometric.com/cpa to confirm their appointment(s). If the candidate is not familiar with the test center location they should ask the customer service representative for directions while they are making the appointment over the phone. There are multiple test centers in some metropolitan areas, so it is important for candidates to be certain of the correct test center location where they are scheduled to take their examination(s).

Those interested in a test run of the Prometric system may also use the telephone call center to schedule a 15-minute generic sample test at the facility prior to examination so they can familiarize themselves with the location and Prometric. There is a $30 fee for this *Test Drive* service.

3. Call the Local Test Center

Some candidates prefer to speak to a customer service representative at the local test center; if this is the case, candidates may call the center directly to make an exam appointment. Calls will only be accepted during business hours, which vary for each test center. Leaving a voicemail message at the local test center is NOT an acceptable method of scheduling. If calling to take two or more sections, candidates should be prepared to identify the dates and times they want to take each section. It is not necessary to make all appointments in one call and the candidate may schedule one appointment at a time. Before calling, the candidate must have an NTS and should have access to it during the call as they will be required to provide the customer service representative with various pieces of information from the NTS.

Candidates will NOT receive written confirmation of their appointment so must write down the date, time, location, and confirmation number for each appointment. Candidates may also visit prometric.com/cpa to confirm their appointment(s). If the candidate is not familiar with the test center location they should ask the customer service representative for directions while they are making the appointment over the phone. There are multiple test centers in some metropolitan areas, so it is important for candidates to be certain of the correct test center location where they are scheduled to take their examination(s).

TESTING INTERNATIONALLY

The international testing format follows the same state board licensure process and the current examination structure. The exam is still only offered in English and is available during the same four testing windows per calendar year as offered to US candidates. There are additional fees that applicants must pay if they wish to take the exam internationally.

Who is eligible?

U.S. citizens and permanent residents living abroad, and citizens and long-term residents of the countries in which the exam is being administered are eligible. In some cases, permanent residents or citizens of neighboring countries may test at international testing centers. The only form of identification that an applicant can use to test internationally is a passport.

Non-US Countries Offering CPA Exam Testing

Japan, Brazil, the United Arab Emirates, Lebanon, Kuwait, and Bahrain

Citizenship Status C = Citizen PR = legal permanent or long term resident	Eligibility to Test in These Countries						
	U.S.	Japan	Brazil	UAE	Lebanon	Kuwait	Bahrain
U.S. C/PR	X	X	X	X	X	X	X
Japan C/PR	X	X					
Antigua/Barbuda C/PR			X				
Argentina C/PR	X		X				
Bahamas C/PR			X				
Barbados C/PR			X				
Belize C/PR			X				
Bolivia C/PR	X		X				
Brazil C/PR	X		X				
Cayman Islands C/PR			X				
Chile C/PR	X		X				
Colombia C/PR	X		X				
Costa Rica C/PR			X				
Dominica C/PR			X				
Dominican Republic C/PR			X				
Ecuador C/PR	X		X				
El Salvador C/PR			X				
French Guiana C/PR	X		X				
Grenada C/PR			X				
Guatemala C/PR			X				
Guyana C/PR	X		X				
Haiti C/PR			X				
Honduras C/PR			X				
Jamaica C/PR			X				
Mexico C/PR			X				
Nicaragua C/PR			X				
Panama C/PR			X				
Paraguay C/PR	X		X				
Peru C/PR	X		X				
St. Kitts/Nevis C/PR			X				
St. Lucia C/PR			X				
St. Vincent/Grenadines C/PR			X				
Suriname C/PR	X		X				
Trinidad & Tobago C/PR			X				
Uruguay C/PR	X		X				
Venezuela C/PR	X		X				
Bahrain C/PR	X			X	X	X	X
Egypt C/PR	X			X	X	X	X
Jordan C/PR	X			X	X	X	X
Kuwait C/PR	X			X	X	X	X
Lebanon C/PR	X			X	X	X	X
Oman C/PR	X			X	X	X	X
Qatar C/PR	X			X	X	X	X
Saudi Arabia C/PR	X			X	X	X	X
UAE C/PR	X			X	X	X	X
Yemen C/PR	X			X	X	X	X
India C/PR	X			X	X	X	X
Any other country in the world C/PR	X						

STEPS FOR APPLYING INTERNATIONALLY*

1. Students must first meet eligibility requirements and apply to a US 'State Board' as long as that state board is one that allows international testing. For states that allow this, please see the list on the next page.
2. Applicant receives their Notice to Schedule.
3. Once approved, the student would then need to complete a separate international registration process on the NASBA website.
4. The applicant must make a commitment to seek CPA licensure upon passing the CPA Exam, and thereafter maintain their status as licensees.
5. Meet citizenship/residency requirements in the jurisdiction in which they are sitting for their exams.
6. Pay additional fees (see below).

*For more on how to apply to sit for the CPA Exam in your non-US country please visit nasba.org/international/international-exam/.

Additional Exam Fees for Testing Internationally

Subject	Additional Amount
Auditing and Attestation (AUD)	$ 356.55
Business Environment and Concepts (BEC)	$ 356.55
Financial Accounting and Reporting (FAR)	$ 356.55
Regulation (REG)	$ 356.55

Changes for the International Exam

Scores for international candidates will be released on the same timeline as domestic scores.

You cannot take your test internationally without a passport. This is most relevant for people living within a testing country or area – in which they must STILL have a passport to demonstrate citizenship and nationality.

Students who are not eligible to test within an approved country's jurisdiction, but are still international (non-US applicant), must report to the United States only and cannot go to a different country to test.

US State Boards that Accept International Applicant Test-takers			
Alaska	Indiana	Nevada	South Carolina
Arizona	Iowa	New Hampshire	South Dakota
Arkansas	Kansas	New Mexico	Tennessee
Colorado	Louisiana	New York	Texas
Connecticut	Maine	North Dakota	Utah
District of Columbia	Massachusetts	Ohio	Vermont
Florida	Michigan	Oklahoma	Virginia
Georgia	Minnesota	Oregon	Washington
Guam	Missouri	Pennsylvania	West Virginia
Hawaii	Montana	Puerto Rico	Wisconsin
Illinois	Nebraska	Rhode Island	Wyoming

TAKING THE EXAMINATION IN GUAM

Regardless of which Board of Accountancy has declared a candidate eligible for the examination, if the candidate intends to take their examination in Guam, they must pay an additional $140 surcharge for each examination section. Residents of Guam who are able to pay at the Guam Computer Testing Center, will incur a reduced surcharge fee of $70. All Guam test-takers must schedule their appointments by either of the following two options:

1. Visit nasba.org/exams/cpaexam/guam/ on the Internet

NASBA operates the Guam computer testing center in cooperation with the Guam Board of Accountancy and Prometric. Before visiting this Web site, candidates should have an NTS and credit card readily available. Once at the website, candidates will be asked to provide information from their NTS and will pay the surcharge using a credit card. After paying the additional surcharge for each examination section, the candidate will need to wait at least 24 hours before scheduling an appointment following the instructions described above.

2. Call the Guam Computer Testing Center: 855-CPA-GUAM or 671-300-7441

The Guam computer testing center is open Monday through Friday from 7:00 a.m. to 4:00 p.m. Guam time. Have your NTS and credit card in front of you when you call. Candidates will be asked to provide information from their NTS and will pay the surcharge using a credit card. After paying the additional surcharge for each examination section, the candidate will need to wait at least 24 hours before scheduling an appointment following the instructions described above.

For Pre-approved Special Testing Accommodations, Call 1-800-967-1139

International Locations Accommodations Phone Numbers:
Japan 0120-34-7737
Latin America 1-443-751-4990
Middle East 31-320-239-530

DO NOT CALL ANY OF THESE NUMBER UNLESS YOU HAVE BEEN PRE-APPROVED FOR SPECIAL TESTING ACCOMMODATIONS BY YOUR BOARD OF ACCOUNTANCY.

If the Board of Accountancy has approved a candidate for special testing accommodations, the information regarding the nature of the accommodation will be sent to NASBA. The type of accommodation will be shown on the candidate's NTS and will be sent to Prometric. Neither the candidate nor the customer service representative may make any changes to the accommodations that have been approved. A candidate requiring special testing accommodations should contact their Board of Accountancy before proceeding if they believe there are any errors on the NTS. If you call to take two or more sections, be prepared to identify the dates, times and locations for each section you wish to take. It is not necessary to make all appointments in one call. If you prefer, you may make one appointment at a time.

Before calling, the candidate must have an NTS and should have access to it during the call as they will be required to provide the customer service representative with various pieces of information from the NTS.

Candidates may visit prometric.com/cpa to confirm their appointment(s). If the candidate is not familiar with the test center location they should ask the customer service representative for directions while they are making the appointment over the phone. There are multiple test centers in some metropolitan areas, so it is important for candidates to be certain of the correct test center location where they are scheduled to take their examination(s).

CHANGES TO APPOINTMENTS

After making an appointment for an examination section, the candidate may find it necessary to change or cancel an appointment. Candidates should be aware that they may be required to pay a penalty or forfeit examination fees, depending on when they notify Prometric of the change or cancellation.

Change the Date, Time or Location of an Appointment

There are three methods to reschedule or change an existing exam appointment:

- Use Prometric's Web scheduling tool located at prometric.com/cpa. The system is available 24 hours a day, seven days a week.
- Call the Prometric Candidate Services Call Center at 1-800-580-9648. The Center is open Monday through Friday from 8:00 a.m. to 8:00 p.m. Eastern time.
- Call the local test center where your appointment is scheduled. If you need to reschedule your appointment, review the table below to determine deadlines and associated fees. Please note that Saturday is considered a business day.

If calling to change an exam date, time or location, the candidate must speak with a staff member and cannot leave a message to reschedule. Candidates testing with special testing accommodations should call 1-800-967-1139 to reschedule. Candidates using a teletypewriter (TTY) should call 1-800-529-3590.

Some types of accommodations are only available at a limited number of test centers. A candidate's Board of Accountancy will have already notified the candidate of this before sending an NTS to a candidate who has requested special accommodations.

Ineligibility

If a candidate's Board of Accountancy informs NASBA that they are no longer eligible to take the Uniform CPA Examination for any reason, the NTS will be cancelled. The candidate will receive a copy of a canceled NTS by United States mail, fax or e-mail, depending on the method identified as the candidate's preferred method for receipt of information.

If the candidate has NOT scheduled an appointment, they do not need to take any other action. If they have scheduled an appointment, NASBA will contact Prometric to cancel the appointment and rescind eligibility. In the event that a candidate is determined to be no longer eligible to take the examination by their Board of Accountancy, examination fees will NOT be refunded.

Refunds

Under most circumstances, NASBA **will not** refund section fees. Additional information on payment of section fees can be found on NASBA's Web site at nasba.org.

Test Center Closings

If severe weather or other local emergency requires a test center to be closed, every attempt will be made to contact candidates scheduled to sit for the exam on that day. If a candidate is unsure of whether or not the test center will be open on their exam day due to inclement weather or other unforeseeable circumstance, the candidate may call their test center directly. If the center is open, it is the candidate's responsibility to keep the appointment. If the center is closed, the candidate will be given the opportunity to reschedule without penalty. If unable to contact the local test center, the candidate may check on the Web at prometric.com/cpa, or call the Candidate Services Call Center at 1-800-580-9648, Monday through Friday, from 8:00 a.m. to 8:00 p.m. Eastern time.

Fees

Fees for the 2017 Exam are as follows:

Application/Qualification Fee paid	(Varies by State)
First time Qualifying and Sitting	Approx. $50-$200
Previously Qualified and Sat (Repeat)	Approx. $25-$75
Section Fees to be Paid Directly to NASBA	**(Uniform)**
Auditing and Attestation	$193.45
Financial Accounting and Reporting	$193.45
Regulation	$193.45
Business Environment and Concepts	$193.45
Total fees paid to NASBA for all four sections	**$773.80**

Credit Status

The Exam utilizes a "rolling" 18-month credit status system. This replaced the conditional credit system of the paper-and-pencil exam. Credit status is established by passing one section of the examination. Once a candidate passes a section of the examination, the candidate will be allowed a maximum of 18 months to pass all remaining sections in order to retain credit on the passed section. If the candidate does not pass all four sections within that 18-month period, the candidate will lose credit for the first section of the exam passed. A new 18-month period will commence with a start date of the next section that was passed. There are state boards that offer exceptions to the above-described 18-month credit status period but for the majority of jurisdictions the 18-month rolling period applies and begins from the date the candidate sits for their first passed exam.

TAKE YOUR EXAMINATION

Arrive Early

Candidates must arrive at the test center at least 30 minutes before the scheduled appointment time for their examination. This allows time to sign in, have a digital photograph taken, be fingerprinted, review the security and test center policies and be seated at the workstation. If a candidate arrives for their scheduled testing appointment any time after the scheduled start time, they may be denied permission to test and will not receive a refund. Therefore, candidates should be sure to arrive at least 30 minutes before their scheduled appointment time to avoid forfeiting all fees for the examination section.

YOU MUST BRING YOUR NOTICE TO SCHEDULE (NTS) WITH YOU

The NTS contains an "Examination Password" that will be entered on the computer before starting the exam as a part of the log-in process. It is important to bring the correct NTS to the testing center as it is possible for a candidate to have more than one active NTS at a time. A candidate will not be admitted into the test center without the correct NTS and will forfeit all examination fees for that section if denied entry for this reason.

Personal Identification

The Uniform CPA Examination employs very strict security measures. One level of security involves identification. **The same form of the candidate's name must appear on the candidate's application, NTS, and on the primary identification presented at the test center.** It is important for candidates to spell and present their names correctly during the application process to assure the correct information is reflected on their Notice to Schedule. If the candidate's name is different from identifications presented at check-in, the candidate will not be permitted to test. Candidates must present two forms of identification, one of which must contain a recent photograph, to test center staff before being allowed into the examination. Each form of identification must bear the candidate's signature and must not be expired. Candidates who do not present valid ID will be barred entry to the exam and exam fees will not be refunded.

You must present *one* of the following primary forms of identification:
- A valid (not expired) state- or territory-issued driver's license with photograph and signature
- A valid (not expired) state- or territory-issued identification card with a recent photograph and signature (Candidates who do not drive may have an identification card issued by the agency which also issues driver's licenses.)
- A valid (not expired) government-issued passport with a recent photograph and signature.
- A United States military identification card with a recent photograph and signature

Your secondary form of identification may be one of the following (or another item from the list above):
- An identification card issued by your Board of Accountancy which includes the same name that appears on the NTS (if applicable to your jurisdiction)
- A valid (not expired) credit card
- A bank ATM card
- A debit card

The following are *UNACCEPTABLE* forms of identification:
- A draft classification card
- A Social Security card
- A student identification card
- A United States permanent residency card (green card)

The secondary form of identification **does not** have to match the information on a candidate's NTS exactly. For example, if a candidate's middle name is printed on their driver's license and NTS but not unexpired ATM card, the driver's license may be used as primary identification while the debit card can serve as secondary identification without issue. It is important to keep this in mind when applying to the state board so that the candidate's name is printed correctly on the NTS.

If the test center staff have questions about the identification presented, the candidate may be asked for additional proof of identity and, if staff are unable to verify identity, the candidate may be refused admission to the exam and will forfeit the examination fee for that section. Admittance to the test center and examination does not imply that the identification presented is valid or that the candidate's scores will be reported if subsequent investigations reveal impersonation or forgery.

Fingerprint Requirement

All CPA Exam candidates are required to have a digital fingerprint taken at Prometric that is used as primary identification for subsequent exam appearances as well as for re-admission to the test center after a break.

Digital fingerprint images will be encrypted and stored electronically together with candidate identification information. Fingerprint images will also be used to detect any attempt to impersonate CPA candidates.

Fingerprinting will be required every time a candidate reports to the test center. In addition, candidates returning to test rooms after breaks will be asked to have their fingerprints taken again for comparison with the fingerprints captured at the beginning of the session. Candidates should keep this in mind if they choose to take breaks during the exam.

At the Test Center

The staff at each test center have been trained in the procedures specific to the Uniform CPA Examination. The staff are there to guide candidates through the guidelines that have been developed by the Boards of Accountancy, NASBA and the AICPA.

1. You must arrive at the test center at least 30 minutes before your scheduled appointment. If you arrive after your scheduled appointment time, you may forfeit your appointment and will not be eligible to have your examination fees refunded.

2. Your examination should begin within 30 minutes of the scheduled start time. If circumstances arise that delay your session more than 30 minutes, you will be given the choice of continuing to wait or rescheduling your appointment.

3. You must place personal belongings, such as a purse or cell phone, in the storage lockers provided by the test center. You will be given the key to your locker which must be returned to the test center staff when you leave. The lockers are very small and are not intended to hold large items. Do not bring anything to the test center unless it is absolutely necessary. Test center personnel will not be responsible for lost or stolen items.

4. You will submit a digital fingerprint that will be used for identification purposes for future Prometric visits or to verify your identity if you leave the testing room for any reason during the exam (like a break or to put your sweater in your locker). Keep your photo ID on you at all times as well but expect your fingerprint to be used as your primary identification within the testing center.

5. You will have a digital photograph taken of your face. (If the digital camera equipment is not working, a Polaroid picture will be taken.)

6. You will be required to sign the test center log book. Each time you exit and re-enter the testing room, you will be required to sign the log book and present your identification.

7. You will be escorted to a workstation by test center staff. You must remain in your seat during the examination, except when authorized to get up and leave the testing room. Except for a standard break at the halfway point of the Exam, any breaks taken (e.g. to use the restroom) will count against the clock.

8. Candidates will be provided with two double-sided, laminated, colored sheets called "noteboards," as well as a fine point marker for making notations. This has replaced the paper and pencil scratch paper provided in the past. You will be directed to write your examination Launch Code (from your NTS) on your noteboards. You will be required to return the noteboards to the test center staff when your exam is complete. If more writing space is required, you may request additional noteboards from the test center staff once you have turned in the original noteboards you received. You must not bring any paper or pencils to the workstation in the testing room.

9. Notify the test center staff if:
    a. You experience a problem with your computer
    b. An error message appears on the computer screen (do not clear the message)
    c. You need additional scratch paper or pencils
    d. You need the test center staff for any other reason

10. When you finish the examination, leave the testing room quietly, turn in your noteboard and sign the test center log book. The test center staff will dismiss you after completing all necessary procedures.

Test Center Regulations

A standardized environment is necessary to ensure that candidates take equivalent but different exams. For this reason, all candidates must follow the same regulations.
- Papers, books, food or purses are not allowed in the testing room.
- Eating, drinking or use of tobacco is not allowed in the testing room.
- Talking or communicating with other candidates is not allowed in the testing room
- Calculators, personal digital assistants or other computer devices are not allowed in the testing room.
- Communication devices (e.g., cell phones, pagers, two-way radios, wireless internet connections to personal digital assistants devices) are not allowed in the testing room.
- Recording devices (audio and video) are not allowed in the testing room.
- You must not leave the testing room without the permission of the test center staff.
- You must be fingerprinted to re-enter the room after any breaks.

A complete list of prohibited items can be found on the AICPA website.

Breaks

Each examination section contains units known as testlets. Each testlet is comprised of either a group of multiple-choice questions or several task-based problems known as simulations. After each testlet, the candidate will be asked if he or she would like to take a non-standardized break (see below for information about the new standardized break). Those who do choose a break must indicate in the software that they will take an optional break and will be asked to leave the testing room quietly and sign the test center log book. Test center staff will confirm that the candidate has completed a testlet before allowing a break. Remember: you do not have to take a break and the clock will keep running if you do (for a non-standardized break)! Therefore, it is recommended that you use break time wisely. Leaving the testing room at any time without exiting the testlet and selecting the break option will result in the candidate being barred from reentry into the testing room and information regarding the candidate's absence will be reported to their Board of Accountancy.

Beginning April 1, 2017, Exam candidates are given a standardized break after the third (of five) testlets. This standardized break is up to 15 minutes and will NOT count against the candidate's time in the Exam. **We recommend that you take this break** to refresh before continuing with the exam.

The standardized break will not count against a candidate's time on the exam, but any other break will count against the time on the exam.

Examination Confidentiality and Break Policy

All candidates must accept the terms of the confidentiality and break policy statement before beginning their examination. The statement must be accepted or the test will be terminated and any exam fees will be forfeited.

Candidate Misconduct, Cheating, Copyright Infringement

The Boards of Accountancy, NASBA and the AICPA take candidate misconduct, including cheating on the Uniform CPA Examination, very seriously. If a Board of Accountancy determines that a candidate is culpable of misconduct or has cheated, the candidate will be subject to a variety of penalties including, but not limited to: invalidation of grades, disqualification from subsequent examination administrations, and civil and criminal penalties. In cases where candidate misconduct or cheating is discovered after a candidate has obtained a CPA license or certificate, a Board of Accountancy may rescind the license or certificate. If the test center staff suspects misconduct, a warning will be given to the candidate for any of the following situations:
- Communicating, orally or otherwise, with another candidate or person
- Copying from or looking at another candidate's materials or workstation
- Allowing another candidate to copy from or look at materials or workstation
- Giving or receiving assistance in answering examination questions or problems
- Reading examination questions or simulations aloud
- Engaging in conduct that interferes with the administration of the examination or unnecessarily disturbing staff or other candidates
- Grounds for confiscation of a prohibited item and warning the candidate include: Possession of any prohibited item (whether or not in use) inside, or while entering or exiting the testing room. This includes use of any prohibited item during a break in a manner that could result in cheating or the removal of examination questions or simulations

Prohibited items include, but are not limited to:
- Books
- Briefcase
- Calculator/Portable Computer
- Calculator Watch
- Camera, Photographic or Scanning Device (still or video)
- Cellular Phone

- Cigarette/Tobacco Product
- Container of any kind
- Dictionary
- Earphone
- Eraser
- Eyeglass Case
- Food or Beverage
- Handbag/Backpack/Hip Pack
- Hat or Visor (except head coverings worn for religious reasons)
- Headset or Audio Earmuffs (if not provided by Testing Center). You may bring soft, foam earplugs with no strings attached for your use. TCAs will inspect the earplugs
- Jewelry – Pendant Necklace or Large Earrings
- Newspaper or Magazine
- Non-Prescription Sunglasses
- Notebook
- Notes in any written form
- Organizer / Day Planner
- Outline
- Pager / Beeper
- Paper (if not provided by Test Center)
- Pen / Pencil (if not provided by Test Center)
- Pencil Sharpener
- Personal Digital Assistant or Other Electronic Device
- Plastic Bag
- Purse/Wallet
- Radio/Transmitter/Receiver
- Ruler/Slide Ruler
- Study Material
- Tape/Disk Recorder or Player
- Umbrella
- Watch
- Weapon of any kind

In addition, jackets, coats, and sweaters are also prohibited; however, if you require a separate sweater or a jacket due to room temperature, it must be worn at all times.

The Boards of Accountancy, NASBA, the AICPA and Prometric use a variety of procedures to prevent candidate misconduct and cheating on the examination. Test center staff are trained to watch for unusual behavior and incidents during the examination. In addition, all examination sessions are audio/videotaped to document the occurrence of any unusual activity and candidate misconduct is reported to Boards of Accountancy on a daily basis.

All examination materials are owned and copyrighted by the AICPA. Any reproduction and/or distribution of examination materials, including memorization, without the express written authorization of the AICPA, is prohibited. This behavior infringes on the legal rights of the AICPA and, in addition to the penalties listed above, the AICPA will take appropriate legal action when any copyright infringements have occurred.

Please see the AICPA's website at *aicpa.org* for a complete list of prohibited items and current information on examination policies.

Grounds for Dismissal

Test center staff may dismiss candidates from the examination or may have scores canceled by the candidate's Board of Accountancy for engaging in misconduct or not following the test center regulations. The following are examples of behavior that will not be tolerated during the examination:

- Repeating acts of misconduct after receiving prior warning(s)
- Attempting to remove or removing examination questions from the testing room by any means
- Copying, writing or summarizing examination questions on any material other than the scratch paper issued to you
- Tampering with computer software or hardware, or attempting to use a computer for any reason other than completing the examination session
- Intentional refusal or failure to comply with instructions of the test center staff
- Attempting to have an impersonator gain admission to the testing room or to substitute for you after a break
- Conduct that may threaten bodily harm or damage to property

RECEIVE YOUR SCORE(S)

Generally, Boards of Accountancy will report scores on a numeric scale of 0-99, with 75 as a passing score. This scale does NOT represent "percent correct." A score of 75 reflects examination performance that represents the knowledge and skills needed to protect the public. A few Boards of Accountancy have elected to report a pass or fail status instead of numeric scores. All questions contained in the examination, including BEC written communication task-based simulations, are formatted to allow responses to be scored electronically. Human graders score selected written communication responses. Candidates receive points for each correct answer to a multiple-choice question.

Similarly, responses to the questions asked in the simulations receive points based on correct answers or correct completion of the presented task. Points are not subtracted for incorrect responses. The points are accumulated according to the relative contributions of each question, which are weighted (see the Uniform CPA Examination Blueprints and skills definition documents for specific content areas and weights, or go to aicpa.org). Overall scores are then adjusted to ensure scores for all candidates (even those who test in different administrations with different examinations) are comparable and equivalent.

When You Should Expect Your Scores

The AICPA sends candidate scores to NASBA. The AICPA will release scores for the exams taken in a window on a specific target date according to the schedule on the following page. However, distribution of scores to the exam takers is the responsibility of the Boards of Accountancy. Each Board of Accountancy sets its own schedule regarding the frequency with which it will approve and release scores.

The AICPA target dates are not guaranteed and may be pushed back due to unforeseen issues. Additionally, BEC scores may be subject to longer delays due to the scoring of Written Communication. Candidates who do not receive their scores should call NASBA at 866-MY-NASBA.

Day of Exam in Testing Window*	Target Release Date Timeline
Day 1-20	11 business days following day 20 of the testing window
Day 21-45	6 business days following day 45 of the testing window
Day 46-Close of Window	6 business days following the close of the testing window
After Close of Window	6 business days after receiving all scoring data for the window

*date the records are received by the AICPA

The Score Review and Appeal Processes

Score Review

Score Review is an independent verification of a candidate's Uniform CPA Examination score, and NOT a re-grading or reconsideration of the candidate's responses on the examination. Because all scores undergo several quality control checks before they are reported, the likelihood of a score change following score review is exceedingly small, **or less than 1%** of all requested score reviews since the inception of the computer-based test. However, the score review option is available to candidates who would like to have their scores checked one more time. Fees apply.

Appeals

If allowed in a candidate's jurisdiction, an option to appeal a failing score may exist. This option enables the candidate to view the questions that he or she answered incorrectly as well as their responses. Such viewing takes place only in an authorized location, under secure conditions, and in the presence of a representative of the candidate's Board of Accountancy. In order to qualify for a score appeal, the candidate must submit a formal request to their Board of Accountancy within 30 days of the date printed on the score report, obtain the Board of Accountancy's approval, and pay the required fee. Contact your Board of Accountancy for specific instructions on the score appeal process. If a candidate is allowed a score appeal, they will be given the opportunity to view the questions they answered incorrectly as well as their responses to those questions. The AICPA will respond to any comments made by the candidate, rescore appealed responses and forward the results to NASBA. NASBA will then forward the scores to the candidate's Board of Accountancy.

RETAKING THE EXAMINATION

Candidates who fail any section of the CPA Exam may retake that section in a future testing window but are not allowed to repeat a failed section within the same two-month testing window. Information on how to retake a failed examination section will be sent to the candidate from their Board of Accountancy with a score report detailing the candidate's performance in each area of that particular exam section. This information may be helpful when preparing to retake any examination sections or in planning for near-term continuing professional education needs. For any questions on retake policies and fees, contact your Board of Accountancy.

ETHICS EXAM

Some jurisdictions require CPA Exam candidates to successfully complete an ethics examination as a requirement of CPA licensure, generally after the candidate has passed all four sections of the exam. The ethics portion is either administered through the AICPA or through continuing education (CPE) provided by your state society of CPAs. Check with your state board for more information on ethics requirements for your jurisdiction.

The CPA Exam

STRUCTURE

The Uniform CPA Examination spans 16 hours and consists of four separate exam parts.

The Uniform CPA Exam
Auditing & Attestation (AUD - 4 hours)
Financial Accounting & Reporting (FAR - 4 hours)
Regulation (REG - 4 hours)
Business Environment & Concepts (BEC - 4 hours)

Examination Content

The content areas for each exam part, along with skills tested, are outlined in the Uniform CPA Examination Blueprints published by the AICPA. For more information about the examination blueprints, visit aicpa.org and choose the "Become a CPA" tab.

Uniform CPA Examination Blueprints

With the 2017 exam the AICPA introduced a set of Uniform CPA Examination Blueprints, which document the minimum level of knowledge and skills needed for initial licensure in content areas and in representative tasks. The blueprints are organized by content AREA, content GROUP, and content TOPIC. Each topic includes one or more representative TASK(s) that a newly licensed CPA may be expected to complete. Each representative task is linked to a SKILL tested in the exam.

Skills are based on Bloom's Taxonomy of Educational Objectives. Critical thinking skills range from the lowest level (Remembering and Understanding) to the highest level (Evaluation), as summarized in the following table.

Skill Levels (beginning with the highest)	
Evaluation	The examination or assessment of problems and use of judgment to draw conclusions.
Analysis	The examination and study of the interrelationships of separate areas in order to identify causes and find evidence to support inferences.
Application	The use or demonstration of knowledge, concepts or techniques.
Remembering and Understanding	The perception and comprehension of the significance of an area utilizing knowledge gained.

The AICPA conducted a Practice Analysis from 2014-2015 in which one main finding was clear: firms expect newly licensed CPAs on their staff to perform at a higher level. The AICPA raised the bar with the revamped 2017 CPA Exam that more authentically tests candidates on the tasks and skill levels that will be required of them as newly licensed CPAs.

Types of Questions

Your score on each exam part is determined by the sum of points assigned to individual questions and simulation parts. Thus, you must attempt to maximize your points on each individual item. To familiarize yourself with the examination's format, functions, and question and response types, review the examination tutorial at aicpa.org. A sample test that contains a few sample multiple-choice questions and simulations for each applicable section is currently available. Neither the tutorial nor the sample test will be available at the test centers and candidates are encouraged to familiarize themselves with the test format prior to taking their first examination.

Multiple Choice Questions

A format is considered objective when it can be graded without subjectivity. Grading objective examinations is a mechanical process that requires little judgment. Any format that can be graded by machine is generally considered objective. Objective formats result in very consistent scores because the acceptability of particular responses is determined before grading begins. The most widely used objective format is multiple-choice (i.e., 4-option questions) because it has a restricted set of alternatives from which the correct answer must be selected. Multiple-choice questions (MCQs) make up 50% of FAR, AUD, REG and BEC.

The multiple-choice questions within each exam part are organized into two groups which are referred to as testlets. The first two testlets of each exam section will contain 31-38 multiple-choice questions per testlet, which are together worth up 50 percent of the exam part. The multiple-choice testlets vary in overall difficulty. A testlet is labeled either 'moderate' or 'difficult' based on its makeup. The questions in a 'difficult' testlet have a higher average level of difficulty than those in a 'moderate' testlet; however, questions of higher difficulty carry a higher point percentage rate therefore fewer must be answered correctly to pass. Every candidate's first multiple-choice testlet in each section will be a 'moderate' testlet. If a candidate scores well on the first testlet, he or she will receive a 'difficult' second testlet. Candidates that do not perform well on the first testlet receive a second 'moderate' testlet. Because the scoring procedure takes the difficulty of the testlet into account, candidates are scored fairly regardless of the type of testlets they receive.

Each multiple-choice testlet contains "operational" and "pretest" questions. The operational questions are the only ones that are used to determine your score. Pretest questions are not scored; they are being tested for future use as operational questions. However, you have no way of knowing which questions are operational and which questions are pretest questions. Therefore, you must approach each question as if it will be used to determine your grade. Of the multiple-choice questions, there are 72 operational and 12 pretest questions in the AUD exam, 66 operational and 11 pretest questions in the FAR exam, 76 operational and 12 pretest questions in the REG exam, and 62 operational and 10 pretest questions in the BEC exam.

Task-Based Simulations

Task-based simulations (TBSs) make up 50% of the FAR, AUD, and REG exams, but only 35% of the BEC exam (with written communications problems taking up the remaining 15%). Each operational TBS in the FAR, AUD, and REG exams is worth approximately 7.1% of the exam score. Each operational TBS in the BEC exam is worth approximately 11.7% of the exam score. The FAR, AUD, and REG sections of the exam each contain 8 task-based simulations. The BEC section includes 4 simulation problems as well as 3 written communication problems, of which 2 are graded. Each of these 2 graded written communications problems is worth approximately 7.5% of the exam score. The actual percentage of total score assigned to each requirement will vary according to its difficulty. Each TBS should be allotted about 10 to 20 minutes to complete, depending on difficulty. Candidates will be required to demonstrate their ability to apply certain skills (application, analysis, or evaluation) in each part of the CPA Exam using task-based simulations. These skills will be tested in a variety of methods such as simulation, or relational case studies, which will test candidates' knowledge and skills using work-related situations. Simulations will require candidates to have basic computer skills, knowledge of common spreadsheet and word processing functions, the ability to use a financial calculator or a spreadsheet to perform standard financial calculations, and the ability to use electronic tools such as databases for research. Therefore, you need to become proficient in the use of these tools to maximize your score on the task-based simulation component of each applicable exam section.

Each TBS contains at least two tabs: the work tab, labeled according to the exhibits used in the TBS (Research, Journal Entry, or Form 1065) and the help tab, labeled Help. The work tab (identified by a pencil icon) is the part of the question that will be graded and contains directions for completion of the task. Some task-based simulations may contain more than one information tab while others may not have any information tabs at all. The help tab provides assistance with the exam software such as instructions on using the provided word processor for written communication problems. While the exam environment closely mirrors common software programs that candidates are likely familiar with, it is recommended that candidates view the help tab for specific instructions on using the exam's provided software.

Document Review Simulations

A new type of simulation was introduced in the July 2016 exam and is known as the Document Review Simulation, or DRS. DRSs are designed to simulate tasks that the candidate will be required to perform as a newly licensed CPA (based on up to two years' experience as a CPA). Each DRS presents a document that has a series of highlighted phrases or sentences that the candidate will need to determine are correct or incorrect. To help make these conclusions, numerous supporting documents, or resources/exhibits, such as legal letters, phone transcripts, financial statements, trial balances and authoritative literature will be included. The candidate will need to sort through these documents to determine what is, and what is not important to solving the problem. Please see the Appendix at the end of this book for more information about DRSs.

Written Communication – BEC

Written communication will be assessed through the use of responses to essay questions, which will be based upon the content topics as outlined in the Blueprints. Candidates will have access to a word processor, which includes a spell check feature. Candidates are encouraged to use the "Help" tab for more information on the word processor functionality as it is similar to but not exactly like popular word processor programs the candidate may already be familiar with.

Research Task Format

FAR, AUD and REG will each contain at least one research problem. If a candidate's exam contains two research problems, it is likely that one of them is a problem being pre-tested.

Candidates will be asked to search through the database to find an appropriate reference that addresses the issue presented in the research problem. A scenario is presented in which the candidate must find his or her answer in the authoritative literature using a pre-determined list of codes (such as Professional Standards or federal taxation code). The candidate will choose the appropriate code title from the drop-down list and then enter a specific reference number applicable to their given scenario.

Authoritative literature for each section appears as follows:

FAR: Candidates will search the FASB ASC (Accounting Standards Codification) for their responses; this section does not have a dropdown menu to select from.

REG: IRC - Internal Revenue Code

AUD: AU-C - Clarified U.S. Auditing Standards

PCAOB – AS - PCAOB Auditing Standards

AT-C - Attestation Services

AR-C - Statements on Standards for Accounting and Review Services

ET - Code of Professional Conduct

BL - Bylaws

VS - Statements on Standards for Valuation Services

CS - Statement on Standards for Consulting Services

PFP - Personal Financial Planning

CPE - Continuing Professional Education

TS – Tax Services

PR – Peer Review Standards

QC - Quality Control

For example, a candidate may be asked the following question:

> A client has entered into an interest rate swap and just learned that it is considered a derivative. The cost was negligible and the entity is trying to determine at what amount to report it on its balance sheet. Identify the location in professional standards that indicates how derivatives should initially be measured.

Using the Authoritative Literature icon at the top of the screen, the candidate will search for keywords associated with the question using the search box, which will pull up all references within the literature to those keywords. From there, the candidate should use the "search within" function to find specific instances of keywords within each subsection. Keywords will be highlighted in the text and the candidate can go through them to find the relevant text that answers the research problem.

In this case, a search for "derivative" and a more detailed search within all references to that topic using the *search within* button would likely bring up FASB ASC 815-10-30-1, which reads:

> All derivative instruments shall be measured initially at fair value.

Using the provided drop-down menu, the candidate would then select the appropriate literature reference from the list (in this case, FASB codification) and enter the codification numbers in the blank boxes. It will look something like this:

> A client has entered into an interest rate swap and just learned that it is considered a derivative. The cost was negligible and the entity is trying to determine at what amount to report it on its balance sheet. Identify the location in professional standards that indicates how derivatives should initially be measured.

Enter your response in the answer fields below.

FASB ASC	815	10	30	1

Research questions will also alert the candidate if they have correctly formatted their answer by displaying a message like "Examples of correctly formatted sections are shown below" or "A correctly formatted IRC subsection is a lower case letter" in a box above the candidate response.

To master research type questions, you can either practice at the below NASBA website, or you can use the Interactive Practice Questions software included in your course.

CPA Exam Candidates: Free Online Access to Professional Literature Package

CPA Exam candidates can get a free six-month subscription to professional literature used in the CPA Examination. This online package includes AICPA Professional Standards, FASB Current Text and FASB Original Pronouncements. Only candidates who have applied to take the CPA Exam and have been deemed eligible by state boards of accountancy will receive access to this package of professional literature. NASBA will verify that a candidate has a valid NTS (Notice to Schedule). A candidate must be in receipt of a valid NTS prior to receiving authorization to the professional literature.

To subscribe visit: https://nasba.org/proflit/

Another good source for Researching Tax Codes for the **Regulation Exam**:

https://www.irs.gov/tax-professionals/tax-code-regulations-and-official-guidance

Testlets

Each section of the exam is presented in 5 testlets. The first 2 testlets contain multiple-choice questions (MCQs) and the last 3 testlets contain task-based simulations. (In the BEC exam, 2 of the last 3 testlets contain task-based simulations and 1 contains written communication problems.) Candidates can go back and forth between different questions within a testlet but cannot go back to previous testlets or review their questions once they have submitted their exam as complete.

Additional facts about the Exam
- You may take 1 part at a time.
- Results are released at various times throughout the exam window.
- In most jurisdictions, candidates must pass all four parts of the Uniform CPA Examination within a "rolling" eighteen-month period, which begins on the date that the first section(s) passed is taken.
- Generally, any credit for any exam part(s) passed outside the eighteen-month period will expire and that section(s) must be retaken.
- Candidates will not be allowed to retake a failed exam part(s) within the same quarter (examination window)
- Candidates will take different, equivalent exams.

Effective Date of Pronouncements (AICPA, 11/12/2015)

Accounting and auditing pronouncements are eligible to be tested on the Uniform CPA Examination in the later of: (1) the first testing window beginning after the pronouncement's earliest mandatory effective date or (2) the first testing window beginning six (6) months after the pronouncement's issuance date. In either case, there is a simultaneous introduction of content related to the new pronouncement and removal of content related to the previous pronouncement.

For the federal taxation area, the Internal Revenue Code and federal tax regulations in effect six months after the enactment date or the change's effective date, whichever is later, are eligible for testing.

For all other subjects covered in the Regulation (REG) and Business Environment and Concepts (BEC) sections, materials eligible to be tested include federal laws in the window beginning six months after their effective date, and uniform acts in the window beginning one year after their adoption by a simple majority of the jurisdictions.

Lecture 0.02
Auditing and Attestation – 4 Hours

Content Allocation

The content areas tested in the AUD section of the exam, as well as the weight given to each content area, are summarized in the following table.

Content Area		Weight
Area I	Ethics, Professional Responsibilities and General Principles	15-25%
Area II	Assessing Risk and Developing a Planned Response	20-30%
Area III	Performing Further Procedures and Obtaining Evidence	30-40%
Area IV	Forming Conclusions and Reporting	15-25%

Skill Allocation

The skills tested in the AUD exam, as well as the weight given to each skill, are summarized in the following table.

Skill	Weight
Evaluation	5-15%
Analysis	15-25%
Application	30-40%
Remembering and Understanding	30-40%

AUD Exam	
Testlet 1 *36 MCQ*	45 min
Testlet 2 *36 MCQ*	45 min
Testlet 3 *2 TBS*	30 min
Testlet 4 *3 TBS*	60 min
Testlet 5 *3 TBS*	60 min
Total Time:	4 hours

Things to consider:
- Use 75 seconds per multiple choice question as a benchmark
- Allocate 15-20 minutes per task-based simulation, depending on complexity
- Plan to use no more than 10 minutes per research question
- Take the standard 15-minute break after the 3rd testlet – it doesn't count against your time.

Uniform CPA Examination Blueprints
Effective January 1, 2018

AUDITING & ATTESTATION (AUD)

The AICPA gives candidates clear guidelines for the knowledge and skills that are tested on the CPA Exam. In the following excerpt we point to the most important information published by the AICPA describing the Exam sections.

The Auditing and Attestation (AUD) exam tests the knowledge and skills that a newly licensed CPA must demonstrate when performing:
- Audits of issuer and nonissuer entities (including governmental entities, not-for-profit entities, employee benefit plans and entities receiving federal grants)
- Attestation engagements for issuer and nonissuer entities (including examinations, reviews and agreed-upon procedures engagements)
- Preparation, compilation and review engagements for nonissuer entities and reviews of interim financial information for issuer entities.

Newly licensed CPAs are also required to demonstrate knowledge and skills related to professional responsibilities, including ethics and independence.

Area I of the AUD section blueprint covers several general topics, including the following:
- Nature and Scope of Engagements – Understanding the nature and scope of the various types of audit and non-audit engagement types, including:
  - Audit Engagements – Financial statement audits as well as other types of audits a newly licensed CPA may perform, such as compliance audits, audits of internal control integrated with an audit of financial statements and audits of entities receiving federal grants
  - Non-audit Engagements – Attestation engagements (including examinations, reviews and agreed-upon procedures engagements), Accounting and Review Services engagements (including preparation, compilation and review engagements) and reviews of interim financial information
- Ethics, Independence and Professional Conduct – Requirements under the AICPA Code of Professional Conduct and professional and independence requirements of the Securities and Exchange Commission (SEC), PCAOB, GAO and DOL
- Terms of Engagement – Preconditions for accepting an audit or non-audit engagement and the terms of engagement and engagement letter
- Engagement Documentation – Requirements for engagement documentation for all types of audit and non-audit engagements
- Communication Requirements – Understanding the requirements for communicating with management, those charged with governance, component auditors and other parties
- Quality Control – Understanding of quality control at the firm and engagement levels

The remaining three areas of the AUD exam blueprint (Areas II, III and IV) cover the activities that a newly licensed CPA must be able to perform when providing professional services related to the types of engagements enumerated above. These sections include the activities relevant for every type of engagement covered in the AUD exam, from the integrated audit of an issuer to a preparation, compilation or review for a small nonissuer, to the audit of a governmental entity. The organization of these sections follows the typical engagement process, from planning through reporting.

Area II of the AUD exam blueprint covers the engagement process from initial planning to risk assessment and designing procedures responsive to risks, including:

- Planning the Engagement – Understanding the engagement strategy and developing a detailed engagement plan
- Understanding an Entity and Its Environment and Understanding Internal Controls Over Financial Reporting – Developing an understanding of an entity and the risks associated with the engagement, understanding an entity's internal controls, and evaluating the effect of internal controls on an engagement
- Assessing Risks and Planning Further Procedures – Identifying and assessing risks of misstatement due to error or fraud and developing appropriate engagement procedures, including understanding and calculating materiality and considering specific engagement risks, as well as incorporating concepts such as group audits, using the work of the internal audit function and the work of specialists

Area III of the AUD exam blueprint covers performing engagement procedures and concluding on the sufficiency and appropriateness of evidence obtained, including performing specific types of procedures (e.g., analytical procedures, observation and inspection, recalculation and reperformance); testing the operating effectiveness of internal controls; performing tests of compliance and agreed-upon procedures, understanding and responding to specific matters that require special consideration (e.g., accounting estimates, including fair value estimates); evaluating and responding to misstatements due to error or fraud and to internal control deficiencies; obtaining management representations; and performing procedures to identify and respond to subsequent events and subsequently discovered facts.

Area IV of the AUD exam blueprint covers identifying the factors that an auditor, accountant or practitioner should consider when reporting on auditing, attestation, compilation, review or compliance engagements, when performing preparation engagements, and when assisting in the preparation of reports for these engagements. This includes other reporting considerations, such as comparative financial statements, consistency, supplementary information and special considerations when performing engagements under Government Auditing Standards.

References – Auditing and Attestation

AICPA Statements on Auditing Standards and Interpretations | Public Company Accounting Oversight Board (PCAOB) Standards (SEC-Approved) and Related Rules, PCAOB Staff Questions and Answers and PCAOB Staff Audit Practice Alerts | U.S. Government Accountability Office Government Auditing Standards | Single Audit Act, as amended Office of Management and Budget (OMB) Audit requirements for Federal Awards (2 CFR 200) | AICPA Statements on Quality Control Standards | AICPA Statements on Standards for Accounting and Review Services and Interpretations | AICPA Statements on Standards for Attestation Engagements and Interpretations | AICPA Audit and Accounting Guides AICPA Code of Professional Conduct | Sarbanes-Oxley Act of 2002 | U.S. Department of Labor (DOL) Guidelines and Interpretive Bulletins re: Auditor Independence | SEC Independence Rules | Employee Retirement Income Security Act of 1974 | The Committee of Sponsoring Organizations of the Treadway Commission (COSO): Internal Control – Integrated Framework | Current textbooks on auditing, attestation services, ethics and independence

AUDITING AND ATTESTATION (AUD)

Area I — Ethics, Professional Responsibilities and General Principles (15–25%)

Content Group/Topic	Skill				Representative Task
	Remembering and Understanding	Application	Analysis	Evaluation	
A. NATURE AND SCOPE					
1. Nature and scope: audit engagements	✓				Identify the nature, scope and objectives of the different types of audit engagements, including issuer and nonissuer audits.
2. Nature and scope: engagements conducted under Government Accountability Office Government Auditing Standards	✓				Identify the nature, scope and objectives of engagements performed in accordance with Government Accountability Office Government Auditing Standards.
3. Nature and scope: non-audit engagements	✓				Identify the nature, scope and objectives of the different types of non-audit engagements, including engagements conducted in accordance with the attestation standards and the accounting and review services standards.
B. ETHICS, INDEPENDENCE AND PROFESSIONAL CONDUCT					
1. AICPA Code of Professional Conduct	✓				Understand the principles, rules and interpretations included in the AICPA Code of Professional Conduct.
	✓				Recognize situations that present threats to compliance with the AICPA Code of Professional Conduct, including threats to independence.
		✓			Apply the principles, rules and interpretations included in the AICPA Code of Professional Conduct to given situations.
		✓			Apply the Conceptual Framework for Members in Public Practice included in the AICPA Code of Professional Conduct to situations that could present threats to compliance with the rules included in the Code.
		✓			Apply the Conceptual Framework for Members in Business included in the AICPA Code of Professional Conduct to situations that could present threats to compliance with the rules included in the Code.
		✓			Apply the Conceptual Framework for Independence included in the AICPA Code of Professional Conduct to situations that could present threats to compliance with the rules included in the Code.

Uniform CPA Examination Section Blueprints: Auditing and Attestation (AUD) | AUD 7

AUDITING AND ATTESTATION (AUD)

Area I — Ethics, Professional Responsibilities and General Principles (15–25%) Continued

Content Group/Topic	Skill				Representative Task
	Remembering and Understanding	Application	Analysis	Evaluation	
B. ETHICS, INDEPENDENCE AND PROFESSIONAL CONDUCT, continued					
2. Requirements of the Securities and the Exchange Commission and the Public Company Accounting Oversight Board	✓				Understand the ethical requirements of the Securities and Exchange Commission and the Public Company Accounting Oversight Board.
	✓				Recognize situations that present threats to compliance with the ethical requirements of the Securities and Exchange Commission and the Public Company Accounting Oversight Board.
		✓			Apply the ethical requirements and independence rules of the Securities and Exchange Commission and the Public Company Accounting Oversight Board to situations that could present threats to compliance during an audit of an issuer.
3. Requirements of the Government Accountability Office and the Department of Labor	✓				Recognize situations that present threats to compliance with the ethical requirements of the Government Accountability Office Government Auditing Standards.
	✓				Recognize situations that present threats to compliance with the ethical requirements of the Department of Labor.
		✓			Apply the ethical requirements and independence rules of the Government Accountability Office Government Auditing Standards to situations that could present threats to compliance during an audit of, or attestation engagement for, a government entity or an entity receiving federal awards.
		✓			Apply the independence rules of the Department of Labor to situations that could present threats to compliance during an audit of employee benefit plans.

Uniform CPA Examination Section Blueprints: Auditing and Attestation (AUD) | AUD 8

AUDITING AND ATTESTATION (AUD)

Area I — Ethics, Professional Responsibilities and General Principles (15–25%) Continued

Content Group/Topic	Remembering and Understanding	Application	Analysis	Evaluation	Representative Task
C. TERMS OF ENGAGEMENT					
1. Preconditions for an engagement	✓				Identify the preconditions needed for accepting or continuing an audit or non-audit engagement.
		✓			Perform procedures to determine whether the preconditions needed for accepting or continuing an audit or non-audit engagement are present.
		✓			Perform procedures to determine whether the financial reporting framework to be applied to an entity's financial statements is acceptable.
		✓			Perform procedures to obtain the agreement of management that it acknowledges and understands its responsibilities for an audit or non-audit engagement.
2. Terms of engagement and engagement letter	✓				Identify the factors affecting the acceptance or continuance of an audit or non-audit engagement.
	✓				Identify the factors to consider when management requests a change in the type of engagement (e.g., from an audit to a review).
		✓			Perform procedures to confirm that a common understanding of the terms of an engagement exist with management and those charged with governance.
		✓			Document the terms of an audit or non-audit engagement in a written engagement letter or other suitable form of written agreement.
D. REQUIREMENTS FOR ENGAGEMENT DOCUMENTATION					
	✓				Identify the elements that comprise sufficient appropriate documentation for an audit or non-audit engagement.
	✓				Identify the requirements for the assembly and retention of documentation for an audit or non-audit engagement.

AUDITING AND ATTESTATION (AUD)

Area I — Ethics, Professional Responsibilities and General Principles (15–25%) Continued

Content Group/Topic	Remembering and Understanding	Application	Analysis	Evaluation	Representative Task
D. REQUIREMENTS FOR ENGAGEMENT DOCUMENTATION, continued					
		✓			Prepare documentation that is sufficient to enable an experienced auditor having no previous connection with an audit engagement to understand the nature, timing, extent and results of procedures performed and the significant findings and conclusions reached.
		✓			Prepare documentation that is sufficient to enable an accountant having no previous connection with a non-audit engagement to understand the nature, timing, extent and results of procedures performed and the significant findings and conclusions reached.
E. COMMUNICATION WITH MANAGEMENT AND THOSE CHARGED WITH GOVERNANCE					
1. Planned scope and timing of an engagement	✓				Identify the matters related to the planned scope and timing of an audit or non-audit engagement that should be communicated to management and those charged with governance.
		✓			Prepare presentation materials and supporting schedules for use in communicating the planned scope and timing of an audit or non-audit engagement to management and those charged with governance.
2. Internal control related matters	✓				Identify the matters related to deficiencies and material weaknesses in internal control that should be communicated to those charged with governance and management for an audit or non-audit engagement and the timing of such communications.
		✓			Prepare written communication materials for use in communicating identified internal control deficiencies and material weaknesses for an audit or non-audit engagement to those charged with governance and management.
3. All other matters	✓				Identify matters, other than those related to the planned scope and timing or deficiencies, and material weaknesses in internal control that should be communicated to management and those charged with governance for an audit or non-audit engagement.

AUDITING AND ATTESTATION (AUD)

Area I — Ethics, Professional Responsibilities and General Principles (15–25%) Continued

Content Group/Topic	Remembering and Understanding	Application	Analysis	Evaluation	Representative Task
F. COMMUNICATION WITH COMPONENT AUDITORS AND PARTIES OTHER THAN MANAGEMENT AND THOSE CHARGED WITH GOVERNANCE					
	✓				Identify matters that should be communicated to component auditors in a group audit engagement.
	✓				Identify matters that should be communicated to parties other than management and those charged with governance (e.g., communications required by law or regulation) for an audit or non-audit engagement.
G. A FIRM'S SYSTEM OF QUALITY CONTROL, INCLUDING QUALITY CONTROL AT THE ENGAGEMENT LEVEL					
	✓				Recognize a CPA firm's responsibilities for its system of quality control for its accounting and auditing practice.
		✓			Apply quality control procedures on an audit or non-audit engagement.

AUDITING AND ATTESTATION (AUD)

Area II — Assessing Risk and Developing a Planned Response (20–30%)

Content Group/Topic	Remembering and Understanding	Application	Analysis	Evaluation	Representative Task
A. PLANNING AN ENGAGEMENT					
1. Developing an overall engagement strategy	✓				Explain the purpose and significance of the overall engagement strategy for an audit or non-audit engagement.
2. Developing a detailed engagement plan		✓			Prepare a detailed engagement plan for an audit or non-audit engagement starting with the prior-year engagement plan or with a template.
		✓			Prepare supporting planning related materials (e.g., client assistance request listings, time budgets) for a detailed engagement plan starting with the prior-year engagement plan or with a template.
			✓		Develop or modify a detailed engagement plan for an audit or non-audit engagement based on planning inputs and constraints.
B. UNDERSTANDING AN ENTITY AND ITS ENVIRONMENT					
1. External factors, including the applicable financial reporting framework		✓			Identify and document the relevant industry, regulatory and other external factors that impact an entity and/or the inherent risk of material misstatement, including the applicable financial reporting framework.
		✓			Document the procedures that were performed to obtain an understanding of the relevant industry, regulatory and other external factors that impact an entity and/or the inherent risk of material misstatement, including the applicable financial reporting framework.
2. Internal factors, including nature of the entity, ownership and governance structures and risk strategy		✓			Identify and document the relevant factors that define the nature of an entity, including the impact on the risk of material misstatement (e.g., its operations, ownership and governance structure, investment and financing plans, selection of accounting policies and objectives and strategies).
		✓			Document the procedures that were performed to obtain an understanding of the relevant factors that define the nature of an entity, including the impact on the risk of material misstatement (e.g., its operations, ownership and governance structure, investment and financing plans, selection of accounting policies, and objectives and strategies).

AUDITING AND ATTESTATION (AUD)

Area II — Assessing Risk and Developing a Planned Response (20–30%) Continued

Content Group/Topic	Remembering and Understanding	Skill — Application	Analysis	Evaluation	Representative Task
C. UNDERSTANDING AN ENTITY'S INTERNAL CONTROL					
1. Control environment and entity-level controls		✓			Identify and document the significant components of an entity's control environment, including its entity-level controls.
		✓			Perform and document the procedures to obtain an understanding of the significant components of an entity's control environment, including its entity-level controls.
2. Flow of transactions and design of internal controls		✓			Perform a walkthrough and document the flow of transactions relevant to an audit of an entity's financial statements, including an audit of an entity's internal controls.
		✓			Perform tests of the design and implementation of internal controls relevant to an audit of an entity's financial statements, including an audit of an entity's internal controls.
			✓		Identify and document the key controls within the flow of an entity's transactions relevant to an audit of an entity's financial statements, including an audit of an entity's internal controls.
				✓	Evaluate whether internal controls relevant to an audit of an entity's financial statements, including an audit of an entity's internal controls are effectively designed and placed in operation.
3. Implications of an entity using a service organization		✓			Identify and document the purpose and significance of an entity's use of a service organization, including its impact on an audit of an entity's financial statements, including an audit of an entity's internal controls.
		✓			Use a service organization report to determine the nature and extent of testing procedures to be performed in an audit of an entity's financial statements, including an audit of an entity's internal controls.

Uniform CPA Examination Section Blueprints: Auditing and Attestation (AUD) | AUD 13

AUDITING AND ATTESTATION (AUD)

Area II — Assessing Risk and Developing a Planned Response (20–30%) Continued

Content Group/Topic	Remembering and Understanding	Skill — Application	Analysis	Evaluation	Representative Task
C. UNDERSTANDING AN ENTITY'S INTERNAL CONTROL, continued					
4. Information Technology (IT) general and application controls		✓			Identify and document an entity's key IT general and application controls, including their impact on the audit of an entity's financial statements, including an audit of an entity's internal controls.
		✓			Perform and document the tests of an entity's IT general and application controls, including controls relevant to the audit of an entity's financial statements, including an audit of an entity's internal controls.
5. Limitations of controls and risk of management override	✓				Understand the limitations of internal controls and the potential impact on the risk of material misstatement of an entity's financial statements.
		✓			Identify and document the risks associated with management override of internal controls and the potential impact on the risk of material misstatement of an entity's financial statements.
D. ASSESSING RISKS DUE TO FRAUD, INCLUDING DISCUSSIONS AMONG THE ENGAGEMENT TEAM ABOUT THE RISK OF MATERIAL MISSTATEMENT DUE TO FRAUD OR ERROR					
			✓		Assess risks of material misstatement of an entity's financial statements due to fraud or error (e.g., during a brainstorming session), leveraging the combined knowledge and understanding of the engagement team.
E. IDENTIFYING AND ASSESSING THE RISK OF MATERIAL MISSTATEMENT, WHETHER DUE TO ERROR OR FRAUD, AND PLANNING FURTHER PROCEDURES RESPONSIVE TO IDENTIFIED RISKS					
1. Impact of risks at the financial statement level		✓			Identify and document the assessed impact of risks of material misstatement at the financial statement level, taking into account the effect of relevant controls.
			✓		Analyze identified risks to detect those that relate to an entity's financial statements as a whole (as contrasted to the relevant assertion level).

Uniform CPA Examination Section Blueprints: Auditing and Attestation (AUD) | AUD 14

AUDITING AND ATTESTATION (AUD)

Area II — Assessing Risk and Developing a Planned Response (20–30%) Continued

Content Group/Topic	Remembering and Understanding	Application	Analysis	Evaluation	Representative Task
E. IDENTIFYING AND ASSESSING THE RISK OF MATERIAL MISSTATEMENT, WHETHER DUE TO ERROR OR FRAUD, AND PLANNING FURTHER PROCEDURES, continued					
2. Impact of risks for each relevant assertion at the class of transaction, account balance and disclosure levels		✓			Identify and document risks and related controls at the relevant assertion level in an entity's financial statements for significant classes of transactions, account balances and disclosures in an entity's financial statements.
			✓		Analyze the potential impact of identified risks and related controls at the relevant assertion level for significant classes of transactions, account balances and disclosures in an entity's financial statements, taking account of the controls the auditor intends to test.
3. Further procedures responsive to identified risks		✓			Develop planned audit procedures that are responsive to identified risks of material misstatement due to fraud or error at the relevant assertion level for significant classes of transactions and account balances.
			✓		Analyze the risk of material misstatement, including the potential impact of individual and cumulative misstatements, to provide a basis for developing planned audit procedures.
F. MATERIALITY					
1. For the financial statements as a whole	✓				Understand materiality as it relates to the financial statements as a whole.
		✓			Calculate materiality for an entity's financial statements as a whole.
		✓			Calculate the materiality level (or levels) to be applied to classes of transactions, account balances and disclosures in an audit of an issuer or nonissuer.
2. Performance materiality and tolerable misstatement	✓				Understand the use of performance materiality and tolerable misstatement in an audit of an issuer or nonissuer.
		✓			Calculate performance materiality or tolerable misstatement for the purposes of assessing the risk of material misstatement and determining the nature, timing and extent of further audit procedures in an audit of an issuer or nonissuer.

AUDITING AND ATTESTATION (AUD)

Area II — Assessing Risk and Developing a Planned Response (20–30%) Continued

Content Group/Topic	Remembering and Understanding	Application	Analysis	Evaluation	Representative Task
G. PLANNING FOR AND USING THE WORK OF OTHERS, INCLUDING GROUP AUDITS, THE INTERNAL AUDIT FUNCTION AND THE WORK OF A SPECIALIST					
	✓				Identify the factors to consider in determining the extent to which an engagement team can use the work of the internal audit function in an audit or non-audit engagement.
	✓				Identify the factors to consider in determining the extent to which an engagement team should use the work of a specialist in an audit or non-audit engagement.
	✓				Identify the factors to consider in determining the extent to which an auditor can use the work of a component auditor in a group audit.
		✓			Determine the nature and scope of the work of the internal audit function that can be used in an audit or non-audit engagement.
		✓			Perform procedures to utilize the work of a specialist to obtain evidence in an audit or non-audit engagement.
		✓			Determine the nature and scope of the work of a component auditor, including the identification of significant components that can be used in a group audit.

AUDITING AND ATTESTATION (AUD)

Area II — Assessing Risk and Developing a Planned Response (20–30%) Continued

Content Group/Topic	Remembering and Understanding	Application	Analysis	Evaluation	Representative Task
H. SPECIFIC AREAS OF ENGAGEMENT RISK					
1. An entity's compliance with laws and regulations, including possible illegal acts	✓				Understand the accountant's responsibilities with respect to laws and regulations that have a direct effect on the determination of material amounts or disclosures in an entity's financial statements for an audit or non-audit engagement.
	✓				Understand the accountant's responsibilities with respect to laws and regulations that are fundamental to an entity's business but do not have a direct effect on the entity's financial statements in an audit or non-audit engagement.
		✓			Perform tests of compliance with laws and regulations that have a direct effect on material amounts or disclosures in an entity's financial statements in an audit or non-audit engagement.
		✓			Perform tests of compliance with laws and regulations that are fundamental to an entity's business, but do not have a direct effect on the entity's financial statements for an audit or non-audit engagement.
2. Accounting estimates, including fair value estimates	✓				Recognize the potential impact of significant accounting estimates on the risk of material misstatement, including the indicators of management bias.
3. Related parties and related party transactions		✓			Perform procedures to identify related party relationships and transactions for an audit or non-audit engagement, including consideration of significant unusual transactions and transactions with executive officers.
			✓		Analyze the potential impact of related party relationships and transactions on the risk of material misstatement for an audit or non-audit engagement, including consideration of significant unusual transactions and transactions with executive officers.

Uniform CPA Examination Section Blueprints: Auditing and Attestation (AUD) | **AUD 17**

AUDITING AND ATTESTATION (AUD)

Area III — Performing Further Procedures and Obtaining Evidence (30–40%)

Content Group/Topic	Remembering and Understanding	Application	Analysis	Evaluation	Representative Task
A. UNDERSTANDING SUFFICIENT APPROPRIATE EVIDENCE					
				✓	Conclude on the sufficiency and appropriateness of evidence obtained during the audit engagement for an issuer or nonissuer.
				✓	Conclude on the sufficiency and appropriateness of evidence obtained during a non-audit engagement based on the objectives and reporting requirements of the engagement.
B. SAMPLING TECHNIQUES					
	✓				Understand the purpose and application of sampling techniques in an audit or non-audit engagement.
		✓			Use sampling techniques to extrapolate the characteristics of a population from a sample of items tested.
C. PERFORMING SPECIFIC PROCEDURES TO OBTAIN EVIDENCE					
1. Analytical procedures			✓		Determine the suitability of substantive analytical procedures to provide evidence to support an identified assertion.
			✓		Develop an expectation of recorded amounts or ratios when performing analytical procedures in an audit or non-audit engagement and determine whether the expectation is sufficiently precise to identify a misstatement in the entity's financial statements or disclosures.
			✓		Perform analytical procedures during engagement planning for an audit or non-audit engagement.
			✓		Perform analytical procedures near the end of an audit engagement that assist the auditor when forming an overall conclusion about whether the financial statements are consistent with the auditor's understanding of the entity.
				✓	Evaluate the reliability of data from which an expectation of recorded amounts or ratios is developed when performing analytical procedures in an audit or non-audit engagement.
				✓	Evaluate the significance of the differences of recorded amounts from expected values when performing analytical procedures in an audit or non-audit engagement.

Uniform CPA Examination Section Blueprints: Auditing and Attestation (AUD) | **AUD 18**

AUDITING AND ATTESTATION (AUD)

Area III — Performing Further Procedures and Obtaining Evidence (30–40%) Continued

Content Group/Topic	Remembering and Understanding	Application	Analysis	Evaluation	Representative Task
C. PERFORMING SPECIFIC PROCEDURES TO OBTAIN EVIDENCE, continued					
2. External confirmations		✓			Prepare external confirmation requests to obtain relevant and reliable evidence in an audit engagement of an issuer or nonissuer, including considerations when using electronic confirmations.
		✓			Use external confirmations to obtain relevant and reliable evidence in an audit engagement of an issuer or nonissuer, including considerations when using electronic confirmations.
			✓		Analyze external confirmation responses in the audit of an issuer or nonissuer to determine the need for follow-up or further investigation.
3. Inquiry of management and others		✓			Inquire of management and others to gather evidence and document the results in an audit or non-audit engagement.
			✓		Analyze responses obtained during structured or informal interviews with management and others and ask relevant and effective follow-up questions during the interview in an audit or non-audit engagement.
4. Observation and inspection			✓		Perform tests of operating effectiveness of internal controls, including the analysis of exceptions to identify deficiencies in an audit of financial statements or an audit of internal control.
				✓	Evaluate evidence through the use of observation and inspection procedures in an audit or non-audit engagement.
5. Recalculation and reperformance		✓			Use recalculation and reperformance to obtain evidence in an audit or non-audit engagement.
6. All other procedures	✓				Identify other procedures in addition to those set out in professional standards, as necessary, to achieve the audit objectives in an audit of an issuer or a nonissuer.
		✓			Perform other procedures in addition to those set out in professional standards, as necessary, to achieve the audit objectives in an audit of an issuer or nonissuer.

AUDITING AND ATTESTATION (AUD)

Area III — Performing Further Procedures and Obtaining Evidence (30–40%) Continued

Content Group/Topic	Remembering and Understanding	Application	Analysis	Evaluation	Representative Task
D. SPECIFIC MATTERS THAT REQUIRE SPECIAL CONSIDERATION					
1. Opening balances		✓			Test whether prior-period closing balances have been correctly brought forward to the current period or restated in the audit of an issuer or nonissuer, including investigation of differences.
2. Investments in securities and derivative instruments	✓				Identify the considerations relating to the measurement and disclosure of the fair value of investments in securities and derivative instruments in an audit of an issuer or nonissuer.
		✓			Test management's assumptions, conclusions and adjustments related to the valuation of investments in securities and derivative instruments in an audit of an issuer or nonissuer.
3. Physical observation of inventory and inventory held by others			✓		Analyze management's instructions and procedures for recording and controlling the results of an entity's physical inventory counting in an audit of an issuer or nonissuer.
				✓	Observe the performance of inventory counting procedures, inspect the inventory and perform test counts to verify the ending inventory quantities in an audit of an issuer or nonissuer.
4. Litigation, claims and assessments		✓			Perform appropriate audit procedures, such as inquiring of management and others, reviewing minutes and sending external confirmations, to detect the existence of litigation, claims and assessments in an audit of an issuer or nonissuer.
			✓		Analyze management's estimate of the liability associated with litigation, claims and assessments in an audit of an issuer or nonissuer.
5. An entity's ability to continue as a going concern	✓				Identify the factors that could cause substantial doubt about an entity's ability to continue as a going concern for a reasonable period of time in an audit of an issuer or nonissuer.

AUDITING AND ATTESTATION (AUD)

Area III — Performing Further Procedures and Obtaining Evidence (30–40%) Continued

Content Group/Topic	Remembering and Understanding	Application	Analysis	Evaluation	Representative Task
D. SPECIFIC MATTERS THAT REQUIRE SPECIAL CONSIDERATION, continued					
6. Accounting estimates, including fair value estimates			✓		Perform procedures to analyze an entity's calculations and detailed support for significant accounting estimates in an audit of an issuer or nonissuer, including consideration of information that contradicts assumptions made by management.
				✓	Evaluate the reasonableness of significant accounting estimates in an audit of an issuer or nonissuer.
E. MISSTATEMENTS AND INTERNAL CONTROL DEFICIENCIES					
		✓			Prepare a summary of corrected and uncorrected misstatements.
			✓		Determine the effect of uncorrected misstatements on an entity's financial statements in an audit or non-audit engagement.
			✓		Determine the effect of identified misstatements on the assessment of internal control over financial reporting in an audit of an issuer or nonissuer.
				✓	Evaluate the significance of internal control deficiencies on the risk of material misstatement of financial statements in an audit of an issuer or nonissuer.

AUDITING AND ATTESTATION (AUD)

Area III — Performing Further Procedures and Obtaining Evidence (30–40%) Continued

Content Group/Topic	Remembering and Understanding	Application	Analysis	Evaluation	Representative Task
F. WRITTEN REPRESENTATIONS					
	✓				Identify the written representations that should be obtained from management or those charged with governance in an audit or non-audit engagement.
		✓			Assist in the preparation of required written representations that should be obtained from management or those charged with governance in an audit or non-audit engagement.
G. SUBSEQUENT EVENTS AND SUBSEQUENTLY DISCOVERED FACTS					
		✓			Perform procedures to identify subsequent events that could affect an entity's financial statements or the auditor's report, including 1) events that occur between the date of the financial statements and the date of the auditor's report and 2) facts that become known to the auditor after the date of the auditor's report in an audit of an issuer or nonissuer.
		✓			Perform procedures to identify subsequent events that could affect an entity's financial statements or the accountant's report, including 1) events that occur between the date of the financial statements and the date of the report and 2) facts that become known to the accountant after the date of the report in a non-audit engagement.
			✓		Determine whether identified subsequent events are appropriately reflected in an entity's financial statements and disclosures in an audit or non-audit engagement.

AUDITING AND ATTESTATION (AUD)

Area IV — Forming Conclusions and Reporting (15–25%)

Content Group/Topic	Remembering and Understanding	Application	Analysis	Evaluation	Representative Task
A. REPORTS ON AUDITING ENGAGEMENTS					
1. Forming an audit opinion, including modification of an auditor's opinion	✓				Identify the factors that an auditor should consider when forming an opinion on an entity's financial statements.
	✓				Identify the type of opinion that an auditor should render on the audit of an issuer or nonissuer's financial statements, including unmodified (or unqualified), qualified, adverse or disclaimer of opinion.
	✓				Identify the factors that an auditor should consider when it is necessary to modify the audit opinion on an issuer or nonissuer's financial statements, including when the financial statements are materially misstated and when the auditor is unable to obtain sufficient appropriate audit evidence.
2. Form and content of an audit report, including the use of emphasis-of-matter and other-matter (explanatory) paragraphs	✓				Identify the appropriate form and content of an auditor's report for an audit of an issuer or nonissuer's financial statements, including the appropriate use of emphasis-of-matter and other-matter (i.e., explanatory) paragraphs.
		✓			Prepare a draft auditor's report starting with a report example (e.g., an illustrative audit report from professional standards) for an audit of an issuer or nonissuer.
3. Audit of internal control integrated with an audit of financial statements	✓				Identify the factors that an auditor should consider when forming an opinion on the effectiveness of internal control in an audit of internal control.
	✓				Identify the appropriate form and content of a report on the audit of internal control, including report modifications and the use of separate or combined reports for the audit of an entity's financial statements and the audit of internal control.
		✓			Prepare a draft report for an audit of internal control integrated with the audit of an entity's financial statements, starting with a report example (e.g., an illustrative report from professional standards).

AUDITING AND ATTESTATION (AUD)

Area IV — Forming Conclusions and Reporting (15–25%) Continued

Content Group/Topic	Remembering and Understanding	Application	Analysis	Evaluation	Representative Task
B. REPORTS ON ATTESTATION ENGAGEMENTS					
1. General standards for attestation reports	✓				Identify the factors that a practitioner should consider when issuing an examination or review report for an attestation engagement.
		✓			Prepare a draft examination or review report for an attestation engagement starting with a report example (e.g., an illustrative report from professional standards).
2. Agreed-upon procedures reports	✓				Identify the factors that a practitioner should consider when issuing an agreed-upon procedures report for an attestation engagement.
		✓			Prepare a draft agreed-upon procedures report for an attestation engagement starting with a report example (e.g., an illustrative report from professional standards).
3. Reporting on controls at a service organization	✓				Identify the factors that a service auditor should consider when reporting on the examination of controls at a service organization.
		✓			Prepare a draft report for an engagement to report on the examination of controls at a service organization, starting with a report example (e.g., an illustrative report from professional standards).

AUDITING AND ATTESTATION (AUD)

Area IV — Forming Conclusions and Reporting (15–25%) Continued

Content Group/Topic	Skill				Representative Task
	Remembering and Understanding	Application	Analysis	Evaluation	
C. ACCOUNTING AND REVIEW SERVICE ENGAGEMENTS					
1. Preparation engagements	✓				Identify the factors that an accountant should consider when performing a preparation engagement.
2. Compilation reports	✓				Identify the factors that an accountant should consider when reporting on an engagement to compile an entity's financial statements, including the proper form and content of the compilation report.
		✓			Prepare a draft report for an engagement to compile an entity's financial statements, starting with a report example (e.g., an illustrative report from professional standards).
3. Review reports	✓				Identify the factors that an accountant should consider when reporting on an engagement to review an entity's financial statements, including the proper form and content of the review report.
		✓			Prepare a draft report for an engagement to review an entity's financial statements, starting with a report example (e.g., an illustrative report from professional standards).

Uniform CPA Examination Section Blueprints: Auditing and Attestation (AUD) | **AUD 25**

AUDITING AND ATTESTATION (AUD)

Area IV — Forming Conclusions and Reporting (15–25%) Continued

Content Group/Topic	Skill				Representative Task
	Remembering and Understanding	Application	Analysis	Evaluation	
D. REPORTING ON COMPLIANCE					
	✓				Identify the factors that an auditor should consider when reporting on compliance with aspects of contractual agreements or regulatory requirements in connection with an audit of an entity's financial statements.
	✓				Identify the factors that a practitioner should consider when reporting on an attestation engagement related to an entity's compliance with the requirements of specified laws, regulations, rules, contracts or grants, including reports on the effectiveness of internal controls over compliance with the requirements.
		✓			Prepare a draft compliance report for an attestation engagement to report on an entity's compliance with the requirements of specified laws, regulations, rules, contracts or grants starting with a report example (e.g., an illustrative report from professional standards).
		✓			Prepare a draft compliance report when reporting on compliance with aspects of contractual agreements or regulatory requirements in connection with an audit of an entity's financial statements starting with a report example (e.g., an illustrative report from professional standards).
E. OTHER REPORTING CONSIDERATIONS					
1. Comparative statements and consistency between periods	✓				Identify the factors that would affect the comparability or consistency of financial statements, including a change in accounting principle, the correction of a material misstatement and a material change in classification.
2. Other information in documents with audited statements	✓				Understand the auditor's responsibilities related to other information included in documents with audited financial statements.
3. Review of interim financial information	✓				Identify the factors an auditor should consider when reporting on an engagement to review interim financial information.

Uniform CPA Examination Section Blueprints: Auditing and Attestation (AUD) | **AUD 26**

AUDITING AND ATTESTATION (AUD)

Area IV — Forming Conclusions and Reporting (15–25%) Continued

Content Group/Topic	Skill Remembering and Understanding	Application	Analysis	Evaluation	Representative Task
E. OTHER REPORTING CONSIDERATIONS, continued					
4. Supplementary information	✓				Identify the factors an auditor should consider when reporting on supplementary information included in or accompanying an entity's financial statements.
5. Single statements	✓				Identify the factors an auditor should consider when reporting on the audit of a single financial statement.
6. Special-purpose and other country frameworks	✓				Identify the factors an auditor should consider when reporting on the audit of financial statements prepared in accordance with a financial reporting framework generally accepted in another country, when the financial statements are intended for use outside of the United States.
	✓				Identify the factors an auditor should consider when reporting on the audit of financial statements prepared in accordance with a special-purpose framework, including cash basis, tax basis, regulatory basis, contractual basis or other basis.
7. Letters for underwriters and filings with the SEC	✓				Identify the factors an auditor should consider when engaged to issue a comfort letter in connection with an entity's financial statements that are included in a securities offering.
	✓				Identify the factors an auditor should consider in connection with audited financial statements of a nonissuer that are included in a registration statement.
8. Alerts that restrict the use of written communication	✓				Identify the factors an auditor should consider when restricting the use of written communication by including an alert when the potential exists for the written communication to be misunderstood or taken out of context.
9. Additional reporting requirements under Government Accountability Office Government Auditing Standards	✓				Identify requirements under Government Accountability Office Government Auditing Standards related to reporting on internal control over financial reporting and compliance with provisions of law, regulations, contracts and grant agreements that have a material effect on the financial statements.

Uniform CPA Examination Section Blueprints: Auditing and Attestation (AUD)   **AUD 27**

State	State Board Web Address	Telephone #
AK	commerce.state.ak.us/occ/pcpa.htm	(907) 465-3811
AL	asbpa.alabama.gov	(334) 242-5700
AR	state.ar.us/asbpa	(501) 682-1520
AZ	azaccountancy.gov	(602) 364-0804
CA	dca.ca.gov/cba	(916) 263-3680
CO	dora.state.co.us/accountants	(303) 894-7800
CT	ct.gov/sboa	(860) 509-6179
DC	pearsonvue.com/dc/accountancy/	(202) 442-4320
DE	dpr.delaware.gov/boards/accountancy/index.shtml	(302) 744-4500
FL	myfloridalicense.com/dbpr/cpa/	(850) 487-1395
GA	sos.state.ga.us/plb/accountancy/	(478) 207-1400
GU	guamboa.org	(671) 647-0813
HI	hawaii.gov/dcca/areas/pvl/boards/accountancy	(808) 586-2696
IA	state.ia.us/iacc	(515) 281-5910
ID	isba.idaho.gov	(208) 334-2490
IL	ilboa.org	(217) 531-0950
IN	in.gov/pla/accountancy.htm	(317) 234-3040
KS	ksboa.org	(785) 296-2162
KY	cpa.ky.gov	(502) 595-3037
LA	cpaboard.state.la.us	(504) 566-1244
MA	mass.gov/reg/boards/pa	(617) 727-1806
MD	dllr.state.md.us/license/occprof/account.html	(410) 230-6322
ME	maine.gov/pfr/professionallicensing/professions/accountants/index.htm	(207) 624-8603
MI	michigan.gov/accountancy	(517) 241-9249
MN	boa.state.mn.us	(651) 296-7938
MO	pr.mo.gov/accountancy.asp	(573) 751-0012
MS	msbpa.state.ms.us	(601) 354-7320
MT	publicaccountant.mt.gov	(406) 841-2389
NC	nccpaboard.gov	(919) 733-4222
ND	state.nd.us/ndsba	(800) 532-5904
NE	nol.org/home/BPA	(402) 471-3595
NH	nh.gov/accountancy	(603) 271-3286
NJ	state.nj.us/lps/ca/accountancy/	(973) 504-6380
NM	rld.state.nm.us/accountancy/index.html	(505) 841-9108
NV	nvaccountancy.com/	(775) 786-0231
NY	op.nysed.gov/cpa.htm	(518) 474-3817
OH	acc.ohio.gov/	(614) 466-4135
OK	oab.state.ok.us	(405) 521-2397
OR	egov.oregon.gov/BOA/	(503) 378-4181
PA	dos.state.pa.us/account	(717) 783-1404
PR	estado.gobierno.pr/	(787) 722-4816
RI	dbr.ri.gov/divisions/accountancy/	(401) 222-3185
SC	llr.state.sc.us/POL/Accountancy	(803) 896-4770
SD	state.sd.us/dol/Boards/accountancy/acc-home.htm	(605) 367-5770
TN	tn.gov/commerce/boards/tnsba/index.shtml	(615) 741-2550
TX	tsbpa.state.tx.us	(512) 305-7800
UT	dopl.utah.gov	(801) 530-6396
VA	boa.virginia.gov	(804) 367-8505
VI	dlca.gov.vi	(340) 773-4305
VT	vtprofessionals.org/opr1/accountants	(802) 828-2837
WA	cpaboard.wa.gov	(360) 753-2585
WI	drl.wi.gov/profession.asp?profid=60&locid=0	(608) 266-5511
WV	boa.wv.gov/Pages/default.aspx	(304) 558-3557
WY	cpaboard.state.wy.us	(307) 777-7551

Section 1 - Audit Standards & Engagement Planning

Corresponding Lectures

Watch the following course lectures with this section:

Lecture 1.01 – Types of Audits
Lecture 1.02 – Clarity Standards
Lecture 1.03 – Generally Accepted Auditing Standards
Lecture 1.04 – Responsibilities of the Auditor under Clarity Standards
Lecture 1.05 – GAAS and Responsibility of Auditor – Class Questions
Lecture 1.06 – Steps in the Audit Process
Lecture 1.07 – Engagement Letter
Lecture 1.08 – Steps in the Audit Process – Class Questions
Lecture 1.09 – Planning Procedures
Lecture 1.10 – Planning Procedures – Class Questions
Lecture 1.11 – Audit Risk, Fraud and Errors
Lecture 1.12 – Consideration of Fraud in the Financial Statements & Fraud Risk Factors
Lecture 1.13 – Audit Risk – Class Questions
Lecture 1.14 – Quality Control
Lecture 1.15 – Research Task Format – Audit
Lecture 1.16 – Engagement Planning – Class Question – DRS
Lecture 1.17 – Audit Risk – Class Question - DRS

EXAM NOTE: *Please refer to the AICPA AUD Blueprint in the Introduction of this book to find a listing of the representative tasks (and their associated skill levels—i.e., Remembering and Understanding, Application, Analysis, and Evaluation) that the candidate should be able to perform based on the knowledge obtained in this section.*

Audit Standards & Engagement Planning

Lecture 1.01

TYPES OF AUDITS

There are several types of audits that may be performed in relation to an entity. These include compliance audits, often performed by governmental or regulatory organizations to determine if the entity is complying with appropriate laws and regulations; operational audits, often performed by internal auditors; and financial statement audits, which may only be performed by CPAs.

Compliance Audits

Compliance audits are performed to determine if an entity is complying with applicable laws and regulations. They are often performed by governmental or regulatory organizations on entities that may be chosen on a random basis or may be selected due to some indication that there may be one or more incidents of noncompliance, such as a tax return with unusual deductions.

- Are they following laws & regulations?
    - o IRS audits
    - o Governmental units to determine compliance with laws and regulations
    - o CPA to determine compliance with provisions of a bond or note agreement

Operational Audits

Operational audits are generally performed by internal auditors to determine if management's policies are being followed appropriately and to evaluate the entity's performance as well as its compliance with internal controls.

- Effectiveness/Efficiency/Economy – done by Internal Auditors, Governmental auditors or CPAs.
    - o Audit a department or division of a corporation to see if meeting organizational goals.
    - o Review by governmental auditors to determine the effectiveness and benefit of specific gov. funded programs.

Financial Statement Audits

Financial statement audits are performed exclusively by CPAs, and are designed to determine if financial statements are fairly presented in accordance with the applicable financial reporting framework. Standards for the performance of financial statement audits are established by the Auditing Standards Board (ASB) of the AICPA for audits of nonpublic entities; by the PCAOB for audits of public entities; and by the IAASB for audits performed under international standards.

- Examination for the purpose of giving an objective opinion as to the fairness of financial statement presentations, in all material respects, that are free from material misstatement, whether due to fraud or error, in conformity with an *Applicable Financial Reporting Framework (AFRF),* such as U.S. Generally Accepted Accounting Principles (GAAP).

A financial reporting framework is a set of criteria used to determine measurement, recognition, presentation, and disclosure of all material items appearing in the financial statements. It determines the form and content of the financial statements. Two examples of applicable financial reporting frameworks include a general purpose framework or a special purpose framework.

A **general purpose framework** is designed to meet the common financial information objectives of a wide range of users. Accounting principles generally accepted in the United States of America (GAAP) is considered a general purpose framework. General purpose frameworks include:
- GAAP, issued by the Financial Accounting Standards Board (FASB)
- International Financial Reporting Standards (IFRS), issued by the International Accounting Standards Board (IASB)
- Statements of Federal Financial Accounting Standards issued by the Federal Accounting Standards Advisory Board for U.S. federal governmental entities
- Statements of Governmental Accounting Standards issued by the Governmental Accounting Standards Board (GASB) for U.S. state and local governmental entities

A **special purpose framework** (OCBOA) is a framework other than GAAP that could include the cash basis (modified cash), tax basis, regulatory agency basis, contractual basis or an "other basis of accounting."

The auditor:
- Possesses the appropriate qualifications to perform the audit.
- Applies **professional skepticism,** an attitude that includes a questioning mind and a critical assessment of audit evidence.
- Complies with relevant ethical requirements.
- Exercises professional judgment throughout the engagement.

To express an opinion on the financial statements, the auditor obtains **reasonable assurance** as to whether the financial statements are free from material misstatement.
- Reasonable Assurance – a high level of assurance, although not equivalent to absolute assurance
    - The scope of the audit is limited to items that are considered material.
    - The auditor cannot look at evidence supporting all information in the financial statements.

To obtain reasonable assurance, the auditor:
- Plans the work
- Properly supervises assistants
- Determine and apply appropriate materiality levels
- Identify and assess risks of material misstatement
    - May be due to error or fraud
    - Based on auditor's understanding of entity and environment
- Obtain sufficient appropriate audit evidence

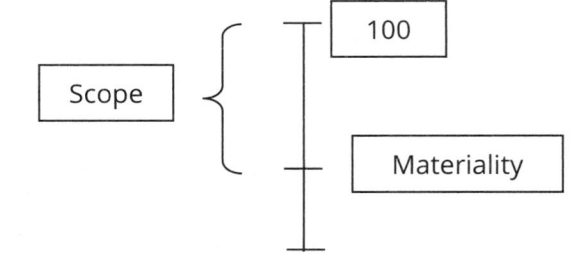

The Steps in an Audit

Prepare for → Obtain Understanding → Assess Risks of Material → Perform Tests → Perform   → Formulate → Issue
The audit   of Client, its Environment, Misstatement and Determine of Controls   Substantive   an Opinion Audit
            including Internal Control Nature, Timing & Extent   Procedures   Report
                                        of Further Procedures

Lecture 1.02

CLARITY STANDARDS

In 2009, the Auditing Standards Board (ASB) began issuing a series of standards referred to as the "clarity" standards, to make **Generally Accepted Auditing Standards** (GAAS) easier to understand and apply. These standards, effective for audits of financial statements for periods ending on or after December 15, 2012, are organized in a uniform manner. These standards were designed to do just that, clarify the auditing standards, make them easier to follow, easier to understand and to increase the convergence with International Standards on Auditing (ISA). These standards apply to audits of nonissuers (Non-public companies) and are issued by the Auditing Standards Board (ASB) of the AICPA.

In anticipation of issuing the clarity standards, the ASB issued a pronouncement that described two levels of requirements that are imposed on auditors, unconditional requirements and presumptively mandatory requirements that apply to an audit performed in accordance with GAAS.

In a standard entitled "Defining Professional Requirements in Statements on Auditing Standards", the ASB describes two types of requirements it imposes on auditors:

- An **unconditional requirement** must be complied with for the auditor to complete an engagement in accordance with GAAS. An auditor is required to comply with an unconditional requirement, which will always include the word "**must**" or the phrase "**is required to**" in every circumstance to which it applies.

- A **presumptively mandatory requirement** is one that the auditor is also expected to comply with in every circumstance to which it applies. In rare circumstances, however, the auditor may depart from a presumptively mandatory requirement if the required procedure would be ineffective, but must document how an alternate procedure was sufficient to achieve the objective of the standard (i.e., the auditor must document an explanation for **not** doing so). A presumptively mandatory requirement will always include the word "**should**."
  - o On some occasions, a standard will include an indication that the auditor **should consider a procedure**.
  - o This establishes a presumptively mandatory requirement to consider the procedure or item being referenced, but does not establish a requirement to perform the procedure.

- These terms apply for Public and Non-Public audits, as well as GAGAS audits.

The clarity project made several changes by introducing some new terminology and definitions (Applicable Financial Reporting Framework, Emphasis-of-matter, Other-matter paragraphs), new requirements (evaluate Applicable Financial Reporting Framework, apply Quality Control procedures at the engagement level) that the auditor must fulfill and some significant changes to the audit report. The clarity project also changed the **format**, with each standard including the following sections:
- Introduction
- Objectives

- Definitions
- Requirements
- Application and Other Explanatory Material

Each standard begins with an **Introduction**, which includes the purpose and scope of each standard. This tells us when the individual standards do or do not apply.

Each standard follows with an indication of the **objective** of that standard (i.e., what requirements are expected to be achieved), which the auditor uses in planning and performing the audit, considering the interrelationships within GAAS, to achieve the overall objectives of the auditor. This assists the auditor:

- In determining if audit procedures in addition to those required are necessary, which will be the case when, in the auditor's judgment, performing the required procedures will not achieve the objective
- In evaluating whether the auditor has obtained sufficient appropriate audit evidence

If audit evidence is not considered sufficient and appropriate, the auditor will determine if it is achievable to obtain sufficient appropriate audit evidence. If not, the auditor will consider the effect on the audit report. In making the determination, however, the auditor will evaluate whether sufficient appropriate audit evidence can be obtained by some combination of:

- Considering evidence obtained in achieving other objectives
- Extending work performed to comply with a requirement, such as by increasing a sample size
- Performing procedures in addition to those required

The auditor may determine that the objective of a relevant standard may not be achievable. This may prevent the auditor from achieving the overall objective of the engagement, which will lead the auditor to either modify the audit report or withdraw from the engagement when allowed under applicable law or regulation. The auditor will fail to meet an objective when:

- The auditor is prevented from complying with relevant requirements.
- The auditor is unable to apply additional audit procedures considered necessary to achieve the objective.

The inability to achieve an objective is considered a **significant finding**, which the auditor is required to document. The auditor is not required to individually document the achievement of each objective, documenting the failure to achieve an objective assists the auditor in evaluating whether the overall objectives of the audit have been achieved.

Each clarified standard next provides **definitions** of terms that are specifically related to that standard.

Each clarified standard then identifies **requirements** in a section that includes all unconditional or presumptively mandatory requirements. As indicated, the auditor is expected to comply with every requirement to achieve the objective of the standard. The only exceptions will apply when:

- An entire section of GAAS does not apply (e.g., the section on reliance on the work of internal auditors is not applicable when the client does not have an internal audit department).
- A specific requirement does not apply because the condition it is intended to provide audit evidence for, does not exist (e.g., the requirement to communicate significant deficiencies and material weaknesses in internal control does not apply when no such weaknesses exist).

The requirements may refer to **application or other explanatory material** included in a final section. This provides guidance, further explanations, and suggestions as to how to go about applying the requirements and, therefore, complying with those standards.

The clarity standards also introduced some **new terminology** and **new definitions,** such as the Applicable Financial Reporting Framework, audit report terminology (Emphasis-of-matter vs. other-matter paragraph) and Group financial audits (division of responsibility), just to mention a few.

Although the clarified standards were predominately intended to make the existing standards easier to understand and apply, they do impose some **new requirements** that the auditor will need to fulfill.

- The auditor is required, for example, **to evaluate the acceptability of the applicable financial reporting framework.** The auditor needs to:
    - ○ Evaluate the **NEEDS** of Users
    - ○ Evaluate whether the applicable framework **MEETS** those needs
    - ○ Evaluate whether it is the **MOST APPROPRIATE FRAMEWORK** under the circumstances
- Management now has 2 major responsibilities added to the audit report (discussed in detail in the Audit Reports section).
- The auditor is also required to apply Quality Control procedures at the engagement level.

There were also significant changes made to both the **form and content of the audit report,** discussed in detail in the Audit Report section.

Lecture 1.03

10 GENERALLY ACCEPTED AUDITING STANDARDS (10 GAAS)

Prior to the issuance of the clarity standards, auditors were required to apply 10 generally accepted audited standards. Under the clarity standards, the 10 GAAS were integrated into the objectives, mentioned above. The PCAOB, which has based its auditing standards on GAAS, has not adopted the clarity standards and, thus, the 10 GAAS still apply to PCAOB (Issuer) audits. In addition, the general concepts still relate to all audits, therefore, they are still important to understand in preparing for the CPA Exam.

The 10 standards are considered overall **measures of the quality** of the auditor's performance. The specific procedures needed to fulfill these standards will vary for each engagement, but the standards themselves are always the same. The GAAS standards are sorted into **three categories**:

- **General standards** – These apply to all aspects of the engagement from acceptance to completion.
- **Fieldwork standards** – These apply only to the portion of the engagement devoted to gathering evidence.
- **Reporting standards** – These apply only to the manner in which the audit report is to be written.

10 GAAS (*Measure of Quality of Auditor's performance*, versus Audit procedures which are Acts to be performed by the auditor.) **(TIPPICANOE)**

3 General Standards
Qualification of auditor and quality of work.

1. <u>T</u>raining & Proficiency
   - "The audit *must* be performed by a person or persons having **adequate technical training and proficiency** as an auditor."
     - o Proper Education in accounting
     - o Knowledge of industry & business
     - o Practical experience
     - o Continuing Professional Education (CPE)

2. <u>I</u>ndependence
   - "In all matters relating to the assignment, an **independence in mental attitude** *must* be maintained by the auditor or auditors."
     - o Ability to act with integrity and objectivity. Independence means you, your spouse, dependent kids, or dependent relatives.

3. Due <u>P</u>rofessional Care
   - **"Due professional care** *must* be exercised in the performance of the audit and the preparation of the report."
     - o **Critical review** of judgement used at every level.
     - o **Skill** and care of a prudent CPA.
       - ▪ Preparation of complete **workpapers.**
       - ▪ Operating without negligence/**Due diligence**.
       - ▪ **Professional Skepticism** – Maintaining an objective attitude during the audit.
       - ▪ Acting with Competency and Diligence.

3 Standards of Fieldwork
How audit is planned and how audit evidence is accumulated and evaluated.

1. <u>P</u>lanning and Supervision
   - "The auditor *must* **adequately plan** the work and *must* **properly supervise** any assistants."

2. <u>I</u>nternal Controls – **Rely** ↑
   - "The auditor *must* obtain a sufficient **understanding** of the entity and the **environment**, including its **internal control**, to assess the risk of material misstatement (**RMM**) of the financial statements whether due to **error or fraud**, and to design the **nature, timing, and extent** of further audit procedures."

   > **Inverse Relationship**

3. <u>C</u>orroborative Audit Evidence – **Substantive Testing** ↓
   - "The auditor *must* obtain **Sufficient Appropriate (Corroborative)** audit **Evidence** by performing **audit procedures** to afford a reasonable basis for an opinion regarding the financial statements under audit."

4 Standards of Reporting

Preparation and content of the audit report
- GAAS audit to check for GAAP.

1. <u>**A**ccounting Principles in Conformity with U.S. GAAP</u>
   - "The report *must* **state** whether the financial statements are presented in conformity with U.S. Generally Accepted Accounting Principles (GAAP)."
     - **Explicitly** stated in report.

2. <u>**N**o new Accounting Principles applied – **Consistency**</u>
   - "The report *must* indentify those circumstances in which such **principles have not been consistently observed** in the current period in relation to the preceding period."
     - Implicit

3. <u>**O**mitted Informative Disclosures – None</u>
   - "Informative disclosures in the financial statements are to be regarded as reasonably **adequate** unless otherwise stated in the report."
     - **Implicit**

4. <u>**E**xpression of an Opinion</u>
   - "The report *must* contain either an expression of **opinion** regarding the financial statements, **taken as a whole**, or an assertion to the effect that an opinion cannot be expressed. When an overall opinion cannot be expressed, the reasons therefore should be stated. In all cases where an auditor's name is associated with financial statements, the report should contain a clear-cut indication of the character of the auditor's work, if any, and the degree of responsibility the auditor is taking."
     - **Explicit**

In summary, the 10 *Generally Accepted Auditing Standards* include (**TIPPICANOE**):
> *General Standards*
>> **T**raining and Proficiency
>> **I**ndependence
>> **P**rofessional Care
> *Standards of Fieldwork*
>> **P**lanning and supervision
>> **I**nternal Controls
>> **C**orroborative Appropriate Audit Evidence
> *Reporting Standards*
>> **A**ccounting Principles in Accordance with GAAP
>> **N**o New Principles – Consistency
>> **O**mitted Disclosures – None
>> **E**xpress an Opinion

RESPONSIBILITIES OF THE AUDITOR (AU-C PREFACE)

A financial audit is an examination whose purpose is to express an opinion on the financial statements of a client. In performing such an engagement, the auditor is expected to follow generally accepted auditing standards (GAAS). These professional attestation standards are promulgated by the Auditing Standards Board (ASB). GAAS are overall **measures of the quality** of the auditor's performance. The specific procedures needed to fulfill these standards will vary for each engagement, but the standards themselves are always the same. Statements on Auditing Standards (SAS) are interpretations of GAAS issued by the Auditing Standards Board of the AICPA.

Qualification of Auditor and Quality of Work

To perform an audit, the auditor is responsible for:
- Having appropriate competence and capabilities in the form of adequate technical *training and proficiency* as an auditor.
- Complying with relevant ethical requirements, including remaining independent from the audit client.
- Maintaining professional skepticism and exercising professional judgment.

Competence and Capabilities

Auditors are responsible for having appropriate competence and capabilities to perform the audit. This is obtained through:
- Proper Education in accounting
- Knowledge of industry & business
- Practical experience
- Continuing professional education (CPE)

While education in accounting is an important component of this requirement, it is also required that the independent auditor have practical and technical experience. Junior auditors with the appropriate education are to be adequately supervised and their work sufficiently reviewed by senior auditors with suitable experience until they have gained the technical experience to work unsupervised.

Relevant Ethical Requirements

While an auditor, presumably, will comply with all of the requirements of the AICPA Code of Professional Conduct, "[t]he auditor must be independent of the entity when performing an engagement in accordance with GAAS...." "The auditor must maintain independence in mental attitude in all matters relating to the audit."
- Ability to act with integrity and objectivity.
- Independence means you, your spouse, dependent kids, and dependent relatvies.

There are circumstances under which an auditor will perform an audit *despite a lack of independence*:
- If GAAS provides for circumstances that allow the auditor to accept the engagement
- The auditor is required by law or regulation to accept the engagement

The Accountant must maintain independence for **attestation engagements (ERAS)**
- **E**xaminations (Audits)
- **R**eviews
- **A**greed-upon procedure engagements and other engagements covered by the attestation standards leading to findings

- **S**pecial reports

Need not be independent for:
- Compilations (when a lack of independence is indicated)
- Taxes
- Consultations
- Financial Statement Preparation Engagement
- Other non-attest services such as bookkeeping or payroll

> Attest Function = Must be Independent
> Independence required for:
> - Audit – Yes
> - Review – Yes
>   - Compilation – No
>   - Taxes – No
>   - Consultation – No
>   - F/S Preparation Engagement

Impair your Independence...

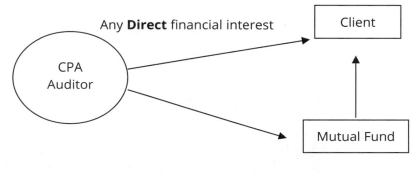

An auditor is also required to comply with those other **ethical requirements that are relevant** to financial statement audit engagements. The standards cite the fundamental principles of professional ethics, which are:
- Responsibilities (ET 0.300.020)
- The public interest (ET 0.300.030)
- Integrity (ET 0.300.040)
- Objectivity and independence (ET 0.300.050)
- Due care (ET 0.300.060)
- Scope and nature of services (ET 0.300.070)

Professional Skepticism and Professional Judgment

All engagements should be planned and performed with professional skepticism. Applying professional skepticism means being alert to information from different sources being contradictory; to the possibility that documentary evidence may not be reliable; and to indications of fraud. In addition, professional skepticism alerts the accountant that, in some circumstances, procedures beyond those required for an engagement may be necessary.

Auditing standards indicate that applying professional skepticism reduces the risks associated with:
- Overlooking unusual circumstances;
- Drawing conclusions from audit procedures that are over-generalized; and
- Making decisions regarding the nature, timing, and extent of audit procedures and evaluating the results of procedures, using inappropriate assumptions.

Auditing standards emphasize the need to apply professional judgment in the interpretation of ethical requirements and auditing standards and when making informed decisions throughout the audit. The auditor plans and performs the audit exercising a degree of professional skepticism and judgment, indicating that the auditor is aware of the possibility that the financial statements might be materially misstated and will be alert to indications, including:
- Some audit evidence may contradict other audit evidence.
- Information may raise questions as to the reliability of documentary evidence and responses to auditor inquiries.
- Conditions may indicate the possibility of fraud.
- There may be a need to apply audit procedures in addition to those required by GAAS.

The auditor applies professional judgment throughout the audit, which should be adequately documented such that an experienced auditor will understand significant judgments made in reaching conclusions. The auditor will apply professional judgment when making decisions related to:
- Materiality;
- Audit risk;
- The nature, timing, and extent of audit procedures to be applied;
- Evaluations as to whether audit evidence is appropriate and sufficient;
- The evaluation of management's judgments; and
- Drawing conclusions from the evidence obtained.

The auditor must exercise **due professional care** in the performance of the audit and the preparation of the report.
- **Critical review** of judgement used at every level.
- **Skill** and care of a prudent CPA.
  - Preparation of complete **workpapers.**
  - Operating without negligence/**Due diligence**.
  - **Professional Skepticism** – Maintaining an objective attitude during the audit.
  - Acting with **Competency and Diligence**.

Sufficient Appropriate Audit Evidence and Audit Risk

The objective of an audit is for the auditor to obtain reasonable assurance in relation to the entity's financial statements and, to do so, the auditor is required to obtain sufficient appropriate audit evidence to reduce audit risk to an acceptably low level. This enables the auditor to draw reasonable conclusions as a basis for expressing an opinion.

Conduct of an Audit in Accordance With GAAS

The AICPA Code of Professional Conduct, at ET 1.310.001, requires an accountant to comply with the professional standards that apply to the services being performed. An auditor is required to comply with all AU-C sections of GAAS that are relevant to the audit, indicated by the fact that the section is in effect and the circumstances addressed by the section exist in the engagement.

Auditing Standards versus Audit Procedures

Auditing standards differ from auditing procedures in that procedures relate to *acts* to be performed, whereas standards deal with *measures of the quality* of the auditor's performance of those acts. Materiality and relative risk underlie the application of all the standards.

Assurance services, as more broadly defined by the AICPA Special Committee on Assurance Services (also referred to as the Elliott Committee), refers to "Independent professional services that improve the quality of information, or its context, for decision makers." Another definition for assurance services, which we will cover in another section, is: an engagement in which an accountant issues a report designed to enhance the degree of confidence of third parties and management about the outcome of an evaluation or measurement of financial statements (subject matter) against an applicable financial reporting framework (criteria). Assurance services include all attestation (including audit/review) services, plus a variety of other services which will be developed in the future. Tax, compilations, compilations and consulting services are not considered assurance services.

Lecture 1.05

CLASS QUESTIONS

Please see the Class Questions and Class Solutions for this Lecture at the end of this Section.

Lecture 1.06

STEPS IN THE AUDIT PROCESS

- Qualification of the auditor & quality of work
- Competency & Capabilities
- Ethical Requirements – Independence & Due Prof care
- Skepticism & Professional Judgment
- Integrity of Management?
- Predecessor Auditor – Successor initiates conversation
- Audit Committee – Communication with
- Engagement Letter

Accepting the Engagement

The first step in planning an engagement is to decide whether to accept the engagement, which will depend on whether the **preconditions for an audit** have been met. There are *two key considerations* in making this decision:

- Determining the acceptability of the applicable financial reporting framework being applied.
- Obtaining management's agreement that it understands and accepts certain responsibilities:
  - Preparation and fair presentation of the financial statements in accordance with the applicable financial reporting framework;
    - Including all appropriate informative disclosures related to a special purpose framework when used to prepare the financial statements;
  - Design, implementation, and maintenance (DIM) of internal control relevant to reliable financial reporting that is free from material misstatement, whether due to fraud or error; and
  - Providing the auditor with access to all relevant information of which management is aware; additional information requested by the auditor; and unrestricted access to entity personnel (no client-imposed scope limit).

A scope limitation imposed by the client prior to acceptance of the engagement that would require the auditor to issue a disclaimer of opinion would generally preclude the auditor from accepting the engagement. The auditor may, but is not required to, accept the engagement in such circumstances if the entity is required to have an audit by law or regulation. The auditor would not be precluded from accepting an engagement because of a scope limitation:

- Imposed by management that will likely result in a qualified opinion; or
- Imposed by circumstances beyond management's control.

The auditor will also want to make certain that the financial statements are auditable. If the accounting records are inadequate, the auditor may not have the ability to gather sufficient appropriate audit evidence, and will have to refuse the engagement.

In addition, an auditor will not wish to associate with an entity that has management that **lacks integrity**. Management has influence over every part of the day-to-day operations of the business and the financial records, and the financial statements are, ultimately, the representation of the management. If the auditor cannot trust the key officers of the business, all evidence related to the financial statements will be subject to serious doubt. Furthermore, one of the required steps toward the end of an audit is to obtain a **client representation letter** from management on certain key items. If the auditor does not trust management, it will be impossible to place reliance on the representations, so the auditor will have to refuse the engagement.

First Year Audits (AU-C 510) (Predecessor Auditor) (Reaudit)

When an auditor accepts an engagement for an initial audit, AU-C Section 510, Opening Balances – Initial Audit Engagements, Including Reaudit Engagements, requires the auditor to pay special attention to beginning balances. An initial audit is the first audit a CPA performs for a client and may involve a variety of circumstances. The auditor may be engaged to audit:

- The financial statements of an entity that has not had its financial statements audited before;
- The financial statements of an entity that's prior year financial statements were audited by a different auditor, referred to as a predecessor, making the new auditor the successor; or
- The financial statements of an entity that had previously been audited by another auditor, referred to as a reaudit.

Beginning balances are significant for a variety of reasons.

- Beginning balance sheet amounts affect items reported on the current period's income statement, statement of cash flows, and statement of changes in stockholders' equity. A misstatement in beginning inventory, for example, will result in a misstatement in the current period's cost of goods sold.
- The auditor is required to determine if accounting principles have been applied on a basis that is consistent with the prior period. The auditor is therefore required to ascertain that the methods applied in the previous period are the same as those being applied in the current period or that changes have been appropriately accounted for and disclosed.
- Opening balances for certain items, such as contingencies and commitments may have ongoing implications that affect the current period's disclosures.

When an auditor accepts an engagement for an initial audit, the auditor will be required to obtain sufficient appropriate audit evidence regarding *opening balances*.

- The auditor will read the entity's most recent financial statements and the predecessor's report, if any, for information regarding:
  - Opening balances (account balances that existed at the beginning of the year) and disclosures (contingencies and commitments)
  - Consistency in the application of the applicable financial reporting framework
- If the prior statements were audited, the auditor should request that management authorize the predecessor to:
  - Allow the successor to review the predecessor's documentation (i.e., read most recent financial statements and the predecessor's report; if modified opinion, evaluate effect on current period financial statements)
  - Respond fully to inquiries by the successor

Once the client has authorized communication, the successor will generally make inquiries of the **predecessor auditor** about several key issues:

- **Reasons for change** – The successor needs to know why the predecessor understands that they are no longer the continuing auditor of the client.
- **Integrity of management** – The predecessor should inform the successor whether they believe management can be trusted.
- **Disagreements during audit** – If any conflicts arose regarding the application of accounting principles or the performance of auditing procedures during the time the predecessor was the auditor of the client, the predecessor should provide necessary details for the successor to understand the nature of the disagreements and how they were resolved.
- **Communication with Management or those charged with Governance**, such as the audit committee, regarding fraud and noncompliance with applicable laws and regulations, including illegal acts, and significant deficiencies and material weaknesses in internal control.

The mnemonic **RID-C** can be used to memorize the four issues to be addressed. Any one of these may cause the successor to get **rid** of the prospective new client and **C** (see) you later!!

If financial statements audited by a predecessor auditor are found to require substantial revision, it is the responsibility of the successor auditor to request that the client arrange a meeting among the three parties to discuss and attempt to resolve the matter.

The predecessor should cooperate as much as possible with the successor. If there is a legitimate reason, such as advice from the predecessor's attorney that causes the predecessor to limit their response or give no response to the successor, the successor should inform the client that the response has been limited. This may affect the decision as to whether to accept the engagement.

In addition to communication with the predecessor, the successor auditor is required to obtain sufficient appropriate audit evidence regarding *opening balances*. The auditor will:

- Determine if prior period closing balances have appropriately been brought forward to the current period;
- Evaluate the appropriateness of the accounting policies that were applied to the opening balances;
- Consider procedures performed during the current period to determine if they provide evidence regarding opening balances; and either:
    - Review the predecessor's documentation regarding opening balances, or
    - Perform specific audit procedures to obtain evidence about opening balances.

If the predecessor's report on the previous period's financial statements included a modified opinion, the successor should evaluate the effect on the current period's financial statements. During the course of the engagement, the successor may become aware of misstatements contained in opening balances that could materially affect the current period's financial statements. If the auditor concludes that the misstatements also affect the current period's financial statements, the auditor should communicate the misstatements to management and those charged with governance. In addition, if the auditor determines that, because of the misstatements, the previous period's audited financial statements may require restatement, the auditor should request that management allow communication between the successor and predecessor regarding the matter.

- The successor should provide the predecessor with whatever information the successor deems appropriate to assist the predecessor in resolving the matter.
- If the client refuses permission or if the circumstances are otherwise not resolved to the satisfaction of the successor, the successor should consider the implications in relation to the current period's audit, including whether the auditor should withdraw from the engagement.

Evidence regarding opening balances may affect the auditor's report on the current period's financial statements. If, for example, the auditor is unable to obtain sufficient appropriate audit evidence regarding opening balances, or if the auditor determines that the opening balances contain a material misstatement that is not appropriately accounted for or disclosed, the auditor will modify the report, expressing a qualified opinion or issuing a disclaimer. The auditor will also issue a qualified or adverse opinion if accounting policies have not been consistently applied or if changes in accounting principles have not been appropriately accounted for and adequately disclosed.

Recurring Audits

When the auditor is engaged for recurring audits, the auditor may determine that the terms of the preceding engagement may or may not need revision. If the terms do not need revision, the auditor should remind the client of the terms of the engagement, which may be done in writing or orally, but should be documented. Indications that the terms of the preceding engagement may need to be revised include:

- Indications that management does not understand the objective and scope of the engagement;
- Revised or special terms;
- Changes to senior management or a significant change in ownership;
- A significant change in the entity's size or the nature of its business;
- Changes to legal or regulatory requirements;
- A change in the applicable financial reporting framework; or
- A change in other reporting requirements.

Management and Those Charged with Governance (AU-C 260)

During the conduct of an audit, there are several items that the auditor is required to communicate regarding the entity. In such cases, the auditor will communicate with **those charged with governance**, which may include management.

- Members of management may serve as executive members of the board of directors.
- In owner-managed entities, management and governance are the same.

Those charged with governance may also include:

- Members of the entity's legal structure, such as company directors.
- Parties external to the entity, such as certain government agencies.
- A collective group of people, such as a Board of Directors.

Management includes those with executive responsibility for the conduct of the entity's organization. Those charged with governance are responsible for overseeing the strategic direction of the entity and the obligations related to accountability.

- In some cases, all of those charged with governance are also involved in managing the entity.
- When that is not the case, there are additional items that are communicated to those charged with governance.

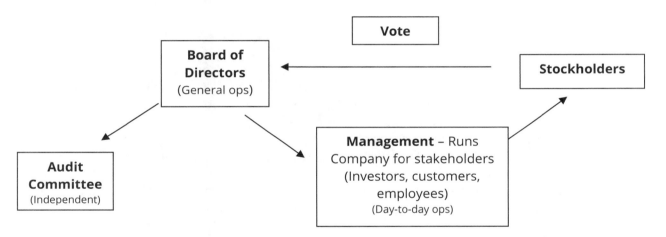

For entities with formal structures, the outside auditor meets with the **audit committee** of the board of directors, which is a sub-committee made up of board members who are not officers or employees of the company (They *must be independent*). The committee members will have no special interest in supporting the financial representations of management, and this provides them with the objectivity necessary to:

- Serve as members of the board of directors that are disinterested in the day-to-day operations (must be Independent).
- Hire and fire the outside auditors.
- Receive their reports and communications.
- Oversee the internal audit function of the company.

Nonissuers, entities that are not subject to the provisions of Sarbanes-Oxley, may not have an audit committee. When that is the case, the individuals who oversee the accounting and financial reporting processes for the entity as well as the audit are considered to be the audit committee. In some cases, this may be only one person.

The prospective auditor negotiates with the audit committee to enter the audit engagement and establish an understanding, which is required to be documented in the form of a written engagement letter or a comparable document, and may be sent to the audit committee for the client's signature.

Communication with those charged with governance is intended to promote a mutual sharing of relevant information. The objectives of establishing such communication are to provide those charged with governance with information about the auditor's responsibilities regarding the audit, including an overview of the planned scope and timing, and to obtain from those charged with governance information relevant to the audit. The auditor will also provide those charged with governance with the auditor's observations arising from the audit that may be relevant to their role in the oversight of the financial reporting process.

Certain matters should be **communicated to those charged with governance**. These communications may be oral or in writing, and may be communicated during the audit or after the audit report is issued. Matters communicated orally should be documented by the auditor. Among the matters the auditor **should** communicate are:

- **Disagreements with management** about accounting policies or audit procedures, including why the auditor believes the appropriate financial reporting framework (AFRF) being applied in the preparation of the financial statements is not the most appropriate under the circumstances.
- **Noncompliance with laws and regulations, including Illegal acts** and significant errors discovered during the audit and fraud involving senior management.
- **Significant accounting policies** adopted or changed by management.
- **Adjustments** proposed by the auditor with a significant impact on the financial statements, including adjusting journal entries (AJEs) and reclassifying journal entries (RJEs), indicating:
  - Uncorrected misstatements and their potential effect, individually and in the aggregate, on the auditor's opinion, requesting that they be corrected; and
  - The effects of uncorrected misstatements from prior periods.
- **Prior discussions with management** before acceptance of the engagement.
- **Problems or significant difficulties** arising during the audit, if any, in obtaining evidence and employee cooperation.
- **Responsibilities** of the auditor under GAAS to form and express an opinion on whether the financial statements are prepared, in all material respects, in accordance with the applicable financial reporting framework, acknowledging:
  - The financial statements have been prepared by management under the oversight of those charged with governance; and
  - Neither management nor those charged with governance are relieved of their responsibilities as a result of the audit.
- **Other information** discussed or dealt with by management when those charged with governance are not all involved in management, including:
  - Corrected misstatements brought to management's attention because of audit procedures;
  - Items discussed with, or communicated to, management regarding significant findings or issues;
  - Auditor views on accounting or auditing matters about which management consulted with other accountants; and
  - Written representations requested by the auditor.
- **Views of the accountant** regarding the qualitative aspects of the entity's significant accounting policies, estimates, and disclosures, including why the auditor might consider accounting practices that are considered acceptable not to be the most appropriate.
- **Estimates** in the accounting records and the process used to obtain them, including fair value estimates, and the basis for the auditor's conclusion about their reasonableness.

The mnemonic **DISAPPROVE** reminds us that audit committees would **disapprove** of an auditor who failed to inform them about these matters.

The auditor will also communicate other findings or issues that, in the auditor's professional judgment, are significant and relevant to those charged with governance in discharging their responsibilities related to the oversight of the financial reporting process.

Those charged with governance should be informed by the auditor as to the form, timing, and expected general content of communications, which may be oral or in writing unless the auditor does not believe that oral communication would be adequate. Any written report, however, should clearly indicate that it is intended solely for the information and use of those charged with government.
- It may also be for the information and use of management, if appropriate; and
- There should be an indication that the report is not intended for the use of anyone other than the parties specified.

There is no need to repeat matters about which "those charged with governance" were notified about in previous audits, and management need not be informed of the above matters, especially since some of the issues may involve questions of management integrity or violations of the law. Also, the auditor should not discuss the detailed audit plan or specific audit procedures with the audit committee or management, since it might reduce the effectiveness of the audit.

Independence and Financial Expertise
Under Sarbanes-Oxley (SOX), the audit committee of an issuer is required to be made up of independent directors, and at least one member of the audit committee is required to be a *financial expert*. If there is not a financial expert on the audit committee, the *reasons* must be disclosed. A **financial expert** has:
- An understanding of GAAP and financial statements
- Experience preparing or auditing comparable financial statements and experience in applying financial statement or audit knowledge to the accounting for estimates, accruals, and reserves
- Experience with internal accounting controls
- An understanding of the functions of the audit committee
  - Need not be a CPA

PCAOB (Public Company) Requirements for Communication with Those Charged With Governance

The PCAOB established requirements for matters to be communicated to those charged with governance when performing an audit of the financial statements of an entity that is subject to Sarbanes-Oxley. The auditor should discuss with the audit committee any significant issues discussed with management regarding appointment or retention of the auditor.

In addition, the auditor should establish an understanding of the terms of the engagement with the audit committee, which should be documented in an engagement letter and executed by the appropriate party on behalf of the entity. The understanding will include the objectives of the engagement, the responsibilities of the auditor, and the responsibilities of management.

In regard to the engagement itself, the auditor should inquire as to whether the audit committee is aware of relevant matters, which may include violations or possible violations of applicable laws or regulations. The auditor will also communicate an overview of the overall audit strategy and timing, as well as significant risks identified during the performance of risk assessment procedures performed in obtaining an understanding of the entity and its environment.

Communication regarding the overall strategy will include:
- Specialized skill or knowledge needed to perform risk assessments, plan or perform the engagement, or evaluate results.
- The extent to which internal auditors will be used in the engagement and to which internal auditors and other personnel will be used under the supervision of the audit committee in the audit of internal control over financial reporting.
- Information about other accounting firms expected to perform audit procedures.
- The basis for concluding that the auditor can serve as principal auditor when parts of the audit are performed by other auditors.

The auditor will also communicate the results of the audit. Matters to be communicated will include the following, as well as the auditor's evaluation of each:
- Significant accounting policies and practices
- Critical accounting policies and practices – those most significant to the entity's financial position and results, and requiring management's most difficult, subjective, or complex judgments
- Critical accounting estimates
- Significant unusual transactions

In addition to the auditor's evaluation of each of the items above, the communication will also include the auditor's evaluation of:
- The financial statement presentation and related disclosures
- New accounting pronouncements with a potential future effect on the entity's financial statements
- Alternative accounting treatments discussed with management

Other matters to be communicated include:
- The auditor's responsibilities for other information in documents containing the audited financial statements
- Difficult or contentious matters for which the auditor sought outside consultation
- Going concern issues
- Uncorrected and corrected mistakes
- Material written communications provided to management
- Modifications to the audit report
- Disagreements with management
- Difficulties in performing the audit

Unlike the communication under GAAS, the auditor is required to submit the communication to those charged with governance prior to issuance of the auditor's report.

Engagement Letter (FACSIMILE)

The auditor is **required** to agree upon the terms of the engagement with the client. The agreement may be with management or with those charged with governance, whichever is appropriate based on the structure of the entity. The auditor is required to obtain management's agreement that it understands and acknowledges its responsibilities, regardless of whether the auditor contracts with management, exclusively with those charged with governance, or exclusively with a third party.

Once the auditor has made the decision to accept the engagement, the auditor is required to send a **written engagement letter** or a comparable written agreement to the client. In it, the auditor will confirm the scope and nature of the engagement and the responsibilities of the various parties. The engagement letter is signed by both the client and the auditor.

The **auditor's** responsibilities include:
- Conducting an audit in accordance with GAAS (this doesn't guarantee that errors and fraud will be detected)
- Informing the client of improvements in control or economy of operations that come to the auditor's attention during the engagement

The **client's** responsibilities include:
- Making available all records
- Not limiting the scope of the auditor's work
- Paying the fee based on the agreed-upon method

The written understanding with the client will also include:
- A statement that, due to the inherent limitations of an audit and internal control, material misstatements may not be detected
- Identification of the applicable financial reporting framework (AFRF)
- Reference to the expected form and content of the report with an indication that the actual report may differ

The auditor is required to establish an understanding with the client and document it through a written communication with the client. This communication is required and is *recommended* to be in the form of an engagement letter or other suitable form, as this reduces the risk of miscommunications between the parties. The understanding includes the following sections:
- Objective and scope of the audit
- *Responsibilities of the Auditor*
- Responsibilities of management
- An indication that, even though the audit is properly planned and performed in accordance with GAAS, there is an unavoidable risk that some material misstatements may not be detected due to the *inherent limitations* of an audit and the inherent limitations of internal control
- The identification of the applicable financial reporting framework
- The expected form and content of any report expected to be issued, accompanied by an indication that circumstances may require the report to differ in form and content
- Other relevant information
- Reporting – expected form and content

Other matters may be referred to in the engagement letter, such as:
- Further elaboration of the scope of the audit
- Communication of the results of the engagement in addition to the audit report
- Matters related to the planning and performance of the engagement, such as the composition of the engagement team
- The anticipation that management will provide written representations
- Management's agreement to provide information on a timely basis to enable the timely completion of the engagement
- Management's agreement to inform the auditor of subsequent events and subsequently discovered facts relevant to the financial statements
- Fees and billing arrangements
- A request for management's acknowledgment, evidenced by their signature on the engagement letter, of receipt of the engagement letter and agreement to its terms

When appropriate, the engagement letter may also include reference to:
- The involvement of other auditors and specialists
- The involvement of internal auditors and other entity staff
- In an initial audit, arrangements to be made with the predecessor
- Restrictions, if any, on the auditor's liability
- The auditor's obligations, if any, to provide audit documentation to other parties
- Additional services to be provided by the auditor
- Any further agreements between the auditor and the entity

The mnemonic **FACSIMILE** can be used to illustrate the elements of the engagement letter.

Fees

Auditor's responsibility (GAAS)

Confirmation of Engagement

Scope & Objective of Engagement (Stmts auditing and obj is an opinion on F/S)

Internal Control (Comm. significant deficiencies and Material weaknesses in I/C)

Management's Responsibility (Prep and fair pres of F/S, Design, Implementation & Maintenance (DIM) of I/C and access to info)

Irregularities - Fraud

i**L**Legal acts – Noncompliance with applicable laws and regulations

Errors

Engagement Letter

Mr. John Apple,
Chairman of the Audit Committee
Budget Co.
555 State Street
San Francisco, California 94133

Dear Mr. Apple,

(Objective and Scope of the Audit)

You have requested that we audit the financial statements of Budget Co., which comprise the balance sheet as of December 31, 20XX, and the related statements of income, changes in stockholders' equity, and cash flows for the year then ended, and the related notes to the financial statements. We are pleased to confirm our acceptance and our understanding of this audit engagement by means of this letter. Our audit will be conducted with the objective of our expressing an opinion on the financial statements.

(Responsibilities of the Auditor)

We will conduct our audit in accordance with auditing standards generally accepted in the United States of America (GAAS). Those standards require that we plan and perform the audit to obtain reasonable assurance about whether the financial statements are free from material misstatement. An audit involves performing procedures to obtain audit evidence about the amounts and disclosures in the financial statements. The procedures selected depend on the auditor's judgment, including the assessment of the risks of material misstatement of the financial statements, whether due to **fraud or error**. An audit also includes evaluating the appropriateness of accounting policies used and the reasonableness of significant accounting estimates made by management, as well as evaluating the overall presentation of the financial statements.

Because of the **inherent limitations** of an audit, together with the inherent limitations of internal control, an unavoidable risk that some material misstatements may not be detected exists, even though the audit is properly planned and performed in accordance with GAAS.

In making our risk assessments, we consider **internal control** relevant to the entity's preparation and fair presentation of the financial statements in order to design audit procedures that are appropriate in the circumstances but not for the purpose of expressing an opinion on the effectiveness of the entity's internal control. However, we will communicate to you in writing concerning any significant deficiencies or material weaknesses in internal control relevant to the audit of the financial statements that we have identified during the audit.

(Responsibilities of Management and Identification of the Applicable Financial Reporting Framework)

Our audit will be conducted on the basis that management acknowledges and understands that they have responsibility:

a. for the preparation and fair presentation of the financial statements in accordance with accounting principles generally accepted in the United States of America;
b. for the design, implementation, and maintenance (DIM) of internal control relevant to the preparation and fair presentation of financial statements that are free from material misstatement, whether due to fraud or error; and
c. to provide us with
    I.   access to all information of which management is aware that is relevant to the preparation and fair presentation of the financial statements such as records, documentation, and other matters;
    II. additional information that we may request from management for the purpose of the audit; and
    III. unrestricted access to persons within the entity from whom we determine it necessary to obtain audit evidence.

As part of our audit process, we will request from management, written confirmation concerning representations made to us in connection with the audit.

(Other Relevant Information)

We will provide you with a **list of schedules** and information needed by our staff during the audit. It is our mutual understanding that in order to meet the audit deadlines, which we have established; your staff will provide that necessary information on a timely basis.
The **fees** for our services will be at our regular per diem rates plus out-of-pocket expenses. Invoices are payable upon presentation.

(Reporting)

We will issue a written report upon completion of our audit of Budget Co.'s financial statements. Our report will be addressed to the board of directors of Budget Co. We cannot provide assurance that an unmodified opinion will be expressed. Circumstances may arise in which it is necessary for us to modify our opinion, add an emphasis-of-matter or other-matter paragraph(s), or withdraw from the engagement.

Please sign and return the attached copy of this letter to indicate your acknowledgment of, and agreement with, the arrangements for our audit of the financial statements including our respective responsibilities.

Sincerely, Roger *Philipp*
Partner
Roger Philipp

Acknowledged and agreed on behalf of Budget Co. by

_____

(Signed)
(Name and Title)
(Date)

The auditor should **not** discuss in detail the audit procedures that will be performed, partly because these procedures will vary depending on the evidence obtained during the engagement, and partly because the effectiveness of many procedures depends on the client not knowing in advance what specific evidence will be examined.

Lecture 1.08

CLASS QUESTIONS

Please see the Class Questions and Class Solutions for this Lecture at the end of this Section.

Lecture 1.09

ENGAGEMENT PLANNING PROCEDURES

Audit planning involves developing an overall strategy for the expected conduct and scope of the audit. The engagement partner and other key members of the engagement team should be involved in the planning of the audit. The engagement team plans the audit to be responsive to the assessment of the risk of material misstatement based on the auditor's understanding of the entity and its environment, including its internal control. The nature, extent and timing of planning will vary with:

- The size and complexity of the entity
- The auditor's experience with the entity
- Knowledge of the entity's business and industry
- Knowledge of the entity and its environment, including internal control

Early appointment of the auditor is preferred and advantageous as it allows the auditor to plan the audit prior to the balance-sheet date; however, an auditor may be appointed at or near year-end as well.

At the beginning of the audit engagement, the auditor will perform **preliminary engagement activities**, including:

- Procedures regarding *acceptance and continuance* of the client relationship and the engagement;
- Evaluation of compliance with relevant *ethical requirements*; and
- Establishing an understanding with the client, documented in the form of an *engagement letter*.

The auditor's **planning activities**, applied in developing the overall strategy, include:

- Identifying characteristics of the engagement that affect the scope of the audit;
- Determining the reporting objectives to plan the nature and timing of communications;
- Considering other factors that the auditor deems significant to the direction of the audit;
- Considering the preliminary activities and relevant knowledge gained from other engagements; and
- Ascertaining the nature, timing, and extent of resources needed to perform the engagement.

The development of a detailed audit plan, including **audit programs**, is required in order to achieve the objectives of the audit. The program ensures that the auditor applies the necessary procedures to verify the financial statement assertions for account balances, classes of transactions, and presentation and disclosure, and to provide support for the auditor's opinion. The plan will include a description of:

- The nature and extent of the risk assessment procedures that are planned to be performed in obtaining an understanding of the entity and its environment and assessing the risks of material misstatement;
- The nature, timing, and extent of further audit procedures determined to be required at the assertion level in response to assessed risks and to the evaluation of audit evidence obtained; and
- Other procedures that are planned to be carried out in order for the engagement to be in compliance with GAAS.

Audit programs are often designed using information from prior engagements or templates, including checklist systems developed by commercial providers, or some combination of the two. Regardless of whether audit programs are developed from prior period programs or from templates, the process requires the consideration of various factors. For example, when developing audit programs from those of the *prior period*:

- The auditor will consider which procedures are required by GAAS to be performed on every engagement.
- The auditor will identify areas that represent more or less risk than in the prior period based on information gathered about the client and its industry during the period.
- The auditor will make certain that the programs are dissimilar enough to avoid the approach being predictable, allowing the client to negate the effectiveness of some aspects of the audit.

When audit programs are developed using templates, the process generally involves the elimination of procedures from the template. Templates and checklists tend to be thorough, taking into account as many circumstances that may affect the audit that the template developer can identify. As a result, the auditor's challenge will be to determine which procedures can be eliminated because they are redundant or unnecessary, improving the efficiency of the engagement, without adversely affecting its effectiveness.

The audit program prepared during early planning should include a list of substantive tests that are planned to be performed later in the engagement; therefore, it is necessary for the auditor to estimate the level at which they'll be assessing RMM.

- This preliminary assessment of RMM is usually based on prior experience with the client or the audits of predecessors.
- The final assessment of RMM won't take place until the auditor gains an understanding of the client and its environment, including its internal control structure.
- If this is different from the preliminary assessment, the audit program will have to be *modified* to increase or decrease the amount of substantive testing to be performed.

As the auditor performs risk assessment procedures, used in obtaining an understanding of the entity and its environment, including its internal controls, the auditor may decide to place a higher or lower reliance on internal controls.

- A *higher reliance* will involve performing tests of controls and, if controls prove to be effective, a reduction in the nature, timing, and extent of further audit procedures to be performed (Rely ↑ Sub ↓).
- A *lower reliance* will mean that the auditor will not perform tests of controls and will enhance the nature, timing, and extent of further audit procedures to be performed (Rely ↓ Sub ↑).

The auditor will also prepare a *time budget* for the engagement. This is accomplished by estimating the amount of time each step in the audit program is expected to require, including time for review and for the engagement team to respond to review comments. The time budget is one means the auditor has of communicating to staff the areas that are perceived to represent the highest risk as these are areas that will generally have the most extensive procedures and will be allocated the most time.

Other factors that will be considered will be the extent to which the auditor will require direct assistance from the client. This will include procedures that the auditor intends to request client personnel to perform or assist in the performance of. It will generally also include a preliminary list of documents that the auditor will be requesting from the client.

Audit Program/Audit Plan

An audit program is a step-by-step list of audit procedures, which is *required* for every GAAS audit. It is designed so that:

- The procedures will achieve specific audit objectives, which relate to management's assertions.
- It supports the auditor's conclusion.
- It describes the nature, timing, and extent of:
    - Risk assessment procedures sufficient to assess the risks of material misstatement (RMM).
    - Further audit procedures at the relevant assertion level for each material class of transactions, account balance, and disclosure.
    - Other procedures to be performed to comply with GAAS.

There are several key considerations in the **development of the audit program**:
- **Materiality**
- **Risk of Material Misstatement (RMM)**
- **Business and Industry considerations**

Materiality

When the auditor expresses an opinion regarding the fair presentation of the financial statements in accordance with the applicable financial reporting framework, it is based on whether the financial statements contain a **material misstatement** that will influence users, or the financial statements are materially misstated as a whole. To express such an opinion, the auditor is required to have an understanding of what is, or is not, material and to establish quantitative measures of what would be considered material in various circumstances.

AU-C 320, Materiality in Planning and Performing an Audit, indicates that the concept of **materiality** is often incorporated in the principles underlying a financial reporting framework in the context of the preparation and fair presentation of the financial statements. The discussion of materiality generally indicates:

- Misstatements and omissions are considered material if they are expected to, individually or in the aggregate, **influence the decisions a user** will make based on the financial statements.
- Surrounding circumstances are considered, including the size and nature of misstatements, in making judgments about materiality.
- Judgments about materiality consider users of financial statements as a group rather than the effects of misstatements on individual users.

The auditor's measurement of materiality is a matter of *professional judgment*, taking into account the anticipated needs of financial statement users. It is applied in the planning of the engagement as well as its performance. The auditor will apply the concept of materiality in:

- Deciding upon the risk assessment procedures to be performed in obtaining an understanding of the entity, its environment, and its internal control;
- Assessing the risks of material misstatement;
- Determining the nature, timing, and extent of further audit procedures; and
- Evaluating identified misstatements in the performance of the engagement and the effects of uncorrected misstatements on the financial statements.

In planning the engagement, the auditor determines materiality in relation to the financial statements, which will be used to determine if the financial statements, taken as a whole, are materially misstated. In addition, separate lower materiality levels may be established for specific classes of transactions, account balances, or disclosures. This would be the case when a misstatement to one of those items that is lower than the materiality level designated for the financial statements, taken as a whole, would influence users of the financial statements.

Materiality is often measured by applying a percentage to some benchmark. Common benchmarks include categories of income, including profit before tax, total revenue, gross profit, or total expenses; total equity; or assets. The selection of an appropriate benchmark will be influenced by a variety of factors, such as:

- The make-up of the elements of the financial statements;
- Items on the financial statements that are expected to be of particular interest to the users;
- The nature of the entity, including its level of maturity, its industry, and the economic environment in which it operates;
- The entity's ownership and organizational structure;
- How the entity is financed; and
- The volatility of the benchmark.

The percentage to be applied to the benchmark is a matter of professional judgement and will take into account the nature of the benchmark. A higher percentage, for example, would be applied to a benchmark based on earnings, such as profit before taxes or gross profit, than would be applied to an item like total revenues.

The auditor must make a preliminary determination of the materiality level, meaning the dollar amount by which financial information can be misstated without the financial statements being considered materially misstated, which would preclude the issuance of an unmodified opinion.

When the materiality level is different for the various financial statements, the **smallest aggregate** dollar amount will be selected. For example, if the materiality level is identified as $10 million on the balance sheet and $3 million on the income statement, the auditor will consider items in the audit to be material if they individually or collectively could result in a misstatement of $3 million or more.

- The auditor plans the audit to obtain **Reasonable Assurance** of detecting misstatements that could be large enough, individually or in the aggregate, to be material to the financial statements.
    - o Materiality is based on Auditor's judgment.
    - o Materiality judgments involve both *Quantitative and Qualitative* considerations.
    - o For planning purposes, materiality is measured using the *smallest aggregate level*.
    - o There is an *inverse relationship* between *audit risk* and the *materiality* consideration.
        - ▪ Assessment of risk as low indicates that an item is less likely to influence users of the financial statements and, thus, a larger misstatement to such an

item will have less effect than a smaller misstatement on a more sensitive
item. Therefore, when risk is low, materiality can be set at a higher level.

- Assessment of risk as high indicates that an item is more likely to influence
  users of the financial statements and, thus, a small misstatement to such an
  item will have a greater impact on users than a larger misstatement on a less
  sensitive item. Therefore, when risk is high, materiality would be set at a low
  level, such that a small misstatement would potentially be considered
  material.

The auditor also determines *performance materiality*, which takes into account that a misstatement
that is not material when considered in relation to the financial statements taken as a whole may
reach that level of materiality when combined with other identified misstatements. As a result,
performance materiality (also referred to as the *tolerable misstatement*) is lower than materiality at
the financial statement level. It is estimated at an amount such that it is probable that the aggregate
of uncorrected and undetected misstatements will not reach the level of financial statement
materiality, causing the financial statements to be materially misstated as a whole.

During the engagement, the auditor may become aware of issues that will change the measurement
of materiality. If, for example, materiality was measured as a percentage of sales and, as a result of
audit procedures applied, the auditor determines that sales were overstated, the auditor will
propose an adjustment to materiality accordingly.

- The decrease in the benchmark will result in a decrease in the measurement of what is
  material.
- This may also result in a decrease to the materiality level assigned to one or more specific
  classes of transactions, account balances, or disclosures.
- Previously identified misstatements that were not considered material may have to be
  reevaluated in relation to the reduced measurement.

If materiality was to be measured at 5% of sales, for example, and the client's trial balance indicated
sales of $5,000,000, a misstatement under $250,000 would not be considered material. A proposed
adjustment reducing sales to $4,500,000 as a result of the overstatement detected by the audit
procedure would reduce the measurement of materiality to $225,000. As a result, a misstatement
between $225,000 and $250,000, which would previously have been considered immaterial, would
now be considered material.

As a result, whenever the auditor proposes an adjustment that would reduce the balance used as
the basis for materiality, misstatements that were originally considered immaterial should be reevaluated to make certain they are still immaterial considering the reduced measurement.

The auditor is required to document:

- Materiality for the financial statements taken as a whole;
- Materiality for specific classes of transactions, account balances, or disclosures, if
  appropriate;
- Performance materiality; and
- Revisions to any of the materiality measurements occurring during the engagement.

Auditors of issuers are required to perform their engagements in accordance with auditing
standards issued by the PCAOB, which include requirements as to how materiality affects the audits
of issuers.

Similar to GAAS, the auditor is required to establish materiality levels for the financial statements as a whole and for particular accounts or disclosures, as well as determining the tolerable misstatement. In addition, similar to GAAS, the auditor is required to reevaluate materiality levels as the audit progresses.

Risk of Material Misstatement – RMM (Control risk & Inherent risk) – The auditor must also make a preliminary assessment of the RMM (the likelihood that the financial statements are materially misstated, which consists of both control risk and inherent risk).
- Inherent risk (IR) is the risk of a material misstatement due to the nature of an element of the financial statements.
- Control risk (CR) is the risk that a material misstatement will not be prevented or detected and corrected on a timely basis due to a lack of effective internal controls.

RMM is considered at the financial statement level as well as at the account balance, class of transaction, and disclosure levels. It is assessed in order to determine the acceptable level of detection risk (DR), which is the risk that a material misstatement will not be detected by the auditor.
- Detection risk is used to determine the amount and types of substantive testing performed by the auditor with the goal of reducing detection risk to an acceptable level. The higher the RMM, the lower the auditor will wish to reduce detection risk.

The audit program prepared during early planning should include a list of substantive tests that are planned to be performed later in the engagement. Therefore, it is necessary for the auditor to estimate the level at which they'll be assessing RMM.
- This preliminary assessment of RMM is usually based on prior experience with the client or the audits of predecessors.
- The final assessment of RMM won't take place until the auditor gains an understanding of the client and its environment, including its internal control structure. If this is different from the preliminary assessment, the audit program will have to be modified to increase or decrease the amount of substantive testing to be performed.

Business and industry – Different businesses have different types of transactions, regulatory environments, accounting policies, and systems of accounting and record keeping, each of which will affect the audit program. Specialized audit manuals developed by the AICPA can provide guidance in developing audit programs meeting the unique requirements of certain industries. In addition, AICPA Accounting Trends and Techniques, an annual publication summarizing disclosures of 600 industrial and merchandising corporations, is a useful source of information when evaluating disclosures.

Planning Considerations

In planning the audit, the auditor should consider:
- The entity's accounting policies and procedures;
- Materiality levels;
- Audit risk and, specifically, the planned assessed level of Risk of Material Misstatements (RMM);
- Matters relating to the entity's business and the industry in which it operates to understand the events and transactions that may have an effect on the client's financial statements;
- The methods used to process accounting information, which influences the design of internal control;
- Financial statement items likely to require adjustment;
- Conditions that may require extension or modification of audit tests; and

- The nature of reports expected to be issued.

The **steps in Planning** an audit include (*Planning Procedures*):
1. **Basic discussions with the client** about the nature of the engagement and the client's business and industry are performed first. In addition, the auditor meets the key employees, or new employees of a continuing client. The overall audit strategy or the timing of the audit may be discussed, but the specific audit procedures should not be.
2. **Review of audit documentation** from previous audits performed by the accounting firm or a predecessor auditor (if the latter makes audit documentation available) will assist in developing an outline of the audit program.
3. **Ask about recent developments** in the company, such as mergers and new product lines, which will cause the audit to differ from earlier years.
4. **Interim financial statements** are analyzed to identify accounts and transactions that differ from expectations (based on factors such as budgets or prior periods). The performance of **analytical procedures** is **mandatory** in the planning of an audit to identify accounts that may be misstated and that deserve special emphasis in the audit program.
5. **Non-audit personnel** of the accounting firm who have provided services (such as tax preparation) to the client should be identified and consulted to learn more about the client.
6. **Staffing** for the audit should be determined and a meeting held to discuss the engagement.
7. **Timing** of the various audit procedures should be determined. For example, internal control testing needs to be performed early in the engagement, inventory counts need to be performed at or near the balance sheet date, and the client representation letter cannot be obtained until the end of the audit fieldwork.
8. **Outside assistance** needs should be determined, including the use of a **specialist** as required (e.g., a tax practitioner, an appraiser for special valuation issues, or an information technology [IT] professional) and the determination of the extent of involvement of the internal auditors of the client.
9. **Pronouncements** reflecting changes in accounting principles and audit standards should be read or reviewed to assist in the development of complete audit programs fitting the unique needs of the client's business and industry.
10. **Scheduling with the client** is needed to coordinate activities. For example, client-prepared schedules need to be ready when the auditor expects to examine them, and the client needs to be informed of dates when they will be prohibited from accessing bank safe deposit boxes to ensure the integrity of counts of securities held at banks.

The mnemonic **BRAINSTOPS** reminds you that an auditor's **brain stops** if they don't plan out the audit carefully before beginning the detailed testing of client records.

The auditor should document the planning of the engagement, including:
- The overall strategy for the audit;
- The audit plan; and
- Any significant changes made to either the overall strategy or the audit plan during the audit engagement, along with the reasons for the changes.

Supervision

The auditor with final responsibility for the audit is responsible for planning the nature, extent and timing of direction and the supervision of assistants—i.e., firm personnel other than the auditor with final responsibility.

- The auditor with final responsibility for the audit may delegate portions of the planning and supervision of the audit to other *firm personnel*. The auditor provides the written audit program and instructions to the assistants.
- Supervision involves directing assistants in accomplishing the audit objectives and subsequently determining whether those objectives were accomplished. Supervision includes:
  - o Instructing assistants.
  - o Reviewing the work performed.
  - o Dealing with differences of opinion among firm personnel.
    - Differences may not be resolved to the satisfaction of all parties.
    - Dissenting parties should document the difference and ask to be disassociated from the matter's resolution.

In some cases, the auditor will determine that specialized skills are needed in the performance of the audit. To seek the assistance of a professional having those skills, who may be on the auditor's staff or who may be external to the auditor's firm, the auditor should have sufficient knowledge to:
- Communicate the objectives of the other professional's work;
- Evaluate whether the procedures performed by the other professional fulfill the auditor's objectives; and
- Evaluate the results.

Lecture 1.10

CLASS QUESTIONS

Please see the Class Questions and Class Solutions for this Lecture at the end of this Section.

Lecture 1.11

AUDIT RISK (AU-C 200)

The **risk** that the auditor may unknowingly **fail to** appropriately **modify the opinion** on financial statements that are **materially misstated**. This is the risk that material errors, fraud, or acts of noncompliance with laws and regulations, including Illegal acts, may cause the financial statements to be materially misstated, and that the auditor will not detect or properly understand them, resulting in the issuance of an inappropriate report. Throughout the engagement, the auditor should carefully consider the issue of audit risk.

Audit risk (AR) is a function of the risk that relevant assertions in the financial statements are materially misstated (RMM) and the risk that the auditor will not detect such material misstatements (DR). Audit risk is the product of two different component risks:
- **Risk of Material Misstatements (RMM)** is the risk that the relevant assertions related to account balances, classes of transactions, or disclosures contain misstatements that could be material to the financial statements when aggregated with other misstatements. (Consists of *Inherent risk (IR)* and *Control risk (CR)*).
  - o **Inherent risk (IR)** – The risk that a material misstatement of an assertion will occur in the absence of any internal controls. This risk is a function of the susceptibility of the various items to being misstated, and cannot be affected by the actions of either the client or auditor. For example, cash is more susceptible to theft than PP&E.
  - o **Control risk (CR)** – The risk that the client's *internal control* structure will fail to prevent or detect and correct a material misstatement on a timely basis. This is a

function of the effort put forth by the client's management to safeguard assets and ensure reliable financial records. As a result, it is affected by the actions of the client but not the auditor.

- **Detection risk (DR)** – The risk that audit procedures will incorrectly lead to a conclusion that a material misstatement does not exist in an account balance when, in fact, such a misstatement does exist. This is a function of the effort put forth by the auditor in performing tests of details of transactions and accounts, and analytical procedures. It is the only risk component that the auditor can affect. It is the risk that the **Auditor** will not detect a misstatement that exists in a relevant F/S assertion. DR can be broken down into its two components:
  - *Test of details risk* **(TD)**
  - *Substantive analytical procedures risk* **(AP)**

Failure of the audit can occur only when the two component risk events occur together. If no misstatement takes place, there is nothing to prevent or detect. If it occurs but is detected by the client's internal control structure, then there is nothing for the auditor to detect. If the misstatement occurs and is not prevented or detected by the client, but the auditor detects it through substantive testing, there will be no misstatement in the financial statements. Only if the misstatement occurs, the client fails to detect it, and the auditor fails to detect it, will audit risk manifest itself in the form of misstated financial statements and the issuance of an inappropriately unmodified opinion.

Audit risk and its two component risks can be expressed non-quantitatively, but the relationship between them is easier to understand when expressed mathematically:

Audit Risk = Inherent Risk × Control Risk × Detection Risk

$$AR = [RMM (IR \times CR) \times DR] \quad \text{or} \quad AR = (IR \times CR) \times (TD \times AP)$$

Acceptable DR = AR / (RMM)

Rely $\downarrow$ RMM $\uparrow$ DR $\downarrow$ SUB $\uparrow$
Rely $\uparrow$ RMM $\downarrow$ DR $\uparrow$ SUB $\downarrow$

Detection risk should bear an inverse relationship to Risk of Material Misstatement (IR × CR). The greater the risk of material misstatement the auditor believes exists, the less the detection risk that can be accepted and vice versa. Regardless of the RMM, however, the auditor should perform substantive procedures for all relevant assertions related to all material classes of transactions, account balances, and disclosures.

Inherent risk and control risk (RMM) differ from detection risk in that they exist independently of the audit, whereas detection risk relates to the auditor's procedures and can be altered by adjusting the nature, timing, and extent of substantive procedures. Thus, the auditor performs the following procedures:

- Determine the acceptable level of audit risk, the risk that the auditor is willing to take, incorporating cost and benefit considerations, that a material misstatement may not be detected by the audit
- Assess the risk of material misstatement by evaluating the inherent risk associated with financial statement elements and assessing control risk based on the auditor's understanding of internal control
- Determine the level of detection risk that is necessary to achieve the desired audit risk

Using the model described above, assume the auditor decides an audit risk of 6% is acceptable, indicating that the auditor is willing to accept that there will be a 6% probability that a material misstatement that would cause the auditor to modify the report will not be detected in the audit.

- The financial statements include assets that are highly susceptible to theft, others that require significant estimates requiring high levels of judgment to determine their carrying values, and other items that are complex or involve very high volumes of transactions.
  - o As a result, the auditor would assess inherent risk as relatively high.
  - o Assume a value of 75%, indicating that there is a 75% probability that the financial statements will be materially misstated if internal controls do not prevent or detect the misstatement and if the auditor does not detect it.

The client has established potentially effective internal controls in some key areas but they are not universal throughout the organization or the processes relevant to financial reporting.

- As a result, the auditor may assess control risk below maximum.
- Assume a value of 80%, indicating that, if a material misstatement does occur, there is an 80% probability that it will neither be prevented nor detected and corrected on a timely basis.
  - o In order to assess control risk below maximum (100%), the auditor is required to perform tests of controls to obtain evidence that the controls that are being relied upon are in place and being executed as designed.
  - o In many cases, the auditor will set control risk at maximum, despite the potential for some effective controls, if the auditor determines it is likely to be more efficient to ignore controls and perform substantive tests that will support a lower detection risk.

Based on an inherent risk of 75% and a control risk of 80%, RMM is 60% (75% × 80%). To achieve an audit risk of 6%, detection risk must be reduced to 10%.

$$RMM = IR \times CR = 75\% \times 80\% = 60\%$$

$$AR = RMM \times DR = 60\% \times 10\% = 6\%$$

Detection risk is a function of the nature, timing, and extent of audit procedures, and, as such, may be changed by the auditor.

The components of the audit risk model may be assessed in quantitative terms, such as percentages, or in non-quantitative terms such as *high, medium,* or *low* risk. The auditor may make a combined assessment of inherent risk and control risk or separate assessments of inherent risk and control risk. Although, the assessment of risk of material misstatement is a matter of professional judgment rather than a precise measurement of risk, the auditor should have an appropriate basis for that assessment. This basis may be obtained through risk assessment procedures performed to obtain an understanding of the entity and its environment, including its internal control, and through the performance of test of controls. There is an inverse relationship between Audit Risk and Materiality.

Fraud and Errors (AU-C 240)

The auditor has specific responsibilities in relation to the detection of **fraud and errors.** The *auditor's responsibility* is to plan and perform the audit to obtain **reasonable assurance** that **no errors or acts of fraud** have caused the financial statements to be **materially misstated**.

A misstatement may refer to any of the following:
- A difference between the amount, classification, or presentation of a reported financial statement element, account, or item and the amount, classification, or presentation that would have been reported under GAAP.
- The omission of a financial statement element, account, or item.
- A financial statement disclosure that is not presented in accordance with GAAP.
- The omission of information required to be disclosed in accordance with GAAP.

Misstatements should not just be evaluated *quantitatively*, but *qualitatively*, such as:
- Misstatements that affect trends of profitability.
- Misstatements that change losses into income.
- Misstatements that affect segment information.
- Misstatements that affect compliance with legal and contractual requirements.

The use of estimates in accounting increases the risk of material misstatements. Because estimates require the application of judgment:
- They are subject to human error.
- They are susceptible to manipulation, resulting in fraudulent financial reporting.

The auditor generally examines samples as a basis for drawing conclusions about a population. Misstatements that are detected in a sample often indicate that comparable misstatements may be present proportionately within the population, implying a likely proportional misstatement of the population.

Material misstatements in the financial statements can result from *errors*, meaning unintentional mistakes, or *fraud*, meaning intentional misbehavior, and both may be *known or likely*.
- **Errors**
  - Unintentional mistakes, misjudgments or omissions of amounts or disclosures.
  - May be due to human error or the incompetency of employees.

- **Two types of fraud (Intentional Acts):**
  Fraud – an intentional act by one or more individuals among management, those charged with governance, employees, or third parties involving the use of deception that results in a misstatement in financial statements that are the subject of an audit.

- **Fraudulent financial reporting** (management fraud, or "cooking the books") – Misrepresentation of facts – Integrity of management.
  - Manipulation, falsification, alteration of accounting records or supporting documents. Inability to produce or locate relevant documents may also be indicative of fraud.
  - Misrepresentation or omission of events, transactions or information.
  - Intentional misapplication of accounting principles.
  - The non-recording of transactions.

- **Misappropriation of assets** – *Defalcation* schemes
  - Embezzlement of funds
  - Theft of other assets
  - Misuse of entity assets

- An auditor evaluates two types of misstatements resulting from errors or fraud. They are *known* or *likely*.
  - **Known misstatements** are misstatements specifically identified during the audit
  - **Likely misstatements** are misstatements that have not been specifically identified, but are considered likely to exist based on audit evidence obtained or due to a difference between management and auditor judgments.
    - Likely misstatements may be based on the assumption that known misstatements identified in a sample are proportionately present in the population.
    - They may be based on the auditor's knowledge of the entity, its industry, or its environment and a disparity with information presented in the financial statements.

The auditor must **communicate** all *known* and *likely* misstatements (even immaterial), identified during the audit, other than those the auditor believes are trivial, to the *appropriate level of management* on a timely basis.
  - Management must correct all known misstatements and should evaluate items for which there are likely misstatements.

The auditor is required to communicate all knowledge or suspicion of fraud to management and/or governance, although the auditor is required to communicate with governance when senior management is involved in the fraud. The communication may be oral or in writing, but should be documented by the auditor. The auditor may want to consult with legal counsel.

Although the auditor cannot ultimately be held responsible for the detection of fraud, the auditor is expected to recognize the possibility that it may occur and that it may result in a material misstatement to the financial statements. In considering fraud while planning an audit, the auditor will consider **three conditions** that are generally assumed to be present whenever a successful fraud occurs, referred to as the **fraud triangle** (below):
- **Reason or Motivation (Incentive/pressure)** – the perpetrator will generally have a reason for having committed the fraud.
  - Personal gain is the most common reason (Incentives).
  - Pressure, such as to meet analysts' expectations, is another common reason.

- **Opportunity** – the perpetrator must have the ability to commit the fraudulent act.
  - A lack of internal controls or internal controls that are not being enforced create opportunity.

- o Some perpetrators have the opportunity because of the authority to override controls or the ability to circumvent controls, such as through collusion.

- **Rationalization** – the perpetrator will generally rationalize the fraudulent act in a manner that is consistent with the perpetrator's belief system.
  - o Some perpetrators **rationalize** their fraudulent acts because they do not believe it is really wrong.
    - ▪ This is usually accompanied by the belief that their action is a common practice.
    - ▪ The commission is sometimes viewed as a means of eliminating an unfair advantage.
  - o Some perpetrators rationalize their fraudulent acts when they perceive they have no choice since the repercussions of not perpetrating the fraud would be too severe, such as the effect on stock price of not meeting an earnings expectation.

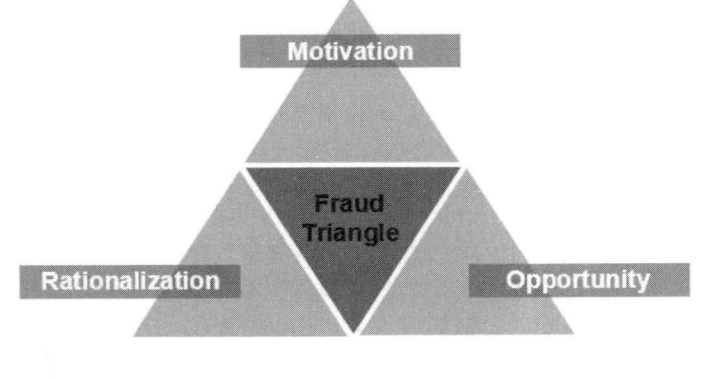

The auditor is also required to communicate knowledge or suspicion of **noncompliance with applicable laws and regulations** (AU-C 250), also referred to as **illegal acts**, to those charged with governance, other than those that are clearly inconsequential. Noncompliance is defined as acts of omission or commission by the entity, either intentional or unintentional, which are contrary to the prevailing laws or regulations. The auditor distinguishes between those with a **direct effect** on the amounts and disclosures in the financial statements, which result in adjusting entries, and those with an **indirect effect** ("others"), which generally result in contingencies.

- Illegal acts with a direct and material effect may include nonpayment of payroll taxes or business license fees.
- Illegal acts with an indirect effect may include antitrust violations, price-fixing, or purchasing securities based on insider information. Other examples include violations of occupational safety laws (OSHA) that might result in financial losses from government fines; or the Foreign Corrupt Practices Act, which makes payment of bribes to foreign officials' illegal and requires publicly held companies to maintain systems of internal control sufficient to provide reasonable assurances that such activities are detected.
- The **auditor's responsibility** is to consider laws that have both a direct effect and those that do not have a direct effect (indirect effect) on the financial statements.
- The auditor should **communicate** with those charged with governance, matters involving noncompliance, other than inconsequential matters, as soon as practicable.
- The **documentation** should include a description of the identified or suspected noncompliance and the results of the discussion with management and those charged with governance and other parties inside or outside the entity.

When noncompliance is identified or suspected, the auditor should obtain an understanding of the nature of the illegal act and the circumstances under which it occurred and any further information that may assist in evaluating the potential impact on the financial statements.

- The matter should be discussed with management or those charged with governance, as appropriate, to determine if support can be provided indicating compliance.
- If compliance cannot be supported and the amount is potentially material, the auditor should consider consulting with legal counsel.

Increased emphasis on professional skepticism – The audit team should begin the engagement with a conscious recognition of the possibility of material misstatement due to fraud. Although the auditor would not accept or continue the relationship if the auditor believed that the client's management lacked integrity, the auditor recognizes that motivation in the form of economic gain or pressure may cause the client to act otherwise. The auditor maintains an understanding of the need to obtain evidence to corroborate management's assertions. The auditor should pay special attention to **fraud risk factors** that increase the probability of fraudulent financial reporting or defalcation.

In addition to information about internal control deficiencies, AU-C section 250, Consideration of Laws and Regulations in an Audit of Financial Statements, requires the auditor to communicate to governance knowledge or suspicion of **noncompliance with applicable laws and regulations,** also referred to as **illegal acts**, other than those that are clearly inconsequential. An entity is not in compliance when, intentionally or unintentionally, it commits acts contrary to prevailing laws or regulations or omits acts required by laws or regulations.

Certain laws and regulations have a **direct effect** on the amounts and disclosures in the financial statements, such as the nonpayment of payroll taxes or, in some jurisdictions, business license fees. These will result in adjusting entries. Others may have an **indirect effect,** such as those that are fundamental to the operations of the business, fundamental to the entity's ability to continue as a going concern, or necessary to avoid a potentially material penalty. These may result in contingencies or may have no financial statement effect, although they may require disclosure.

In obtaining an understanding of an entity and its environment, including its internal controls, the auditor will obtain a general understanding of the legal and regulatory framework under which the entity operates and how it complies with that framework. The entity should have a system under which all laws and regulations to which the entity is subject are identified, interpreted, and complied with.

Consideration of Fraud in a Financial Statement Audit (AU-C 240)

The auditor's responsibilities for the detection of material misstatements due to fraud are met through the performance of **various steps** during different phases of the audit. Standards require the auditor to perform the following:

- **Understand** the nature and characteristics of fraud (above)
- Hold a "**brainstorming**" session with engagement staff to discuss the risks of material misstatements due to fraud:
  - How and where financial statements might be susceptible to fraud, how management could perpetrate and conceal fraudulent financial statements, and how assets could be misappropriated; and
  - Consider known internal and external factors affecting **Motivation (Incentives /pressures)** for fraud, **Opportunities** and a culture or environment that enables management or others to **Rationalize** committing fraud.
  - Exercise **Professional Skepticism**.

- The auditor is required to **obtain the information** needed to identify risks of material misstatement due to fraud.
  - Inquiry of management and others about knowledge or suspicion of fraud, management's understanding of the risk of fraud, and programs and controls established to mitigate risks.
  - Evaluation of results of analytical procedures performed in the planning of the audit.
  - Consideration of fraud risk factors, which are events or conditions that create reasons or motivation to commit fraud, the opportunity to commit fraud, or the attitudes that allow the rationalization of committing fraud (see table).
  - Consider other information

- The auditor will also evaluate the results of analytical procedures performed in the planning of the audit, consider the identified fraud risk factors and whatever other information is available to the auditor. On that basis, the auditor will **Identify risks** that may result in a material misstatement to the financial statements due to fraud:
  - Information gathered is evaluated considering size, complexity, and ownership attributes of entity.
  - Information is evaluated as to *pervasiveness* of fraud risk factors, whether they affect the financial statements as a whole or specific account balances or classes of transactions and related assertions.
  - The auditor applies professional judgment in the consideration of:
    - Whether the *type of risk* indicates misappropriation of assets or fraudulent financial reporting.
    - Whether the risk is of sufficient *magnitude* to cause a material misstatement.
    - The *likelihood* that the risk will result in a material misstatement.

One of the most common ways in which financial statements are fraudulently misstated is through the overstatement of revenue. As a result, the auditor is required to presume that **revenue recognition** represents a risk of material misstatement. In addition, the auditor recognizes that, due to the potential of **management override of controls,** there would not necessarily be evidence of specific risks of material misstatement due to fraud.

- Once the auditor has identified factors that represent the risks of material misstatement of the financial statements, the auditor will **evaluate those risks** in light of the entity's internal controls.
    - Controls may be specific to identified risks or broadly intended to prevent, deter, and detect fraud.
    - The auditor considers whether controls mitigate identified risks.

- The auditor will **determine the nature, timing, and extent** of substantive procedures needed to respond to the results of the assessments.
    - The auditor may change the overall way the audit is conducted.
    - The auditor may change the nature of procedures to obtain more reliable evidence; the timing of procedures, such as by performing tests of balances closer to the balance sheet date; or the extent of procedures to obtain more evidence to derive more conclusive results.
    - The auditor should perform procedures in recognition of the risk of management override of controls. The auditor may:
        - Examine journal entries and other adjustments;
        - Review accounting estimates for bias; or
        - Evaluate the business rationale for significant unusual transactions.
- The auditor will then **evaluate the audit evidence obtained.** In accumulating the evidence, the risk of material misstatement due to fraud is assessed throughout the audit. The auditor will:
    - Evaluate results of analytical procedures performed as substantive tests or as part of overall review for indications of risks of material misstatement not identified previously;
    - Evaluate accumulated results of procedures at or near date of auditor's report; and
    - Consider if identified misstatements may be indicative of fraud.
        - Even if not material, the auditor should consider the implications.
        - If material, or potentially material, the auditor should attempt to obtain additional evidence, consider the implication on other aspects of the audit, discuss the matter with the appropriate level of management, and consider suggesting that the client consult legal counsel.
    - When risk is very high, the auditor may consider withdrawing from the engagement taking into account:
        - Implications about the integrity of management; and
        - The level of cooperation from governance.

- The auditor is required to **Communicate** knowledge or suspicion of fraud to management and governance on a timely basis.
    - Any evidence of the existence of fraud should be communicated to management.
    - Fraud involving senior management and fraud resulting in a material misstatement should be communicated to those charged with governance.
        - Discuss with an appropriate level of management at least **ONE level above** those involved.
    - Risks that have internal control implications should be communicated if they represent significant deficiencies or material weaknesses in internal control.
    - Disclosure to third parties may be appropriate:
        - To comply with legal or regulatory requirements;
        - To a successor auditor when responding to inquiries;
        - To respond to a subpoena; or

- To a funding agency when required of an entity receiving governmental financial assistance.

- The auditor is required to **document the consideration of fraud**, including:
    - The brainstorming session;
    - Procedures performed to obtain information used to identify risks of material misstatement due to fraud;
    - Identified risks of material misstatement;
    - Reasons revenue recognition was not considered a fraud risk factor, if appropriate;
    - Results of procedures performed in response to risk of management override of controls;
    - Other factors drawing the auditor to the conclusion that additional procedures were required; and
    - The nature of communication about fraud.

The auditor should pay special attention to **fraud risk factors** that increase the probability of *fraudulent financial reporting or defalcation*. Analysis of fraud risk factors provides only a general indication as to the existence of a material misstatement. The auditor must specifically assess fraud risk by identifying and evaluating fraud risk factors. Keep in mind the employees Motivation (Incentives/Pressures), Opportunities, and Attitudes/Rationalizations as they relate to the different categories.

EXAMPLES OF FRAUD RISK FACTORS
Misstatements Arising from *Fraudulent Financial Reporting*

Incentives/Pressure (Motivation)	Opportunities	Attitudes/Rationalizations
1. Threats to financial stability or profitability • Decline in margins along with high degree of competition or sales saturation • High vulnerability to rapid changes (e.g., technology, product obsolescence, interest rates) • Declines in customer demand and business failures in industry or economy • Threat of bankruptcy, foreclosure, or takeover due to operating losses • Recurring negative cash flows from operations along with reported earnings and growth • Rapid growth or unusual profitability, especially when compared to others • New accounting, statutory, or regulatory requirements **2. Pressure to meet requirements or expectations of third-party excessive** • Creditors or analysts have profitability or trend expectations, particularly if aggressive • Need for additional debt or equity to remain competitive • Difficulty in meeting exchange listing requirements or debt covenants • Potential adverse effect of poor financial results on pending transactions **3. Threats to personal financial situations of management or directors** • Significant financial interests in the entity • Compensation largely contingent on financial results • Personal guarantees of entity debts **4. Excessive pressure by management or governance to meet financial targets**	**1. Opportunities due to the nature of the entity or industry** • Significant related-party transactions not in the ordinary course of business • Entity has ability to dictate terms or conditions to suppliers or customers, which could result in inappropriate transactions) • Accounts based on significant estimates involving subjective judgments or uncertainties • Significant, unusual, or highly complex transactions, especially near period end • Significant international operations across with differing business environments and cultures • Significant bank accounts or operations in tax haven jurisdictions **2. Management not monitored effectively** • Management dominated by a single person or small group without compensating controls • Ineffective oversight by governance **3. Organizational structure complex or unstable** • Difficulty in determining organization or individuals with controlling interest in entity • Overly complex structure • High turnover of senior management, counsel, or board members **4. Deficiencies in internal control** • Inadequate monitoring of controls • Ineffective accounting, internal audit, or information technology staff; or high turnover • Accounting and information systems that are not effective	**1. Factors allowing governance, management, or employees to engage in fraudulent activities** • Ethical standards not effectively communicated, implemented, supported, or enforced • Nonfinancial management inappropriately participate in selecting accounting principles or determining estimates • History of violations of securities or other laws • Management has excessive interest in maintaining or increasing stock price • Aggressive or unrealistic forecasts provided to analysts and others • Management fails to correct significant deficiencies on a timely basis • Management interested in minimizing earnings for tax reasons • Recurring use of materiality by management in attempts to justify marginal or inappropriate accounting • Strained relationship with current or predecessor auditor

EXAMPLES OF FRAUD RISK FACTORS
Misstatements Arising from _Misappropriation of Assets_

Incentives/Pressures (Motivation)	Opportunities	Attitudes/Rationalizations
1. **Pressure created by personal financial obligations of management or employees with access to assets**	1. **Assets particularly susceptible due to characteristics or circumstances**	**Attitudes or behavior of those with access to assets susceptible to misappropriation**
2. **Adverse relationship between the entity and employees with access to assets**	• Large amounts of cash processed or on hand	• Disregard for need for monitoring or reducing risks
• Known or anticipated layoffs	• Inventories consisting of small, high-value, or high-demand items	• Disregard for internal control
• Changes to compensation or benefit plans	• Assets easily convertible such as bearer bonds, diamonds, or computer chips	• Behavior indicating displeasure or dissatisfaction with company or its treatment of employees
• Promotions, compensation, or other rewards inconsistent with expectations	• Fixed assets that are small or marketable	• Changes in behavior or lifestyle that indicate assets may have been misappropriated
	2. **Inadequate internal controls over assets, including inadequate**	
	• Segregation of duties	
	• Monitoring of employees with access to assets	
	• Recordkeeping for assets	
	• System for authorizing or approving transactions	
	• Physical safeguarding of assets	
	• Reconciliation of assets	
	• Documentation of transactions, such as credits for merchandise returns	
	• No requirement for mandatory vacations for key employees	
	• Management understanding of information technology (IT) to properly oversee IT staff	
	• Controls over access to automated records	

If the auditor determines the financial statements are materially misstated, they should propose adjustments to the client. If the client fails to make these adjustments, the auditor will issue a qualified or adverse opinion on the financial statements due to the departure from GAAP. If the auditor is unable to obtain sufficient appropriate evidence to determine if errors or fraud have material effects on the financial statements, the auditor will issue a qualified opinion or disclaimer due to the scope limitation.

The auditor should pay attention to the way the client handles information about fraud. If management fails to take action against the responsible party and doesn't move to limit the risk of a repeat of errors and fraud causing material misstatement, the auditor must consider the implications as it relates to management's integrity and may have to withdraw from the engagement. The auditor also must withdraw if the client refuses to accept an audit report that has been modified due to errors or fraud on the financial statements.

CLASS QUESTIONS

Please see the Class Questions and Class Solutions for this Lecture at the end of this Section.

QUALITY CONTROL (SQCS)

A CPA **firm must** establish a system of quality control designed to provide it with reasonable assurance that the firm and its personnel comply with professional standards and applicable regulatory and legal requirements, and that the firm or engagement partners issue reports that are appropriate in the circumstances. These standards are explicitly limited in their application to a firm's accounting and auditing practice. Although these quality control standards may be applied to other segments of a firm's practice, the standards do not require it.

A system of quality control consists of policies designed to achieve these objectives and the procedures necessary to implement and monitor compliance with those policies. SQCS (Statements on Quality Control Standards), issued by the ASB, apply to an accounting and auditing practice.
- A practice that performs audit, attestation, compilation, review, and other services for which standards have been set.
- Only applies to engagements governed by standards set by the Auditing Standards Board (ASB) or the Accounting and Review Services Committee (ARSC) of the AICPA.

Quality control standards complement those that are applied primarily at the individual level (such as the Code of Professional Conduct). Each **CPA firm** is different: the specific procedures depend on the size of the firm, the nature of the practice, the organizational structure and cost-benefit considerations. The 6 Elements of Quality control include (**HEAL-ME**):
- **Human Resources (Personnel management)** – The firm should establish policies and procedures for effective hiring, development, assignment, and advancement of staff.
- **Ethical Requirements – (Independence)** The firm should establish procedures to ensure that independence is maintained in attest engagements, and that there is an appropriate means for identifying potential independence difficulties involving staff members. The purpose is to ensure that the firm will always be able to act with integrity and objectivity in the performance of work.
- **Acceptance and continuance of client relationships and specific engagements** – The firm should establish policies and procedures to be followed before the acceptance of new clients and engagements and to determine if continued association with existing clients is warranted. The primary purpose is to ensure that the firm only associates with clients whose managements have integrity.
- **Leadership responsibilities for quality within the firm ("tone at the top")** – The firm's leadership must assume ultimate responsibility for the firm's quality control.
- **Monitoring** – The firm should establish procedures to verify that it is complying with the above standards. Specific individuals should be assigned responsibility for the administration of policies and procedures, but all members of the firm are responsible for compliance.
- **Engagement performance** – The firm should establish policies and procedures to ensure that it meets applicable professional standards in the performance of its engagements.

Policies and procedures also need to be established:

- o For resolving differences of opinions within the engagement team.
- o So that the confidentiality, safe custody, integrity, accessibility, and retrievability of engagement documentation are maintained.

Although an effective quality control system is conducive to compliance with GAAS, deficiencies in or instances of noncompliance with a firm's quality control system do not, in and of themselves, indicate that an engagement was not performed in accordance with the applicable professional standards.

To evaluate the quality control of a firm according to the above standards, either the PCAOB, in the case of auditors of public entities, or another CPA professional, in the case of auditors of nonpublic entities, will review and critique the firm's policies and procedures. These are known as **peer review** programs. Written communication of the firm's quality control policies and procedures to firm personnel is not required, but is recommended.

Quality Control (HEAL-ME)	**GAAS**
- Conduct of all professionals within **CPA firm** on ALL engagements →	- Each individual Audit engagement
Human Resources (Personnel management) **E**thical Requirements – (Independence) **A**cceptance and continuance of client relationships and specific engagements **L**eadership responsibilities for quality within the firm ("tone at the top") **M**onitoring **E**ngagement performance	Auditor → **TIPPICANOE**

Quality Control for an Engagement Conducted in Accordance with GAAS (AU-C 220)

A CPA is required to implement quality control procedures at the engagement level to give the auditor reasonable assurance of:
- Compliance with professional standards and applicable laws and regulations.
- The issuance of a report that is appropriate under the circumstances.

Specific requirements in relation to an audit engagement include:
- The engagement partner's responsibility for the overall quality of the engagement
- Alertness to the risk of noncompliance with ethical requirements
- Procedures related to acceptance and continuance of the client relationship and the audit engagement
- Considerations related to assigning personnel to the engagement
  - o May involve the use of personnel with specialized skills
  - o May involve the use of external specialists
- Engagement performance
- Monitoring of the engagement

- Engagement documentation that includes:
  - Issues identified and resolutions related to compliance with ethical requirements
  - Conclusions regarding compliance with independence requirements
  - Conclusions regarding acceptance and continuance
  - Nature, scope, and conclusions of consultations during the engagement

Quality control requirements for engagement performance indicate the engagement partner's responsibilities for:

- Direction, supervision, and performance of the engagement in compliance with professional standards, applicable legal and regulatory requirements, and firm policies and procedures.
- Issuance of a report that is appropriate under the circumstances.
- Reviewing the results of the engagement to evaluate the sufficiency of appropriate audit evidence to support conclusions reached and the report issued.
- Consultations among engagement team members to resolve difficult or contentious matters.
- Making certain that an engagement quality review is performed when called for by firm policy.
- Making certain that firm policies are followed in dealing with differences of opinion among members of the engagement team.

Lecture 1.15

RESEARCH TASK FORMAT

Research is tested in its own independent task-based simulation problem. Each Audit exam will include at least 1 research type TBS. The Candidates will be asked to search through the database to find an appropriate reference that addresses the issue presented in the research problem. A scenario is presented in which the candidate must find his answer in the authoritative literature using a pre-determined list of codes. The candidate will choose the appropriate code title from the drop-down list and then enter a specific reference number applicable to their given scenario.

Using the Authoritative Literature, the candidate will search for keywords associated with the question using the search box, which will pull up all references within the literature to those keywords. From there, the candidate should use the "search within" function to find specific instances of keywords within each subsection. Keywords will be highlighted in the text and the candidate can go through them to find the relevant text that answers the research problem.

Research questions will also alert the candidate if they have correctly formatted their answer by displaying "Your response is correctly formatted" in a box below the candidate response if the candidate has entered reference numbers correctly. For example, single-digit reference numbers (such as "paragraph 3") may be formatted as a two-digit response (such as "paragraph "03"). A good tool is to also use the Authoritative Literature to look up answers to other TBS in the exam, for example, if they ask you about an audit report, use the Authoritative Literature to assist you in solving this type of TBS.

The Authoritative literature for Audit has the most choices available. We have provided an example for the most frequently tested code sections below.

AUDIT Professional Authoritative Literature for Research Questions

The first step in performing a research question for the AUD exam is to determine what set of standards the question relates to. Standards tested on the AUD exam include Statements on Auditing Standards (SAS) for nonpublic U.S. entities, **AU-C**; auditing standards for public U.S. entities, **PCAOB-AS**; Statements on Standards for Attestation Engagements (SSAE), **AT-C**; Statements on Standards for Accounting and Review Services (SSARS) standards for reviews, compilations, or preparation engagements of nonpublic entities, **AR-C**; the AICPA Code of Professional Conduct, **ET**; the bylaws applicable to members of the AICPA, **BL**; standards for valuation services, **VS**; standards for consulting services, **CS**; standards for personal financial planning services, **PFP**; requirements for continuing professional education, **CPE**; tax services, **TS**, peer review standards, **PR**, and quality control standards, **QC**.

AU-C U.S. Clarified Auditing Standards for financial statement audits of nonpublic entities. The primary source of authoritative literature for the performance of an audit of a non-public entity in the U.S. consists of **Statements on Auditing Standards (SAS)** issued by the Auditing Standards Board (ASB), the senior technical body of the AICPA designated to issue pronouncements on auditing matters applicable to the preparation and issuance of audit reports for nonissuers.

In performing a research question related to auditing standards for nonpublic entities, after determining that the appropriate source will be SASs, the **AU-C literature**, the next step would be to determine which section of the standards the information is likely to be included in.

The sections of the **clarified auditing standards** for *nonpublic entities* are:

AU-C 200 – Overall objectives of the independent auditor and the conduct of an audit in accordance with GAAS
AU-C 210 – Terms of engagement
AU-C 220 – Quality control for an engagement conducted in accordance with GAAS
AU-C 230 – Audit documentation
- AU-C 9230 – Audit documentation – auditing interpretation of section 230
AU-C 240 – Consideration of fraud in a financial statement audit
AU-C 250 – Consideration of laws and regulations in an audit of financial statements
AU-C 260 – The auditor's communication with those charged with governance
AU-C 265 – Communicating internal control related matters identified in an audit
- AU-C 9265 – Communicating internal control related matters identified in an audit – auditing interpretation of section 265
AU-C 300 – Planning an audit
AU-C 315 – Understanding the entity and its environment and assessing the risks of material misstatement
AU-C 320 – Materiality in planning and performing an audit
AU-C 330 – Performing audit procedures in response to assessed risks and evaluating the audit evidence obtained
AU-C 402 – Audit considerations relating to an entity using a service organization
AU-C 450 – Evaluation of misstatements identified during the audit
AU-C 500 – Audit evidence
- AU-C 9500 – Audit evidence – auditing interpretation of section 500
AU-C 501 – Audit evidence – Specific consideration for selected items
AU-C 505 – External confirmations
AU-C 510 – Opening balances – Initial audit engagements, including reaudit engagements
AU-C 520 – Analytical procedures
AU-C 530 – Audit sampling

AU-C 540 – Auditing accounting estimates, including fair value accounting estimated, and related disclosures

AU-C 550 – Related parties

AU-C 560 – Subsequent events and subsequently discovered facts

AU-C 570 – The auditor's consideration of an entity's ability to continue as a going concern

- AU-C 9570 – The auditor's consideration of an entity's ability to continue as a going concern – auditing interpretation of section 570

AU-C 580 – Written representations

AU-C 585 – Consideration of omitted procedures after the report release date

AU-C 600 – Special considerations – Audits of group financial statements including the work of component auditors

- AU-C 9600 – Special considerations – Audits of group financial statements including the work of component auditors – auditing interpretation of section 600

AU-C 610 – Using the work of internal auditors

AU-C 610A – The auditor's consideration of the internal audit function in an audit of financial statements

AU-C 620 – Using the work of an auditor's specialist

- AU-C 9620 – Using the work of an auditor's specialist – auditing interpretation of section 620

AU-C 700 – Forming an opinion and reporting on financial statements

- AU-C 9700 – Forming an opinion and reporting on financial statements – auditing interpretation of section 700

AU-C 705 – Modifications to the opinion in the independent auditor's report

AU-C 706 – Emphasis-of-matter paragraphs and other-matter paragraphs in the independent auditor's report

AU-C 708 – Consistency of financial statements

AU-C 720 – Other information in documents containing audited financial statements

AU-C 725 – Supplementary information in relation to the financial statements as a whole

- AU-C 9725 – Supplementary information in relation to the financial statements as a whole – auditing interpretation of section 725

AU-C 730 – Required supplementary information

AU-C 800 – Special considerations – Audits of financial statements prepared in accordance with special purpose frameworks

AU-C 805 – Special considerations – Audits of single financial statements and specified elements, accounts, or items of a financial statement

- AU-C 9805 – Special considerations – Audits of single financial statements and specified elements, accounts, or items of a financial statement – auditing interpretation of section 805

AU-C 806 – Reporting on compliance with aspects of contractual agreements or regulatory requirements in connection with audited financial statements

AU-C 810 – Engagements to report on summary financial statements

AU-C 905 – Alert that restricts the use of the auditors written communication

AU-C 910 – Financial statements prepared in accordance with a financial reporting framework generally accepted in another country

AU-C 915 – Reports on application of requirements of an applicable financial reporting framework

AU-C 920 – Letters for underwriters and certain other requesting parties

AU-C 920A – Letters for underwriters and certain other requesting parties

AU-C 925 – Filings with the U.S. Securities and Exchange Commission under the Securities Act of 1933

AU-C 930 – Interim financial information

AU-C 935 – Compliance audits

Once the appropriate section has been identified, scanning the section, if relatively short, or using a word search, if the section is longer, will generally be sufficient to quickly identify the specific paragraph being sought.

> **Sample research question:**
> Identify the section of professional standards that describes from whom written representation should be obtained.
> **Answer:** Written representations are considered a form of audit evidence. Written representations is the title of AU-C 580, which is where the answer is most certainly to be found. Scrolling in that section, under requirements, the first caption is "Management From Whom Written Representations Are Requested" and paragraph AU-C 580.09 indicates "The auditor should request written representations from management with appropriate responsibilities for the financial statements and knowledge of the matters concerned."
> **Solution: AU-C 580.09**

The **Public Company Accounting Oversight Board**, or **PCAOB-AS** - is a nonprofit corporation established by Congress to oversee the audits of **public entities**, referred to as *issuers*, in order to protect investors and the public interest by promoting informative, accurate, and independent audit reports. The **PCAOB-AS** standards have been codified and are organized as follows:

General Auditing Standards

1000 – General Principles and Responsibilities
    AS 1001: Responsibilities and Functions of the Independent Auditor
    AS 1005: Independence
    AS 1010: Training and Proficiency of the Independent Auditor
    AS 1015: Due Professional Care in the Performance of Work

1100 – General Concepts
    AS 1101: Audit Risk
    AS 1105: Audit Evidence
    AS 1110: Relationship of Auditing Standards to Quality Control Standards

1200 – General Activities
    AS 1201: Supervision of the Audit Engagement
    AS 1205: Part of the Audit Performed by Other Independent Auditors
    AS 1210: Using the Work of a Specialist
    AS 1215: Audit Documentation
    AS 1220: Engagement Quality Review

1300 – Auditor Communications
    AS 1301: Communications with Audit Committees
    AS 1305: Communications About Control Deficiencies in an Audit of Financial Statements

Audit Procedures

2100 – Audit Planning and Risk Assessment
    AS 2101: Audit Planning
    AS 2105: Consideration of Materiality in Planning and Performing an Audit
    AS 2110: Identifying and Assessing Risks of Material Misstatement

2200 – Auditing Internal Control Over Financial Reporting

AS 2201: An Audit of Internal Control Over Financial Reporting That Is Integrated with An Audit of Financial Statements

2300 – Audit Procedures in Response to Risks – Nature, Timing, and Extent

AS 2301: The Auditor's Responses to the Risks of Material Misstatement

AS 2305: Substantive Analytical Procedure

AS 2310: The Confirmation Process

AS 2315: Audit Sampling

2400 – Audit Procedures for Specific Aspects of the Audit

AS 2401: Consideration of Fraud in a Financial Statement Audit

AS 2405: Illegal Acts by Clients

AS 2410: Related Parties

AS 2415: Consideration of an Entity's Ability to Continue as a Going Concern

2500 – Audit Procedures for Certain Accounts or Disclosures

AS 2501: Auditing Accounting Estimates

AS 2502: Auditing Fair Value Measurements and Disclosures

AS 2503: Auditing Derivative Instruments, Hedging Activities, and Investments in Securities

AS 2505: Inquiry of a Client's Lawyer Concerning Litigation, Claims, and Assessments

AS 2510: Auditing Inventories

2600 – Special Topics

AS 2601: Consideration of an Entity's Use of a Service Organization

AS 2605: Consideration of the Internal Audit Function

AS 2610: Initial Audits – Communications Between Predecessor and Successor Auditors

2700 – Auditor's Responsibilities Regarding Supplemental and Other Information

AS 2701: Auditing Supplemental Information Accompanying Audited Financial Statements

AS 2705: Required Supplementary Information

AS 2710: Other Information in documents Containing Audited Financial Statements

2800 – Conducting Audit Procedures

AS 2801: Subsequent Events

AS 2805: Management Responsibilities

AS 2810: Evaluating Audit Results

AS 2815: The Meaning of "Present Fairly in Conformity with Generally Accepted Accounting Principles:

AS 2820: Evaluating Consistency of Financial Statements

2900 – Post-Audit Matters

AS 2901: Consideration of Omitted Procedures After the Report Date

AS 2905: Subsequent Discovery of Facts Existing at the Date of the Auditor's Report

Auditor Reporting

3100 – Reporting on Audits of Financial Statements

AS 3101: Reports on Audited Financial Statements

AS 3110: Dating of the Independent Auditor's Report

3300 – Other Reporting Topics
AS 3305: Special Reports

AS 3310: Special Reports on Regulated Companies

AS 3315: Reporting on Condensed Financial Statements and Selected Financial Data

AS 3320: Association with Financial Statements

Matters Relating to Filings Under Federal Securities Laws
AS 4101: Responsibilities Regarding Filings Under Federal Securities Statutes

AS 4105: Reviews of Interim Financial Information

Other Matters Associated with Audits
AS 6101: Letters for Underwriters and Certain Other Requesting Parties

AS 6105: Reports on the Application of Accounting Principles

AS 6110: Compliance Auditing Considerations in Audits of Recipients of Governmental Financial Assistance

AS 6115: Reporting on Whether a Previously Reported Material Weakness Continues to Exist

---

Sample research question:

Assume that you are assigned to the audit of Roger Corporation, an issuer company. Your firm is performing its first integrated audit for the company, and the partner on the engagement has asked you to research professional standards to identify the factors that should be considered in planning the audit and may affect the firm's audit procedures. Identify and insert the reference in the following box.

Answer: An audit of internal control over financial reporting that is integrated with an audit of financial statements is the topic of AS 2201. Scrolling quickly down that section, there is a heading "Planning the Audit", under which paragraph 2201.09 indicates "The auditor should properly plan the audit of internal control over financial reporting and properly supervise the engagement team members. When planning an integrated audit, the auditor should evaluate whether the following matters are important to the company's financial statements and internal control over financial reporting and, if so, how they will affect the auditor's procedures – "

Solution: PCAOB AS 2201 Par. 09

AT-C: Attestation Engagements (SSAE)
When a CPA performs an attestation engagement, the authoritative literature is the **Statements on Standards for Attestation Engagements (SSAEs)**, which are issued by senior technical bodies of the AICPA designated to issue pronouncements on attestation matters. The primary objective of attestation standards (AT-C) is to provide guidance for performing and reporting on attestation engagements.

Although attestation engagements are not audits of financial statements, to which SASs apply, or reviews of financial statements, to which SSARS apply, they are similar in many respects. Attestation engagements consist of *examinations*, in which the accountant expresses an opinion; *reviews*, in which the accountant expresses a conclusion; and *agreed-upon procedures* engagements, in which the accountant expresses findings. They are distinct from audits and reviews of financial statements in that, instead of comparing financial information to an applicable financial reporting framework, attestation engagements involve reporting on the reliability of subject matter or an assertion about the subject matter, as measured against suitable and available criteria.

The **Attestation Standards (AT-C)** are organized as follows:

AT-C Introduction
AT-C Glossary
AT-C 100 – Common Concepts
- AT-C 105 – Concepts common to All Attestation Engagements

AT-C 200 – Level of Service (ERA)
- AT-C 205 – Examination Engagements
- AT-C 210 – Review Engagements
- AT-C 215 – Agreed-Upon Procedures Engagements

AT-C 300 – Subject Matter
- AT-C 305 – Prospective Financial Statements
- AT-C 310 – Reporting on Pro Forma Financial Information
- AT-C 315 – Compliance Attestation
- AT-C 320 – Reporting on an Examination of Controls at a Service Organization Relevant to User Entities' Internal Control Over Financial Reporting
- AT-C 395 – Management's Discussion and Analysis

Sample research question:

In anticipation of a merger, the president of Welcore Inc., a nonpublic audit client of your firm, would like to present a projection to shareholders that is intended to present what the president believes to be the likely impact of the transaction. The president has asked you to perform an examination of the projection so that you can express an opinion as to whether the prospective financial information is presented in accordance with the guidelines for the presentation of prospective financial information, as established by the AICPA, and whether the assumptions underlying the projection are suitably supported and provide a reasonable basis for the president's projection, given the hypothetical assumptions regarding the business combination. Which section of the Professional Standards addresses this issue?

Answer: Prospective financial statements are addressed in AT- C Section 305, entitled "Prospective Financial Information". Scrolling down that section, there is a heading entitled "Objectives of an Examination Engagement". Paragraph .07 under that heading begins with "In conducting an examination of prospective financial information, the objectives are..."

Solution: AT-C 305.07

AR-C: Statements on Standards for Accounting and Review Services (SSARS) apply to

preparation engagements, compilations and reviews of *nonpublic* company financial statements. They do not cover preparing a trial balance, assisting in adjustments, consulting on accounting or tax matters, preparing tax returns, preparing manuals, and processing financial data, which are considered bookkeeping services. They apply exclusively to nonpublic entities, also referred to as nonissuers.

SSARS concern the preparation of financial statements for a client, which does not involve the issuance of a report, or the compilation or review of financial statements, both of which do require the accountant to issue a report. The principals and requirements related to preparation, compilation, and review engagements are not limited to financial statements. They may also be applied to engagements for the preparation, compilation, or review of financial information.

SSARS also provides guidance on the compilations and reviews of comparative financial statements, pro forma financial information, and personal financial statements included in written personal financial plans.

SSARS, like the other standards, have been codified.

The sections of the standards related to preparation engagements, compilations, and reviews are (**AR-C**):

AR-C 60 – General Principles for Engagements Performed in Accordance With Statements on Standards for Accounting and Review Services

AR-C 70 – Preparation of Financial Statements

AR-C 80 – Compilation Engagements

AR-C 90 – Review of Financial Statements

   • AR-C 9090 – Review of Financial Statements – Accounting and Review Services Interpretation of Section 90

AR-C 120 – Compilation of Pro Forma Financial Information

Sample research question:

The president of Enright Corporation, a client, asked you to perform a review of the financial statements for the current year only. You have completed your fieldwork and find you can issue an unmodified review report. Which section of the Professional Standards indicates what, is required to be included in an unmodified review report for the financial statements of a single year?

Answer: Reviews of financial statements are the subject matter of AR-C section 90. Scrolling in AR-C Section 90, There is a heading entitled "Reporting on the Financial Statements" followed by a sub-heading entitled "Accountant's Review Report". Paragraph 39 under that sub-heading begins with "The written review report should include…"

Solution: AR-C 90.39

ET-Code of Professional Conduct (CODE)

The AICPA Code of Professional Conduct (**ET**) was created to provide guidance and rules to all members of the AICPA—those in public practice, in industry, in government, and in education—in the performance of their professional responsibilities. It includes principles and rules as well as interpretations and guidance. The principles provide a framework upon which the rules are based, which in turn govern the performance of professional responsibilities.

The Code is divided into 4 chapters consisting of a preface that applies to all members, part 1 for members in public practice, part 2 for members in business, and part 3 for other members. A rule is specific in a numbered paragraph, followed by interpretations and guidance. As an example, the Independence rule is in part 1 and is paragraph 1.200.001. The rule is followed by "Interpretations under the Independence Rule" in paragraphs 1.200.005 through 1.297.030.03.

The Code has been codified as follows:

Preface – All Members
>   ET 0.100 – Overview of the Code of Professional Conduct
>   ET 0.200 – Structure and Application of the AICPA Code
>   ET 0.300 – Principles of Professional Conduct
>   ET 0.400 – Definitions
>   ET 0.500 – Nonauthoritative Guidance
>   ET 0.600 – New, Revised, and Pending Interpretations and Other Guidance

Part 1 – Members in Public Practice
>   ET 1.000 – Introduction
>   ET 1.100 – Integrity and Objectivity
>   ET 1.200 – Independence
>   ET 1.300 – General Standards
>   ET 1.310 – Compliance With Standards

ET 1.320 – Accounting Principles
ET 1.400 – Acts Discreditable
ET 1.500 – Fees and Other Types of Remuneration
ET 1.600 – Advertising and Other Forms of Solicitation
ET 1.700 – Confidential Information
ET 1.800 – Form of Organization and NAME

Part 2 – Members in Industry
ET 2.000 – Introduction
ET 2.100 – Integrity and Objectivity
ET 2.300 – General Standards
ET 2.310 – Compliance With Standards
ET 2.320 – Accounting Principles
ET 2.400 – Acts Discreditable

Part 3 – Other Members
ET 3.100 – Introduction
ET 3.400 – Acts Discreditable

Sample research question:
You work with a CPA firm as an assistant. The senior on the XYZ audit has asked you to determine whether you are eligible to work on the XYZ audit since he knows that you own 100 shares of XYZ worth $700 in total. He has asked you to research the following: He thinks that he recalls the issue relates to whether you are or are not a "covered member." He would like you to find the definition of a covered member in the professional standards. What section and paragraph addresses the definition of a covered member.

Answer: Definitions are provided in the preface to the Code of Professional Conduct in section ET 0.400. The definitions are listed in alphabetical order and "Covered member" is defined in paragraph .12.
Solution: ET 0.400.12

BL-Bylaws
Bylaws of the American Institute of Certified Public Accountants **(BL)**, governing matters of membership and governance of the Institute. Contained in the same publication as the Code of Professional Conduct.

The sections of the Bylaws are as follows:

BL 100 – Name and Purpose
BL 200 – Admission to, and Retention of, Membership and Association
BL 300 – Organization and Procedure
BL 400 – Financial Management and Controls
BL 500 – Meetings of the Institute and the Council
BL 600 – Election of Council, Board of Directors, and Officers of the Institute
BL 700 – Termination of Membership and Disciplinary Sanctions
BL 800 – Amendments
BL 900 - General

VS-Statements on Standards for Valuation Services

The AICPA Statement on Standards for Valuation Services **(SSVS)** establishes standards for AICPA members who are engaged to, or, as part of another engagement, estimate the value of a business (including not-for-profit entities or activities), business ownership interest, security, or intangible asset. Although the SSVS have been codified, there is only one section, VS 100, Valuation of a Business, Business Ownership Interest, Security, or Intangible Asset.

CS-Statement on Standards for Consulting Services

The AICPA Statement on Standards for Consulting Services **(SSCS)** provides behavioral standards for the conduct of consulting services. The SSCS includes the General Standards found in Rule 201 of the AICPA Professional Code of Conduct plus three additional standards found in Rule 203, including Client Interest, Understanding with the Client and Communication with the Client. Consulting services differ fundamentally from the CPA's function of attesting to the assertions of other parties. In an attest service, the practitioner expresses a conclusion about the reliability of a written assertion that is the responsibility of another party, the asserter. In a consulting service, the practitioner develops the findings, conclusions, and recommendations presented. The nature and scope of work is determined solely by the agreement between the practitioner and the client. Generally, the work is performed only for the use and benefit of the client.

The only section of SSCS is CS 100, Statements on Standards for Consulting Services.

PFP-Personal Financial Planning

The AICPA Statement on Standards in Personal Financial Planning Services **(PFP)** establishes responsibilities in providing personal financial planning services. The only section of PFP is PFP 100, Statement on Responsibilities in Personal Financial Planning Practice.

CPE-Continuing Professional Education

The AICPA Statement on Standards for Continuing Professional Education Programs **(CPE)** establishes a framework for the development, presentation, measurement, and reporting of CPE programs and thereby help to ensure that accounting professionals receive the quality continuing professional education necessary to satisfy their obligations to serve the public interest.

TS-Tax Services

The AICPA's Statements on Standards for Tax Services (SSTSs) are enforceable tax practice standards for members of the AICPA. The SSTSs apply to all members regardless of the jurisdictions in which they practice and the types of taxes with respect to which they are providing services. The SSTSs are organized into the following sections from which to choose:
- TS 100 – Tax Return Positions
- TS 200 – Answers to Questions on Returns
- TS 300 – Certain Procedural Aspects of Preparing Returns
- TS 400 – Use of Estimates
- TS 500 – Departure From a Position Previously Concluded in an Administrative Proceeding or Court Decision
- TS 600 – Knowledge of Error – Return Preparation and Administrative Procedures
- TS 700 – Form and Content of Advice to Taxpayers

PR-Peer Review Standards

The Standards for Performing & Reporting on Peer Reviews and Interpretations provide information on administering, planning, performing, reporting on and the acceptance of peer reviews of CPA firms (and individuals) enrolled in the AICPA Peer Review Program.

QC-Quality Control Standards

The AICPA Statements on Quality Control Standards **(SQCSs)** govern quality control standards established by the AICPA. The AICPA's Quality Control Standards do not address the quality-control ramifications of the Sarbanes-Oxley Act nor do they address the quality control ramifications of the PCAOB standards that must be followed by auditors of issuers. NOTE: the CPA exam will cover only those standards currently in force.

There is only one section of the SQCS, QC 10, A Firm's System of Quality Control.

Sample research question:

Assume that you are employed by Wilson & Wilson CPAs. One of the partners has asked you to research the professional standards for the section that identifies the elements of a firm's quality control standards. Identify the section and place the reference in the box below.

Answer: QC 10A.17

Use this chart for Audit Research questions

Professional Standards Selections	
AU-C	U.S. Auditing Standards
PCAOB-AS	PCAOB Auditing Standards
AT-C	Attestation Services
AR-C	Statements on Standards for Accounting & Review Services
ET	Code of Professional Conduct
BL	Bylaws
VS	Statements on Standards for Valuation Services
CS	Statement on Standards for Consulting Services
PFP	Personal Financial Planning
CPE	Continuing Professional education
TS	Tax Services
PR	Peer Review Standards
QC	Quality Control Standards

Lecture 1.16

CLASS QUESTIONS

Please see the Class Questions and Class Solutions for this Lecture at the end of this Section.

Lecture 1.17

CLASS QUESTIONS

Please see the Class Questions and Class Solutions for this Lecture at the end of this Section.

CLASS QUESTIONS

Work through the below Class Questions while following along with the respective lectures. Once this is complete, you can begin independently practicing what you've learned by quizzing yourself on this course section in your Interactive Practice Questions (IPQ), which can be found in your online Student Dashboard. Your IPQ simulates the computer-based testing experience, and will also help you understand how concepts are applied to the exam. Each question includes answer explanations from expert CPAs that will help you determine why you answered a question correctly or incorrectly. This is key to your success on the CPA Exam.

Lecture 1.05

1. Which of the following best describes what is meant by the term generally accepted auditing standards for a PCAOB audit?

    a. Rules acknowledged by the accounting profession because of their universal application.
    b. Pronouncements issued by the Auditing Standards Board.
    c. Measures of the quality of the auditor's performance.
    d. Procedures to be used to gather evidence to support financial statements.

2. To exercise due professional care an auditor should

    a. Critically review the judgment exercised by those assisting in the audit.
    b. Examine all available corroborating evidence supporting management's assertions.
    c. Design the audit to detect all instances of noncompliance (illegal acts).
    d. Attain the proper balance of professional experience and formal education.

3. Because of the risk of material misstatement, an audit of financial statements in accordance with generally accepted auditing standards should be planned and performed with an attitude of

    a. Objective judgment.
    b. Independent integrity.
    c. Professional skepticism.
    d. Impartial conservatism.

Lecture 1.08

4. Before accepting an engagement to audit a new client, a CPA is required to obtain

    a. An understanding of the prospective client's industry and business.
    b. The prospective client's signature to the engagement letter.
    c. A preliminary understanding of the prospective client's control environment.
    d. The prospective client's consent to make inquiries of the predecessor auditor, if any.

5. Before accepting an audit engagement, a successor auditor should make specific inquiries of the predecessor auditor regarding the predecessor's

    a. Opinion of any subsequent events occurring since the predecessor's audit report was issued.
    b. Understanding as to the reasons for the change of auditors.
    c. Awareness of the consistency in the application of GAAP between periods.
    d. Evaluation of all matters of continuing accounting significance.

6. An auditor would least likely initiate a discussion with those charged with governance of an audit client concerning

    a. The methods used to account for significant unusual transactions.
    b. The maximum dollar amount of misstatements that could exist without causing the financial statements to be materially misstated.
    c. Indications of fraud and noncompliance committed by a corporate officer that were discovered by the auditor.
    d. Disagreements with management as to accounting principles that were resolved during the current year's audit.

Lecture 1.10

7. During the initial planning phase of an audit, a CPA most likely would

    a. Identify specific internal control activities that are likely to prevent fraud.
    b. Evaluate the reasonableness of the client's accounting estimates.
    c. Discuss the timing of the audit procedures with the client's management.
    d. Inquire of the client's attorney as to whether any unrecorded claims are probable of assertion.

8. Which of the following procedures would an auditor most likely perform in planning a financial statement audit?

    a. Inquiring of the client's legal counsel concerning pending litigation.
    b. Comparing the financial statements to anticipated results.
    c. Examining computer-generated exception reports to verify the effectiveness of internal control.
    d. Searching for unauthorized transactions that may aid in detecting unrecorded liabilities.

Lecture 1.13

9. As the acceptable level of detection risk decreases, the assurance directly provided from

    a. Substantive tests should increase.
    b. Substantive tests should decrease.
    c. Tests of controls should increase.
    d. Tests of controls should decrease.

10. Which of the following audit risk components may be assessed in nonquantitative terms?

	Control risk	Detection risk	Inherent risk
a.	Yes	Yes	No
b.	Yes	No	Yes
c.	Yes	Yes	Yes
d.	No	Yes	No

11. Which of the following are conditions that make up the fraud triangle?

	Rationalization	Opportunity	Motivation
a.	Yes	Yes	Yes
b.	Yes	No	Yes
c.	No	Yes	Yes
d.	No	No	No

12. If an auditor discovers fraud that they consider immaterial, to whom should they report this?

    a.   Report the fraud to those charged with governance.
    b.   Report the fraud directly to the Public Company Oversight Board.
    c.   Report the fraud to management at least one level below those involved in the fraud.
    d.   Not report it to anyone as it is considered immaterial.

13. The nature and extent of a CPA firm's quality control policies and procedures depend on

	The CPA firm's size	The nature of the CPA firm's practice	Cost benefit considerations
a.	Yes	Yes	Yes
b.	Yes	Yes	No
c.	Yes	No	Yes
d.	No	Yes	Yes

CLASS SOLUTIONS

1. (**c**) As implied by the term "standard", generally accepted auditing standards (GAAS) represent benchmarks against which to measure the quality of the auditor's performance. GAAS includes rules (a) that are acknowledged by the accounting profession as well as procedures used to gather evidence (d), which enable the auditor to achieve quality. GAAS for audits of nonissuers are communicated to the profession in the form of pronouncements issued by the Auditing Standards Board (b). For a PCAOB audit, pronouncements are issued by the PCAOB.

2. (**a**) In exercising due professional care, the auditor exercises judgment and reviews the judgments of assistants. An auditor examines samples of, rather than all, evidence corroborating financial statement assertions (b) and designs the audit to detect instances of noncompliance (illegal acts) that have the potential of resulting in a material misstatement, not all instances (c). The auditor is required to attain the proper balance of professional experience in achieving the standard related to competence, not due professional care (d).

3. (**c**) GAAS require the auditor to plan and perform the audit with an attitude of professional skepticism, which includes the need to maintain objectivity in applying judgments throughout the audit (a). The auditor is required to be independent and to act with integrity (b) in the performance of the engagement in order to meet the auditor's responsibility to the users of financial information, but not specifically due to the risk of material misstatement and there is no requirement that an auditor apply impartial conservatism (d).

4. (**d**) In determining whether to accept an engagement, an auditor is required to make certain that the client does not have management that lacks integrity. One means of making such a determination is through communication with the predecessor auditor, if there is one. Failure to consent to communication with the predecessor may indicate a lack of integrity. The auditor is required to have or obtain an understanding of the client's industry and business (a), but not as a prerequisite to acceptance. The auditor is required to document an understanding with the client, which would be done upon acceptance of the engagement but not before (b). The auditor obtains an understanding of a client's internal control, including the control environment (c), in the performance of the audit but is not required to do so before acceptance.

5. (**b**) The primary objective of communicating with a predecessor auditor is to enable the successor to determine if the client's management lacks integrity. The predecessor's understanding of the reasons for the change in auditors may be relevant as the change may have been due to a disagreement about accounting principles or a scope limitation, which might affect the successor's evaluation. A predecessor would not necessarily be aware of events subsequent to the issuance of the predecessor's report (a). In addition, although the predecessor did have to ascertain that accounting principles were consistently applied in the prior and immediately preceding period, the predecessor would not be aware as to whether they continued to be applied on a consistent basis (c). Although the successor may make inquiries of a predecessor regarding matters of continuing accounting or auditing significance (d), the auditor is not required to do so.

6. (**b**) The maximum dollar amount of misstatements that could exist without causing the financial statements to be materially misstated is a matter of the auditor's professional judgment and would not be discussed with the entity's governance. The auditor may discuss methods used to account for unusual transactions (a) to evaluate whether or not the auditor considers them appropriate. Indications of fraud and noncompliance (illegal acts) (c) may be discussed with management, governance, or both, depending on the nature of the instance and the level of employee or management that was involved. The auditor will also discuss disagreements with management as to accounting principles (d) during the audit to make certain that governance is aware, in case management is not acting in accordance with its authority.

7. (**c**) Although all of the alternatives represent activities of the auditor, discussing the timing of audit procedures with the client's management is the only activity that would be performed during the initial planning phase of the audit. The auditor will identify specific control activities likely to prevent fraud (a) while obtaining an understanding of the entity and its environment, including its internal control, performed after initial planning. The auditor will evaluate the reasonableness of client estimates (b) while obtaining and evaluating audit evidence, and will also inquire of the client's attorney regarding unrecorded claims and other contingencies (d) while obtaining audit evidence, generally near the end of the process.

8. (**b**) The auditor compares the client's financial statements to anticipated results as a means of identifying areas that differ from expectations and may be indications of risks of material misstatement. Examining computer-generated exception reports to verify the effectiveness of internal control (c) is a test of controls that would be performed when the auditor, upon obtaining an understanding of internal control, decides to rely on it. Making inquiries of the client's legal counsel (a) and searching for unauthorized transactions in the search for unrecorded liabilities (d) are procedures that would be performed while gathering and evaluating audit evidence, subsequent to planning.

9. (**a**) The auditor performs substantive tests to address detection risk. When detection risk is higher than acceptable, it is decreased by increasing substantive testing. Substantive testing can be decreased (b) when the risk of material misstatement is low and a high level of detection risk is acceptable. Tests of controls (c and d) are performed in the evaluation of control risk and are not related to detection risk.

10. (**c**) Control risk and inherent risk are components of the risk of material misstatement (RMM). RMM and detection risk are components of audit risk. All may be expressed in quantitative or nonquantitative terms.

11. (**a**) The Association of Certified Fraud Examiners has identified three characteristics necessary for a fraud scheme to be successful, referred to as the fraud triangle. The conditions that make up the fraud triangle are: a reason or incentive to commit the fraud, the opportunity through a lack of controls or an ability to override or circumvent controls, and the ability to rationalize the fraud. If one or more of these conditions does not exist (b, c, and d), it is not likely that the fraudulent act will be successful.

12.   (**a**) There is no materiality threshold in determining when awareness or suspicion of fraud must be communicated by the auditor to those charged with governance, such as the audit committee (d). In any circumstance where fraud is either detected or suspected, the auditor is required to communicate it accordingly. It is up to those charged with governance to determine what course of action is appropriate based on the auditor's communication. It is governance who will decide if the fraud should be disclosed to a regulator, such as the PCAOB (b). The auditor's communication should be made to a level of management at least one above those involved, not one level below (c).

13.   (**a**) A firm is required to maintain a system of quality control to assure that it is complying with all applicable standards and issuing only reports that are appropriate under the circumstances. The nature and extent of a firm's policies and procedures are affected by the size of the firm since a firm with one professional would not, for example, require the same policies and procedures for staying current on auditing standards as a firm with many professional staff. It is affected by the nature of the practice since quality control standards apply to accountants performing reviews as well as those performing audits. Finally, cost-benefit considerations are generally taken into account in establishing policies and procedures of almost any variety, as a firm would not want to apply more resources preventing a problem that will not be particularly costly or problematic if it were not prevented.

Lecture 1.13

TASK-BASED SIMULATIONS

Task-Based Simulation 1

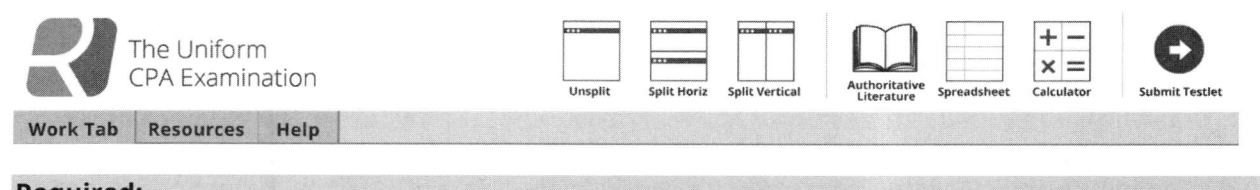

Required:

Items 1 through 15 pertain to an auditor's risk analysis of an entity. Select the best answer for each item.

Bond, CPA, is considering audit risk at the financial statement level in planning the audit of Toxic Waste Disposal (TWD) Company's financial statements for the year ended December 31, 20X6. TWD is a privately owned entity that contracts with municipal governments to remove environmental wastes. Audit risk at the financial statement level is influenced by the risk of material misstatements, which may be indicated by a combination of factors related to management, the industry, and the entity.

Required:

Based only on the information below, indicate whether each of the following factors (Items 1 through 15) would most likely increase (I) decrease (D) or have no effect (N) on audit risk and the risk of material misstatement.

Items to be answered:

Company Profile

1. This was the first year TWD operated at a profit since 20X2 because the municipalities received increased federal and state funding for environmental purposes.

2. TWD's Board of Directors is controlled by Mead, the majority stockholder, who also acts as the chief executive officer.

3. The internal auditor reports to the controller and the controller reports to Mead.

4. The accounting department has experienced a high rate of turnover of key personnel.

5. TWD's bank has a loan officer who meets regularly with TWD's CEO and controller to monitor TWD's financial performance.

6. TWD's employees are paid biweekly.

7. Bond has audited TWD for four years.

Recent developments

8. During 20X6, TWD changed its method of preparing its financial statements from the cash basis to generally accepted accounting principles.

9. During 20X6, TWD sold one half of its controlling interest in United Equipment Leasing (UEL) Co. TWD retained significant interest in UEL.

10. During 20X6, litigation filed against TWD in 20X1 alleging that TWD discharged pollutants into state waterways was dropped by the state. Loss contingency disclosures that TWD included in prior years' financial statements are being removed for the 20X6 financial statements.

11. During December 20X6, TWD signed a contract to lease disposal equipment from an entity owned by Mead's parents. This related party transaction is not disclosed in TWD's notes to its 20X6 financial statements.

12. During December 20X6, TWD completed a barter transaction with a municipality. TWD removed waste from a municipally owned site and acquired title to another contaminated site at below market price. TWD intends to service this new site in 20X7

13. During December 20X6 TWD increased its casualty insurance coverage on several pieces of sophisticated machinery from historical cost to replacement cost.

14. Inquiries about the substantial increase in revenue TWD recorded in the fourth quarter of 19X6 disclosed a new policy. TWD guaranteed to several municipalities that it would refund the federal and state funding paid to TWD if any municipality fails federal or state site clean-up inspection in 20X7.

15. An initial public offering of TWD's stock is planned for late 20X7.

Task-Based Simulation 2

The Uniform CPA Examination	Unsplit	Split Horiz	Split Vertical	Authoritative Literature	Spreadsheet	Calculator	Submit Testlet

Work Tab | Resources | Help

Required:

Green, CPA, is considering audit risk, including fraud risk, at the financial statement level in planning the audit of National Federal Bank (NFB) Company's financial statements for the year ended December 31, 20X5. Audit risk at the financial statement level is influenced by the risk of material misstatements, which may be indicated by a combination of factors related to management, the industry, and the entity. In assessing such factors Green has gathered the following information concerning NFB's environment.

Company profile

NFB is a federally insured bank that has been consistently more profitable than the industry average by marketing mortgages on properties in a prosperous rural area, which has experienced considerable growth in recent years. NFB packages its mortgages and sells them to large mortgage investment trusts. Despite recent volatility of interest rates, NFB has been able to continue selling its mortgages as a source of new lendable funds.

NFB's board of directors is controlled by Smith, the majority stockholder, who also acts as the chief executive officer. Management at the bank's branch offices has authority for directing and controlling NFB's operations and is compensated based on branch profitability. The internal auditor reports directly to Harris, a minority shareholder, who also acts as chairman of the board's audit committee.

The accounting department has experienced little turnover in personnel during the five years Green has audited NFB. NFB's formula consistently underestimates the allowance for loan losses, but its controller has always been receptive to Green's suggestions to increase the allowance during each engagement.

Recent developments

During 20X5, NFB opened a branch office in a suburban town thirty miles from its principal place of business. Although this branch is not yet profitable due to competition from several well-established regional banks, management believes that the branch will be profitable by 20X7. Also, during 20X5, NFB increased the efficiency of its accounting operations by installing a new, sophisticated computer system.

Items to be answered:

Based only on the information above, indicate by marking the appropriate button whether the following factors indicate an increased or decreased audit risk.

Factor	Increased audit risk	Decreased audit risk
1. Branch management authority	○	○
2. Government regulation	○	○
3. Company profitability	○	○
4. Demand for product	○	○
5. Interest rates	○	○
6. Availability of mortgage funds	○	○
7. Involvement of principal shareholder in management	○	○
8. Branch manager compensation	○	○
9. Internal audit reporting relationship	○	○
10. Accounting department turnover	○	○
11. Continuing audit relationship	○	○
12. Internal controls over accounting estimates	○	○
13. Response to proposed accounting adjustments	○	○
14. New unprofitable branch	○	○
15. New computer system	○	○

Task-Based Simulation 3

The Uniform
CPA Examination

| Unsplit | Split Horiz | Split Vertical | Authoritative Literature | Spreadsheet | Calculator | Submit Testlet |

Work Tab   **Resources**   **Help**

Required:

Dodd, CPA, audited Adams Company's financial statements for the year ended December 31, 20X2. On November 1, 20X3, Adams notified Dodd that it was changing auditors and that Dodd's services were being terminated. On November 5, 20X3, Adams invited Hall, CPA, to make a proposal for an engagement to audit its financial statements for the year ended December 31, 20X3.

Required:

1. What procedures concerning Dodd should Hall perform before accepting the engagement?

2. What additional procedures should Hall consider performing during the planning phase of this audit (after acceptance of the engagement) that would **not** be performed during the audit of a continuing client?

Task-Based Simulation 4

The Uniform
CPA Examination

Unsplit   Split Horiz   Split Vertical   Authoritative   Spreadsheet   Calculator   Submit Testlet
                                              Literature

Research | Help

Johnson & Johnson, CPAs, is considering accepting an engagement to perform an audit for a new client whose prior period financial statements had been audited by another CPA. Johnson & Johnson would like to make certain that they understand the auditor's objective in conducting an initial audit engagement.

1. Which title of Professional Standards addresses this issue & will be helpful in understanding the auditor's objectives in conducting an initial audit engagement?

2. Enter the exact section and paragraph with helpful information.

Use this chart for Audit Research questions

Professional Standards Selections	
AU-C	U.S. Auditing Standards
PCAOB-AS	PCAOB Auditing Standards
AT-C	Attestation Services
AR-C	Statements on Standards for Accounting & Review Services
ET	Code of Professional Conduct
BL	Bylaws
VS	Statements on Standards for Valuation Services
CS	Statement on Standards for Consulting Services
PFP	Personal Financial Planning
CPE	Continuing Professional education
TS	Tax Services
PR	Peer Review Standards
QC	Quality Control Standards

Task-Based Simulation 5

The Uniform
CPA Examination

Unsplit   Split Horiz   Split Vertical   Authoritative Literature   Spreadsheet   Calculator   Submit Testlet

Research | Help

Bill Barlow, CPA, is in the final stages of an audit of a client's financial statements. During the course of the engagement, certain significant matters came to Bill's attention that he was either required to, or felt it was necessary to, communicate to those charged with governance. Some of these matters were communicated orally and some were communicated in writing. Bill is trying to determine what is required to be documented in regard to these communications.

1. Which title of Professional Standards addresses this issue & will be helpful in understanding the documentation requirements for matters communicated with governance?

2. Enter the exact section and paragraph with helpful information.

Task-Based Simulation 6

The Uniform
CPA Examination

Unsplit   Split Horiz   Split Vertical   Authoritative Literature   Spreadsheet   Calculator   Submit Testlet

Research | Help

Fred Flintstone is a staff accountant at Granite, Rubble, & Dino, CPAs and is working on his first audit engagement. He has heard a lot of conflicting information about the auditor's responsibility for fraud in a financial statement audit engagement and wants to clarify what the actual responsibilities are.

1. Which title of Professional Standards addresses this issue & will be helpful in understanding the auditor's responsibility for fraud in a financial statement audit?

2. Enter the exact section and paragraph with helpful information.

Task-Based Simulation 7

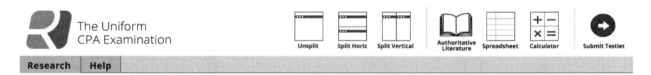

Hardy & Hale have recently decided to get together to form their own firm in which they will be performing financial statement audits. They are in the process of developing a quality control policies and procedures and want to make certain that they are complying with applicable standards. They realize that first they should have an understanding of the firm's objectives in establishing a system of quality control.

1.   Which title of Professional Standards addresses this issue & will be helpful in understanding the objectives of a system of quality control?

2.   Enter the exact section and paragraph with helpful information.

Task-Based Simulation 8

An auditor has reached a preliminary understanding regarding an engagement to audit a publicly-held entity. The auditor wants to make certain that the understanding with the entity's audit committee includes all of those components required.

1.   Which title of Professional Standards addresses this issue & will be helpful in understanding what must be included in the auditor's understanding established with the audit committee of a publicly-held entity in anticipation of an audit?

2.   Enter the exact section and paragraph with helpful information.

TASK-BASED SIMULATION SOLUTIONS

Task-Based Simulation Solution 1

1.   D   Increased federal and state funding providing a profitable year would decrease audit risk and risk of material misstatement since management will have less of a need to overstate profits.

2.   I   Control of the board of directors by a majority stockholder who is also the chief executive officer (management is dominated by a single individual) gives one individual the opportunity to circumvent internal controls, increasing audit risk and the risk of material misstatement.

3.   I   The internal auditor should report directly to the board of directors or the audit committee. Reporting to the controller and indirectly to the majority stockholder increases audit risk and the risk of material misstatement.

4.   I   A high turnover of personnel in the accounting department results in a greater likelihood of errors and may indicate problems, increasing audit risk and the risk of material misstatement.

5.   D   Regular meetings between the controller and a bank loan officer increase the likelihood that problems will be detected and communicated, decreasing audit risk and the risk of material misstatement.

6.   N   The frequency with which employees are paid has no impact on audit risk or the risk of material misstatement.

7.   D   A continuing auditor will have greater familiarity with the client and their business and industry, decreasing audit risk and the risk of material misstatement.

8.   I   Changing the method of accounting, even to a more favorable method, increases the likelihood of errors, increasing audit risk and the risk of material misstatement.

9.   I   Selling one-half of a controlling interest in another company means that the equity method would be applied instead of the preparation of consolidated financial statements. This would increase audit risk due to the reduced ability to obtain information and also increase the risk of material misstatement.

10.   D   The elimination of a loss contingency due to a lawsuit being dropped eliminates the possibility of understating a potential liability reducing audit risk and the risk of material misstatement.

11.   I   Entering into a significant related party transaction increases the possibility that the transaction will not be properly accounted for, increasing audit risk and the risk of material misstatement.

12.   I   Acquiring title to a contaminated site is an unusual transaction and creates a contingent liability, depending on the nature of the contamination. As a result, both audit risk and the risk of material misstatement are increased.

13.   N   Insurance coverage would have little to no effect on audit risk and the risk of material misstatement.

14.   I   Guaranteeing a refund to municipalities failing federal or state clean-up inspection creates a contingent liability and increases audit risk.

15.   I   With an initial public offering planned; there is greater incentive to overstate profitability and financial position, increasing audit risk.

Task-Based Simulation Solution 2

Factor	Increased audit risk	Decreased audit risk
Branch management authority	●	○
Government regulation	○	●
Company profitability	○	●
Demand for product	○	●
Interest rates	●	○
Availability of mortgage funds	○	●
Involvement of principal shareholder in management	○	●
Branch manager compensation	●	○
Internal audit reporting relationship	○	●
Accounting department turnover	○	●
Continuing audit relationship	○	●
Internal controls over accounting estimates	●	○
Response to proposed accounting adjustments	○	●
New unprofitable branch	●	○
New computer system	●	○

1. I Since branch managers have the authority to direct and control the entity's operations and are compensated based on branch performance, they have an incentive to commit fraud and represent a fraud risk factor that increases audit risk.

2. D Government regulation indicates another level of oversight, which reduces audit risk.

3. D When an entity is profitable, it has less incentive to commit fraudulent financial reporting, reducing audit risk.

4. D A strong demand for an entity's product, as indicated by its ability to continue selling despite volatile interest rates, reduces the incentive for fraudulent financial reporting, reducing audit risk.

5. I The fact that interest rates are volatile increase the likelihood that an error will be made in making interest calculations and in reporting interest related transactions. This increases audit risk, due to the increased possibility of errors, but does not represent a fraud risk factor.

6. D The availability of mortgage funds facilitates the entity's ability to do business profitably, reducing the incentive for fraudulent financial reporting and reducing audit risk.

7. D In general, when an owner is involved in management, it increases oversight over employees and decreases the risk of fraud.

8. I Since branch managers are compensated on the basis of branch performance, they would be incentivized to overstate branch results representing a fraud risk factor that increases audit risk.

9. D The fact that the internal auditors report to an independent member of the board of directors increases their independence and their potential effectiveness. This reduces the likelihood that violations of internal controls will go undetected, reducing audit risk.

10.   D   A lack of turnover of accounting personnel indicates that existing personnel will be more familiar with the transactions and policies of the entity and are less likely to make errors, reducing audit risk.

11.   D   A long-term relationship between auditor and client increases the auditor's familiarity with the client and has the potential of increasing the effectiveness of the auditor's risk assessment, reducing audit risk.

12.   I   The fact that estimates of loan losses are consistently understated indicates, as a minimum, that the company does not have effective policies when it comes to developing estimates, increasing audit risk. Such underestimates may be intentional on the part of management to improve the appearance of results, indicating a fraud risk factor.

13.   D   The fact that the client responds favorably to the auditor's proposed adjustments indicates that the entity is at least willing to issue financial statements that are fairly presented, reducing audit risk.

14.   I   The acquisition of an unprofitable branch may have the tendency to make results look unfavorable and, as a result, management may be motivated to minimize the negative impact by overstating the unprofitable branch's results. This represents a fraud risk factor that increases audit risk.

15.   I   A new computer system increases the likelihood of error as personnel become familiar with the system. This increases audit risk.

Task-Based Simulation Solution 3

1. The procedures Hall should perform before accepting the engagement include the following:
   a. Hall should explain to Adams the need to make an inquiry of Dodd and should request permission to do so.
   b. Hall should ask Adams to authorize Dodd to respond fully to Hall's inquiries.
   c. If Adams refuses to permit Dodd to respond or limits Dodd's response, Hall should inquire as to the reasons and consider the implications in deciding whether to accept the engagement.
   d. Hall should make specific and reasonable inquiries of Dodd regarding matters Hall believes will assist in determining whether to accept the engagement, including specific questions regarding:
      - Facts that might bear on the integrity of management;
      - Disagreements with management as to accounting principles, auditing procedures, or other similarly significant matters;
      - Dodd's understanding as to the reasons for the change of auditors;
      - Communications to the audit committee regarding fraud, noncompliance (illegal acts), and internal control related matters.
   e. If Hall receives a limited response, Hall should consider its implications in deciding whether to accept the engagement.

2. The additional procedures Hall should consider performing during the planning phase of this audit that would not be performed during the audit of a continuing client may include the following:
   a. Hall may apply appropriate auditing procedures to the account balances at the beginning of the audit period and, possibly, to transactions in prior periods.
   b. Hall may make specific inquiries of Dodd regarding matters Hall believes may affect the conduct of the audit, such as
      - Audit areas that have required an inordinate amount of time;
      - Audit problems that arose from the condition of the accounting system and records.
   c. Hall may request Adams to authorize Dodd to allow a review of Dodd's working papers.
   d. Hall should document compliance with firm policy regarding acceptance of a new client.
   e. Hall should start obtaining the documentation needed to create a permanent working paper file.

Task-Based Simulation Solution 4

| AU-C | 510 | .04 |

Task-Based Simulation Solution 5

| AU-C | 260 | .20 |

Task-Based Simulation Solution 6

| AU-C | 240 | .05 |

Task-Based Simulation Solution 7

| QC | 10A | .12 |

Task-Based Simulation Solution 8

| PCAOB | AS 1301 | Par .05 |

DOCUMENT REVIEW SIMULATIONS

Lecture 1.16
Document Review Simulation 1

R/ The Uniform CPA Examination

| Unsplit | Split Horiz | Split Vertical | Authoritative Literature | Spreadsheet | Calculator | Submit Testlet |

Work Tab   **Resources**   **Help**

Scroll down to complete all parts of this task.

Background

You are an experienced senior associate of Shipley LLC, a large national auditing firm. You have just been assigned to the Financial Statement audit of Daley Company ("Daley"), a non-issuer, for the year ended 20X6. Although Daley is a new client for you, Shipley LLC has been performing the audit for more than a decade.

Company Profile

Daley Company is a manufacturer of premium stuffed animals and other soft infant toys, and has been in existence for nearly thirty-five years. Daley has a strong presence in the high-end infant and toy markets. One of Daley's signature competitive advantages is that their classically themed products all include hand-made elements, and are known to be high quality. Daley owns its own manufacturing facility, located in Nebraska. Daley has historically experienced solid growth, at times into the double digits, which has slowed in recent years. The company is divided into several divisions, which are aligned with its major product lines. In 20X4, Daley entered a contract to produce stuffed animal versions of characters from Timmy Tiger, a popular young child's television show.

Marketing

Daley operates in a highly competitive industry, which has experienced increased competition from newer companies that are able to mass produce less expensive, more "trendy" products. The company's distribution channel consists of high-end boutiques and toy stores. Daley has resisted the trend to sell through big box stores or through large online retailers. Its products are only sold and shipped in the lower 48 states of the USA. Consistent with industry practice, Daley follows a policy of FOB destination.

Management

The company is a family run partnership, with two generations of the Washington family currently involved in operations. There is a five-member audit committee, which is comprised of both family members and business associates of the partners. There is also a seven-member Board of Directors, which is comprised of family members with a partnership interest in the company, but who are not involved in the day-to-day operations of Daley.

President and CEO, Thomas Washington, is one of the founding partners. He has been a successful businessman throughout his career. However, he has recently been butting heads with his son, Mark Washington, who was recently named Executive Vice President of the company. The two have differing visions for the future of the company and different ideas about how to remain competitive. The CFO, MaryAnn Washington Sparks, has held that role for three years. Both Mark and MaryAnn have "grown up" in the company by working at a stream of increasingly responsible roles. The Vice President of Marketing, Henry Washington, is Thomas' brother. Henry's son Fred also works in the Finance department as Controller, but does not get along well with MaryAnn and frequently complains about his compensation and about being passed over for the role of CFO.

Engagement

The previous senior associate on the engagement, George Smith, participated in the audit of Daley Company for the past three years. George began work on this year's interim controls update and audit planning. However, due to medical problems, George was neither able to complete his work, nor finish reviewing the work of his staff, and is now on an extended medical leave.

Daley has provided you with its draft balance sheets and income statements. You must review the prior year audit program and work papers, the interim work performed, and the client's draft financial statements in order to prepare the audit program for 20X6.

Review the prior year audit program. Based on the review of the prior year's audit program, draft financial statements, and the interim fieldwork update memo, analyze each step of the assets section of the Proposed 20X6 Audit Program. Revise the Proposed 20X6 Audit Program, correcting any errors, adding any necessary steps, and removing any inappropriate or unnecessary items. Ensure that the 20X6 audit program is appropriate, given the information provided.

To revise the Proposed 20X6 Audit Program, click on each segment of underlined text below and select the needed correction, if any, from the list provided. If the underlined text is already correct in the context of the document, select [Original text] from the list. If removal of the entire underlined text is the best revision to the document, select [Delete text] from the list.

If a procedure is required other than the one indicated in the original text, the appropriate procedure should be selected from the remaining items in the list.

Proposed 20X6 Audit Program

Daley Company
Year ended December 31, 20X6
Year-end Audit

Accounts Receivable:

1. Obtain a summary schedule of all Accounts Receivable accounts. Agree each account balance to the Trial Balance. Tie the schedule total to the Financial Statements.

2. Confirm balances > $79,200. Investigate any discrepancies.

3. Examine Allowance for Doubtful Accounts for preciseness and consistency with company policy.

4. Trace receivables greater than the materiality threshold to subsequent cash collections in 20X6.

5. Vouch one receivable to original sales transaction documents. Investigate any discrepancies.

6. Inquire about discounting and factoring of balances.

7. Review cutoff of sales, sales returns, and cash receipts.

8. No other audit procedures required.

Notes Receivable:

9. Obtain a summary schedule of all Notes Receivable accounts. Agree each account balance to the Trial Balance. Tie the schedule total to the Financial Statements.

10. Confirm interim balances. Investigate any discrepancies.

11. Inquire about discounting and factoring of items.

12. Trace Notes Receivable > $79,200 to subsequent cash collections in 20X6.

13. Examine Allowance for Doubtful Accounts for preciseness and consistency with company policy.

14. Inquire about new loan agreements.

15. No other audit procedures required.

Items for Analysis

Accounts Receivable:

Obtain a summary schedule of all Accounts Receivable accounts. Agree each account balance to the Trial Balance. Tie the schedule total to the Financial Statements.

1. Choose an option below:

    - [Original text] Obtain a summary schedule of all Accounts Receivable accounts. Agree each account balance to the Trial Balance. Tie the schedule total to the Financial Statements.

    - [Delete text]

    - Obtain a summary schedule of all Accounts Receivable accounts. Tie the schedule total to the Financial Statements.

    - Obtain a summary schedule of all Accounts Receivable accounts. Agree each account balance to the Trial Balance.

    - Obtain a summary schedule of all Accounts Receivable accounts. Agree each account balance to the Trial Balance. Foot/recalculate all manual totals on the summary schedule. Test foot spreadsheet totals. Tie the schedule total to the Financial Statements.

    - Obtain a summary schedule of all Accounts Receivable accounts. Agree each account balance to the Trial Balance. Foot/recalculate all totals on the summary schedule. Tie the schedule total to the Financial Statements.

Confirm balances > $79,200. Investigate any discrepancies.

2. Choose an option below:

    - [Original text] Confirm balances > $79,200. Investigate any discrepancies.

    - [Delete text]

    - Confirm all balances. Investigate any discrepancies.

    - Confirm balances for all receivables new in fiscal year 20X6. Investigate any discrepancies.

    - Confirm balances for all receivables new in fiscal year 20X6 > $79,200. Investigate any discrepancies.

    - Confirm 100% of individually material receivables and a sample of the remaining balances.

    - Confirm 100% of individually material receivables and a sample of the remaining balances. Investigate any discrepancies.

Examine Allowance for Doubtful Accounts for preciseness and consistency with company policy.

3. Choose an option below:

    - [Original text] Examine Allowance for Doubtful Accounts for preciseness and consistency with company policy.

    - [Delete text]

    - Examine Allowance for Doubtful Accounts for preciseness and consistency with company policy. Recalculate the Allowance for Doubtful Accounts to ensure that company policy is being followed. Investigate and document any digressions from policy. Examine the aging of Accounts Receivable to determine the preciseness of the allowance.

    - Examine Allowance for Doubtful Accounts for reasonableness and consistency with company policy. Recalculate the Allowance for Doubtful Accounts to ensure that company policy is being followed. Investigate and document any digressions from policy. Examine the aging of Accounts Receivable to determine the adequacy of the allowance.

    - Examine Allowance for Doubtful Accounts for preciseness and consistency with company policy. Investigate and document any digressions from policy. Examine the aging of Accounts Receivable to determine the preciseness of the allowance.

    - Examine Allowance for Doubtful Accounts for reasonableness and consistency with company policy. Investigate and document any digressions from policy. Examine the aging of Accounts Receivable to determine the reasonableness of the allowance.

Trace receivables greater than the materiality threshold to subsequent cash collections in 20X6.

4. Choose an option below:

    - [Original text] Trace receivables greater than materiality threshold to subsequent cash collections in 20X6.

    - [Delete text]

    - Trace receivables greater than materiality threshold to subsequent cash collections in 20X5.

    - Trace receivables greater than materiality threshold to subsequent cash collections in 20X5 and 20X6.

    - Trace receivables greater than materiality threshold to subsequent cash collections in 20X6 and 20X7.

    - Trace receivables greater than materiality threshold to subsequent cash collections in 20X7.

Vouch one receivable to original sales transaction documents. Investigate any discrepancies.

5. Choose an option below:

    - [Original text] Vouch one receivable to original sales transaction documents. Investigate any discrepancies.

    - [Delete text]

    - Vouch all Accounts Receivable to original sales transaction documents. Investigate any discrepancies.

- Vouch new Accounts Receivable to original sales transaction documents. Investigate any discrepancies.

- Vouch all prior year Accounts Receivable to original sales transaction documents. Investigate any discrepancies.

Inquire about discounting and factoring of balances.

6. Choose an option below:

- [Original text] Inquire about discounting and factoring of balances.

- [Delete text]

- Inquire about pledging and factoring of balances.

- Inquire about pledging and discounting of balances.

- Inquire about pledging, discounting, and factoring of balances.

- Inquire about pledging, discounting, factoring, and confirming of balances.

Review cutoff of sales, sales returns, and cash receipts.

7. Choose an option below:

- [Original text] Review cutoff of sales, sales returns, and cash receipts.

- [Delete text]

- Review cutoff of sales and cash receipts.

- Review cutoff of sales and sales returns.

- Review cutoff of cash receipts and sales returns.

No other audit procedures required.

8. Choose an option below:

- [Original text] No other audit procedures required.

- Reperform calculations to evaluate reasonableness of balances in Accounts Receivable and Allowance for Doubtful Accounts and to understand account trends.

- Perform analytical procedures on Accounts Receivable and Allowance for Doubtful Accounts to evaluate reasonableness of balances and to understand account trends.

- Observe and inquire about the staff's process for determining the proper balance in Accounts Receivable and Allowance for Doubtful Accounts to evaluate reasonableness of balances and to understand account trends.

- Inspect original documents to evaluate reasonableness of balances in Accounts Receivable and Allowance for Doubtful Accounts and to understand account trends.

Notes Receivable:

Obtain a summary schedule of all Notes Receivable accounts. Agree each account balance to the Trial Balance. Tie the schedule total to the Financial Statements.

9. Choose an option below:

   - [Original text] Obtain a summary schedule of all Notes Receivable accounts. Agree each account balance to the Trial Balance. Tie the schedule total to the Financial Statements.

   - [Delete text]

   - Obtain a summary schedule of all Notes Receivable accounts. Tie the schedule total to the Financial Statements.

   - Obtain a summary schedule of all Notes Receivable accounts. Agree each account balance to the Trial Balance.

   - Obtain a summary schedule of all Notes Receivable accounts. Agree each account balance to the Trial Balance. Foot/recalculate all manual totals on the summary schedule. Test foot spreadsheet totals. Tie the schedule total to the Financial Statements.

   - Obtain a summary schedule of all Notes Receivable accounts. Agree each account balance to the Trial Balance. Foot/recalculate all totals on the summary schedule. Tie the schedule total to the Financial Statements.

Confirm interim balances. Investigate any discrepancies.

10. Choose an option below:

   - [Original text] Confirm interim balances. Investigate any discrepancies.

   - [Delete text]

   - Confirm year-end balances. Investigate any discrepancies.

   - Confirm interim payments. Investigate any discrepancies.

   - Confirm year-end payments. Investigate any discrepancies.

   - Confirm year-end transactions. Investigate any discrepancies.

Inquire about discounting and factoring of items.

11. Choose an option below:

   - [Original text] Inquire about discounting and factoring of balances.

   - [Delete text]

   - Inquire about pledging, discounting, and factoring of balances.

   - Inquire about pledging, discounting, factoring, and confirming of balances.

   - Inquire about pledging and factoring of balances.

   - Inquire about pledging and discounting of balances.

Trace Notes Receivable > $79,200 to subsequent cash collections in 20X6.

12. Choose an option below:

- [Original text] Trace Notes Receivable > $79,200 to subsequent cash collections in 20X6.

- [Delete text]

- Trace Notes Receivable > $79,200 to subsequent cash collections in 20X7.

- Trace Notes Receivable > $10,600 to subsequent cash collections in 20X6.

- Trace Notes Receivable > $10,600 to subsequent cash collections in 20X7.

- Examine payment received on Notes Receivable in 20X7.

Examine Allowance for Doubtful Accounts for preciseness and consistency with company policy.

13. Choose an option below:

- [Original text] Examine Allowance for Doubtful Accounts for preciseness and consistency with company policy.

- [Delete text]

- Examine Allowance for Doubtful Accounts for reasonableness and consistency with company policy. Recalculate the Allowance for Doubtful Accounts to ensure that company policy is being followed. Investigate and document any digressions from policy. Examine the aging of Notes Receivable to determine the adequacy of the allowance.

- Examine Allowance for Doubtful Accounts for preciseness and consistency with company policy. Investigate and document any digressions from policy. Examine the aging of Notes Receivable to determine the preciseness of the allowance.

- Examine Allowance for Doubtful Accounts for preciseness and consistency with company policy. Recalculate the Allowance for Doubtful Accounts to ensure that company policy is being followed. Investigate and document any digressions from policy. Examine the aging of Notes Receivable to determine the preciseness of the allowance.

- Examine Allowance for Doubtful Accounts for reasonableness and consistency with company policy. Investigate and document any digressions from policy. Examine the aging of Notes Receivable to determine the reasonableness of the allowance.

Inquire about new loan agreements.

14. Choose an option below:

- [Original text] Inquire about new loan agreements.

- [Delete text]

- Review new loan agreements.

- Vouch new loan agreements.

- Trace new loan agreements to the balance sheets.

- Agree new loan agreements to the balance sheets.

No other audit procedures required.

15. Choose an option below:

- [Original text] No other audit procedures required.

- Inquire of management about loans to management and other related parties, especially those that have any unique terms. Determine the business purpose of the transaction. Evaluate whether any notes require disclosure in the financial statements.

- Inquire of management about loans to management and other related parties, especially those that have any unique terms. Determine the business purpose of the transaction and verify that it has been approved by the Board of Directors. Evaluate whether any notes require disclosure in the financial statements.

- Inquire of management about loans to management and other related parties, especially those that have unique terms. Determine the business purpose of the transaction and verify that it has been approved by the Board of Directors.

- Inquire of management about loans to management and other related parties greater than the materiality threshold. Determine the business purpose of the transaction and verify that it has been approved by the Board of Directors. Evaluate whether any notes require disclosure in the financial statements.

Resources/Exhibits

Interim Update Memo

To: Jack Lincoln, Engagement Partner
From: George Smith, Senior Associate
Re: Daley Company Interim Fieldwork Results
Date: December 15, 20X6

1. Risk assessments for Daley Company have historically been set at low for the revenue cycle. There have been no modifications to the controls during the fiscal year. During tests of controls, we noted six instances out of ten where there were errors when we vouched amounts in the subledger to original sales documents. We noted that revenue was consistently recorded at FOB shipping point.

2. Risk assessments for Daley Company have historically been set at low for the purchasing cycle. There have been no modifications to the controls during the fiscal year. No exceptions were noted during tests of controls.

3. Consistent with the audits of the last five years, we recommend setting materiality at 5% of net income, or $79,200.

4. During our interviews with Finance Department staff, several of them mentioned the increasing amount of disagreements between the Controller and CFO. The number of arguments seems to have increased from the prior year.

5. We met with senior management (CEO, Executive Vice President, and CFO). It was noted that both net sales and net income amounts were significantly lower than budgeted for the first ten months of the fiscal year. The CEO stated that this is due to the company's new ventures, such as the Timmy Tiger product line. The Executive Vice President stated that the disappointing results were due to the closing of several high-end brick and mortar stores, which were major customers for Daley.

Minutes of Special Meeting

Daley Company
Minutes of Special Meeting of December 20, 20X6

Members Present: All seven members present.

Agenda items:
1. Approval of Thomas Washington's recommendation to immediately cease production of all Timmy Tiger products. Mark Washington recommended against this action.
2. Approval of interest-free, open-ended loan of $225,000 to MaryAnn Washington Sparks.
3. Approval of agreement to a settlement in harassment suit against Henry Washington by former employee.

Actions taken:
1. Agenda item #1 not approved.
2. Agenda item #2 not approved.
3. Agenda item #3 approved by majority.

Draft Financial Statements

Daley Company
Income Statements - Draft for Discussion Purposes Only
For the years ended December 31, 20X6 and 20X5

	20X6	20X5
Sales, net of returns & allowances	2,850,700	4,760,200
Less: Cost of goods sold	(1,498,900)	(1,666,100)
Net sales	1,351,800	3,094,100
Compensation expense	824,600	819,500
Legal expense	250,000	47,000
Utilities expense	79,530	72,600
Lease expense	120,000	120,000
Depreciation expense	9,200	89,500
Other expense	31,900	36,700
Total expense	1,315,230	1,185,300
Net operating revenue	36,570	1,908,800
Gain on sale	400,000	
Income taxes	228,000	324,100
Net revenue	208,570	1,584,700

Daley Company
Balance Sheets - Draft for Discussion Purposes Only
December 31, 20X6 and 20X5

	20X6	20X5
Current Assets:		
Cash & Cash Equivalents	2,534,360	2,996,130
Accounts Receivable	540,200	290,800
Less: Allowance for Doubtful Accounts	10,800	5,800
Prepaid Expenses	76,700	65,270
Inventory (at LCM)	3,180,620	2,070,600
Notes Receivable	475,000	250,000
Total Current Assets	6,817,680	5,678,600
Long-Term Assets:		
Buildings, at cost	-	1,250,000
Less: Accumulated Depreciation	(833,300)	(833,000)
Furniture & Fixtures	92,000	90,000
Less: Accumulated Depreciation	(36,200)	(27,000)
Total Long-Term Assets	(777,500)	480,000
Total Assets	6,040,180	6,158,600

	20X6	20X5
Current Liabilities:		
Accounts Payable	337,040	307,130
Current Portion of Long-Term Debt	300,000	300,000
Taxes Payable	225,300	200,100
Accrued Expenses	42,600	29,700
Accrued Vacation	15,000	10,000
Total Current Liabilities	919,940	846,930
Long-Term Liabilities:		
Notes Payable	1,100,000	1,400,000
Total Liabilities	2,019,940	2,246,930
Common Stock	400,000	400,000
Retained Earnings	4,220,240	4,011,670
Dividends Paid	(600,000)	(500,000)
Total Equity	4,020,240	3,911,670
Total Liabilities and Equity	6,040,180	6,158,600

Prior Year Audit Program

Daley Company
Year ended December 31, 20X5
Year-end Audit

Accounts Receivable

- Obtain a summary schedule of all Accounts Receivable accounts. Agree each account balance to the Trial Balance. Tie the schedule total to the Financial Statements.

- Confirm balances > $79,200. Investigate any discrepancies.

- Examine Allowance for Doubtful Accounts for preciseness and consistency with company policy.

- Trace receivables greater than the materiality threshold to subsequent cash collections in 20X6.

- Vouch one receivable to original sales transaction documents. Investigate any discrepancies.

- Inquire about discounting and factoring of balances.

- Review cutoff of sales, sales returns, and cash receipts.

Notes Receivable:

- Obtain a summary schedule of all Notes Receivable accounts. Agree each account balance to the Trial Balance. Tie the schedule total to the Financial Statements.

- Confirm balances. Investigate any discrepancies.

- Inquire of management about discounting and factoring of items.

- Trace Notes Receivable > $79,200 to subsequent cash collections in 20X6.

- Examine Allowance for Doubtful Accounts for preciseness and consistency with company policy.

- Inquire about new loan agreements.

Lecture 1.17
Document Review Simulation 2

The Uniform CPA Examination

Unsplit | Split Horiz | Split Vertical | Authoritative Literature | Spreadsheet | Calculator | Submit Testlet

Work Tab | Resources | Help

Scroll down to complete all parts of this task.

Company

Hydrojet, Inc., is a manufacturer of jet boats and personal watercraft, with headquarters in northern Florida. Personal watercraft are manufactured at the Florida facility. The company's jet boats are manufactured at a Mexico facility. Finished goods are sold primarily to independent marine stores throughout the United States.

In its ninth year of operations, Hydrojet has experienced two years of declining jet boats sales after a period of rapid growth. The overall market demand for jet boats has declined and many competitors have filed for bankruptcy in recent years. Due to several innovations, the demand for personal watercraft has declined only slightly. Tough new federal emissions regulations further threaten industry profitability.

Engagement

The year under audit is year 2. This is the first year that Hydrojet has engaged Cutt, Paste, and Semele, CPAs, to perform the annual audit of its financial statements. The prior audit firm is upset that they have lost the audit client. However, they indicate that no disagreements with management have occurred. The audit committee indicates that they changed firms because they wanted to institute a policy of no more than five consecutive years with the same audit firm. A senior accountant from the prior audit firm took an accounting position with Hydrojet on September 1.

Facility Tour

The CFO gives your audit team a tour of the Florida facility. During the tour, you note that parts of the facility seem to require some minor repairs.

You note that the finished watercraft inventory is kept in a lot enclosed only by a chain-link fence. The CFO explains that the company has not had any problems with theft of its products owing to its rural location. You also note several of these watercrafts are much dustier than others.

The CFO comments on the collegiality of the workforce. However, in your tour of the office, you overhear two clerical employees complaining about their rate of pay. While in the lunch room, you overhear several other employees recounting war stories about a recent accounting software upgrade, noting how fortunate it was that the accounting department staff is not required to take vacations annually—or the upgrade still might not be finished.

Task

Amend the memo for the team leader of this audit, documenting the risk of material misstatement as appropriate. To revise the document, click on each segment of underlined text below and select the needed correction, if any, from the list provided. If the underlined text is already correct in the context of the document, select [Original text]. If none of the statements are appropriate in the context of the document, select [Delete text].

Memo Excerpt

To: Adrian Cutt, Audit Team Leader
From: Ben Paste, Staff
Re: Preliminary List of Risk of Material Misstatements
Date: September 3, Year 2

Adrian:

Here is a list of risks of material misstatements to date.

A. Jet boats are manufactured at a Mexico facility. This may pose (1) no unforeseen risk. (2) We need not change our audit plan owing to this circumstance.

B. Finished goods are sold primarily to independent marine stores throughout the United States. This may pose (3) no unforeseen risk. (4) We need not change our audit plan owing to this circumstance.

C. Hydrojet, in its ninth year of operations, has experienced two years of declining jet boat sales after a period of rapid growth. The overall market demand for jet boats also has declined and many competitors have filed for bankruptcy in recent years. This may pose (5) no unforeseen risk. (6) We need not change our audit plan owing to this circumstance.

D. Due to several innovations, the demand for personal watercraft has declined only slightly. This may pose (7) no unforeseen risk. (8) We need not change our audit plan owing to this circumstance.

E. To help achieve a 25% increase in sales goal, the CEO has changed the sales staff's compensation from salaried to commission based. This may pose (9) no unforeseen risk. (10) We need not change our audit plan owing to this circumstance.

F. Unhappy with past sales performance, the CEO plans to terminate relationships with several retail outlets and identify new retail outlets for distribution of its product lines. This may pose (11) no unforeseen risk. (12) We need not change our audit plan owing to this circumstance.

G. Hydrojet's bank has placed strict new covenants on the company's renewed line of credit. This may pose (13) no unforeseen risk. (14) We need not change our audit plan owing to this circumstance.

H. A senior accountant from the prior audit firm has taken an accounting position with Hydrojet. This may pose (15) no unforeseen risk. (16) We need not change our audit plan owing to this circumstance.

I. While in the lunch room, several employees were overheard recounting war stories in connection with a recent accounting software upgrade. This may pose (17) no unforeseen risk. (18) We need not change our audit plan owing to this circumstance.

J. The accounting department staff is not required to take vacations. This may pose (19) no unforeseen risk. (20) We need not change our audit plan owing to this circumstance.

Ben

Items for Analysis

Jet boats are manufactured at a Mexico facility. This may pose no unforeseen risk.

1. Choose an option below:

   - [Original text] no unforeseen risk.

   - a financial statement level risk.

   - a relevant assertion level risk.

Jet boats are manufactured at a Mexico facility. We need not change our audit plan owing to this circumstance.

2. Choose an option below:

   - [Original text] We need not change our audit plan owing to this circumstance.

   - [Delete text]

   - Significant changes in the operating and economic environment may reveal previously unknown weaknesses.

   - New personnel may not be adequately trained in internal control processes.

   - New or revamped information systems are relatively untested.

   - The internal controls may not be sufficiently scalable for rapid growth.

   - Foreign operations add another layer of complexity.

   - This suggests management is not very focused on internal controls, causing concern about the tone at the top.

Finished goods are sold primarily to independent marine stores throughout the United States. This may pose no unforeseen risk.

3. Choose an option below:

   - [Original text] no unforeseen risk.

   - a financial statement level risk.

   - a relevant assertion level risk.

Finished goods are sold primarily to independent marine stores throughout the United States. We need not change our audit plan owing to this circumstance.

4. Choose an option below:

   - [Original text] We need not change our audit plan owing to this circumstance.

   - [Delete text]

   - Significant changes in the operating and economic environment may reveal previously unknown weaknesses.

   - New personnel may not be adequately trained in internal control processes.

   - New or revamped information systems are relatively untested.

   - The internal controls may not be sufficiently scalable for rapid growth.

   - Foreign operations add another layer of complexity.

- This suggests management is not very focused on internal controls, causing concern about the tone at the top.

Hydrojet, in its ninth year of operations, has experienced two years of declining jet boat sales after a period of rapid growth. The overall market demand for jet boats also has declined and many competitors have filed for bankruptcy in recent years. This may pose no unforeseen risk.

5. Choose an option below:

- [Original text] no unforeseen risk.

- a financial statement level risk.

- a relevant assertion level risk.

Hydrojet, in its ninth year of operations, has experienced two years of declining jet boat sales after a period of rapid growth. The overall market demand for jet boats also has declined and many competitors have filed for bankruptcy in recent years. We need not change our audit plan owing to this circumstance.

6. Choose an option below:

- [Original text] We need not change our audit plan owing to this circumstance.

- [Delete text]

- Significant changes in the operating and economic environment may reveal previously unknown weaknesses.

- New personnel may not be adequately trained in internal control processes.

- New or revamped information systems are relatively untested.

- The internal controls may not be sufficiently scalable for rapid growth.

- Foreign operations add another layer of complexity.

Due to several innovations, the demand for personal watercraft has declined only slightly. This may pose no unforeseen risk.

7. Choose an option below:

- [Original text] no unforeseen risk.

- a financial statement level risk.

- a relevant assertion level risk.

Due to several innovations, the demand for personal watercraft has declined only slightly. We need not change our audit plan owing to this circumstance.

8. Choose an option below:

- [Original text] We need not change our audit plan owing to this circumstance.

- [Delete text]

- New personnel may not be adequately trained in internal control processes.

- New or revamped information systems are relatively untested.

- The internal controls may not be sufficiently scalable for rapid growth.

- New sales outlets introduce new potential for a fraudulent entity to take advantage of Hydrojet, under the guise of a legitimate outlet.

- New technology may cause obsolescence in existing inventory.

- Changes to conform to compliance requirements may not be executed accurately, as all personnel might not understand their duties under the new requirements sufficiently.

To help achieve a 25% increase in sales goal, the CEO has changed the sales staff's compensation from salaried to commission based. This may pose no unforeseen risk.

9. Choose an option below:

- [Original text] no unforeseen risk.

- a financial statement level risk.

- a relevant assertion level risk.

To help achieve a 25% increase in sales goal, the CEO has changed the sales staff's compensation from salaried to commission based. We need not change our audit plan owing to this circumstance.

10. Choose an option below:

- [Original text] We need not change our audit plan owing to this circumstance.

- [Delete text]

- New personnel may not be adequately trained in internal control processes.

- New or revamped information systems are relatively untested.

- The internal controls may not be sufficiently scalable for rapid growth.

- Disgruntled employees might be motivated to commit fraud or theft.

- Sales staff on commission might be motivated to commit fraud that they would not consider on salary.

- Managers with significant bonus opportunities based on profits might be motivated to commit fraud.

- Foreign operations add another layer of complexity—for example, taxes, currency exchange, and additional regulatory bodies.

- New sales outlets introduce new potential for a fraudulent entity to take advantage of Hydrojet, under the guise of a legitimate outlet.

- This suggests management is not very focused on internal controls, causing concern about the tone at the top.

Unhappy with past sales performance, the CEO plans to terminate relationships with several retail outlets and identify new retail outlets for distribution of its product lines. This may pose no unforeseen risk.

11. Choose an option below:

- [Original text] no unforeseen risk.

- a financial statement level risk.

- a relevant assertion level risk.

Unhappy with past sales performance, the CEO plans to terminate relationships with several retail outlets and identify new retail outlets for distribution of its product lines. We need not change our audit plan owing to this circumstance.

12. Choose an option below:

- [Original text] We need not change our audit plan owing to this circumstance.

- [Delete text]

- New personnel may not be adequately trained in internal control processes.

- New or revamped information systems are relatively untested.

- The internal controls may not be sufficiently scalable for rapid growth.

- Disgruntled employees might be motivated to commit fraud or theft.

- Sales staff on commission might be motivated to commit fraud that they would not consider on salary.

- Unrealistic goals may motivate employees to report false results.

- Foreign operations add another layer of complexity—for example, taxes, currency exchange, and additional regulatory bodies.

- New sales outlets introduce new potential for a fraudulent entity to take advantage of Hydrojet, under the guise of a legitimate outlet.

- This suggests management is not very focused on internal controls, causing concern about the tone at the top.

Hydrojet's bank has placed strict new covenants on the company's renewed line of credit. This may pose no unforeseen risk.

13. Choose an option below:

- [Original text] no unforeseen risk.

- a financial statement level risk.

- a relevant assertion level risk.

Hydrojet's bank has placed strict new covenants on the company's renewed line of credit. We need not change our audit plan owing to this circumstance.

14. Choose an option below:

- [Original text] We need not change our audit plan owing to this circumstance.

- [Delete text]

- Significant changes in the operating and economic environment may reveal previously unknown weaknesses.

- New personnel may not be adequately trained in internal control processes.

- New or revamped information systems are relatively untested.

- The internal controls may not be sufficiently scalable for rapid growth.

- Disgruntled employees might be motivated to commit fraud or theft.

- Sales staff on commission might be motivated to commit fraud that they would not consider on salary.

- Managers with significant bonus opportunities based on profits might be motivated to commit fraud.

- Foreign operations add another layer of complexity—for example, taxes, currency exchange, and additional regulatory bodies.

- New sales outlets introduce new potential for a fraudulent entity to take advantage of Hydrojet, under the guise of a legitimate outlet.

- This suggests management is not very focused on internal controls, causing concern about the tone at the top.

A senior accountant from the prior audit firm has taken an accounting position with Hydrojet. This may pose no unforeseen risk.

15. Choose an option below:

- [Original text] no unforeseen risk.

- a financial statement level risk.

- a relevant assertion level risk.

A senior accountant from the prior audit firm has taken an accounting position with Hydrojet. We need not change our audit plan owing to this circumstance.

16. Choose an option below:

- [Original text] We need not change our audit plan owing to this circumstance.

- [Delete text]

- New personnel may not be adequately trained in internal control processes.

- An employee of the audit firm formerly with the client could be in the position of auditing his or her own work.

- An employee of the client formerly with the audit firm would know how to thwart some of the audit procedures.

- This suggests management is not very focused on internal controls, causing concern about the tone at the top.

While in the lunch room, several employees were overheard recounting war stories in connection with a recent accounting software upgrade. This may pose no unforeseen risk.

17. Choose an option below:

- [Original text] no unforeseen risk.

- a financial statement level risk.

- a relevant assertion level risk.

While in the lunch room, several employees were overheard recounting war stories in connection with a recent accounting software upgrade. We need not change our audit plan owing to this circumstance.

18. Choose an option below:

- [Original text] We need not change our audit plan owing to this circumstance.

- [Delete text]

- Known weaknesses in internal control suggest unknown weaknesses in internal control exist.

- New personnel may not be adequately trained in internal control processes.

- New or revamped information systems are relatively untested.

- The internal controls may not be sufficiently scalable for rapid growth.

- Sales staff on commission might be motivated to commit fraud that they would not consider on salary.

- Managers with significant bonus opportunities based on profits might be motivated to commit fraud.

- Unrealistic goals may motivate employees to report false results.

- This suggests management is not very focused on internal controls, causing concern about the tone at the top.

The accounting department staff is not required to take vacations. This may pose no unforeseen risk.

19. Choose an option below:

- [Original text] no unforeseen risk.

- a financial statement level risk.

- a relevant assertion level risk.

The accounting department staff is not required to take vacations. We need not change our audit plan owing to this circumstance.

20. The accounting department staff is not required to take vacations. Choose an option below:

- [Original text] We need not change our audit plan owing to this circumstance.

- [Delete text]

- Significant changes in the operating and economic environment may reveal previously unknown weaknesses.

- Foreign operations add another layer of complexity—for example, taxes, currency exchange, and additional regulatory bodies.

- New sales outlets introduce new potential for a fraudulent entity to take advantage of Hydrojet, under the guise of a legitimate outlet.

- New technology may cause obsolescence in existing inventory.

- New technology may make existing inventory obsolete.

- Changes to conform to compliance requirements may not be executed accurately, as all personnel might not understand their duties under the new requirements sufficiently.

- This suggests management is not very focused on internal controls, causing concern about the tone at the top.

Resources/Exhibits

Excerpt from Consultant's Business Projection Report

Eager to revive Hydrojet's profitability, the Board of Directors has implemented several new changes, starting with the hiring of a new CEO, lured away from a major competitor.
To further protect its bottom line, the Board of Directors has restructured the CEO's and CFO's compensation packages, to include a substantial bonus based on the company's net profits, effective for year 3.

The new CEO is optimistic and ambitious and has set a goal of a 25% increase in sales for year 3. To help achieve this goal, the CEO has changed the sales staff's compensation from salaried to commission-based. Unhappy with past sales performance, the CEO plans to terminate relationships with several retail outlets and identify new retail outlets for distribution of its product lines.

Excerpt from Bank Correspondence

First State Bank
2900 Prosperous Way
Eventide, CA 00910

Due to recent declining trends, we have initiated stricter covenants applicable to all business debt. This includes Hydrojet's line of credit, renewed June 30, year 2.

Excerpt from Board of Director's Minutes

On April 17, Hydrojet uncovered embezzlement by Patricia Poplar, a payroll clerk. The clerk's scheme was to add hours to her timesheet after approval, during processing of the timecards. The company was fortunate to discover the theft while the employee was out sick for two days. The CFO indicates that while this discovery was unexpected, he is confident that this was an isolated occurrence.

DOCUMENT REVIEW SIMULATION SOLUTIONS

Document Review Simulation Solution 1

Proposed 20X6 Audit Program
Daley Company
Year ended December 31, 20X6
Year-end Audit

Accounts Receivable:

1. Obtain a summary schedule of all Accounts Receivable accounts. Agree each account balance to the Trial Balance. Foot/recalculate all totals on the summary schedule. Tie the schedule total to the Financial Statements.

2. Confirm 100% of individually material receivables and a sample of the remaining balances. Investigate any discrepancies.

3. Examine Allowance for Doubtful Accounts for reasonableness and consistency with company policy. Recalculate the Allowance for Doubtful Accounts to ensure that company policy is being followed. Investigate and document any digressions from policy. Examine the aging of Accounts Receivable to determine the adequacy of the allowance.

4. Trace receivables greater than materiality threshold to subsequent cash collections in 20X7.

5. Vouch new Accounts Receivable to original sales transaction documents. Investigate any discrepancies.

6. Inquire about pledging, discounting, and factoring of balances.

7. Review cutoff of sales, sales returns, and cash receipts.

8. Perform analytical procedures on Accounts Receivable and Allowance for Doubtful Accounts to evaluate reasonableness of balances and to understand account trends.

Notes Receivable:

9. Obtain a summary schedule of all Notes Receivable accounts. Agree each account balance to the Trial Balance. Foot/recalculate all totals on the summary schedule. Tie the schedule total to the Financial Statements.

10. Confirm year-end balances. Investigate any discrepancies.

11. Inquire about pledging, discounting, and factoring of balances.

12. Trace Notes Receivable > $10,600 to subsequent cash collections in 20X7.

13. Examine Allowance for Doubtful Accounts for reasonableness and consistency with company policy. Recalculate the Allowance for Doubtful Accounts to ensure that company policy is being

followed. Investigate and document any digressions from policy. Examine the aging of Notes Receivable to determine the adequacy of the allowance.

14. Review new loan agreements.

15. Inquire of management about loans to management and other related parties, especially those that have any unique terms. Determine the business purpose of the transaction and verify that it has been approved by the Board of Directors. Evaluate whether any notes require disclosure in the financial statements.

EXPLANATIONS:

Accounts Receivable:

1. Obtain a summary schedule of all Accounts Receivable accounts. Agree each account balance to the Trial Balance. Foot/recalculate all totals on the summary schedule. Tie the schedule total to the Financial Statements.

The correct procedure is the sixth answer choice, "Obtain a summary schedule of all Accounts Receivable accounts. Agree each account balance to the Trial Balance. Foot/recalculate all totals on the summary schedule. Tie the schedule total to the Financial Statements." The summary schedule of all Accounts Receivable will include a list of all the different Accounts Receivable accounts within the various locations and divisions of the entity, with subtotals for each group of related accounts. Each of the accounts will also be listed on the Trial Balance and the accountant will make certain that each balance on the Trial Balance is in agreement with the balance on the schedule. The accountant will verify the clerical accuracy of the schedule by footing or recalculating all of the balances on the schedule to make certain that an error was not made or that the total was not fraudulently misstated. The accountant will also make certain that the amount on the Financial Statements, which will be the total, agrees with the total on the schedule to make certain that the Financial Statements are accurate.

The first, fourth, and fifth alternatives include some, but not all of the appropriate procedures. The third alternative is also incorrect because it does not have the accountant performing any procedures in relation to the schedule.

2. Confirm 100% of individually material receivables and a sample of the remaining balances. Investigate any discrepancies.

The correct procedure of "Confirm 100% of individually material receivables and a sample of the remaining balances. Investigate any discrepancies." This procedure satisfies the audit objectives of Rights & Obligations and Existence. Shipley Company found six errors out of ten during its interim controls testing of the revenue cycle. It also noted that revenue was consistently recorded at FOB shipping point. However, Daley's accounting policy is to record revenue at FOB destination. Based upon these results, Shipley should increase its risk assessment for the revenue cycle from low to medium or high. As a result, Shipley will have to increase the amount of its year-end audit work since it cannot rely on controls in this area as it did previously. Due to the need for an increased amount of substantive procedures in conjunction with the decrease in materiality threshold, the auditor should confirm individually material receivables and a sample of the remaining balances. PPS sampling (discussed in another section) is ideal for this situation. While $79,200 is the materiality threshold for the statements as a whole, it is too large for the threshold for consideration of individual items within A/R; two mistakes of $70,000 in individual items could distort A/R materially. On the other hand, confirming 100% of A/R balances might not be necessary; the client may have many small balances that, even in the aggregate, are immaterial. By confirming individually material receivables and a sample of the remaining balances, the audit is both effective and efficient. The auditor should always investigate any discrepancies.

3. Examine Allowance for Doubtful Accounts for reasonableness and consistency with company policy. Recalculate the Allowance for Doubtful Accounts to ensure that company policy is being followed. Investigate and document any digressions from policy. Examine the aging of Accounts Receivable to determine the adequacy of the allowance.

The correct procedure is "Examine Allowance for Doubtful Accounts for reasonableness and consistency with company policy. Recalculate the Allowance for Doubtful Accounts to ensure that company policy is being followed. Investigate and document any digressions from policy. Examine the aging of Accounts Receivable to determine the adequacy of the allowance." This procedure satisfies the audit objective of Allocation, Accuracy & Valuation. Since the company's policy for determining the Allowance for Doubtful Accounts is an accounting estimate, the auditor is not examining for precision, but rather for reasonableness. The auditor should always recalculate the Allowance for Doubtful Accounts to ensure that company policy is being followed. An auditor should always investigate and document any digressions from policy. The auditor should examine the aging of Accounts Receivable to determine the adequacy of the allowance.

4. Trace receivables greater than materiality threshold to subsequent cash collections in 20X7.

The correct procedure is "Trace receivables greater than materiality threshold to subsequent cash collections in 20X7," which satisfies the audit objective of Allocation, Accuracy & Valuation. If a receivable has a balance as of the end of the entity's fiscal period, collection must occur, at the earliest, in the next period. As a result, the auditor needs to look at cash collections in the period following the year under audit. The proper fiscal year for the audit procedure is 20X7. It is likely that the auditor did not accurately update this procedure from the prior year audit program.

5. Vouch new Accounts Receivable to original sales transaction documents. Investigate any discrepancies.

The correct procedure is "Vouch new Accounts Receivable to original sales transaction documents. Investigate any discrepancies." This procedure satisfies the audit objectives of Existence, and Rights & Obligations. For previous audits, control risk was assessed at low for the revenue cycle. However, based on the number of errors found during interim control testing, and the fact that Daley Company is consistently recording revenue at FOB shipping point, instead of following its policy of recording revenue at FOB destination, Shipley cannot rely heavily on Daley's revenue cycle controls. Shipley will need to perform a greater number of substantive tests than in the past. The auditor can, however, rely on prior year testing for prior year items. The auditor should only vouch new receivables to original sales transaction documents. The auditor should always investigate any discrepancies.

6. Inquire about pledging, discounting, and factoring of balances.

The correct procedure is "Inquire about pledging, discounting, and factoring of balances," which satisfies the audit objectives of Rights & Obligations and Presentation & Disclosure. The auditor does not need to inquire about confirming balances, as that is an audit procedure that Shipley performs.

7. Review cutoff of sales, sales returns, and cash receipts.

The original procedure of "Review cutoff of sales, sales returns, and cash receipts" is correct. This procedure satisfies the audit objective of Rights & Obligations. All three areas of sales, sales returns, and cash receipts should be examined for proper cutoff.

8. Perform analytical procedures on Accounts Receivable and Allowance for Doubtful Accounts to evaluate reasonableness of balances and to understand account trends.

The correct procedure is "Perform analytical procedures on Accounts Receivable and Allowance for Doubtful Accounts to evaluate reasonableness of balances and to understand account trends." This procedure satisfies the audit objectives of Completeness and Allocation, Accuracy & Valuation. To evaluate reasonableness of balances and understand account trends, the auditor performs analytical procedures, such as ratio analysis.

Notes Receivable:

9. Obtain a summary schedule of all Notes Receivable accounts. Agree each account balance to the Trial Balance. Foot/recalculate all totals on the summary schedule. Tie the schedule total to the Financial Statements.

The correct procedure is "Obtain a summary schedule of all Notes Receivable accounts. Agree each account balance to the Trial Balance. Foot/recalculate all totals on the summary schedule. Tie the schedule total to the Financial Statements," which satisfies the audit objective of Allocation, Accuracy and Valuation. The auditor needs to agree each account on the summary schedule to the trial balance to ensure that the numbers being audited agree to the company's accounting records. The auditor needs to tie the schedule total to the financial statements to ensure that the amounts audited are equal to those amounts presented on the financial statements. The auditor needs to foot all totals on the summary schedule. Even if the source of the schedule is a spreadsheet, the spreadsheet formulas may contain errors. Since this lead schedule ties to the final financial statements, the auditor must ensure that all of the totals are correct.

10. Confirm year-end balances. Investigate any discrepancies.

The correct procedure is "Confirm year-end balances. Investigate any discrepancies."   This procedure satisfies the audit objectives of Rights & Obligations, Existence and Allocation, Accuracy & Valuation. The auditor should confirm year-end balances, and not payments or transactions that occur during the fiscal year.

11. Inquire about pledging, discounting, and factoring of balances.

The correct procedure is "Inquire about pledging, discounting, and factoring of balances," which satisfies the audit objectives of Rights & Obligations and Presentation & Disclosure. The auditor does not need to inquire about confirming balances, as that is an audit procedure that Shipley performs.

12. Trace Notes Receivable > $10,600 to subsequent cash collections in 20X7.

The correct procedure is "Trace Notes Receivable > $10,600 to subsequent cash collections in 20X7." This procedure satisfies the audit objectives of Allocation, Accuracy & Valuation. Shipley has used 5% of net income as its materiality threshold in past years' audits of Daley, which has consistently yielded a dollar amount of approximately $79,200. However, based on Daley's draft financial statements, 5% of net income for 20X6 would be $10,600. The auditor needs to look at cash collections in the period following the year under audit. Therefore, the proper fiscal year for the audit procedure is 20X7. The auditor may not have appropriately updated this procedure from the prior year audit program. The auditor should note that since Notes Receivable are likely longer term than trade Accounts Receivable, the auditor should look for partial payments made in the subsequent period, but may not find an entire note's balance paid off.

13. Examine Allowance for Doubtful Accounts for reasonableness and consistency with company policy. Recalculate the Allowance for Doubtful Accounts to ensure that company policy is being followed. Investigate and document any digressions from policy. Examine the aging of Notes Receivable to determine the adequacy of the allowance.

The correct procedure is "Examine Allowance for Doubtful Accounts for reasonableness and consistency with company policy. Recalculate the Allowance for Doubtful Accounts to ensure that company policy is being followed. Investigate and document any digressions from policy. Examine the aging of Notes Receivable to determine the adequacy of the allowance." This procedure satisfies that audit objective of Allocation, Accuracy & Valuation. Since the company's policy for determining the Allowance for Doubtful Accounts is an accounting estimate, the auditor is not examining for precision, but rather for reasonableness. The auditor should always recalculate the Allowance for Doubtful Accounts to ensure that company policy is being followed. An auditor should always investigate and document any digressions from policy. The auditor should examine the aging of Notes Receivable to determine the adequacy of the allowance.

14. Review new loan agreements.

The correct procedure is "Review new loan agreements," which satisfies the audit objectives of Existence and Presentation & Disclosure. The auditor needs to review, rather than just inquire about, the terms of any new loan agreements. The agreements themselves can't be vouched, traced, or agreed to the balance sheets; only the amounts can be agreed to the Trial Balance, and the sum of all Notes Receivable would tie to the balance sheets.

15. Inquire of management about loans to management and other related parties, especially those that have any unique terms. Determine the business purpose of the transaction and verify that it has been approved by the Board of Directors. Evaluate whether any notes require disclosure in the financial statements.

The correct procedure is "Inquire of management about loans to management and other related parties, especially those that have any unique terms. Determine the business purpose of the transaction and verify that it has been approved by the Board of Directors. Evaluate whether any notes require disclosure in the financial statements." This procedure satisfies the audit objective of Presentation & Disclosure. The addition of this procedure is necessary as the auditor should always review for transactions with related parties, paying attention to any unique terms. In fact, the minutes of the special December 20, 20X6, meeting indicate that a $225,000 loan to the CFO was not verified by the Board of Directors. However, the balance of Notes Receivable increased by exactly that amount. The auditor needs to assess this situation with skepticism. A related party transaction may require disclosure in the notes to the financial statements.

Document Review Simulation Solution 2

To: Adrian Cutt, Audit Team Leader
From: Ben Paste, Staff
Re: Preliminary List of Risk of Material Misstatements
Date: September 3, Year 2

Adrian:

Here is a list of risks of material misstatements to date.

A. Jet boats are manufactured at a Mexico facility. This may pose (1) a financial statement level risk. (2) Foreign operations add another layer of complexity.

B. Finished goods are sold primarily to independent marine stores throughout the United States. This may pose (3) no unforeseen risk. (4) We need not change our audit plan owing to this circumstance.

C. Hydrojet, in its ninth year of operations, has experienced two years of declining jet boat sales after a period of rapid growth. The overall market demand for jet boats also has declined and many competitors have filed for bankruptcy in recent years. This may pose (5) a financial statement level risk. (6) Significant changes in the operating and economic environment may reveal previously unknown weaknesses.

D. Due to several innovations, the demand for personal watercraft has declined only slightly. This may pose (7) a relevant assertion level risk. (8) New technology may cause obsolescence in existing inventory.

E. To help achieve a 25% increase in sales goal, the CEO has changed the sales staff's compensation from salaried to commission-based. This may pose (9) a relevant assertion level risk. (10) Sales staff on commission might be motivated to commit fraud that they would not consider on salary.

F. Unhappy with past sales performance, the CEO plans to terminate relationships with several retail outlets and identify new retail outlets for distribution of its product lines. This may pose (11) a relevant assertion level risk. (12) New sales outlets introduce new potential for a fraudulent entity to take advantage of Hydrojet, under the guise of a legitimate outlet.

G. Hydrojet's bank has placed strict new covenants on the company's renewed line of credit. This may pose (13) a financial statement level risk. (14) Managers with significant bonus opportunities based on profits might be motivated to commit fraud.

H. A senior accountant from the prior audit firm has taken an accounting position with Hydrojet. This may pose (15) no unforeseen risk. (16) We need not change our audit plan owing to this circumstance.

I. While in the lunch room, several employees were overheard recounting war stories in connection with a recent accounting software upgrade. This may pose (17) a financial statement level risk. (18) New or revamped information systems are relatively untested.

J. The accounting department staff is not required to take vacations. This may pose (19) a financial statement level risk. (20) This suggests management is not very focused on internal controls, causing concern about the tone at the top.

Explanations

1. [Mexico facility] <u>This may pose a financial statement level risk.</u>

   - No unforeseen risk. Foreign operations add another layer of complexity.

   - **A financial statement level risk.** Minimal foreign operations typically involve currency transactions. An entire facility in a foreign country impacts many financial statement accounts in various ways (for example, valuation, presentation, and disclosure) as well as adding possible confusion in terms of culture and language. Editors' Note: While the scenario is similar to another simulation, the items requiring responses are different. The examiners frequently use the same scenarios with different questions.

   - A relevant assertion level risk. Minimal foreign operations typically involve currency transactions. An entire facility in a foreign country impacts many financial statement accounts in various ways (for example, valuation, presentation, and disclosure) as well as adding possible confusion in terms of culture and language.

2. [Mexico facility] <u>Foreign operations add another layer of complexity.</u>

   - We need not change our audit plan owing to this circumstance. Foreign operations add another layer of complexity.

   - [Delete text] An appropriate comment is among those available for response.

   - Significant changes in the operating and economic environment may reveal previously unknown weaknesses. The use of the foreign facility does not suggest a significant change from operations in previous years.

   - New personnel may not be adequately trained in internal control processes. The use of the foreign facility does not suggest inadequate training.

   - New or revamped information systems are relatively untested. The use of the foreign facility does not suggest information systems that are relatively untested.

   - The internal controls may not be sufficiently scalable for rapid growth. The use of the foreign facility does not suggest internal controls without scalability.

   - **Foreign operations add another layer of complexity.** Minimal foreign operations typically involve currency transactions. An entire facility in a foreign country impacts many financial statement accounts in various ways (for example, valuation, presentation, and disclosure) as well as adding possible confusion in terms of culture and language. Editors' Note: While the scenario is similar to another simulation, the items requiring responses are different. The examiners frequently use the same scenarios with different questions.

   - This suggests management is not very focused on internal controls, causing concern about the tone at the top. The use of the foreign facility does not suggest an inappropriate tone at the top.

3. [independent marine stores] <u>No unforeseen risk.</u>

   - **No unforeseen risk.** Sales to independent parties are considered the norm.

   - A financial statement level risk. Sales to independent parties are considered the norm.

- A relevant assertion level risk. Sales to independent parties are considered the norm.

4. [independent marine stores] We need not change our audit plan owing to this circumstance.

   - **We need not change our audit plan owing to this circumstance.** Sales to independent parties are considered the norm.

   - [Delete text] An appropriate comment is among those available for response.

   - Significant changes in the operating and economic environment may reveal previously unknown weaknesses. Sales to independent parties is not a change from operations in previous years.

   - New personnel may not be adequately trained in internal control processes. Sales to independent parties do not suggest inadequate training.

   - New or revamped information systems are relatively untested. Sales to independent parties do not suggest new or revamped information systems.

   - The internal controls may not be sufficiently scalable for rapid growth. Sales to independent parties do not suggest internal controls without scalability. Transactions with related parties would merit added procedures.

   - Foreign operations add another layer of complexity. Sales to independent parties do not suggest foreign operations are falsely reported. No mention is made that the independent stores are foreign.

   - This suggests management is not very focused on internal controls, causing concern about the tone at the top. Sales to independent parties are considered the norm. Transactions with related parties would merit additional procedures.

5. [2 years of declining jet boat sales] <u>A financial statement level risk.</u>

   - No unforeseen risk. A significant decline in revenue will have a ripple effect to all areas of operations.

   - **A financial statement level risk.** A significant decline in revenue will have a ripple effect to all areas of operations.

   - A relevant assertion level risk. A significant decline in revenue will have a ripple effect to all areas of operations.

6. [2 years of declining jet boat sales] <u>Significant changes in the operating and economic environment may reveal previously unknown weaknesses.</u>

   - We need not change our audit plan owing to this circumstance. A significant decline in revenue will have a ripple effect to all areas of operations.

   - [Delete text] An appropriate comment is among those available for response.

   - **Significant changes in the operating and economic environment may reveal previously unknown weaknesses.** A significant decline in sales will have a ripple effect to all areas of operations. As pressure comes from declining sales, management might be tempted to misstate financial position to ensure continued credit and to support managers' bonuses. Sales staff working on commission might be tempted to inflate sales just to maintain the same level of compensation. Operations personnel might get increasing pressure to contain costs, resulting in lower quality products or raw materials from questionable sources. Also, any existing fraud or theft may come to light; for instance, the decline in jet boat sales will make it more difficult for any existing lapping of receivables to continue. That the overall market demand for jet boats also has declined and many competitors have filed for bankruptcy in recent years points to a significant change.

- New personnel may not be adequately trained in internal control processes. The decline in jet boat sales does not suggest inadequate training. While an argument could be made that training might be curtailed if lower revenues continue for long, there is a better response available.

- New or revamped information systems are relatively untested. The decline in jet boat sales does not suggest new or revamped information systems.

- The internal controls may not be sufficiently scalable for rapid growth. The decline in jet boat sales is the opposite of rapid growth. A decline of jet boats does not suggest internal controls without scalability.

- Foreign operations add another layer of complexity. The decline in jet boat sales does not suggest foreign operations are falsely reported.

7. [several innovations—obsolescence] <u>A relevant assertion level risk.</u>

- No unforeseen risk. Innovations may cause obsolescence in existing inventory.

- A financial statement level risk. Innovations may cause obsolescence in existing inventory. The valuation of existing inventory must be considered in light of the presumably diminished demand for craft with the old technology. This risk generally would be limited to inventory valuation assertions.

- **A relevant assertion level risk.** Innovations may cause obsolescence in existing inventory. The valuation of existing inventory must be considered in light of the presumably diminished demand for craft with the old technology. This risk generally would be limited to inventory valuation assertions.

8. [several innovations—obsolescence] <u>New technology may cause obsolescence in existing inventory.</u>

- We need not change our audit plan owing to this circumstance. The valuation of existing inventory must be considered in light of the presumably diminished demand for craft with the old technology.

- [Delete text] An appropriate comment is among those available for response.

- New personnel may not be adequately trained in internal control processes. Innovations do not suggest personnel training is inadequate.

- New or revamped information systems are relatively untested. Innovations do not suggest the new or revamped information systems is untested.

- The internal controls may not be sufficiently scalable for rapid growth. Innovations do not suggest internal controls without scalability.

- New sales outlets introduce new potential for a fraudulent entity to take advantage of Hydrojet, under the guise of a legitimate outlet. Innovations do not suggest the new sales outlets will commit fraud.

- **New technology may cause obsolescence in existing inventory.** The valuation of existing inventory must be considered in light of the presumably diminished demand for craft with the old technology.

- Changes to conform to compliance requirements may not be executed accurately, as all personnel might not understand their duties under the new requirements sufficiently. Innovations do not suggest that the compliance requirements are likely to be misunderstood by employees.

9. [Sales commission-based] <u>A relevant assertion level risk.</u>

   - No unforeseen risk. Sales staff on commission might be motivated to commit fraud that they would not consider on salary.

   - A financial statement level risk. Sales staff on commission might be motivated to commit fraud that they would not consider on salary.

   - **A relevant assertion level risk.** Sales staff on commission might be motivated to commit fraud that they would not consider on salary. This risk generally would be limited to revenue cycle and payroll accounts.

10. [Sales commission-based] <u>Sales staff on commission might be motivated to commit fraud that they would not consider on salary.</u>

    - [Delete text] An appropriate comment is among those available for response.

    - We need not change our audit plan owing to this circumstance. Sales staff on commission might be motivated to commit fraud that they would not consider on salary.

    - New personnel may not be adequately trained in internal control processes. Sales staff on commission does not suggest inadequate personnel training.

    - New or revamped information systems are relatively untested. Sales staff on commission does not suggest the information systems are untested.

    - The internal controls may not be sufficiently scalable for rapid growth. Sales staff on commission does not suggest internal controls without scalability.

    - Disgruntled employees might be motivated to commit fraud or theft. While sales staff might be disgruntled by the new compensation model, there is a better response available.

    - **Sales staff on commission might be motivated to commit fraud that they would not consider on salary.** Sales staff newly working on commission might be tempted to inflate sales just to maintain the same level of compensation.

    - Managers with significant bonus opportunities based on profits might be motivated to commit fraud. The manager's bonus is based on net profit, not sales. Sales staff on commission does not suggest managers committing fraud.

    - Foreign operations add another layer of complexity—for example, taxes, currency exchange, and additional regulatory bodies. Sales staff on commission does not suggest are foreign operations are reported falsely.

    - New sales outlets introduce new potential for a fraudulent entity to take advantage of Hydrojet, under the guise of a legitimate outlet. Sales staff on commission does not suggest new sales outlets commit fraud.

    - This suggests management is not very focused on internal controls, causing concern about the tone at the top. Sales staff on commission, by itself, does not suggest an inappropriate tone at the top.

11. [new retail outlets] <u>A relevant assertion level risk.</u>

- No unforeseen risk. New sales outlets introduce new potential for a fraudulent entity to take advantage of Hydrojet, under the guise of a legitimate outlet.

- A financial statement level risk. New sales outlets introduce new potential for a fraudulent entity to take advantage of Hydrojet, under the guise of a legitimate outlet. This risk generally would be limited to revenue cycle and commission accounts.

- **A relevant assertion level risk.** New sales outlets introduce new potential for a fraudulent entity to take advantage of Hydrojet, under the guise of a legitimate outlet. This risk generally would be limited to revenue cycle and commission accounts.

12. [new retail outlets] <u>New sales outlets introduce new potential for a fraudulent entity to take advantage of Hydrojet, under the guise of a legitimate outlet.</u>

- [Delete text] An appropriate comment is among those available for response.

- We need not change our audit plan owing to this circumstance. New sales outlets introduce new potential for a fraudulent entity to take advantage of Hydrojet, under the guise of a legitimate outlet.

- New personnel may not be adequately trained in internal control processes. New sales outlets do not suggest personnel may be inadequately trained.

- New or revamped information systems are relatively untested. New sales outlets do not suggest information systems may be untested.

- The internal controls may not be sufficiently scalable for rapid growth. New sales outlets do not suggest internal controls without scalability.

- Disgruntled employees might be motivated to commit fraud or theft. New sales outlets do not suggest disgruntled employees might commit fraud or theft.

- Sales staff on commission might be motivated to commit fraud that they would not consider on salary. New sales outlets do not suggest sales staff might commit fraud or theft.

- Unrealistic goals may motivate employees to report false results. New sales outlets do not suggest employees might report false results.

- Foreign operations add another layer of complexity—for example, taxes, currency exchange, and additional regulatory bodies. New sales outlets do not suggest foreign operations are reported inappropriately.

- **New sales outlets introduce new potential for a fraudulent entity to take advantage of Hydrojet, under the guise of a legitimate outlet.** Unless the screening process for new outlets is effective, Hydrojet risks, at best, ending up with sales outlets comparable to the ones it sought to replace, and at worst, ending up with monetary losses and damage to its reputation from association with a fraudulent entity.

- This suggests management is not very focused on internal controls, causing concern about the tone at the top. New sales outlets, by themselves, do not suggest an inappropriate tone at the top.

13. [strict bank covenants] <u>A financial statement level risk.</u>

- No unforeseen risk. Pressure to keep the line of credit might result in management being tempted to misstate the financial statements.

- **A financial statement level risk.** Pressure to keep the line of credit might result in management being tempted to misstate the financial statements. These misstatements could occur anywhere in the financial statements that management would think the misstatements would be undetected.

- A relevant assertion level risk. Pressure to keep the line of credit might result in management being tempted to misstate the financial statements. These misstatements could occur anywhere in the financial statements that management would think the misstatements would be undetected.

14. [strict bank covenants] <u>Managers with significant bonus opportunities based on profits might be motivated to commit fraud.</u>

- [Delete text] An appropriate comment is among those available for response.

- We need not change our audit plan owing to this circumstance. Pressure to keep the line of credit might result in management being tempted to misstate the financial statements.

- Significant changes in the operating and economic environment may reveal previously unknown weaknesses. Stricter bank covenants might be a significant change in the operating environment, but there is a better response available.

- New personnel may not be adequately trained in internal control processes. A change in a line of credit does not suggest inadequate personnel training.

- New or revamped information systems are relatively untested. A change in a line of credit does not suggest information system are relatively untested.

- The internal controls may not be sufficiently scalable for rapid growth. A change in a line of credit does not suggest internal controls without scalability.

- Disgruntled employees might be motivated to commit fraud or theft. A change in a line of credit does not suggest misconduct by disgruntled employees.

- Sales staff on commission might be motivated to commit fraud that they would not consider on salary. A change in a line of credit does not suggest misconduct by sales staff.

- **Managers with significant bonus opportunities based on profits might be motivated to commit fraud.** Pressure to keep the line of credit might result in management being tempted to misstate the financial statements.

- Foreign operations add another layer of complexity—for example, taxes, currency exchange, and additional regulatory bodies. A change in a line of credit does not suggest foreign operations are not appropriately recorded.

- New sales outlets introduce new potential for a fraudulent entity to take advantage of Hydrojet, under the guise of a legitimate outlet. A change in a line of credit does not suggest that new sales outlets are likely to commit fraud.

- This suggests management is not very focused on internal controls, causing concern about the tone at the top. While management might focus less on internal controls in their interest to maintain the line of credit, there is a better response available. A change in a line of credit, by itself, does not suggest the tone at the top is inappropriate.

15. [prior auditor hired] <u>No unforseen risk.</u>

- **No unforeseen risk.** Businesses frequently recruit accountants from CPA firms. This accountant was not recruited from the firm performing the audit this year, but rather from the firm that performed the audit of last year's financial statements.

- A financial statement level risk. Businesses frequently recruit accountants from CPA firms.

- A relevant assertion level risk. Businesses frequently recruit accountants from CPA firms.

16. [prior auditor hired] <u>We need not change our audit plan owing to this circumstance.</u>

- [Delete text] An appropriate comment is among those available for response.

- **We need not change our audit plan owing to this circumstance.** Businesses frequently recruit accountants from CPA firms. This accountant was not recruited from the firm performing the audit this year, but rather from the firm that performed the audit of last year's financial statements.

- New personnel may not be adequately trained in internal control processes. The degree of personnel training is unlikely to be adversely impacted by hiring an accountant from a CPA firm.

- An employee of the audit firm formerly with the client could be in the position of auditing his or her own work. The accountant was not recruited from HydroJet to work for Cutt, Paste, and Semele, CPAs, but rather from the firm that performed the audit of last year's financial statements to work for Hydrojet.

- An employee of the client formerly with the audit firm would know how to thwart some of the audit procedures. This accountant was not recruited from Cutt, Paste, and Semele, CPAs, but rather from the firm that performed the audit of last year's financial statements.

- This suggests management is not very focused on internal controls, causing concern about the tone at the top. Hiring an accountant from a CPA firm suggests that the employee is competent. Hiring competent employees of all sorts suggests an appropriate tone at the top. Also, hiring competent accountants generally improves internal control.

17. [accounting software upgrade] <u>A financial statement level risk.</u>

- <u>No </u>unforeseen risk. New or revamped information systems are relatively untested.

- **A financial statement level risk.** New or revamped information systems are relatively untested. Information system weaknesses could result in errors that pervade all aspects of the financial statements.

- A relevant assertion level risk. New or revamped information systems are relatively untested. Information system weaknesses could result in errors that pervade all aspects of the financial statements.

18. [accounting software upgrade] <u>New or revamped information systems are relatively untested.</u>

- [Delete text] An appropriate comment is among those available for response.

- We need not change our audit plan owing to this circumstance. New or revamped information systems are relatively untested. Information system weaknesses could result in errors that pervade all aspects of the financial statements.

- Known weaknesses in internal control suggest unknown weaknesses in internal control exist. An accounting software upgrade does not suggest known weaknesses in internal control.

- New personnel may not be adequately trained in internal control processes. Inadequate training would aggravate risks caused by information system weaknesses, but this is not the best response.

- **New or revamped information systems are relatively untested.** Information system weaknesses could result in errors that pervade all aspects of the financial statements. A new system could act in an unanticipated manner if insufficiently tested.

- The internal controls may not be sufficiently scalable for rapid growth. Internal control weaknesses would aggravate risks caused by information system weaknesses, but this is not the best response. New computer systems typically are better able to handle scalability issues; a new computer system does not suggest internal controls without scalability.

- Sales staff on commission might be motivated to commit fraud that they would not consider on salary. Sales staff intent to commit fraud would aggravate risks caused by information system weaknesses, but this is not the best response.

- Managers with significant bonus opportunities based on profits might be motivated to commit fraud. Managers' intent to commit fraud would aggravate risks caused by information system weaknesses, but this is not the best response.

- Unrealistic goals may motivate employees to report false results. Employee intent to report false results would aggravate risks caused by information system weaknesses, but this is not the best response.

- This suggests management is not very focused on internal controls, causing concern about the tone at the top. It is rather a stretch to assume the exchange of such "war stories" means the tone at the top is inappropriate. Few major information technology changes are smooth.

19. [vacations] <u>A financial statement level risk.</u>

- No unforeseen risk. Minimum mandatory vacations for accounting staff is a typical internal control.

- **A financial statement level risk.** Minimum mandatory vacations for accounting staff is a typical internal control. Internal control weaknesses could result in errors that pervade all aspects of the financial statements.

- A relevant assertion level risk. Minimum mandatory vacations for accounting staff is a typical internal control. Internal control weaknesses could result in errors that pervade all aspects of the financial statements.

20. [vacations] <u>This suggests management is not very focused on internal controls, causing concern about the tone at the top.</u>

- [Delete text] An appropriate comment is among those available for response.

- We need not change our audit plan owing to this circumstance. Minimum mandatory vacations for accounting staff is a typical internal control. Internal control weaknesses could result in errors that pervade all aspects of the financial statements.

- Significant changes in the operating and economic environment may reveal previously unknown weaknesses. The lack of mandatory vacations does not suggest a significant change.

- Foreign operations add another layer of complexity—for example, taxes, currency exchange, and additional regulatory bodies. The lack of mandatory vacations does not suggest foreign operations are problematic.

- New sales outlets introduce new potential for a fraudulent entity to take advantage of Hydrojet, under the guise of a legitimate outlet. The lack of mandatory vacations does not suggest new sales outlets might commit fraud.

- New technology may cause obsolescence in existing inventory. The lack of mandatory vacations does not suggest new technology is causing obsolescence in inventory.

- Changes to conform to compliance requirements may not be executed accurately, as all personnel might not understand their duties under the new requirements sufficiently. The lack of mandatory vacations does not suggest trouble with compliance requirements.

- **This suggests management is not very focused on internal controls, causing concern about the tone at the top.** Minimum mandatory vacations for accounting staff is a typical internal control. It is easily implemented and relatively inexpensive. Not having such a basic control causes concerns about the tone at the top.

Section 2 - Professional Responsibilities and Ethics

Corresponding Lectures

Watch the following course lectures with this section:

Lecture 2.01 – AICPA Code of Professional Conduct
Lecture 2.02 – AICPA Code of Professional Conduct (Continued)
Lecture 2.03 – AICPA Code of Professional Conduct (Continued)
Lecture 2.04 – Consulting Services Standards
Lecture 2.05 – Sarbanes-Oxley Act (SOX)
Lecture 2.06 – AICPA Code of Professional Conduct – Class Questions
Lecture 2.07 – Private Securities Litigation Reform Act, PCAOB
                     Standards, SEC, GAO and DOL
Lecture 2.08 – Professional Responsibilities – Class Questions
                     (Continued)

EXAM NOTE: *Please refer to the AICPA AUD Blueprint in the Introduction of this book to find a listing of the representative tasks (and their associated skill levels—i.e., Remembering and Understanding, Application, Analysis, and Evaluation) that the candidate should be able to perform based on the knowledge obtained in this section.*

Professional Responsibilities & Ethics

AICPA CODE OF PROFESSIONAL CONDUCT

There are a number of ways in which CPAs may distinguish themselves. Every CPA is required to obtain a CPA certificate, which is issued by the state to which the CPA applies and is administered by that state's board of accountancy. In addition, a CPA may be a member of the AICPA; a member of a state society of CPAs; and a member of various professional organizations, some of which are based on ethnicity, such as the Philippine Institute of CPAs (PICPA) and the National Association of Black Accountants (NABA), while others are based on some other factor, such as the segment of the profession in which its members operate like the Association of Governmental Accountants (AGA) or the Institute of Management Accountants (IMA).

A CPA may also be subject to various regulators such as the SEC or the PCAOB. Each of these agencies, organizations, regulators, and societies have rules and guidelines that affect the behavior of CPAs. One of the most comprehensive is the **AICPA Code of Professional Conduct (Code) (ET – for research)**. Many sets of rules and codes of ethics related to accountants are largely based on the Code, which is regularly tested on the CPA exam.

While the consequences of violating the Code will not be more severe than the loss of the CPA's membership in the AICPA, which is why the rules and guidelines are expressed as obligations of "members," violations of other codes of conduct (state board of accountancy) may result in a prohibition against performing certain types of services, the inability to serve certain regulated clients, or, in some cases, the suspension or loss (revocation) of the CPA certificate. This could result from the commission of a felony or the filing of a fraudulent tax return, whether for the CPA or for a client.

In addition to the Code, a CPA will consider the ethical requirements of all applicable bodies and agencies, which may include:
- State societies
- State boards of accountants and related regulatory agencies
- The SEC, PCAOB, GAO, and DOL
- Taxing authorities

The Code is organized in **4 parts**: the Preface, which is applicable to all members; Part 1, which is applicable to members in public practice; Part 2, which applies to members in industry; and Part 3, which applies to all other members, including those retired or unemployed.

Each part is divided into topics. The **Preface** (applicable to all members) is divided into **six** topics consisting of:
- 0.100 – Overview of the code of Professional Conduct
- 0.200 – Structure and Application of the AICPA code
- 0.300 – Principles of Professional Conduct
- 0.400 – Definitions
- 0.500 – Nonauthoritative Guidance
- 0.600 – New, Revised, and Pending Interpretations and Other Guidance

The topics and subtopics or sections are similarly numbered and named in each of the remaining three parts. All of the enumerated topics and subtopics apply to Part 1, Members in Public Practice.

Fewer apply to Part 2, Members in Industry, and only two apply to Part 3, Other Members. The subtopics are as follows:

- **Part 1** – Members in **Public Practice**
    - 1.000 – Introduction
    - 1.100 – Integrity and Objectivity
    - 1.200 – Independence
    - 1.300 – General Standards
    - 1.310 – Compliance With Standards
    - 1.320 – Accounting Principles
    - 1.400 – Acts Discreditable
    - 1.500 – Fees and Other Types of Remuneration
    - 1.600 – Advertising and Other Forms of Solicitation
    - 1.700 – Confidential Information
    - 1.800 – Form of Organization and Name

- **Part 2** – Members in **Industry**
    - 2.000 – Introduction
    - 2.100 – Integrity and Objectivity
    - 2.300 – General Standards
    - 2.310 – Compliance With Standards
    - 2.320 – Accounting Principles
    - 2.400 – Acts Discreditable

- **Part 3 – Other Members**
    - 3.100 – Introduction
    - 3.400 – Acts Discreditable

Preface

The preface, applicable to *all members*, consists of **six topics:**

Topic 100 – Provides an **overview**, including an explanation of the structure of the Code; a requirement that members adhere to the Code's **rules** based on an understanding of the rules and the voluntary actions of the CPA; an indication that CPAs are expected to follow **interpretations**, and may be required to justify departures from them; and an indication that, when a CPA has multiple professional roles, the highest and most restrictive level of standards should be applied.

Topic 200 – Describes the **structure** of the Code and indicates its **applicability** to the services performed by a CPA. It indicates that, with few exceptions, the Code applies to all professional services performed by a CPA, except when rules identify services to which they do not apply. This topic also describes how certain terms are interpreted in a section related to drafting conventions.
- Rules requiring a member to **consider** something are requiring the CPA to *think about* the matters being addressed.
- Rules requiring a member to **evaluate** something are requiring the CPA to *measure a matter's significance.*
- Rules requiring a member to **determine** something are requiring the CPA to establish a *conclusion* related to a matter or make a decision in relation to it.

In addition, a CPA will apply professional judgment in determining whether or not to perform a procedure or take an action that the Code indicates that the CPA should consider.

Topic 300 – Describes the **principles** embedded in the Code. In the preamble, it reminds CPAs of their responsibility of *self-discipline* exceeding the simple compliance with applicable laws and regulations; *responsibilities to the public, to clients, and to colleagues*; and a commitment to *act with honor* despite the possibility of personal sacrifice that may result. Various principles support these premises:

- *Responsibilities* – Requires the application of sensitive professional and moral judgment at all times and cooperation with other members of the profession to improve the art of accounting, to maintain the public's confidence in the profession, and to carry out the profession's responsibility for self-governance.
- *Public Interest* – Requires a commitment to professionalism and acting in a manner that serves the public interest and honors the trust that the public has in the accounting profession. The public interest is the collective well-being of the community of people and institutions that are served by the accounting profession, which requires the accountant to act with integrity when confronted by conflicts among various stakeholders and perform services applying integrity, objectivity, and due professional care.
- *Integrity* – Requires that the highest level of integrity be applied through the CPA's honesty and candor, within the constraints of client confidentiality, and an unwillingness to subordinate service or the public trust to personal gain or advantage.
- *Objectivity and Independence* – Requires independence, both in *fact* and in *appearance*, when performing auditing and other attestation services, for which standards require independence, and that the CPA remain free of conflicts of interest and exercise impartiality and intellectual honesty in the performance of all professional services.
- *Due Care* – Requires compliance with technical and ethical standards while continuing to endeavor to improve the CPA's competence and quality of services, which is accomplished through a commitment to learning throughout the CPA's professional life, and diligence in the provision of professional services enabling performance to the best of the CPA's ability. Due care also requires a CPA to remain competent and to understand the limitations to that competence, which may result in consultation or the referral of services, and to adequately plan and supervise all professional activities for which the CPA is responsible.
- *Scope and Nature of Services* – Requires the CPA to evaluate whether or not services can be performed in a manner consistent with the principles of the Code by practicing in a firm with appropriate quality control policies and procedures commensurate with the services being performed; making certain that services performed for an audit client do not create a conflict of interest; and that activities in which the CPA participates are appropriate for members of the CPA profession.

Topic 400 – Provides **definitions** of terms that are used throughout the Code.

Topic 500 – Specifies that only the Code is authoritative and that guidance provided by the staff of the Professional Ethics Division of the AICPA is **nonauthoritative guidance**.

Topic 600 – Indicates the status of **new, revised, or pending interpretations and other guidance**. It specifies that new or revised authoritative interpretations and other guidance are effective as of the last day of the month in which the pronouncement or notice is published in the Journal of Accountancy.

Part 1

Part 1 is applicable to members in **public practice**, including government auditors who are part of a governmental audit agency responsible for auditing governments or component units of them, provided the auditor is either elected directly by the voters or appointed with removal subject to oversight or approval by a legislative body. When a CPA is serving both as a member in public practice and as a member in industry, both Parts 1 and 2 will apply.

Topic 1.000 – Introduction

This topic introduces a conceptual framework approach to applying the Code. It provides a member with a means of evaluating compliance with the code when confronted with a decision or other circumstance that is not directly addressed. Applying the conceptual framework approach cannot overcome a clear violation of the rules or interpretations of the Code. It can, however, assist the CPA in determining if the Code has been violated when it is not necessarily clear.

The *conceptual framework approach* involves a 3-step process:
- **Identify threats** that may interfere with the CPA's ability to remain in compliance with the Code. The CPA may, for example, be considering entering into a relationship that is not prohibited but that raises the possibility of a conflict of interest. The existence of one or more threats does not necessarily indicate that the CPA is in violation of the Code, but requires that the threat or threats be evaluated.

- **Evaluate the significance of identified threats**, both individually and in the aggregate, to determine if they are at an acceptable level. A threat is considered to be at an acceptable level when a reasonable and informed third party would conclude that the Code was not violated. The evaluation will consider qualitative and quantitative factors and should take into account existing safeguards that are in place and may reduce the threat to an acceptable level.

- **Identify and apply safeguards** to those threats that are not at an acceptable level. In some cases, a single safeguard may eliminate more than one threat while, in others, it may require several safeguards to reduce a single threat to an acceptable level. In cases where safeguards cannot be implemented to reduce the threat or threats to an acceptable level, providing those specific professional services would result in the member's compliance with the Code being compromised, the member should determine if declining or discontinuing the service or resigning from the engagement would be appropriate.

Threats

There are **seven categories of threats** identified in Topic 1.210 of the Code. They are not mutually exclusive in that a single threat may fall under more than one category. Threats are evaluated both individually and in the aggregate. The categories are:

- The threat of **self-review** exists when the accountant performs some form of evaluation of matters that were previously influenced by the accountant's judgment, such as when an accountant is performing an attest service in relation to a client's financial statements when the accountant's firm performed bookkeeping services for that client. The self-review threat is the threat that the accountant will assume a level of reliability without performing an appropriate level of testing or other due diligence.

- An **advocacy** threat exists when the accountant's actions effectively promote a client's interests or position. This would be the case if the accountant is:

- o   Providing forensic accounting services to the client in a conflict with third parties.
- o   Providing investment advice for an officer, director, or shareholder holding 10% or more of the client's shares.
- o   Promoting or underwriting the client's securities, or acting as a registered agent for the client.
- o   Endorsing the products or services of a client.

It does not result from testifying as a fact witness or defending the results of a professional service performed for the client. Advocacy is covered in detail in Topic 1.140.

- The threat of an **adverse interest** exists when the interests of the client are in conflict with the interests of the accountant, which may inhibit the accountant from applying objectivity. This would be the case, for example, if the client and the accountant were involved in, or anticipating, litigation against each other.

- The threat of **familiarity** results from a close and longstanding relationship with a client, potentially causing the accountant to become too sympathetic to the client's interests or too trusting of the client's work or products. Examples of the types of relationships that create a familiarity threat include:
  - o   The spouse, a family member, or a close friend of an engagement team member is employed by the client.
  - o   The member has a close and significant business relationship with an officer, director, or significant shareholder of the client.
  - o   Senior firm personnel have a long-standing relationship with the client.

- The threat of **undue influence** results from attempts by management or others to exercise an excessive amount of influence over the accountant. This may involve:
  - o   A client's threat to replace the accountant as a result of a disagreement.
  - o   A client exerting pressure to limit an engagement to reduce fees.

- The threat of **self-interest** occurs when the accountant has the opportunity to obtain a potential benefit from an interest in, or another relationship with, a client. This would be the case if:
  - o   The accountant has a financial interest in the client, the value of which may be affected by the results of the service being performed.
  - o   The accountant enters into an arrangement that involves a contingent fee rather than one that is predetermined.
  - o   The accountant relies excessively on the fees earned from the client.

- The threat of **management participation** occurs when the accountant takes on the role of management for the client or performs management functions on behalf of the client. Assuming management responsibilities will generally impair a member's independence in relation to a client but will not necessarily, otherwise, indicate a violation of the Code. A member may still perform professional services for such a client provided the services do not require the accountant to be independent.

- The performance of management functions does not impair independence as long as the member is not assuming management responsibility. The accountant may, for example, design a client's system of internal control provided the client takes responsibility for all decisions involving the allocation or use of resources, and the general requirements for the performance of nonattest services in section 1.295 of the Code, discussed later in this chapter, have been met. This includes designating someone from the client's organization, preferably a member of senior management, who will take responsibility for the services performed by the CPA.

Safeguards

Safeguards are controls that eliminate or reduce threats, ranging from prohibitions against circumstances that create threats to procedures that counteract the potential risk associated with a threat. Safeguards are considered effective if they eliminate a threat or reduce it to an acceptable level.

There are a number of factors that determine if safeguards are likely to be effective. The factors include the circumstances surrounding the situation, whether threats are identified properly, whether safeguards are designed appropriately, who applies the safeguards and who are subject to them, and how they are applied and the consistency with which they are applied.

Certain safeguards are imposed on the accountant by **requirements of the profession, or by legislation or regulation**. Examples include:
- Education, training, and continuing professional education (CPE) requirements
- Professional standards, combined with monitoring and disciplinary processes and external reviews of the firm's quality control
- Legislation
- Requirements related to competency and experience

Other safeguards result from **client characteristics or policies**. These, which act in combination with other safeguards, might include:
- Client personnel with an appropriate combination of skill, knowledge, and experience to oversee professional services provided by the accountant
- A tone at the top that emphasizes a commitment to fair reporting, compliance with laws and regulations, and ethical conduct
- Client governance related to the accountant's services that is structured and designed for appropriate decision making, oversight, and communication
- Policies limiting the client's use of the accountant for services that impair independence, encourage noncompliance with ethical requirements, or would not serve the public interest

Safeguards may be **implemented by the firm**. These may be many and varied, including:
- Leadership that stresses the importance of ethical behavior and acting in the interest of the public
- Policies and procedures designed to:
    o Implement and monitor quality control
    o Monitor compliance with firm policies
    o Monitor the firm's reliance on revenues from a single client
- Training and timely communication of firm policies and procedures
- Designating an appropriate individual from senior management to oversee the firm's quality control
- Disciplinary policies designed to encourage compliance with policies and procedures, and to empower staff to communicate noncompliance
- Discussing independence and ethics with the client's audit committee or the client's governance, and establishing policies and procedures for independence-related communication
- Disclosing to the audit committee the nature of services being provided and their related fees

- Consulting with interested third parties
- Rotation of senior attest engagement personnel
- Use of another firm to re-perform and take responsibility for portions of engagements

Another safeguard that can be initiated by the firm would be to establish a **consultation function**. It would be staffed with experts in accounting, auditing, independence, or other relevant issues. They would assist the attest engagement team in assessing issues that are highly technical, require a great deal of judgment, or for which there is no guidance. They would also assist the engagement team in resisting undue pressure from the client when there are disagreements regarding those matters.

Ethical Conflicts

Ethical conflicts may arise as a result of various circumstances, but most relate to a circumstance where internal or external pressures create obstacles that interfere with following an appropriate course of action; where conflicts arise in applying relevant professional and legal standards, such as when reporting suspected fraud may be a violation of client confidentiality rules; or some combination of these.

Departures from rules or laws may require justification when the member believes them to be appropriate in the circumstances. Members may suffer consequences, however, when resolution is not achieved in a manner that permits compliance with all applicable rules and laws.

A CPA should consider consulting with others within their employing firm or organization before taking a course of action. If a course of action is not effective and an ethical conflict is not resolved, regardless of whether consultation occurred or not, the accountant should consider consulting with others or obtaining advice from a professional body or from legal counsel. When conflicts remain unresolved, it is likely that the CPA will be in violation of one or more rules and the CPA should consider whether it is appropriate to continue a relationship with the engagement team, assignment, client, firm, or employer.

Topic 1.100 – Integrity and Objectivity

In performance of **any** professional service, a member shall maintain objectivity and integrity, avoid conflicts of interest, and not knowingly misrepresent facts or subordinate their judgment to others.

Topic 1.110 – Conflicts of Interest

Conflicts of interest arise when a CPA is performing professional services related to a matter for two or more clients with conflicting interests or when the interests of the CPA or the CPA's firm conflict with those of the client. Before accepting an engagement or a relationship, the CPA should evaluate a potential conflict of interest by identifying:
- The relationships among parties involved and the natures of their relevant interests, which may change during the course of the engagement; and
- The nature and implications of the service being provided.

Safeguards may reduce the threat of a conflict of interest to an acceptable level. Maintaining separate engagement teams, for example, with clear policies and procedures for maintaining confidentiality may be an adequate safeguard to reduce the threat of a conflict of interest to a reasonable level when the conflict arises from performing services for two or more clients with conflicting interests related to the subject matter of the engagements.

Serving as a director on the board of an entity may create a conflict of interest if the entity, such as a bank, enters into or considers transactions with the CPA's clients. The member may consider limiting the relationship to a consulting arrangement, excluding transactions that may involve the CPA's clients. If, however, the CPA does serve as a director, threats and safeguards should be evaluated to make certain that threats are at an acceptable level.

When a conflict of interest does exist, even when threats are reduced to an acceptable level, the accountant is *required to disclose* the nature of the conflict to clients and others affected by it and to obtain their consent for the performance of the professional services.

Topic 1.120 – Gifts and Entertainment

Offering gifts or entertainment to a client or accepting gifts or entertainment from a client may create various threats to the CPA's compliance with the Code, including threats associated with self-interest, familiarity, and undue influence. Threats cannot be reduced to an acceptable level when the offer or acceptance of gifts is in violation of member or client policies or applicable laws, rules, or regulations if the member is aware of the violation or is unaware due to recklessness.

Threats may be reduced to an acceptable level when gifts or entertainment are *reasonable* in the circumstances when considering such factors as the nature of the item, the occasion giving rise to it, the cost, and other facts and circumstances surrounding it.

Topic 1.130 – Preparing and Reporting Information

In order to comply with the rule regarding integrity and objectivity, a member who is responsible for recording, maintaining, preparing, approving, or presenting information has an obligation to adhere to the relevant reporting framework when there is one. When there is not, the accountant should apply professional judgment, taking into consideration the purpose for which the information is being presented and the audience it is intended for. The information should not be presented in a manner intended to mislead, nor should there be omissions that cause the information to be misleading.

Making materially false and misleading entries in an entity's financial statements or records, or permitting or directing another to do so; failing to correct materially false and misleading financial statements or records of an entity with the authority to do so; and signing a document containing false and misleading information, or permitting or directing another to do so, create threats to compliance with the rule regarding integrity and objectivity that could not be reduced to an acceptable level.

Differences of opinion between a member and supervisors or other individuals within the member's organization may create self-interest, familiarity, or undue influence threats to the members' ability to comply with the integrity and objectivity rules as a result of the potential of subordinating the member's judgment. A supervisor, for example, may take a position that the member believes is not in compliance with standards, represents a material misstatement of facts, or violates applicable laws or regulations. In such cases, threats cannot be reduced to an acceptable level and the member should:
- Discuss concerns with the supervisor.
- Discuss concerns with an appropriate higher level of management within the member's organization when the difference of opinion cannot be resolved through discussion with the supervisor. Appropriate actions in response might involve:
    - Correcting the information.
    - Informing those to whom the information has already been given of the correct information.

- If the member concludes that appropriate actions are not taken, the member should follow certain safeguards to *reduce or eliminate the threats* to an acceptable level:
  - Consult with an appropriate professional organization or body.
  - Determine if the member's organization has internal policies and procedures for reporting differences of opinion.
  - Determine whether the member is responsible for communicating with third parties, such as regulatory agencies, keeping confidentiality requirements in mind.
  - Consult with legal counsel.
  - Document an understanding of the facts, the matters involved, and the conversations held, identifying the parties with which they were held.

If threats can be reduced to an acceptable level, the member will discuss conclusions with the other party and take no further action.

Upon a conclusion that no safeguards can eliminate the threats or reduce them to an acceptable level, the member should not be willing to continue to be associated with the information, consider whether it is appropriate to continue in a relationship with the organization and should take steps to eliminate exposure to having subordinated judgment.

Pressure may be explicitly or implicitly placed upon a member to breach the rules of conduct, the rules related to integrity and objectivity most commonly. Pressure may be imposed by colleagues or supervisors within the member's organization or from external sources, such as customers or vendors, lenders, or others. A member should neither yield to such pressure resulting in a breach to the Code nor exert pressure on others such that a breach may result.

Pressure may relate to any combination of:
- Conflicts of interest;
- Presentation or suppression of information;
- Performing tasks without an appropriate level of competence or due care;
- Advancing the interests of those with financial interests; and
- Gifts and entertainment.

The member should make a determination whether the pressure could result in a breach, consulting with others, as appropriate, taking into consideration the implications of the interpretation "Confidential Information Obtained from Employment or Volunteer Activities." If the member concludes that the pressure would result in a breach, there are a number of safeguards that may be considered. The member might:
- Try to resolve the matter by discussing it with the individual exerting the pressure.
- Discuss the matter with a supervisor or parties at a higher level, such as management, internal and independent auditors, or members of those charged with governance.
- Request a change in responsibilities, removing the member from the influence of the party exerting the pressure.
- Expose the matter using the mechanisms within the organization, such as whistleblower policies.
- Consult with legal counsel.

If the member determines that the pressure to breach cannot be eliminated, the member should not undertake, or should cease undertaking, the activity that would result in the breach and consider whether to remain involved in a relationship with the organization. The member should also document an understanding of the facts, the matters involved, the conversations held, identifying the parties with which they were held, and how the matters were addressed.

Topic 1.140 – Client Advocacy

When performing certain nonattest services for a client, such as tax or consulting services, the member may be in position to act as an advocate for the client in supporting the client's position on accounting or financial reporting issues to other engagement team members or to standard setters or regulators. These services may pose threats to the member's ability to comply with the integrity and objectivity rules that should be evaluated.

Topic 1.150 – Use of a Third-Party Service Provider

Use of a third-party service provider in a professional engagement may expose the third party to confidential information posing a threat to the member's ability to comply with the integrity and objectivity rules. Before disclosing confidential client information to a third-party service provider, the member should inform the client, preferably in writing.

Topic 1.200 – Independence

A member in public practice shall be independent in the performance of professional services when independence is required by applicable professional standards.

Independence is the ability to act with **integrity and objectivity** and applies to a *covered member and to the member's immediate family,* including the member's spouse or spousal equivalent, and all dependents, whether related or not. A **covered member** would be any of the following:
- A member of an attest engagement team or an individual in a position to influence the attest engagement
- A partner, partner equivalent, or manager providing more than 10 hours of nonattest services to the attest client within a fiscal year
- A partner or partner equivalent in the same office in which the lead engagement partner for the attest engagement practices
- The firm and its employee benefit plan
- An entity under the control of any one of the other covered members described and two or more of those individuals or entities acting together
- With agreed-upon procedure engagements only, covered members may be limited to those participating in or directly supervising the engagement, and individuals consulting with the engagement team on technical or industry-related issues.

A covered member:
- Must maintain independence for certain engagements (**ERAS**)
    - **E**xaminations – Audits
    - **R**eviews - Conclusions
    - **A**greed-upon procedure engagements leading to findings
    - **S**pecial reports

Attest Function = Must be Independent
Independence required for:
• Audit – Yes
• Review – Yes
o Taxes – No
o Compilation – No
o Preparation eng's – No
o Consultation – No

- Need not be independent for:
  - Taxes
  - Consultations
  - Preparation engagements
  - Compilations (when a lack of independence is indicated)

- Independence should be maintained in both:
  - **Fact** – State *"of mind"*
  - **Appearance** – How it appears to the public

The Code provides some specific guidance as to certain events, circumstances, or conditions that will create threats to independence that cannot be reduced to an acceptable level. If, for example, a member has any direct financial interest in a client, independence is impaired and no safeguards could reduce the threat to independence to an acceptable level.

When events, circumstances, or conditions that might impair independence *are not addressed* directly in the Code, *the member is required to apply the conceptual framework approach*, applied in the same manner as the conceptual framework approach related to the Code itself.

Topic 1.210 – Conceptual Framework Approach

Rules of conduct incorporated in the Code provide indications as to when independence is in fact impaired, such as a *direct financial interest* in a client or having the authority to sign checks on a client's bank account. Even when a CPA has not engaged in any activity or relationship that would specifically impair independence, however, threats to independence may be at an unacceptable level.

Threats to independence are considered to be at an acceptable level when a reasonable and informed third party, aware of the relevant information, would conclude that the member's independence is not impaired. As a result, the member will focus on the *appearance* of independence when applying the conceptual framework.

Threats to independence include:
- **Adverse interest threat** – When a member's interests are in opposition to the clients, such as when they are involved in, or anticipating, litigation, the member may not act objectively.

- **Advocacy threat** – A member may compromise independence when promoting a client's position, depending on the degree to which the member promotes it. This may be the case when the member is promoting the client's securities in an initial public offering, serving as an expert witness on behalf of the client, or representing the client in tax court or elsewhere.

- **Familiarity threat** – A long relationship with a client may make a member sympathetic to a client's interests or accepting of the client's work or product, such as when there has been a history of work that has been essentially error-free in the past. The degree to which this occurs may cause a threat to the member's independence, particularly when an immediate family member or close relative holds a key position with the attest client; a partner of the firm, or the equivalent, has been on the engagement team for the attest engagement for an extended period of time; or a member of the engagement team's firm has recently been a director or officer of the attest client or has a close friend in a key position.

- **Management participation threat** – A member who serves as an officer or director of an attest client; accepts responsibility for the design, implementation, or maintenance of internal control for an attest client; or hires, supervises, or terminates employees of the attest client, creates a management participation threat to independence. An auditor, for example, may decide to ignore a significant deficiency in internal control when the auditor's firm has accepted responsibility for their design and implementation of internal control. When this is the case, of course, the accountant would not be independent since accepting responsibility for the design and implementation of internal control involves assuming a management responsibility. Doing so raises the management participation threat to an unacceptable level in relation to independence. In such a case, no safeguards would be able to reduce the threat to an acceptable level.

- **Self-interest threat** – When a member may benefit from an interest in, or relationship with, an attest client, a self-interest threat to independence is created. The benefit may be financial or nonfinancial, including a direct financial interest or material indirect financial interest in an attest client; a loan from the client, an officer or director, or a significant shareholder of the attest client; an excessive reliance on fees from a single attest client; or a material joint venture or business arrangement with an attest client.

- **Self-review threat** – When a member or the member's firm performs nonattest services for an attest client, there is the possibility that either the member will not test the information with an appropriate level of due diligence, or may overlook an error or other discrepancy to preserve the reputation of the firm and the relationship with the client, creating a self-review threat to the member's independence.

- **Undue influence threat** – An undue influence threat is the threat that the member will subordinate judgment to a third party as a result of a third party's reputation or expertise, aggressive or dominant personality, or attempts to coerce or exercise excessive influence; or to someone associated with the attest client due, perhaps, to a threat to replace the member or the member's firm over a disagreement, pressure to reduce procedures as a means of reducing fees, or receiving gifts from the attest client or related parties.

Similar to the approach used in evaluating threats to compliance with the Code, the member will evaluate safeguards to determine if there are those that are already in place that reduce threats to independence to an acceptable level. If threats are not already reduced to an acceptable level, the member will evaluate other safeguards that may be implemented that may so reduce it.

The member will consider safeguards imposed by the requirements of the profession or by laws or regulations; those resulting from client characteristics or policies; and those implemented by the firm.

AICPA Code of Professional Conduct (Continued)

Topic 1.220 – Accounting Firms

When a firm is part of a **network** of firms, all firms within that network are required to comply with the independence rules in relation to an attest client of any of the firms within that network if the use of the audit or review report for the client is not restricted. In other cases, the covered member should consider any threats to independence that the covered member knows of or has reason to believe may be created by the interests or relationships of other firms within the network.

A firm is considered to be part of a network of firms if the firms cooperate to enhance their ability to provide professional services through cross referrals and other means and has one or more of the following additional characteristics:

- A common brand name or initials that are part of the firm name
- Common control through ownership or management
- Sharing of profit and costs with the exception of certain costs such as those of operating the association and other costs that are not material to the firm
- Collaboration to create a common business strategy that member firms are held accountable for implementing
- Sharing of significant professional resources, such as systems and staff
- Uniform quality control policies monitored and enforced by the association

A covered member may also be part of an **alternative practice structure** (**APS**), which is required to comply with independence rules; is required to be organized in a form allowed by applicable laws, rules, and regulations; and is required to comply with the rules in the Code related to the form of an organization and its name (1.800).

An APS is an organization in which a firm provides attest services while other professional services are performed by another public or private organization that is closely aligned, such as a CPA firm with a closely aligned consulting entity. Independence rules apply to both covered members and direct superiors in an APS.

- Covered members include employed and leased individuals otherwise having the characteristics of a covered member.
- Direct superiors are covered members who can directly control the activities of an engagement partner or manager.

Indirect superiors, those one or more levels above direct superiors, can impair independence by having a material relationship with an attest client that is prohibited as a financial interest (1.240); acts as a trustee or executor (1.245); has a prohibited loan (1.260); maintains joint closely held investments with the attest client (1.265); or is involved in any of a variety of specific relationships. An indirect superior may, however, perform nonattest services that would be prohibited to the firm performing attest services without impairing independence.

When an attest firm allows members of another firm which is not independent of an attest client to participate in an attest engagement, threats to independence cannot be reduced to an acceptable level and the attest firm's independence will be impaired. Members of the non-independent firm, however, may serve in a capacity similar to that of an internal auditor as long as the firm complies with auditing standards.

A member whose independence becomes impaired after the issuance of a report may reissue the report provided the member or the member's firm does not perform procedures associated with updating or dual dating the report.

An indemnification clause in an engagement letter, in which an attest client holds the member harmless from liability resulting from knowing misrepresentations by management does not impair independence. Independence would be impaired, however, if an attest firm indemnifies an attest client from liability arising directly or indirectly from the acts of the attest client. An alternative dispute resolution clause in an engagement letter would not impair independence.

Topic 1.230 – Unpaid Fees

When fees for services that were performed *more than one year* before the date of the current-year report remain unpaid, this creates a threat to independence that cannot be reduced to an acceptable level. This is true even if the fees have not been billed to the client and if the client has signed a note for the amount owed. This does not apply, however, to unpaid fees due from a client in bankruptcy.

Topic 1.240 – Financial Interests

In general, a member who possesses or has a commitment to acquire a ***direct or material indirect*** *financial interest* in an attest client creates a self-interest threat that cannot be reduced to an acceptable level and the member's independence would be impaired. The same would be true if a partner or professional employee of the firm, including the partner's immediate family or any group of those individuals acting together, owned more than *5 percent* of an attest client during the period of the attest engagement.

Certain other financial interests may or may not create threats to independence that cannot be reduced to acceptable level, impairing independence.
- Threats to independence may be reduced to an acceptable level when a member *receives an unsolicited direct or indirect financial interest in an attest client*, such as through a gift that is not material to the member, if the member applies two safeguards:
  o The financial interest is disposed of within 30 days of learning of the interest, or sooner if practicable; and
  o The member does not participate on the attest engagement team during the period in which the covered member does not have the right to dispose of the financial interest.

- Ownership of shares of a *mutual fund* constitutes a direct financial interest in the mutual fund. Ownership of the underlying investments of the mutual fund may be direct or indirect, depending on the proportion of the mutual fund owned by the member and the diversity of the mutual fund's holdings.
  o Ownership of 5% or less of a diversified mutual fund results in an immaterial indirect financial interest in its investments.
  o Ownership of more than 5% of a diversified fund, or an ownership interest in an undiversified fund, should be evaluated to determine if the member holds a material indirect interest.

- Financial interests in *retirement, savings, compensation, or similar firm-sponsored plans* may be direct or indirect financial interests, based on circumstances.
  o Investments in a firm-sponsored plan are direct financial interests of the firm.
  o The ability to supervise or participate in a plan's investment decisions creates a direct financial interest while the inability to do so results in an indirect financial interest.

- o Financial interests held by a defined benefit plan are only considered the financial interest of a member who is a trustee or otherwise supervises or participates in the plan's investment decisions.
  - o Allocated shares held in an employee stock ownership plan (ESOP) are indirect financial interests until the member has the right to dispose of the allocated shares of the ESOP.
  - o Interests resulting from share-based compensation arrangements, including rights to acquire equity interests and restricted stock awards are direct financial interests even if they are not vested or exercisable.

- A *partnership interest* is a direct financial interest in a general or a limited partnership.
  - o A general partner has a direct financial interest in the partnership's financial interests.
  - o A limited partner has an indirect financial interest in the partnership's financial interests unless the limited partner controls the partnership, supervises or participates in the partnership's investment decisions, or has the ability to replace the general partner or participate in investment decisions, in which case the interest is direct.

- An ownership interest in a *limited liability company* (LLC) is a direct financial interest in the LLC.
  - o The managing member and those with the ability to control, supervise, or participate in the LLC's investment decisions have direct financial interests in the LLC's financial interests.
  - o Others without the ability to control, supervise, or participate in the LLC's investment decisions have indirect financial interests.

- The account owner of a *Section 529 plan* (Education savings plan) has a direct financial interest in the plan, but beneficiaries do not have a direct or indirect financial interest in the plan.

Topic 1.245 – Trusts and Estates

If an estate or trust has any direct or any material indirect financial interest in an attest client, a threat to the member's independence would not be at an acceptable level if the member served as trustee of the trust, or executor or administrator of the estate, during the period of the professional engagement if any of the following also applied:
- The member had the authority to make investment decisions for the trust or estate;
- The trust or estate either owned, or was committed to acquire, an equity interest in excess of 10% of the attest client's outstanding equity securities; or
- The value of the equity interest in the attest client exceeded 10% of the total assets of the trust or estate.

When the CPA is the grantor of a trust, the trust and its investments are considered direct financial interests of the CPA, even if the trust is a blind trust, if the trust's investments ultimately revert to the CPA, or if the CPA:
- Can amend or revoke the trust;
- Has the authority to control the trust; or
- Has the ability to participate in, or supervise, the trust's investment decisions.

If none of those circumstances apply, the CPA has a direct financial interest in the trust and an indirect financial interest in the trust's underlying investments.

Topic 1.250 – Participation in Employee Benefit Plans

When a CPA is a participant in an employee benefit plan that is either sponsored by an attest client or is, itself, an attest client, independence is generally impaired due to the self-interest threat. The threat would be reduced to an acceptable level, however, in certain circumstances the CPA is a participant in a public employee retirement plan that is sponsored by more than one governmental organization, one of which is the employer of the CPA. In addition:

- The CPA is required as an employee to participate in the plan, which is offered to all employees in comparable positions;
- The CPA does not influence or control key aspects of the plan such as investment strategy, benefits, or other management activities; and
- The CPA may not serve in a role prohibited by ET 1.275, *Current Employment or Association with an Attest Client*.

When, as a result of an immediate family member's employment, that family member is a participant in a plan that is an attest client or is sponsored by an attest client, the requirements of ET 1.270, *Family Relationships with Attest Clients*, are to be complied with.

Topic 1.255 – Depository, Brokerage, and Other Accounts

A firm may have funds on deposit at an attest client that is a bank or similar depository institution without impairing its independence as long as the firm concludes that the likelihood that the institution will experience financial difficulties is remote. An individual's independence would not be impaired as long as:

- The balance on deposit is fully insured; or
- The aggregate of uninsured amounts is not material to the individual; or
- Uninsured amounts that are considered material are reduced to an amount that is not material within 30 days of when it became, or becomes, material to the individual.

When a CPA maintains brokerage or other accounts with an attest client that is an insurance company, investment advisor, broker-dealer, bank, or other member of the financial services industry, impairment of independence may be avoided if certain safeguards are in place:

- The attest client is providing services applying its normal terms, procedures, and requirements; and
- Any risk of loss, such as from the client's bankruptcy, insolvency, fraud or illegal acts, or other circumstances, is not material to the individual after considering protections from federal, state, or other insurers or from other sources.

An insurance policy from a stock or mutual life insurance company is not considered a financial interest unless the policy offers the policy holder an investment option. Holding such a policy would create a self-interest threat to independence only if the policy was not obtained under the issuing entity's normal terms, procedures, and requirements.

When a CPA holds an insurance policy with an investment option, independence may be impaired.

- If not obtained under the insurer's normal terms, procedures, and requirements, threats to independence would not be at an acceptable level.
- When obtained under the insurer's normal terms, procedures, and requirements, a direct financial interest would be created if the CPA participates in or oversees investment decisions and the self-interest threat would be at an unacceptable level

Topic 1.260 – Loans, Leases, and Guarantees

Loans to or from an attest client, an officer or director of an attest client, or an individual owning 10% or more of an attest client's outstanding ownership interests create a *self-interest threat* that may not be at an acceptable level. Unsecured loans that are not material to the CPA's net worth, home mortgage loans, and secured loans will not raise the threat to an unacceptable level if certain safeguards are all in place:

- The loan was obtained under the institutions normal terms, procedures, and requirements.
- The loan was obtained prior to the institution becoming an attest client; from a lender that was not an attest client but was subsequently sold to an attest client; or prior to the CPA becoming a covered member.
- The loan has been maintained as current at all times as long as the borrower has been a covered member and there have been no changes to the terms of the loan not provided for in the original agreement.
- The estimated value of collateral at least equals the outstanding balance of the home mortgage or secured loan.

Obtaining one of the following from a lending institution under its normal lending procedures, terms, and requirements would *not impair* a CPA's independence as long as the CPA is in compliance with the terms of the agreement at all times:

- Automobile loans or leases collateralized by the automobile;
- Loans fully collateralized by the cash surrender value of an insurance policy or cash deposits at the same institution; or
- Credit cards and overdraft protection with an aggregate balance of no more than $10,000 after payment of the most recent monthly statement, made within the grace period.

A *lease arrangement* with an attest client would not raise threats to an unacceptable level if all of the following safeguards are in place:

- The lease meets the criteria to be accounted for as an operating lease under GAAP;
- The terms and conditions are comparable to other similar leases; and
- All payments are made in accordance with the lease terms.

Topic 1.270 – Family Relationships with Attest Clients

In general, members of a CPA's **immediate family,** which include the CPA's spouse or spousal equivalent, and all dependents, whether related or not, are required to comply with the independence rules to avoid impairing the independence of the CPA. Any financial interests of immediate family members are attributed to the CPA, including when determining the materiality of an indirect financial interest. Without impairing a CPA's independence, an immediate family member may:

- Be employed by an attest client provided it is not in a key position, which would create the threats of management participation, familiarity, and self-interest.
- Participate in an employee benefit plan that is an attest client or is sponsored by an attest client as long as the family member is not in a key position with the client, the plan is offered to all employees in comparable positions, the family member is not part of the plan's governance, and the family member does not participate in or oversee investment decisions.
- Participate in a retirement plan that is not an attest client or sponsored by an attest client but that holds an investment in an attest client provided:
  - The CPA does not participate in, and cannot influence, the attest engagement;
  - The family member has no investment options that do not involve an investment option in an attest client; and

○ If given the opportunity to invest in other than in attest client or an attest client investment option, the family member disposes of financial interests in attest clients as soon as is practicable, no later than 30 days after the option becomes available.

Actions and circumstances related to **close relatives**, which are parents, siblings, and nondependent children, may also result in an impairment of a member's independence. This would be the case if either a member of the engagement team, or an individual in a position to influence the engagement team or any partner or partner equivalent in the office of the engagement has a close relative:

- In a key position with the attest client during the period covered by the engagement or during the period of the engagement; or
- With a financial interest in the attest client that is known or believed to be material to the relative or enables the relative to exercise significant influence over the attest client.

Topic 1.275 – Current Employment or Association with an Attest Client

When a member is employed or associated with an attest client as a director, officer, employee, promoter, underwriter, voting trustee, or trustee of a pension or profit-sharing plan during the period covered by financial statements or during the period of the professional engagement, the familiarity, management participation, advocacy, or self-review threats will be raised to an unacceptable level and independence will be impaired. The member may serve as an adjunct faculty member for an attest client educational institution provided the member:

- Is not in a key position with the educational institution;
- Does not participate on, nor can influence, the engagement team;
- Is employed by the educational institution in a non-tenured or part-time position;
- Is not a participant in an employee benefit plan to the extent that it is not required; and
- Does not assume management responsibilities or set policy for the institution.

Threats would be at an acceptable level if a member's association with an attest client consisted of:

- Serving as an honorary director or trustee for an attest client not-for-profit organization provided the position is clearly honorary and held in name only; the member does not vote or otherwise participate in board or management responsibilities; and, if named in letterheads or materials that are circulated externally, is identified as an honorary director or trustee.
- Serving on the advisory board of an attest client provided the responsibilities are truly advisory in nature; the advisory board is neither authorized to make nor does it appear to make management decisions; and the advisory board is distinct from the decision-making body with a minimum of common members.
- Serving on a committee established to study possible changes in the form of an attest client county government, or the government of the state in which the attest client county government resides, and advising the county government client.
- Serving as the treasurer for a mayoral campaign when the attest client is the candidate's political party or the municipality in which the candidate is running. Independence would be impaired, however, if the campaign organization itself was the attest client.

A CPA may not serve on the engagement team, or be in a position to influence the engagement team, of an attest client at which the CPA had been employed as an officer, director, promoter, underwriter, voting trustee, or trustee for the entity's pension or profit sharing trust during any portion of the period or periods to which the attest engagement applies.

Independence will not be impaired if a CPA fails to disassociate from an attest client before becoming a covered member if certain safeguards are all met:
- The member discontinues participation in the client's employee health and welfare plans unless the client is legally required to allow the member to participate and the member pays 100% of the cost of participation on a current basis;
- The member discontinues participation in all other employee benefit plans and disposes of all vested benefits from the plan at the earliest date permitted by the plan;
  - Disposal is not required if the member would be subject to a significant penalty
  - The covered member must not participate on the attest engagement team or be in a position to influence the engagement.
- The member disposes of any direct and any material indirect financial interest in the client;
- The member collects or repays any loans to or from the client' and
- The covered member evaluates whether other relationships with the attest client create additional threats that must be addressed.

Seeking or discussing *potential employment* or other association with an attest client, including receiving a specific offer of employment, would impair independence unless:
- The circumstances are promptly reported to an appropriate party at the firm; or
- The individual discontinues participation in the engagement or providing services to the attest client until either the offer is rejected or employment with the client is no longer being sought.

A member who leaves from a CPA firm to take a key position with an attest client would potentially have created the threat of familiarity, self-interest, undue influence, or management participation. Independence will be impaired unless:
- Amounts due to the member from the firm are not material to the firm;
- The member has no remaining capital balance in the CPA firm;
- The member cannot influence the firm's operations or financial position; and
- The member is not associated with the firm and does not participate, or appear to participate, in the firm's business once employed or associated with the attest client, even if compensated for doing so.

In addition, the ongoing engagement team should consider whether to modify engagement procedures. If the member left the firm within one year of an engagement, an appropriate firm member should review the subsequent attest engagement and ascertain that an appropriate level of professional skepticism was applied, considering:
- The position the member holds with the attest client'
- The position the member held with the firm; and
- The nature of services performed by the member for the attest client while associated with the firm.

Employment with Audit Client

- **Prior to leaving:**
  - Must inform audit firm of conversations with client about possible employment.
  - Immediately be removed from the audit.
  - Once removed, the audit firm must review the work performed by the departed auditor.

- **After employed by the audit client:**
  - Audit firm must consider modifying the audit plan.
  - Assure remaining audit team is objective.

- The next annual audit must be separately reviewed by an audit firm professional uninvolved in the audit.

Topic 1.280 – Memberships

Although memberships do create or enhance threats associated with management participation, self-review, and self-interest, they do not necessarily impair independence.
- A pro rata share of a club's equity or debt securities held by a CPA belonging to an attest client social club would not be considered a direct financial interest if the club membership is essentially a social matter.
- Membership in an attest client trade association would not impair independence unless the CPA serves in an inappropriate position, as indicated in ET section 1.275, such as a director, officer, or employee during the period covered by the financial statements subject to the attest engagement or during the period of the engagement.

Threats associated with membership in a common interest realty association (CIRA) that is an attest client would not impair independence if:
- The association performs public safety, road maintenance, and utility functions, similar to a local government;
- The CPA's annual assessment is not material to either the CPA or the CIRA's budget;
- Liquidation of the CIRA would not result in a distribution to the CPA; and
- The CPA would not be liable to the CIRA's creditors if it were to become insolvent.

Subject to those restrictions related to depository accounts and loans, membership in an attest client credit union would not impair the CPA's independence if membership was based on the CPA's qualifications or characteristics other than the fact that the CPA provides professional services to the credit union. If membership is due to providing professional services to the credit union, independence would be impaired.

Topic 1.285 – Gifts and Entertainment

Offering a gift to, or accepting a gift from, an attest client, an individual in a key position with an attest client, or an individual owning 10% or more of an attest client's outstanding equity may impair independence if the threats of undue influence or self-interest are increased to an unacceptable level. To avoid impairing independence:
- A gift may only be accepted from an attest client if it is clearly insignificant to the recipient.

- Being entertained by an attest client is acceptable if it is reasonable under the circumstances.
- A CPA may only offer gifts or entertainment to a client that is reasonable under the circumstances.

In determining if a gift or entertainment is reasonable under the circumstances, the CPA will consider:
- The nature of the item and the occasion giving rise to it;
- The cost or value;
- The nature, value, and frequency of other gifts or entertainment offered or accepted;
- Whether business was actively conducted before, during, or after entertainment;
- Whether or not other attest clients participated; and
- The individuals from the attest client involved.

Topic 1.290 – Actual or Threatened Litigation

Litigation, whether actual or the expressed intention to begin litigation may create an adverse interest or a self-interest threat that could be at an unacceptable level. The materiality of such actual or threatened litigation to the CPA, the CPA's firm, and to the client should be evaluated by the CPA in making a determination. Whether or not independence is impaired will depend on the facts and circumstances surrounding each situation and will require the CPA to apply professional judgment.

Some, but not all, actual or threatened **litigation between a CPA and an attest client** will impair independence. Independence will not be impaired by litigation that is not related to the client's attestation engagement and is not material to either the CPA or the attest client. Examples of litigation that will *impair independence* include:
- Deficiencies in audit work performed for the attest client alleged by its present management.
- Allegations by the CPA of fraud or deceit by management.

Any threats to a CPA's independence due to actual or threatened litigation is eliminated when the parties reach final resolution and the matter no longer affects the relationship with the attest client. This is a matter of the CPA's professional judgment.

Lecture 2.03

AICPA Code of Professional Conduct (Continued)
Part 1

Topic 1.295 – Performance of *Nonattest* Services and Independence
Many CPA firms provide a variety of nonattest services for their attest clients, the most common of which include bookkeeping; tax compliance; and nontax disbursement services; such as payroll services. The performance of nonattest services may create *self-review, management participation, or advocacy threats to independence.* When significant threats to independence exist during either the period during which the professional engagement is being performed, or the period covered by the financial statements that are the subject of the attest service, they must be reduced to an acceptable level or independence will be impaired.

Certain nonattest services, and certain conditions under which nonattest services are performed create threats to independence that cannot be reduced to an acceptable level. These will not prevent the CPA from performing an attest service for such a client if:

- The nonattest services were performed prior to the period in which the attest services were performed;
- The nonattest services relate to periods prior to the periods covered by the financial statements that are the subject of the attest services; and
- The financial statements for the period during which the nonattest services were performed were attested to by another CPA.
    - If the attest engagement is an audit, the prior financial statements were audited by another CPA.
    - If the attest engagement is a review, the prior financial statements were audited or reviewed by another CPA.

In addition to bookkeeping, tax compliance, and payroll, other nonattest services include advisory services; appraisal, valuation, and actuarial services; benefit plan administration; business risk and corporate finance consulting; executive or employee recruiting; forensic accounting; information systems design, implementation, or integration; Internal audit; and investment advisory or management services. Preparing the financial statements for an attest client and performing a cash-to-accrual conversion or reconciliations as part of the financial statement closing process are also nonattest services.

Although a CPA may not perform certain nonattest services for an attest client because they create threats to independence that cannot be reduced to an acceptable level, many nonattest services may be performed for an attest client **without impairing independence**. In order to make certain that independence is not impaired when performing nonattest services for an attest client, the CPA will address **three distinct components** of the Code.

1. The CPA will evaluate the *cumulative effect* of all nonattest services being performed for the client, using a conceptual framework approach, to determine if threats to independence are at an acceptable level.

2. The CPA will apply the *three general requirements* for performing nonattest services enumerated in the Code.

3. The CPA will evaluate the *specific services* being performed to make certain that none of them individually raise threats to independence to an unacceptable level.

1. Cumulative Effect of Multiple Nonattest Services
When a CPA performs multiple nonattest services for an attest client, the self-review and management participation threats may be elevated and the accountant should evaluate whether or not they are at an acceptable level and, if they are not at an acceptable level, whether safeguards that are in place, or that may be put into effect, will reduce them to an acceptable level.

- The **self-review threat** is the threat that occurs when a CPA uses the results of performing a service for a client, such as bookkeeping services, as a component of another service, such as a review or an audit of the client's financial statements, without appropriately evaluating the service previously performed, including the judgments made while performing that service.

- The **management participation threat** is the threat that the CPA will assume management responsibilities.

The three general requirements for performing nonattest services for an attest client are designed to reduce the self-review and management participation threats to an acceptable level. The fact that the three general requirements have been complied with does not, however, eliminate the need to evaluate the services performed in relation to all potential threats to independence as well as the cumulative effect of multiple nonattest services being performed for the attest client.

2. Apply the 3 General Requirements for Performing Nonattest Services

The performance of nonattest services for an attest client increases threats to the CPA's independence and the CPA should apply safeguards to avoid impairment. Specific nonattest services that a CPA may perform for an attest client raise threats to independence to an unacceptable level, which cannot be reduced to an acceptable level through the implementation of safeguards. When that is not the case, however, complying with the general requirements will reduce threats to an acceptable level.

The general requirements fall into **three categories**:

A. The client must accept its responsibilities;

B. The accountant's responsibilities must be limited; and

C. A written understanding must be established with the client.

A. Client Responsibilities

The first of the general requirements is that the client and its management must agree to assume all management responsibilities. **Management responsibilities** involve:
- Leading and directing an entity; and
- Making decisions regarding human, financial, and intangible resources, including their acquisition, use, control, and disposal.

Examples of management responsibilities that the auditor may **NOT assume** include:
- Setting policy or strategic direction for the client;
- Directing, or taking responsibility for, the actions of client employees;
- Authorizing, executing, or completing transactions, or having the authority to do so;
- Preparing source documents;
- Having custody of client assets;
- Deciding upon which recommendations of the CPA or others should be implemented;
- Reporting to those charged with governance on behalf of management;
- Serving as a stock transfer or escrow agent, registrar, general counsel, or in a similar role for an attest client;
- Accepting responsibility for a client project;
- Accepting responsibility for the preparation and fair presentation of the entity's financial statements in accordance with an applicable financial reporting framework (AFRF);
- Accepting responsibility for designing, implementing, or maintaining (DIM) internal control; and
- Performing monitoring procedures by evaluating internal controls on an ongoing basis.

In addition, management must *accept responsibility for oversight* of the nonattest service being performed by the accountant for the client. The client does this by designating an individual with appropriate skill, knowledge, and experience, preferably someone in senior management, to fulfill the role. The party is not required to be able to perform the service but should have an adequate understanding to oversee it.

The client must also agree to *evaluate the adequacy and results* of the service performed and *accept responsibility* for the results of the service.

B. Limitation on Accountant's Responsibilities

In order to maintain independence, the accountant **may not** assume any management responsibilities. In addition, the accountant must be satisfied that the client will be able to meet the criteria it agrees to in the form of accepting all management responsibilities and the oversight and responsibility for the nonattest services being performed by the accountant on its behalf.

The accountant should also be satisfied that **the client will**:
- Make an informed judgment in regard to the result of the service; and
- Accept responsibility for significant judgments and decisions for which it has responsibility.

C. Written Understanding

In order to preserve independence, the accountant must enter into an understanding with a client regarding the nonattest services to be performed. The understanding is *required to be in writing* and is generally in the form of an **engagement letter**. It is required to include:
- The objectives of the engagement;
- The services to be performed;
- An acknowledgement by the client that it is accepting its responsibilities;
- An indication of the CPA's responsibilities; and
- Limitations on the engagement, if any.

3. Nonattest Services that Do or Do Not Impair Independence

As indicated, certain nonattest services, and certain conditions under which nonattest services are performed create threats to independence that cannot be reduced to an acceptable level. The AICPA Code of Professional Conduct has **provided guidance** for when the accountant is performing certain **types of nonattest services**. These include:
- Advisory services
- Appraisal, valuation, and actuarial services
- Benefit plan administration
- Bookkeeping, payroll, and other disbursements
- Business risk consulting
- Corporate finance consulting
- Executive or employee recruiting
- Forensic accounting
- Information systems design, implementation, or integration
- Internal audit
- Investment advisory or management
- Tax services
- Attestation services

Advisory Services

When a CPA provides advisory services to a client, the management participation and self-review threats are affected. These threats will be at an acceptable level, however, if the services are exclusively advisory in nature and the accountant does not assume any management responsibilities.

Without raising threats to an unacceptable level, **a CPA may**:
- Provide advice, resources for research, and make recommendations to management to assist it in performing its functions and making its decisions;
- Attend board meetings as an advisor with no voting rights;
- Provide interpretations of financial statements, forecasts, or other analyses; or

- Advise management regarding its anticipated plans, strategies, or relationships.

Appraisal, Valuation, and Actuarial Services

When a CPA provides appraisal, valuation, and actuarial services, the management participation and self-review threats are affected. When these services both involve a significant degree of subjectivity and are material to the client's financial statements, either individually or in combination with other valuation, appraisal, or actuarial services, threats would not be at an acceptable level and could not be reduced to an acceptable level by the application of safeguards.

Valuations of ESOPs or business combinations, and appraisals of assets or liabilities generally require a significant degree of subjectivity and impair independence if the results are material to the client's financial statements. An actuarial valuation of pension or postemployment benefit liabilities do not generally require a significant degree of subjectivity and would not raise threats to independence to an unacceptable level. In addition, appraisals, valuations, and actuarial services that are performed for nonfinancial statement purposes would not raise threats to an unacceptable level.

Benefit Plan Administration

When a CPA provides benefit plan administration services, the management participation and self-review threats are affected. Without raising threats to an unacceptable level, however, **a CPA may**:
- Communicate summary plan information to a trustee of the plan;
- Provide management advice regarding the application and impact of provisions in a plan document;
- Process transactions initiated by plan participants or approved by administrators such as processing investment or benefit elections, processing changes in contributions to the plan, performing data entry, preparing participant confirmations, and processing distributions and loans;
- Prepare account valuations for plan participants; and
- Prepare and transmit participant statements.

Threats, however, would be raised to an unacceptable level and the accountant would not be able to reduce them to an acceptable level through the application of safeguards if the accountant (**Cannot do**):
- Makes policy decisions for management;
- Interprets plan provisions for a participant without management concurrence;
- Disburses funds on behalf of the plan;
- Has custody of plan assets; or
- Serves in a fiduciary capacity, as defined in ERISA.

Bookkeeping, Payroll, and Other Disbursements

When a CPA provides bookkeeping, payroll and other disbursement services, the management participation and self-review threats are affected. Without raising threats to an unacceptable level, however, **a CPA may**:
- Record transactions, for which the client has approved or determined the account classification, in the client's general ledger;
- Post transactions, coded by the client, to the client's general ledger;
- Prepare financial statements based on the client's trial balance;
- Post entries that have been approved by the client to the client's trial balance;
- Propose entries or changes to the financial statements that are reviewed by the client, provided the accountant is satisfied that the nature and financial statement impact are understood by the client, before posting;

- Generate unsigned checks from information provided and approved by the client;
- Process payroll for a client based on payroll records that have been provided and approved by the client;
- After client review and authorization, transmit payroll or other disbursement information to a bank, provided:
    - Prior to transmission, the client has made arrangements to limit such payments as to amounts and payee; and
    - Once transmitted, the client has authorized the bank to process the information; and
- Prepare a bank, accounts receivable, or other reconciliation.

Threats, however, would be raised to an unacceptable level and the accountant would not be able to reduce them to an acceptable level through the application of safeguards if the accountant (**Cannot do**):

- Determines or changes, without prior approval from the client, journal entries, coding, classifications, or accounting records;
- Authorizes or approves transactions;
- Prepares source documents, such as purchase orders or invoices, or makes changes to them without client approval;
- Accepts responsibility for authorizing client payments, other than certain electronic payroll tax payments provided certain requirements are complied with;
- Accepts responsibility as a check signer;
- Has custody of client funds; or makes credit or banking decisions for the client; or
- Approves invoices from vendors for payment.

Business Risk Consulting
When a CPA provides business risk consulting services, the management participation and self-review threats are affected. Without raising threats to an unacceptable level, however, **a CPA may**:

- Assist management in assessing its business risk control processes; or
- Recommend, and assist in the implementation of, improvements to the client's business risk control processes.

Threats, however, would be raised to an unacceptable level and the accountant would not be able to reduce them to an acceptable level through the application of safeguards if the accountant (**Cannot do**):

- Makes or approves business risk decisions; or
- Presents considerations of business risk to the board of directors on behalf of management.

Corporate Finance Consulting
When a CPA provides corporate finance consulting services, the advocacy, management participation, and self-review threats are affected. Without raising threats to an unacceptable level, however, **a CPA may**:

- Assist management in developing corporate strategies and identifying capital sources, based on client criteria;
- Introduce sources of capital to the client, based on client criteria;
- Assist management in determining effects of potential transactions with possible buyers, sellers, or providers of financing;
- Advise the client during negotiations and assist the client in drafting its offering documents;
- Participate, in an advisory capacity, in transaction negotiations; or
- Be named as the client's financial adviser in a private placement memorandum or an offering document.

Threats, however, would be raised to an unacceptable level and the accountant would not be able to reduce them to an acceptable level through the application of safeguards if the accountant (**Cannot do**):

- Commits the client to a transaction;
- Consummates a transaction on behalf of a client;
- Acts as promoter, underwriter, broker-dealer, or guarantor of client securities;
- Acts as distributor of a client's private placement memorandum or offering documents; or
- Maintains custody of the client's securities.

Executive or Employee Recruiting

When a CPA provides executive or employee recruiting services, the management participation and self-review threats are affected. Without raising threats to an unacceptable level, however, **a CPA may**:

- Recommend candidate specifications or a position description to the client;
- Solicit and screen candidates who conform to client criteria;
- Recommend candidates who appear qualified based on client criteria; and
- Participate, in an advisory capacity, in hiring or compensation discussions.

Threats, however, would be raised to an unacceptable level and the accountant would not be able to reduce them to an acceptable level through the application of safeguards if the accountant (**Cannot do**):

- Commits the client to employee compensation or benefit arrangements; or
- Hires or terminates client employees.

Forensic Accounting

A CPA may provide forensic accounting services, consisting of investigative services and litigation services. Investigative services include all forensic services that do not involve litigation and affect the management participation and self-review threats to independence. Litigation services pertain to actual or potential proceedings, legal or regulatory, before a trier of facts to resolve a dispute between parties. Litigation services include expert witness services, litigation consulting services, and other related services.

- In general, performing *expert witness* services increases the advocacy threat to an unacceptable level that could not be reduced to an acceptable level by safeguards.
  - Threats would be at an acceptable level if the services were being performed for a large group of plaintiffs or defendants, including the client; and
  - The clients make up less than 20% of the members of the group, no client is designated as lead plaintiff or defendant, and no client has sole decision-making authority to determine who will serve as expert witness.
- Acting as a *"fact witness"* is not considered a nonattest service and would not impair an accountant's independence if the accountant responds to requests for providing an opinion regarding matters within the accountant's expertise.

Litigation consulting services, in which the accountant provides advice about facts, issues, or strategy, elevate the advocacy and management participation threats to independence. Provided that the general requirements for performing nonattest services have been met, threats would be at an acceptable level and independence would not be impaired. Subsequent agreement to serve as an expert witness, however, elevates threats to an unacceptable level, which could not be reduced to an acceptable level through the application of safeguards.

The advocacy threat would also be raised to an unacceptable level, which could not be reduced to an acceptable level through the application of safeguards, if the accountant is serving as a trier of fact, special master, court-appointed expert, or arbitrator in a matter involving a client. Threats, on the other hand, would be at an acceptable level if the accountant agrees to serve as a mediator in a circumstance where the accountant is facilitating negotiations in which the parties are reaching their own agreement.

Information Systems Design, Implementation, or Integration
Performing information systems design, implementation, or integration services affect the management participation and self-review threats to the accountant's independence. Threats would not be elevated to an unacceptable level if the accountant performs any of the following services (**A CPA may**):
- Installation or integration of a client's financial information system that was designed or developed by parties other than the accountant;
- Assisting the client in establishing a *chart of accounts* and formats for financial statements in the client's financial information system;
- Designing, developing, installing, or integrating an information system that is not related to the client's accounting records or financial statements;
- Training or instructing client employees in regard to the information and control systems; or
- Performing network maintenance, updating virus protection, applying routine updates and patches, or configuring user settings based on requests from management.

Threats to independence would be at an unacceptable level and would not be able to be reduced to an acceptable level by safeguards if the accountant (**Cannot do**):
- Designs or develops the client's financial information system;
- Makes modifications to source code related to the client's financial information system, unless inconsequential;
- Supervises client personnel in the operation of the client's financial information system; or
- Operates a client network.

Internal Audit
Internal audit services consist of assisting the client in its internal audit, or internal control activities. If a client outsources its internal control activities to the accountant, such that the accountant essentially manages the client's internal audit activities, including accepting responsibility for the **d**esign, **i**mplementation, and **m**aintenance (DIM) of internal control, threats to independence would not be at an acceptable level and applying safeguards could not reduce threats to an acceptable level.

Other than outsourcing services, the CPA may assist the client in performing financial and operational internal audit activities provided, to the accountant's satisfaction, management:
- Designates someone to be responsible for the internal audit function who possesses suitable skills, knowledge, and experience, preferably from within senior management;
- Makes all decisions regarding the scope, risk, and frequency of internal control activities, including those performed by the CPA or by others;
- Evaluates all findings and results that emanate from the internal audit activities, whether performed by the accountant or others; and
- Evaluate the adequacy of the procedures performed and the results of those procedures.

Activities that the **CPA may not perform** without raising threats to an unacceptable level, without the ability to reduce them to an acceptable level by applying safeguards, include:

- Performing ongoing evaluations or control activities that affect either the execution of transactions or ensuring that they are properly executed and accounted for;
- Performing routine activities related to an ongoing compliance or quality control function in connection with client operating or production processes;
- Performing routine operations built into the client's business process, such as separate evaluations on the effectiveness of specific significant controls;
- Providing the primary basis for management's assertions regarding the design or operating effectiveness of internal controls;
- Determining which recommendations for the improvement of the client's internal control system should be implemented, if any;
- Reporting to the board of directors on behalf of management in regard to the internal control function;
- Taking responsibility for, or approving, the internal audit work plan, including scope, priorities, and frequency of performance; or
- Taking a *management role* in relation to the client.

Evaluating whether components of a client's internal control system have been put in place and are operating properly is part of the monitoring process. Ongoing evaluations that are incorporated in the client's system are the responsibility of management and would raise the management participation threat to an unacceptable level that could not be adequately reduced by the application of safeguards. The performance of separate evaluations, applied periodically to determine if controls are present and functioning, do not create a significant management participation threat to independence.

Because of the nature of internal audit services, the accountant will be required to apply judgment in determining when threats have been raised to an unacceptable level and whether or not they can be reduced to an acceptable level through the application of safeguards.

Performing services that are normally associated with the attest function, such as confirming accounts receivable or analyzing fluctuations in account balances, are not internal audit services and do not impair the accountant's independence, even when they exceed the scope of the accountant's responsibilities for the nature of attest service being performed for the client.

Investment Advisory or Management
When a CPA provides investment advisory or management services, the management participation and self-review threats are affected. Without raising threats to an unacceptable level, however, **a CPA may:**

- Apply client criteria, such as rate of return, to recommend an allocation of funds among various investments or asset classes;
- Maintain records of the client's portfolio, prepare reports, and provide analysis of investments in comparison with third party benchmarks;
- Evaluate the management of the portfolio to assess if managers are following the client's investment policy guidelines, meeting the client's investment objectives, and conforming to the client's parameters, including its risk tolerance;
- Submit to a broker-dealer the client's investment selection provided the client has consented to the submission and authorized the broker-dealer to execute the transaction.

Threats, however, would be raised to an unacceptable level and the accountant would not be able to reduce them to an acceptable level through the application of safeguards if the accountant (**Cannot do**):

- Makes investment decisions on behalf of the client'
- Has discretionary authority over client investments;
- Executes a transaction to trade a client's investments; or
- Has custody of client assets, even temporarily.

Tax Services

Tax services include:

- Tax return preparation or transmittal;
- Transmittal of a tax payment to a taxing authority
- Signing and filing a tax return or having a power of attorney limited strictly to tax matters; and
- Representing a client before a taxing authority in an administrative proceeding.

Preparing a tax return and transmitting the return and related payment to a taxing authority may create or increase the management participation and self-review threats to independence. In such circumstances, the accountant's independence would not be impaired if the accountant does not have control or custody over client assets. In addition, the individual designated to oversee the tax services must review and approve the tax return and related payments; and if the return is required to be signed for filing, signs the tax return prior to it being transmitted by the accountant to the taxing authority.

In addition, provided certain conditions are met, signing and filing a tax return on behalf of a client, assuming the accountant has the legal authority to do so, **would not impair** the accountant's independence. Nor would:

- Serving as the client's authorized representative in an administrative proceeding; or
- Having a power of attorney that is limited strictly to tax matters.

Representing a client in court to resolve a tax dispute would raise threats to independence to an unacceptable level and applying safeguards would not be able to reduce threats to an acceptable level.

Attestation Services

Independence requirements apply to the performance of all attest services, including services performed in accordance with **attestation standards**. The CPA is not required to be independent of an individual or entity engaging the CPA to perform an attestation engagement if the individual or entity is not the responsible party, the party responsible for the assertion to which the accountant is attesting. Modifications to the independence requirements in relation to the attestation standards include:

- Restrictions on nonattest services only apply to those nonattest services performed in relation to the subject matter of the nonattest services.
- Covered members who must comply with the independence requirements in an agreed-upon procedures engagement may be limited to those participating on the engagement; those who directly supervise the engagement partner or partner equivalent; and individuals consulting with the engagement team regarding technical or industry-related issues relevant to the engagement.

Topic 1.300 – General Standards

A member must comply with the following standards for all professional engagements:
- Only accept engagements expected to be completed with ***professional competency***.
- Exercise ***due professional care***.
- Adequately ***plan and supervise*** engagements.
- Obtain ***sufficient relevant data*** to afford a reasonable basis for conclusions and recommendations.

A member who performs auditing, review, compilation, consulting services, tax or other services shall comply with standards promulgated by bodies designated by Council. The bodies include:
- FASB
- GASB
- PCAOB (SOX)
- IASB for IAS
- AICPA bodies
  - ARSC – Accounting and Review Services Committee
  - ASB – Auditing Standards Board
  - Management Consulting Standards Executive Committee
  - Attestation Standards
  - Tax Executive Committee
  - Forensic and Valuation Services Executive Committee
  - Personal Financial Planning Executive Committee

A member may not provide positive or negative assurance that financial statements are in conformity with a financial reporting framework (GAAP, IASB, PCAOB, GASB, and FASAB statements) if statements contain departures from that framework having a material effect on statements taken as a whole except when unusual circumstances would make financial statements *misleading* if the requirements of the framework had been followed. May depart from GAAP/GASB w/o modifying report if new legislation or a new form of business transaction exists.

Topic 1.400 – Acts Discreditable

A member should NOT commit certain acts that are discreditable to the profession. These might include:
- Discrimination and harassment in employment practices
- Failing to file a tax return or pay a tax liability
- Retaining client records to enforce payment of a bill.
- Providing a fee estimate to a client for services, when the accountant expects the actual fee to be substantially higher (Deliberate underbidding).
- Negligence in the preparation of Financial Statements.
- Filing a fraudulent tax return for self or client.
- Commission of a Felony.
- Noncompliance with applicable requirements of governmental bodies; commissions, or other regulatory agencies when operating within their jurisdiction, including the SEC, Federal Communications Commission, or the PCAOB;
- Solicitation or disclosure of CPA examination questions and answers.
- False, misleading, or deceptive acts in promoting or marketing professional services
- Inappropriate use of the CPA credential

Topic 1.500 – Fees and Other Types of Remuneration

A member may NOT prepare an original or amended tax return for a contingent fee or accept contingent fees for services involving, or from a client for whom the CPA performs such services:

- An audit or review
- A compilation of financial statements expected to be used by third parties without indicating the lack of independence
- An examination of prospective financial statements

Contingent fees are permitted when performing certain tax-related services, including:

- Representing a client in an examination of an income tax return
- Filing an amended income tax return claiming a refund:
    - Based on a tax issue subject to a test case or an evolving position
    - In an amount greater than the threshold for review by the Joint Committee on Internal Revenue Taxation or state taxing authority

A member may accept commissions and referral fees only if both:

- Non-attest engagement client.
- Payment fully disclosed to client.

No commission may be accepted if the accountant is required to be independent for the service provided.

Topic 1.600 – Advertising and Other Forms of solicitation

A member may NOT engage in false, misleading, or deceptive advertising.

Topic 1.700 – Confidential Information

Information is considered confidential, not privileged. Must not reveal information without client permission with certain **exceptions:**

- Valid subpoena or summons.
- Inquiry by AICPA trial board.
- A request made as part of a Quality control peer review program.

A CPA may not give information to another CPA as a professional courtesy and may not take copies of client files when leaving the firm.

Topic 1.800 – Form of Organization and Name

A member may practice public accounting in any form of organization that is permitted by law or regulation with characteristics consistent with those approved in resolutions of the AICPA Council.

- Form and name should not be misleading.
- A firm cannot designate itself as "members of the AICPA" unless all of its CPA OWNERS are members of the AICPA.
- An individual may practice in name of a former partnership for up to 2 years (applies when all other partners have died or withdrawn).
- A firm name may include names of past partners.

Part 2

Part 2 is applicable to members in **private industry**. A member who is both in private industry and public practice, the requirements applicable to a member in public practice will apply.

Topic 2.000 – Introduction

This topic indicates that this part applies to members in private industry. It also requires a conceptual framework approach to determining when threats to compliance with the Code are at an acceptable level and when they require the application of safeguards to eliminate the threat or reduce it to an acceptable level. The conceptual framework is comparable to that for members in public accounting.

Topic 2.100 – Integrity and Objectivity

As is true for members in public accounting, those in private industry shall maintain objectivity and integrity, avoid conflicts of interest, and not knowingly misrepresent facts or subordinate judgment in the performance of any professional service.

Topic 2.300 – General Standards

A member must comply with the following standards for all professional engagements:
- Only accept engagements expected to be completed with professional competency.
- Exercise due professional care.
- Adequately plan and supervise engagements.
- Obtain sufficient relevant data to afford a reasonable basis for conclusions and recommendations.

Topic 2.400 – Acts Discreditable

A member should NOT commit certain acts that are discreditable to the profession. These might include:
- Violations of laws related to discrimination or harassment in the workplace.
- Solicitation or disclosure of CPA examination questions and answers.
- Nonpayment of a tax liability or not filing a return
- Preparing financial statements in a negligent manner

Part 3

Part 3 is applicable to members who are **neither in public accounting or private industry**, such as a member who is *retired or unemployed*.

Topic 3.000 – Introduction

This topic indicates that this part applies to members who are neither in public accounting or private industry.

Topic 3.400 – Acts Discreditable

A member should NOT commit certain acts that are discreditable to the profession. These might include:
- Violations of laws related to discrimination or harassment in the workplace.
- Solicitation or disclosure of CPA examination questions and answers.
- Nonpayment of a tax liability or not filing a return
- Disclosing confidential information obtained as a result of previous relationships

CONSULTING SERVICES STANDARDS (SSCS NO.1)

Consulting services consist of advisory services, implementation services, product services or even providing technical assistance in implementing a new IT system. Independence need not be maintained, but the consultant must act with integrity and objectivity. A written or oral understanding with the client should be established.

- General standards of the profession, which apply to all services performed by the CPA
  - Professional Competence (T)
  - Due professional care (P)
  - Planning & supervision (P)
  - Sufficient relevant data (C)

Additional general standards apply specifically to consulting services:

- Client interest – must act with integrity & objectivity (need NOT be independent) while seeking to fulfill client's objectives.
- Understanding with client – written or oral agreement to perform engagement.
- Communication with client:
  - Disclose conflicts of interest.
  - *Cite reservations* about potential benefits of engagement.
  - Provide findings in appropriate oral or written form.

STATEMENTS ON STANDARDS IN PERSONAL FINANCIAL PLANNING SERVICES (PFP FOR RESEARCH PURPOSES)

CPAs often help clients by performing personal financial planning services, which involves assisting clients in identifying and establishing *personal financial goals and resources*. The services may include such activities as cash flow, risk and management, retirement, or investment planning; estate, gift, and wealth transfer planning; elder planning; charitable planning, education planning; or tax planning.

A CPA performing personal financial planning (PFP) services is required to adhere to the requirements of Statements on Standards in Personal Financial Planning Services (SSPFPS), issued by the AICPA if the CPA:

- Represents to the public or clients that PFP services are being provided;
- Performs activity that require registration as an investment advisor under federal or state jurisdictions; or
- Sells a product or service as a result of the engagement.

A CPA performing PFP services is only required to be independent if also performing attest services for that client, which require independence. The CPA will evaluate the services performed and the relationship with the client in the context of the independence requirements under the AICPA Code of Professional Conduct.

A CPA performing PFP services should adhere to certain *general requirements*. These include:

- Compliance with all applicable ethical requirements
- Possession of knowledge of PFP principles and skills adequate to allow the CPA to identify client goals, analyze relevant information, apply appropriate approaches, and develop recommendations using professional judgment.
- Evaluation of potential conflicts of interest regarding the engagement.

- Compliance with applicable laws and regulations.

Prior to the engagement, the CPA should disclose in writing all compensation that the CPA and its firms or affiliates will receive, including any compensation alternatives.

SSPFPS address **five issues** in relation to PFP services. These include:
- *Planning the engagement*
- *Obtaining and analyzing information*
- *Developing and communicating recommendations*
- *Implementation engagements*
- *Monitoring and updating engagements*

They also provide guidance when either working with, or using advice provided by, another service provider.

Planning

The primary planning related requirement is for the CPA to make certain that the client is informed, in writing, of the scope and nature of the services and the CPA's compensation for them. The written communication, required to be documented in the CPA's file, will include other relevant aspects of the engagement, such as:
- Objectives
- Roles and responsibilities of the CPA, of the client, and of others, including other service providers
- Timing
- Constraints or scope limitations
- Conflicts of interest
- The CPA's responsibilities, if any, for implementation, monitoring, or updating proposals

Obtaining and Analyzing Information

A CPA performing PFP services is required to use *professional judgment* in the collection and analysis of information and in determining if sufficient information has been or can be obtained and analyzed to achieve the engagement's objectives. If sufficient information does not exist or cannot be obtained, the engagement should be modified or terminated.

Analysis of information obtained should include evaluation of the reasonableness of significant estimates and assumptions, use of assumptions that are consistent with one another, and the relationship of other PFP activities performed by the CPA or others.

Developing and Communicating Recommendations

Recommendations should be made that are consistent with the objectives of the engagement, derived from analysis of relevant information, including the client's goals and financial circumstances. Communication with the client should include significant assumptions and estimates.

Documentation should include:
- Client's goals
- Significant assumptions and estimates
- Limitations on work performed

- Recommendations and any qualifications to the recommendations

Implementation Engagements

When engaged to assist the client in implementing PFP recommendations, the understanding with the client should be documented and should include the roles and responsibilities of the CPA, the client, and of other service providers. Documentation will include a summary of decisions being implemented, recommended actions taken, and limitations on work performed in the implementation engagement.

Written communication with the client should also include the CPA's responsibility, if any, for:
- Selecting products or service providers or acquiring products; establishing selection criteria; or coordinating or reviewing the performance of other service providers.
- Identifying and evaluating selection criteria in terms of the client's objectives and any constraints that may result from the client's circumstances or other factors.
- Recommending products, indicating information gathered to evaluate conformity to selection criteria, adequate to communicate the recommendations and their evaluation and any compensation received for making the recommendations.

Monitoring and Updating Engagements

When involved in monitoring, the CPA should document services provided, including the frequency and period used to measure progress toward stated objectives, monitoring criteria being used, criteria related to the achievement of objectives that are being monitored, and evaluation of the progress toward achieving the client's objectives.

When involved in an updating engagement, documentation of the nature and extent of services will include whether or not objectives, information, and assumptions remain valid; and the effect of revising certain recommendations on the client's ability to achieve other PFP objectives.

Other Service Providers

When a CPA refers another service provider in relation to PFP services, the CPA should consider the service provider's professional qualifications and should communicate, in writing, any compensation for making the referral and the extent to which the CPA will or will not evaluate the work of the other service provider.

When using the advice of another service provider, a CPA providing PFP services should understand the impact of the advice. If the CPA has evaluated the advice, the CPA need not communicate concurrence but should communicate in writing any circumstances in which the CPA does NOT concur.

VALUATION SERVICES (VS FOR RESEARCH PURPOSES)

Valuation services (**VS**) may involve valuation of businesses, ownership interests, securities, or intangible assets and may be provided to businesses, individuals, attorneys and other CPAs or performed within the course of a CPA's duties in certain instances. Valuation services are covered under the AICPA's *Statements on Standards for Valuation Service (VS)*. Examples of typical valuation services include:
- Purchase price allocations for business combinations (FASB ASC 805).

- Goodwill impairment analysis (FASB ASC 350).
- Valuation of stock-based compensation (FASB ASC 718).
- Estate and gift tax planning and reporting.
- Charitable donations.
- Mergers and acquisitions or purchases/sales of businesses.
- Due diligence.
- Employee stock options/stock ownership plans.

Statements on Valuation Services **do not** cover:
- Audits, compilations, and reviews.
- Use of values that are client-provided or from a third party.
- Engagements to determine the value of economic damages.
- Mechanical computations of value that do not involve the application of valuation approaches.

Performance of valuation services **require**:
- Professional competence
- Objectivity
- Disclosure of potential conflicts of interest
- An understanding with the client
- Disclosure of assumptions and limiting conditions, and scope restrictions or limitations in the report

The accountant will issue either a detailed report or a summary report for a valuation engagement, and a calculation report for a calculation engagement.

TAX SERVICES (TS for Research Purposes)

Statements on Standards for Tax Services (**TS**) guide a member in the performance of tax services, which include recommending a tax position to a client or preparing or signing a client's tax return. The practitioner should determine and comply with standards established by the applicable tax authority for recommending tax return positions or preparing or signing tax returns. TS establish minimum standards for recommending a tax position or preparing or signing a tax return for those jurisdictions that either do not have formal standards or have standards that are not as strict as those imposed by TS.
- The practitioner should not recommend a position or prepare or sign a tax return taking a position that the practitioner does not have a good faith belief that has *substantial authority* in favor of its being sustained on the basis of the merits of the position.
- The practitioner may recommend a tax return position if the practitioner concludes that there is a reasonable basis for the position and advises the taxpayer to appropriately disclose the position.
- The practitioner may also prepare or sign a tax return that takes a position that the practitioner concludes has a reasonable basis and is appropriately disclosed.
- The practitioner should advise the client regarding potential penalties related to tax positions taken and the possibility of avoiding penalties through adequate disclosure.

Each tax jurisdiction may have its own reporting and disclosure standards. Those that the practitioner should be familiar with include:
- **More likely than not** indicates that there is a greater than 50% likelihood that the position will be sustained on the basis of its merits.

- **Substantial authority** indicates that those authoritative sources supporting the position are substantial in relation to those opposing the position, often requiring approximately 40% likelihood that the position will be sustained on the basis of its merits.
- **Realistic possibility** of success indicates that the practitioner believes that there is approximately a 1/3 likelihood that the position will be sustained on the basis of its merits.
- **Reasonable basis** indicates the practitioner believes that one or more credible authorities support the position and that the position is not frivolous or patently improper.
    - The standard is not satisfied if the position is merely arguable.
    - A reasonable basis is often associated with a 20% likelihood that the position will be sustained on the basis of its merits.

The **Substantial Authority** standard is considered to be an approximately 40% likelihood of success. So, to put the likelihoods in order:

- *More likely than not* standard > 50% probability of success if tax position is challenged
- *Substantial authority* standard ≈ 40% probability of success (≈ approximately)
- *Realistic possibility* of success ≈ 33% (1/3) probability of success
- *Reasonable basis* standard ≈ 20% probability of success.

A position taken may conflict with a position that previously resulted from an administrative proceeding (tax audit) or court decision, provided taxpayer is not be bound to the specified treatment in later tax returns.

When providing tax advice to clients:

- Any written communication should comply with standards of taxing authorities.
- It should be assumed that advice will affect the reporting or disclosure of transactions on the client's tax returns and should consider standards for return reporting and disclosure and potential consequences of the position, such as penalties.
- The CPA need not inform the client of subsequent developments affecting advice previously given.

Before signing, the CPA makes a reasonable effort to obtain information necessary to answer all questions on the return.

Without obtaining verification, the CPA *may rely on information obtained from the taxpayer* or others but may not ignore indications that the information is incorrect, incomplete, or inconsistent with the CPA's knowledge of the client.

- Client estimates may be used if the CPA believes them to be reasonable.
- Estimates should be presented such that it is clear they are estimates.

The CPA may become aware of an error on a previously filed return or in a return that is subject to an administrative proceeding, or that a required return was not filed. The CPA may not inform the taxing authority without permission from the client, but should:

- Promptly inform the client
- Advise the client, orally or in writing, of the potential error

A CPA should consider withdrawal from an engagement where a client has failed to correct an error in a prior return and should evaluate a continued relationship with the client. The CPA should take steps to avoid repeating the error if it is deemed appropriate to prepare the current return.

- The CPA should request that the client inform a taxing authority of an error when representing the client in an administrative proceeding.

- Failure to obtain permission may result in withdrawal from the engagement and evaluation of the client relationship.

PRIVACY ACTS

Congress passed certain laws that are designed to protect individuals from professionals or institutions that may use their client or customer information in an appropriate manner. The Gramm-Leach–Bliley Act requires tax planners and tax preparers to notify clients about the information that will be obtained and policies for protecting the client's information. The Financial Services Modernization Act of 1999 prohibits a financial institution from sharing client information, other than with other financial institutions, without first obtaining the customer's consent.

Federal Privacy Disclosure Rules – Gramm-Leach-Bliley Act

- When performing tax planning, financial planning or tax returns, the Federal Trade Commission (FTC) requires certain disclosures be made either in writing or electronically to all clients.
  - The categories of personal info to be collected, disclosed and to which third parties this info may be disclosed.
  - The CPA's policy on sharing info of past clients and the policy regarding protecting the confidentiality, security and integrity of the info.

The Financial Services Modernization Act of 1999

- Prohibits financial institutions from sharing private personal info to nonaffiliated third parties without prior notice to the client. Can still share with other financial institutions and its affiliates.

WORKING PAPERS (AUDIT DOCUMENTATION)

The accountant, not the client, owns the working papers that an accountant creates during an engagement. Nevertheless, the accountant must maintain **confidentiality**, and cannot provide the papers or information obtained during engagements to other parties without the permission of the client (it should be noted that client confidentiality does not preclude a CPA from providing access to other members of his/her firm). There are some **exceptions** to confidentiality, including:
- **Valid subpoena** – the accountant must honor a valid court order to turn over information.
- **IRS administrative subpoena.**
- **Court order** (unless rare state with privilege statute).
- **Quality control peer review** – The accountant may allow other accountants and the PCAOB to see confidential information in connection with a valid program of peer review.

Common law does not recognize the concept of **privilege**, which would allow the accountant to refuse to honor a court subpoena. A small number of states have enacted privilege statutes, and the federal government now recognizes working papers developed in connection with the preparation of a tax return to be privileged in certain circumstances. Nevertheless, privilege may not be used if the accountant has already provided some of the information requested in the subpoena, and the purpose of privilege is to protect the client, not the accountant, so the accountant may not assert privilege even where privilege statutes exist if the client waives the privilege.

SARBANES-OXLEY ACT (SOX)

Sarbanes-Oxley Act (SOX) was created to restore investor's confidence. Established the **P**ublic **C**ompany **A**ccounting **O**versight **B**oard (**PCAOB**) to regulate auditors of public companies – subject to SEC oversight. SOX led to *"integrated audits"* in which auditors' report on audits of both the financial statements and on internal control over financial reporting for public audit clients. This eliminated a significant portion of the accounting profession's system of self-regulation. The PCAOB is a private-sector, nonprofit corporation, created by the Sarbanes-Oxley Act of 2002, to oversee the auditors of public companies, or **issuers**, in order to protect the interests of investors and further the public interest in the preparation of informative, fair, and independent audit reports.

In some cases, nonissuers not subject to the requirements of SOX may nonetheless request an audit conducted in accordance with PCAOB standards. AU-C 700 reminds practitioners that, in such cases, the auditor is still required to also conduct the audit in accordance with generally accepted accounting standards (GAAS).

Relevant provisions follow:

Title I – Public Accounting Oversight Board (sections)

- **101** – Establishes the Board (PCAOB), which consists of 5 full time members, 2 of which are CPAs, all appointed by the SEC.
- **102** – Requires public accounting firms to register with the Board in order to issue or participate in the issuance of an audit report for an issuer.
- **103** – Authorizes the Board to establish audit standards, quality control standards, and ethics standards to be used by registered public accounting firms in the preparation and issuance of audit reports. The board also inspects, investigates, and disciplines public accounting firms and enforces compliance with the act.
  - Standards either by the AICPA (ASB) or the PCAOB or a combination of the two.
  - Must keep workpapers for 7 years from report release date.
  - A second partner is required to review all audit reports.
  - Audit reports must describe the scope of testing for I/C.
- **104** – Provides for Quality Control *Peer Review Inspections* to be conducted by the Board:
  - Must be performed every year for firms that provide more than 100 audit reports annually.
  - At least every 3 years if 100 or less annually
    - A written report of findings, including deficiencies discovered, is provided to the SEC and made available to the public.
- **105** – Gives Board authority to conduct investigations and obtain all relevant info.
  - Power to suspend auditors, revoke the registration of the accounting firm, or impose penalties for violations or for unwillingness to cooperate with an investigation.
  - Provisions apply to both domestic and foreign auditors.
  - Monetary penalties for violation of board rules or securities law capped at $100K for an individual and $2M for an entity (if intentional breach $750K and $15M).
- **106** – Regulates foreign public accounting firms furnishing an audit report to an issuer and requires them to comply with board requests.
- **107** – Gives SEC oversight and enforcement authority over the Board and its decisions.
- **108** – Amends the Securities Act of 1933 to allow the SEC, which has the authority to establish accounting standards, to adopt the accounting standards established by a standard setting body that meets certain qualifications, such as the FASB.

- o   Required study of accounting principles, including content, structure, and standard-setting process.
- o   Made recommendations to FASB, resulting in development of the Codification, and adopted FASB standards as amended by SEC pronouncements.
- **109** – Calls for funding of the Board and the designated accounting standard-setting body (FASB) to be funded from fees imposed upon public companies.

Title II – Auditor Independence

- **201** – *Prohibits* any registered public accounting firm from providing the following non-audit services to Audit clients:
  - o   Bookkeeping or other services related to the accounting records.
  - o   Financial info systems design or implementation.
  - o   Appraisal or valuation services, or providing fairness opinions or contribution-in-kind reports.
  - o   Actuarial services.
  - o   Internal audit outsourcing services.
  - o   Management functions or human resources.
  - o   Broker or dealer investment advisor or investment banking services.
  - o   Legal services and expert services that are unrelated to the audit.
  - o   Any other service the board determines impermissible.
    - ▪   Tax services are still permissible if preapproved by the audit committee and disclosed to the SEC.
    - ▪   May still perform these services to nonaudit clients or to private companies.
- **202** – Requires the issuer's audit committee to preapprove all auditing and non-auditing services to be provided to an issuer.
  All nonaudit services that are not prohibited are also required to be preapproved unless they are considered de minimis. De minimis nonaudit services entail fees that do not exceed 5% of the total fees paid to the auditor. In addition, the client must not have recognized the services as nonaudit services at the time of the engagement and the services were promptly brought to the attention of the audit committee and approval was obtained prior to the completion of the audit.
- **203** – Establishes mandatory and substantive rotation of audit partner and partner responsible for review every 5 years (not audit firm rotation).
- **204** – Requires audit firm to report to the audit committee:
  - o   Critical accounting policies and practices
  - o   Alternative accounting treatments within GAAP discussed with management
  - o   Material written communications between auditor's firm and management of the issuer
- **205** – Defines the term audit committee and indicates that the entire board of directors is considered the audit committee when one has not been designated.
- **206** – Prohibits the audit firm from providing audit services for issuer if the CEO, controller, CFO, CAO or any person serving in the equivalent capacity was employed in the audit practice of the accounting firm during the one-year period prior to the audit.

Title III – Corporate Responsibility

- **301** – Makes audit committee, which must be independent, responsible for appointment, compensation and oversight of any audit work performed by the audit firm. Allows the SEC to de-list any issuer not in compliance with title III.

- **302** – Requires principal executive and principal financial officers to certify, in each annual or quarterly report:
    - That they reviewed the report
    - The report does not contain any untrue statement of material fact or omission of a material fact
    - Financial position and results of operations are fairly presented

  Officers also certify that they:
    - Are responsible for establishing and maintaining effective internal control
    - Have evaluated the effectiveness of the controls within 90 days prior to the report
    - Have presented their conclusions as to the effectiveness of internal control

  Signing officers required to disclose to auditors and audit committee:
    - Significant deficiencies in the design or operation of internal controls
    - Any fraud, regardless of whether or not material, that involves management or employees involved in internal controls

Report of signing officers also indicates changes in internal controls over financial reporting.
- **303** – Prohibits an officer or director of an issuer to fraudulently influence, coerce, manipulate, or mislead the auditor.
- **304** – Requires executives of an issuer to forfeit any bonus or incentive based pay or profits from the sale of stock, received in the 12 months period after the date of issuance of financial statements subject to an earnings restatement (**Claw-back Policy**).
- **305** – The SEC may bar any person who has violated federal securities laws from serving as an officer or director of an issuer.
- **306** – Prohibits trading by officers and directors during blackout periods established between the end of a quarter and the earnings report date.

Title IV – Enhanced Financial Disclosures

- **401** – Requires all financial statements prepared in accordance with GAAP to reflect all material adjustments identified by the auditors.
    - Also required the SEC to establish standards to address off-balance sheet transactions.
    - Result was rules for consolidation of variable interest entities
- **402** – Prohibits personal loans to directors and executive officers.
- **403** – Requires directors, officers, and principal shareholders to disclose the amount of all equity securities in which they hold a beneficial interest and any changes in their interests since the previous filing.
- **404** – Requires that management acknowledge its responsibility for establishing and maintaining adequate internal control over financial reporting and that management assess the effectiveness of internal control as of the end of the period. Also *requires the auditor to examine the design and operating effectiveness of internal control over financial reporting to provide a sufficient basis to report on management's assessment.*
    - The auditor should conduct the attestation in a manner consistent with the Statements on Standards for Attestation Engagements and PCAOB Standards
    - Note that the auditor is not attesting to the effectiveness or the efficiency of internal control but on management's assessment of internal control.
    - The Act does not specify a date by which the auditor's report is to be submitted.

- **405** – Exempts investment companies registered under the Investment Company Act of 1940 from sections 401, 402, and 404.
- **406** – Requires an issuer to disclose whether or not it has adopted a code of ethics for senior financial officers and, if not, the reasons for not having done so.
- **407** – Must disclose whether at least 1 member of its audit committee is a "financial expert."
- **408** – Provides for enhanced review of periodic disclosures by Board.
- **409** – Requires issuers to disclose material changes in the financial condition or operations on a rapid and current basis.

Title V – Analyst Conflict of Interest

Title VI – Commission Resources and Authority

Title VII – Studies and Reports

Title VIII – Corporate and Criminal Fraud Accountability

Title IX – White Collar Crime Penalty Enhancements

- **906** – Requires that management certify that the reports filed with the SEC (10Q, 10K) comply with relevant securities laws and also fairly present, in all material respects, the financial condition and results of operations of the company.
  Note: Violations of rules of the PCAOB are treated as violations of the Securities Exchange Act of 1934 with its penalties, and the Act contains provisions for future rule-making.

Lecture 2.06

CLASS QUESTIONS

Please see the Class Questions and Class Solutions for this Lecture at the end of this Section.

Lecture 2.07

PRIVATE SECURITIES LITIGATION REFORM ACT OF 1995

Although the Private Securities Litigation Reform Act of 1995 was primarily designed to limit frivolous lawsuits related to the securities laws, it imposes requirements on an auditor to perform certain tests and to notify the SEC of noncompliance with applicable laws and regulations.

- **Imposes requirements to include audit tests to detect (RIG):**
  - o **R**elated party transactions.
  - o **I**llegal acts (noncompliance with Laws and Regulations)
  - o **G**oing concern doubts.

- **Requires quick notice of illegal acts (noncompliance with laws and regulations) unless clearly inconsequential.**
  - o Auditor must inform board of directors within 1 business day.

- o Board must notify SEC by next business day.
- o Auditor must resign or notify SEC within 1 business day after that, if board fails to notify SEC and provide auditor with proof of notice (auditor cannot be sued privately for negative effect of SEC notice on the company's securities).

CORPORATE AND CRIMINAL FRAUD ACCOUNTABILITY ACT OF 2002

The SEC has stepped up its monitoring of public companies under the Corporate and Criminal Fraud Accountability Act of 2002. This Act has significant influence on the auditor's professional environment concerning the detection of fraud. Provisions include:
- Auditors are required to maintain all audit working papers for 7 years.
- It is a felony to knowingly destroy or create documents (including audit working papers) to impede, obstruct or influence any existing or contemplated federal investigation.
- The statute of limitations on securities fraud claims is extended to 5 years from the fraud, or 2 years after the fraud was discovered.
- Employees of CPA firms (and audit clients) are extended whistleblower protection that would prohibit the employer from taking certain actions against employees. Whistleblower employees are also granted a remedy of special damages and attorney's fees.
- Securities fraud by CPA's (and audit clients) is punishable of up to 10 years in prison.

PCAOB STANDARDS (AS)

As a result of numerous incidents involving fraudulent financial reporting involving such companies as Enron, WorldCom, Global Crossing, and others, Congress passed the Sarbanes-Oxley Act. One of the numerous provisions of Sarbanes-Oxley established the Public Company Accounting Oversight Board, or PCAOB. The **PCAOB** is a nonprofit corporation established by Congress to oversee the audits of **public entities**, referred to as *issuers*, in order to protect investors and the public interest by promoting informative, accurate, and independent audit reports.

As a prerequisite to performing an audit of an issuer, a public accounting firm must register with the PCAOB. The PCAOB also performs inspections, conducts investigations and disciplinary proceedings of registered firms and sanctions firms, when necessary.

The **inspections** include:
- Inspection and review of selected audit and review engagements.
- An evaluation of the sufficiency of the quality control system of the CPA firm, and how the system is documented and communicated.
- Perform other tests of the audit, supervisory and quality control procedures as considered necessary.

At the completion of the inspection, a written report is then sent to the SEC and any other appropriate regulatory agency. The content of the report is made available to the public, but quality control system criticisms are not made public unless the firm doesn't address the issues within 12 months.

The PCAOB is responsible for standards for issuers related to:
- Auditing
- Attestation
- Quality Control
- Ethics Standards (independence) and (integrity & objectivity).

The **PCAOB** originally issued auditing standards, referred to as AS 1 through AS 18. They have since been codified and are organized as follows

General Auditing Standards

1000 – General Principles and Responsibilities

AS 1001: Responsibilities and Functions of the Independent Auditor – Requires the auditor to comply with PCAOB standards and distinguishes between the auditor's responsibilities and those of management.

AS 1005: Independence – Requires the auditor to be independent in mental attitude in all matters relating to the engagement.

AS 1010: Training and Proficiency of the Independent Auditor – Requires the auditor to have adequate technical training and proficiency as an auditor.

AS 1015: Due Professional Care in the Performance of Work – Requires the auditor to apply due professional care in the planning and performance of the engagement and in the preparation of the report.

1100 – General Concepts

AS 1101: Audit Risk – Requires the auditor to consider risk in both an integrated audit and in an audit of financial statements, consisting of audit risk, which is made up of the risk of material misstatement and detection risk (RMM & DR).

AS 1105: Audit Evidence – Describes what constitutes and requires the auditor to perform procedures to obtain *sufficient appropriate* audit evidence.

AS 1110: Relationship of Auditing Standards to Quality Control Standards – Requires the auditor's firm to establish quality control policies and procedures to provide reasonable assurance that the firm will comply with applicable PCAOB standards in the performance of its audit engagements.

1200 – General Activities

AS 1201: Supervision of the Audit Engagement – Requires the auditor to supervise the engagement team to assure that work is performed as directed and that conclusions reached are supported.

AS 1205: Part of the Audit Performed by Other Independent Auditors – Indicates when an auditor may serve as a principal auditor and the effect on the auditor's procedures and the report in circumstances when the auditor does and does not make reference to the other auditor in the report.

AS 1210: Using the Work of a Specialist – Provides guidance to auditors using a specialist when performing an audit under PCAOB standards.

AS 1215: Audit Documentation – Requires the auditor to establish a written record to support conclusions reached and all representations made by the auditor, including those in the audit report.

AS 1220: Engagement Quality Review – Requires that audit engagements, reviews of interim financial, and attestation engagements be subjected to an engagement quality review and concurring approval of issuance.

1300 – Auditor Communications

AS 1301: Communications with Audit Committees – Requires the auditor to communicate to the audit committee relevant information regarding the audit, including the overall strategy and timing, and obtain any information relevant to the audit from the audit committee.

AS 1305: Communications About Control Deficiencies in an Audit of Financial Statements – Requires the auditor to communicate all significant deficiencies and material weaknesses detected during the audit, in writing, to management and the audit committee prior to the issuance of the auditor's report on the financial statements.

Audit Procedures

2100 – Audit Planning and Risk Assessment

AS 2101: Audit Planning – Requires the auditor to plan the audit so that it can be conducted effectively, including the establishment of an overall audit strategy and an audit plan that incorporates planned risk assessment procedures and planned responses to identified risks of material misstatement.

AS 2105: Consideration of Materiality in Planning and Performing an Audit – Requires the auditor to consider quantitative and qualitative factors in determining what constitutes a potential material misstatement to the financial statements and to plan and design audit procedures that are expected to be effective in detecting them.

AS 2110: Identifying and Assessing Risks of Material Misstatement – Establishes guidelines for the performance of risk assessment procedures, enabling the auditor to obtain an understanding of the entity and its environment, including its internal control, as a basis for designing and applying responses to identified risks of material misstatement.

2200 – Auditing Internal Control Over Financial Reporting

AS 2201: An Audit of Internal Control Over Financial Reporting That Is Integrated with An Audit of Financial Statements – Establishes requirements for engagements in which the auditor is engaged to examine management's assessment of internal control that is relevant to financial reporting.

2300 – Audit Procedures in Response to Risks – Nature, Timing, and Extent

AS 2301: The Auditor's Responses to the Risks of Material Misstatement – Requires the auditor to design and implement appropriate responses to identified risks of material misstatement including responses that have an overall effect on how the audit is conducted and the effects on the nature, timing, and extent of audit procedures to be performed.

AS 2305: Substantive Analytical Procedure – Establishes guidelines for circumstances in which the auditor is using analytical procedures as substantive tests based on the nature of the assertion begin tested, the existence of predictable relationships among data, the availability of reliable information upon which to base expectations, and the precision of expectations developed by the auditor.

AS 2310: The Confirmation Process – Defines the confirmation process; discusses the relationship of confirmations to the assessment of audit risk; identifies factors affecting the reliability of confirmations; indicates alternative procedures to be applied when responses to confirmations are not received; addresses the evaluation of the results of confirmation procedures; and specifically addresses the confirmation of accounts receivable.

AS 2315: Audit Sampling – Provides guidance for the planning, performing, and evaluating of audit samples.

2400 – Audit Procedures for Specific Aspects of the Audit

AS 2401: Consideration of Fraud in a Financial Statement Audit – Establishes requirements and provides direction to address the auditor's responsibility to obtain reasonable assurance that the financial statements are not materially misstated as it relates to fraud.

AS 2405: *Illegal Acts by Clients* – Establishes the auditor's responsibility for considering the possibility of illegal acts by a client and guidance on the auditor's responsibility when a possible illegal act is detected.

AS 2410: *Related Parties* – Establishes requirements for the auditor's consideration of the client's identification of related parties and related party transactions, as well as how they are accounted for and disclosed.

AS 2415: *Consideration of an Entity's Ability to Continue as a Going Concern* – Establishes the auditor's responsibility to evaluate whether there is substantial doubt as to an entity's ability to continue as a going concern for a reasonable period of time, including auditing procedures to be performed and any reporting responsibilities.

2500 – Audit Procedures for Certain Accounts or Disclosures

AS 2501: *Auditing Accounting Estimates* – Establishes guidance regarding obtaining sufficient appropriate audit evidence to support significant estimates in the financial statements.

AS 2502: *Auditing Fair Value Measurements and Disclosures* – Establishes standards to be applied in regard to obtaining sufficient appropriate audit evidence related to the measurement and disclosure of assets, liabilities, and components of equity that are presented or disclosed at fair value.

AS 2503: *Auditing Derivative Instruments, Hedging Activities, and Investments in Securities* – Provides guidance to the auditor on planning and performing procedures related to the accounting for and reporting on derivative instruments and hedging activities, addressing the assertions of existence or occurrence, completeness, rights and obligations, valuation or allocation, and presentation and disclosure.

AS 2505: *Inquiry of a Client's Lawyer Concerning Litigation, Claims, and Assessments* – Requires the auditor to perform certain procedures to obtain evidence about litigation, claims, and assessments, including inquiries of client management; obtaining a description and evaluation of litigation, claims, and assessments from management; examining relevant documents; obtaining written assurance from management regarding disclosure of unasserted claims; and requesting that management send an inquiry letter to lawyers consulted or retained in relation to those matters.

AS 2510: *Auditing Inventories* – Indicates that the observation of inventories is a generally accepted audit procedure and places a burden on the auditor to justify the opinion expressed on the financial statements when inventory has not been observed.

2600 – Special Topics

AS 2601: *Consideration of an Entity's Use of a Service Organization* – Provides guidance to auditors of entities that use service organizations that become part of its information system and for auditors that issue reports related to the processing of transactions by a service organization for use by the auditors of the entity using it.

AS 2605: *Consideration of the Internal Audit Function* – Provides guidance to the auditor on the consideration of the work of internal auditors in forming an opinion on the financial statements and for obtaining direct assistance from internal auditors in performing the audit in accordance with PCAOB standards.

AS 2610: *Initial Audits* – Communications Between Predecessor and Successor Auditors – Requires an auditor in an initial engagement to communicate with the predecessor auditor as a prerequisite for accepting the engagement and establishes guidance for communication with the predecessor when the auditor discovers misstatements in financial statements reported on by the predecessor.

2700 – Auditor's Responsibilities Regarding Supplemental and Other Information

AS 2701: Auditing Supplemental Information Accompanying Audited Financial Statements – Requires the auditor to perform audit procedures in relation to supplemental information to support an opinion as to whether or not the supplemental information is fairly stated.

AS 2705: Required Supplementary Information – Provides guidance to auditors as to the nature of procedures to apply to supplemental information required by the FASB, GASB, or FASAB and indicates when the auditor is required to report on required supplemental information.

AS 2710: Other Information in Documents Containing Audited Financial Statements – Establishes requirement for auditor to read other information included in documents that include the financial statements, excluding registrations statements filed with the SEC, to make certain that there are no inconsistencies with information included in the audited financial statements.

2800 – Conducting Audit Procedures

AS 2801: Subsequent Events – Requires the consideration of subsequent events by management and evaluation by the auditor, including those representing conditions existing at the balance sheet date and requiring adjustment to the financial statements, and those representing conditions that came into existence after the balance sheet date and requiring disclosure.

AS 2805: Management Responsibilities – Requires the auditor to obtain written representations from management as a component of an audit performed in accordance with PCAOB standards, including guidance as to specific representations to be obtained.

AS 2810: Evaluating Audit Results – Provides guidance to the auditor in making a determination as to the appropriateness and sufficiency of audit evidence.

AS 2815: The Meaning of "Present Fairly in Conformity with Generally Accepted Accounting Principles - Requires the auditor to determine, based on the requirements of the SEC, the accounting principles applicable to the company under audit and requires the auditor to determine if the principles applied by the entity are generally accepted, are appropriate under the circumstances, and if the financial statements are informative in relation to matters that will affect the use of the financial statements.

AS 2820: Evaluating Consistency of Financial Statements – Requires the auditor to evaluate the consistency of the financial statements, provides guidance for the evaluation, and describes the effects of the evaluation on the auditor's report.

2900 – Post-Audit Matters

AS 2901: Consideration of Omitted Procedures After the Report Date – Requires the auditor to evaluate whether the opinion expressed can be supported despite the omitted procedure and, if not, requires the auditor to perform the procedure or a satisfactory alternative. If unable to do so, the auditor should consult with legal counsel as to responsibilities and the best course of action. If performance indicates that facts existing at the financial statement date would have affected the report, the auditor should follow the guidance in AS 2905.

AS 2905: Subsequent Discovery of Facts Existing at the Date of the Auditor's Report – Upon discovery of facts not known to the auditor at the date of the report that would have been investigated if known at the time, requires the auditor to determine if the information is reliable and if it existed as of the date of the report. If so, the auditor is further required to determine if the information would have affected the auditor's report and if there are parties likely to be relying on the financial statements that would attach importance to the information. Requires the auditor, upon making such a determination, to work with the client and perform procedures to make certain that the report is not inappropriately relied upon.

Auditor Reporting

3100 - Reporting on Audits of Financial Statements

AS 3101: Reports on Audited Financial Statements – Provides guidelines for the preparation of a standard audit report, circumstances calling for a modified report, and guidelines as to how the report will be modified.

AS 3110: Dating of the Independent Auditor's Report – Requires the auditor to date the report no earlier than the date on which *sufficient appropriate audit evidence* is obtained and provides guidance for reporting events occurring after the date of the report but before its issuance and the reissuance of a report.

3300 – Other Reporting Topics

AS 3305: Special Reports – Provides guidance for preparing reports related to financial statements prepared in accordance with a comprehensive basis of accounting other than GAAP; related to specified elements, accounts, or items of a financial statement; to compliance with aspects of contractual agreements or regulatory requirements; to presentations designed to comply with contractual agreements or regulatory provisions; and related to financial information presented in prescribed forms or requiring a prescribed form or report.

AS 3310: Special Reports on Regulated Companies – Requires reports on regulated companies to address whether the financial statements present fairly, in all material respects, the financial position of the entity as of the balance sheet date and the results of its operations and cash flows for the period then ended in conformity with accounting principles generally accepted in the United States of America unless statements are for filing with its supervisory agency.

AS 3315: Reporting on Condensed Financial Statements and Selected Financial Data – Provides guidance for reporting on condensed information presented by a public entity that I required to provide complete audited financial statements to a regulatory agency at least annually and for reporting on selected financial data derived from audit financial statements presented in a document containing audited financial statements.

AS 3320: Association with Financial Statements – Specifies that an accountant is associated with financial statements upon consenting to the inclusion of the auditor's name in a report, document, or written communication containing the statements, whether audited or unaudited.

Matters Relating to Filings Under Federal Securities Laws

AS 4101: Responsibilities Regarding Filings Under Federal Securities Statutes – Establishes the auditor's responsibility for financial representations in documents filed under federal securities statutes.

AS 4105: Reviews of Interim Financial Information – Establishes standards and provides guidance related to the nature timing, and extent of procedures that should be performed in a review of interim financial information.

Other Matters Associated with Audits

AS 6101: Letters for Underwriters and Certain Other Requesting Parties – Provides guidance for performing engagements to provide comfort letters to underwriters and others in relation to financial statements and financial information included in registration statements filed with the SEC.

AS 6105: Reports on the Application of Accounting Principles – Provides guidance to an accountant preparing a written report on the application of accounting principles to specified transactions, or the type of opinion that may be rendered on a particular entity's financial statements or providing oral advice to be used by a principal to a transaction in determining how accounting principles apply to a specific transaction or the type of opinion that may be rendered on a particular entity's financial statements.

AS 6110: *Compliance Auditing Considerations in Audits of Recipients of Governmental Financial Assistance* – Provides guidance to an auditor engaged to audit a governmental entity under PCAOB standards and to report on compliance with laws and regulations under Government Auditing Standards.

AS 6115: *Reporting on Whether a Previously Reported Material Weakness Continues to Exist* – Allows an auditor to report on whether a previously reported material weakness continues to exist if the auditor has audited the entity's financial statements and internal control or has been engaged to do so.

SECURITIES AND EXCHANGE COMMISSION (SEC), GOVERNMENT ACCOUNTABILITY OFFICE (GAO) AND THE DEPARTMENT OF LABOR (DOL)

While a CPA will follow the requirements of the AICPA Code of Professional Conduct in making a determination as to whether or not independence is impaired, certain engagements also require the accountant to comply with the requirements of a regulatory body.

- If a CPA practices before the Securities and Exchange Commission and performs audits of issuers, the requirements of the Public Company Accounting Oversight Board apply;

- If performing an audit of a nonfederal governmental agency or an entity receiving governmental financial assistance, the engagement is performed in accordance with Generally Accepted Government Auditing Standards and must comply with the ethical requirements of the Government Accountability Office Government Auditing Standards; and

- An accountant performing audits of employee benefit plans are required to comply with the independence requirements of the Department of Labor.

The Securities and Exchange Commission (SEC)

"The mission of the SEC is to protect investors, maintain fair, orderly, and efficient markets, and facilitate capital formation." As will be discussed in Regulation (REG), the Securities Act of 1933 and the Securities and Exchange Act of 1934 were designed to protect the public from potentially unscrupulous practices of publicly traded companies. They established the SEC and gave it the authority to require publicly-held companies to issue audited financial statements, designate the acceptable basis or bases of accounting for publicly-held companies, and oversee auditors of publicly-held companies.

The SEC has designated the PCAOB to regulate auditors of publicly-held entities and to develop and maintain auditing standards applicable to their audits. In some cases, the requirements imposed are **more restrictive** than those imposed on auditors of nonpublic entities, such as the prohibition against performing almost any nonassurance services for an audit client and the requirement to disclose audit and nonaudit fees earned. In most cases, however, the Auditing Standards Board (ASB) of the AICPA has evaluated GAAS with the intention of eliminating as many differences between those requirements and those of the PCAOB as is reasonably possible.

INDEPENDENCE STANDARDS OF THE GOVERNMENT ACCOUNTABILITY OFFICE (GAO)

The GAO is an agency of Congress responsible for investigating how the federal government spends taxpayer money. It is also responsible for setting generally accepted government auditing standards (GAGAS), which are issued in a document referred to as the "**Yellow Book.**"

The Yellow Book is broken down into sections that include:
- Government Auditing – Foundation and Ethical Principles
- Standards for Use and Application of GAGAS
- General Standards
- Standards for Financial Audits
- Standards for Attestation Engagements
- Fieldwork Standards for Performance Audits
- Reporting Standards for Performance Audits

The General Standards include the GAO's separate, and somewhat **more restrictive, independence requirements** that apply when performing an engagement in accordance with GAGAS. It indicates that: *"In all matters relating to the audit work, the audit organization and the individual auditor, whether government or public, must be independent."* This includes independence of mind, indicating that the auditor is free of influence that might compromise the auditor's judgment, and independence in appearance so that users of the financial information will consider it reliable.

To provide assurance that an auditor is **independent** both in mind and in appearance, GAGAS incorporates an independence conceptual framework that can be applied in making a determination as to whether or not independence has been impaired. An auditor evaluates independence, applying the framework, whenever facts or circumstances create threats to independence. The approach is very similar to that incorporated into the independence requirements for nongovernmental auditors in the AICPA code of Professional Conduct.

Similar to the approach for evaluating independence indicated in AICPA professional standards, government auditors are expected to:
- Identify threats to independence
- Evaluate the significance of the threats, individually and collectively
- Apply safeguards to eliminate or mitigate the threats such that they are reduced to an acceptable level

The framework is applied by first identifying facts and circumstances that create **threats to independence**. There are 7 categories of threats in the **Yellow Book** to independence:
- A **self-interest** threat occurs when the auditor has a financial or other interest in the entity that might affect the auditor's judgment.
- A **self-review** threat occurs when the extent of nonattest services performed by the auditor for the client raise a question as to whether the auditor will be reviewing judgments and estimates that the auditor participated in the development of.
- A **bias** threat occurs when the auditor is not objective about the client. This may result from the relationship between the auditor and client. It may also be a result of the beliefs of the auditor, which may be political, religious, or philosophical, and that may or may not conform to the objectives, mission, or operations of the client.
- A **familiarity** threat occurs as a result of the duration and closeness of the relationship between the auditor and the client. This includes the threat that the client may anticipate

what may be emphasized by the auditor and may be able to effectively deceive the auditor as a result.

- An **undue influence** threat occurs when factors or parties separate from the client might create influence or pressure that may affect the auditor's judgments in regard to the client.
- A **management participation** threat occurs when the auditor takes on the role of management or performs management functions for the client.
- A **structural** threat occurs when the audit entity is connected to the government entity in such a way that may impair the auditor's ability to remain objective in the performance of the engagement or reporting of the results.

If the threat to independence results from the performance of nonattest services, the auditor will first determine if the service was prohibited. If so, independence is impaired and the auditor will not be able to perform the engagement. If the threat does not result from the performance of nonattest services, or if the nonattest services were not prohibited, the auditor will consider the magnitude of threats.

Prohibited nonattest services include:
- Performing *management responsibilities*, such as strategic planning for the entity, developing entity program policies, directing employees, making decisions regarding the acquisition, use or disposition of resources, custody of assets, reporting to governance, accepting responsibility for internal controls, and voting in the management committee or board of directors;
- Performing certain *accounting functions without obtaining management approval,* such as determining or changing journal entries, authorizing or approving transactions, preparing or altering source documents, and accepting responsibility for the preparation or fair presentation of the financial statements;
- Providing *internal audit assistance* in the form of setting policies, strategic direction, or scope for the internal audit function, or performing internal control procedures;
- *Accepting responsibility* for the design, implementation, or maintenance (DIM) of internal control, or its monitoring;
- Participation in *information technology services* including the design, development, or alteration of IT systems that manage aspects of the operations that will be audited, or operating or supervising the operation of such a system;
- Providing *valuation services* that impact information included in the financial statements; or
- Performing specific *additional services* related to non-tax disbursements, benefit plan administration, investment advisory or management, corporate finance, executive or employee personnel, and business risk consulting.

The auditor will consider threats individually and in the aggregate to determine if they are at an acceptable level, which would not impair the auditor's ability to perform and report on the engagement objectively. If threats are not at an acceptable level, the auditor will consider **safeguards** against those threats. Safeguards are policies and procedures instituted by the auditor to address threats to independence. Safeguards may include:
- Consulting with other auditors, regulators, or other independent third parties;
- Disclosing the nature and extent of services that could potentially impair independence to those responsible for governance and discussing independence issues with them; and
- Using an outside auditor to participate in the audit by performing or reperforming parts of it, or by reviewing the work performed.

The client can also initiate policies and procedures designed to create safeguards. These may include:

- Requiring appointment of the auditor to be approved by parties who are not part of management;
- Establishing procedures for selecting providers of nonaudit services designed to enhance objectivity; and
- Oversight of the auditor's services by governance.

If safeguards are sufficient to reduce threats to an acceptable level, the auditor will document the analysis and may perform the audit engagement. If safeguards are not sufficient, the auditor's independence is impaired and the auditor may not perform the engagement.

In addition to establishing the above framework for evaluating independence, the GAO has established independence requirements and guidelines for audit organizations that are located within the entities they audit; audit organizations performing nonaudit services for the entities they audit; and documentation that is necessary to support the auditor's conclusions and demonstrate appropriate consideration to the auditor's independence.

An auditor that works within the entity that is being audited is **considered independent** if the head of the audit organization meets all of certain criteria:

- Is accountable to the head or deputy head of the entity or its governance;
- Reports results to both the head or deputy head and governance;
- Is organizationally outside of the staff or line-management function of the audited unit;
- Has access to governance; and
- Is removed from the political process sufficiently to avoid fear of political reprisal.

An auditor may perform nonaudit services for the entity under audit provided that auditor has assurance that management will perform all of the following in relation to the nonaudit service:

- Assume all management responsibility;
- Oversee the service, designating an individual within the organization with the appropriate characteristics to effectively do so;
- Evaluate the adequacy and results of the service; and
- Accept responsibility for the results.

To support the auditor's consideration of independence, **documentation** should include:

- Threats to independence and the safeguards applied;
- The safeguards applied if the audit organization is structurally located within a government unit and is considered independent as a result of those safeguards;
- Consideration of management's ability to oversee nonaudit services provided; and
- The understanding with the audited entity regarding the performance of nonaudit services.

DEPARTMENT OF LABOR INDEPENDENCE REQUIREMENTS (DOL)

Employee benefit plans must be audited in accordance with the Employee Retirement Income Security Act of 1974 (ERISA), as enforced by the Department of Labor (DOL). ERISA indicates that the audit is to be performed by an *independent* qualified public accountant (IQPA) and, in the DOL's view, "an accountant's independence is at least of equal importance to the professional competence he or she brings to an engagement to render an opinion and issuing a report on the financial statements of an employee benefit plan." The DOL Independence requirements are a bit **more restrictive** than the AICPA requirements.

The rule specifies three types of relationships that will impair an accountant's independence. The requirements apply to the accountant and the accountant's firm and relate to the period of the engagement as well as the period covered by the engagement. **Independence is impaired** by:
- Having, or committing to acquiring, any direct financial interest or any material indirect financial interest in the plan
- Acting as the plan's, or plan sponsor's, promoter, underwriter, investment advisor, voting trustee, director, officer, or employee
- Maintaining financial records for the plan

Independence is not impaired if the accountant is engaged by the plan's sponsor for a professional engagement, provided it does not involve an activity that is prohibited. In addition, independence is not impaired if the plan uses the services of an actuary that is associated with the accountant.

Lecture 2.08

CLASS QUESTIONS

Please see the Class Questions and Class Solutions for this Lecture at the end of this Section.

CLASS QUESTIONS

Work through the below Class Questions while following along with the respective lectures. Once this is complete, you can begin independently practicing what you've learned by quizzing yourself on this course section in your Interactive Practice Questions (IPQ), which can be found in your online Student Dashboard. Your IPQ simulates the computer-based testing experience, and will also help you understand how concepts are applied to the exam. Each question includes answer explanations from expert CPAs that will help you determine why you answered a question correctly or incorrectly. This is key to your success on the CPA Exam.

Lecture 2.06

1. According to the standards of the profession, which of the following circumstances will prevent a CPA performing audit engagements from being independent?

    a. Obtaining a collateralized automobile loan from a financial institution client.
    b. Litigation with a client relating to billing for consulting services for which the amount is immaterial.
    c. Employment of the CPA's spouse as a client's director of internal audit.
    d. Acting as an honorary trustee for a not-for-profit organization client.

2. Which of the following reports may be issued only by an accountant who is independent of a client?

    a. Standard report on an examination of a financial forecast.
    b. Report on consulting services.
    c. Compilation report on historical financial statements.
    d. Compilation report on a financial projection.

3. Which of the following statements is correct regarding an accountant's working papers?

    a. The accountant owns the working papers and generally may disclose them as the accountant sees fit.
    b. The client owns the working papers but the accountant has custody of them until the accountant's bill is paid in full.
    c. The accountant owns the working papers but generally may not disclose them without the client's consent or a court order.
    d. The client owns the working papers but, in the absence of the accountant's consent, may not disclose them without a court order.

4. According to the ethical standards of the profession, which of the following acts is generally prohibited?

    a. Issuing a modified report explaining a failure to follow a governmental regulatory agency's standards when conducting an attest service for a client.
    b. Revealing confidential client information during a quality review of a professional practice by a team from the state CPA society.
    c. Accepting a contingent fee for representing a client in an examination of the client's federal tax return by an IRS agent.
    d. Retaining client records after an engagement is terminated prior to completion and the client has demanded their return.

5. According to the ethical standards of the profession, which of the following acts is generally prohibited?

    a. Purchasing a product from a third party and reselling it to a client.
    b. Writing a financial management newsletter promoted and sold by a publishing company.
    c. Accepting a commission for recommending a product to an audit client.
    d. Accepting engagements obtained through the efforts of third parties.

6. Which of the following services may a CPA perform in carrying out a consulting service for a client?

    I. Analysis of the client's accounting system.
    II. Review of the client's prepared business plan.
    III. Preparation of information for obtaining financing.

    a. I and II only.
    b. I and III only.
    c. II and III only.
    d. I, II, and III.

7. Per the Sarbanes Oxley act (SOX) title II, which of the following non-audit services to audit clients, are not prohibited from being performed by a registered public accounting firm?

    a. Bookkeeping services.
    b. Appraisal or valuation services.
    c. Internal audit services.
    d. Tax services.

8. The profession's ethical standards most likely would be considered to have been violated when a CPA represents that specific consulting services will be performed for a stated fee and it is apparent at the time of the representations that the

    a. Actual fee would be substantially higher.
    b. Actual fee would be substantially lower than the fees charged by other CPAs for comparable services.
    c. CPA would not be independent.
    d. Fee was a competitive bid.

9. According to the profession's standards, which of the following statements is correct regarding the standards a CPA should follow when recommending tax return positions and preparing tax returns?

    a. A CPA may recommend a position that the CPA concluded is frivolous as long as the position is adequately disclosed on the return.
    b. A CPA may recommend a position in which the CPA has a good faith belief that the position has substantial authority in favor of its being sustained if challenged.
    c. A CPA will usually not advise the client of the potential penalty consequences of the recommended tax return position.
    d. A CPA may sign a tax return as preparer knowing that the return takes a position that will not be sustained if challenged.

Lecture 2.08

10. According to the AICPA Code of Professional Conduct, which of the following activities results in an act discreditable to the profession?

   a. A CPA solicits recent Uniform CPA Examination questions without written authorization from the AICPA.
   b. A CPA signs a document containing immaterial false and misleading information, or permits or directs another CPA to do so.
   c. A CPA who is engaged to perform a government audit neglects to follow certain government auditing requirements and discloses in the audit report the fact that such requirements were **not** followed and the reasons for it.
   d. A CPA fails to give a client copies of the CPA's workpapers related to a completed and issued work product upon the client's request because the client has not paid fees payable to the CPA for the work product.

11. When a former partner of a registered public accounting firm who left the firm two years ago accepts a financial reporting oversight role at an issuer audit client, the independence of the registered public accounting firm is considered impaired **unless** which of the following is true?

   a. The former partner discloses the relationship to the issuer audit client's board of directors.
   b. The former partner was employed by the registered public accounting firm for a period of 2 years or less.
   c. The former partner has no remaining capital balance in the registered public accounting firm.
   d. The former partner exerts only limited influence over the registered public accounting firm's operations and financial policies.

12. An auditor has performed certain bookkeeping and other nonattest services that are not prohibited by the AICPA Code of Professional Conduct for a potential audit client. The auditor has established and documented an understanding with the client and the client has agreed to assume all management responsibility, to oversee the services and designate an individual within the organization to do so, to evaluate the adequacy of the services, and accept responsibility for the results. Which of the following is correct?

   a. The auditor may conduct the audit under GAAS but additional requirements must be met.
   b. The auditor may conduct the audit under PCAOB standards, but must disclose the performance of the services.
   c. The auditor may conduct the audit under GAGAS, but must disclose the performance of the services.
   d. The auditor may not perform the audit under GAGAS.

13. The controller of a small utility company has interviewed audit firms proposing to perform the annual audit of their employee benefit plan. According to the guidelines of the Department of Labor (DOL), the selected auditor must be

    a. The firm that proposes the lowest fee for the work required.
    b. Independent for purposes of examining financial information required to be filed annually with the DOL.
    c. Included on the list of firms approved by the DOL.
    d. Independent of the utility company and **not** relying on its services.

14. Which of the following services would constitute a management function under Government Auditing Standards, and result in the impairment of a CPA's independence if performed by the CPA?

    a. Developing entity program policies.
    b. Providing methodologies, such as practice guides.
    c. Providing accounting opinions to a legislative body.
    d. Recommending internal control procedures.

CLASS SOLUTIONS

1. **(c)** A collateralized automobile loan is a normal transaction for a financial institution and, provided the terms are comparable to those offered to other customers, such a loan would not impair an auditor's independence (a). Although litigation with a client might generally impair an auditor's independence, that would not be the case if it is immaterial (b). Not-for-profit organizations often name individuals as honorary trustees in order to add credibility to the organization or attract supporters. As long as the position is honorary, however, and the CPA is not assuming management responsibilities and is not involved in governance, independence would not be impaired (d). Independence might be impaired if a CPA's spouse is the director of the audit client's internal audit function. The CPA may be inclined, for example, to accept the results of work done by the client's internal auditors without the same level of due diligence that might be applied if the auditor had no relationship with the director.

2. **(a)** An engagement to report on an examination of a financial forecast is an attest engagement that is also an assurance engagement, requiring the auditor to be independent. An auditor is not required to be independent to perform a nonattest engagement, such as a consulting engagement (b). Compilations are not assurance engagements, whether they are compilations of historical financial statements or financial projections. An accountant may perform a compilation engagement despite a lack of independence as long as the lack of independence is clearly indicated in the compilation report (c and d).

3. **(c)** The CPA, not the client, owns an accountant's working papers (b and d). The accountant's working papers, however, contain information obtained in a professional engagement, which is considered confidential information and generally may only disclose them with the client's permission (a). In some cases, however, such as in response to a valid subpoena or court order, the accountant may disclose them.

4. **(d)** An auditor would be required to issue a modified report, not prohibited from doing so, if a government regulatory agency's standards were not followed when conducting an attest engagement (a). There are several circumstances under which it is permissible to reveal confidential client information including doing so in response to a court subpoena and as part of a quality review of the auditor's practice (b). Although an auditor may not accept a fee that is contingent on the results of an audit or on the amount of a tax refund, a contingent fee may be accepted in regard to tax matters based on the results of a proceeding like an examination (c). Refusing to return a client's records after the termination of an engagement and the demand of the client would be considered an act that is discreditable to the profession and prohibited by the profession's ethical standards.

5. **(c)** A CPA may accept a commission only if it is from a client for which the CPA does not provide attest services and is disclosed to the client. A CPA may not accept a commission from an audit client. Many CPA firms earn revenues by buying products from third parties and selling them to clients (a) and through publishing, including newsletters that are promoted and sold by a publishing company (b). In addition, many CPAs obtain clients as a result of efforts of third parties, although the CPA is still required to evaluate whether or not to accept the client relationship.

6.   (**d**) A consulting engagement may take a wide variety of forms and is ultimately dictated by the needs of the client and the capabilities of the CPA. CPAs often analyze accounting systems for clients, usually for the purpose of suggesting improvement (I). They also review business plans for clients (II) and assist clients in preparing information to be used to obtain financing (III). As a result, all three are consulting services that may be performed by a CPA.

7.   (**d**) The Sarbanes Oxley act specifically prohibits any registered public accounting firm from providing many non-audit services to audit clients. Tax services are permissible if preapproved by the audit committee and disclosed to the SEC. The list of prohibited services includes:
- Bookkeeping or other services related to the accounting records.
- Financial info systems design or implementation.
- Appraisal or valuation services, fairness opinions.
- Actuarial services.
- Internal audit outsourcing services.
- Management functions or human resources.
- Broker or dealer investment advisor or investment banking services.
- Legal services and expert services unrelated to the audit.

8.   (**a**) Deliberate underbidding is an act discreditable to the profession. A CPA is permitted to perform work for a lower fee than others might charge (b). A CPA does not require independence to perform consulting services (c). Competitive bidding is an acceptable means of obtaining business (d).

9.   (**b**) A tax preparer should never take a position the preparer believes is frivolous. The standard for adoption of a position is that there be substantial authority in favor of its being sustained if challenged. If the CPA believes that there are potential penalties from adopting a certain position, the client should be advised of this potential. A tax preparer should not sign a return that takes a position the CPA believes will not withstand a challenge.

10. (**a**) According to ET 1.400, acts discreditable to the profession include soliciting or disclosing CPA exam questions and answers. Signing a document that contains a misstatement that is immaterial would not be an act discreditable to the profession (b). Nor would failing to comply with auditing requirements in an engagement provided the noncompliance was appropriately disclosed (c). Failure to return a client's records due to nonpayment of fees would be an act discreditable to the profession but refusing to make copies of the accountant's workpapers is not (d).

11. (**c**), It would be considered a conflict of interest if a firm performs an audit of an issuer if someone with financial reporting oversight responsibility was employed by the firm and participated in any capacity in the audit during the 1-year period preceding the date of the initiation of the audit. In addition, the former firm member may have no remaining capital balance in the firm. It is not sufficient for the former firm member to inform the client's board of directors (a). It makes no difference how long the firm member was employed by the firm (b). The former partner may not be in position to exert any influence over the accounting firm without impairing independence (d).

12. (**a**) An auditor may perform certain nonattest services for an attest client provided the auditor establishes and documents an understanding with the client under which the client agrees to assume all management responsibility, oversee the services and designate an appropriately qualified individual to do so, evaluate the adequacy of the services, and accept responsibility for the results. In addition, however, when an auditor is performing multiple nonattest services for an attest client, the auditor is also required to apply the conceptual framework to determine if the effect of the aggregate of the nonattest services raises one of seven threats to independence to an unacceptable level. In general, an auditor may not perform nonattest services for an audit client under PCAOB standards. Certain nonattest services, such as tax planning services, may be performed for an audit client if they are approved in advance by the client's audit committee, who is responsible for making certain that the services do not impair the auditor's independence (b). An auditor may perform certain nonattest services that are not specifically prohibited for an audit client under GAGAS provided the client agrees to assume all management responsibility, oversee the services and designate an appropriately qualified individual to do so, evaluate the adequacy of the services, and accept responsibility for the results. The services need not be disclosed to users of the financial statements and no additional requirements need be met (c). An auditor may perform certain nonattest services that are not specifically prohibited for an audit client under GAGAS provided the client agrees to assume all management responsibility, oversee the services and designate an appropriately qualified individual to do so, evaluate the adequacy of the services, and accept responsibility for the results. No additional requirements need be met (d).

13. **(b)** The DOL requires an auditor to be independent when auditing an employee benefit plan and prohibits the auditor from having a direct or material indirect interest in the plan or its sponsor; from serving as promoter, underwriter, investment advisor, voting trustee, director, officer, or employee of the plan or the sponsor; or from maintaining financial records for the plan. There is no requirement that the audit be performed by the firm quoting the lowest fee (a). Nor is there a list of approved firms (c). Relying on the services of the sponsor utility company does not impair the auditor's independence and, in fact, the auditor may not have a choice of utility provider (d).

14. **(a)** Management functions are defined under Government Auditing Standards similarly to how they are defined under the AICPA Code of Professional Conduct and involve making decisions involving the strategic direction of the entity and making decisions regarding the acquisition, use, or disposition of resources. This would include developing entity program policies as this involves establishing strategy for the entity. Providing methodologies from which management may choose (b); providing accounting opinions to a legislative body enabling them to make better decisions (c); and recommending internal control procedures, which management may or may not implement (d), are not considered management functions and would not impair independence.

TASK-BASED SIMULATIONS

Task-Based Simulation 1

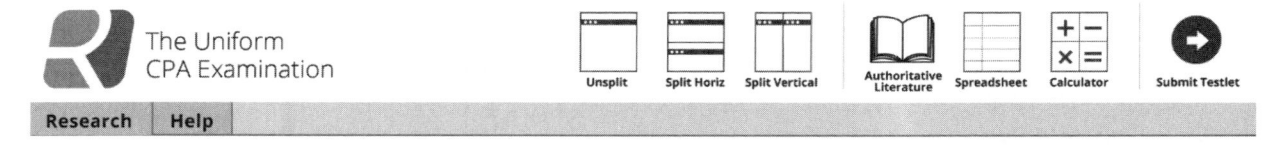

X.L. Family, CPA, just learned that his cousin's daughter is employed as a factory assistant at a manufacturing plant that is a client and he is trying to determine if his independence has been impaired.

1. Which title of Professional Standards addresses this issue & will be helpful in understanding whether or not his independence has been impaired?

2. Enter the exact section and paragraph with helpful information.

Task-Based Simulation 2

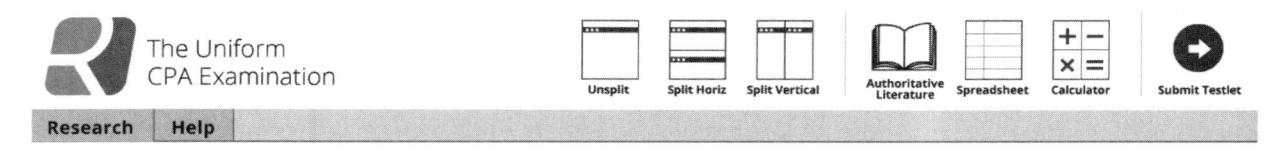

Arnold Stallone, CPA, is planning on selling his practice and practice for auditions of American Idol. He is wondering whether or not he can give information to a potential buyer without obtaining permission from his clients.

1. Which title of Professional Standards addresses this issue & will be helpful in understanding whether or not information about clients can be disclosed?

2. Enter the exact section and paragraph with helpful information.

Task-Based Simulation 3

A CPA is planning the audit of an issuer entity and is trying to determine what preliminary engagement activities should be performed.

1. Which title of Professional Standards addresses this issue & will be helpful in understanding what preliminary engagement activities should be performed?

2. Enter the exact section and paragraph with helpful information.

TASK-BASED SIMULATION SOLUTIONS

Task-Based Simulation Solution 1

ET	1.270.100.02

Task-Based Simulation Solution 2

ET	1.700.050.01

Task-Based Simulation Solution 3

PCAOB	AS 2101	Par .06

Section 3 - Internal Control

Corresponding Lectures

Watch the following course lectures with this section:

Lecture 3.01 – Internal Control

Lecture 3.02 – 5 Components of Internal Control (CRIME)

Lecture 3.03 – Understanding the Internal Control Structure

Lecture 3.04 – Sarbanes-Oxley Act and Basic Concepts

Lecture 3.05 – Internal Control – Class Questions

Lecture 3.06 – Operating Cycles: Revenue Cycle

Lecture 3.07 – Operating Cycles: Spending Cycle

Lecture 3.08 – Operating Cycles: Personnel and Payroll

Lecture 3.09 – Operating Cycles: Investing, Financing, Production and Conversion Cycles

Lecture 3.10 – Operating Cycles – Class Questions

Lecture 3.11 – Documentation of Internal Control Structure

Lecture 3.12 – Documentation of Internal Control Structure – Class Questions

Lecture 3.13 – Internal Control Reports and Communications, Financial Statement Audit

Lecture 3.14 – Internal Control Reports and Communications, Attestation Engagement

Lecture 3.15 – Internal Control Reports and Communications, PCAOB Audit

Lecture 3.16 – Internal Control Reports and Communications – Class Questions

Lecture 3.17 – Internal Control – Class Question – DRS

EXAM NOTE: *Please refer to the AICPA AUD Blueprint in the Introduction of this book to find a listing of the representative tasks (and their associated skill levels—i.e., Remembering and Understanding, Application, Analysis, and Evaluation) that the candidate should be able to perform based on the knowledge obtained in this section.*

Internal Control

INTERNAL CONTROL

The Steps in an Audit

Prepare for → Obtain Understanding → Assess Risks of Material → Perform Tests → Perform → Formulate → Issue
The audit   of Client, its Environment, Misstatement and Determine of Controls   Substantive   an Opinion   Audit
                 including Internal Control   Nature, Timing & Extent   Procedures   Report
                                               of Further Procedures

AU-C 315, Understanding the Entity and Its Environment and Assessing the Risks of Material Misstatements, requires the auditor to perform ***risk assessment procedures*** to assess risk of material misstatement (RMM) at both the financial statement level and the assertion level. It also requires the entity to obtain an understanding of ***internal control*** relevant to the audit.

The **objective** of AU-C 315 is for the auditor to identify and assess the risks of material misstatement (RMM), whether due to *fraud or error*, at the financial statement and relevant assertion levels through ***understanding*** the entity and its environment, including the entity's **internal control**, thereby providing a basis for designing and implementing responses to the assessed risks of material misstatement.

Auditors of entities that **do not report** to the SEC, often referred to as **nonissuers**, are required to follow GAAS, issued by the Auditing Standards Board (ASB) of the AICPA. These standards require the auditor to obtain and document an understanding of the client's internal controls in order to assess the risk of material misstatement (RMM) of the financial statements, which consists of inherent risk (IR) and control risk (CR). The auditor then uses the RMM to determine the extent to which detection risk (DR) must be reduced to reduce audit risk (AR) to an acceptable level.
- When an auditor believes that the nature, timing, or extent of substantive testing can be limited as a result of effective internal control, the auditor must perform tests of controls to verify that they are operating effectively as designed and intended.
- The auditor draws a conclusion, based on tests of controls, as to whether or not the controls can be relied upon for the **entire period** for which controls were tested.

Auditors of entities that **do report** to the SEC, often referred to as **issuers**, are also required to obtain an understanding of internal control. Like auditors of nonissuers, they are required to obtain and document the understanding in order to assess the risk of material misstatement of the financial statements and to plan and perform the audit. Sarbanes-Oxley, however, requires auditors of issuers to perform an **integrated audit** of both internal control over financial reporting and of the financial statements. As a result, in addition to obtaining sufficient evidence to support the auditor's control risk assessment, the auditor is required to obtain sufficient evidence to support an ***opinion on internal control over financial reporting (ICFR)*** as of a **specific point in time**, the date of the financial statements.

Auditors of both issuers and nonissuers may conclude either that internal controls are not sufficiently reliable to limit the nature, timing, or extent of substantive testing or that the cost of testing controls exceeds the potential benefit. In either case, the auditor will not perform tests of controls for the purpose of reducing RMM and will, instead, perform substantive tests based on CR set at maximum.

Setting CR at maximum means that the auditor believes that if an error or fraud were to occur, there is a 100% probability that the entity's internal control will neither prevent it nor detect it to allow correction on a timely basis. When the auditor also is performing an examination of internal control (always the case in the audit of an issuer) the auditor is required to perform tests of the operating effectiveness of internal controls--even when controls are not expected to be effective or the cost of testing controls is expected to exceed the cost reductions in substantive testing.

- An entity's internal control cannot be considered effective if one or more material weaknesses exist.
- The auditor must plan and perform the examination to obtain reasonable assurance as to whether or not material weaknesses exist as of the specified date.
- Material weaknesses may exist when the financial statements are not materially misstated.

Controls are evaluated at the **entity level**, seeking assurance as to the general reliability of the financial reporting process and the desire and intention of the entity to operate in an ethical environment, free of fraud and significant errors, with systems and procedures to provide assurance as to the *three primary objectives* of a system of internal control (**ACE**):

- **A**ccurate & Reliable financial reporting
- **C**ompliance with applicable laws and regulations
- **E**fficient and effective operations

Controls are also evaluated at the **assertion level**. When management is presenting financial statements, there are various assertions embedded in which management is indicating that the financial information contains certain characteristics. When a misrepresentation may result in a material misstatement to the financial statements, the assertion affected is considered a relevant assertion. When performing an audit, the auditor is required to obtain sufficient appropriate audit evidence to support every relevant assertion this can be accomplished by:

- Demonstrating through the use of tests of controls that internal controls are sufficient to prevent a material misstatement in regard to that assertion or to detect and correct such a misstatement on a timely basis;
- Obtaining evidence through the performance of substantive tests to demonstrate that the information presented is free of material misstatement, regardless of the existence of internal controls; or
- Some combination of those approaches, which is most frequently the case.

There are several assertions, some of which overlap one another, classified into three categories. The first 5 assertions relate to **Events and Transactions** that occurred during the period of audit, as generally presented on an entity's *income statement* (**CPA-CO**). They are:

- **Completeness** – All events or transactions pertaining to the entity that occurred.
- **Period Cutoff** – All events and transactions have been reported in the appropriate period (Everything is reported in the right Period).
- **Accuracy** – The events or transactions have been reported in the appropriate amounts.
- **Classification** – All events and transactions are included in appropriate accounts or categories.
- **Occurrence** – The event or transaction, which pertains to the entity, did occur (It happened).

Just remember that if all revenue and expenses are properly reported, the **CPA-CO** will have no problem preparing your taxes.

The next 4 assertions relate to **Account Balances**, amounts reported as of the date of the financial statements, as generally presented on the *balance sheet* (**RACE**). They are:

- **Rights and Obligations** – The entity has rights to those items reported as assets and liabilities are the obligations of the entity (they are ours).
- **Allocation and Valuation** – All assets, liabilities, and equity related items are reported in amounts that are appropriate as of the date of the financial statements (Amount is correct).
- **Completeness** – All assets, liabilities, and equity that should have been reported are included on the financial statement.
- **Existence** – Assets, liabilities, and equity reported on the financial statements exist as of the financial statement date (They are real).

Of course, if an entity has a healthy balance sheet, it is running at good **RACE**.

The final 5 assertions relate to the **Presentation** of the financial statements and the financial statement **Disclosures (RACOU–n (Raccoon)**. They are:

- **Rights and Obligations** – All information presented and disclosed is related to events, transactions, and other matters that pertain to the entity (It all Took place).
- **Accuracy and Valuation** – Both financial and nonfinancial information is fairly presented, properly disclosed, and provides appropriate amounts (We Know it is all correct).
- **Completeness** – All information that should be presented is disclosed (It is All included).
- **Occurrence** – Disclosed events, transactions and other matters have occurred and pertain to the entity.
- **Understandability and Classification** – Financial information is appropriately presented and described and disclosures are expressed in a clear manner (Everything is Clear).

Raccoons (RACOU-n's) are always presenting and disclosing my garbage at night!!

The auditor is looking for the presence of useful controls: the strengths in the system. The system is primarily formed by those controls designed by management that relate to the financial statement assertions and which are meant to produce **accurate financial records** and **safeguarding of assets**. Those controls designed to enable **adherence to laws and regulations** and **promote efficiency** in the organization are usually not relevant to the financial statement assertions.

To ensure that only sales that actually occurred are recorded in the sales journal, the occurrence assertion, the entity may establish a control requiring that sales be recorded in the sales journal only when there is a customer order form, a sales order form, a shipping report, and an invoice, all of which agree as to the goods that were sold and the price to be received for them. To ensure that all sales that actually occur are recorded, the completeness assertion, the entity may require the use of prenumbered sales order forms and account for all forms, including making certain that none are out of sequence.

The most commonly used framework to benchmark internal controls in the US is *Internal Control – Integrated Framework* developed by COSO. COSO describes internal control as:

> *A process, effected by the entity's board of directors, management, and other personnel designed to provide reasonable assurance regarding the achievement of objectives in the*

*categories of (1) Accurate and reliable financial reporting, (2) Compliance with applicable laws and regulations, and (3) Effectiveness and efficiency of operations (**ACE**).*

- Management is responsible for the development, implementation and maintenance (DIM) of Internal controls. The auditor seeks reasonable assurance that Internal controls are achieving certain **Objectives (ACE):**
  - o **A**ccurate & Reliable financial reporting
  - o **C**ompliance with laws and regulations
  - o **E**ffectiveness and efficiency of operations

The mnemonic **ACE** will remind management that it should try to establish a strong internal control structure so as to have an ACE in the hole.

The primary interest of the outside auditor is in the first objective, accurate and reliable financial reporting, which relate to the fair presentation of the financial statements being audited. The second goal, compliance with laws and regulations, is primarily relevant to **compliance auditing**, which may occur in connection with audits under government auditing standards.   The financial statement auditor would, however, be concerned about compliance with those laws and regulations that could have a material direct or indirect effect on the financial statements. The third goal, promoting effectiveness and efficiency of operations, is generally not addressed by the financial statement auditor, but is addressed in consulting engagements and **operational audits**.

Lecture 3.02

5 COMPONENTS OF INTERNAL CONTROL

AU-C 315 requires the auditor to obtain an understanding of all **5 components of internal control** under COSO in order to evaluate the design of relevant controls and determine whether they have been implemented; assess the risk of material misstatement; and design the nature, timing and extent of further audit procedures.

ELEMENTS OF INTERNAL CONTROL: (CRIME)

Control *Environment* (CHOPPER)

The first component of the COSO framework is the control environment, also referred to as the tone at the top. The control environment sets the tone of an organization, influencing the control consciousness of its people. It is the foundation for all other components of internal control, providing discipline and structure. Control environment factors include the following (**CHOPPER**):
- **Commitment to competence** – Effective control requires a sincere interest on the part of the employees in performing good work.
- **Human resource policies & practices** – A company can minimize the control difficulties created by new employees by sound hiring and training policies for employees.
- **Organizational structure** – A company that operates all over the world has different internal control problems than one operating entirely within a single building.
- **Participation of those charged with Governance** – An audit committee of the board of directors that actively monitors the internal audit function produces a more attentive management on such matters.
- **Philosophy of management & mgt operating style** – The belief (or lack of it) in the importance of internal control by management will affect the seriousness with which it is

taken by the rest of the employees. This is especially the case when decision-making in the company is dominated by a single individual.

- **Ethical values & Integrity** – Honest employees will be less likely to cause internal control difficulties related to fraud and improve the opportunity for those resulting from errors to be effectively detected.
- **Responsibility assignment** – The manner in which authority, responsibility and accountability is assigned to different employees determines the controls that will be needed. Again, the domination of decision-making by a single individual holds significance, since such power makes it extremely difficult for internal control to be trusted.

COSO has indicated that there are *five principles* related to the control environment. They indicate that management and those charge with governance:

1. Demonstrate a commitment to integrity and ethical values;
2. Exercise their oversight responsibility;
3. Establish structure, authority, and responsibility;
4. Demonstrate a commitment to competence; and
5. Enforce accountability.

The auditor is responsible for determining if the control environment, influenced by management with the oversight of those charged with governance, has established an honest culture, promoting ethical behavior. The control environment, consisting of what are referred to as *entity-level controls*, should provide a foundation for the overall internal control structure, including the other components and for assuring that internal controls are not undermined by deficiencies in the control environment.

Entity-level controls deal with company-wide issues and set the tone of the organization, involve the assignment of authority and responsibility, and address conduct. Entity-level controls include a mission statement that is part of the entity's culture; a code of conduct that applies to all members of the organization, including management; organization charts and job descriptions that indicate the roles of individuals within the organization; and the behavior of management and executives, which is often considered one of the more significant components.

The auditor obtains knowledge of entity-level controls through inquiries made of management and others and through observations. The auditor can often learn a great deal about the control environment by simply observing the relationship between employees and their supervisors and management and, in particular, if employees at all levels are shown an appropriate level of respect.

Risk Assessment

An entity's risk assessment for financial reporting purposes is its identification, analysis, and management of risks relevant to the preparation of financial statements that are fairly presented in conformity with GAAP or whatever financial reporting framework that will be applied in the preparation. Risk assessment includes risks that may affect an entity's ability to properly record, process, summarize, and report financial data. Risk assessment, for example, may address how the entity considers the possibility of unrecorded transactions or identifies and analyzes significant estimates recorded in the financial statements.

Risks relevant to financial reporting include external and internal **factors,** such as the following:
- Changes in the operating environment
- New personnel

- New or revamped information systems
- Rapid growth
- New technology
- New lines of business, products, or activities
- Corporate restructurings
- Foreign operations
- Changes to accounting pronouncements
- Changes to the economic environment

COSO has indicated that there are *four principles* related to risk assessment. They indicate that management and those charged with governance:
1. Specify suitable objectives;
2. Identify and analyze risk;
3. Assess fraud risk; and
4. Identify and analyze significant change.

Control Activities

Control activities are policies and procedures that help ensure that management directives are carried out. The focus of control activities may be one of the following:
- **P**erformance reviews – Controls involving the evaluation of performance against some criteria such as comparting actual amounts to budgeted amounts, comparing current period results to those of prior years, or evaluating financial data in relation to nonfinancial data.
- **I**nformation processing – Controls that prevent the processing of information unless certain criteria are met, such as the matching of certain documentation before recording a sale. In an information technology, or IT, environment, there are general controls that relate to the overall operation of the system, including the structure of the organization and access to information; and application controls that relate to specific functions being performed.
- **P**hysical controls – Controls that limit access to assets.
- **S**egregation of duties – Controls that involve assigning different people responsibilities for **authorizing** transactions, **recording** transactions, maintaining **custody** of assets, and performing reconciliations or **comparisons**. It is intended to reduce the opportunities to allow any person to be in a position to both *perpetrate and conceal errors or fraud* in the normal course of their duties (**ARCC-S**).
  - **A**uthorization of transactions
  - **R**ecording (posting) of transactions
  - **C**ustody of assets
  - **C**omparisons
    - **S**egregation of duties

In addition to identifying control activities, the auditor will have to determine if they are relevant to the audit. Some will be relevant in the professional judgment of the auditor. This will be the case, for example, when the auditor determines that a control activity reduces the risk of material misstatement in relation to a management assertion and:
- The auditor has a basis for testing the control activity to determine if it was properly designed and being applied properly during the period under audit; and
- The nature, timing, and extent of further audit testing can be reduced as a result of relying on the control activity if the tests of controls indicate that it is effective.

There may also be certain risks that could result in a material misstatement to the financial statements that cannot be evaluated on the basis of substantive evidence alone. This might be the case, for example, for a class of transactions that is processed automatically with a minimum of manual intervention and where much of the information related to the initiation, authorization, recording, processing, and reporting is in electronic form. The reliability of information derived from such transactions would be dependent on the controls related to the processing of those transactions.

COSO has indicated that there are *three principles* related to control activities. They indicate that management and those charged with governance:
1. Select and develop control activities;
2. Select and develop general controls over technology; and
3. Deploy controls through policies and procedures.

Information and Communication

The information and communication component of internal control relates to the flow of information to and from the entity as well as within the entity. Information should flow in all directions so that management's directives can be properly communicated to those who are expected to work toward achieving them and so that management can obtain feedback to determine if objectives are being achieved.

Communication with external parties facilitates the flow of goods and services and enhances the efficiency with which business can be conducted. It also enables parties and other entities with which an entity does business to assist in the enforcement of the entity's internal controls. If business customers are informed, for example, that all sales are expected to be reported on a specific pre-numbered sales form, customers may prevent a sales person from taking an order without completing such a form, which may be done for inappropriate purposes.

The auditor is concerned, in particular, with information systems relevant to financial reporting. The auditor, as a result, should obtain an understanding related to how:
- *Info system* consists of the methods and records used to *record, process, summarize and report* Co.'s transactions and to maintain accountability for the related accounts.
- *Communication* involves establishing individual duties and responsibilities relating to internal control and making them known to involved personnel.
- Transactions are initiated, authorized, and processed; and how transactions, events, and conditions are reported, including which components are performed manually and which are performed electronically.
- Accountability is maintained for assets, liability, and equity, including the maintenance of records supporting information or specific items in the financial statements.
- The incorrect processing of transactions is identified and resolved.
- Recurring and nonrecurring journal entries, unusual transactions, and other adjustments are identified and prepared.
- System overrides or bypasses to controls are processed and accounted for.
- Information is transferred from the processing systems to the general ledger.
- Events and conditions, other than transactions, that are relevant to financial reporting, including depreciation and amortization of assets and collectibility of receivables, are identified, and how information is captured.
- Financial statements are prepared, including the development of estimates.
- Information that is required to be disclosed is identified, accumulated, recorded, processed, summarized, and properly reported.

COSO has indicated that there are *three principles* related to information and communication. They indicate that management and those charge with governance:
1. Use relevant information;
2. Communicate internally; and
3. Communicate externally.

Monitoring

Monitoring activities are the means by which management determines if internal controls are being followed and if they are effective. Controls are monitored thorough some combination of ongoing activities, which are generally part of recurring activities such as the supervision of employees; and separate evaluations.

When the entity has an internal audit function, understanding the role it plays contributes to the auditor's understanding of the entity and its environment, and, in particular, its internal control. In some circumstances, the auditor may use the work performed by the entity's internal auditor's either to modify the nature, timing, or extent of other audit procedures to be performed, or to assist in the performance of audit procedures under the oversight of the auditor.

In addition to obtaining an understanding of how the entity monitors its internal controls, the auditor should also obtain an understanding of the information that is used in the entity's monitoring activities, the sources of that information, and the basis upon which the reliability of the information is evaluated.

COSO has indicated that there are *two principles* related to monitoring. They indicate that management and those charge with governance:
1. Conduct ongoing and/or separate evaluations; and
2. Evaluate and communicate deficiencies.

One way of remembering the 5 components of internal control is:
- **C**ontrol activities
- **R**isk assessment
- **I**nformation and communication
- **M**onitoring
- Control **E**nvironment

The mnemonic **CRIME** reminds management that it would be a crime not to consider all of the internal control elements when designing the system.

OBTAINING AN UNDERSTANDING OF THE ENTITY'S INTERNAL CONTROL STRUCTURE (AU-C 315)

An auditor performs the following procedures to obtain and apply an understanding of internal control to an audit:

Step 1 – Obtain an understanding of the design of all five components of the entity's internal control (CRIME) through the performance of risk assessment procedures.

Step 2 – Document the understanding of Internal Control.

Step 3 – Assess Risk of Material Misstatement (RMM) which consists of inherent risk (IR) and control risk (CR). RMM = IR × CR).

Step 4 – Develop an audit strategy to either:

- o (**RELY?**) *Perform tests of control* (TofC) to determine if CR is *below maximum*, reducing RMM below the level of IR and allowing for the modification of the nature, timing, and extent of further audit procedures (sub tests): or
- o (**NOT Rely**) Decide **NOT** to perform tests of controls, assessing CR at the *maximum level* as if the control did not exist, and measuring RMM as being equal to IR.

Step 5 – Reassess Risk of Material Misstatement and evaluate results.

- o For controls for which tests of controls were performed, evaluate results to reassess RMM and determine if it is appropriate to modify the nature, timing, and extent of further audit procedures.

Step 6 – Document conclusions and determine the effect on the planned substantive procedures. At this point, the audit program needs to be developed or revised for further audit procedures.

1. Understand the Design of CRIME by performing Risk Assessment Procedures

(what is the form?)

Have the controls been **IMPLEMENTED** (put into use?). To evaluate the implementation of a control means to determine whether a control is actually being used by the entity. The auditor first considers the design of the control. If the control is improperly designed, it may represent a material weakness in the entity's internal control.

An auditor obtains an understanding of the entity and its environment, including its internal control (CRIME) through the performance of **risk assessment procedures**. These are procedures designed to provide the auditor with an adequate understanding to enable the auditor to effectively assess the risk of material misstatement of the financial statements. Risk assessment procedures include:

- *Analytical procedures* (Using high level data)
- **Inquiries** of management and others within the entity, including inquiries of internal auditors.
- **Inspection** (of documents and records)
- **Observation** (the application of specific controls)

Most of the information that an auditor obtains about an entity's internal controls will initially be the result of *inquiries* made of the entity's management and others who the auditor believes can provide relevant information. If the auditor is a continuing auditor, much information will be derived from reviewing prior period engagement files. When obtaining an understanding of controls that are relevant to the audit, however, the auditor may not rely exclusively on inquiries to evaluate the design of those controls and to determine whether they have been *implemented*.

The auditor will initially evaluate the design of the control, usually based on information derived from inquiries, to determine whether it has the potential of reducing RMM. If not, the control is not relevant to the audit and no determination will be made as to whether it has been implemented. If so, however, the auditor can determine if the control has been implemented and if it is operating as it was designed only by performing a **walk through**. This involves applying some means other than inquiry, such as observing the control being applied, performing analytical procedures to determine if the control is producing the appropriate results, or the inspection of documents or other items that will provide evidence that the control is in place.

- While performing a walk through, as described above, provides information about the design and implementation of a control, it is not sufficient to determine if the control was operating effectively throughout the period being audited or to rely on the control as a basis for modifying the nature, timing, and extent of further audit procedures.
- If the auditor intends to rely on the control as a basis for modifying the nature, timing, and extent of further audit procedures, the auditor is required to determine if the control was operating effectively throughout the affected period through the performance of tests of controls.

In the course of obtaining an understanding of internal control, the auditor may identify control deficiencies, weaknesses in internal control that might allow errors to occur without the ability to identify and correct them on a timely basis. Identified deficiencies will be evaluated to determine if they are *significant deficiencies* or *material weaknesses*, both of which must be communicated to management and those charged with governance.

The auditor makes a determination as to which procedures to apply when obtaining different aspects of the understanding. Not all procedures will apply to each aspect and procedures other than those specified may also prove helpful to the auditor in identifying risks of material misstatement. These other procedures may include reviewing information from external sources, or making inquiries of parties outside the entity but with the cooperation of the entity.

The knowledge obtained through risk assessment procedures is used to:
- Identify the types of potential misstatements (Errors or Fraud).
- Consider factors that affect the risk of material misstatements.
- Design tests of controls and substantive procedures.
  - As part of obtaining an understanding of internal control sufficient to plan the audit, the auditor should evaluate whether the client's programs and controls that address the identified risks of material misstatement due to fraud have been suitably designed and implemented.
  - Determine if these have been **Implemented (Placed into operation)**.
    - Understanding **doesn't** require evaluating their **operating effectiveness**.

The goal of this understanding is to identify those controls that might reduce the risk of misstatements. If the auditor believes that these controls can be relied upon, tests of controls will be performed to evaluate their operating effectiveness. Assuming they prove effective, the auditor will be able to reduce substantive testing.

Notice, however, that the auditor is only trying to determine what controls have been **implemented** (are being used), and is **not** determining whether the controls have been **operating effectively**. The latter is only necessary in a financial statement audit if the auditor plans to rely on the controls. The auditor's main concern is whether, and how, a specific control prevents, detects, and corrects material misstatements in relevant assertions. Once the auditor has gained an understanding of the internal control structure, they may decide to assess the Risk of Material Misstatement high (not rely on internal control), in which case there is no point in determining whether the controls are effective.

The techniques available to the auditor to gain information about a client's internal control structure include:

- Prior audits – Reviewing audit documentation that document the internal control structure of the client in prior years.
- Reperformance – Applying the control that the client personnel presumably performed to determine if the procedure was performed properly.
- Inquiry – Asking management and other client personnel to describe the controls that they are currently using.
- Inspection – Examining documents that are used in internal control, such as authorization forms and procedures manuals.
- Observation – Watching employees perform their jobs.

Keep in mind that the auditor is initially interested in the form, but is ultimately interested in the **substance** of the controls. Often, inquiry and inspection will provide the auditor with information about controls that have been designed, but **observation** will reveal that these controls aren't actually being enforced by management. Observation is especially critical in determining whether controls involving **segregation of duties** are being implemented in practice, and not just in theory.

2. Document Understanding of Internal Control

The auditor is required to document key elements of the understanding of the entity and its environment, as well as each of the 5 components of internal control (CRIME), the sources of information from which the understanding was obtained, and the risk assessment procedures performed. The form is influenced by the size and complexity of the entity.

There are no specific requirements as to how the understanding of internal control is documented other than the requirement to document the understanding of all five components. There are different techniques that are commonly used for documenting the auditor's understanding of the internal control structure. These are (**FIND**):

- *Flowchart* – This is a visual depiction of the internal control structure that shows a process from beginning to end and indicates which departments or groups of employees are responsible for each function, what documents are used and how they are distributed and disposed of, and the interaction among departments or groups of employees. This form of documentation is particularly helpful in determining if there is adequate segregation of duties as well as tracing documents through the system. Flowcharting requires knowledge of specialized symbols but does a good job of giving the auditor a sense of the flow and sequence of transactions in the client entity.

- Testing on the CPA exam has been limited to reading flowcharts and then answering conventional questions about strengths and weaknesses in the internal control structure, and has never involved their preparation.
- Historically, exam questions have been written so that the candidate could understand flowcharts provided, even if they had no prior knowledge of the standard meaning of the various symbols, and we do not suggest using your valuable study time in an attempt to learn all the symbols.

- **Internal Control Questionnaire (ICQ)** – This is usually in the form of a series of questions that can be answered with a simple **yes or no**. They are usually designed so that a yes answer indicates that a control is properly in place (strength) and a no answer indicates a potential weakness. An advantage is that it easily identifies potential weaknesses in internal control but it is difficult to develop a complete and comprehensive questionnaire and it is difficult to obtain an understanding of the flow of the system using it.
  - This is the most structured of the approaches and is the easiest for an inexperienced staff member in an audit to utilize.
  - It is also a very popular area of testing on the CPA exam.

- **Narrative or Memorandum** – This form of documentation, often referred to as the *narrative approach*, is in the form of a detailed written description of the internal control structure. It generally describes the system in a manner similar to how it is depicted in a flowchart but with words rather than symbols. This makes it easier for a user to understand the flow of the system and the interrelationships among departments and employees that are part of it. It does not clearly indicate whether there is adequate segregation of duties, however, and it is often difficult to visualize the flow of documentation.
  - This approach can be cumbersome and is not commonly used.
  - It is tested very infrequently on the CPA exam.

- **Decision table/tree** – Parts of an internal control structure may require a client employee to choose from several alternative actions depending on the conditions faced, and documenting such activities. This may best be accomplished by preparing a decision table that lists each possible condition and the actions that will result from each (depicts the logic of an operation or process). It uses Yes/No questions and each answer will direct the user to the next relevant question. This is, however, a limited tool that cannot effectively document the entire structure.

| NO – RMM ↑ (Sub Approach) |
| YES – RMM ↓ (Combined Approach) |

3. Assessing Risk of Material Misstatement (RMM)

The auditor should perform the risk assessment to identify and assess the risks of material misstatement at the financial statement level and at the relevant assertion level for classes of transactions, account balances, and disclosures.

The auditor first assesses risk of material misstatement at the financial statement level by evaluating the entity's ability to prepare financial statements that are fairly presented in accordance with the applicable financial reporting framework. This will include factors such as the auditor's perception of the competency of the entity's accounting personnel; an evaluation of the entity's ability to develop estimates and interpret accounting principles; whether the auditor considers management aggressive or believes management is under pressure to achieve difficult financial goals; if the industry or the economy has created particular challenges; or if the entity is seeking financing or anticipating entering into a substantial transaction. Any of these or a variety of other factors may increase the risk that the financial statements, taken as a whole, will be materially misstated.

The auditor may use either a *substantive approach,* in which substantive procedures are emphasized, or a combined approach, in which both tests of controls and substantive procedures are used.
- The auditor needs to
    - Identify the risks.
    - Relate the identified risks to the types of potential misstatements that could occur at the relevant assertion level.
    - Consider whether the risks are so significant that they could result in a material misstatement of the financial statements.
    - Consider the likelihood (probability) that the identified risks could result in material misstatements on the financial statements.

If the risk assessment is based on an expectation that controls are operating effectively, the auditor should test the operating effectiveness of controls (TofC) that have been determined to be suitably designed to prevent or detect material misstatements.
- Intend to Rely?
  The risk assessment may **NOT** include an expectation that controls operate effectively when (*Substantive approach*):
    - Controls appear **inadequate / Ineffective/ weak.**
    - Auditor believes that performing extensive substantive procedures is likely to be more *cost effective* than performing tests of controls. **(Cost/benefit – inefficient).**

If the controls **appear effective**, tests of controls will be performed when (*Combined approach*):
- The auditor's risk assessment includes an expectation of ***operating effectiveness of controls*** because the likelihood of material misstatement is lower if the control operates effectively *(Cost effective)* or
- When ***substantive procedures alone*** do not provide sufficient audit evidence.

Since tests of controls alone are not normally sufficient upon which to base an audit opinion, the further audit procedures will be composed of a *combination* of tests of controls and substantive procedures. Thus, the decision to perform tests of controls will be made when the auditor believes that a combination of tests of controls and a decreased scope of substantive procedures is likely to be more cost effective than performing more extensive substantive procedures. The overall approach here, as it relates to controls is to
- Identify controls that are relevant to specific assertions that are likely to prevent or detect material misstatements, and
- Perform tests of controls to evaluate the effectiveness of those controls.

The auditor also assesses risk at the financial statement level by identifying those items that may have a propensity for misstatement. This may be individual accounts, such as items on the balance sheet; classes of transactions, such as items on the income statement; or disclosures, including footnotes as well as descriptions and notations on the financial statements themselves. Items will represent a greater risk of misstatement for a variety of reasons. It may be *due to error* as a result of:
- The difficulty of obtaining information needed to accurately record the transaction; or

- The complexity of the requirements for accounting for an item.

An item may be more susceptible to *fraud* because:
- It is a valuable item that might be misappropriated by employees or others;
- It is an item for which it is easy to conceal a misstatement; or
- A misstatement to the item has the potential of influencing other actions such as the payment of a commission or the earning of a bonus based on performance.

Once items that are susceptible to misstatement are identified, risk of material misstatement is assessed at the relevant assertion level. The fact that an item is likely to be misstated will generally affect all of the assertions and the risk should be analyzed accordingly. For example:

- For an entity that might have a tendency to *overstate results* because it is competing in the capital markets, sales may be likely to be overstated and the auditor will be concerned about:
  - Occurrence, since the entity may record sales that did not occur;
  - Cutoff, since the entity may record sales from the next period in the current period;
  - Accuracy, since the entity may record sales in amounts greater than the actual transactions; and
  - Classification, since the entity may wish to characterize the proceeds from the issuance of debt or from the sale of assets that do not generate revenues into sales.
  - The auditor would not be concerned about completeness, however, since an entity wishing to overstate sales would not omit sales.

- For an entity that might have a tendency to *understate results* for the purpose of avoiding taxation, sales may be likely to be understated and the auditor will be concerned about:
  - Completeness, since the entity may omit sales;
  - Cutoff, since the entity may postpone the recognition of sales that occurred this period until the next period; and
  - Valuation, since sales may be reported at amounts lower than the actual amounts.
  - The auditor would be less concerned about occurrence, since an entity intending to understate sales is not likely to report sales that did not occur; and
  - The auditor would be less concerned with classification, since an entity intending to understate sales is not likely to include items that are not properly reported as sales in that category.

4. Tests of Controls (Develop an Audit Strategy)

Develop an audit strategy to either:

- *Perform tests of control* to determine if CR is below maximum, reducing RMM below the level of IR and allowing for the modification of the nature, timing, and extent of further audit procedures (sub tests): or
- Decide not to perform tests of controls, assessing CR at the *maximum level* as if the control did not exist, and measuring RMM as being equal to IR.

To test the effectiveness of the design and operation of a control (what is the substance?). The auditor must consider *how* the control was applied, the *consistency* with which it was applied and *by whom* it was applied. Tests of controls generally consist of 4 types of procedures (**RIIO**).
  - Testing the Cycles for **ARCC's** by doing **RIIO**

There are 4 *Procedures* for testing controls (**RIIO**).

- **Reperformance** – The auditor applies the control that the client personnel presumably performed to determine if the procedure was performed properly. Reperformance, which also includes recalculation, may involve the auditor performing a reconciliation to determine if the result is the same as that derived by the entity or may involve re-footing an invoice to make certain that amounts have been calculated correctly.

- **Inspection** – The auditor examines controls, documents and reports that provide documentary evidence. For example, the auditor might examine paid invoices to make certain they have been properly cancelled to avoid paying the same invoice more than once.

- **Inquiry** – The auditor asks client personnel involved in controls to state how effectively certain controls were enforced. For example, the auditor might ask the accounting personnel if they handled any cash or signed checks in the course of the year.

- **Observation** – The auditor watches client personnel performing their regular functions to see if they follow the controls that were designed and implemented. For example, the auditor might observe the distribution of pay checks to see if appropriate procedures for verifying employees are being followed.

These different types of tests of controls can be very effective in determining if a system features appropriate **segregation of duties**. In general, however, the most effective type of test of control is observation.

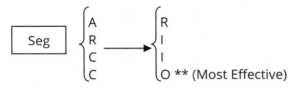

Items susceptible to misstatement due to error or fraud are generally identified by applying a "What Could Go Wrong" analysis, applied at the assertion level and taking into consideration the auditor's understanding of the entity's internal control. For example, the auditor may be evaluating the occurrence assertion in relation to sales. The following may result:

- The auditor determines that, since sales personnel are highly incentivized by a liberal commission system, they may be motivated to overstate sales reported to the company and, as a result, reported by the company.

- The response to the auditor's question: "What could go wrong?" is that sales personnel may submit paperwork for sales that did not actually occur.

- The auditor will next try to determine if there are controls that would either prevent the recording of sales that did not occur or would cause them to be detected and corrected on a timely basis.
  - The controls may be built into the system, which the auditor can determine by reviewing the documented understanding.
  - Otherwise, the auditor will inquire as to whether management has considered the possibility and developed a separate control, of which the auditor is not yet aware, to deal with the issue.

If there are not controls to deal with the issue that are either built into the system or have been separately developed and implemented, the auditor would likely conclude that a control deficiency has been identified. The auditor will evaluate the control deficiency, determining if it is a *significant deficiency* or a *material weakness* and, if so, make certain to include it in a communication to those charged with governance. In addition, however, the auditor will evaluate what further audit procedures will provide evidence that recorded sales did actually occur.

- The auditor will develop an audit program with procedures designed to verify that the information reported on the financial statements is correct.

- To test the assertion of occurrence, the auditor will likely select a sample from the population of recorded sales and trace them to supporting documentation to verify that they actually occurred.

If there are controls intended to deal with the issue, the auditor will evaluate the design of the controls and make a determination as to whether the design is suitable and if the control is likely to be effective. If not, the auditor will not attempt to verify that the control has been implemented as it is irrelevant. If, however, the control is expected to be effective, the auditor will perform some form of **walk through** involving observing the control, inspecting documents, or performing analytical procedures.

The auditor will then determine an audit strategy:

- The auditor may decide **Not to Rely** on the controls related to a relevant assertion.
  - RMM will be equal to the assertion's inherent risk under the assumption that there are no relevant controls in place.
  - The auditor will develop a program to test the assertion by applying *substantive audit procedures* that the auditor believes will provide sufficient appropriate audit evidence.

- The auditor may decide to **Rely** on the controls related to the relevant assertion.
  - RMM will be reduced from IR, taking into account the effect of CR being below the maximum.
  - The auditor will *perform tests of the controls* selecting from a population that covers the entire period during which the auditor is anticipating that the controls were in place.

If the auditor plans to use audit evidence about the operating effectiveness of controls obtained in prior audits and the controls have not changed since they were last tested, the auditor should test the operating effectiveness of such controls at least **once in every three years**. The auditor will determine that controls have not changed since they were last tested through the performance of risk assessment procedures.

5. Reassess RMM to Determine DR

Based on the results of the tests of controls the auditor will determine whether it is necessary to modify the scope of substantive procedures. If tests of control reveal that the system *operates as expected*, there will generally be no need to change the scope of planned substantive procedures. Conversely, if the system does not operate as effectively as expected, the scope of substantive procedures for the relevant assertions involved will increase (thereby decreasing detection risk).

- DR tells you how much substantive testing to do
- Must do substantive testing (adjust Audit Program for Substantive tests)
- AR / (IR × CR) = DR

When an auditor decides to rely on controls, tests of controls are performed to determine if the controls were working effectively as they were designed for the period under audit.

If, based on the tests of controls, the auditor concludes that the controls are **effective**, the nature, timing, and extent of further audit procedures in relation to that assertion will be reduced.

If, however, based on the tests of controls, the auditor cannot conclude that the controls are effective, CR will be reset **to maximum** and the auditor will develop an audit program to test the assertion applying substantive audit procedures as if there were no controls related to the assertion and as if no test of controls had been performed.

Since the most expensive and inefficient alternative is to perform tests of controls, only to determine that the controls are not reliable, the auditor will do a ***cost/benefit analysis*** before deciding to perform tests of controls. In performing the analysis:
- The auditor will estimate the cost of performing a substantive audit without performing tests of controls.
- The auditor will estimate the cost of performing tests of controls.
- The auditor also estimate the cost of the reduced substantive testing that will be performed if the controls prove to be reliable.
- Finally, the auditor will estimate the likelihood that the controls to be tested are likely to be effective.

The auditor will then:
- Add the cost of performing tests of controls to the cost of reduced substantive testing and multiply the total by the probability that the controls will be effective.
- Add the cost of performing tests of controls to the cost of the unreduced substantive testing and multiply the total by the probability that controls will not be reliable, which is 100% minus the probability used previously.
- The total of those two amounts will be compared to the cost of performing substantive tests exclusively.

The lower of the two amounts will determine the strategy to be taken.

Tests of controls alone are not normally considered sufficient evidence upon which to base an audit opinion. As a result, even when tests of controls prove that controls can be relied upon, further audit procedures may be reduced but will *not be eliminated*. In many cases, the auditor will use ***dual purpose testing,*** which consists of tests that are designed to test the effectiveness of controls while providing evidence as to the fairness or correctness of an element of the financial statements by supporting one of management's assertions.
- When the results are satisfactory, the auditor will conclude that the control may be relied upon and the evidence obtained is sufficient to support the assertion, eliminating the need for further testing.
- When the results are not satisfactory, the auditor will conclude that the control may not be relied upon and will determine the nature, timing, and extent of further audit procedures that will be necessary to support the assertion.

6. Document Conclusions and Develop or Revise Audit Programs

The auditor is *required* to communicate significant deficiencies and material weaknesses to management and those charged with governance. The basis for risk assessment must *always* be documented. The auditor needs to document:

- The assessment of the risks of material misstatement at the financial statement and relevant assertion levels;
- The basis for that assessment;
- Significant risks identified and related controls evaluated; and
- Risks identified that require tests of controls to obtain sufficient audit evidence and the related controls evaluated.

The auditor will *document* the procedures performed and the conclusions reached such that others will understand what procedures were performed, what items were tested and how they were selected, the evidence gathered, and the conclusions drawn.

In addition, the auditor will develop audit programs to indicate the further audit procedures that the auditor believes are necessary and appropriate in order to draw a conclusion related to a management assertion.

Lecture 3.04

SARBANES-OXLEY ACT (SOX)

SOX created a variety of regulations and eliminated a significant portion of the accounting profession's system of self-regulation. Some issues include:

- Section 302 is entitled "Corporate Responsibility for Financial Reports" and requires that the principal executive officer and the principal financial officer, or their equivalents, certify as to certain items on each annual or quarterly report:
  - The signing officer has reviewed the report
  - Based on the signer's knowledge, the report does not contain a material untrue statement or omit a material fact
  - Based on the signer's knowledge, the financial statements and other information are fairly presented
- In addition, the signing officers certify that:
  - They are responsible for establishing and maintaining internal controls
  - They have designed those controls to ensure the receipt of all relevant information during those periods in which periodic reports are being prepared
  - They have evaluated the effectiveness of internal controls within 90 days prior to the report
  - They have presented their conclusions about the effectiveness of internal controls in the report
- Officers are also required to report to auditors and to the audit committee:
  - All significant deficiencies that could adversely affect the reporting process and any material weaknesses
  - Any fraud (whether material or not) involving management or employees with a role in internal controls

Basic Concepts and Internal Control Limitations

Regardless of the good intentions of management, even a strong control environment combined with excellent control activities is subject to certain **inherent limitations (COCO)**:

- **Collusion** – Control activities that depend on segregation of duties will not be effective if those engaged in the segregated functions conspire with one another.
- **Override by management** – Since management designs and implements the system of internal control, it is in a position to override it, so that even an effective internal control structure cannot be expected to prevent intentional misbehavior by management. This is one of the reasons the auditor must establish the integrity of management before accepting the engagement. It is also important to establish whether employee personnel have ever been asked to override systems of internal control by management.
- **Competence/Human error** – If control procedures are erroneously applied, they will not be effective. Internal control cannot be expected to prevent mistakes in human judgment (misjudgment).
- **Obsolescence** – A good internal control structure may cease to be effective due to changes in the company's operations or size, changes in technology, or other changes affecting the way the entity's business is transacted.

It is essential to keep in mind the concept of **reasonable assurance** as it relates to internal control, taking into account the **cost/benefit factor**. Even if it were possible to design a perfect system of internal control, management would not do so, since there are costs involved in any action, and the costs of the internal control structure should not exceed the benefits. As a result, management may sometimes reasonably refuse to remedy a deficiency in internal control that it knows exists.

The auditor is required to respond to management override of controls – Because management is often in a position to override controls in order to commit financial-statement fraud, the standard includes procedures to test for management override of controls on every audit. It should be noted that even a properly planned and performed audit may not detect a material misstatement resulting from fraud because of (1) concealment aspects of fraudulent activity, including the fact that fraud often involves collusion or falsified documents, and (2) the need to apply professional judgment in the identification or evaluation of *fraud risk factors* and other conditions.

Lecture 3.05

CLASS QUESTIONS

Please see the Class Questions and Class Solutions for this Lecture at the end of this Section.

Lecture 3.06

OPERATING CYCLES AND THE FLOW OF TRANSACTIONS

An auditor divides the audit down into different cycles that make up the flow of transactions for the entire company. All related accounts within each cycle are audited together. Within each cycle, the auditor is concerned with what each specific *employee* does, the *documents* they handle and how each document relates to the *segregation* of ARCC'S (Authorization, Recording, Custody and Comparison). Controls have a function of either **Preventing** misstatements before they occur (most effective) or **Detecting and Correcting** misstatements that have already occurred (less expensive to implement, but could detect too late).

In obtaining an understanding of an entity's internal control, the auditor will identify the different **types of transactions or events** that occur on an ongoing basis and that affect the entity's operations or its financial position. The auditor will then obtain an understanding of various components and in particular:

- Initiation (**S**tart) – The auditor should determine what event or circumstance initiates a transaction. Sales transactions, for example, may be initiated when the entity's sales force make calls to their regular customers or when customers call in orders as they identify their needs.

- **A**uthorization – Before an entity will commit resources to meet its obligations in a transaction or to respond to an event or circumstance, it will want to determine that the counterparty to the transaction is a legitimate party with the intent and ability to perform or that the event or circumstance is real.

- **C**ompletion or execution – The entity should have policies and procedures to make certain that its obligations in transactions and its responses to recurring events and circumstances are being performed in accordance with management's directives. This will include the flow of documents, services, goods, and other resources throughout the system.

- **R**ecording – The entity should have a system for making certain that all transactions, events, or circumstances that affect operations or financial position are properly captured and reflected in the entity's financial records.

- Verifications (**E**valuate **D**efenses) – Each system should have checks and balances to make certain that each function within the system is performed properly and in the appropriate sequence. This may involve policies such as those requiring the shipping department to compare a customer's purchase order with an internal sales order and to a list of goods transferred from stores before shipping the goods. It may also involve accounting for the sequence of pre-numbered documents, checking for authoritative signatures, or periodically reconciling recorded amounts to physical assets. These verifications may occur throughout a system.

It should be easy to remember that a good system of internal control is **SACRED** to a business.

When the auditor obtains an understanding of each of the systems applied to recurring transactions, often referred to as cycles, the auditor is concerned with what each specific employee does, the documents they handle, and whether there is appropriate segregation of duties. The duties to be *segregated* are the **a**uthorization of transactions, the **r**ecording of those transactions, **c**ustody of the resources that are associated with that transaction, and **c**omparison or reconciliation of the recorded amounts to the physical resources (ARCC).

Some controls are considered **preventative,** designed to minimize the possibility that misstatements will occur. Although a preventative approach has the tendency to be the most effective, it is not always feasible to develop controls that will be effective at preventing a misstatement, particularly one that results from fraud, and in many cases, the cost of developing an effective preventative control will exceed the benefit that can be derived from it. Other controls are designed to be **corrective** in that they are designed to identify misstatements that may occur due to errors or fraud and establish a means of correcting them on a timely basis. These, of course, have their limitations in that they may not be effective for a fraudulent misstatement that is cleverly concealed and may identify a misstatement after a negative impact has already occurred.

When evaluating the system for a particular cycle, the focus will be on the accounts balances or classes of transactions that are affected. The *revenue cycle* will generally result in a debit to cash or accounts receivable and a credit to sales, while the *purchasing cycle* will result in a debit to purchases in a periodic system, or to inventory in a perpetual system, and a credit to accounts payable. For the account affected, the auditor will evaluate whether or not a step or process within the system supports one or more of management's assertions.

- A requirement that each recorded sale be supported by an order signed by a customer supports management's assertion of occurrence in that having a signed purchase order provides evidence that a sale did occur.

- A policy that the accounting clerk notify a supervisor whenever an internally generated sales order is presented out of sequence supports the assertion of completeness in that tracing all sales orders to the accounting records will provide evidence that all sales transactions have been recorded.

REVENUE CYCLE (SALES REVENUE / ACCOUNTS RECEIVABLE / CASH RECEIPTS)

The revenue cycle of a business consists of sales, billings, and collections. In order to properly segregate the incompatible functions of authorization, recording, and custody, the activities may include **specific employees** with each of the following duties. This list should be reviewed simply to make sure you are comfortable with the meaning of each job title:

- **Sales clerk** – Accepts orders from customers and prepares written sales orders using internal prenumbered, preprinted forms (PPN) (recording).
- **Credit manager** – Approves customer credit on orders (authorization).
- **Warehouse clerk** – Holds goods in inventory awaiting requests for shipment (custody).
- **Shipping clerk** – Removes items from inventory to ship to customer (custody).
- **Billing clerk** – Prepares sales invoices to send to customers (recording).
- **Receivables clerk** – *Posts* sales and collections to individual customer accounts based on sales invoices and remittance advices, respectively (recording).
- **General ledger bookkeeper** – *Posts* journal entries for sales and collections (recording).
- **Mail room clerk/receptionist** – Opens mail containing customer checks (or cash) and remittance advices, prepares a prelist of checks, referred to as a remittance listing, and directs these items to appropriate parties within the system (custody).
- **Cashier** – Receives checks, prepares deposit slip, and deposits funds at the bank (custody).
- **Cash receipts clerk** – Receives remittance listing and posts to cash receipts journal (recording).
- **Receiving clerk** – Receives all goods that are being returned and returns them to inventory (custody).
- **Treasurer** – Approves credit memos for returns and write-offs of uncollectible accounts (authorization).
- **Controller/Internal Audit** – Bank reconciliations and analyses of past-due accounts receivable should be performed by individuals independent of cash receipts and disbursements (comparison).

A system may not necessarily include all of the above employees, and sometimes a function may be performed by another employee or one of the above employees identified by a different title. For example, all of the clerks involved in recording may simply be called bookkeepers. Also, the system will include periodic reconciliations, such as reconciling the bank account, that may be performed by virtually any employee who is not involved in the preparation of either of the two types of records being compared and does not have custody of resources being compared to recorded amounts. . A key aspect of **segregation of duties** is that an employee who is responsible for **one** of the three functions (authorization, recording, custody) should **not** be involved in either of the **other two**.

Some of the **documents** and records that are commonly seen in the revenue cycle include the following. This list, like that of individuals within the system, is being presented simply to ensure that you will be familiar with the purpose of each when mentioned on the exam:

- **Sales order** – The list of goods ordered by the customer along with the prices to be charged. Even if a customer has submitted their own purchase order, a sales order will be prepared, since these are prenumbered and make it possible to periodically account for orders to be sure they were processed.
- **Bill of lading** – The shipping document that is signed by the carrier, often a trucker, accepting goods from the shipping clerk.
- **Sales invoice** – The bill that is prepared and sent to the customer after shipment to request payment. Before doing so, the billing clerk should compare the sales order and bill of lading to ensure they are in agreement.
- **Sales register (journal)** – A book in which sales invoice information is posted. Cash register records provide similar information for retail outlets and other cash businesses.
- **Subsidiary receivables ledger** – A book that lists the outstanding receivables with a separate record for each customer.
- **Remittance advice** – The document included in an envelope with the check or other form of payment to indicate the purpose of the check.
- **Remittance listing** – A summary of the money received that day. This may be called a prelist in some cases, and is prepared by the employee first receiving the cash, which is usually the mail room clerk.
- **Cash receipts journal** – A book in which the remittance listings are posted.
- **Deposit slip** – The document signed or stamped by the bank to acknowledge receipt of checks and that is periodically reconciled to postings into the cash receipts journal by an independent employee.
- **Bank Reconciliation** – Comparison of the cash balance according to the entity's books to the amount indicated by the bank that it is holding on behalf of the entity (book to physical).

The purpose of most other documents and records can be determined by seeing the context in which they are being used on the exam.

Ultimately, the reason an auditor cares about the internal control structure is that it relates to whether the **financial statement assertions** are correct and therefore may be relied upon. The assertions are discussed in detail in another section, but some specific applications of these assertions are frequently tested in discussing the revenue cycle. Examples related to each assertion follow (**U-PERCV**):

- ***U*nderstandability & Classification** – Transactions and events have been recorded in the proper accounts and information is presented and described clearly.
- ***P*resentation & Disclosure –** Management asserts that all sales to employees have been properly identified in the statements and notes as related party transactions. The auditor may review sales invoices for specific sales to employees and then trace these invoices to the general ledger entry to see if they are posted to the "due from employees" account.
- ***E*xistence or Occurrence (Vouching) –** Management asserts that all sales that have been recorded actually have taken place (be sure not to confuse this with the previous assertion). The auditor may select a sales invoice and vouch from the sales invoice to the

bill of lading in order to ensure that items billed to customers were based on actual shipments.

- **Rights & Obligations** – Management asserts the right to collect receivables. An auditor can vouch from postings in the subsidiary receivables ledger for a specific client back to the sales order, bill of lading, and sales invoice, in order to establish that the goods were ordered, shipped, and billed, giving the company the right to collect.
- **Completeness (Tracing) & Cutoff** – Management asserts that it has recorded all sales that have taken place. The auditor may select a bill of lading and then trace from the bill of lading to the sales invoice in order to ensure that all shipped goods have been billed to customers.
- **Valuation, Allocation & Accuracy** – Management asserts that receivables are likely to be collected. The auditor can test the process of credit approval before shipment in order to determine that the company is only shipping to customers likely to pay.

Another way to look at the assertions:

As indicated, the auditor's understanding of the system of internal control is to determine if the financial statement assertions are correct and may be relied upon. In relation to sales for events and transactions (**CPA-CO**):

- **C**ompleteness – All sales that occurred were recorded. The auditor will evaluate whether prenumbered sales order forms are being used and if the sequence of forms is being accounted for in which case a gap in the sequence may indicate an unrecorded transaction.
- **P**eriod Cutoff – All transactions are recorded in the appropriate period. The auditor will determine if there is a process for identifying when goods were shipped, in the case of goods sold with fob shipping terms, or received, in the case of goods sold with FOB destination terms, and if the accounting department has a process for making certain that sales are reported in the appropriate period.
- **A**ccuracy – All transactions are recorded in the appropriate amount. The auditor will determine if the recording of sales involves comparing the quantities on customer order forms to internally prepared sales order forms and to goods shipped as well as whether there is a process for checking the mathematical accuracy of documents.
- **C**lassification (**S**orted) – Amounts reported as sales include only sales of the entity's goods or services in the ordinary course of business and do not include proceeds from transactions that should not appropriately be reported as sales. The auditor will evaluate whether there is a means of preventing transactions that are not with a customer and are not accompanied by appropriate sales forms from being included in sales.
- **O**ccurrence – Each recorded sale actually occurred. The auditor will evaluate whether those responsible for recording are required to have some form of verification, such as a sales order signed by the customer, to indicate that a sale actually occurred as a prerequisite for its being recorded.

In relation to accounts receivable balances (**RACE**):

- **R**ights and obligations – All amounts reported as accounts receivable are owed to the entity. The auditor will want to make certain that receivables are supported by sales orders and shipping documents indicating that the entity has met its performance obligations and is entitled to the payment.
- **A**llocation and Valuation – The amounts reported represent the amounts that the entity is actually owed. The auditor will evaluate this in the same manner as accuracy for sales.
- **C**ompleteness – All receivables are included in the amount reported. The auditor will evaluate this in the same manner as completeness for sales.

- *E*xistence – All reported accounts receivable are actual claims that resulted from sales. The auditor will evaluate this in the same manner as occurrence for sales.

In obtaining an understanding, the auditor should consider activities that may occur outside of the entity. For example, the company may direct customers to send payments directly to a bank lockbox instead of to the company itself, thereby eliminating access to cash and checks by any of the employees in the revenue cycle. This obviously strengthens the internal control over cash receipts.

Segregation of Duties in the Revenue Cycle

For proper segregation of duties, authorization of transactions, the recording function, and custody of assets should be kept separate.

- The functions of authorizing sales on account and authorizing credits to accounts receivable that may result from sales discounts, sales returns, sales allowances, or write offs, should be segregated.
- The function of authorizing sales, recording accounts receivable, and having custody of inventory should be segregated.
- The functions of the cashier who has **custody** of the cash, the **recording** of cash receipts, and preparing the bank reconciliation (**comparison**) should be segregated. In businesses that handle large amounts of cash during the normal course of operations, obtaining bonds (insurance and background searches) for employees who handle cash is a common practice. Employee knowledge that bonding companies often prosecute those accused of dishonest acts can act as an effective deterrent to theft and fraud.
- Employees responsible for authorizing sales approval, issuance of credit memos and bad debt write-offs should be denied access to cash.

Revenue Cycle
- Customer **Purchase Order**
- **Sales Order** → Multiple Copies (PPN)

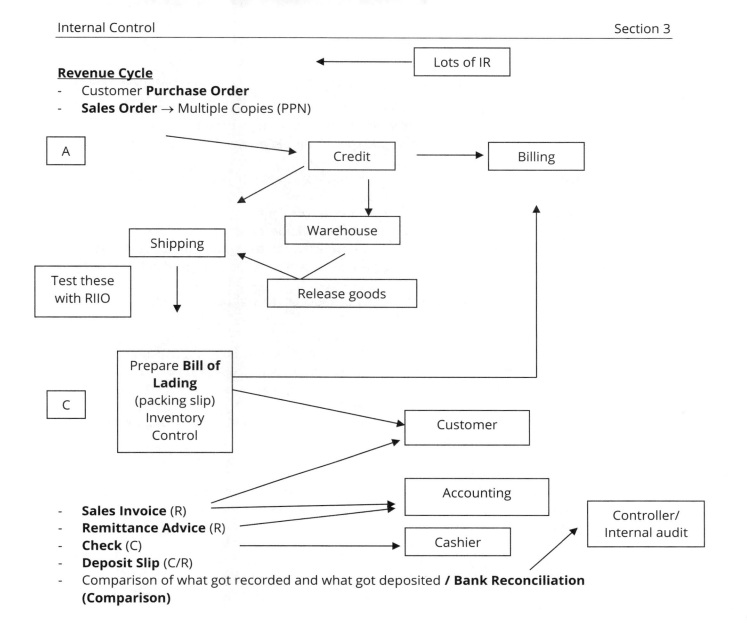

- **Sales Invoice** (R)
- **Remittance Advice** (R)
- **Check** (C)
- **Deposit Slip** (C/R)
- Comparison of what got recorded and what got deposited **/ Bank Reconciliation (Comparison)**

SPENDING CYCLE (PURCHASES/ ACCOUNTS PAYABLE / CASH DISBURSEMENTS)

The spending cycle of a business consists of ordering goods or services, receiving or using them, and paying for them. In order to properly segregate the incompatible functions of authorization, recording, and custody, the activities may include specific **employees** with each of the following duties:

- **Purchasing manager** – Approves purchase requests before they are processed and negotiates terms with vendors (authorization).
- **Purchasing clerk** – Places orders with vendors (recording).
- **Receiving clerk** – Receives delivery of goods from vendors (custody).
- **Payables clerk** – Prepares payment voucher which is the basis for authorizing the issuance of a check to the vendor after verifying the accuracy of the vendor invoice and comparing supporting documents (recording).
- **Payables manager** – Oversees the Posting of vouchers to appropriate purchase records (recording).
- **Treasurer** – Signs and mails check for payment (custody).
- **Shipping department** – Sends goods back to vendors when goods are nonconforming or a right to cancel an order is being exercised by the company (custody).

The **documents** most often discussed on the exam include:

- **Purchase requisition** – The internal request by the department in need for goods to be ordered by the purchasing department.
- **Purchase order** – The external form mailed to the vendor to request that goods be delivered to the company.
- **Receiving report** – The document prepared in the receiving department and signed by the carrier to acknowledge the goods that have been delivered to the company.
- **Purchase (vendor) invoice** – The document received from the vendor indicating the goods the vendor claims to have shipped. This is the same document that is known as the sales invoice when considered from the vendor's side of the transaction.
- **Invoice register** – A book listing invoices received from vendors.
- **Payment voucher** – The document prepared by the payables clerk to request that a check be issued for payment to a vendor.
- **Purchase journal (or voucher register)** – A book listing all of the payment vouchers generated by the company.

There are certain issues involving the various purchase documents that are commonly repeated on the exam:

- When the **purchase order** is prepared by the purchasing clerk to send to the vendor, additional copies of the order are sent to the receiving department to authorize them to accept delivery of the goods and the payables department to enable them to do appropriate comparisons later. The receiving department copy does **not include quantities** for the goods ordered so as to ensure that the receiving department will perform an independent count of the goods delivered instead of relying on the purchase order numbers. The payables clerk compares the purchase order and receiving report with the vendor invoice to ensure they agree before preparing the payment voucher.
- The **check** for payment is usually prepared by a clerk in the treasury department who doesn't have signature authority. They will provide the unsigned check along with the payment voucher and supporting document to the treasurer for signature. The treasurer makes sure the check agrees with the voucher and other documents before signing. **Immediately after signing**, the treasurer cancels the supporting documents (so

that they won't accidentally be processed again at a later time), places the check in the envelope, seals it, and arranges for mailing.

The auditor should look for specific applications of the different control activities to the spending cycle. Commonly-tested examples of auditing procedures used to understand the internal control structure related to spending include (**PRAISE**):

- **P**hysical controls – Verify that all goods are received by the receiving department and returns are shipped by the shipping department.
- **R**ecording – Verify that receiving reports are prepared for all goods received and that debit memos are prepared for all goods that are returned.
- **A**uthorization – Select individual cancelled checks and vouch them to the purchase orders, receiving reports, vendor invoices, and payment vouchers.
- **I**ndependent checks – Verify that the client periodically performs inventory counts and reconciles amounts on hand to inventory records so as to know when inventory has been lost or stolen.
- **S**egregation of duties – Use inquiry and observation to determine that there is a separation of the functions of (1) authorization of purchases and payments, (2) recording of purchase orders and posting to the purchase journal, and (3) custody of inventory and checks for payment.
- **E**valuate performance – Determine if the client uses a standard costing system that generates variances, enabling them to identify actual cost numbers that may be incorrect.

Just as in the case of the revenue cycle, the auditor is primarily concerned with the relationship of the various control activities to the various management assertions. Similarly to the revenue cycle, tracing through the system in the normal order (from source documents to postings in books and records) is an attempt to verify the **completeness** of the records, while vouching in reverse order (from books and records back to source documents) is an attempt to verify the **existence or occurrence** of all the transactions that are reflected in the records.

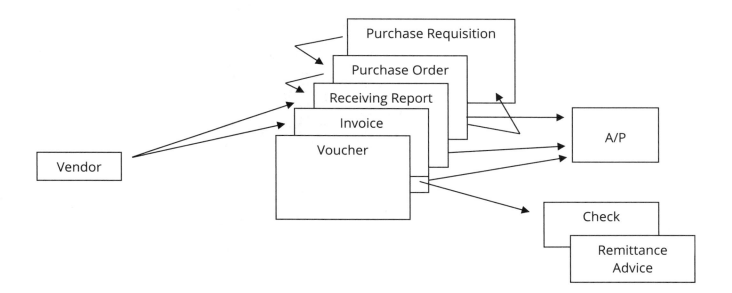

Segregation of Duties in the Purchases and Spending Cycle

For proper segregation of duties, authorization of transactions, the recording function, and custody of assets should be kept separate.

- The functions of authorizing purchases, receiving goods purchased, and recording the purchase should be segregated.
- The cash functions should be segregated. Authorizing payment for purchases, recording payments, access to checks, and reconciliation of the bank account should be segregated.
- Individuals with authority to approve vouchers for payment should not have access to unused purchase orders.

Lecture 3.08

PERSONNEL & PAYROLL CYCLE

The personnel cycle of a business normally is segregated between different departments:

- **Personnel** – This is the **authorization** department that is responsible for hiring of new employees, approval of changes in pay rates, and termination of employees.
- **Payroll** – This is the **recording** department that performs the calculation of payroll amounts. They will examine and then update records based on authorization forms for hiring, firing, and pay rates received from personnel, and will calculate payroll based on time sheets and other reports approved by appropriate supervisors in the various operational departments of the company. They update pay records and prepare vouchers for the amount of payment. They may also be involved in the preparation of pay checks as long as they do not have the ability to sign them and do not receive custody of signed but unclaimed pay checks that have not been voided.
- **Treasurer** – This is the **custody** department that is responsible for the signing and distribution of pay checks to employees, and unclaimed paychecks should always be retained within this same department until they are either distributed or voided. If payment of wages is in cash, employees should be required to sign a receipt for the amount received.
- **Controller** – **Comparison** – Bank Reconciliation.

Personnel (Authorize)	Payroll (Recording)	Treasurer (Custody)	Controller (Comparison)
Hire	Calculate Pay	Signs and distributes checks	Bank Reconciliation
Fire		Custody of cash	
Salary Rates			

Key Documents

The key documents generated in this cycle include:

- Personnel records;
- Hiring and deduction authorization forms (W-4);
- Time cards;
- Payroll register;
- Paychecks;
- Payroll cost allocation; and
- Bank reconciliations.

Description of the Personnel and Payroll Cycle

Personnel Department (HR)

The personnel department is involved with the **personnel records** and all the **hiring forms**, including the **deduction forms** for payroll deductions. The personnel department approves changes in pay rates and deductions from employee salaries.

The personnel department is also involved in the termination process. It is essential that the personnel department promptly sends employees' termination notices to the payroll department.

Employee

The employee prepares a **time card**, and submits it to the supervisor for authorization. The time card is then sent to the payroll department.

Payroll Department

The payroll department examines authorization forms from the personnel department for new employees and adds the employees' names to the payroll processing program. The payroll department promptly updates the records for changes in deductions, pay rates, and terminations. The payroll department enters all the time card and wage rate information into the **payroll register**. **Payroll checks** are prepared by the payroll department and submitted to the treasurer for signature.

The payroll department also prepares a **payroll cost allocation** based on the time card information. The payroll cost allocation is used to distribute payroll costs over the various accounts affected.

Treasurer

The treasurer receives the checks from the payroll department and signs them. The treasurer is responsible for distribution of paychecks. Unclaimed paychecks should remain in the custody of the treasurer. Unclaimed checks should **not** be returned to the payroll department.

Controller

As an overall verification of custody controls over cash, the controller should prepare monthly **bank reconciliations** to verify that there were no errors made in recording receipts in the cash receipts journal.

Segregation of Duties in the Personnel and Payroll Cycle

For proper segregation of duties, authorization of transactions, the recording function, and custody of assets should be kept separate.
- The functions of authorizing the hiring of personnel, payroll processing (recording) and distributing payroll checks (custody) should be segregated.
- The functions of authorizing payroll rate changes and payroll processing (recording) should be segregated.
- Payroll checks should be prepared by the payroll department and signed by the treasurer, segregating recording and custody.

Service Organizations

Many companies use various types of service bureaus to assist them with the processing of routine transactions. Certain transactions, like payroll, may require a particular expertise and can often be processed more efficiently by an entity that specializes in that type of transaction. One of the most common types of service bureaus processes the payroll of various customer entities.

When an entity uses one of these service bureaus, also referred to as **service organizations,** AU-C section 402, Audit Considerations Relating to an Entity Using a Service Organization, provides guidance as to the impact on an audit. It defines a service organization as "an organization or segment of an organization that provides services to user entities that are relevant to those user entities' internal control over financial reporting."

The objective of the "user auditor" (the auditor of the client using the services of the service organization), are to obtain an understanding of the nature and significance of the services provided, and evaluate their effect on the user entity's internal control in order to assess the risks of material misstatement, and to design and perform audit procedures responsive to those risks.

Since the auditor is not in a position to examine the activities of such an outside organization, they will often need to rely on reports of the auditor of the service organization itself, referred to as the **service auditor**. The latter will usually issue a report on the internal control structure that the former may consider in assessing the internal control structure of the client. The report on internal control structure by the service organization's auditor will describe the services of the organization that are covered by the report and a description of the auditor's procedures. This will enable the auditor of one of the service organization's customers to understand the overall impact of the service organization's work on the internal control structure of the customer. Before relying on such a report, the auditor should be satisfied as to the competence and independence of the service auditor, and the adequacy of the standards under which the report was issued.

The report of the service organization's auditor will assist the customer's auditor in gaining an understanding of the internal control structure of the customer, to the extent it depends on the service organization's work. This will not, however, be considered a basis for determining the effectiveness of the customer's internal control structure, so the use of the report is not a division of responsibility. As a result, there must be **no** reference to the auditor of the service organization in the audit report on the financial statements of the customer.

Transactions processed by **service organization** (payroll processing) (AU-C 402/AT-C 320)
- TofC in place at client.
- TofC in place at service organization by another auditor.
  - Report on whether controls have been implemented and controls operating effectiveness.
- Get report from the other Auditor (service auditor).
  - *Expresses an opinion* on management's assertions regarding:
    - Management's description of the service organization's system fairly presents the system that was designed and implemented during the period.
    - The controls related to the control objectives stated in management's description were suitably *designed and operated effectively* during the period.
  - The report also includes a description of the tests of controls and the results of those tests that were performed by the service auditor.
  - Description of the Scope and nature of procedures performed.

- o   ID party specifying objectives.
- o   ID purpose of engagement.
- o   ID parties Intended use.
- A service auditor should inquire of management about subsequent events.

As part of obtaining an understanding of the internal controls of a client using a service organization, the auditor should *obtain an understanding* as to *how* the client uses the service organization. The understanding will include:
- The nature of the services provided;
- The significance of the services to the user entity;
- The effect on the user entity's internal control;
- The nature and materiality of transactions that are processed by the service organization;
- Interaction between the activities of the user entity and of the service organization;
- The nature of the relationship between the entities; and
- Contractual terms for activities performed by the service organization.

The auditor will also evaluate the internal controls established by the user entity to administer the relationship with the service organization. The entity may, for example, have controls to verify the accuracy of the output of the service organization. The auditor will use the understanding of the nature and significance of the services provided by the service organization, along with the entity's related controls, to identify and assess risks of material misstatement that may result.

In some cases, the auditor will be unable to obtain a sufficient understanding of the nature and significance of the relationship with a service organization using the resources available through the user entity. In such cases, the auditor will obtain a sufficient understanding by performing one or more of the following:
- Obtaining and reading a type 1 or type 2 report, if available;
- Obtain information from contact with the service organization, through the user entity;
- Apply procedures directly to the operations of the service organization; or
- Use the work of another auditor applying procedures designed to obtain the necessary information.

There are *two reports* that the auditor of a service organization may issue:

- **A type 1 report** is a report on management's description of the service organization's system of controls and the suitability of the **design of** the controls. It consists of:
    - o   Management's description of the system;
    - o   Management's written assertion that, in all material respects, based on appropriate criteria,
        - ▪   The description of the system fairly presents the system that was designed and implemented as of a specified date and
        - ▪   Controls related to objectives stated in management's description were suitably designed to achieve those objectives; and
    - o   A report from the auditor of the service organization, referred to as the service auditor, expressing an opinion in relation to management's written assertions.

- **A type 2 report** is a report on management's description of the service organization's system of controls and the suitability of the **design of and the operating effectiveness** of the controls. It consists of:
    - o   Management's description of the system;
    - o   Management's written assertion that, in all material respects, based on appropriate criteria,

- The description of the system fairly presents the system that was designed and implemented as of a specified date,
- Controls related to objectives stated in management's description were suitably designed to achieve those objectives, and
- The controls related to the specified objectives were *operating effectively* throughout the specified period; and

o A report from the auditor of the service organization, referred to as the service auditor, expressing an opinion in relation to management's written assertions and describing the *tests of controls* performed and the *results* of those tests.

To rely upon a type 1 or type 2 report, the auditor should:
- Determine that the date of a type 1 report, or the period covered by a type 2 report is appropriate for the auditor's needs;
- Evaluate whether the evidence provided by the report is appropriate and sufficient for the purpose of obtaining an understanding of the user's internal control; and
- Determine if the user entity has developed controls that are complementary to those of the service organization that address risks of material misstatement relating to relevant assertions in the user's financial statements.

When the auditor of the user entity intends to rely on the controls at the service organization, they must be subjected to tests of controls, which may be accomplished by:
- Obtaining and reading a type 2 report;
- Applying tests of controls at the service organization; or
- Using another auditor to perform tests of control at the service organization.

If the auditor's test of controls consists of obtaining and reading a type 2 report, the auditor will evaluate the report to determine:
- Whether it is for an appropriate period;
- Whether there are complementary controls at the user entity identified by the service organization as addressing risks of material misstatement and, if so, determining if those controls have been designed and implemented and applying tests of controls to them;
- If the time period covered by tests of controls is adequate and evaluating the length of time since testing; and
- Whether tests of controls performed by the service auditor provide sufficient appropriate audit evidence to support the user auditor's risk assessment.

Lecture 3.09

INVESTING & FINANCING CYCLE

The **investing and financing** cycle deals with transactions involving acquisition and disposal of assets other than inventory and transactions with creditors and shareholders. Lately the exam has done significant testing on Derivatives in the TBS section of the Audit exam. Substantive testing for derivatives will be covered in more detail in the audit evidence section.

Since there are typically very few transactions in these areas in a typical year for a client, an auditor will often find it most efficient to ignore the internal control structure and simply test the few transactions that took place. In this case, the auditor will:
- Not test the controls;
- Assess risk of material misstatement at the same level as inherent risk, assuming that control risk is at the maximum level, generally resulting in a high RMM; and

- Reduce detection risk by performing extensive substantive tests.

In those less frequent cases where a large number of transactions have occurred, the auditor may find it more efficient to rely on the internal control structure rather than test the numerous transactions that took place. In this case, the auditor will:
- Test the controls to determine their effectiveness;
- Reduce the risk of material misstatement based on the results of the tests of controls; and
- Accept higher detection risk by performing only limited substantive tests.

As with the other cycles, the auditor is concerned with the relationship of the internal control procedures to the management assertions on the financial statements. Examples of controls that support the assertions with regard to **investments** include (**PERCV**):
- **Presentation & Disclosure** – The controller determines that securities are classified in the records correctly as trading securities, available-for-sale securities, or held-to-maturity securities, based on management decisions as to the intent of holding them.
- **Existence or Occurrence** – The treasurer vouches the agreement of broker advices on purchases with cancelled checks.
- **Rights & Obligations** – Securities on hand are examined by senior management to ensure that they are registered in the name of the company.
- **Completeness & Cutoff** – The internal auditor makes a list of securities in bank safe deposit boxes and compares them with the securities listed in the records.
- **Valuation, Allocation & Accuracy** – The controller compares current market prices with the listed values of securities.

Applying the **RACE** mnemonic for account balances:
- **R**ights and obligations – Management examines investment securities to verify that they are registered in the name of the entity or confirms such with custodians of the investments.
- **A**llocation and Valuation – The recorded values of investments are periodically compared to current market prices.
- **C**ompleteness – The investments on hand and held by custodians are periodically reconciled to their recorded amounts.
- **E**xistence – The entity maintains physical custody of investments in a secure physical location or they are maintained in the custody of a trustee, which can be confirmed.

The procedures will typically be applied by management or other employees at a very high level, reflecting the extremely large value and great danger of fraud in connection with marketable securities. Requiring two officers to be involved in access is common. In fact, it is generally best to have an independent trustee maintain possession of securities so that they are safeguarded from all misappropriation by company employees.

AU-C 501 presents guidance on auditing **Derivative instruments**, hedging activities, and investments in both debt and equity securities. Applicable accounting standards are in the FASB Codification, Topic 815, Derivatives and Hedging.

Internal Controls

Inherent risk associated with investments, particularly marketable securities, is generally high, largely due to the fact that their value is readily determinable and they are frequently easily transferrable.

Inherent Risk Assessment (IR): Factors affecting inherent risk in this area include:
- Management's investment objectives
- Complexity of the security or derivative instrument
- Whether the transaction giving rise to the security involved cash
- The entities with the security or derivative in question
- Whether the derivative is stand-alone or an embedded feature of a separate agreement
- External factors affecting management's assertions such as credit, market and legal risks
- Evolving GAAP with respect to derivatives and investments
- Reliance on outside parties
- Assumptions about future conditions

Internal controls reduce control risk such that, regardless of a high inherent risk, risk of material misstatement can be reduced. When internal controls in relation to investments are expected to reduce control risk below the maximum, reducing the risk of material misstatement, specific controls are associated with management assertions and tests of controls are performed to gather evidential matter regarding their operating effectiveness.

Control Risk Assessment (CR): Identify specific controls applicable to assertions and gather evidential matter regarding their operating effectiveness (tests of controls). Examples of controls include:
- Monitoring of investment activities and reporting by independent control staff;
- Senior management approval of transactions;
- Accurate risk measurement systems for investments and derivatives;
- Regular reconciliations to control account balances;
- Definitions and regular reviews of limits and constraints on investment activities; and
- Regular reviews of controls by senior management or some independent body.
  - As CR↑ (increases) the auditor's acceptable level of DR↓ (decreases), which means the auditor will perform MORE ↑ Substantive Testing.

Substantive Procedures (discussed in more detail in Audit Evidence)
Since derivatives are required to be reported at fair value, the auditor is required to evaluate whether the fair values of investments in derivatives have been determined appropriately, using an acceptable valuation method. Substantive procedures in the area of investments in Derivatives should be designed to test management's assertions with regard to (**PERCV**):
- **Presentation & Disclosure** – This will involve **reading disclosures** to make certain they are in compliance with GAAP; determining if securities have been pledged as collateral for indebtedness through **inquiries** and **inspection** of documents; and determining that investments are appropriately classified through inquiries of management.
- **Existence** – This may involve the **inspection** of securities on hand; **confirmations** with brokers or other third parties either holding securities or who may be counter-parties; **reviewing** documents; and, when appropriate, **inspecting** documentation of settlement or realization.
- **Rights & Obligations** – This may involve the **review** of documents and **confirmations** with counterparties.
- **Completeness** – This may involve **review** of minutes of the board of directors or others responsible for governance; **tests of subsequent transactions** for evidence of realization or

settlement; **confirmations** with counterparties, financial institutions, brokers, and others; and **evaluating beginning amounts** for disposition of inclusion in ending amounts.

- **Valuation:**
  - o For valuation based on cost:
    - ▪ Inspection of documentation
    - ▪ Confirmation
  - o For valuation based on financial results of investee:
    - ▪ Obtaining audit evidence supporting investee's results
    - ▪ Reading available financial statements of investee
  - o For valuation based on fair value:
    - ▪ Obtaining quoted market prices on exchanges when available
    - ▪ Obtaining quoted market prices from broker-dealers for unlisted securities
    - ▪ Obtaining estimates, including those using models like Black-Scholes

An entity uses derivatives as hedges to protect itself against various risks that may be inherent in the assets or liabilities they hold, in anticipated transactions, or other aspects of their business. The purpose of the hedge is to shift the risk to a counterparty. For example:

- An entity with a fixed rate receivable may be concerned that fluctuations in interest rates will affect its fair value. They might enter into an interest rate swap in which they will pay out interest at a fixed rate, to offset the interest received, and receive interest from the counterparty at a variable rate.
  - o As a result, they will always be paying the market rate of interest and changes in the fair value of the note will be offset by changes in the fair value of the derivative used as a hedge.
  - o This would be considered a **fair value hedge.**
- An entity with a variable rate receivable may be concerned about the uncertainty of future cash inflows due to fluctuations in the interest rate. They might enter into an interest rate swap in which they will pay out interest at a variable rate, to offset the interest received, and receive interest from the counterparty at a fixed rate.
  - o As a result, regardless of changes in the market interest rate, the entity will receive a steady and predictable stream of interest cash inflows.
  - o This would be considered a **cash flow hedge**.

A cash flow hedge may also be used to transfer risk associated with a forecasted transaction. A company planning to purchase goods or services from a foreign supplier may enter into a forward exchange contract to make certain that a change in the foreign currency exchange rates does not adversely affect the cash flows associated with the transaction.

In order to apply hedge accounting to a derivative instrument, at the inception management must designate the derivative as a hedge; formally document the hedging relationship, the entity's risk management strategy for using the hedge, and the method of assessing its effectiveness; and have the expectation that the hedge will be highly effective. The auditor should gather evidence that management has met these requirements. In addition:

- For fair value hedges, the auditor should obtain evidence to support the recorded change in the hedged item that is attributable to the hedged risk.
- For a cash flow hedge of a forecasted transaction, the auditor should obtain evidence that supports management's determination that the forecasted transaction will probably occur. Support may include evidence:
  - o Regarding the frequency of similar past transactions.
  - o Supporting the entity's ability to execute the transaction.
  - o Indicating the loss that might result if the transaction does not occur.

      o Supporting the likelihood that substantially different transactions might be used to achieve the same business purpose.

Most testing related to **Property, plant, and equipment** transactions concerns itself with the different types of controls that reduce the risk of misstatement. In a good internal control structure, the internal audit staff will periodically inspect physical assets. This cycle includes acquisitions, disposals and depreciation expense. Among the **objectives** are:

- Verifying the *existence* of recorded assets by Vouching from records to the physical assets. This can assist in identifying unrecorded disposals.
- Verifying the completeness of acquisitions by Tracing from the physical assets to the records. This can assist in identifying unrecorded acquisitions.

A common problem involves the recording of equipment purchases in expense accounts, especially for repairs and maintenance. Besides the tracing of physical assets to records mentioned above, the internal audit staff may also examine the relevant accounts and compare them with budgeted amounts, since large variances may indicate the expensing of costs that should have been capitalized.

PRODUCTION AND CONVERSION CYCLE

The **production and conversion cycle** deals with manufacturing operations. Most of the controls are similar to those in the purchasing and spending cycle, since inventory may be involved in both cycles, the difference being whether they were manufactured or purchased. Acquisition of, and accounting for, raw materials purchased in a manufacturing process would be similar to merchandise inventory in a nonmanufacturing entity.

Examples of controls related to the management assertions for manufactured inventory include:

- **Presentation & Disclosure –** Direct labor charged to individual time tickets is compared to the total direct labor charged to work-in-process, in order to ensure direct labor costs have not been charged to manufacturing overhead.
- **Existence or Occurrence** – Perpetual inventory records are compared with goods on hand.
- **Completeness & Cutoff –** Forms used for material requisitions are prenumbered and periodically accounted for.
- **Valuation, Allocation & Accuracy** – Subsidiary records are periodically reconciled to inventory control accounts.

Using the mnemonic **RACE** for account balances:

- **R**ights and obligations – Terms of notes, lines of credit, and other debt instruments are evaluated to determine if inventories have been pledged as collateral.
- **A**llocation and Valuation – Allocations of salaries and wages to inventory are reviewed to make certain appropriate amounts are included.
- **C**ompleteness – Forms used for the acquisition of raw materials and other items are prenumbered and all numbers are accounted for.
- **E**xistence – Perpetual inventory records are regularly reconciled to goods in inventory to make certain that recorded amounts are still on hand.

As with the purchasing and spending cycle, the objectives within the production and conversion cycle include properly recording and executing transactions. In addition, an especially difficult objective of internal control with respect to manufacturing processes is maintaining proper custody as raw materials become work-in-process and then finished goods. In contrast, inventory in a merchandising company normally only goes from the receiving department to inventory when acquired and then from inventory to the shipping department when sold.

Lecture 3.10

CLASS QUESTIONS

Please see the Class Questions and Class Solutions for this Lecture at the end of this Section.

Lecture 3.11

DOCUMENTING THE INTERNAL CONTROL STRUCTURE

An auditor is **required to** document the understanding of a client's internal control. There is no specific means of documentation required and the auditor may select any method, or combination of methods, that best suits the needs of the auditor in being able to apply the understanding to result in an audit that is both efficient and effective.

Internal Control Questionnaire (ICQ) Yes (strength) / No (weakness) questions covering all control activities:

One common form of documentation is the **internal control questionnaire** (**ICQ**). A questionnaire always phrases questions in a form that requires a **yes or no** answer for each question, with a yes answer indicating the presence of a potentially useful control, and a no response indicating a weakness. This is consistent with the emphasis of the auditor on finding **strengths** in the system to rely on.

A well-designed questionnaire will include questions related to each of the different types of control activities (from the PRAISE mnemonic) that may be utilized in an internal control structure. There is no perfect questionnaire that can be memorized for the exam, but the following list includes questions that can be adapted to individual TBS types of questions (these questions should be made more precise by referring to documents and personnel that are used in the specific department that is being tested). For each of the six activities, two potential questions are provided, since recommended solutions usually have contained around 12 questions spread over all the activities (**PRAISE**):

- **Physical controls** – Is proper security maintained over valuable department assets? Are there adequate safeguards over unused documents?
- **Recording** – Are transactions documented as to all relevant terms and descriptions? Are documents prenumbered and periodically accounted for?
- **Authorization** – Are transactions authorized by personnel at least one level above the request level? Are the third parties involved in transactions approved in advance?
- **Independent checks** – Are documents compared to verify their agreement before transactions are executed? Are records periodically reconciled to related documents?
- **Segregation of duties** – Is the principal function of the department (Authorization, Recording, or Custody) independent of each of the other two functions?
- **Evaluate performance** – Are there written department policies and procedures? Are unusual or uncompleted transactions periodically investigated?
- **Segregation of duties** – Are the principal functions of each process, authorization, recording, custody, and comparison (ARCC) independent of one another?
  - **Authorization** – Are transactions authorized by personnel at least one level above the request level?

   o **Recording** – *Are transactions documented as to all relevant terms and descriptions? Are documents prenumbered and periodically accounted for?*

   o **Custody** of assets – Is custody limited to those with a need to have access? Are those with access subjected to bonding or appropriate background checks?

   o **Comparison** – Are physical assets periodically reconciled to recorded amounts? Are normal activities, such as bank deposits, subject to comparisons of recorded amounts to support documents, such as comparing daily deposits to remittance listings or reconciling amounts in cash registers?

Normally, it is possible to identify at least one document, record, or asset to fit each question. Thus, a questionnaire involving the production cycle might ask, "Is proper security maintained over work-in-process inventories?" One involving the payroll cycle might ask, "Is proper security maintained over signature plates?"

- **To prepare ICQ/Narrative**
  - What cycle are you in?
  - Key controls (ARCCS).
  - For each document.
    - PPN? (Preprinted, pre-numbered, numerical sequence).
    - Information on the document?
    - Send copies to whom?

Among the biggest challenges of using an ICQ is the preparation of the questionnaire itself. In order to be effective, the auditor must understand the nature of the cycle being evaluated well enough to be able to include a question about every control that should be included in the system in order for internal controls to be effective. If the auditor neglects to include a question about a control that may be considered necessary to support one of management's assertions, there will not be a "no" answer to indicate to the auditor that there is a control deficiency.

The preparation of an ICQ involves the application of a systematic process that begins with identifying the system that is being evaluated. The auditor then determines what account balances or classes of transactions are affected by that system. Sales and accounts receivable are affected by the revenue cycle, for example, while inventory and accounts payable is affected by the purchases cycle.

Once the auditor has identified which account balances and classes of transactions are affected by the cycle being evaluated, the auditor should next determine where in the cycle (SACRED) there should be controls for each of the assertions relevant to that account balance or class of transaction. In the sales or revenue cycle, for example, evidence that a transaction occurred will primarily be created during the initiation (Start) of a transaction.

- The auditor will determine what evidence would indicate that a recorded transaction actually occurred, which may be a sales order from the customer.
- The auditor will then devise a question that will indicate that such evidence is obtained in the initiation of a sales transaction.

It should be kept in mind that there may be evidence regarding one or more assertions in several of the phases of the cycle. In addition, there are many ways in which evidence may be created and obtained. As a result, questions must be made general enough to accommodate the client's system, since the questionnaire is developed before the auditor knows the client's system, yet specific enough to make certain that there are, in fact, controls that are designed to prevent errors or fraud, or to detect and correct them on a timely basis.

In order for a questionnaire to be effective, the auditor will also have to anticipate the forms that the client should use, how many copies of each form will be needed, and how those copies should be distributed. Without this information, a question with a yes or no answer is unlikely to provide the auditor with information about forms that are used and their disposition, an essential element of internal control. The auditor also needs to determine what information should be on each form so that appropriate questions can be formulated.

The auditor will also have to design the questionnaire to identify any circumstances where there is not appropriate segregation of duties. This may require the auditor to anticipate what individual, or what department, within the client's organization should have responsibility for each component so that a question with a yes or no answer can be developed.

Flowcharts and Narratives are other potentially effective forms of internal control documentation. Both perform essentially the same function in that both a flowchart and a narrative generally describe each step in a cycle in sequence; identifies the party or department responsible for performing the procedure; indicates what forms enter the cycle, such as a customer's purchase order, or are created in the cycle, such as a material requisition form, how many copies are created, and how those copies are distributed; and most other aspects of the cycle. While the narrative uses a written description, however, the flowchart uses a diagram to describe the same process.

- An *advantage of the narrative* is that it is easy to understand and often provides users a clearer view of the flow of a system and the interaction among the participants than other forms of documentation. Disadvantages, however, are that it is often difficult to identify whether responsibilities are properly segregated and it may be difficult to trace the flow of documents.
- An *advantage of flowcharts* is that it is immediately clear whether there is appropriate segregation of duties and the flow of documents can be readily seen. A disadvantage is that, since most flowcharts are organized by department, the flow of a transaction may not be readily determinable.

Candidates are often asked to *identify strengths or weaknesses* in internal control based on a narrative or a flowchart. These questions are best handled by the following process:
- Examine each symbol in the flowchart or each sentence in the narrative.
- Determine if the symbol or sentence represents a control activity (PIPS).
- Identify the assertion that the control activity relates to (CPA-CO or RACE).
- Evaluate whether the control activity is likely to be effective in providing assurance that an error or fraud will not cause a misrepresentation related to the assertion if the control activity is operating effectively.
- Based on which of the components of the cycle is affected (ARCC), ascertain that it is not being performed in the same department or by the same party performing an incompatible function.

SYMBOL	DESCRIPTION	SYMBOL	DESCRIPTION
	Manual Operation (Prepare, compare or match)		Manual Input (keyboard)
	Computer Operation or Process (Print P.O)		Input or Output (general ledger)
	Document (Invoice, p.o., error listing)		Magnetic Tape (Master payroll data file)
	On Page Connector (to connect to a different location on the page without drawing a connecting line)		Off Page Connector (from Customer)
	A decision – (granting credit, If, then, else)		Off-line storage (file by name, date, order number)
	Magnetic disc storage (customer credit file)		On-line storage (disc, drum)

Lecture 3.12

CLASS QUESTIONS

Please see the Class Questions and Class Solutions for this Lecture at the end of this Section.

INTERNAL CONTROL REPORTS AND COMMUNICATIONS

Auditors have a responsibility to communicate with management and those charged with their clients' governance regarding certain internal control matters. Those responsibilities vary, depending on the nature of the engagement.

Under GAAS

- o **1 –** An auditor of nonissuers is required to communicate identified weaknesses in internal control.
- o **2 –** An auditor may be engaged to perform an examination of internal control as of a specified date or for a period of time (Integrated audit).
  - ▪ Such an engagement may only be accepted when integrated with an audit of the entity's financial statements.
  - ▪ As a result of such an engagement, the auditor issues a report on the effectiveness of the entity's internal control.

Under PCAOB

- o **3 –** An auditor of issuers is required to report on management's assertion regarding the effectiveness of internal control as of a specified date.

GAAS I/C Reports		PCAOB
1. Financial Statement Audit	**2. GAAS Engagement (Integrated audit)**	**3. PCAOB Audit**
GAAS (AU-C 265)	GAAS (AU-C 940) **"Audited** in accordance with GAAS"	PCAOB AS 2201 **"Audited** in accordance with standards of the PCAOB"
Controls → Rely on	All Controls	All Controls
No Opinion → Disclaimer	Opinion → Mgt maintained effective I/C over financial reporting	Opinion → Mgt maintained effective I/C over financial reporting
Letter of Recommendation (LOR)		
- Purpose of audit = opinion on financial statements but not on Internal Controls	*Inherent limitations* that I/C may not prevent/ detect and correct misstatements *Projection* subject to risks	*Inherent limitations* that I/C may not prevent/ detect and correct misstatements *Projection* subject to risks
- Definition of significant deficiency & material weakness		
- Identify significant deficiency & Material Weaknesses		
- Limited use statement (No general public viewing – giving it to management. Limited because you only looked at controls you rely on).	For General Distribution	For General Distribution
Written Comm Req'd to Mgt: govn (w/l 60 days) Control deficiency: YES** NO Significant deficiency: YES YES Material weakness: YES YES ** If auditor thinks it warrants attention	**To Mgt chrgd governan (by report release date)** YES NO (60 days) YES YES YES YES	**To Mgt To audit comm (by report release date)** YES NO YES YES YES YES

1. Internal Control Reports for a Financial Statement Audit under GAAS (AU-C 265)

Communicating Internal Control Related matters identified in an Audit of Financial Statements (AU-C 265) (In connection with Nonpublic Companies – Nonissuers)

The auditor obtains an understanding of a client's internal control as part of the understanding of the entity and its environment, for the purpose of assessing the risk of material misstatement (RMM) of the financial statements and to determine the nature, timing, and extent of further audit procedures. During the course of obtaining that understanding, the auditor may become aware of deficiencies in internal control. **AU-C section 265** requires the auditor to communicate to those charged with governance and management deficiencies in internal control that, in the auditor's judgment, are sufficiently important to merit their attention.

"A **deficiency** in internal control exists (**Control deficiency**) when the design or operation of a control does not allow management or employees, in the normal course of performing their assigned functions, to prevent, or detect and correct misstatements on a timely basis." As indicated, a deficiency may be in **design or operation**.
- A deficiency in *design* occurs when either a needed control has not been put into place, or a control that has been put into place is not designed to mitigate the risk it was intended to address.
- A deficiency in *operation* occurs when either a well-designed control is not operating as designed or the individual responsible for performing the control lacks the authority or ability to perform it effectively.

In addition to deficiencies identified while the auditor is obtaining an understanding of internal control, the auditor may identify control deficiencies during risk assessment. When an auditor assesses RMM as moderate to high for a management assertion, it implies that either:
- Inherent risk is high and of a nature that an effective control could not be designed and effectively put into operation.
- Inherent risk is high and of a nature that an effective control could be designed and effectively put into operation, but that is not the case due to a deficiency in design or operation.

When an auditor becomes aware of deficiencies in internal control, the auditor will evaluate them to determine if they amount to **material weaknesses** or **significant deficiencies**.
- <u>**A material weakness**</u> is defined as "a deficiency, or combination of deficiencies, in internal control, such that there is a reasonable possibility that a *material misstatement* of the entity's financial statements will not be prevented, or detected and corrected, on a timely basis."
- <u>**A significant deficiency**</u> is defined as "a deficiency, or combination of deficiencies, in internal control that is less severe than a material weakness yet important enough to merit attention by those charged with governance."

Two factors that the auditor will consider when evaluating a <u>**control deficiency**</u> to determine if it is a significant deficiency or a material weakness, are *probability and magnitude*. In general, when a control deficiency exists, the auditor evaluates the likelihood that it will result in a misstatement to the financial statements. The likelihood of a misstatement might be:
- Remote
- Reasonably possible
- Probable

In addition, the magnitude of misstatement that might result might be either:
- Immaterial
- Material

Clearly, a deficiency in a control that should prevent, or detect and timely correct, a misstatement that would not be material and is only remotely likely to occur would be neither a significant deficiency nor a material weakness. A deficiency in a control that should prevent, or detect and timely correct, a misstatement that would cause the financial statements, taken as a whole, to be materially misstated and is probably going to occur would clearly be a material weakness. Evaluation of anything in between is a matter of auditor judgment.

If an auditor determines that a deficiency, or combination of deficiencies, is not a material weakness, the auditor should consider if prudent officials, having the same knowledge of the facts and circumstances, would draw the same conclusion.

Material weaknesses are indicated by:
- Ineffective oversight by those charged with governance.
- Restatements of prior years' financial statements due to material misstatements due to error or fraud.
- Material misstatements that would have not been detected by the company's internal control, but were identified by the auditor.
- Fraud by senior management, whether material or immaterial.

Although identifying such deficiencies is not an objective of the audit, the auditor must notify the client, management and those **charged with Governance (board, audit committee)**, in writing of any significant deficiencies or material weaknesses that come to the auditor's attention. This requirement includes significant deficiencies and material weaknesses that were previously communicated and have not yet been resolved. The communication is best made by the *report release date*, but should be made no later than **60 days** after the report release date. They may also be communicated during the audit, if the auditor sees fit.

The communication of significant deficiencies and material weaknesses is required to be in writing. The written communication should:
- State that the **purpose** of the audit was to report on the financial statements and not to provide assurance on the effectiveness of internal control.
- Indicate that the auditor is not expressing an opinion on the effectiveness of internal control.
- Include a statement that the auditor's consideration of internal control was not designed to identify all significant deficiencies or material weaknesses.
- Include the **definition** of material weaknesses and, if applicable, significant deficiencies.
- *Identify* which matters noted are considered significant deficiencies and which are material weaknesses.
- State that the communication is intended solely for management, those charged with governance, and others within the organization, and is NOT intended for any others (**Limited Use statement**).

A written report indicating that *no material weaknesses* were identified may be issued; however, a written report indicating that *no significant deficiencies* were identified may not be issued.

Those charged with Governance is defined as the persons with responsibility for overseeing the strategic direction of the entity and obligations related to the accountability of the entity. This may include the board of directors and audit committee. The internal control report is generally issued to Management and those charged with Governance.

In addition to the written communication to governance, per the clarity standards, the auditor is required to provide the following to an appropriate level of management on a timely basis:
- A written communication indicating significant deficiencies and material weaknesses that the auditor intends to communicate to the audit committee or those charged with governance.
- A written or oral communication indicating other deficiencies in internal control that:
  - Have not been communicated to management by others
  - Are sufficiently important to merit management's attention

The following is an illustrative of a written communication to management and those charged with governance designed to meet the requirements for communicating internal control related matters identified in a financial statement audit.

INTERNAL CONTROL REPORT
(F/S Audit)

To: Management, the Audit Committee and the Board of Directors (Governance)

(Date: no later than **60 days** after the report release date)

In planning and performing our audit of the financial statements of ABC Company as of and for the year ended December 31, 20XX, in accordance with auditing standards generally accepted in the United States of America, we considered ABC Company's internal control over financial reporting (internal control) as a basis for designing our auditing procedures that are appropriate in the circumstances for the purpose of expressing our opinion on the financial statements, but not for the purpose of expressing an opinion on the effectiveness of the Company's internal control. Accordingly, we do not express an opinion on the effectiveness of the Company's internal control.

Our consideration of internal control was for the limited purpose described in the preceding paragraph and was not designed to identify all deficiencies in internal control that might be significant deficiencies or material weaknesses and therefore, significant deficiencies or material weaknesses may exist that were not identified. However, as discussed below, we identified certain deficiencies in internal control that we consider to be *material weaknesses* [*and other deficiencies that we consider to be* significant deficiencies].

A deficiency in internal control exists when the design or operation of a control does not allow management or employees, in the normal course of performing their assigned functions, to prevent, or detect and correct, misstatements on a timely basis. A material weakness is a deficiency, or a combination of deficiencies, in internal control, such that there is a reasonable possibility that a material misstatement of the entity's financial statements will not be prevented, or detected and corrected, on a timely basis. We consider the following deficiencies to be material weaknesses in internal control:

   [*Describe the material weaknesses that were identified and an explanation of their potential effects.*]

[*A significant deficiency is a deficiency, or combinations of deficiencies, in internal control that is less severe than a material weakness, yet important enough to merit attention by those charged with governance. We consider the following deficiencies in the Company's internal control to be significant deficiencies.*]

   [*Describe the significant deficiencies that were identified and an explanation of their potential effects.*]

This communication is intended solely for the information and use of management, [*identify the body or individuals charged with governance*], others within the organization, and [*identify any specified governmental authorities to which the auditor is required to report*] and is not intended to be, and should not be used by anyone other than these specified parties.

L. Rosenthal, CPA
Santa Monica, CA
April 8, 20XX

Lecture 3.14

2. Engagement to Examine Internal Control *Integrated* with an Audit of Financial Statements under GAAS (AU-C 940)

An Examination of an Entity's Internal Control Over Financial Reporting (ICFR) that is Integrated with an Audit of its Financial Statements (**Nonissuer**).

AU-C Section 940, An Audit of Internal Control Over Financial Reporting (ICFR) that is Integrated with an Audit of Financial Statements provides guidance to be applied by the auditor of a nonissuer when accepting an engagement to report on the entity's internal controls. Whereas an auditor of a nonissuer may accept such an engagement but is not required to do so, an audit of an issuer under PCAOB standards requires the auditor to perform an *integrated engagement* and report on internal controls.

- The auditor will normally examine the **effectiveness** of internal control over financial reporting as of the end of the entity's fiscal year.
  - o The examination may be as of a different date, which should correspond to the date of the balance sheet being audited.
  - o The examination may be for the period of time covered by the financial statements being audited.
- In all cases, the engagement should only be performed for an examination that is integrated with an audit of the entity's financial statements, including the use of the same measure of **materiality.**

The objective of an examination is to **form an opinion** as to the **effectiveness** of internal control over financial reporting (ICFR). The auditor obtains a written assertion from management as to the effectiveness of ICFR. Management's refusal to provide such an assertion is a scope limitation that cannot be overcome.

- The accountant should withdraw from the integrated engagement if allowed to do so by law or regulation.
- If not allowed to do so, the auditor will issue a disclaimer of opinion.

In an integrated engagement, the auditor is required to obtain **sufficient appropriate evidence** to obtain **reasonable assurance** as to whether **material weaknesses** exist as of the date of management's assertion. In performing the examination, the auditor uses the same criteria as management uses in evaluating the effectiveness of internal control over financial reporting.

- Internal control over financial reporting cannot be effective if one or more material weaknesses exist.
- A material weakness may exist even though the financial statements are not materially misstated.
- The auditor is not required to search for internal control deficiencies that are not material weaknesses.

An engagement to examine internal control may only be accepted if management agrees to certain conditions:

- Accepting responsibility for the effectiveness of internal control.
- Evaluating internal control effectiveness using suitable and available criteria.
- Supporting its assertion about the effectiveness of internal control with sufficient appropriate evidence.
- Providing its assertion regarding the effectiveness of internal control in a report accompanying the auditor's report.

An integrated audit is planned and performed to meet the objectives of *both* the audit of the entity's financial statements and the examination of the entity's internal control over financial reporting. As a result, tests of controls should be designed to provide sufficient appropriate evidence to support:

- The auditor's opinion on the effectiveness of internal control as of the end of the period.
- The degree to which the auditor has decided to rely on the entity's internal control to reduce the assessed risk of material misstatement.

The planning of the examination takes into account the auditor's risk assessment, used to identify significant accounts and disclosures, as well as relevant assertions. The auditor should also evaluate whether controls address risks of fraud, including those identified in the discussion among engagement staff held as part of the audit.

- As is true in the audit, the auditor pays more attention to those areas representing greater risk.
- Tests of controls would not be performed when a deficiency in a control would not cause a material misstatement to be more than remote.

In both the audit of the financial statements and the examination of internal control, the auditor uses a **top-down approach:**

- First, the auditor assess risk at the *financial statement level.*
  - Incorporates use of the auditor's overall understanding of internal control.
  - Concentrates on **entity level controls,** including controls over:
    - The control environment
    - Management override
    - Company's risk assessment process
    - Monitoring results
    - Assessing business risk
    - Monitoring the activities of the audit committee
    - The period-end financial reporting process.

- Next, the auditor directs attention to significant accounts and disclosures and their relevant assertions.
  - Attention is directed to accounts, disclosures, and assertions that present a greater than remote possibility of material misstatement.
  - The understanding of risks in the entity's processes is verified, often through the performance of **walkthroughs:**
    - May include Reperformance or recalculation, inquiry, inspection of documents and observation (**RIIO**).

The auditor identifies potential deficiencies in design or operation.

- Controls that address risks of material misstatement in each of the relevant assertions is selected for testing:
  - The auditor performs tests of the effectiveness of both the design and the operation of controls.
  - Testing designed to provide evidence appropriately based for the degree of risk represented by a potential deficiency.

The auditor evaluates the severity of identified deficiencies, which consist of their ***magnitude and their probability:***

- A material weakness has the potential of causing a material misstatement to the financial statements.

- A material weakness indicates at least a reasonable possibility that controls will not prevent the misstatement, nor detect and correct it on a timely basis.

As a result of the examination, the auditor forms an opinion on the effectiveness of the entity's internal control over financial reporting and evaluates management's assertion regarding the internal control contained in a report that accompanies the auditor's report. Management's **report** should contain:
- Acknowledgment of management's responsibility for internal control;
- A description of what was examined, such as controls related to preparing financial statements in accordance with GAAP;
- Identification of the criteria used to evaluate internal control, such as those established by the report of the Committed of Sponsoring Organizations of the Treadway Commission (COSO) entitled Internal Control – Integrated Framework;
- Management's assertion regarding the effectiveness of the entity's internal control.
- A description of any material weaknesses; and
- The date of the assertion.

The auditor should also obtain **written representations** from management, some of which will repeat items in the report. Representations will indicate:
- Management's responsibility for internal control;
- An indication that management has performed an assessment of the entity's ICFR based on a set of criteria that is identified;
- That management's assessment did not incorporate the results of procedures performed by the auditor;
- Management's assessment of ICFR as of a specified date;
- An indication that management has informed the auditor of all deficiencies in ICFR, whether deficiencies in design or operation, separately indicating significant deficiencies and material weaknesses;
- Any fraud either resulting in a material misstatement to the financial statements or involving senior management, management, or other employees involved in ICFR, even if the fraud does not result in a material misstatement to the financial statements;
- An indication as to whether significant deficiencies and material weaknesses previously identified have been resolved, indicating those that have not; and
- An indication as to any changes to ICFR made subsequent to the date being reported on, including any corrective action taken by management.

The auditor *forms an opinion* on the effectiveness of ICFR through the consideration of various factors, including:
- Tests of controls performed for the examination of ICFR, as well as any additional tests of controls performed in relation to the audit of the financial statements.
- Misstatements detected during the course of the audit of the financial statements.
- Deficiencies identified.
- Reports issued by internal auditors.
- The results of substantive procedures performed in the audit of the financial statements, including:
  - The auditor's risk assessment;
  - Findings related to noncompliance with applicable laws and regulations;
  - Related party transactions and complex or unusual transactions;
  - Indications of management bias in the selection of accounting principles or in the development of estimates; and
  - The nature and extent of misstatements detected.

- Management's report.

At the conclusion of the engagement, the auditor communicates certain matters to management and those charged with governance. The communication includes all material weaknesses and significant deficiencies identified by the auditor, including those that may have been identified in a previous period but have not yet been corrected. It should be in writing and made by the date on which the auditor's report is released.

- The auditor also issues a written report to management within **60 days** of the report release date.
- It includes all deficiencies, including those that are not material weaknesses or significant deficiencies.

The auditor issues a **report on internal control** that includes certain elements:

- A title that includes the word "independent."
- An appropriate addressee.
- An *introductory* paragraph containing:
    o The identity of the entity whose ICFR was audited with an indication that ICFR has been audited;
    o The date as of which the ICFR was assessed; and
    o The criteria against which it was measured.

- A section with the subheading "*Management's Responsibility for Internal Control Over Financial Reporting*" that indicates management's responsibilty for:
    o The design, implementation, and maintenance of effective ICFR;
    o Assessing the effectiveness of ICFR; and
    o Providing management's report on ICFR.

- A section with the subheading "*Auditor's Responsibility*": that indicates:
    o The auditor's responsibility to express an opinion on the entity's ICFR based on the audit;
    o That the engagement was conducted in accordance with GAAS, which requires the auditor to plan and perform the audit to obtain reasonable assurance about the effectiveness of ICFR;
    o A description of the audit stating that the auditor performed procedures to obtain evidence about the existence of material weaknesses, that the auditor applied judgment in determining what procedures to perform; and that the audit included obtaining an understanding of ICFR and testing and evaluating its design and operation; and
    o An indication that the auditor believes that the examination sufficiently supports the opinion.
- A section with the subheading "*Definition and Inherent Limitations of Internal Control Over Financial Reporting*" that includes the definition of internal control with an indication of its inherent limitations.
- A section with the subheading "*Opinion*" that contains the auditor's opinion.
- The auditor's signature, the city and state in which the auditor operates, and the date of the report.

An unmodified report will appear as follows:

INDEPENDENT AUDITOR'S REPORT (AU-C 940)

To: Management, the Audit Committee and the Board of Directors

Report on Internal Control Over Financial Reporting

We have **audited** Asher Company's internal control over financial reporting as of December 31, 20XX, based on [*identify criteria, such as those established in Internal Control—Integrated Framework issued by the Committee of Sponsoring Organizations of the Treadway Commission (COSO)*].

Management's Responsibility for Internal Control Over Financial Reporting

Asher Company's management is responsible for designing, implementing, and maintaining (DIM) effective internal control over financial reporting, and for its assessment about the effectiveness of internal control over financial reporting, included in the accompanying [indicate title of management's report].

Auditor's Responsibility

Our responsibility is to express an opinion on Asher Company's internal control over financial reporting based on our audit. We conducted our examination in accordance with auditing standards generally accepted in the United States of America. Those standards require that we plan and perform the audit to obtain reasonable assurance about whether effective internal control over financial reporting was maintained in all material respects.

An audit of internal control over financial reporting involves performing procedures to obtain evidence about whether a material weakness exists. The procedures selected depend on the auditor's judgment, including the assessment of the risks that a material weakness exists. An audit includes obtaining an understanding of internal control over financial reporting and testing and evaluating the design and operating effectiveness of internal control based on the assessed risk.

We believe that the audit evidence we have obtained is sufficient and appropriate to provide a basis for our audit opinion.

Definition and Inherent Limitations of Internal Control Over Financial Reporting

An entity's internal control over financial reporting is a process effected by those charged with governance, management, and other personnel, designed to provide reasonable assurance regarding the preparation of reliable financial statements in accordance with [*indicate the applicable financial reporting framework such as accounting principles generally accepted in the United States of America*]. An entity's internal control over financial reporting includes those policies and procedures that (1) pertain to the maintenance of records that, in reasonable detail, accurately and fairly reflect the transactions and dispositions of the assets of the company; (2) provide reasonable assurance that transactions are recorded as necessary to permit preparation of financial statements in accordance with [*the applicable financial reporting framework indicated above*], and that receipts and expenditures of the entity are being made only in accordance with authorizations of management and those charged with governance; and (3) provide reasonable assurance regarding prevention, or timely detection and correction of unauthorized acquisition, use, or disposition of the entity's assets that could have a material effect on the financial statements.

Because of its *inherent limitations*, internal control over financial reporting may not prevent, or detect and correct misstatements. Also, projections of any assessment of the effectiveness to future periods are subject to the risk that controls may become inadequate because of changes in conditions, or that the degree of compliance with the policies or procedures may deteriorate.

Opinion

In our opinion, Asher Company maintained, in all material respects, effective internal control over financial reporting as of December 31, 20XX, based upon [*identify criteria*].

Report on Financial Statements

We have also audited, in accordance with auditing standards generally accepted in the United States of America, the [*identify financial statements audited*] of Asher Company, and our report dated [*date of report, which should be the same dates as the report on ICFR*] expressed [*indicate nature of opinion*].

G Ruiz, CPA
San Francisco, CA
[Date]

The following is an example of a **Combined** Unmodified Opinion on Internal Control and an Unmodified Audit Opinion on the Financial Statements based on the AICPA's Clarified standards (Note: The audit report portion will be covered in another section) (**Nonissuer**)

Independent Auditor's Report

To: Management, the Audit Committee and the Board of Directors (Governance)

Report on the Financial Statements and Internal Control
We have **audited** the accompanying financial statements of Roger Company, which comprise the balance sheet as of December 31, 20XX, and the related statements of income, changes in stockholder's equity, and cash flows for the year then ended, and the related notes to the financial statements. **We also have <u>audited</u> Roger Company's internal control over financial reporting as of December 31, 20XX, based on [identify criteria].**

Management's Responsibility for the Financial Statements AND Internal Control Over Financial Reporting
Roger Company's management is responsible for the preparation and fair presentation of these financial statements in accordance with accounting principles generally accepted in the United States of America; this includes the design, implementation, and maintenance of effective internal control relevant to the preparation and fair presentation of these financial statements that are free from material misstatement, whether due to error of fraud. **Management is also responsible for its assertion about the effectiveness of internal control over financial reporting, included in the accompanying [title of management's report].**

Auditor's Responsibility
Our responsibility is to express an opinion on these financial statements **and an opinion on Roger Company's internal control over financial reporting based on our audits.** We conducted our audits in accordance with auditing standards generally accepted in the United States of America. Those standards require that we plan and perform the audits to obtain reasonable assurance about whether the financial statements are free of material misstatement **and whether effective internal control over financial reporting was maintained in all material respects.**

An audit of financial statements involves performing procedures to obtain audit evidence about the amounts and disclosures in the financial statements. The procedures selected depend on the auditor's judgment, including assessment of the risks of material misstatement of the financial statements, whether due to fraud or error. In making those risk assessments, the auditor considers internal control relevant to the entity's preparation and fair presentation of the financial statements in order to design audit procedures that are appropriate in the circumstances. An audit of financial statements also includes evaluating the appropriateness of accounting policies used and the reasonableness of significant accounting estimates made by management, as well as evaluating the overall presentation of the financial statements.

An audit of internal control over financial reporting involves performing procedures to obtain evidence about whether a material weakness exists. The procedures selected depend on the auditor's judgment, including the assessment of the risk that a material weakness exists. An audit of internal control over financial reporting involves obtaining an understanding of internal control over financial reporting and testing and evaluating the design and operating effectiveness of internal control over financial reporting based on the assessed risk.

We believe that the audit evidence we have obtained is sufficient and appropriate to provide a basis for our audit opinions.

Definitions and Inherent Limitations of Internal Control Over Financial Reporting
An entity's internal control over financial reporting is a process effected by those charged with governance, management, and other personnel, designed to provide reasonable assurance regarding the preparation of reliable financial statements in accordance with [applicable financial reporting framework, such as accounting principles generally accepted in the United States of America]. An entity's internal control over financial reporting includes those policies and procedures that (1) pertain to the maintenance of records that, in reasonable detail, accurately and fairly reflect the transactions and dispositions of the assets of the entity; (2) provide reasonable assurance that transactions are recorded as necessary to permit preparation of financial statements in accordance with [applicable financial reporting framework, such as accounting principles generally accepted in the United States of America], and that receipts and expenditures of the entity are being made only in accordance with authorizations of management and those charged with governance; and (3) provide reasonable assurance regarding prevention, or timely detection and correction of unauthorized acquisition, use, or disposition of the entity's assets that could have a material effect on the financial statements.

*Because of its **inherent limitations**, internal control over financial reporting may not prevent, or detect and correct misstatements. Also, projections of any assessment of effectiveness to future periods are subject to the risk that controls may become inadequate because of changes in conditions, or that the degree of compliance with the policies or procedures may deteriorate.*

Opinions
In our opinion, the financial statements referred to above present fairly, in all material respects, the financial position of Roger Company as of December 31, 20XX, and the results of its operations and its cash flows for the year then ended in accordance with accounting principles generally accepted in the United States of America. **Also in our opinion, Roger Company maintained, in all material respects, effective internal control over financial reporting as of December 31, 20XX, based on [identify criteria].**

[Auditor's signature]
[Auditor's city and state]
[Date of the auditor's report]

Report Modifications

There are several reasons that an auditors report on ICFR may be modified. Examples include:

- The identification of material weaknesses;
- An incomplete or improper management report;
- A scope limitation;
- Reference to the report of a component auditor; or
- The inclusion of other information in management's report.

Material Weaknesses

Unless there is a limitation on the scope of the engagement, when material weaknesses are identified, the auditor will express an *adverse opinion* on the effectiveness of an entity's ICFR. The report will include a definition of a material weakness and a statement that one or more material weaknesses have been identified.

- The report will also identify material weaknesses described in management's assessment of ICFR.
- When material weaknesses identified by the auditor are not included in management's assessment, the report will be modified to so indicate.

The auditor will also determine the impact, if any, on the opinion on the financial statements and should disclose whether or not the opinion has been affected.

- This may be disclosed in an other-matter paragraph; or
- It may be disclosed in the paragraph identifying the material weakness that was omitted form management's assessment.

The report will include all of the same components as an unmodified report up through the section providing the definition of ICFR and its inherent limitations. Instead of an opinion paragraph following, the remainder of the report will appear as follows:

Basis for Adverse Opinion

A *material weakness* is a deficiency, or a combination of deficiencies, in internal control over financial reporting, such that there is a reasonable possibility that a material misstatement of the entity's financial statements will not be prevented, or detected and corrected, on a timely basis. The following material weakness has been identified and included in the accompanying [*title of management's report*].

[*Identify the material weakness described in management's report*.]

Adverse Opinion

In our opinion, because of the effect of the material weakness described in the *Basis for Adverse Opinion* paragraph on the achievement of the objectives of [*identify criteria*], Asher Company has *not maintained effective internal control over financial reporting* as of December 31, 20XX, based upon [*identify criteria*].

Report on Financial Statements

We have also audited, in accordance with auditing standards generally accepted in the United States of America, the [*identify financial statements audited*] of Asher Company, and our report dated [*date of report, which should be the same dates as the report on ICFR*] expressed [*indicate nature of opinion*]. We considered the material weakness identified above in determining the nature, timing, and extent of audit procedures applied in our audit of the 20XX financial statements, and this report does not affect such report on the financial statements.

G Ruiz, CPA
San Francisco, CA
[Date]

Incomplete or Incorrect Management Report

Management's report may be missing one or more of the elements required to be included by auditing standards. When this is the case, the auditor will request that management revise the report. If management refuses to do so, the auditor will include an *other-matter* paragraph describing the reason the auditor considers the report deficient. If management's report neglects to dislose one or more material weakness, the auditor will issue an *adverse opinion*.

Scope Limitations

When a scope limitation is imposed on the auditor after acceptance of the engagement, the audior should either *withdraw* from the engagement or express a *disclaimer of opinion*. If the scope limitation consists of the client's refusal to provide an assertion regarding the effectiveness of ICFR, the auditor is required to withdraw and will only issue a disclaimer if not allowed to withdraw as a result of law or regulation.

When an auditor issuing a disclaimer of opinion on ICFR has identified one or more material weakness, the disclaimer should define a material weakness and provide a description of any material weaknesses identified.

Making Reference to the Report of a Component Auditor

When an entity includes one or more components, the ICFR of which was audited by a component auditor, the auditor responsible for the report, the engagement auditor, will use the same criteria in determining whether or not to refer to the report of the component auditor as used when reporting on the audit of group financial statements.

Reference should not be made to a component auditor unless the engagement auditor is satisfied that the component auditor conducted an audit in accordance with GAAS, or with the provisions of the PCAOB, if appropriate; and that the component auditor has issued a report on ICFR that is not restricted.

Additional Information in Management's Report

In some circumstances, management's report, or the document containing management's report, will also include additional information. When this is the case:
- The auditor should disclaim an opinion in reference to the additional information; and
- The auditor should read the additional information to make certain that it does not contain information that is inconsistent with management's report or a misstatement of fact.

Lecture 3.15

3. An Audit of Internal Control that is Integrated with an Audit of Financial Statements – PCAOB AS 2201

When auditing the financial statements of entities that report to the SEC under the 1934 act (issuers) and are subject to the requirements of the Public Company Accounting Oversight Board (**PCAOB**), the auditor will have to also perform an audit of internal control over financial reporting (**ICFR**) that is *Integrated* with an audit of financial statements in order to determine that management has complied with Rules 404a & b of the Sarbanes-Oxley Act of 2002.
- Rule 404a requires the annual report to include a report on internal control indicating management's responsibility for internal control and management's assessment of internal control's effectiveness.
- Rule 404b requires the auditor to report on management's assessment of internal control.
  - The auditor does not report on the efficiency or the effectiveness of internal control but reports on management's assessment of it.
  - The Act does not specify a date by which the auditor's report is to be submitted.

The standards for audits of ICFR under AU-C Section 940 were written to apply the guidance in PCAOB AS 2201 to nonissuers. The requirements and guidance are almost identical and, as a result, the information provided will reflect only those **differences** between AS 2201 and AU-C Sectoin 940.

One major difference is that AS 2201 is a *requirement* and auditors of issuers are required to perform an examination of internal control that is integrated with a financial statement audit, which expresses an opinion as of the date of the financial statements. An examination under GAAS, however, is performed only if the auditor is engaged to do so.

While most requirements are the same, under AS 2201, an auditor has greater responsibilities for the **communication** of internal control deficiencies:
- **Material weaknesses** *must* be communicated to management and the audit committee in writing prior to the issuance of the auditor's report on internal control over financial reporting.

- **Significant deficiencies** identified by the auditor *must* also be communicated in writing to the audit committee prior to the issuance of the auditor's report on internal control.
- The auditor should also communicate **control deficiencies** that are not significant deficiencies or material weaknesses to managerment in writing on a timely basis.

AS 2201 also provides slightly different definitions of control deficiencies and material weaknesses.

- AS 2201 indicates that a control deficiency "exists when the design or operation of a control does not allow management or employees, in the normal course of performing their assigned functions, to prevent or detect misstatements on a timely basis," while GAAS indicates a control deficiency as existing "when the design or operation of a control does not allow management or employees, in the normal course of performing their assigned functions, to prevent, or detect **and correct**, misstatements on a timely basis."
- The definition of a *material weakness* is also different for the same reason.

The only minor difference between an auditor's report on internal control prepared as a result of the GAAS standards and one issued as a result of AS 2201 is the definition of internal control, which uses the one provided with AS 2201.

Following is an example of the unmodified report (unqualified opinion) on ICFR for a PCAOB Audit that would be issued if **separate reports** on the financial statements and Internal control are issued.

REPORT OF INDEPENDENT REGISTERED PUBLIC ACCOUNTING FIRM
on Internal Control over Financial Reporting (PCAOB AS 2201)

The Board of Directors and Shareholders of ABC Inc.

We have **audited** ABC, Inc.'s internal control over financial reporting **as of** January 31, 20X8, based on criteria established in *Internal Control–Integrated Framework* issued by the Committee of Sponsoring Organizations of the Treadway Commission (the COSO criteria). ABC Inc.'s management is responsible for maintaining effective internal control over financial reporting, and for its assessment of the *effectiveness* of internal control over financial reporting included in the accompanying "Management's Report to Our Shareholders." Our responsibility is to express an opinion on the company's internal control over financial reporting based on our audit.

We conducted our audit in **accordance with the standards of the Public Company Accounting Oversight Board (United States)**. Those standards require that we plan and perform the audit to obtain reasonable assurance about whether effective internal control over financial reporting was maintained in all material respects. Our audit included obtaining an understanding of internal control over financial reporting, assessing the risk that a material weakness exists, testing and evaluating the design and operating effectiveness of internal control based on the assessed risk, and performing such other procedures as we considered necessary in the circumstances. We believe that our audit provides a reasonable basis for our opinion.

A company's internal control over financial reporting is a process designed to provide reasonable assurance regarding the reliability of financial reporting and the preparation of financial statements for external purposes in accordance with generally accepted accounting principles. A company's internal control over financial reporting includes those policies and procedures that (1) pertain to the maintenance of records that, in reasonable detail, accurately and fairly reflect the transactions and dispositions of the assets of the company; (2) provide reasonable assurance that transactions are recorded as necessary to permit preparation of financial statements in accordance with generally accepted accounting principles, and that receipts and expenditures of the company are being made only in accordance with authorizations of management and directors of the company; and (3) provide reasonable assurance regarding prevention or timely detection of unauthorized acquisition, use, or disposition of the company's assets that could have a material effect on the financial statements.

Because of its *inherent limitations*, internal control over financial reporting may not prevent or detect misstatements. Also, projections of any evaluation of effectiveness to future periods are subject to the risk that controls may become inadequate because of changes in conditions, or that the degree of compliance with the policies or procedures may deteriorate.

In our opinion, ABC, Inc. maintained, in all material respects, effective internal control over financial reporting as of January 31, 20X8, based on the COSO criteria.

We also have audited, in accordance with the standards of the Public Company Accounting Oversight Board (United States), the consolidated balance sheets of ABC, Inc. as of January 31, 20X8 and 20X7, and the related consolidated statements of income, shareholders' equity, and cash flows for each of the three years in the period ended January 31, 20X8 and our report dated March 26, 20X8 expressed an unqualified opinion thereon.

W. Philipp, CPAs,
SF, CA
March 26, 20X8

The following is an example of a **combined** Unmodified audit report (unqualified opinion) on the financial Statements and an unqualified Internal Control opinion (Note: The audit report portion will be covered in another section) (**Issuer**).

REPORT OF INDEPENDENT REGISTERED PUBLIC ACCOUNTING FIRM (ISSUER)

To the Audit Committee and Stockholders of Roger Company

[*Introductory paragraph*]

We have **audited** the accompanying balance sheets of Roger Company as of December 31, 20X8 and 20X7, and the related statements of income, stockholders' equity and comprehensive income, and cash flows for each of the years in the three-year period ended December 31, 20X8. ***We also have audited Roger Company's internal control over financial reporting as of December 31, 20X8, based on criteria established in Internal Control – Integrated Framework issued by the Committee of Sponsoring Organizations of the Treadway Commission (COSO).*** Roger Company's management is responsible for these financial statements, ***for maintaining effective internal control over financial reporting, and for its assessment of the effectiveness of internal control over financial reporting, included in the accompanying [title of management's report].*** Our responsibility is to express an opinion on these financial statements ***and an opinion on the company's internal control over financial reporting based on our audits.***

[*Scope paragraph*]

We conducted our audits in accordance with the standards of the Public Company Accounting Oversight Board (United States). Those standards require that we plan and perform the audits to obtain reasonable assurance about whether the financial statements are free of material misstatement ***and whether effective internal control over financial reporting was maintained in all material respects.*** Our audits of the financial statements include examining, on a test basis, evidence supporting the amounts and disclosures in the financial statements, assessing the accounting principles used and significant estimates made by management, and evaluating the overall financial statement presentation. ***Our audit of internal control over financial reporting included obtaining an understanding of internal control over financial reporting, assessing the risk that a material weakness exists, and testing and evaluating the design and operating effectiveness of internal control based on the assessed risk. Our audits also included performing such other procedures as we considered necessary in the circumstances***. We believe that our audits provide a reasonable basis for our opinions.

[*Definition paragraph*]

A company's internal control over financial reporting is a process designed to provide reasonable assurance regarding the reliability of financial reporting and the preparation of financial statements for external purposes in accordance with generally accepted accounting principles. A company's internal control over financial reporting includes those policies and procedures that (1) pertain to the maintenance of records that, in reasonable detail, accurately and fairly reflect the transactions and dispositions of the assets of the company; (2) provide reasonable assurance that transactions are recorded as necessary to permit preparation of financial statements in accordance with generally accepted accounting principles, and that receipts and expenditures of the company are being made only in accordance with authorizations of management and directors of the company; and (3) provide reasonable assurance regarding prevention or timely detection of unauthorized acquisition, use, or disposition of the company's assets that could have a material effect on the financial statements.

[*Inherent limitations paragraph*]

Because of its inherent limitations, internal control over financial reporting may not prevent or detect misstatements. Also, projections of any evaluation of effectiveness to future periods are subject to the risk that controls may become inadequate because of changes in conditions, or that the degree of compliance with the policies or procedures may deteriorate.

[*Opinion paragraph*]

In our opinion, the financial statements referred to above present fairly, in all material respects, the financial position of Roger Company as of December 31, 20X8 and 20X7, and the results of its operations and its cash flows for each of the years in the three-year period ended December 31, 20X8, in conformity with accounting principles generally accepted in the United States of America. ***Also in our opinion, Roger Company maintained, in all material respects, effective internal control over financial reporting as of December 31, 20X8, based on criteria established in Internal Control—Integrated Framework issued by the Committee of Sponsoring Organizations of the Treadway Commission (COSO).***

Aaron & Co. CPAs
San Francisco, California, United States of America
February 20X9.

Previously Reported Weaknesses under PCAOB AS 6115

Under PCAOB AS 6115, the auditor of an issuer may be engaged to report on whether a previously reported *internal control weakness* continues to exist. In such an engagement, the auditor obtains reasonable assurance about whether the weakness continues to exist as of a date specified by management and issues a report to that effect.

The standards for such an engagement involve:
- Planning the engagement.
- Obtaining an understanding of internal control over financial reporting.
- Testing and evaluating whether a material weakness continues to exist.
- Form an opinion on whether a previously reported material weakness continues to exist.

Lecture 3.16

CLASS QUESTIONS

Please see the Class Questions and Class Solutions for this Lecture at the end of this Section.

CLASS QUESTIONS

Work through the below Class Questions while following along with the respective lectures. Once this is complete, you can begin independently practicing what you've learned by quizzing yourself on this course section in your Interactive Practice Questions (IPQ), which can be found in your online Student Dashboard. Your IPQ simulates the computer-based testing experience, and will also help you understand how concepts are applied to the exam. Each question includes answer explanations from expert CPAs that will help you determine why you answered a question correctly or incorrectly. This is key to your success on the CPA Exam.

Lecture 3.05

1. Which of the following is not a component of an entity's internal control?

    a. Control risk.
    b. Control activities.
    c. Monitoring.
    d. Control environment.

2. In obtaining an understanding of an entity's internal control in a financial statement audit, an auditor is required to obtain knowledge about the

	Operating effectiveness of controls	Implementation of controls
a.	Yes	Yes
b.	No	Yes
c.	Yes	No
d.	No	No

3. When an auditor increases the assessed level of control risk (Risk of Material Misstatement) because certain control activities were determined to be ineffective, the auditor would most likely increase the

    a. Extent of tests of controls.
    b. Level of detection risk.
    c. Extent of tests of details.
    d. Level of inherent risk.

4. Which of the following is not a step in an auditor's assessment of Control Risk (Risk of Material Misstatement)?

    a. Evaluate the effectiveness of internal control with tests of controls.
    b. Obtain an understanding of the entity's information system and control environment.
    c. Perform tests of details of transactions to detect material misstatements in the financial statements.
    d. Consider whether controls can have a pervasive effect on financial statement assertions.

5. After obtaining an understanding of internal control and assessing the risk of material misstatement, an auditor decided to perform tests of controls. The auditor most likely decided that

    a. It would be efficient to perform tests of controls that would result in a reduction in planned substantive tests.

    b. Additional evidence to support a further reduction in the risk of material misstatement is **not** available.

    c. An increase in the assessed level of the risk of material misstatement is justified for certain financial statement assertions.

    d. There were many internal control weaknesses that could allow misstatements to enter the accounting system.

6. In assessing Risk of Material Misstatement (Control Risk), an auditor ordinarily selects from a variety of techniques, including

    a. Inquiry and recalculation.

    b. Reperformance and observation.

    c. Comparison and confirmation.

    d. Inspection and verification.

7. Which of the following most likely would not be considered an inherent limitation of the potential effectiveness of an entity's internal control?

    a. Incompatible duties.

    b. Management override.

    c. Mistakes in judgment.

    d. Collusion among employees.

8. When considering internal control, an auditor should be aware of the concept of reasonable assurance, which recognizes that

    a. Internal control may be ineffective due to mistakes in judgment and personal carelessness.

    b. Adequate safeguards over access to assets and records should permit an entity to maintain proper accountability.

    c. Establishing and maintaining internal control is an important responsibility of management.

    d. The cost of an entity's internal control should not exceed the benefits expected to be derived.

Lecture 3.10

9. Sound internal control dictates that immediately upon receiving checks from customers by mail, a responsible employee should

    a. Add the checks to the daily cash summary.

    b. Verify that each check is supported by a prenumbered sales invoice.

    c. Prepare a duplicate listing of checks received.

    d. Record the checks in the cash receipts journal.

10. Tracing shipping documents to prenumbered sales invoices provides evidence that

   a. No duplicate shipments or billings occurred.
   b. Shipments to customers were properly invoiced.
   c. All goods ordered by customers were shipped.
   d. All prenumbered sales invoices were accounted for.

11. In testing controls over cash disbursements, an auditor most likely would determine that the person who signs checks also

   a. Reviews the monthly bank reconciliation.
   b. Returns the checks to accounts payable.
   c. Is denied access to the supporting documents.
   d. Is responsible for mailing the checks.

12. For effective internal control, the accounts payable department generally should

   a. Stamp, perforate, or otherwise cancel supporting documentation after payment is mailed.
   b. Ascertain that each requisition is approved as to price, quantity, and quality by an authorized employee.
   c. Obliterate the quantity ordered on the receiving department copy of the purchase order.
   d. Establish the agreement of the vendor's invoice with the receiving report and purchase order.

13. An auditor most likely would assess control risk (risk of material misstatement) at a high level if the payroll department supervisor is responsible for

   a. Examining authorization forms for new employees.
   b. Comparing payroll registers with original batch transmittal data.
   c. Authorizing payroll rate changes for all employees.
   d. Hiring all subordinate payroll department employees.

14. The purpose of segregating the duties of hiring personnel and distributing payroll checks is to separate the

   a. Authorization of transactions from the custody of related assets.
   b. Operational responsibility from the recordkeeping responsibility.
   c. Human resources function from the controllership function.
   d. Administrative controls from the internal accounting controls.

15. In meeting the control objective of safeguarding of assets, which department should be responsible for

	Distribution of paychecks	Custody of unclaimed paychecks
a.	Treasurer	Treasurer
b.	Payroll	Treasurer
c.	Treasurer	Payroll
d.	Payroll	Payroll

16. The auditor may observe the distribution of paychecks to ascertain whether

   a. Pay rate authorization is properly separated from the operating function.
   b. Deductions from gross pay are calculated correctly and are properly authorized.
   c. Employees of record actually exist and are employed by the client.
   d. Paychecks agree with the payroll register and the time cards.

17. Which of the following departments most likely would approve changes in pay rates and deductions from employee salaries?

   a. Personnel.
   b. Treasurer.
   c. Controller.
   d. Payroll.

Lecture 3.16

18. Which of the following statements is correct concerning significant deficiencies in an audit?

   a. An auditor is required to search for significant deficiencies during an audit.
   b. All significant deficiencies are also considered to be material weaknesses.
   c. An auditor may communicate significant deficiencies during an audit or after the audit's completion.
   d. An auditor may report that **no** significant deficiencies were noted during an audit.

19. In an integrated audit, which of the following is defined as a weakness in internal control that is less severe than a material weakness but important enough to warrant attention by those responsible for oversight of the financial reporting function?

   a. Control deficiency.
   b. Unusual weakness.
   c. Unusual deficiency.
   d. Significant deficiency.

20. An engagement to examine internal control will generally

    a. Require procedures that duplicate those already applied in assessing risk of material misstatement during a financial statement audit.

    b. Increase the reliability of the financial statements that have already been audited.

    c. Be more extensive in scope than the assessment of Risk of Material Misstatement made during a financial statement audit.

    d. Be more limited in scope than the assessment of Risk of Material Misstatement made during a financial statement audit.

21. How do the scope, procedures, and purpose of an examination of internal control compare to those for obtaining an understanding of internal control and assessing risk of material misstatement as part of an audit?

	Scope	**Procedures**	**Purpose**
a.	Similar	Different	Similar
b.	Different	Similar	Similar
c.	Different	Different	Different
d.	Different	Similar	Different

22. For an issuer (public) company audit of internal control, walkthroughs provide the auditor with primary evidence to

	Evaluate the effectiveness of the design of controls	**Confirm whether controls have been implemented**
a.	Yes	Yes
b.	Yes	No
c.	No	Yes
d.	No	No

CLASS SOLUTIONS

1. (**a**) The five components of internal control are the control environment (d), risk assessment, control activities (b), information and communication, and monitoring (c). Control risk is the risk that internal control will not prevent a misstatement due to error or fraud or detect and correct it on a timely basis. It is not a component of internal control.

2. (**b**) The auditor obtains an understanding of internal controls by performing risk assessment procedures that include inquiry, analytical procedures, observation, review of documents, and various other procedures. They are designed to enable the auditor to identify deficiencies in design or in operation, including whether or not controls have been implemented. Tests of controls, which are designed to evaluate the operating effectiveness of controls, are performed only for those controls on which the auditor intends to rely.

3. (**c**) An increase in control risk as a result of the ineffectiveness of a control, increases the risk of material misstatement. In order to maintain a level of audit risk that is sufficiently low, the auditor will be required to decrease, rather than increase, detection risk (b), which is likely to result in an increase in the extent of tests of details. Tests of controls are performed in order to determine whether or not controls can be relied upon (a) and inherent risk is the risk associated with the element of financial reporting and is not within the control of the auditor (d).

4. (**c**) Control risk is the risk that internal control will not prevent material misstatements, whether due to error or fraud, nor detect and correct them on a timely basis. The auditor determines control risk by obtaining an understanding of internal control (b), considering whether controls can have a pervasive effect on financial statement assertions (d), and, for those that can, perform tests of controls to evaluate their effectiveness (a). The assessment of control risk will be used to determine the risk of material misstatement (RMM) of the financial statements, which will be used to determine the nature, timing, and extent of tests of details to be performed.

5. (**a**) An auditor performs tests of controls in relation to those controls that are expected to be effective in the prevention, or detection and correction, of potential material misstatements, which would provide evidence supporting a reduction in RMM (b). If the results prove that they are effective, planned substantive testing can be reduced. An increase in RMM for certain assumptions would apply if tests of controls did not provide evidence that the controls tested were effective or if the auditor decided not to rely on controls, increasing control risk to maximum (c). Controls would not be tested if the auditor believed that there were weaknesses that would allow misstatements, but substantive testing would be increased (d).

6. (**b**) Although an auditor will generally make inquiries in assessing RMM, recalculation is a substantive test, not a risk assessment procedure nor a test of controls (a). Reperformance, such as of a control procedure, and observation are both risk assessment procedures used in assessing RMM. Comparison and confirmation (c) are both substantive procedures and, while inspection may be either a risk assessment procedure or a substantive test, verification is generally more closely associated with substantive testing (d).

7. (**a**) Management override, mistakes in judgment, and collusion among employees (b, c, and d) are all inherent limitations of internal control. Even a well-designed and effectively operating system of internal control cannot prevent errors that result from mistakes in judgment (c) or fraud that results from management override of controls (b) or collusion among employees (d). Incompatible duties, which may result from a lack of sufficient employees, is a deficiency in the design of internal control, not an inherent limitation.

8. (**d**) The concept of reasonable assurance recognizes that there is a cost associated with establishing and maintaining internal controls, which should not exceed the benefit derived from having the control, as opposed to absolute assurance, which would disregard the cost of controls. The fact that internal control may be ineffective due to mistakes or carelessness is an inherent limitation of internal control, one of the reasons we can obtain reasonable, but not absolute assurance as to the effectiveness of internal control (a). While safeguards over access to assets and records do permit proper accountability (b) and establishing and maintaining internal control is an important responsibility of management (c), neither is related to the concept of reasonable assurance.

9. (**c**) Immediately preparing a duplicate list of checks received provides a degree of accountability as one forwarded to the accounting department can be used to verify that the appropriate amount has been deposited by the person responsible for making the deposit, who would receive the other copy. A daily cash summary (a) is likely to be completed at the end of each day, not immediately upon receiving checks in the mail. Recording the checks in the journal (d) and verifying that each check is supported by a prenumbered sales invoice (b) are both performed as part of the vouching and recording processes, not immediately upon receiving the checks.

10. (**b**) Tracing shipping documents to prenumbered sales invoices verifies that all goods shipped have been invoiced. If not, there would be no invoice to match selected shipping documents. Duplicate shipments would be detected by tracing all shipping documents to customer orders and duplicate billings would be detected by tracing all billings to shipping documents (a). Tracing customer orders to shipping documents could determine if all goods ordered by customers were shipped (c) and accounting for the sequence of all sales invoices in the sales journal will determine if all sales invoices were accounted for (d).

11. (**d**) For proper segregation of duties, the person reviewing the bank reconciliation should not have any other duties in relation to cash (a). Once checks are signed, they become negotiable and the person signing them should not relinquish custody to accounts payable (b) or anyone else. The person should, instead, mail the checks to the recipients. The person signing checks needs access to supporting documents to determine if the disbursement is authorized and appropriate (c).

12. (**d**) The person signing checks will cancel supporting documents (a). The purchasing department will ascertain that requisitions are approved by an authorized employee (b) and obliterate the quantity ordered on the receiving department's copy of the purchase order so that they will be required to count the goods received (c). To verify that a voucher or check should be prepared, the accounts payable department will match the vendor's invoice to the purchase order, to make certain that the goods were ordered, and the receiving report to make certain they were received.

13.   (**c**) The payroll department supervisor will examine authorization forms for new employees to make certain they are not paying nonexistent or unauthorized employees (a) and will compare payroll registers to original batch transmittal data to verify that the amount paid is correct (b). The payroll department supervisor will also have responsibility for hiring subordinate employees for that department (d). It is the responsibility of personnel, or human resources, however, to institute payroll rate changes that are ordinarily instituted by the employee's department.

14.   (**a**) Hiring personnel is essentially authorizing that the individual be paid and distribution of payroll checks is custody of related assets, which would be incompatible duties. While hiring personnel is an operational responsibility, distributing payroll checks is not part of the record keeping process (b). While hiring personnel is a human resource function, distributing payroll checks is a function of the treasury, not the controller (c). Segregation of duties is an internal accounting control and an administrative control, which often overlap (d).

15.   (**a**) The treasurer's department is responsible for the custody of the entity's cash. Once paychecks are signed, they are the equivalent of cash and should remain in the custody of the treasurer who should distribute them. Unclaimed paychecks are also the equivalent of cash and should remain in the custody of the treasurer. Payroll is responsible for preparing the checks but should not have custody of them once they are signed.

16.   (**c**) The auditor can determine if pay rate authorization is properly separated from the operating function by determining who is responsible for operations and making certain that the same party is not responsible for pay rate authorizations (a). The auditor can determine if deductions are proper by recalculation (b) and can determine if paychecks agree with the payroll register and time cards by tracing a sample of paychecks to the supporting time cards and also to the payroll register (d). Observing the distribution of paychecks will allow the auditor to see who is receiving them to determine that they actually exist and appear to be employed by the client.

17.   (**a**) The personnel, or human resources, department will generally approve pay rate changes that are recommended by operating personnel, and deductions from employees' salaries. The treasurer has custody of the cash, which should be segregated from authorization of transactions (b), the controller (c) and payroll (d) are responsible for the recordkeeping function, which should also be segregated from authorization of transactions.

18.   (**c**) An auditor obtains an understanding of internal control as part of the understanding of the entity and its environment, not for the purposes of identifying significant deficiencies (a). Significant deficiencies are control deficiencies that are not material weaknesses (b) but are significant enough that the auditor believes they should be brought to the attention of the client. The auditor may report that no material weaknesses were detected as it is assumed that a material weakness would be detected if the auditor met the requirements of standards. Since the auditor is not required to search for significant deficiencies, however, there is no guarantee that they will all be identified.

19.   (**d**) A control deficiency is any deficiency in internal control, which could be a material weakness, a significant deficiency, or neither (a). Although an entity may have an unusual weakness (b) or an unusual deficiency (c), those are not terms associated with the auditor's understanding of internal control. Standards define a significant deficiency as a control deficiency that is not as severe as a material weakness but significant enough to merit the attention of management.

20. **(c)** In the assessment of RMM, the auditor will only test those controls that are expected to be relied upon, more limited in scope than an examination of internal control, not the other way around (d). In an examination of internal control, the auditor expresses an opinion in relation to the effectiveness of internal control, requiring an engagement more extensive in scope. The examination of internal control may require additional procedures but does not require the performance of duplicate procedures (a). The examination of internal control is conducted for the purpose of expressing an opinion related to the effectiveness of internal control and is not related to the auditor's opinion on the financial statements (b).

21. **(d)** The scope of an examination of internal control is different, in fact more extensive, than that for the assessment of RMM since it requires more extensive tests of controls. The procedures are the same in both although, as indicated, there will generally be more procedures, specifically tests of controls, in the examination of internal control. The purpose is different in that the purpose of the examination is to express an opinion while the purpose of the understanding is to determine the nature, timing, and extent of further substantive procedures to be performed in the audit.

22. **(a)** Walkthroughs are used by the auditor in obtaining an understanding of internal control. They may involve inquiry, observation, document inspection, recalculation, and reperformance and are used to identify deficiencies in design and to determine if controls have been put into operation.

Lecture 3.12

TASK-BASED SIMULATIONS

Task-Based Simulation 1

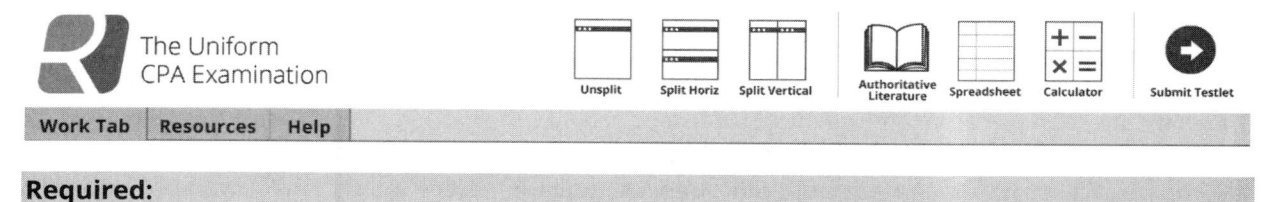

| Work Tab | Resources | Help |

Required:

An auditor's working papers include the narrative description below of the cash receipts and billing portions of Southwest Medical Center's internal control.

Southwest is a healthcare provider that is owned by a partnership of five physicians. It employs 11 physicians, including the five owners, 20 nurses, five laboratory and X-ray technicians, and four clerical workers. The clerical workers perform such tasks as reception, correspondence, cash receipts, billing, accounts receivable, bank deposits, and appointment scheduling. These clerical workers are referred to in the narrative as "office manager.," "clerk #1," "clerk #2," and "clerk #3." Assume that the narrative is a complete description of the system.

NARRATIVE

About two-thirds of Southwest's patients receive medical services only after insurance coverage is verified by the office manager and communicated to the clerks. Most of the other patients pay for services by cash or check when services are rendered, although the office manager extends credit on a case-by-case basis to about 5% of the patients.

When services are rendered, the attending physician prepares a pre-numbered service slip for each patient and gives the slip to clerk #1 for pricing. Clerk #1 completes the slip and gives the completed slip to clerk #2 and a copy to the patient.

Using the information on the completed slip, clerk #2 performs one of the following three procedures for each patient:
- Clerk #2 files an insurance claim and records a receivable from the insurance company if the office manager has verified the patient's coverage, or
- Clerk #2 posts a receivable from the patient on clerk #2's PC if the office manager has approved the patient's credit, or
- Clerk #2 receives cash or a check from the patient as the patient leaves the medical center, and clerk #2 records the cash receipt.

At the end of each day, clerk #2 prepares a revenue summary.

Clerk #1 performs correspondence functions and opens the incoming mail. Clerk #1 gives checks from insurance companies and patients to clerk #2 for deposit. Clerk #2 posts the receipt of patients' checks on clerk #2's PC patient receivable records and insurance companies' checks to the receivables from the applicable insurance companies. Clerk #1 gives mail requiring correspondence to clerk #3.

Clerk #2 stamps all checks "for deposit only" and each day prepares a list of checks and cash to be deposited in the bank. (this list also includes the cash and checks personally given to clerk #2 by patients.) Clerk #2 keeps a copy of the deposit list and gives the original to clerk #3.

Clerk #3 personally makes the daily bank deposit and maintains a file of the daily bank deposits. Clerk #3 also performs appointment scheduling for all of the doctors and various correspondence functions. Clerk #3 also maintains a list of patients whose insurance coverage the office manager has verified.

When insurance claims or patient receivables are not settled within 60 days, clerk #2 notifies the office manager. The office manager personally inspects the details of each instance of nonpayment. The office manager converts insurance claims that have been rejected by insurance companies into patient receivables. Clerk #2 records these patient receivables on clerk #2's PC and deletes these receivable from the applicable insurance companies. Clerk #2 deletes the patient receivables that appear to be uncollectible from clerk #2's PC when authorized by the office manager. Clerk #2 prepares a list of patients with uncollectible balances and gives a copy of the list to clerk #3, who will not allow these patients to make appointments for future services.

Once a month an outside accountant posts clerk #2's daily revenue summaries to the general ledger, prepares a monthly trial balance and monthly financial statements, accounts for the pre-numbered service slips, files payroll forms and tax returns, and reconciles the monthly bank statements to the general ledger. This accountant reports directly to the physician who is the managing partner.

All four clerical employees perform their tasks on PCs that are connected through a local area network. Each PC is accessible with a password that is known only to the individual employee and the managing partner. Southwest uses a standard software package that was acquired from a software company and that cannot be modified by Southwest's employees. None of the clerical employees have access to Southwest's check writing capabilities.

Items to be answered:

A.   Using only the information in the narrative, describe the **strengths** in Southwest's internal control that an auditor most likely could consider in assessing control risk below the maximum level.

B.   Using only the information in the narrative, describe the **weaknesses** in Southwest's internal control that could permit material misstatements to occur in the financial statements. In addition, for each weakness, identify one internal control activity that most likely could help correct that weakness.

Use the following format for requirement **B**:

Weaknesses	Internal control activities

Task-Based Simulation 2

R The Uniform
CPA Examination

Unsplit   Split Horiz   Split Vertical   Authoritative Literature   Spreadsheet   Calculator   Submit Testlet

| Work Tab | Resources | Help |

Required:

You are working for Roger S.P. CPAs. The following partially completed flowchart depicts part of Asher Inc., your client's revenue cycle. Some of the flowchart symbols are labeled to indicate controls and records. For each symbol numbered **1** through **13**, select one response from all the answer lists below. Each response in the lists may be selected once or **not** at all.

Items to be answered:

Operations and controls
A. Enter shipping data
B. Verify agreement of sales order and shipping document
C. Write off accounts receivable
D. To warehouse and shipping department
E. Authorize account receivable write-off
F. Prepare aged trial balance
G. To sales department
H. Release goods for shipment
I. To accounts receivable department
J. Enter price data
K. Determine that customer exists
L. Match customer purchase order with sales order
M. Perform customer credit check
N. Prepare sales journal
O. Prepare sales invoice

Documents, journals, ledgers, and files
P. Shipping document
Q. General ledger master file
R. General journal
S. Master price file
T. Sales journal
U. Sales invoice
V. Cash receipts journal
W. Uncollectible accounts file
X. Shipping file
Y. Aged trial balance
Z. Open order file

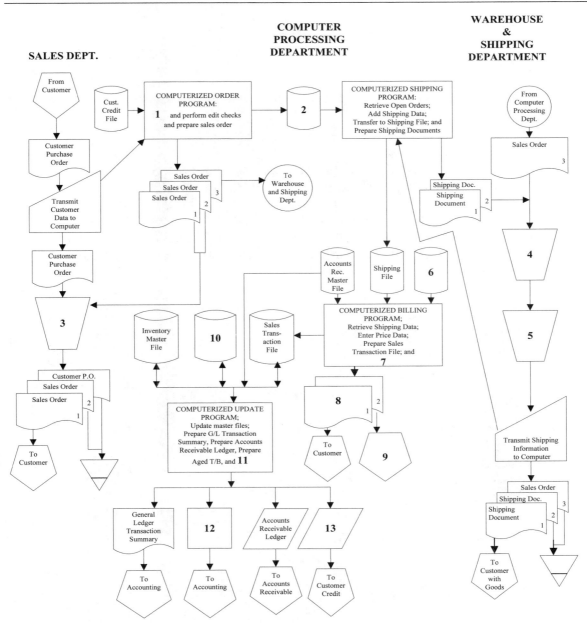

Task-Based Simulation 3

The Uniform
CPA Examination

Unsplit | Split Horiz | Split Vertical | Authoritative Literature | Spreadsheet | Calculator | Submit Testlet

Work Tab | **Resources** | **Help**

Required:

The flowchart below depicts the activities relating to the purchasing, receiving, and accounts payable departments of Lottie Company, Inc.

Based only on the flowchart, describe the internal control procedures (**strengths**) that most likely would provide reasonable assurance those specific internal control objectives for the financial statement assertions regarding purchases and accounts payable will be achieved. Do not describe weaknesses in the internal control.

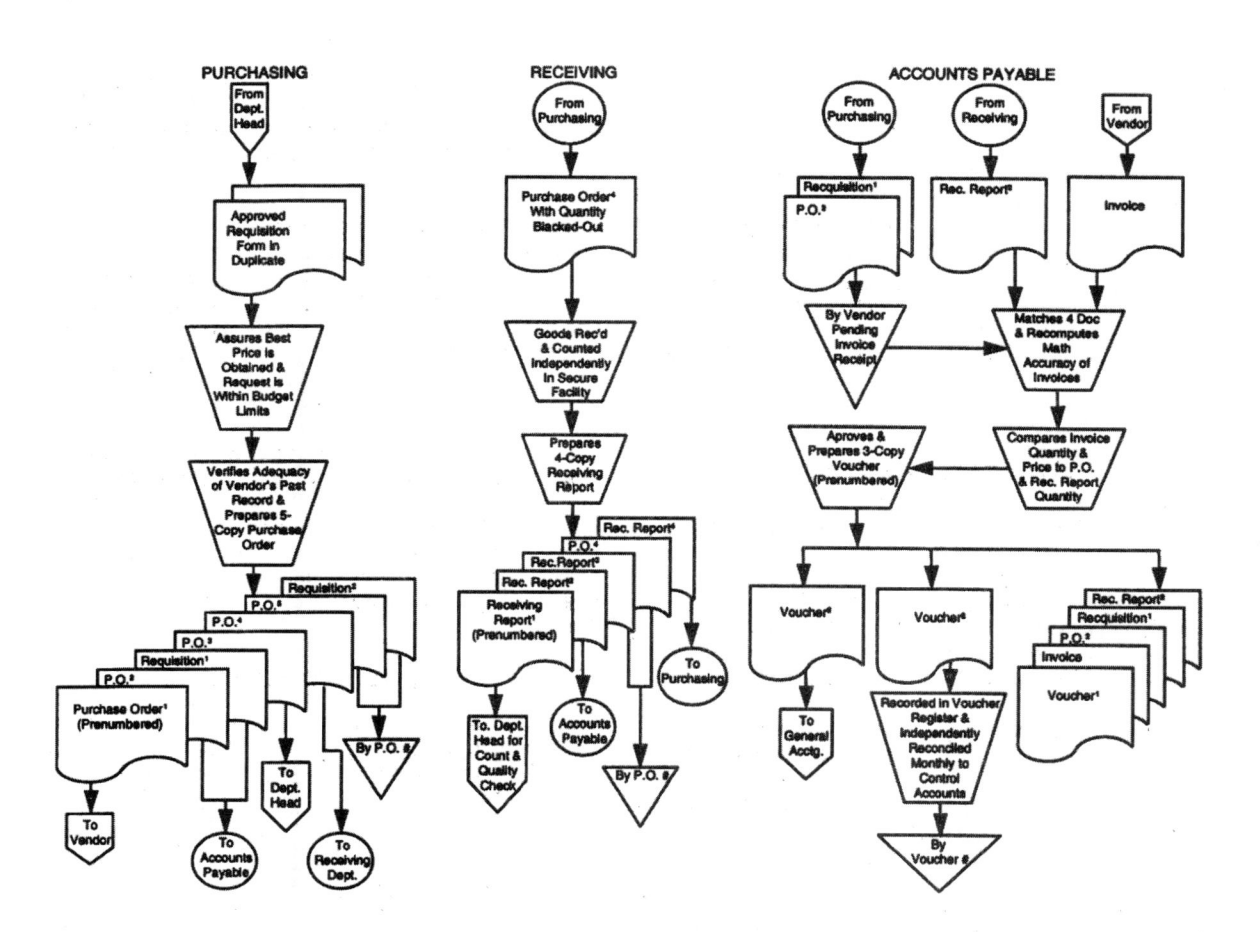

Task-Based Simulation 4

Background:

Darren, CPA, is auditing the financial statements of Menter, Inc. for the year ended January 31, 20X5. Darren has compiled a list of possible errors and irregularities that may result in the misstatement of Menter Inc. financial statements, and a corresponding list of internal control procedures that, if properly designed and implemented, could assist Menter Inc. in preventing or detecting the errors and irregularities.

Required:

For each possible error and irregularity numbered **1 through 15,** select one internal control procedure from the answer list that, if properly designed and implemented, most likely could assist Menter Inc. in preventing or detecting the errors and irregularities. Each response in the list of internal control procedures may be selected once, more than once, or not at all.

Possible Errors and Irregularities

1. Invoices for goods sold are posted to incorrect customer accounts.
2. Goods ordered by customers are shipped, but are **not** billed to anyone.
3. Invoices are sent for shipped goods, but are **not** recorded in the sales journal.
4. Invoices are sent for shipped goods and are recorded in the sales journal, but are **not** posted to any customer account.
5. Credit sales are made to individuals with unsatisfactory credit ratings.
6. Goods are removed from inventory for unauthorized orders.
7. Goods shipped to customers do **not** agree with goods ordered by customers.
8. Invoices are sent to allies in a fraudulent scheme and sales are recorded for fictitious transactions.
9. Customers' checks are received for less than the customers' full account balances, but the customers' full account balances are credited.
10. Customers' checks are misappropriated before being forwarded to the cashier for deposit.
11. Customers' checks are credited to incorrect customer accounts.
12. Different customer accounts are each credited for the same cash receipt.
13. Customers' checks are properly credited to customer accounts and are properly deposited, but errors are made in recording receipts in the cash receipts journal.
14. Customers' checks are misappropriated after being forwarded to the cashier for deposit.
15. Invalid transactions granting credit for sales returns are recorded.

Items to be answered:

Internal Control Procedures

A. Shipping clerks compare goods received from the warehouse with the details on the shipping documents.

B. Approved sales orders are required for goods to be released from the warehouse.

C. Monthly statements are mailed to all customers with outstanding balances.

D. Shipping clerks compare goods received from the warehouse with approved sales orders.

E. Customer orders are compared with the inventory master file to determine whether items ordered are in stock.

F. Daily sales summaries are compared with control totals of invoices.

G. Shipping documents are compared with sales invoices when goods are shipped.

H. Sales invoices are compared with the master price file.

I. Customer orders are compared with an approved customer list.

J. Sales orders are prepared for each customer order.

K. Control amounts posted to the accounts receivable ledger are compared with control totals of invoices.

L. Sales invoices are compared with shipping documents and approved customer orders before invoices are mailed.

M. Pre-numbered credit memos are used for granting credit for goods returned.

N. Goods returned for credit are approved by the supervisor of the sales department.

O. Remittance advices are separated from the checks in the mailroom and forwarded to the accounting department.

P. Total amounts posted to the accounts receivable ledger from remittance advices are compared with the validated bank deposit slip.

Q. The cashier examines each check for proper endorsement.

R. Validated deposit slips are compared with the cashier's daily cash summaries.

S. An employee, other than the bookkeeper, periodically prepares a bank reconciliation.

T. Sales returns are approved by the same employee who issues receiving reports evidencing actual return of goods.

Task-Based Simulation 5

The Uniform
CPA Examination

Unsplit	Split Horiz	Split Vertical	Authoritative Literature	Spreadsheet	Calculator	Submit Testlet

Work Tab   **Resources**   **Help**

Background:

Guillermo, CPA, has been engaged to audit the financial statements of Cecilia Computer Outlets, Inc., a new client. Cecilia is a privately owned chain of retail stores that sells a variety of computer software and video products. Cecilia uses an in-house payroll department at its corporate headquarters to compute payroll data, and to prepare and distribute payroll checks to its 300 salaried employees. Guillermo is preparing an internal control questionnaire to assist in obtaining an understanding of Cecilia's internal control and in assessing risk of material misstatement.

Required:

Prepare a "Payroll" segment of Guillermo's internal control questionnaire that would assist in obtaining an understanding of Cecilia's internal control and in assessing risk of material misstatement.

Do **not** prepare questions relating to cash payrolls, computer applications, payments based on hourly rates, piecework, commissions, employee benefits (pensions, health care, vacations, etc.), or payroll tax accruals other than withholdings.

Use the format in the following example:

Question	Yes	No
Are paychecks prenumbered and accounted for?		

Task-Based Simulation 6

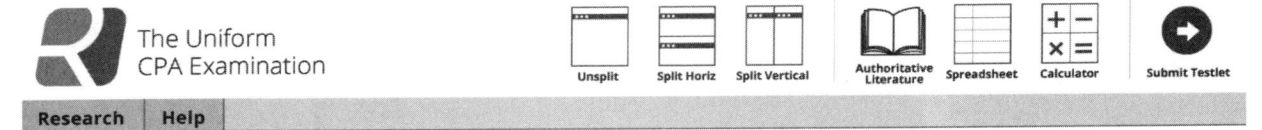

Bowie, CPA, has obtained an understanding of his audit client's internal controls and is in the process of documenting the understanding. In addition to overviews of how the system works and its various control activities, Bowie wants to be certain of complying with documentation requirements under GAAS.

1. Which title of Professional Standards addresses this issue & will be helpful in understanding the requirements for documenting the understanding of an audit client's internal controls relevant to reliable financial reporting?

2. Enter the exact section and paragraph with helpful information.

Task-Based Simulation 7

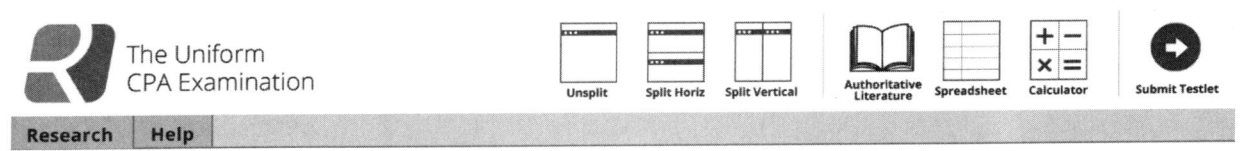

Good, Better, & Best, CPAs, has audited the financial statements of A Very Fine Co and, in the process identified several significant deficiencies in internal control. There are a couple of issues that may be difficult to explain and they are wondering by what date they are required to provide the written communication regarding internal control related matters.

1. Which title of Professional Standards addresses this issue & will be helpful in understanding when the written communication is required?

2. Enter the exact section and paragraph with helpful information.

Task-Based Simulation 8

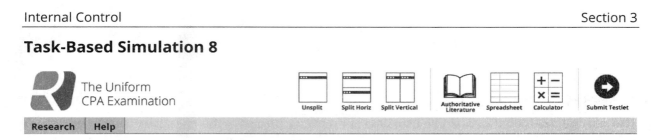

Robertson, CPA, has performed an examination of a client's internal control for the purpose of issuing a report on internal control. Robertson is requesting certain written representations from management and is concerned about overlooking something important.

1. Which title of Professional Standards addresses this issue & will be helpful in understanding what written representations Robertson should request in relation to a report on internal control?

2. Enter the exact section and paragraph with helpful information.

Task-Based Simulation 9

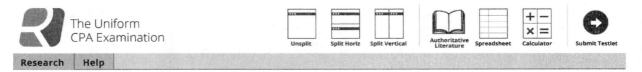

Ben Diemma, CPA, is performing an audit of internal control over financial reporting that is integrated with an audit of the financial statements of a publicly-held client. Ben is trying to determine which controls should be tested.

1. Which title of Professional Standards addresses this issue & will be helpful in understanding which controls should be tested in an audit of internal controls that is integrated with an audit of financial statements?

2. Enter the exact section and paragraph with helpful information.

TASK-BASED SIMULATION SOLUTIONS

Task-Based Simulation Solution 1

The strengths can be described by using the sentence or phrase in the narrative. The weaknesses will generally relate to something that is not being done that should be or to a lack of segregation of duties. For each weakness, a control activity that could correct the weakness should be identified.

1. Some of the **strengths** in internal control that could be considered in assessing control risk below the maximum level include:

    *   Patients receive medical services only after insurance coverage is verified by the office manager and communicated to the clerks.

    *   The physician rendering services completes a pre-numbered medical slip that is used for recording revenue and is given to the patient as a receipt.

    *   Clerk #2 gives a list of patients with uncollectible balances to clerk #3 to prevent them from making appointments for future services.

    *   An outside accountant who is independent from the revenue generating and revenue reporting functions accounts for the pre-numbered service slips on a monthly basis.

    *   A bank reconciliation is prepared monthly by an outside accountant who is independent from the revenue generating and revenue reporting functions.

    *   Only the individual employees and the managing partner know computer passwords.

    *   The employees cannot modify computer software.

    *   None of the employees who are involved in the revenue generating and revenue recording functions have access to check writing capabilities.

2. Some of the **weaknesses** in internal control that could result in material misstatements in the financial statements, along with control activities that could correct the weaknesses, include:

    *   The office manager does not have strict guidelines as to procedures to be performed or limits to be used when granting credit.

    *   Objective credit limits should be established and a formal credit check should be performed before credit is extended.

    *   The office manager both approves the extension of credit and approves the write-off of uncollectible patient receivables.

    *   The approval of credit and the write-off of uncollectible amounts should be separated with write-offs approved by one of the partners.

    *   There is no independent verification of clerk #1's pricing procedures.

    *   Another employee, such as clerk #3, should be assigned the responsibility of verifying clerk #1's pricing procedures.

    *   Clerk #2 performs many incompatible functions including:

        o   Receiving cash and checks directly from patients

        o   Receiving checks from patients and insurance companies through the mail

- o Preparing the daily revenue summary

- o Preparing the daily bank deposit

- o Maintaining the accounts receivable records with the ability to add or delete information without proper authorization

- o Notifying the office manager when insurance claims and patient receivables are not settled within 60 days

- o Preparing a list of patients with uncollectible balances

- Someone who does not receive cash or checks should prepare the daily revenue summary and the daily deposit.

- Checks received through the mail should be stamped by clerk #1 who opens the mail with the remittance advices, copies of the checks, or a list of the checks given to clerk #2.

- Someone who does not have access to cash and checks should perform recording accounts receivable and deleting uncollectible accounts.

- The office manager should be notified when insurance claims and patient receivables are not settled within 60 days by someone who does not maintain accounts receivable records.

- Someone who does not maintain accounts receivable records should prepare the list of patients with uncollectible balances.

- Uncollectible patient receivables are not determined on the basis of established objective criteria.

- Objective criteria should be established for the write-off of uncollectible patient receivables.

- There is no follow-up in the form of phone calls, letters, or collections agencies in relation to uncollectible accounts.

- Procedures, including the use of phone calls, letters, or collections agencies, should be used to follow up on uncollectible patient receivables.

- An aged trial balance of patient receivables is not prepared and reconciled to the general ledger.

- An aged trial balance of patient receivables should be prepared by someone other than clerk #2 and reviewed by one of the partners.

- Rejected insurance claims are automatically converted to patient receivables

- Rejected insurance claims should be reviewed by one of the partners and follow-up procedures should be implemented to determine why the claims were rejected.

- There is no investigation of insurance claims that are not settled within 60 days.

- Insurance claims that have not been settled within 60 days should be reviewed by one of the partners and follow-up procedures should be implemented to determine why the claims have not be settled.

Task-Based Simulation Solution 2

1.   M   The inputs to the #1 include the customer credit file and customer data and the output includes the sales order. It would be logical that the customer's credit would be checked before the sales order would be completed and all information necessary to do so is available – ***Perform customer credit check***

2.   Z   Sales orders are prepared just before the symbol for #2 and using #2 as an input, open orders are retrieved. It would be logical that the sales orders would be stored in an open order file and that the file would be used for retrieving open orders – ***Open order file***

3.   L   The customer purchase order and copies of the sales order are inputs and outputs for #3. It seems logical that the purchase order would be matched to the sales order in this step – ***match customer purchase order with sales order***

4.   B   The inputs to #4 include the shipping documents and the sales order. It would be logical that the sales order and the shipping document would be compared to verify that they agree –***Verify agreement of sales order and shipping document***

5.   H   Once the shipping documents and sales order have been compared to verify agreement, the goods can be shipped –***Release goods for shipment***

6.   S   The accounts receivable master file, the shipping file, and #6 are inputs to a process that involves entering price data. In order to do so, the master price file must be input, making it #6 – ***Master price file***

7.   O   Inputs to #7 include the accounts receivable master file, the shipping file, and the master price file. The process includes retrieving shipping data, entering price data, and preparing a sales transaction file. Since goods have already been shipped by this time, it would be appropriate to prepare a sales invoice so that the customer can be billed – ***Prepare sales invoice***

8.   U   Since the sales invoice is being prepared in step #7, the sales invoice must be an output from the process – ***Sales invoice***

9.   I   In addition to sending a copy of the sales invoice to the customer, it must be sent to the accounts receivable department so that it can be entered as a receivable on the customer's record – ***To accounts receivable department***

10.   Q   The inventory master file, the sales transaction file, and #10 are inputs to a process that involves updating the master files, preparing a general ledger transaction summary, preparing the accounts receivable ledger, and preparing an aged trial balance. The general ledger transaction summary could not be prepared without the general ledger master file as an input –***General ledger master file***

11.   N   With the sales transaction file as an input to the process, it would make sense that the sales journal would be prepared – ***prepare sales journal***

12.   T   Since the sales journal is being prepared as part of the process leading to #12, the sales journal must be an output. The sales journal would be forwarded to accounting – *Sales journal*

13.   Y   Since the process leading to #13 includes preparing an aged trial balance, the aged trial balance must be an output. The aged trial balance would be forwarded to customer credit – *Aged trial balance*

Task-Based Simulation Solution 3

The best way to approach this question is to follow the flowchart in order, beginning with the purchasing department, followed by receiving, and accounts payable. Determine what is occurring at each step and describe it unless it is either irrelevant or inappropriate. If you are not certain whether or not a step is appropriate, include a description of it.

Purchasing

- Proper authorization for purchase requisitions is required from the department head.

- Requisitions are checked against budget limits before preparation of a purchase order.

- The adequacy of each vendor's past record is verified.

Receiving

- The receiving department uses a purchase order without quantities requiring that an actual count be made.

- A secure facility is used to limit access to goods during the receiving activity.

- The department head of the requisitioning department verifies the quantity and quality of goods received.

Accounts Payable

- Requisitions, purchase orders, and receiving reports are matched against invoices as to quantities, prices, and mathematical accuracy.

- The voucher register is reconciled to control accounts on a monthly basis.

- All supporting documentation is required before invoice is sent to treasurer for payment.

General

- The purchasing, receiving, and accounts payable functions are segregated.

Task-Based Simulation Solution 4

1.   C   With monthly statements mailed to all customers with outstanding balances, an incorrect posting of an invoice to a customer's account is likely to be noticed by the customer and brought to the appropriate party's attention.

2.   G   By starting with the population of shipping documents and comparing them to sales invoices when goods are shipped, any good shipped that are not billed will result in shipping documents that will not be able to be matched to an invoice.

3.   F   To determine if all sales invoices are recorded in the sales journal, the auditor can check for missing numbers if the sales invoices are prenumbered or can work from a population of all sales invoices and trace them to the sales journal. In addition, the auditor can compare a summary of daily sales to the amount recorded for that day in the sales journal to determine if there are unrecorded invoices.

4.   K   By comparing control totals of invoices to amounts posted to the accounts receivable ledger, it can be ascertained that all invoices are posted to someone's account.

5.   I   To avoid making sales to individuals with unsatisfactory credit ratings, the company can require that all credit sales be to customers who have already been approved and are listed on an approved list or require authorization from an appropriate party with credit granting authority.

6.   B   Removal of goods from inventory for unauthorized orders can be prevented if the custodian of goods in the warehouse is not allowed to release the goods without an approved sales order.

7.   D   Shipping nonconforming goods to customers can be avoided if shipping clerks are required to compare goods that are about to be shipped to the customer's sales order.

8.   L   Recording of invoices for fictitious transactions can be detected by tracing recorded transactions from the sales journal to the underlying shipping documents to make certain that the invoices represent goods that were actually shipped.

9.   P   By comparing total amounts posted to the accounts receivable ledger to validated bank deposit slips, the auditor can determine that amounts posted to the accounts were actually deposited and did not represent amounts greater than what was actually received.

10.   C   If customers' checks are misappropriated before being forwarded to the cashier for deposit, they will not be entered as reductions to the customers' accounts. As a result, when monthly statements are mailed to the customers, they will detect the fact that their balance is overstated.

11.   C   If customers' checks are credited to incorrect customers' accounts, those making the payment will notice that their balance is overstated when they receive the monthly statements mailed to all customers with outstanding balances.

12.   P   If different customer accounts are each credited for the same cash receipt, the total credits posted to the accounts receivable ledger will exceed the amount deposited which can be detected by comparing the total amount posted to the validated deposit slip.

13.   S   If errors are made in recording receipts in the cash receipts journal, the bank account will not reconcile. These errors can be detected if someone other than the person making the errors reconciles the bank account.

14.   P   If customers' checks are misappropriated after being forwarded to the cashier for deposit, the amount deposited will be lower than the amount credited to the customers' accounts and can be detected by comparing the two amounts.

15.   N   Granting credit for invalid sales returns can be avoided if the supervisor of the sales department approves all returns of goods for credit.

Task-Based Simulation Solution 5

Payroll
Internal Control Questionnaire

Question	Yes	No

1. Are paychecks prenumbered and accounted for?

2. Are discretionary payroll deductions and withholdings authorized in writing by employees?

3. Are the employees who perform each of the following payroll

Functions independent of the other five functions?

- o Personnel and approval of payroll changes
- o Preparation of payroll data
- o Approval of payroll
- o Singing of paychecks
- o Distribution of paychecks
- o Reconciliation of payroll account

4. Are changes in standard data on which payroll is based (hires, separations, salary changes, promotions, deduction and withholding changes, etc.) promptly input to the system to process payroll?

5. Is gross pay determined by using authorized salary rates and time and attendance records?

6. Is there a suitable chart of accounts and/or established guidelines for determining salary account distribution and for recording payroll withholding liabilities?

7. Are clerical operations in payroll preparation verified?

8. Is payroll preparation and recording reviewed by supervisors or internal audit personnel?

9. Are payrolls approved by a responsible official before payroll checks are distributed?

10. Are payrolls disbursed through an imprest account?

11. Is the payroll bank account reconciled monthly to the general ledger?

12. Are payroll bank reconciliations properly approved and differences promptly followed up?

13. Is the custody and follow-up of unclaimed salary checks assigned to a responsible official?

14. Are differences reported by employees followed up on a timely basis by persons not involved in payroll preparation?

15. Are there procedures (e.g. tickler files) to assure proper and timely payment of withholdings to appropriate bodies and to file required information returns?

Task-Based Simulation Solution 6

| AU-C | 315 | .33 |

Task-Based Simulation Solution 7

| AU-C | 265 | .13 |

Task-Based Simulation Solution 8

| AU-C | 940 | .57 |

Task-Based Simulation Solution 9

| PCAOB | AS 2201 | Par .39 |

Lecture 3.17

DOCUMENT REVIEW SIMULATION

Document Review Simulation 1

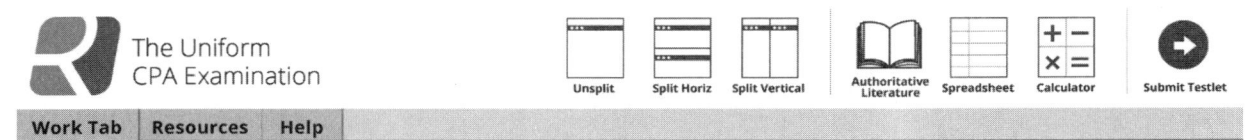

Scroll down to complete all parts of this task.

Major Manufacturing has four manufacturing departments: extrusion, press, welding, and forging. Work in each department is finished at the fiscal year end for extensive cleaning and repairs, so there is no work in process inventory at the fiscal year end. Materials move through only one manufacturing department.

The year under audit is year 2. This is the second year that Major has engaged Cutt, Paste & Semele, CPAs, to perform the annual audit of its financial statements.

Major uses an in-house payroll department at its corporate headquarters to compute payroll data, and to prepare and distribute payroll checks to its 517 employees. Payroll for salaried, commissioned, and hourly employees is processed bi-weekly. Rates and working conditions for manufacturing hourly employees are negotiated during the union contract negotiations when renewing contracts, typically annually. Other employees typically have rate changes 90 days after their hire date and then once annually on June 30. The controller, Bob Clough, indicates that nothing has changed in payroll processing since the previous year's audit. Based on documentation from the previous year's audit, an intern, Irene Inverness, has prepared a draft of the payroll segment of an internal control questionnaire to assist in obtaining an understanding of Major's internal control and in assessing risk of material misstatement. Other segments of the questionnaire will address questions relating to cash payrolls, computer applications, employee benefits (pensions, health care, vacations, etc.), and payroll tax accruals other than withholding.

Amend the questionnaire that Irene has drafted, as appropriate. To revise the document, click on each segment of underlined text below and select the needed correction, if any, from the list provided. If the underlined text is already correct in the context of the document, select "original text." If none of the statements are appropriate in the context of the document, select "delete text."

Major Manufacturing
Internal Control Questionnaire—Payroll Segment
May 5, year 2

	Question	**Yes**	**No**
A.	Are paychecks pre-numbered and accounted for?	○	○
B.	Are discretionary payroll deductions and withholdings authorized in writing by employees?	○	○
C.	(1) <u>Are garnishment documents filed for subsequent review</u>?	○	○
D.	Are the employees who perform each of the following payroll functions independent of the other listed functions?		
	• (2) <u>Hiring, separations, and assignment of parking spaces</u>	○	○
	• Preparation of payroll data	○	○
	• (3) <u>Printing of payroll checks</u>	○	○
	• Approval of payroll	○	○
	• (4) <u>Signing of paychecks</u>	○	○
	• Reconciliation of payroll account	○	○
E.	Are hires, separations, and promotions promptly input to the system to process payroll?	○	○
F.	Are changes in salary, commissions, and wage rates promptly input to the system to process payroll?	○	○
G.	Are changes in deductions and withholdings promptly input to the system to process payroll?	○	○
H.	(5) <u>Is gross pay determined by using authorized salary and wage rates and attendance records</u>?	○	○
I.	Is there a suitable chart of accounts and/or established guidelines for determining compensation account distribution and for recording payroll withholding liabilities?	○	○
J.	Are clerical operations in payroll preparation verified?	○	○
K.	Is payroll preparation and recording reviewed by supervisors or internal audit personnel?	○	○
L.	Are payrolls approved by a responsible official before payroll checks are distributed?	○	○
M.	(6) <u>Is the payroll clerk bonded</u>?	○	○
N.	Is the payroll bank account reconciled monthly to the general ledger?	○	○
O.	Are payroll bank reconciliations properly approved and differences promptly followed up?	○	○
P.	(7) <u>Is the custody and follow-up of unclaimed salary checks assigned to a responsible official</u>?	○	○
Q.	Are differences reported by employees followed up on a timely basis by persons not involved in payroll preparation?	○	○
R.	(8) <u>Are there procedures (e.g. tickler files) to ensure proper and timely payment of withholdings to appropriate bodies</u>?	○	○

Items for Analysis

<u>Are garnishment documents filed for subsequent review?</u>

1. Choose an option below:

   - [Original text] Are garnishment documents filed for subsequent review?

   - [Delete text]

   - Are garnishment claims compared to employee data?

   - Are garnishment claims verified with employees?

   - Are garnishment claims compared to employee data and documents filed for subsequent review?

   - Are garnishment claims compared to employee data and verified with employees?

   - Are garnishment claims verified with employees and documents filed for subsequent review?

   - Are garnishment claims compared to employee data, verified with employees, and documents filed for subsequent review?

<u>Hiring, separations, and assignment of parking spaces</u>

2. Choose an option below:

   - [Original text] Hiring, separations, and assignment of parking spaces.

   - [Delete text]

   - Hiring and separations

   - Hiring, assignment of parking spaces, and approval of salary, commissions, and wage rates.

   - Separations and approval of salary, commissions, and wage rates.

   - Hiring and approval of salary, commissions, and wage rates.

   - Hiring, separations, and approval of salary, commissions, and wage rates.

<u>Printing of payroll checks.</u>

3. Choose an option below:

   - [Original text] Printing of payroll checks.

   - [Delete text]

   - Approval of salary, commissions, and wage rates.

   - Transfer of money from an operating bank account to the payroll bank account.

   - Custody of undistributed signed paychecks.

   - Distribution of paychecks.

Signing of paychecks.

4. Choose an option below:

    - [Original text] Signing of paychecks.

    - [Delete text]

    - Distribution of paychecks.

    - Custody of undistributed signed paychecks.

    - Signing and distribution of paychecks.

    - Signing of paychecks and custody of undistributed signed paychecks.

    - Distribution of paychecks and custody of undistributed signed paychecks.

    - Signing and distribution of paychecks and custody of undistributed signed paychecks.

Is gross pay determined by using authorized salary, commissions, and wage rates and time and attendance records?

5. Choose an option below:

    - [Original text] Is gross pay determined by using authorized salary and wage rates and attendance records?

    - [Delete text]

    - Is gross pay determined by using authorized salary, commissions, and wage rates and time records?

    - Is gross pay determined by using authorized salary and wage rates and attendance and time records.

    - Is gross pay determined by using authorized salary, commissions, and wage rates and attendance and time records.

    - Is gross pay determined by using authorized salary, commission, and wage rates and attendance, sales, and time records?

Is the payroll clerk bonded?

6. Choose an option below:

    - [Original text] Is the payroll clerk bonded?

    - [Delete text]

    - Does the human resources manager review commission calculations periodically?

    - Does the payroll clerk update the salary, wage, and commission rates daily?

    - Are payrolls disbursed through an imprest account?

    - Does the A/P clerk distribute the signed paychecks?

Is the custody of unclaimed salary checks assigned to a responsible official?

7. Choose an option below:

   - [Original text] Is the custody of unclaimed salary checks assigned to a responsible official?

   - [Delete text]

   - Is the follow-up on unclaimed salary checks assigned to a responsible official?

   - Is the custody of and follow-up on unclaimed salary checks assigned to a responsible official?

   - Is the custody of unclaimed paychecks assigned to a responsible official?

   - Is the follow-up on unclaimed paychecks assigned to a responsible official?

   - Is the custody of and follow-up on unclaimed paychecks assigned to a responsible official?

Are there procedures (e.g. tickler files) to ensure proper and timely payment of withholdings to appropriate bodies?

8. Choose an option below:

   - [Original text] Are there procedures (e.g. tickler files) to ensure proper and timely payment of withholdings to appropriate bodies?

   - [Delete text]

   - Are there procedures (e.g. tickler files) to ensure proper and timely filing of required information returns?

   - Are there procedures (e.g. tickler files) to ensure proper and timely payment of withholdings to appropriate bodies and to file required information returns?

   - Are hourly employees' timecards sent to the human resources department for approval?

   - Are hourly employees' timecards sent to the payroll clerk for approval?

   - Are hourly employees' timecards sent to the treasurer for approval?

Excerpt from prior year work paper

Major Manufacturing
FYI: Select client personnel contact information
Prepared by: Ben Paste
Date: April 27, year 1
Assisted by:
Date:
Reviewed by:
Date:

Name	Title	Extension	e-mail
Alice Adams	A/P clerk	526	aadams@majormfg.com
Ralph Carter	Receiving clerk	333	ralphc@majormfg.com
Bob Clough	Controller	256	RClough@majormfg.com
Sally Lund	Office manager	116	slund@majormfg.com
James Marvin	Maintenance specialist	555-2652	jmarvin@marormfg.com
Sam Sligh	Shipping clerk	355	ssligh@majormfg.com
Trixie Townsend	Treasurer	563	trixie@majormfg.com
Patricia Wells	Purchasing department head	256	pwells@majormfg.com

<u>Excerpt from prior year work paper</u>

Major Manufacturing
Payroll Overview
Prepared by: Ben Paste
Date: May 2, year 1
Assisted by: Ian Inman
Date: April 27, year 1
Reviewed by: *BC*
Date: *1-3-r2*

Each Major employee is paid bi-weekly at latest by the Friday following the end of the pay period under one of three models: hourly, salary, and salary with a commission element. When year-end changes, vacation or sickness among personnel involved in completion of the payroll, or holidays do not interfere, payroll usually is processed before this deadline, so paychecks typically are distributed at the Wednesday afternoon shift change.

Hourly employees are paid based on their hourly rates with a premium for the second shift They receive time and half for more than 40 hours up to 48 hours and double time for more than 48 hours in a work-week. The work week begins with the start of shift change (3:00) on Sunday for second shift and the end of shift change (3:30) on Sunday for the first shift.

Salaried staff aside from sales staff are paid a base salary based on attendance.

Sales staff are paid a base salary. They also get a commission ultimately based on collected sales revenues over an annual minimum. Rather than wait until the annual minimum is reached, a conservatively annualized projection of sales to date is made each month and compared to the annual minimum. If the projection is over the annual minimum, payments for that month are made in the first pay period of the next month. Sales staff receive a commission calculation statement each month.

As Major has few write-offs of accounts receivable, sales staff receive an advance of the commission element of their compensation when an order ships. If an invoice is unpaid for 90 days, the commission paid on that sale is subtracted from commissions for the current month, but not from the base salary. The sales staff receives the commission when the overdue invoices are paid in full, if paid within 12 months of the original invoice date, but not on settlements or amounts paid in bankruptcy.

When the sales staff separate from the company, the advance is not paid, but commissions accrue on previously made sales. These commissions are paid once payment is received from the related customers. If the sales staff separate from the company, with a net negative balance due to unpaid invoices, whether the advance is excused is decided on a case by case basis.

DOCUMENT REVIEW SIMULATION SOLUTION

Document Review Simulation Solution 1

Major Manufacturing
Internal Control Questionnaire—Payroll Segment
May 5, year 2

	Question	Yes	No
A.	Are paychecks pre-numbered and accounted for?	○	○
B.	Are discretionary payroll deductions and withholdings authorized in writing by employees?	○	○
C.	(1) <u>Are garnishment claims compared to employee data and documents filed for subsequent review</u>?	○	○
D.	Are the employees who perform each of the following payroll functions independent of the other listed functions?		

- (2) <u>Hiring, separations, and approval of salary, commissions, and wage rates</u>
- Preparation of payroll data
- (3) [Delete text]
- Approval of payroll
- (4) <u>Signing and distribution of paychecks and custody of undistributed signed paychecks</u>
- Reconciliation of payroll account

		Yes	No
	Preparation of payroll data	○	○
	(3) [Delete text]	○	○
	Approval of payroll	○	○
	Signing and distribution...	○	○
		○	○
	Reconciliation of payroll account	○	○
E.	Are hires, separations, and promotions promptly input to the system to process payroll?	○	○
F.	Are changes in salary, commissions, and wage rates promptly input to the system to process payroll?	○	○
G.	Are changes in deductions and withholdings promptly input to the system to process payroll?	○	○
H.	(5) <u>Is gross pay determined by using authorized salary, commission, and wage rates and attendance, sales, and time records</u>?	○	○
I.	Is there a suitable chart of accounts and/or established guidelines for determining compensation account distribution and for recording payroll withholding liabilities?	○	○
J.	Are clerical operations in payroll preparation verified?	○	○
K.	Is payroll preparation and recording reviewed by supervisors or internal audit personnel?	○	○
L.	Are payrolls approved by a responsible official before payroll checks are distributed?	○	○
M.	(6) <u>Are payrolls disbursed through an imprest account</u>?	○	○
N.	Is the payroll bank account reconciled monthly to the general ledger?	○	○
O.	Are payroll bank reconciliations properly approved and differences promptly followed up?	○	○
P.	(7) <u>Is the custody of and follow-up on unclaimed paychecks assigned to a responsible official</u>?	○	○
Q.	Are differences reported by employees followed up on a timely basis by persons not involved in payroll preparation?	○	○

R.   (8) <u>Are there procedures (e.g. tickler files) to ensure proper and timely payment of withholdings to appropriate bodies and to file required information returns?</u>   ○   ○

EXPLANATIONS:

1.   Are garnishment claims compared to employee data and documents filed for subsequent review?

Garnishment claims are compared to employee data to ensure that the claim actually relates to the employee in question. Garnishment documents are kept for subsequent review in case the employee takes issue with the withholding as well as regular annual audits. Garnishment claims are court orders to apply money or property due a debtor to the debtor's creditor. The employer generally is obligated to send the amount of the garnishment to the creditor regardless of whether the employee verifies it. While an employer might notify employees of pending garnishment claims received, garnishment claims generally are not verified with employees. If there is a question concerning the authenticity of a garnishment document, the employer is more likely to verify a garnishment with the issuing court, not the employee. If an employee disputes a garnishment, the employee must make the counter-claim to the court issuing the garnishment, not the employer. Internal control questionnaires typically are designed so that 'yes' answers are items for the auditor to skip and 'no' answer are items for the auditor to consider. As a 'yes' answer to a question involving employee verification of garnishments would suggest the attention of the auditor when it would be inappropriate, a question involving employee verification of garnishments is unlikely.

2.   Hiring, separations, and approval of salary, commissions, and wage rates.

Hiring, separations, and approval of salary, commissions, and wage rates typically all are performed by the personnel (or human resources) department. These authorization duties are not incompatible with each other, but each of them are incompatible with other tasks in the list that involve record-keeping, custody, and reconciliation. The human resources department also might assign parking spaces. As the assignment of parking spaces generally is irrelevant to internal controls, it is inappropriate for an internal control questionnaire.

3.   [Delete text]

None of the options is needed in a list of incompatible duties, given the other items in the list (as amended). The printing of payroll checks need not be separated from the preparation of payroll data; as a matter of convenience and expediency, the payroll clerk often prints (but does not sign) payroll checks in small entities; in a large entity, a treasury clerk would do so. The approval of salary, commissions, and wage rates need not be separated from the hiring and separation functions. The signing of paychecks need not be separated from the transfer of money from an operating bank account to the payroll bank account, the custody of undistributed signed paychecks, nor the distribution of paychecks; these tasks are all custody of assets.

4. Signing and distribution of paychecks and custody of undistributed signed paychecks.

    The treasurer typically signs and distributes paychecks and retains custody of any undistributed signed paychecks. These three duties should be separated from the record-keeping duties of the payroll clerk and the authorization duties of the human resources department. While each of these duties or any combination of two of these duties also are appropriate to keep separate from the authorization, record-keeping, and reconciliation functions, it is best that the questionnaire ask about all of these duties.

5. Is gross pay determined by using authorized salary, commission, and wage rates and attendance, sales, and time records?

    Wage calculations usually involve multiplying wages rates by time worked—rather than attendance. Salary calculations usually involve salary rates and attendance records, rather than time or commission records. Commission calculations involve commission rates and sales records. Either a question including all six of these components or multiple questions each asking about one component is most appropriate in the circumstances.

6. Are payrolls disbursed through an imprest account?

    A payroll imprest account is a bank account dedicated to employee compensation payments. Most employers have this easily employed and inexpensive internal control. It typically has a small continual balance. Just before paychecks (written on this account) are disbursed, the exact amount of the payroll is deposited (or transferred) into the imprest account. This simplifies the bank reconciliation—there are few deposits, only checks for compensation are disbursed from this account, and the balance per books is always the same. A bond is an insurance policy that reimburses the employer for losses related to that employee's theft or fraud. Typically, companies bond employees who have custody of assets (such as a treasurer) or have access to customers' assets (such as a locksmith). Employees with record-keeping duties (such as an A/P clerk) rarely are bonded. Typically, the human resources manager is not the person to review payroll calculations. It is more likely that an internal auditor, the payroll clerk's supervisor, or a sales manager would review commission calculations—with the sales manager's review being sporadic rather than periodic. As payroll is processed bi-weekly, updating the rates daily seems excessive, unless the quantity of updates would overwhelm the payroll process function if not updated frequently. With annual changes for 517 employees being the norm, daily updates to rates seems extreme. Typically, internal controls are designed to separate the incompatible duties of authorization, record-keeping, custody of assets, and reconciliation. The A/P clerk is involved in record-keeping and so should not have custody of assets (such as signed checks). Internal control questionnaires typically are designed so that 'yes' answers are items for the auditor to skip and 'no' answer are items for the auditor to consider. As a 'yes' answer to this question (Does the A/P clerk distribute the signed paychecks?) would require the attention of the auditor, this question is unlikely.

7. Is the custody of and follow-up on unclaimed paychecks assigned to a responsible official?

    Both the custody of any signed check and follow-up on any unclaimed check (paycheck or regular check) is of concern to an auditor. Aside from issues surrounding custody of the asset, unclaimed paychecks could be due to fictitious employees. The use of the phrase 'salary checks' ignores paychecks issued to hourly employees. While the questionnaire preparer may not intend to differentiate between the two, the questionnaire reader may do so. The paychecks for both salaried and hourly employees are of concern to the auditor.

8. Are there procedures (e.g. tickler files) to ensure proper and timely payment of withholdings to appropriate bodies and to file required information returns?

Both the proper and timely payment of withholdings to appropriate bodies and filing of required information returns are of concern to the auditor. Timecards generally are approved by the employee's supervisor, who is in the best position to know if it is accurate, rather than the human resources department, the payroll clerk, or the treasurer. Internal control questionnaires typically are designed so that 'yes' answers are items for the auditor to skip and 'no' answer are items for the auditor to consider. As a 'yes' answer to the presented questions on timecard approval would require the attention of the auditor, these questions are unlikely. A tickler file (paper or electronic) generally is organized by date; task reminders of importance to the owner (tax return preparation, subscription renewal, holiday party preparation, etc.) are put into the file whenever thought of and the file owner refers to the file periodically to ensure projects are completed in a timely fashion. A reminder can be as simple as a flyer from last year's scout jamboree sponsored by the business or as elaborate as a list of physical inventory preparation tasks employing a multi-disciplinary team.

Section 4 – Audit Evidence

Corresponding Lectures

Watch the following course lectures with this section:

Lecture 4.01 – Audit Evidence
Lecture 4.02 – Audit Risk, F/S Level and Assertion Level
Lecture 4.03 – Management's Assertions
Lecture 4.04 – Analytical Procedures
Lecture 4.05 – Substantive Testing vs. Internal Control Testing
Lecture 4.06 – Audit Evidence – Class Questions
Lecture 4.07 – Financial Statement Accounts – Cash
Lecture 4.08 – Financial Statement Accounts – Receivables
Lecture 4.09 – Financial Statement Accounts – Investments in Securities and Derivatives
Lecture 4.10 – Financial Statement Accounts – Inventories
Lecture 4.11 – Financial Statement Accounts – PP&E and Current Liabilities
Lecture 4.12 – Financial Statement Accounts – L/T Debt, Stockholders Equity and Payroll
Lecture 4.13 – Financial Statement Accounts – Class Questions
Lecture 4.14 – Audit Program / Audit Plan
Lecture 4.15 – Audit Program / Audit Plan – Class Questions
Lecture 4.16 – Management Representation Letter and Attorney Letter
Lecture 4.17 – Related Party Transactions, Specialists, Internal Auditors, Estimates and Subsequent Events
Lecture 4.18 – Audit Evidence - Class Questions
Lecture 4.19 – Audit Evidence - Class Question - DRS

EXAM NOTE: *Please refer to the AICPA AUD Blueprint in the Introduction of this book to find a listing of the representative tasks (and their associated skill levels—i.e., Remembering and Understanding, Application, Analysis, and Evaluation) that the candidate should be able to perform based on the knowledge obtained in this section.*

Audit Evidence

AUDIT EVIDENCE

The Steps in an Audit

Prepare for → Obtain Understanding → Assess Risks of Material → Perform Tests → *Perform* → Formulate → Issue
the Audit   of Client, its Environment,   Misstatement and Determine   of Controls   *Substantive*   an Opinion   Audit
              including Internal Control   Nature, Timing & Extent   *Procedures*   Report
                                           of Further Procedures

AU-C 500 requires an auditor to design and perform audit procedures that are appropriate in the circumstances for the purpose of obtaining **sufficient appropriate audit evidence.**

As discussed in Internal Controls, based on the understanding, the auditor will determine the **nature**, **timing**, and **extent** of the substantive tests necessary to gather enough appropriate evidence. **Sufficiency** relates closely to the **extent** of testing, and **Appropriateness** relates to the **nature** (timing is a matter of recognizing that tests at year-end provide stronger evidence than reliance on tests applied to interim data).

Sufficient Appropriate Audit Evidence is needed:
- **Sufficiency** relates to the *quantity* **(extent)** of corroborative evidence obtained. The amount is based on the auditor's judgment.
  - Must rely on evidence that is **Persuasive rather than Conclusive** due to the limitations of an audit.
  - The auditor must be aware of the fact that the **cost** of obtaining evidence may, in some circumstances, exceed the **benefit** obtained by having it (**Cost/Benefit** tradeoff).

Sufficiency relates to the **amount** of evidence that is obtained. The auditor will have to consider both the costs and benefits of obtaining evidence (high cost alone cannot be a proper reason to omit a test, however). The quantity of evidence required is affected by both the risk of material misstatement and the quality of evidence. The decision as to sufficiency will be based on the determination of the **acceptable level of detection risk (DR)**:

Acceptable DR = AR / (RMM)

RMM = IR × CR

As the RMM decreases due to the identification of effective internal controls in that phase of the audit, the acceptable level of detection risk increases, meaning the auditor can reduce the amount of substantive testing. Both sufficiency and the appropriateness of audit evidence should be considered when assessing risks and designing audit procedures.
- **Appropriateness** relates to the measure of the *quality* **(nature)** of the audit evidence, including its relevance and reliability in providing support for the conclusions on which the auditor's opinion is based.
  - **Relevance** – Evidence is relevant if it provides evidence in support of a relevant assertion (**U-PERCV**).

- ○ **Reliability/Faithful Representation** – The reliability of audit evidence, which determines the degree to which it is persuasive to the auditor, is influenced by its **source and nature**.
  - ▪ Persuasiveness of evidence is based on its **source:**
    1. Directly obtained by auditor (*auditor developed* – Inventory observation)
    2. Obtained from outsider (*Outside* – Bank confirmations)
    3. Prepared by outsider but obtained from client (*outside/inside* – bank statements)
    4. Prepared by client (*Inside* – client sales invoices)
       - ▫ Concerned with accuracy and completeness when using info provided by the client

As indicated in **AU-C Section 500**, the **reliability** of audit evidence is directly related to the **source** from which it is obtained, the conditions under which it is developed and acquired, and its form. Evidence obtained by an auditor, ranking from the most reliable to the least, may come from the following sources.

1. Audit evidence may be obtained **directly by the auditor**, such as through the observation of the application of a control or walking around the factory facilities to inspect manufacturing equipment. This is more reliable than audit evidence obtained indirectly or by inference, such as through an inquiry about the application of a control.
2. The reliability of audit evidence is increased when it is obtained from independent sources **outside** the entity, such as confirmations received directly by the auditor from financial institutions or from customers of the client, as opposed to information received from the client.
3. Evidence that originated **outside** the entity but is provided from **inside** the entity, such as a customer invoice or a bank statement provided to the auditor by the client, is more reliable than information that is both received from the entity and prepared by the entity.
4. The reliability of **inside** audit evidence that is generated **internally** is increased when the related controls, including those imposed by the entity, over its preparation and maintenance, are effective.
5. Audit evidence in documentary form, whether paper, electronic, or other medium, is more reliable than evidence obtained orally. A contemporaneously written record of a meeting, for example, is more reliable than a subsequent oral representation of the matters discussed.

Audit evidence provided by original documents is more reliable than audit evidence provided by photocopies, facsimiles, or documents that have been filmed, digitized, or otherwise transformed into electronic form, the reliability of which may depend on the controls over their preparation and maintenance.

When evaluating the reliability of evidence, the auditor should keep in mind that fraudulent misstatement of the financial statements may mean that management may have the ability to alter internal documents, from category 4, or external documents within the client's control, as in category 3, making this evidence less reliable than that received from outsiders. Evidence received from outsiders, however, may also be compromised as a result of collusion.

The higher the level of validity of evidence, the lower the likelihood that a material misstatement will not be detected by the auditor, reducing the achieved level of DR in the audit. An audit with a low acceptable level of DR will normally require that the auditor seek the highest level of persuasiveness possible. No audit can rely entirely on client-prepared accounting data.

Keep in mind, however, that the auditor may rely in part on evidence obtained with any level of persuasiveness. The representation letter, for example, is obtained in every audit even though it represents the lowest level of persuasiveness due to the absence of any effective internal control over management.

Audit Evidence – AU-C Section 500 defines audit evidence as all the information used by the auditor in arriving at the conclusions on which the audit opinion is based, including the information contained in the *accounting records* underlying the financial statements and *other information*. This includes:
- **Accounting Records** – Checks, invoices, contracts, the general and subsidiary ledgers, journal entries and other adjustments, worksheets, spreadsheets, and other records that support cost allocations, computations, reconciliations, and disclosures.
  - Underlying accounting data alone is **not** sufficient appropriate evidence upon which to base the auditor's opinion.

- **Other Information - Corroborative Evidence** – Minutes of various meetings of the board of directors and others; confirmations; information obtained by the auditor in developing an understanding of the entity and its environment, such as comparable data about competitors to use for benchmarking purposes; and information obtained by the auditor through the performance of audit procedures, such as inquiry, observation, and inspection of documents.

The auditor uses judgment to evaluate both the sufficiency and appropriateness of audit evidence. The auditor should also consider the:
- Significance and likelihood of potential misstatements.
- Effectiveness of management's responses and controls.
- Experience gained during previous audits.
- Results of audit procedures performed.
- Source, reliability, and persuasiveness of audit evidence obtained.
- Understanding of the entity and its environment.

Lecture 4.02

AUDIT RISK, FINANCIAL STATEMENT LEVEL AND RELEVANT ASSERTION LEVEL

As indicated in AU-C Section 315, the purpose of obtaining an understanding of the entity and its environment, including its internal control is to identify and assess risks of material misstatement, whether due to fraud or error, at the *financial statement level* and *relevant assertion levels* to provide a basis for designing and implementing responses.

The auditor will assess the risk of material misstatement (RMM) at the **financial statement level**, which considers the environment in which the entity is operating to determine if there are factors that would make the financial statements of the entity more or less likely to be materially misstated. This is referred to as *inherent risk (IR).* As IR increases, RMM gets higher as well.

The client can reduce RMM at the financial statement level by designing, implementing, and maintaining (DIM) internal controls over financial reporting (ICFR) that promote the preparation of financial statements that are fairly presented in accordance with the applicable financial reporting framework. Internal controls increase the likelihood that errors or fraud will be prevented or that they will be detected and corrected on a timely basis so that financial statements will not be materially misstated.

When internal controls are not adequately designed or implemented, there is a risk that a material misstatement may occur that will not be prevented or detected and corrected on a timely basis by internal controls. This is referred to as **control risk (CR)** and, similar to IR, a higher CR results in a higher RMM.

Although it is not actually a mathematical formula, if each risk could be measured as a probability, some percentage up to 100%, RMM would equal IR × CR. For example, if IR is 50%, indicating that there is a 50% probability that the information will be misstated if there are no internal controls to prevent or detect and correct it:

- If CR is 100%, indicating that there are no controls in place to prevent or detect such a misstatement, there is a 50% likelihood that the financial information will be misstated.

- If CR is 50%, the information is likely to be misstated 50% of the time due to inherent risk, but 50% of the times that it is, internal controls will prevent or detect and correct the misstatement, meaning the information will only be misstated 25% of the time.

Examples of controls that may _reduce CR and RMM_ at the financial statement level may include:

- Making certain that personnel involved in the reporting process are properly qualified with appropriate education and experience, are adequately trained and supervised, and have the resources for education;

- Management establishing a tone at the top that encourages honesty and integrity and adherence to a code of conduct that encourages good behavior;

- An accounting and reporting system that is appropriate for the nature of the entity and the complexity of its accounting; and

- An atmosphere of transparency in which reasonable objectives are set and employees are evaluated based on their achievements.

Audit risk is the risk that the auditor will issue an opinion that is inappropriate under the circumstances. This occurs when the evidence obtained causes the auditor to express a more favorable opinion than would have been expressed if the auditor had all of the facts. Audit risk consists of a number of components, each of which has its own implications.

Audit Risk (AR = IR × CR × DR)
- RMM (Risk of Material Misstatement = IR × CR)
  - IR = Inherent Risk
  - CR = Control Risk

- **Detection risk** – The probability that the auditor's substantive tests will not detect material misstatements (AP × TD)
  - AP = risk associated with analytical procedures (that they will not be effective in detecting material misstatements)
  - TD = risk associated with tests of details (that they will not be effective in detecting material misstatements)

- In order to keep audit risk (AR) at an acceptable level, the greater the risk of material misstatement (RMM), the lower the detection risk (DR) that can be accepted, and the greater the extent of substantive procedures required.

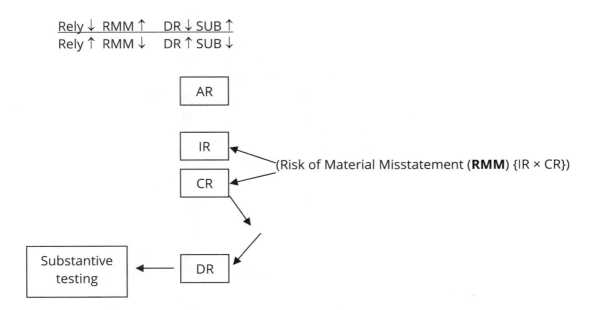

In order to reduce **audit risk** to an acceptably low level, the auditor should respond to the assessed level of risk in two ways: at the financial statement level and at the relevant assertion level.

At the **financial statement level**, the auditor will consider the users of the financial statements and the purposes for which they will be used, to determine if management may have an incentive to overstate or understate results of operations and financial position. In addition, the auditor will consider the economic and industry conditions, management compensation arrangements, financing arrangements and the state of the capital markets, changes in entity management or other key personnel, and a variety of other relevant factors in determining if there is an increased or decreased risk that the entity may issue materially misstated financial statements.

- To address the risks of material misstatement at the **financial statement level,** some of the auditor's responses to reduce audit risk to an acceptably low level may include:
  - o An increased need for professional skepticism of the audit team.
  - o Consider assigning more experienced staff with specialized skills or even the use of specialists.
  - o The auditor may supervise staff more closely.
  - o Incorporate more unpredictability in audit procedures.
  - o Adjust the nature, timing, and extent of further audit procedures (such as shifting interim substantive testing to year-end substantive testing) when the control environment is weak.
    - ▪ When RMM is high because of deficiencies in the entity's internal controls, the auditor may respond by performing more procedures near the end of the period, rather than at an interim date; applying more substantive procedures in order to obtain more extensive audit evidence; and increasing the scope of the audit by increasing the number of locations to be included.

- The auditor should design and perform further audit procedures whose ***nature, timing, and extent*** are responsive to the assessed risks of material misstatement at the **relevant assertion level.** The auditor should consider:
  - The significance and probability that a material misstatement will occur.
  - The characteristics of the class of transactions, account balance or disclosure involved.
  - The nature of the controls used (manual vs. automated).
  - Whether the auditor expects to test the operating effectiveness of the controls in preventing or detecting material misstatements.
    - ***Nature*** *of audit procedures* (appropriateness) – this includes both its *purpose* (test of control vs. substantive procedures) and its *type* (I-CORRIIA). The nature of audit procedures is the *most important* consideration in responding to assessed risks.
      - The higher the auditor's assessment of RMM, the lower the acceptable level of DR.
      - Lower DR is achieved by obtaining audit evidence that is more *Relevant & Reliable*.

    - ***Timing*** *of audit tests* – this refers to *when* the audit procedures are performed as well as the period or date for which the audit evidence is applicable.
      - Tests may be performed at an interim date or at period end.
      - The higher the auditor's risk assessment (RMM), the closer to period-end substantive procedures should be performed.

    - ***Extent*** *of audit procedures* (sufficiency) – this refers to the *quantity* of a specific audit procedure to be performed. This is based on auditor's judgment and the auditor should consider the tolerable misstatement, the assessed risk of material misstatement and the degree of assurance that is sought.
      - The higher the auditor's risk assessment (RMM), the greater the extent of audit procedures.
      - This may mean more procedures or larger sample sizes to which procedures are applied.

To address risk at the assertion level, the auditor will consider the individual elements of financial reporting. Operating items and account balances will be scrutinized to determine if they represent risk of material misstatement and, if so, the type of likely misstatement. This then allows the auditor to determine which assertions are most affected and what procedures will be most effective in obtaining evidence that either will or will not support the assertion.

Assets like inventory may represent risk if they are susceptible to theft, in which case the auditor will concentrate on the *existence assertion.*
- The auditor will determine if there are control procedures in place that can be relied upon and that, if operating as designed, would effectively prevent theft.
- The auditor may apply substantive procedures, such as comparing physical observations of inventory to recorded amounts and performing analytical procedures to determine if the relationships among inventory, cost of sales, and gross profits are reasonable.
- Transactions like sales may be misstated due to the use of numerous shipping arrangements under various shipping terms, increasing the likelihood that a sale will be

recognized on an inappropriate date. In this case, the auditor will concentrate effort on the *cutoff assertion*.

- The auditor will determine if there are control procedures in place that can be relied upon and that, if operating as designed, would assure that sales are recognized in the appropriate period.
- The auditor may apply substantive procedures such as tracing recorded transactions surrounding the end of the period to shipping or receiving documents while evaluating shipping terms and tracing shipping and receiving documents surrounding the end of the period to the journals to determine if they were reported in the appropriate period.

As mentioned earlier, the auditor may use either a *substantive approach,* in which substantive procedures are emphasized, or a *combined approach*, in which both tests of controls and substantive procedures are used.

- For certain relevant assertions and risks, only substantive procedures will be performed. This may occur because either there are no effective controls or because it would *not be efficient* (cost/benefit) to test the operating effectiveness of controls.
  - Substantive procedures should be performed for each material transaction class, account balance, and disclosure item.
  - In situations where a significant amount of information is initiated, authorized, recorded, processed, or reported electronically, substantive procedures alone may not be sufficient.

- In other situations, both tests of the operating effectiveness of controls and substantive procedures are used. Typically, if controls are operating effectively, less assurance will be required from substantive procedures.
  - The auditor will perform tests of controls to obtain evidence as to whether or not controls are functioning effectively as designed.
    - If so, the auditor can reduce the amount of substantive testing considered necessary, often increasing the efficiency of the audit.
    - If not, the auditor will not be able to rely on them and will not be able to reduce the amount of substantive testing, resulting in an inefficient audit.
    - As a result, the auditor may elect not to perform tests of controls due to the inefficiency of performing substantive tests exclusively.
  - Tests of controls are required in circumstances when substantive testing alone cannot provide sufficient evidence to adequately reduce the risk of material misstatement.
    - There may not be documentary evidence to support a transaction, such as an unsolicited donation to a not-for-profit organization.
    - No substantive tests can provide meaningful evidence of the fairness and the auditor may be required to rely on the internal controls surrounding the transaction, such as contributions received, to obtain reasonable assurance that an item is not materially misstated.

Management's Assertions (U-PERCV) (Financial Statements) →	Objectives →	Audit Procedures (I-CORRIIA) (Substantive Tests)

MANAGEMENT'S ASSERTIONS (AU-C 315)

Management's Assertions (AU-C 315) are representations made by management in the financial statements being audited.

Management makes implicit or explicit assertions regarding the recognition, measurement, presentation, and disclosure of information in the financial statements and related disclosures. All of the procedures applied in an audit are directed toward the eventual goal of expressing an opinion on the financial statements. The auditor should always keep in mind the **management assertions** that are represented in the financial statements. These assertions can be summarized as follows (**COCA-CURVE**)

- **Completeness**
    - All transactions and events that should have been recorded have been recorded.
    - All assets, liabilities, and equity interests that should have been recorded have been recorded.
    - All disclosures that should have been included in the financial statements have been included.
- **Occurrence**
    - Transactions and events that have been recorded have occurred and pertain to the entity.
    - Disclosed events, transactions, and other matters have occurred and pertain to the entity.
- **Cutoff**
    - Transactions and events have been recorded in the correct accounting period.
- **Accuracy**
    - Amounts and other data relating to recorded transactions and events have been recorded appropriately.
    - Financial and other information is disclosed fairly and in appropriate amounts.
- **Classification**
    - Transactions and events have been recorded in the proper accounts.
    - Financial information is appropriately presented and described.
- **Understandability**
    - Disclosures are clearly expressed.
- **Rights and Obligations**
    - The entity holds or controls the rights to assets, and liabilities are the obligations of the entity.
    - Disclosed events, transactions, and other matters pertain to the entity.
- **Valuation and Allocation**
    - Assets, liabilities, and equity interests are included in the financial statements at appropriate amounts, and any resulting valuation or allocation adjustments are appropriately recorded.
    - Financial and other information is disclosed fairly and in appropriate amounts.
- **Existence**
    - Assets, liabilities, and equity interests exist.

The auditor should use relevant assertions in assessing risks by considering the different types of potential misstatements that may occur, and then designing further audit procedures that are responsive to the assessed risks. To identify relevant assertions, the auditor should determine the *source* of likely potential misstatements in each significant class of transactions, account balance,

and presentation and disclosure. In determining whether a particular assertion is relevant, the auditor should evaluate:
- The nature of the assertion.
- The volume of transactions or data related to the assertion.
- The nature and complexity of the systems used to process information supporting the assertion.

The Management Assertions are grouped within three main categories:
- Assertions about **classes of transactions and events** for the period under audit (income statement) (**CPA-CO**).
- Assertions about **account balances** at the period end (balance sheet) (**RACE**).
- Assertions about **presentation and disclosure** (financial statements) (**RACOU**-n).
  - *Raccoons (RACOU-n's)* are always presenting and disclosing my garbage at night!!

Classes of Transactions & Events (CPA-CO)	Account Balances at year-end (RACE)	Presentation & Disclosures (RACOU-n) (Raccoon)
Completeness	*Rights and Obligations*	*Rights and Obligations*
Period Cutoff	*Allocation and Valuation*	*Accuracy and Valuation*
Accuracy	*Completeness*	*Completeness*
Classification	*Existence*	*Occurrence*
Occurrence		*Understandability and Classification*

When solving CPA exam questions that call for lists of procedures, the most efficient approach may be to group the 11 objectives into six groups. These six groups can then be applied to any area. They are **U-PERCV**, as follows:
- **Understandability & Classification** – Management asserts that information is presented and described clearly, and transactions and events have been recorded in the Proper Accounts.
- **Presentation & Disclosure** – Management asserts that all accounts are presented in the proper sections of the financial statements and that all necessary informative disclosures have been made.
- **Existence or Occurrence** – Management asserts that all assets, liabilities, and equity interests listed on the balance sheet exist, and disclosed transactions and events that have been recorded have occurred and pertain to the entity.
- **Rights & Obligations** – Management asserts that it is the legal owner of all assets listed on the financial statements, and that the liabilities represent legal obligations of the entity. Also, that all disclosed events pertain to the entity.
- **Completeness & Cutoff** – Management asserts that ALL assets, liabilities, equity interests, transactions and events have been recorded and ALL disclosures that should have been included have been included. Transactions and events have been recorded in the Correct accounting period (CUTOFF).

- **Valuation, Allocation & Accuracy** – Management asserts that amounts are valued using a method in accordance with generally accepted accounting principles, and that revenues and expenses are allocated to the proper periods. Recorded transactions and disclosures have been recorded appropriately.

Audit Objectives

- The Auditor develops specific audit objectives in order to substantiate assertions that are material to the financial statements.

Audit Procedures (Substantive Tests) (AU-C 330)

There are a variety of audit procedures the auditor may use to obtain audit evidence. Some procedures are more appropriate for tests of controls, some for substantive testing, and some may be used for either or both. In addition, when selecting procedures for substantive testing purposes, some are more appropriate for *tests of details* and others are more appropriate for *tests of balances*.

- Two categories of Substantive tests
  - *Test of details* of transactions & events, account balances & presentation & disclosures (**TD**-Test of Details risk)
  - *Analytical procedures* (**AP**-Analytical Procedures risk)

Tests of details refer to tests designed to verify the account balances, the transactions (income statement) and presentation and disclosures that occurred during the year and were the source of the account balances.

Analytical procedures refer to examination of the relationship between different numbers and nonfinancial information to identify unusual relationships, which may indicate misstated amounts. Substantive procedures are *required* for each material transaction class, account balance, and disclosure item.

Audit procedures should be used by an auditor to obtain an understanding of the entity and its environment, including its internal control (*risk assessment procedures*), to test the operating effectiveness of controls (*tests of controls*), and to detect material misstatements (*substantive procedures*). The auditor should obtain evidence to draw reasonable conclusions on which to base an opinion, by performing the following **audit procedures:**

- **Risk assessment procedures** are performed to obtain an understanding of the entity and its environment, including its internal control, to assess the risk of material misstatement (RMM) at the financial statement and relevant assertion levels. They do not provide a sufficient basis for the auditor's opinion.
- **Tests of controls** are performed to test the *operating effectiveness* of controls in preventing or detecting material misstatements at the relevant assertions level. They are necessary when the auditor's risk assessment presumes controls are operating effectively or if substantive procedures alone do not provide sufficient appropriate audit evidence.
- **Substantive procedures** should be used to detect material misstatements through tests of details and analytical procedures for all relevant assertions related to each material class of transactions, account balance, and disclosure. These are used regardless of the assessed risk of material misstatement.

No audit can be performed without including substantive tests of details. **Audit procedures** (acts to be performed) are used as risk assessment procedures, tests of controls, and substantive procedures. The following is a list of types of procedures **(I-CORRIIA):**

- **In*quiry*** (e.g., written inquiries and oral inquiries)
  The auditor can make **inquiries** of management and others. Inquiries may be written or oral and may be used in obtaining an understanding of the entity and its environment, including its internal controls; to learn about accounting policies and procedures, such as how estimates are developed and capitalization policies; how balances were derived, including the sources used for developing measurements or the methodology for determining balances; or any other matters that the auditor believes a response to which will provide audit evidence.

- ***Confirmation*** (e.g., accounts receivable)
  Audit evidence obtained directly from parties outside the entity (discussed later).

- ***Observation*** (e.g., observation of inventory count, observation of control activities)
  The auditor can **observe** activities, such as the performance of processes, to determine if internal controls have been implemented and are being applied effectively. The auditor can also observe the taking of a physical count of inventory to both obtain evidence about the existence of inventory and to verify the accuracy of the counts.

- ***Recalculation*** (e.g., checking the mathematical accuracy of documents or records)
  The auditor may **recalculate** information included in the financial statements, such as recalculating depreciation expense and accumulated depreciation to compare it to the client's amounts.

- **R*eperformance*** (e.g., reperforming the aging of accounts receivable)
  The auditor can actually perform processes to determine the outcome and compare that outcome to information provided by the client. The auditor can **reperform** an internal control procedure, for example, to determine if the procedure would be effective in preventing a material misstatement from occurring or detecting it so that it can be corrected on a timely basis.

- **In*spection of tangible assets*** (e.g., inventory items)
  The auditor can **inspect assets** to verify that they are in appropriate condition and that they are the same as described by the entity.

- **In*spection (Examination) of records or documents*** (e.g., invoice for an equipment purchase transaction)
  The auditor can **inspect documents** to determine if they have been interpreted and recorded properly. The information on the document may be ***traced*** from the source document into the books and records to check for completeness, such as tracing the inventory quantity from a count sheet directly into the books and records. Performing the test in the other direction, however, is called *vouching*. This occurs when the information is ***vouched*** from the books back to the source documents, to check for existence or occurrence. An example would be vouching the inventory quantity from the books back to the inventory count sheets.

- o **Tracing – Completeness**
- o **Vouching – Existence or Occurrence**

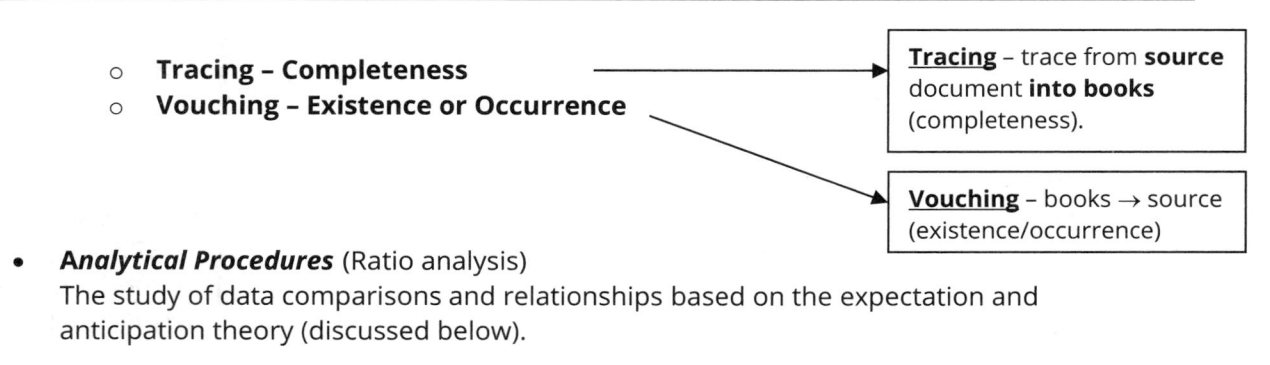

Tracing – trace from **source** document **into books** (completeness).

Vouching – books → source (existence/occurrence)

- **Analytical Procedures** (Ratio analysis)
  The study of data comparisons and relationships based on the expectation and anticipation theory (discussed below).

A nice way to remember the audit procedures is that I love to travel the world, and **I** have even been to **Korea** (**I-CORRIIA**).

Lecture 4.04

ANALYTICAL PROCEDURES (AP) (AU-C 520)

Analytical procedures (AP) (AU-C 520) (e.g., scanning numbers for reasonableness, calculating ratios)

- Expectation/Anticipation Theory
- Relationships between numbers

Analytical procedures (AP) are audit procedures that involve the auditor developing an expectation based on knowledge that may have been obtained from a variety of sources. This expectation is then compared to client representations and the degree to which they match will provide the auditor with evidence as to the reliability of management's representation. The reliability of the expectation, which is generally a function of the source of information used by the auditor to develop it, and its precision determine the reliability of the evidence obtained.

The decision by the auditor as to what tests of details to apply will depend on the level of detection risk that must be achieved and the availability of appropriate evidence. Observation, for example, may not be possible for an intangible asset, such as goodwill, which does not represent a physical asset that can be observed, and may not be necessary when the risk of material misstatement is assessed at a low level and the auditor is willing to accept evidence obtained from other sources to provide sufficient substantive information.

The objective of tests of details is to detect material misstatements in the financial statements. Since the balances at the financial statement date often depend heavily on transactions occurring near the end of the year, the auditor must be careful about the decision to perform substantive tests at interim dates. This can increase **incremental audit risk** and should be avoided unless the acceptable level of detection risk is relatively high or the accounts are such that year-end balances are reasonably predictable.

In some cases, tests of details **cannot** be performed until after the close of the fiscal year under audit. Examples include the search for unrecorded liabilities (since the auditor must know what was recorded to perform such a search) and obtaining a management representation letter (since such a letter must be dated as of the audit completion date). Other tests must be performed as close to the balance sheet date as possible, such as the counts of inventory and marketable securities on hand.

In selecting appropriate audit procedures, the auditor may consider the relationship between cost and usefulness. However, in situations where there is no appropriate alternative procedure, difficulty or expense are NOT valid reasons for choosing to omit necessary audit procedures.

Assume, for example, that an auditor had determined from the previous period's audit that the entity leased its facitlities under an operating lease and that the lease, which had a remaining term of several periods, had an anniversary date that fell on July 1, the middle of the client's fiscal year, and that the lease called for an annual increase of 3% as of the anniversary date.
- Rent in the previous period was $20,000 per month for the first 6 months, or $120,000, and $20,600 per month for the latter 6 months, or $123,600, for a total of $243,600.
- Rent in the current period is expected to be $20,600 per month for the first 6 months, or $123,600, and $21,218 per month in the latter 6 months, or $127,308, for a total of $250,908.

In addition, the auditors obtained personal knowledge about the client by visiting the client during the period and from periodic discussions with management. As a result, the auditor is confident that:
- The client did not move its location during the period;
- The client did not sublet any part of their facilities during the period; and
- The client had no need to rent any additional facilities.

As a result, the auditor can establish an expectation that the client will report rent expense of $250,908. If the client reports rent expense of $250,908 for the period, due to the reliability and precision of the auditor's expectation, the auditor is likely to conclude that rent expense is not materially misstated and that no further audit procedures are required.

If, on the other hand, the auditor knew, from having performed the previous period's audit, that the client had reported $30,000,000 in sales in the previous period and, based on public documents published by the Bureau of Labor and Statistics, that the client's industry saw a 5% rise during the previous fiscal period, the auditor may establish an expectation of approximately $31,500,000 for the current year's sales. Without considering actions taken by the client, such as new products introduced, old ones discontinued, or marketing efforts; actions of competitors; and other factors, the expectation is neither precise nor reliable.
- If the client were to report sales of $32,000,000, the auditor would not likely be sufficiently confident that it was not materially misstated without performing other procedures.
- Those procedures may relate to tests of internal controls surrounding the reporting of sales, tests of the details of the transactions recorded as sales, or some combination of both.

AU-C Section 520, Analytical Procedures, indicates that an auditor should consider various factors before deciding to use AP as a substantive test to support amounts reported for classes of transactions or account balances.

Analytical procedures refer to comparisons between amounts reported on the client's financial statements and the client's expectations developed from a combination of financial and nonfinancial information. A basic premise underlying the use of analytical procedures is that plausible relationships can be expected to exist among data. For example, **payroll tax expense** and **payroll expense** can be expected to have a relationship that reflects the relevant tax rates, and **actual costs** in a manufacturing company can be expected to have a relationship to the **standard costs** established for these categories. These might show up in variance reports that would indicate unusual deviations and fluctuations.

In general, relationships involving *income statement accounts* are more predictable than those involving only balance sheet accounts. For example, there isn't any necessary relationship between **equipment** and **accumulated depreciation on equipment** (except that the accumulated depreciation won't exceed the total cost), but there should be a predictable relationship between **equipment** and **depreciation expense on equipment** that reflects the average useful life of the assets, since that is a basis for the calculation of annual expense.

There are five basic types of comparisons that may be performed as analytical procedures (**CRAFT**):

- **Client vs. Industry** – A client's financial data can be expected to have some plausible relationship to industry averages. A client's sales, for example, may have a tendency to rise and fall at the same time the revenues of competitors in the industry change.
- **Related Accounts** – Certain accounts are closely associated with each other and have a range of expected relationships. Interest expense, for example, should approximate the weighted average of liabilities for the period to the weighted average effective interest rate paid by the entity.
- **Actual vs. Budget** – Results during the year should have a plausible relationship to budgets, allowing for the inevitable variances. Actual payroll expenses, for example, should be reasonably close to budgets for payroll, given the control management has over the level of hiring.
- **Financial vs. Non-financial** – Certain non-financial measures are clearly associated with dollars of revenues or costs. Number of passenger miles flown during the year, for example, should have a predictable relationship to airline revenues.
- **This year vs. Prior** – In the absence of extreme changes in the company and with appropriate adjustments for normal growth and changes to the entity's environment, income statement amounts for the current period should be closely associated with those from previous years of the company. Rent expense, for example, will be similar to the previous year in the absence of major changes in company size or alteration of the ratio of purchased to leased assets.

The mnemonic **CRAFT** will remind the auditor to craft different types of analytical procedures in order to achieve the objectives of the audit.

Keep in mind that, in all cases, the compared data should include at least one amount from the actual results of the period under audit. It would make no sense, for example, to compare prior year actual amounts with the current year budgeted amounts, even though they are likely to have a plausible relationship, since neither set of numbers is included in the financial statements of the current period.

Analytical procedures may be performed at three different times during an audit:

- **Planning** – In planning the audit, the application of analytical procedures to the interim financial data can help the auditor gain a basic understanding of the client's business and identify unusual relationships between data that suggest the need for greater amounts of testing of certain accounts. Since the auditor has not yet begun to examine the details of the client's information, the procedures will be applied to data that are aggregated at a high level. Analytical procedures used during the planning phase of the audit are considered risk assessment procedures and are **required**.

- **Substantive** – Analytical procedures may be performed as substantive tests to reduce detection risk in the audit. For certain assertions, these procedures may be sufficient to satisfy the requirements of the audit, eliminating the need to perform tests of details of transactions and accounts (discussed in another module). The decision to use analytical procedures instead of tests of details is made based on the auditor's judgment as to the relative efficiency and effectiveness of the two types of substantive tests. The use of analytical procedures during the substantive testing phases of the audit is **optional**.

When using *analytical procedures in **substantive testing**,* the auditor should complete the following steps:
1. Determine the suitability of particular substantive analytical procedures for given assertions.
2. Evaluate the reliability of data from which the auditor's expectations are developed.
3. Develop an expectation for a recorded amount or ratio that is based on recorded amounts.
4. Evaluate whether the expectation is sufficiently precise to identify a misstatement that may cause the financial statements to be materially misstated.
5. Determine the amount of discrepancy between the recorded amount or ratio and the auditor's expectation that would not require further investigation.
6. Compare the recorded amounts or ratios with the expectations.
7. Investigate any significant differences from the expectations.

- **Overall review** – At the conclusion of the audit, analytical procedures are applied to the data in order to identify relationships that were not identified earlier in the audit engagement. This assists the auditor in assessing conclusions reached and in evaluating the overall financial statement presentations. If these procedures suggest the presence of misstated account balances, the auditor may have to return to the client and perform additional substantive tests of details to satisfactorily complete the engagement. The use of analytical procedures during the overall review of the audit is **required**.
  - These AP should be performed by the manager or partner with overall knowledge of the client's business and industry.
  - The ultimate purpose of these AP is to form an overall conclusion as to whether the financial statements are consistent with the auditor's understanding of the entity.

Some of the most popular **ratios** that are the basis for analytical procedures include:
- **Current ratio** – Current assets divided by current liabilities.
- **Quick ratio** – Quick assets (cash + marketable securities + accounts receivable) divided by current liabilities.
- **Receivables turnover** – Credit sales for the year divided by the average level of accounts receivable.
- **Inventory turnover** – Cost of sales for the year divided by the average level of inventory.
- **Debt-equity ratio** – Total liabilities divided by stockholders' equity.

These ratios can be compared with comparable ratios for prior years, budgets, industry averages, or other benchmarks to identify data that may be materially misstated. In addition, these ratios may be useful in making other determinations necessary in an audit. For example:
- A current ratio of less than 1 may indicate an upcoming inability to pay debts as they come due within the current year that may lead the auditor to have substantial doubt as to the client's ability to continue as a going concern for a reasonable period of time.
- A very low inventory turnover ratio may identify slow-moving or obsolete inventory that needs to be written down or off in the valuation of ending inventory.

It is very important to understand the ratios and the Purpose or Use for the ratios. Some of the frequently tested ratios include:

Ratio	Formula	Purpose or Use

Liquidity – Measures of the company's short-term ability to pay its maturing obligations.

1. Working Capital	Current assets – Current liabilities	Measures the company's solvency
2. Current ratio	$\dfrac{\text{Current assets}}{\text{Current liabilities}}$	Measures short-term debt-paying ability
3. Quick or acid-test ratio	$\dfrac{\text{Cash, marketable securities, and receivables (net)}}{\text{Current liabilities}}$	Measures immediate short-term liquidity
4. Current cash debt coverage ratio	$\dfrac{\text{Net cash provided by operating activities}}{\text{Average current liabilities}}$	Measures a company's ability to pay off its current liabilities in a given year from its operations

Activity – Measures how effectively the company uses its assets

5. Receivables turnover	$\dfrac{\text{Net credit sales}}{\text{Average trade receivables}}$	Measures liquidity of receivables
6. Inventory turnover	$\dfrac{\text{Cost of goods sold}}{\text{Average inventory}}$	Measures liquidity of inventory
7. Asset turnover	$\dfrac{\text{Net sales}}{\text{Average total assets}}$	Measures how efficiently assets are used to generate sales
8. Number of days' supply in average inventory	= 360 / Inventory Turnover **or** = Average (ending) inventory / Average daily cost of goods sold	Measures number of days required to sell inventory
9. Number of days' sales in average receivables	= 360 / Receivables Turnover	Measures number of days required to collect receivables

Ratio	Formula	Purpose or Use

Profitability – Measures of the degree of success or failure of a given company or division for a given period of time.

10. Profit margin on sales (Gross margin)	$\dfrac{\text{Net income}}{\text{Net sales}}$	Measures net income generated by each dollar of sales
11. Rate of return on assets	$\dfrac{\text{Net income}}{\text{Average total assets}}$	Measures overall profitability of assets
12. Rate of return on common stock equity (Return on equity)	$\dfrac{\text{Net income minus preferred dividends}}{\text{Average common stockholders' equity}}$	Measures profitability of owners' investment
13. Earnings per share	$\dfrac{\text{Net income minus preferred dividends}}{\text{Weighted shares outstanding}}$	Measures net income earned on each share of common stock
14. Price-earnings ratio	$\dfrac{\text{Market price of stock}}{\text{Earnings per share}}$	Measures the ratio of the market price per share to earnings per share
15. Payout ratio	$\dfrac{\text{Cash dividends}}{\text{Net income}}$	Measures percentage of earnings distributed in the form of cash dividends

Coverage – Measures of the degree of protection for long-term creditors and investors.

16. Debt to equity	$\dfrac{\text{Total debt}}{\text{Stockholders' equity}}$	Shows creditors the corporation's ability to sustain losses
17. Debt to total assets	$\dfrac{\text{Total debt}}{\text{Total assets}}$	Measures the percentage of total assets provided by creditors
18. Times interest earned	$\dfrac{\text{Income before interest expense and taxes}}{\text{Interest expense}}$	Measures ability to meet interest payments as they come due
19. Cash debt coverage ratio	$\dfrac{\text{Net cash provided by operating activities}}{\text{Average total liabilities}}$	Measures a company's ability to repay its total liabilities in a given year from its operations
20. Book value per share	$\dfrac{\text{Common stockholders' equity}}{\text{Outstanding shares}}$	Measures the amount each share would receive if the company were liquidated at the amounts reported on the balance sheet

Lecture 4.05

SUBSTANTIVE TESTING VS. INTERNAL CONTROL TESTING

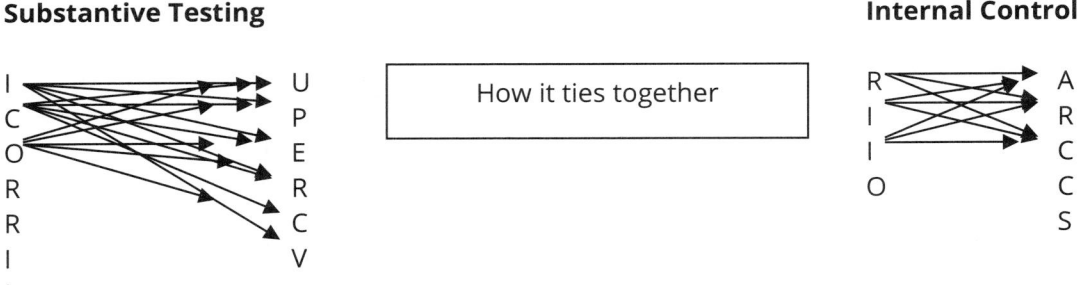

Substantive Testing   **Internal Control**

To understand the application of the assertions to the audit of individual accounts, let's look at an example involving **inventory (RACE):**

- **R**ights and obligations
  - ○ The auditor may determine that the entity has adequate controls to reasonably assure that only inventory to which the entity has rights is recorded, in which case the auditor will perform tests of controls to make certain that the controls are operating as designed.
  - ○ The auditor may obtain evidence about the entity's rights to inventory by tracing inventory purchases to supporting documentation.

- **A**llocation and valuation
  - ○ The auditor may determine that the entity's procedures for measuring and recording inventory reasonably assure that inventory is fairly measured and valued in accordance with GAAP, in which case the auditor will perform tests of controls to make certain that procedures are being followed as designed.
  - ○ The auditor may obtain evidence that inventory is appropriately reported at the lower of cost or net realizable value by performing tests involving recalculation to determine if the client has made appropriate calculations.
  - ○ The auditor may perform substantive analytical procedures to obtain satisfaction that inventory is fairly stated by comparing amounts reported as inventory and cost of sales, as well as the relationships to sales and accounts payable to expectations.

- **C**ompleteness
  - ○ The auditor may determine that the entity has adequate controls to reasonably assure that all inventories to which the entity has rights are recorded, in which case the auditor will perform tests of controls to make certain that the controls are operating as designed.
  - ○ The auditor may obtain evidence that all inventory that is owned is recorded by tracing items in inventory to the accounting records to make certain that they have been recorded.

- **E**xistence
  - The auditor may determine that recorded inventory actually exists by observing the physical inventory.
  - The auditor may obtain evidence that recorded inventories exist by obtaining written confirmations from warehouses storing inventory on behalf of the entity.

Applying the **U-PERCV** approach:
- **U**nderstandability & Classification – To verify that transactions and events have been recorded in the proper accounts and are clearly described, the auditor would read the financial statements and trace purchases into the purchases journal.
- **P**resentation & Disclosure – To verify that all necessary disclosures have been made and that inventory is classified properly, the auditor will read the financial statements and notes.
- **E**xistence or Occurrence – To verify that the inventory exists, the auditor will observe the physical count of inventory.
- **R**ights and obligations – To verify that the client owns the inventory, the auditor will examine vendor invoices.
- **C**ompleteness & Cutoff – To verify that that the client has included all inventory owned by them at year-end, the auditor will perform cutoff tests of receiving and shipping occurring in the days surrounding the balance sheet date.
- **V**aluation, Allocation & Accuracy – To verify that the client is properly accounting for the inventory at the lower of cost or net realizable value, the auditor will review supplier catalogs in order to estimate the replacement cost of the inventory on hand.

With respect to income accounts, such as sales and purchases, the auditor will examine and compare documents related to the transactions. In general, documents will be traced through the system in the **normal order** of processing to verify **completeness**, and will be vouched in **reverse order** to determine **existence or occurrence**. For example, comparing shipping documents to sales invoices verifies that all shipments have been billed (completeness) and comparing sales invoices to shipping documents verifies that all bills are for goods actually shipped (existence or occurrence).

Two Different Audit Approaches
- **Test of Balances (Balance Sheet)**
  - Many transactions, small dollar amounts
    - Cash, A/R, Inventory, A/P
- **Test of Transactions (Income Statement)**
  - Few transactions, large dollar amounts
    - Investments, PP&E, Bonds, N/P, stockholders' equity

OPENING BALANCES (AU-C 510) – INITIAL AUDIT ENGAGEMENTS, INCLUDING REAUDIT ENGAGEMENTS

The auditor is required to obtain *Sufficient Appropriate audit evidence* about whether the opening balances contain misstatements that materially affect the current period's financial statements. Therefore, when an auditor initially accepts an engagement to audit the financial statements of an entity, or when the auditor is engaged to reaudit the financial statements of a period that were previously audited, the auditor has specific concerns to be addressed:
- Whether or not opening balances are fairly stated.
- Whether or not accounting principles have been applied consistently in the current period in relation to the preceding period.

The auditor should read the entity's most recent financial statements and the audit report, if any, thereon, to identify information that may be relevant to opening balances, disclosures, and consistency. In addition, the auditor should obtain sufficient appropriate audit evidence regarding opening balances, including:
- Whether prior period balances have been correctly brought forward to the current period.
- Whether opening balances reflect the application of appropriate accounting policies.
- Whether audit procedures provide sufficient appropriate audit evidence relevant to opening balances, and whether they have been applied consistently.

If the auditor is unable to obtain sufficient appropriate audit evidence regarding opening balances, the auditor should issue a modified opinion or a disclaimer of opinion, as appropriate.

Lecture 4.06

CLASS QUESTIONS

Please see the Class Questions and Class Solutions for this Lecture at the end of this Section.

Lecture 4.07

FINANCIAL STATEMENT ACCOUNTS: (THINK OF I-CORRIIA)

To develop an audit plan for specific items on the financial statements, the auditor will determine which assertions apply, based on whether the item being examined is a class of transactions, an account balance, or a disclosure or presentation related item. The auditor will also identify which assertions are relevant assertions in that a misrepresentation could result in a material misstatement to the financial statements. For each relevant assertion:
- If the auditor is planning to test controls, the auditor will identify the controls that support the assertion, determine how to test them, and determine what substantive procedures will be performed if controls prove to be reliable.
- If the auditor is not planning to test controls, the auditor will determine the substantive tests that will provide evidence that will support that assertion.

Cash & Cash Equivalents

In obtaining evidence about cash and cash equivalents, the auditor will first evaluate whether there is reason to believe that cash and cash equivalents is misstated at the financial statement element or account balance level. The auditor will consider the amount reported as cash and cash

equivalents and apply analytical procedures to determine if the amount seems reasonable considering, for example:
- The normal pattern of expenditures experienced by the entity;
- The entity's policies for maintaining minimum and maximum balances in cash and cash equivalents, and for cash reserves, along with the means of maintaining balances within that range; and
- The entity's policies for authorizing expenditures.

Objectives
- o Adequate I/C
- o Rights and obligations (cash is not restricted).
- o Allocation and valuation (cash recorded in the appropriate amount).
- o Completeness (all cash included).
- o Existence (cash balances actually exist).
- Confirmation – bank reports balances of deposits and loans
- Bank reconciliation
- Bank cutoff statement
- **Kiting** – attempt to overstate cash by showing deposit in current year and disbursement per books in subsequent year.

Applying the **RACE** approach (Account balance)**:**

Rights and Obligations
The accounts containing cash and cash equivalents are owned by the entity and are not encumbered or otherwise restricted by parties outside the entity. A misrepresentation in relation to rights and obligations might occur if there is an account included in cash and cash equivalents that is subject to an externally imposed restriction or is pledged as collateral for an obligation of the entity.
- Bank confirmations to verify account holder.
- Bank confirmations to identify restrictions.

Allocation and Valuation
The amounts reported as cash and cash equivalents are accurately measured. A misrepresentation in relation to valuation and allocation might occur if the amount of either cash on hand or cash on account was overstated or understated.
- Bank confirmations to verify balance per bank.
- Review bank reconciliations to corroborate amounts.
- Reconcile summary schedules to general ledger.
- Obtain bank cutoff statement to verify amounts on bank reconciliation.
- Observation of cash and cash equivalents on hand at balance sheet date.
- Test translation of foreign currency balances.

Completeness
All cash and cash equivalents that are owned by the entity are included in the reported balance. A misrepresentation in relation to completeness might occur if cash on account or on hand that is attributed to the entity is not reported.
- Perform analytical procedures to determine if amounts and volume of transactions match expectations.
- Bank confirmations to banks with closed accounts to identify unreported balances.

Existence

The amount reported as cash and cash equivalents represents cash and cash equivalents that are either on hand or on account. A misrepresentation in relation to existence might occur if the entity reported accounts held with financial institutions that did not exist or reported cash on hand that did not exist, such as petty cash accounts.

- Bank confirmations to balances.
- Observation of cash and cash equivalents on hand at balance sheet date.

There are various *forms of evidence* the auditor may use in the audit of cash and cash equivalents. Some will be obtained from the client, some directly from outside sources, and some may result from the direct actions of the auditor. Evidence the auditor may use includes:

- Bank statements received by the client and provided to the auditor;
- Bank statements related to accounts closed during the period received by the client and provided to the auditor;
- Bank cutoff statements, bank statements that are for a relatively short period beginning with the first transaction after the last bank statement provided to the entity at the end of its fiscal period, received directly by the auditor;
- Bank reconciliations prepared by the client;
- Bank confirmations from all institutions with which the entity has accounts and for which the entity had accounts that had been closed, obtained directly by the auditor from each financial institution;
- Observation of cash and cash equivalents on hand at balance sheet date; and
- Minutes of meetings of those responsible for governance to identify authorization for opening, closing, or encumbering cash or cash equivalents.

Applying the **PERCV** approach:

Presentation & Disclosure

- Review disclosures for compliance with GAAP
- Inquire about compensating balance requirements and restrictions

Existence or Occurrence

- Confirmation/observation
- Count cash on hand
- Prepare bank transfer schedule (kiting)

In seeking evidence that cash and cash equivalents exist, the auditor will determine if there are controls in place that would provide assurance that reported cash balances actually did exist. These controls might include:

- Periodic reconciliation of reported cash balances to bank statements or other statements of account received from account holders performed by an appropriate party; or
- Periodic test counts of petty cash both on prescribed dates, such as at the end of each month, and on randomly selected dates to enhance the possibility of detecting fraudulent use.

Substantive procedures the auditor may perform in relation to existence may include:

- Inspection – The auditor may inspect the bank reconciliations prepared by the entity, matching bank statements received from financial institutions by the entity to each reported account to verify the existence or the accounts;

- Observation – The auditor may either observe the counting of petty cash accounts and other cash on hand or will perform independent counts to verify that petty cash amounts reported on the balance sheet actually exist; and
- Confirmation – The auditor may obtain confirmations and bank cutoff statements directly from institutions holding cash accounts on behalf of the entity to verify that the reported accounts actually exist.

Rights & Obligations
- Review cutoffs (receipts and disbursements)
- Review passbooks, bank statements

In seeking evidence that the entity had rights to all cash and cash equivalents that are reported as such on the financial statements, the auditor will determine if there are controls in place that would provide assurance that amounts reported as cash and cash equivalents have not been encumbered and are the rightful property of the entity. These might include:
- Policies established by those responsible for governance limiting the authority to encumber cash or cash equivalents;
- Instructions from those responsible for governance to financial institutions to inform governance of any encumbrances placed on cash or cash equivalent accounts; and
- Accounting policies requiring that the encumbering of cash or cash equivalent accounts requires their reclassification out of cash and cash equivalents into an appropriate asset category.

Substantive procedures the auditor may perform in relation to rights and obligations may include:
- Confirmation – The auditor may obtain confirmations directly from institutions holding cash accounts on behalf of the entity to verify that there are no encumbrances affecting the accounts held at that institution;
- Inquiry – The auditor may inquire as to whether there are any encumbrances that have been placed on any accounts containing cash or cash equivalents; and
- Inspection – The auditor may read minutes of meetings of those charged with governance to determine if the encumbrance of any cash or cash equivalent accounts have been authorized.

Completeness & Cutoff
- Perform analytical procedures
- Review bank reconciliation
- Obtain bank cutoff statement to verify reconciling items on bank reconciliation

In seeking evidence that the entity has reported all cash and cash equivalents, the auditor will determine if there are controls in place that would provide assurance that all cash and cash equivalents owned by the entity are reported. These might include:
- Policies and procedures related to the receipt and depositing of cash to make certain that it is deposited into accounts that are owned and reported by the entity; and
- Periodic high-level reviews by management of cash receipts and disbursements to determine if reported amounts are reasonable in relation to expected and known levels of activity experienced by the entity.

Substantive procedures the auditor may perform in relation to completeness may include:
- Confirmation – The auditor may obtain confirmations directly from institutions in which the entity held accounts that were closed during the period;

- Inquiry – The auditor may inquire of management as to whether there are any accounts in which the entity is holding cash or cash equivalents that are not included in amounts reported on the financial statements; and
- Analytical Procedures – The auditor may compare the amounts and the volume of transactions to the auditor's expectations.

Valuation, Allocation & Accuracy
- *Foot* (adding) summary schedules
- Reconcile summary schedules to general ledger
- Test translation of any foreign currencies

In seeking evidence that the entity has reported all cash and cash equivalents in appropriate amounts, the auditor will determine if there are controls in place that would provide assurance that all cash and cash equivalents owned by the entity are reported. These might include:
- Periodic reconciliation of reported cash balances to bank statements or other statements of account received from other account holders performed by an appropriate party; and
- Periodic test counts of petty cash.

Substantive procedures the auditor may perform in relation to valuation and allocation may include:
- Confirmation – The auditor may obtain confirmations directly from institutions in which the entity holds accounts and compare the balance as of the end of the accounting period to the amount used in the bank reconciliation;
- Inspection – The auditor may inspect bank reconciliations to determine that all amounts are correct and agree with amounts in the trial balance and on the financial statements;
- Recalculation – The auditor will obtain a bank cutoff statement for each cash and cash equivalent account held at an institution and perform a reconciliation to verify that amounts for deposits in transit, outstanding checks, and other issues that required time for clearance that were reported on the bank reconciliation at the end of the period either cleared the account or were otherwise resolved;
- Recalculation – The auditor may prepare a summary of all cash and cash equivalents and trace the amount to the trial balance and, ultimately, to the amount reported on the financial statements;
- Recalculation – The auditor may verify accuracy of conversion of foreign currency balances into the reporting currency; and
- Observation – The auditor may observe cash and cash equivalents on hand at balance sheet date.

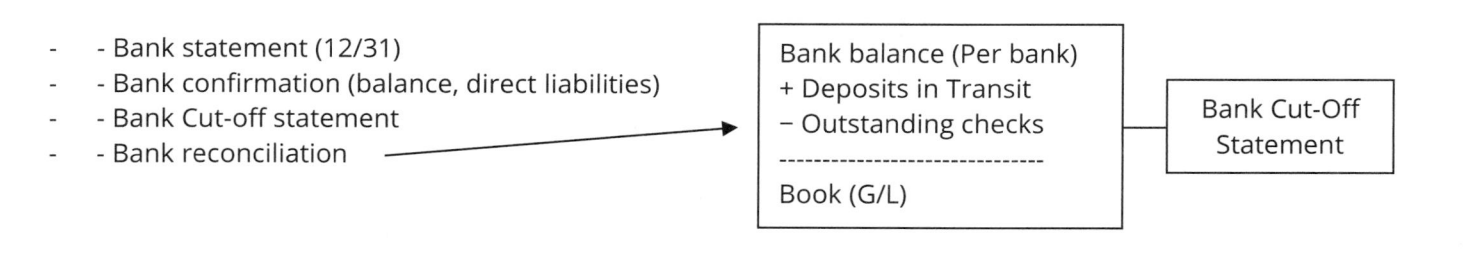

Cash and cash equivalents are particularly susceptible to fraud. Of all fraud schemes, misappropriation of assets is the most common and the asset that is most frequently misappropriated is cash. This is done in a variety of ways.

- Cashiers and others may be stealing cash receipts. This is evaluated as part of the understanding of the revenues and cash receipts systems.
- Employees and others may be stealing cash from cash registers, petty cash accounts, or other areas in which there may be cash that is accessible. The entity's policies regarding cash receipts and the handling of petty cash will be evaluated to determine the entity's susceptibility.
- Employees and others may be stealing cash by causing the entity to make inappropriate cash disbursements in the form of overpayments, payments without the receipt of goods or services, payments to phantom entities or employees, and others. The auditor evaluates these in the various tests related to cash disbursements as part of the audit of expenses and the handling of other expenditures.
- Management may overstate cash using some technique, such as kiting, to hide the overstatement.

Kiting is a special type of fraud used by management to overstate cash and cash equivalents at the end of the period. It is accomplished by making transfers from one of the entity's accounts to another, recording the increase in the recipient account at the end of the current fiscal period and recognizing the decrease in the disbursing account at the beginning of the subsequent period. Provided the checks did not clear the disbursing account before the year-end, the disbursements would simply not be recorded and, as a result, would not be a reconciling item. The deposits to the recipient accounts, however, will be reported as deposits in transit that will be shown as clearing the account shortly after year-end on the cutoff statement.

One common way in which kiting can be detected is when the auditor prepares a schedule of intercompany bank transfers. Using such a schedule, the auditor can verify that the reduction in the disbursing account is recorded in the same period as the increase in the recipient account.

Intercompany bank transfer schedule (12/15 – 1/15)

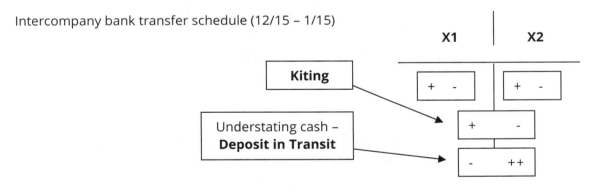

The auditor still wants to confirm banks with no balance because a loan payable with the bank may exist.

There aren't many complications in the audit of cash. Cash on hand is usually verified by performing a count at the balance sheet date. In performing the audit of cash in bank, the auditor will examine the bank statements sent to the client, including a **cutoff statement**, sent directly by the bank to the auditor, with a closing date a couple of weeks following the year-end (to ensure that outstanding checks and deposits in transit have cleared within a reasonable period of time).

The auditor will also obtain a **standard bank confirmation** directly from the bank. The information that will be provided includes:
- Balances in all deposit accounts as of the balance sheet date.

- Outstanding loan balances at that date.
- Collateral agreements on loans (including agreements to maintain compensating balances in cash accounts).

The bank will only send such a confirmation at the request of the client, but since the information is provided directly to the auditor by the bank, it has a higher level of persuasiveness than bank statements and other information examined by the auditor at the client's premises. One concern is that the specific bank employee preparing the form may not be aware of all the financial relationships the client has with the bank, in which case the information provided to the auditor may be incomplete.

An auditor will also be examining the **statement of cash flows** that must accompany the other financial statements. Since this statement is derived entirely from transactions affecting the balance sheet and income statement, one of the auditor's responsibilities is to reconcile the amounts on the statement of cash flows to the information on the two source statements.

Special attention must be paid to transfers made by the client between different bank accounts around the balance sheet date. The auditor will prepare an **interbank transfer schedule** that includes all checks written from one of the client's accounts to another for the few days surrounding year-end.

The **Interbank Transfer schedule** might look as follows:

	Bank Accounts		Disbursement Date		Receipt Date	
Check			Per	Per	Per	Per
No.	From	To	Books	Bank	Books	Bank
576	East Bank	West Bank	Dec 30	Jan 4	Dec 30	Jan 3
583	West Bank	East Bank	Jan 3	Jan 2	Dec 30	Dec 31

The auditor will examine each transfer with the intention of identifying:
- **Deposits in transit** at the balance sheet date.
- Evidence of **kiting** of checks.

With respect to deposits in transit, the auditor wants to make sure that these are listed on the bank reconciliation in determining the correct balance of the receiving account (so that the total cash in bank will not be understated). In the normal sequence, the check will first be written from the disbursing account and posted to the cash disbursements journal (or check register) on that date.

Thus, the **disbursement date per books should be the earliest date** of the four. The check may then be transmitted to another location for deposit, which will cause a delay in the deposit of the check at the receiving bank. A **deposit in transit** occurs when the **disbursement per books** occurred **before year-end** but the **receipt per bank** occurred **after** year-end.

Kiting is an attempt by the client to overstate total cash in the bank by reporting a receipt in the current period without reporting the equivalent disbursement. **Kiting** occurs when the **disbursement per books** occurred **after year-end** but the **receipt** (per books and/or per bank) occurred **before** year-end (Check #583 above).

Lecture 4.08

Receivables

Objectives

- Adequate I/C.
- Rights and obligations (the entity has a legitimate claim to receivables).
- Allocation and valuation (receivables are presented at net realizable value (**NRV**)).
- Completeness (all receivables are reported).
- Existence (receivables actually exist).

In obtaining evidence about receivables, the auditor will first evaluate whether there is reason to believe that receivables are misstated at the financial statement element or account balance level. The auditor will consider the amount reported as accounts receivable and apply analytical procedures to determine if the amount seems reasonable. Based on the auditor's knowledge of the client's collection policies and the strictness with which they are enforced, the auditor will develop an expectation for the number of days' sales in accounts receivable:

- If the client has policies that are strictly enforced, the auditor may be able to develop an expectation that is adequately precise and adequately reliable to establish a very narrow expectation range.
    - o   If the client's reported amount is within that range, it would be considered strong evidence that the balance was not materially misstated, reducing the timing, extent, and nature of further audit procedures to be applied.
    - o   If the client's reported amount falls outside the range, the auditor will make inquiries to determine if there is a reasonable explanation, such as a large customer being given extended terms, or if it is indicative of a potential misstatement.

- If the client's policies are not clearly established or strictly enforced, the relationship between accounts receivable and sales is not predictable in a manner that is either precise or reliable.
    - o   The auditor would not obtain any meaningful evidence by performing such analytical procedures; and
    - o   The auditor may determine that the lax policies represent a control deficiency and potentially a significant deficiency or material weakness.

The auditor may also apply an analytical procedure to the allowance for doubtful accounts if the relationship between accounts receivable and the allowance is predictable. This will also depend, to a degree, on how strictly the entity enforces its collection policies and the degree to which it is systematic in determining when accounts will be written off, turned over to collection, or subjected to some other action.

Applying the **RACE** approach (Balance Sheet)**:**

Rights and Obligations
The entity is entitled to the proceeds from the collections of the receivables. A misrepresentation in relation to rights and obligations might occur if the entity was acting as an agent in the sale of goods and is, therefore, not entitled to the proceeds or if receivables have been used as collateral, invalidating the entity's claim to the proceeds from collection.

- Accounts receivable confirmations.
- Tracing receivables to documentation of sales transactions.

Allocation and Valuation

The amounts reported as receivables are accurately measured. A misrepresentation in relation to valuation and allocation might occur if receivables are overstated, perhaps because of misappropriated cash receipts or understated due to an unrecorded sale.

- Accounts receivable confirmations.
- Tracing receivables to subsequent collections.
- Review of process for estimating allowance for uncollectible accounts.
- Analytical procedures to evaluate the reasonableness of receivables.

Completeness

All receivables to which the entity is entitled to the proceeds from collection are included in the reported balance. A misrepresentation in relation to completeness might occur if a receivable due to the entity was not recorded, perhaps as a result of an unrecorded sale transaction.

- Trace sales transactions to recorded accounts receivable.
- Analytical procedures to evaluate the reasonableness of receivables.

Existence

The amount reported as receivables represent claims for cash or other financial instruments that are enforceable against other parties. A misrepresentation in relation to existence may occur if the entity records sales and the related receivables from transactions that did not actually occur.

- Accounts receivable confirmations.
- Tracing receivables to documentation of sales transactions.
- Tracing receivables to subsequent collections.

There are various *forms of evidence* the auditor may use in the audit of receivables. Some will be obtained from the client, some directly from outside sources, and some may result from the direct actions of the auditor. Evidence the auditor may use includes:

- Prenumbered sales invoices, shipping reports, and documents related to the selection of merchandise from inventory prepared internally by the entity;
- Customer purchase orders received by the entity from the customer and provided to the auditor by the entity;
- Aged analyses of accounts receivable used as a basis for determining the appropriate balance in the allowance for doubtful accounts;
- Correspondence between the entity and the customer regarding a receivable;
- Sales invoices and periodic statements sent by the entity to its customers;
- Confirmations sent directly from the customer to the auditor; and
- Evidence of subsequent collection.

Applying the **PERCV** approach:

Presentation & Disclosure

- Review disclosures for compliance with GAAP
- Inquire about pledging, discounting
- Review loan agreements for pledging, factoring

Existence or Occurrence

- Confirmation
- Inspect notes
- Vouch (examine shipping documents, invoices, credit memos)

In seeking evidence that receivables exist, the auditor will determine if there are controls in place that would provide assurance that reported receivables actually do exist. These controls might include:
- Information processing controls requiring that supporting documents that evidence a sale are evaluated and matched before recognizing receivables; and
- Periodic evaluations by management to verify that past due accounts and write-offs are not due to nonexistent customers.

Substantive procedures the auditor may perform in relation to existence may include:
- Inspection – The auditor may inspect the documentation that supports a receivable, including the customer purchase order, entity sales order, shipping documents, documents requesting that the goods be moved from inventory to shipping, and sales invoices to verify that the transactions creating the receivables actually occurred;
- Observation – The auditor may trace receivables to subsequent collections; and
- Confirmation – The auditor may obtain confirmations directly from customers to verify that reported amounts are actually owed to the entity.

Rights and Obligations
- Review cutoffs (sales, cash receipts, sales returns)
- Inquire about factoring of receivables

In seeking evidence that the entity had rights to all receivables that are reported on the financial statements, the auditor will determine if there are controls in place that would provide assurance that the entity is entitled to collections from amounts reported as receivables that the receivables have not been encumbered. These might include:
- Policies established by those responsible for governance limiting the authority to borrow using receivables as collateral; and
- Information processing controls requiring that supporting documents that evidence a sale are evaluated and matched before recognizing receivables.

Substantive procedures the auditor may perform in relation to rights and obligations may include:
- Inspection – The auditor may inspect the documentation that supports a receivable including the customer purchase order, entity sales order, shipping documents, documents requesting that the goods be moved from inventory to shipping, and sales invoices to verify that the transactions creating the receivables were satisfied by the entity;
- Observation – The auditor may trace receivables to subsequent collections; and
- Confirmation – The auditor may obtain confirmations directly from customers to verify that reported amounts are actually owed to the entity.

Completeness & Cutoff
- Perform analytical procedures

In seeking evidence that the entity has reported all receivables, the auditor will determine if there are controls in place that would provide assurance that all receivables owned by the entity are reported. These might include:
- Using prenumbered forms for all transactions and accounting for all numbers missing from a particular sequence; and
- Periodic high-level reviews by management of receivable balances in relation to sales to determine if reported amounts are reasonable in relation to expected and known levels of activity experienced by the entity.

Substantive procedures the auditor may perform in relation to completeness may include:

- Confirmation – The auditor may obtain confirmations directly from customers to verify that all amounts owed to the entity are reported.
- Recalculation – The auditor may account for the sequence of all prenumbered documents that are used in the process to make and record sales on account.
- Observation – The auditor may trace shipping documents for transactions occurring near the end of the period to the accounting records to make certain that there is a proper cutoff and that all sales and receivables were recognized in the appropriate period:
  - The auditor may account for the numerical sequence of all shipping documents to make certain that all shipments are accounted for.
  - The auditor may trace shipping documents to sales invoices to make certain that all goods shipped have been billed to the customer.
  - The auditor may account for the numerical sequence of all sales invoices to make certain that all sales are accounted for.
  - The auditor may trace sales invoices to the sales journal to make certain that all sales have been recorded.
- Analytical Procedures – The auditor may compare the amounts reported as receivables to the auditor's expectations that are based on the auditor's knowledge of the entity's receivable policies and its reported sales for the period.

Valuation, Allocation & Accuracy

- Foot subsidiary ledger
- Reconcile subsidiary ledger to general ledger
- Examine subsequent cash receipts
- Age receivables to test adequacy of allowance for doubtful accounts
- Discuss adequacy of allowance for doubtful accounts with management and compare to historical experience

In seeking evidence that the entity has reported all receivables in appropriate amounts, the auditor will determine if there are controls in place that would provide assurance that all receivables to which the entity is entitled are reported at appropriate amounts. These might include:

- Receivables are regularly evaluated to determine if accounts should be written down or off;
- Discrepancies reported by customers are investigated on a timely and appropriately thorough basis; and
- Periodic high-level reviews by management to determine if receivables seem reasonable in relation to the entity's volume of activity.

Substantive procedures the auditor may perform in relation to valuation and allocation may include:

- Confirmation – The auditor may obtain confirmations directly from customers verifying the amounts that are owed to the entity;
- Recalculation or Inspection – The auditor may either obtain an aged analysis of the client's receivables and calculate an estimated amount for the allowance for doubtful accounts to be compared to the client's balance, or the auditor may review the client's aged analysis to determine if the allowance was properly calculated and reported; and
- Observation – The auditor may trace amounts reported as receivables to subsequent collections.

External Confirmations (AU-C 505)

External confirmations are considered one of the more reliable sources of audit evidence. As indicated:
- Audit evidence obtained directly from parties outside the entity, like external confirmation, is more reliable than evidence obtained from within the entity; and
- Evidence in documentary form is more reliable than evidence obtained orally.

External confirmations may be used for a variety of audit purposes, including:
- Confirmations to banks regarding bank balances and related transactions.
- Confirmations to customers to verify accounts receivable amounts and terms.
- Confirmations to vendors to verify accounts payable amounts and terms.
- Confirmations to warehouses to verify existence of inventories or other assets being held for the entity.
- Confirmations to brokers or investment firms to verify existence and balances of investment securities held on behalf of the entity.
- Confirmations to lenders to verify amounts due and terms.

AU-C Section 505, External Confirmations, *requires* the auditor to use external confirmations for accounts receivable, unless:
- The overall accounts receivable balance is not material;
- The use of external confirmations is not expected to be effective; or
- RMM at the relevant assertion level is low and the auditor can address the assessed risk through the use of other planned substantive procedures.

When using external confirmations, the auditor is required to maintain control over various aspects of the confirmation process. Specifically, the auditor should:
- Determine the information to be confirmed or requested.
- Select the appropriate party to whom to address the confirmation.
- Design the confirmation requests to make certain:
  - They are addressed to the appropriate responding party.
  - Responses are provided directly to the auditor.
- Send the requests, including follow-up requests.

*There are **three types of confirmations:***

- **Negative** confirmations, in which the customer is asked to respond only if the amount is incorrect.
  - No need to respond.
  - The auditor does not expect the request to be ignored.
  - A low exception rate expected.
  - No news is good news.   **RMM ↓ (CR↓)**
  - Most applicable for small balances.
  - Provides *implicit evidence.*

- **Positive** (RSVP) confirmations, in which the customer is asked to verify the correctness of the amount on the confirmation.
  - Requires a response.
  - Most applicable for large balances.   **RMM ↑ (CR↑)**
  - Provides *Explicit evidence.*

- **Blank** confirmations, a special form of *positive confirmation*, in which the customer is asked to provide an amount without being told the value on the client's records.

Factors that may suggest the need for positive or blank confirmations may include:
- A large balance
- An active account
- Delinquency
- High assessed level of Risk of Material Misstatement (RMM)
- The expectation that the customer will not pay attention to a negative confirmation

One problem with the use of positive confirmations is that some parties may not respond or may do so, but not on a timely basis. Methods that *encourage a higher response* may include:
- The use of clear language on the confirmation;
- Sending the confirmation to a specific individual;
- Identifying the entity being audited;
- Having the client sign the confirmation request by hand;
- Setting a deadline for a response;
- Sending second requests; and
- Calling addressees to obtain oral confirmation and request a response to the written confirmation.

When an addressee **does not respond** to a positive confirmation, there are various actions an auditor may take, including:
- Sending second confirmation requests;
- Asking the client to contact the addressee to request a response;
- Review related transactions in subsequent periods, such as cash receipts in relation to accounts receivable;
- Inspect supporting documents, such as a customer's purchase order and shipping documents;
- Examine correspondence between the addressee and the client; or
- Consider an audit adjustment.

AU-C 505 also suggests that when reconciliation of aggregate balances to positive or blank confirmation requests proves difficult, confirmation of single transactions, such as individual invoices, may be a suitable alternative.

Due to the inherent risks associated with e-mail or FAX responses to requests for confirmation of accounts receivable, mailed returns of the original request and verification by telephone in the case of faxed or emailed responses, are considered preferable.

If management refuses to allow the auditor to perform external confirmation procedures, the auditor should seek evidence to determine if management's reasons are valid and reasonable.
- If so, the auditor will evaluate the effect on the risk of material misstatement and apply alternative audit procedures.
- If not, or if the auditor is not able to obtain sufficient appropriate audit evidence applying alternative audit procedures, the auditor should:
    - Communicate with those in charge of governance; and
    - Evaluate the implications on the audit and on the auditor's report.

One fraud risk factor associated with receivables is the possibility of **lapping**. Lapping occurs when cash received on account is misappropriated, resulting in the overstatement of a customer's account. When cash is subsequently received from another customer, a portion is allocated to the customer whose account is overstated, resulting in an overstatement of the latter customer's account.

This type of fraud can best be prevented by appropriate segregation of duties since, to be successful, the person misappropriating the cash receipts will also have to be able to influence how receipts are applied to accounts. A lack of segregation of duties or collusion will make this type of fraud more likely to occur.

Because the overstatement of a customer's balance moves from one customer to another as collections are received, this type of fraud may be very difficult to detect. There are two factors that make it more readily detectable:
- If the perpetrator commits this type of fraud on a repetitive basis, which is often the case, the amount of overstatement and the number of accounts affected will increase to a point where it will be difficult to conceal; and
- If the amount is material and the company has clear credit and collection policies that are strictly enforced, the relationship between accounts receivable and sales will change, which should alert management or the auditor to a potential problem.

Lapping of A/R – Attempt to cover theft of receivables collection by posting subsequent collection from another customer to that subsidiary account.

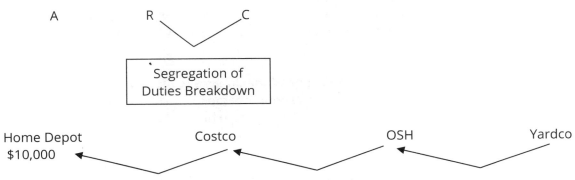

(Payment from Costco gets credited to Home Depot, OSH gets credited to Costco, etc)

Although confirmations provide the strongest evidence of the **existence** of the receivable, keep in mind that there are other management assertions that need to be verified, and other procedures may be more appropriate to achieve additional audit objectives:
- **Valuation** – The fact that a customer has confirmed a balance does not prove they will pay it. The best evidence of the valuation of the receivable is **subsequent collection** (since the audit is likely to continue more than 30 days following the balance sheet date, most sales under terms of net 30 will be collected before the auditor's report has to be issued). Other valuation procedures include inspecting the **aging** of receivables and examining **credit ratings** of customers to determine if the allowance for uncollectibles is sufficient.
- **Completeness** – Since the primary concern of the auditor with respect to receivables is **overstatement**, and special emphasis is placed on confirming large account balances claimed by the client, confirmations cannot be expected to provide significant information about understated receivables. Also, a customer is not as likely to inform the auditor if the balance is understated, since the customer benefits from the amount being too low. The best evidence of completeness is to perform **cutoff** tests on shipments occurring immediately before and after the balance sheet date, to ensure that all sales taking place during the year have been recorded in sales and accounts receivable. In addition, **tracing**

of shipping documents to sales invoices will help verify that all shipped goods have been billed to customers, and the examination of the **numerical sequence** of shipping documents and sales invoices will ensure that documents have not been lost and, as a result, not been posted to sales.

The auditor should perform tests to ensure that **lapping** of receivables is not taking place.
- Lapping is used by a receivables bookkeeper to disguise the theft of collections from customers.

The technique involves the following:
- A check or cash payment from a customer on a receivable is misappropriated (stolen) by the bookkeeper or another employee in collusion with the bookkeeper.
- Since deposits are periodically reconciled to postings in the receivables records, payment cannot be posted to the customer's account.
- So that the customer won't complain about the failure to be credited for payment (exposing the theft), the bookkeeper posts a later payment from a second customer to that first customer's account.
- This, of course, now causes the second customer's account to be misstated, but the bookkeeper simply posts a payment from a third customer after that to the second customer's account.
- Of course, this complicated scheme must be continued indefinitely to cover the theft, but in companies that frequently receive payments of the same amount from different customers (for instance, a cable company that has standard monthly rates), it may be possible to steal several payments and cover them easily with later payments of equal amount.

In a strong internal control structure, the segregation of the duties of **collection and posting** will make lapping more difficult, and periodic rotation to another employee of the responsibility of posting to receivables records will prevent the bookkeeper from being able to indefinitely cover such thefts.

The substantive test by the auditor that is most likely to detect lapping involves a **comparison** of the dates on checks deposited to the bank with the posting dates in the receivables records, since lapping will always require that "covering" payments be from a later collection.

Uncollectible Accounts Receivable

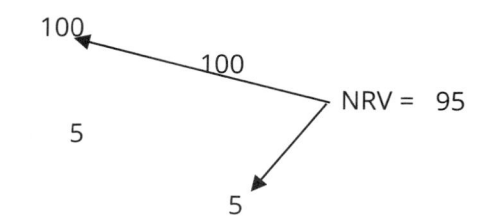

A/R	100
Sales Revenue	100
	NRV = 95
Bad Debt expense	5
Allowance for Uncollectible	
accounts (Doubtful accounts)	5

Lecture 4.09

Investments In Securities and Derivatives (AU-C 501)

In obtaining evidence about investments in securities and derivatives, the auditor will first evaluate whether there is reason to believe that investments are misstated at the financial statement element or account balance level. The auditor will consider the entity's policies for retaining and investing working capital, for accumulating funds for long-term or short-term investment purposes, and related to distributions to shareholders. The auditor may also look at investment-related income to determine if it seems reasonable in relation to the level of investment reported by the entity.

Objectives

- Adequate I/C
- Rights and obligations (Entity owns investments)
- Allocation and valuation (investment is reported at appropriate amount)
- Completeness (all investments reported)
- Existence (investments exist)

Applying the **RACE** approach (Account Balance):

Rights and Obligations

The entity owns the investments that are reported. A misrepresentation in relation to rights and obligations might be the inclusion on the balance sheet of investments that are held on behalf of others and are not the property of the entity.
- Inspect underlying agreements
- Trace to documentation supporting acquisition
- Confirm significant terms with counterparties and holders
- Review bank confirmations for evidence of use as collateral

Allocation and Valuation

The amounts reported as investments are accurately measured. A misrepresentation in relation to valuation and allocation might occur if investments that are required to be reported under the equity method are not, if investments in derivatives or in marketable trading or available-for-sale securities are not reported at fair value, or if investments in held-to-maturity marketable debt securities are not reported at amortized cost.
- Confirm significant terms with counterparties and holders
- Compare to market values for financial instruments with observable market data
- Test amortization of discount or premium
- Review financial statements of major investees

Completeness

All investments in securities and derivatives owned by the entity are included in the amount or amounts reported on the balance sheet. A misrepresentation in relation to completeness might occur if the entity held investments that were excluded from the balance sheet.
- Reconcile dividends received to publicly available information
- Obtain confirmations from counterparties regarding the absence of side agreements
- Confirm holdings with 3rd party custodians

Existence

The amount reported as investments in securities and derivatives are actual investments in the custody of the entity or in the custody of a third party on behalf of the entity. A misrepresentation in relation to existence might be the inclusion on the balance sheet of investments that have already been sold or the recording of an expenditure for an expense or other item as an investment.

- Confirm with 3rd party custodians
- Reconcile to interest and dividends received
- Physically observe securities in the client's custody
- Trace to acquisition documentation

There are various *forms of evidence* the auditor may use in the audit of investments in securities and derivative instruments. Some will be obtained from the client, some directly from outside sources, and some may result from the direct actions of the auditor. Evidence the auditor may use includes:

- Stock certificates and bonds held by the entity;
- Contracts with counterparties related to derivative instruments;
- Communication between the entity and third parties holding investment securities on behalf of the entity;
- Activity and settlement statements from third parties with custody of investment securities on behalf of the entity and from third parties charged with administering derivatives;
- Minutes of meetings of those charged with governance authorizing activities involving investments in securities and derivatives;
- Management's analyses used to determine if investments, other than those reported at fair value, have been impaired;
- Client schedules of investments and investment activity;
- Bank statements and cancelled checks evidencing payments for purchases and deposits from sales of investments in securities and derivatives; and
- Confirmations sent directly from issuers of investment securities, counterparties to derivative instruments, and custodians of securities on behalf of the entity.

Using the **PERCV** approach:

Presentation & Disclosure

- Review disclosures for compliance with GAAP
- Inquire about pledging
- Review loan agreements for pledging
- Review management's classification of securities
- Inquire about derivatives to understand the economic substance (see Derivatives below)

Existence or Occurrence

- Confirmation of securities held by third parties
- Inspect and count
- Vouch (to available documentation)

In seeking evidence that investments exist, the auditor will determine if there are controls in place that would provide assurance that reported investments actually do exist. These controls might include:

- Controls requiring that all securities remain in the custody of the treasurer's department or, when in the custody of a third party, that only the treasurer's department has the ability to authorize purchase or sale transactions; and
- Security instruments are kept in a secure location.

Substantive procedures the auditor may perform in relation to existence may include:

- Confirmation – The auditor may obtain confirmations directly from third parties holding investment securities on behalf of the entity, from counterparties to derivative instruments, and from issuers of investment securities held by the entity;
- Inspection – The auditor may inspect the investment securities that are in custody of the client; and
- Reperformance – The auditor may trace recorded investments to purchase documents, evidence of payment, and authorizations from those charged with governance.

Rights & Obligations

- Review cutoffs (examine transactions near year-end)
- Confirmation of significant terms with counterparties and holders
- Inspect underlying agreements
- Consider findings from other audit procedures

In seeking evidence that the entity had rights to all investments in securities and derivative instruments that are reported on the financial statements, the auditor will determine if there are controls in place that would provide assurance that the entity has not either used the investments as collateral or is otherwise not entitled to the rights associated with the investments.

In most cases, rights and obligations is not a high-risk assertion in relation to these items. The entity will generally have custody of investment securities, or they will be held in custody for the entity, where possession is evidence of ownership. A lender, requiring investment securities as collateral, will generally take possession of the security instruments, or they will be put into a custodianship that is not accessible by the client. Controls might include:

- Policies established by those responsible for governance limiting the authority to borrow using investments as collateral; and
- Periodic evaluation of the reasonableness of investment income in relation to the investments owned by the entity.

Substantive procedures the auditor may perform in relation to rights and obligations may include:

- Inspection – The auditor may inspect stock certificates, bonds, and other securities maintained in the entity's possession;
- Inspection – The auditor may inspect the documentation that supports transactions occurring near the end of the period to make certain that the cutoff is appropriate and that all transactions were reported in the appropriate period;
- Confirmation – The auditor may obtain confirmations from holders of investment securities on behalf of the client, counterparties to derivative instruments, and issuers of investment instruments;
- Inspection – The auditor may inspect agreements and documents with counterparties to derivative instruments; and
- Analytical Procedures – The auditor may evaluate the reasonableness of investment income in relation to the entity's investment activity.

Completeness & Cutoff

- Perform analytical procedures
- Reconcile dividends received to published records
- Confirmation by counterparties or holders concerning existence of undisclosed side-agreements
- Tests to determine existence of undisclosed instruments
- Inspection of documents to determine existence of undisclosed embedded derivatives
- Comparing beginning account detail with ending account detail
- Review of board minutes

In seeking evidence that the entity has reported all investments in securities and derivative instruments, the auditor will determine if there are controls in place that would provide assurance that all investments owned by the entity are reported. These might include:

- Periodic reconciliation of investment securities held to amounts reported on the financial statements; and
- Trace dividends, interest, or other investment income received to investment securities that are reported on the financial statements.

Substantive procedures the auditor may perform in relation to completeness may include:

- Confirmation – The auditor may obtain confirmations directly from third parties holding securities on behalf of the entity, counterparties to derivative instruments, and closely-held issuers of securities owned by the entity;
- Analytical Procedure – The auditor may evaluate the reasonableness of interest, dividend, and other investment income in relation to the investments held;
- Inspection – The auditor may review agreements with counterparties to derivative instruments and other documents related to investment activities to determine if there are imbedded derivatives;
- Inspection – The auditor may review the client's schedule reconciling beginning balances in investment accounts to ending balances, tracing increases and decreases to supporting documentation; and
- Inspection – The auditor may review minutes of meetings of management and those charged with governance authorizing transactions involving investments.

Valuation, Allocation & Accuracy

- Foot summary schedules
- Reconcile summary schedules to general ledger
- Test amortization of premiums and discounts
- Determine the market value for trading and available-for-sale securities
- Review audited financial statements of major investees

In seeking evidence that the entity has reported all investments in securities and derivative instruments in appropriate amounts, the auditor will determine if there are controls in place that would provide assurance that all investments are properly accounted for. These might include:

- For equity method investments, policies for obtaining information about investee earnings and policies and procedures for making adjustments to balances of equity method investments;
- For investments measured at amortized cost, policies and procedures for calculating amortization of discount or premium and verification of its accuracy;
- For investments reported at amortized cost and under the equity method, policies and procedures to identify factors that may indicate an impairment and for measuring and recording an impairment that is determined to have occurred;

- Policies and procedures for obtaining information about fair value for those investments reported at fair value; and
- Policies for measuring fair value when level 1 inputs are not available, including means of determining adjustments to fair values for investments whose fair value is measured using level 2 inputs and the valuation techniques applied for investments whose fair value is measured using level 3 inputs.

Substantive procedures the auditor may perform in relation to valuation and allocation may include:

- Recalculation – The auditor may independently determine market value for investments in trading securities, available-for-sale securities, and other investments reported at fair value;
- Inspection – The auditor may obtain audited financial statements of investees accounted for under the equity method to verify the amount of earnings and adjustments to the investment reported by the entity;
- Inspection – The auditor may review statements from financial institutions, counterparties to derivative instruments, or other parties designated as administering derivative instruments to verify fair value;
- Recalculation – The auditor may recalculate interest and dividend income that should have been earned on investments reported by the entity and compare to amounts received and reported;
- Recalculation – The auditor may foot and cross foot schedules of investments maintained by the client and trace balances to the general ledger and the financial statements; and
- Analytical Procedure – The auditor may evaluate the relationship between investment income and amounts reported as investments to determine if it seems reasonable.

When auditing investments, the auditor will verify the **rights and obligations** assertion by determining the client's ownership of the securities (this also can be considered proof of the **existence** of the investments). There are two principal techniques that will be used:

- **Confirmation** – For securities that are being held by independent custodians (such as brokerage firms), the auditor will obtain confirmation of the client's ownership of securities directly from the custodians. Note that confirmation cannot be with the investee companies themselves, since they will usually list the custodian as the owner of all shares held by that custodian on behalf of all their clients.
- **Observation** – The auditor will perform a count of securities that are held by the client. In many cases, these securities are kept in a safe deposit box at the bank, and the auditor will accompany the client to the bank to open the box and perform the count.

A count of securities at the bank should be performed as close to the balance sheet date as possible, and the auditor must be concerned about the possibility of securities being added or removed in the time interval between the date of the count and the balance sheet date. The bank cannot access the box directly, nor will it know what might have been added or removed during a visit to the bank by the client. Nevertheless, the auditor can ensure that the securities in the box at the balance sheet date were identical to those at the time of the count by simply directing the client not to access the box during the time interval between the count and the balance sheet date, and the auditor can examine the bank record of the dates on which access to the box was obtained by the client.

For example, if the year ends December 31, and the auditor performs the count on January 5, the auditor will look at the access record of the bank, and if the last access before the count date was December 30, will know that the contents of the box are identical to those at the balance sheet date. If the auditor chooses to perform the count on December 27, the client can be directed not to access the box in the remaining days of the year, and the auditor can later contact the bank to verify that no access occurred between December 27 and December 31.

Investments, other than those accounted for under the **equity method** of accounting, are valued on the basis of one of two approaches:
- Some are valued on the basis of the ***investee's financial results***. When this is the case, the auditor should:
  - o Obtain and read the investee's financial statements and accompanying audit report.
  - o If financial information is not audited or otherwise not acceptable, the auditor should apply audit procedures to the financial statements or arrange for another auditor to do so.
  - o Obtain sufficient appropriate audit evidence for factors not recognized in the investee's financial statements or assets with fair values significantly different from carrying amounts.
  - o Evaluate the effect of a potential lack of comparability when the investee's financial information is for a period other than that of the financial statements of the reporting entity.

- Derivatives and some other investment securities are valued at ***fair value***. When this is the case, the auditor should:
  - o Evaluate whether methods used for determining fair value are consistent with requirements, if any, of the applicable financial reporting framework.
  - o Determine if methods used by brokers or dealers are appropriate when values are obtained from such sources.
  - o Obtain evidence to support management's assertions about fair value determined using a valuation model, when appropriate.

For derivative instruments accounted for as hedges, the auditor will generally apply additional procedures:
- The auditor will evaluate the hedged item and the derivative being used as a hedge to determine if the relationship is appropriate;
- The auditor will review the client's documentation to verify that all of the requirements for reporting a derivative as a hedge have been met;
- The auditor will evaluate the client's analysis used to determine if the derivative will be accounted for as a fair value hedge or a cash flow hedge; and
- The accountant will verify amounts reported as the fair value of the derivative instrument at the financial statement date and will test the application of the accounting approach being used by the entity.

AU-C Section 501, Audit Evidence – Specific Considerations for Selected items, requires the auditor to apply certain approaches when obtaining evidence related to the value of investments.

- For investments with a value that is based on the entity's performance, such as equity method investments, the auditor should:
  - o Read the investee's financial statements and, if appropriate, the audit report associated with them;
  - o Apply auditing procedures, or arrange for another auditor to do so, in relation to investee financial statements that are either not audited or for which the audit report is unsatisfactory;

- Obtain evidence to support amounts, including fair values, that are materially different from amounts on investee financial statements; and
- Evaluate the effects of a difference in the period covered by the financial statements of the investee and the period covered by the reporting entity's financial statements.

- For derivative instruments and investments measured at fair value, the auditor should:
  - Determine if the method used for determining fair value by the reporting entity is consistent with the requirements of the applicable financial reporting framework for determining fair value;
  - Obtain an understanding of the valuation techniques applied by third-party sources of fair value to determine their appropriateness; and
  - Obtain evidence supporting management's valuation when determined using a valuation model, including whether or not the model is appropriate.

AU-C Section 501 also requires the auditor to evaluate management's conclusions regarding whether or not investments have been impaired and obtain evidence supporting any impairment adjustment reported, including a determination as to whether or not the requirements of the applicable financial reporting framework have been appropriately applied. It also requires the auditor to obtain evidence about unrealized increases or decreases in the fair values of derivatives recognized or disclosed due to the derivative's ineffectiveness.

Think of *Derivatives* and Hedging instruments (FASB ASC Topic 815)
  A derivative is a financial instrument with the following three characteristics (**SUN**):

- **S̲ettlement is for a net amount** – A derivative will be settled at a future date with an exchange of cash or assets that are in amounts equivalent to the difference between the relative positions of the parties to the derivative.
  - In an interest rate swap, for example, the parties do not pay one another the different interest amounts, but one party pays the difference between the amounts to the other.
  - In a forward exchange contract, the parties do not actually exchange currencies, but one party pays the difference in value between the currencies to the other.

- **U̲nderlying and Notional amount** –The total amount at which a derivative will be settled is determined by applying one or more underlyings to one or more notional amounts or payment provisions.
  - An underlying is a specified interest rate, security price, commodity price, foreign exchange rate, price or rate index or other variable that is applied to the notional amount to determine the value of a party's position.
  - The notional amount is the number of units, which may be currency units, shares, bushels, pounds, or some other unit.
    - In an interest rate swap, it is the principal balance upon which interest is calculated.
    - In a forward exchange contract, it is the number of foreign currency units that the contract is for.

- **N̲o net investment** – At the time the derivative contract is entered into, there is either no initial investment by either side, or the amount of the initial net investment is smaller than would ordinarily be required for a comparable response to changes in market factors.

- In the case of an interest rate swap or forward exchange contract, the parties each believe they are in the more favorable position and the only cost is that of establishing and documenting the understanding between the parties.
- In the case of a stock option, the investor is paying substantially less than the cost of the underlying shares, but will experience comparable gains and losses as the value of the shares fluctuate.

- Examples include:
  - **Option contract** (Has *right* but *not obligation* to purchase/sell in the future)
    - Put option – right to sell shares
    - Call option – right to acquire shares in the future
  - **Futures contracts** (Has *right and obligation* to deliver/purchase foreign currency or goods in the future, through an exchange, at a price set today)
  - **Forward contracts** (similar to a futures contract but between the parties without the use of an exchange)
  - **Swaps**, such as interest rate swaps (contracts to exchange cash flows based on underlying values)

Hedging activities are defensive strategies to protect an entity against the risk of adverse price or interest rate movements on certain assets, liabilities or anticipated transactions. Among the substantive procedures performed, the auditor should gather evidence to determine whether management:
- Complied with GAAP hedge accounting requirements
- Expected that the hedging strategy would be "highly effective"
- Periodically assessed the hedge's ongoing effectiveness

The auditor verifies the assertion of **allocation or valuation** with respect to investments in various ways:
- **Trading (HFT) and Available-for-sale (AFS) securities (debt only)** – Since these are reported at market value, the auditor will verify the prices at the balance sheet date through a public source of information, such as the Wall Street Journal.
- **Held-to-maturity securities** – Since these are carried at amortized cost, the auditor will recompute the amortization.
- **Equity method investments** – Investments in companies over which the client has significant influence are adjusted for income and dividends of the investee, and the auditor will obtain the financial statements of the investee company to verify the amounts utilized.
- **Investment income** – To verify reported dividend and interest income, the auditor will (1) examine dividend and interest record books produced by investment advisory services, such as Moody's Investment Service, and (2) perform analytical procedures to determine the reasonableness of the relationship between investment income and investments.

At time of purchase of Investment

Investment	X	
Cash		X

Unrealized Gain (at year end)

Allowance for Increase	X	
Unrealized Gain		X (Trading- *I/S* / AVS – *OCI*)

Marketable Debt Securities

Trading securities (HFT)	Available for sale (AFS)	Held to maturity
Balance Sheet:		
Current only	Current/non-current	Non-current
Debt only	Debt only	Debt only
FMV	FMV	Amortized cost
	Cum *Unrealized gains/losses in equity as accumulated other comprehensive income	

Stmt of Comprehensive Income:		
INCOME:		
*Unrealized gains/losses		
Realized gain/loss	Realized gain/loss	Realized gain/loss
Interest income	Interest income	Interest income
	Non-temporary decline in value	Non-temporary decline in value
OTHER COMP INCOME: (OCI)	Unrealized gains/losses	

Cash Flows:		
Operating activity	Investing activity	Investing Activity

Auditing Accounting Estimates, Including Fair Value Accounting Estimates, and Related Disclosures (AU-C 540)

Generally accepted accounting principles require companies to use **"fair value"** for measuring, presenting, and disclosing various accounts (e.g., investments in trading or available-for-sale securities, assets and liabilities acquired in a business combination, assets and liabilities exchanged in nonmonetary transactions, derivatives, impaired assets, and financial instruments for which the entity has elected the fair value option). Fair value is generally considered to be the amount at which an asset could be sold in a current transaction between willing parties, or the amount that would have to be paid to transfer a liability. Auditing fair values is similar to that of other estimates in that a combination of three approaches is often used: (1) review and test management's process, (2) independently develop an estimate, or (3) review subsequent events.

The auditor will consider estimates when performing risk assessment procedures by obtaining an understanding of:
- Requirements of the applicable financial reporting framework regarding estimates.
- How management determines when estimates are necessary for the recognition or disclosure of items in the financial statements.
- How management develops accounting estimates and the data upon which they are based.

Based on the understanding, the auditor will evaluate the risk of material misstatement of estimates and will undertake one or more of the following, taking into account the nature of the accounting estimate:

- Determine whether events up to the date of the auditor's report provide evidence regarding the estimate.
- Test the methods and assumptions used by management and the data on which they are based.
- Test the operating effectiveness of controls over the development of accounting estimates.
- Develop an expectation in the form of a point or range of estimates to use as a basis for evaluating management's estimate.

In addition, when estimates represent significant risks of material misstatement to the financial statements, the auditor will apply additional procedures:

- Address the effects of **estimation uncertainty,** including whether management has considered alternative assumptions and whether management's assumptions are reasonable.
- Evaluate management's decision to recognize or not recognize accounting estimates and the basis used for measurement.
- Evaluate the reasonableness of the accounting estimates.
- Determine if disclosures are in compliance with the applicable financial reporting framework.
- Review decisions and estimates to evaluate for potential management bias.

The auditor will also document the basis for the auditor's conclusions about the reasonableness of estimates giving rise to significant risks and indicators of possible management bias.

Lecture 4.10

Inventories (AU-C 501)

Observation – Verify Existence

In obtaining evidence about inventories, the auditor will first evaluate whether there is reason to believe that inventories are misstated at the financial statement element or account balance level. The auditor will consider the amount reported as inventories and apply analytical procedures to determine if the amount seems reasonable. Based on the auditor's knowledge of the client's inventory policies, such as reorder points and economic order quantities, the availability of inventories, their shelf lives, the relationship between sales and cost of sales, inventory turnover, and various other factors, the auditor will establish an expectation for the amount of inventory the client should have on hand, which will be compared to the amount reported by the client.

Objectives

- Adequate I/C
- Rights and obligations (Inventory is owned by entity)
- Allocation and valuation (Quantities are correct and properly priced)
- Completeness (All inventory is included)
- Existence (Inventory actually exists)

Applying the **RACE** approach (Account balance)**:**
Rights and Obligations
The entity owns the inventories. A misrepresentation in relation to rights and obligations might be the inclusion on the balance sheet of inventory held on consignment on behalf of another entity or including purchased inventory in transit that is shipped under a destination contract.
- Trace inventories to purchase documents
- Perform search and obtain bank confirmations to determine if inventory is pledged as security
- Review consignment agreements to identify inventory not owned

Allocation and Valuation
The amounts reported as inventory are accurately measured. A misrepresentation in relation to valuation and allocation might occur if inventory is overstated, perhaps due to the failure to apply the lower of cost or net realizable rule, or understated because of inventory that was incorrectly counted during the inventory count.
- Evaluate the entity's procedures for valuing inventory
- Determine replacement cost and recalculate floor and ceiling to evaluate lower of cost or market measurements
- Verify that inventory counts match quantities in the accounting records
- Evaluate obsolete and slow-moving inventory for potential adjustment
- Perform analytical procedures to evaluate the reasonableness of inventories and the relationships to accounts payable and cost of sales

Completeness
All inventory owned by the entity and held for sale in the ordinary course of business is included in the amount reported on the balance sheet. A misrepresentation in relation to completeness might occur if inventory that the company owned was excluded from the inventory balance, such as inventory sold and in transit that was shipped under a destination contract.
- Evaluate inventory counting procedures to make certain that all inventory is counted
- Trace inventory counts to accounting records
- Identify inventory held by employees, consignees, and warehouses
- Analytical procedures to evaluate the reasonableness of receivables

Existence
The amount reported as inventories are existing goods held for sale in the ordinary course of business. A misrepresentation in relation to existence might be the inclusion on the balance sheet of inventory that has already been sold or goods in transit that are not yet, or no longer, the property of the entity.
- Observe the physical count of inventories
- Confirm with warehouses and consignees with custody of the entity's inventories

There are various *forms of evidence* the auditor may use in the audit of inventories. Some will be obtained from the client, some directly from outside sources, and some may result from the direct actions of the auditor. Evidence the auditor may use includes:
- Purchase orders and receiving reports indicating that the inventory was ordered and received;
- Reconciliations of perpetual inventory records to periodic physical counts taken by the client;
- Agreements with consignees and consignors;

- Confirmations from warehouses, consignees, and others that may be holding inventory on behalf of the entity;
- Client inventory count sheets;
- Bank confirmations indicating whether there are any collateral arrangements involving the entity's inventories; and
- The auditor's personal observation of inventory.

Applying the **PERCV** approach**:**

Presentation & Disclosure

- Review disclosures for compliance with GAAP
- Inquire about pledging
- Review purchase commitments

Existence or Occurrence

- Confirmations of consigned inventory and inventory in warehouses
- Observe inventory count

In seeking evidence that inventories exist, the auditor will determine if there are controls in place that would provide assurance that reported inventories actually do exist. These controls might include:

- Controls limiting access to inventory to authorized parties to prevent inventory theft;
- Information processing controls that provide assurance that all inventory recorded in perpetual inventory records have been purchased and title and risk of loss has transferred to the entity;
- Periodic counts by the entity to verify that amounts included in the inventory records continue to exist; and
- Counting procedures that indicate what items have been counted to avoid counting the same inventory multiple times.

Substantive procedures the auditor may perform in relation to existence may include:

- Inspection – The auditor will observe the entity's physical count of inventory and perform test counts;
- Inspection – The auditor will trace recorded inventory items to materials requisitions, purchase orders, and receiving reports;
- Inspection – Evaluate purchases and sales of inventory near the end of the period, including shipping terms, to determine if it is appropriately included in, or excluded from, inventory; and
- Confirmation – The auditor will obtain confirmations directly from warehouses, consignees, and others having possession of the entity's inventory.

When inventory is material, **AU-C Section 501**, Audit Evidence – Specific Considerations for Selected Items, requires the auditor to attend the physical inventory count for the purpose of obtaining evidence regarding the existence of inventory and its condition. While attending the physical inventory count, the auditor should:

- Evaluate instructions and procedures;
- Observe the performance of count procedures;
- Inspect inventory; and
- Perform test counts.

Having obtained evidence about the accuracy of the inventory count, the auditor will also perform procedures to determine if the physical counts are accurately reported in the accounting records. If the count is performed on a date other than the date of the financial statements, the auditor will also obtain evidence to determine that changes between the count date and the date of the financial statements have been properly reflected.

When the auditor is unable to attend the physical count, alternate procedures should be applied including the performance of test counts on alternate dates, applying audit procedures to transactions occurring between the count date and the date of the financial statements.

When inventory that is in the custody of third parties is material, AU-C Section 501 requires the auditor to either request confirmations from the third parties or perform an inspection of the inventory or other procedures as the auditor considers appropriate under the circumstances.

Rights & Obligations
- Review cutoffs (sales, sales returns, purchases, purchase returns)

In seeking evidence that the entity had rights to all inventories that are reported on the financial statements, the auditor will determine if there are controls in place that would provide assurance that the entity has not recorded inventory held on consignment as owned inventory and that inventory has not been encumbered. These might include:
- Policies established by those responsible for governance limiting the authority to borrow using inventory as collateral; and
- Information processing controls requiring that entries to the perpetual inventory records be supported by appropriate documentation, including purchase orders and receiving reports.

Substantive procedures the auditor may perform in relation to rights and obligations may include:
- Inspection – The auditor will inspect the documentation that supports an inventory purchase including materials requisitions, purchase orders, and receiving reports;
- Inspection – The auditor will inspect agreements and documents related to transactions with consignors and consignees to verify that inventory sent out on consignment is included and that inventory received on consignment is not included in the inventory balance;
- Inspection – The auditor will inspect UCC filings and public records that may indicate a secured interest in the entity's inventories; and
- Confirmation – The auditor will obtain confirmations from financial institutions, providing information as to whether inventory has been pledged as collateral for a financing arrangement.

Completeness & Cutoff
- Perform test counts and compare with client's counts/summary
- Inquire about consigned inventory
- Perform analytical procedures
- Account for all inventory tags and count sheets

In seeking evidence that the entity has reported all inventory, the auditor will determine if there are controls in place that would provide assurance that all inventory owned by the entity are reported. These might include:
- Performing periodic counts of inventory and verifying that all items counted are included in the inventory records;

- Instructions for tagging and counting inventories to make certain all items are counted; and
- Use of prenumbered receiving reports with a reconciliation to identify any receiving reports that did not result in an entry to inventory.

There are various forms of evidence the auditor may use to test completeness. Some will be obtained from the client, some directly from outside sources, and some may result from the direct actions of the auditor. Evidence the auditor may use includes:
- Prenumbered materials requisitions, purchase orders, and receiving reports;
- Correspondence between the entity warehouses, consignees, and other third parties holding the entity's inventories; and
- The auditor's personal observations.

Substantive procedures the auditor may perform in relation to completeness may include:
- Confirmation – The auditor will obtain confirmations directly from warehouses, consignees, and other third parties holding the entity's inventory;
- Recalculation – The auditor will account for the sequence of all prenumbered documents that are used in the processes related to the purchases and sales of inventory to make certain all are included in the accounting records;
- Reperformance – Perform test counts of inventory and trace them to inventory count sheets to verify that all inventory is included;
- Inspection – Evaluate purchases and sales of inventory near the end of the period, including shipping terms, to determine if it is appropriately included in, or excluded from, inventory; and
- Inquiry and Observation – Identify and inspect inventory held by employees; and
- Observation – The auditor will observe the counting of inventory, perform test counts, and verify that all items counted are included in the inventory records.

Valuation, Allocation & Accuracy
- Foot and extend summary schedules
- Reconcile summary schedules to general ledger
- Test inventory costing method
- Determine that inventory is valued at lower of cost or market, which is net realizable value for all inventories except those valued under LIFO, and those calculated under the retail inventory method.
- Examine inventory quality (salable condition)
- Test inventory obsolescence
- Periodic vs. Perpetual inventory system for valuation

In seeking evidence that the entity has reported all inventories in appropriate amounts, the auditor will determine if there are controls in place that would provide assurance that all inventories are reported at the lower of cost or net realizable value. These might include:
- Adequate review and supervision of the data entry process to provide assurance that amounts are being input accurately;
- Periodic evaluations of inventory to identify slow moving, damaged, or obsolete inventories; and
- Periodic comparisons to net realizable value to verify that inventories are properly reported.

There are various forms of evidence the auditor may use to test valuation and allocation. Some will be obtained from the client, some directly from outside sources, and some may result from the direct actions of the auditor. Evidence the auditor may use includes:
- Invoices for the purchases of inventory; and
- Sales prices for inventory and costs associated with disposal.

Substantive procedures the auditor may perform in relation to valuation and allocation may include:
- Observation – Trace amounts reported in inventory to invoices from suppliers to verify cost;
- Recalculation – Use information about sales prices and costs of disposition to calculate net realizable value and compare it to cost to determine if the entity has reported inventory at the lower of cost or net realizable value;
- Observation – Evaluate slow-moving and obsolete inventory to determine if an adjustment is required; and
- Analytical Procedure – Compare the relationship of sales to cost of sales and cost of sales to inventories to the auditor's expectations based on knowledge of the client's inventory policies to determine if the amount reported as inventory seems reasonable.

Goods in Transit

When a company buys or sells goods, the shipping terms will determine whether or not they are included in that entity's inventory while the goods are in transit. Although there are numerous factors that differentiate shipping contracts, most fall into one of two categories:
- **Shipping contracts, FAS** (free alongside) **shipping point or FOB** (free onboard), in which title transfers from the seller to the buyer when goods are delivered by the seller to a common carrier; and
- **Destination contracts, FAS destination or FOB destination**, in which title transfers from the seller to the buyer when goods are delivered by a common carrier to the buyer.

FOB shipping point

- Title passes to the buyer when the seller delivers the goods to a common carrier (shipped).
- Included in buyer's books at year-end.

FOB destination

- Title passes to the buyer when the buyer receives the goods from the common carrier (received).
- Included in seller's books until received by buyer.

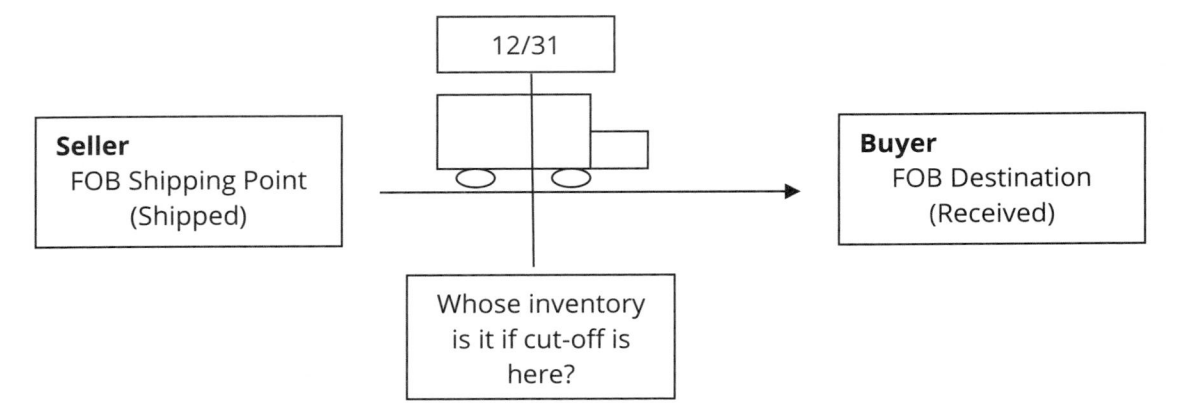

In a perpetual system, inventory purchases are debited to Inventory. The quantity on hand can be determined at any point in time.

At time of purchase:

Inventory	100	
A/P		100

As sales occur:

A/R	150	
Sales Revenue		150

COGS	100	
Inventory		100

In verifying the **existence or occurrence** of inventory, the auditor will observe physical inventory during the physical count of goods. If the client has a strong **perpetual** inventory system, this count can be performed at various dates and different batches of inventory can be counted at different times. The auditor will compare counts to the inventory records as of the date of the count and reconcile between the dates of the counts and the date of the financial statements.

Assuming the auditor does not find errors involving inventories reported in the previous period, which would require a prior period adjustment, the primary type of error an auditor may find will be an *overstatement or an understatement of inventory*. In the case of an *overstatement*, the auditor will propose a journal entry reducing ending inventory and increasing cost of goods sold:

Cost of goods sold	100	
Inventory		100

If the auditor detects an *understatement,* the entry above will be reversed.

When RMM with respect to inventory is high, especially when the client uses a **periodic** inventory system, the count must be made at the balance sheet date, or as close to it as possible.

During the count, to support the **existence** assertion, the auditor should examine items that are in the listed inventory count and, on a test basis, trace those amounts to the inventory tags on actual goods. In addition, the auditor can obtain evidence to support the **completeness** assertion by tracing some of the inventory tags to the inventory records.

In addition to the count, the auditor must perform **cutoff** tests for receiving and shipping that occurred around the balance sheet date, again to ensure that inventory is complete.

In order to verify the **rights and obligations** assertion with respect to inventory, the auditor will examine vendor invoices and other evidence of the purchase of the goods by the client. In addition, the auditor must inspect **loan agreements** to determine if any inventory has been pledged as collateral for a loan or assigned to a creditor for value. Since any such actions require disclosure in the financial statements or notes, this procedure also contributes to verifying the assertions related to **presentation and disclosure**.

Proving **Allocation and valuation** requires several different procedures:
- Vendor invoices are examined to determine that correct prices have been recorded for inventory purchases.
- For manufactured inventory, an examination of standard cost rates (especially for overhead that is applied to inventory costs) is necessary.
- *Inventory turnover rates* should be examined to identify slow-moving and obsolete inventory that may need to be written off or written down to net realizable value.
- Inquiries should be made of production supervisors and inventory control personnel about slow-moving or obsolete inventory as well.
- The auditor can recalculate the net realizable value for performing a lower of cost or market evaluation.

Lecture 4.11

Property Plant and Equipment (PP&E – Fixed Assets)

In obtaining evidence about property, plant, and equipment and identifiable intangibles, which will collectively be referred to as **fixed assets**, the auditor will first evaluate whether there is reason to believe that fixed assets are misstated at the financial statement element or account balance level. Based on the auditor's knowledge of the entity and its industry, along with knowledge obtained in previous engagements, the auditor will determine if there has been a change in capacity, indicating an increase or decrease in the overall fixed assets held by the entity, whether any fixed assets were near the end of their useful lives, in which case disposals and replacements may have occurred, and whether the related depreciation and the balance in accumulated depreciation seem appropriate.

Objectives
- Adequate I/C
- Rights and obligations (Fixed assets are owned by the entity)
- Allocation and valuation (Assets are properly valued, including proper capitalization of costs, depreciation or amortization, and impairments)
- Completeness (All fixed assets are included)
- Existence (Fixed assets actually exist)

Applying the **RACE** approach (Account Balance):

Rights and Obligations

The entity owns the fixed assets that are reported. A misrepresentation in relation to rights and obligations might be the inclusion on the balance sheet of assets being used under an operating lease as a fixed asset.

- Trace additions to purchase documents
- Perform search and obtain bank confirmations to determine if fixed assets are pledged as security

Allocation and Valuation

The amounts reported as fixed assets are accurately measured. A misrepresentation in relation to valuation and allocation might occur if fixed assets are not being depreciated appropriately or if costs incurred that should have been capitalized, such as delivery or installation of a fixed asset, has been charged to expense.

- Evaluate the entity's procedures for capitalizing costs
- Determine if there is an indication of impairment and whether the assets have been appropriately evaluated
- Test depreciation and amortization calculations

Completeness

All fixed assets owned by the entity are included in the amounts reported on the balance sheet. A misrepresentation in relation to completeness might occur if the entity held fixed assets that had incorrectly been recorded as repairs and maintenance expense.

- Observe fixed assets and trace additions to accounting records
- Perform analytical procedures to determine reasonableness of fixed assets

Existence

The amount reported as fixed assets are actual assets in the custody of the entity. A misrepresentation in relation to existence might be the inclusion on the balance sheet of fixed assets that have been sold, capitalizing an expenditure that should have been recognized as an expense, or recording an acquisition that did not occur or was not on behalf of the entity.

- Observe fixed assets

There are various *forms of evidence* the auditor may use in the audit of fixed assets. Some will be obtained from the client, some directly from outside sources, and some may result from the direct actions of the auditor. Evidence the auditor may use includes:

- Legal documents, state filings, and contracts that evidence rights represented by identifiable intangible assets;
- Invoices, purchase agreements, shipping records, and other documents related to the acquisition of fixed assets;
- Sales agreements, escrow statements, and closing statements related to the disposal of fixed assets;
- Client schedules reporting fixed asset holdings along with related depreciation and amortization;
- Property tax bills and insurance policies;
- Minutes of meetings of management or those charged with governance authorizing acquisitions or disposals of fixed assets; and
- Bank confirmations indicating whether fixed assets have been used as collateral for loans.

Applying the **PERCV** approach:

Presentation & Disclosure

- Review disclosures for compliance with GAAP
- Inquire about liens and restrictions
- Review loan agreements for liens and restrictions

Existence or Occurrence

- Inspect additions
- Vouch additions
- Review any leases for proper accounting (Capital vs. Operating)
- Perform search for unrecorded retirements

In seeking evidence that fixed assets exist, the auditor will determine if there are controls in place that would provide assurance that reported fixed assets actually do exist. These controls might include:

- Policies and procedures requiring all disposals of fixed assets to be approved by those charged with governance or an appropriate level of management;
- Policies limiting access to fixed assets to appropriate parties;
- Means of anchoring or otherwise securing fixed assets to prevent theft; and
- Periodic reconciliation of schedules of fixed assets maintained by the entity to actual observations of fixed assets.

Substantive procedures the auditor may perform in relation to existence may include:

- Observation – The auditor may physically observe fixed assets to ascertain their existence;
- Confirmation – The auditor may obtain confirmations directly from warehousemen who may be holding inventory or fixed assets for the entity;
- Inspection – The auditor may inspect purchase documents for items purchased during the period;
- Inspection – The auditor may inspect insurance policies and property tax bills to make certain that reported fixed assets are listed when appropriate;
- Inspection – The auditor may review agreements between the entity and other parties or regulators granting the entity rights associated with identifiable intangible assets; and
- Inspection – The auditor may trace cash receipts that are from sources other than revenues to verify that all sales of fixed assets have been properly recorded.

Rights & Obligations

- Review minutes for approval of additions

In seeking evidence that the entity had rights to all fixed assets that are reported on the financial statements, the auditor will determine if there are controls in place that would provide assurance that the entity has not either used fixed assets as collateral or is not entitled to the rights associated with identifiable intangibles, or that the entity has not recognized as an asset property that is subject to an operating lease.

Substantive procedures the auditor may perform in relation to rights and obligations may include:

- Inspection – The auditor may inspect purchase documents, including escrow or closing statements, as appropriate;
- Inspection – The auditor may inspect insurance policies and property tax bills to determine if fixed assets are properly included;

- Confirmation – The auditor may obtain confirmations from financial institutions requesting information about fixed assets that may have been used as collateral; and
- Inspection – The auditor may perform a UCC search to determine if any fixed assets have been encumbered with parties other than the entity's financial institutions providing confirmations.

Completeness & Cutoff

- Perform analytical procedures
- Vouch major entries to repairs and maintenance expense

In seeking evidence that the entity has reported all fixed assets, the auditor will determine if there are controls in place that would provide assurance that all fixed assets owned by the entity are reported. These might include:

- Capitalization policies that are communicated and enforced to make certain that all capital expenditures are reported as such instead of being expensed;
- Policies requiring appropriate approval for removal of fixed assets from fixed asset schedules; and
- Periodic comparisons of fixed assets to schedules of fixed assets and amounts reported on the financial statements.

Substantive procedures the auditor may perform in relation to completeness may include:

- Observation – The auditor may physically inspect fixed assets and trace them to fixed asset schedules and to the financial statements;
- Analytical Procedure – The auditor may evaluate the reasonableness of fixed assets taking into account the entity's volume of activity;
- Inspection – The auditor may review insurance policies and property tax statements to make certain that all fixed assets listed are reported on the financial statements; and
- Inspection – Evaluate amounts reported as repairs and maintenance expense to verify that no amounts that should have been capitalized have been recognized as expense.

Valuation, Allocation & Accuracy

- Foot summary schedules
- Reconcile summary schedules to general ledger
- Recalculate deprecation

In seeking evidence that the entity has reported all fixed assets in appropriate amounts, the auditor will determine if there are controls in place that would provide assurance that all fixed assets are properly accounted for. These might include:

- Appropriate policies for determining when expenditures will be reported as repairs and maintenance expense and when they should be capitalized;
- Evaluation and periodic re-evaluation of useful lives, salvage values, and allocation methods applicable to depreciable fixed assets and amortizable identifiable intangibles; and
- Policies and procedures appropriate to identify events and circumstances that may indicate that an asset has been impaired.

Substantive procedures the auditor may perform in relation to valuation and allocation may include:

- Recalculation – The auditor may independently recalculate depreciation and amortization expense for the period, along with the resulting balances in the allowance for doubtful accounts;
- Inspection – The auditor may review purchase documents, escrow or closing statements, and other documents to determine if amounts were properly capitalized;
- Inspection – The auditor may review charges to repairs and maintenance expense for the period to determine if amounts that should have been capitalized have been recognized as expense;
- Observation – The auditor may inspect fixed assets to determine if they appear to be in use and working as intended so that impairment losses are not required to be recognized;
- Recalculation – The auditor may foot and cross foot schedules of fixed assets, depreciation expense, and accumulated depreciation and recalculate amounts included on the schedules; and
- Analytical Procedure – The auditor may evaluate whether amounts recorded upon the acquisition of fixed assets approximate the auditor's expectations for such items.

Beginning Balance

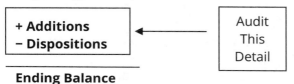

| + Additions |
| – Dispositions |

Audit This Detail

Ending Balance

Since there are generally relatively few transactions involving fixed assets and identifiable intangibles, the auditor will generally use a **test of transactions** approach in which the emphasis is on changes during the year.

With respect to reported additions of fixed assets during the year, the auditor will inspect purchase documents that support these additions to verify **valuation**, then observe the actual fixed assets to verify **existence**. In the case of real property, deeds generally consist of a legal conveyance of rights, but sales price and related mortgage acquisition costs are rarely specified. As to **completeness**, the auditor will examine repairs and maintenance accounts to determine if any expenditures for property and equipment were incorrectly expensed.

With respect to retirements, the auditor is primarily concerned with **existence**, and will obtain listings of property and then try to locate the actual assets to be certain there are no unrecorded retirements of assets. The auditor will also examine the journal entries made for retirements in order to ensure that the correct amounts were removed from relevant accounts, supporting the **valuation** assertion. This is one of the few entries that results in a debit to accumulated depreciation. Such a debit can only result from one of the following:

- Removal of accumulated depreciation upon retirement or sale of an asset;
- Correction of an excessive entry for depreciation expense made previously; or
- Costs incurred to extend the useful life of the asset.

For assets that were owned for the entire year, the auditor's main concern will be with depreciation. The auditor will review the computations of depreciation expense and consider the appropriateness of the useful lives and methods to verify **allocation and valuation**, and will then review the posting of these amounts to the proper categories in order to verify **presentation and disclosure.**

When auditing intangible assets, verification of **rights and obligations** is achieved through the inspection of records for those that were purchased as well as those that resulted from expenditures to acquire or defend legal intangibles, such as patents. Of course, these inspections also provide evidence of **valuation.**

In addition, amortization entries will be reviewed for mathematical accuracy, and the auditor will consider evidence that intangibles may have been impaired in value and need to be written off. This also relates to valuation.

For goodwill, the auditor is concerned with **existence or occurrence**, since only goodwill purchased as part of the acquisition of a business may be recorded, and **allocation and valuation**, both as it relates to the correct computation of the original goodwill and the amortization over an appropriate life.

Current Liabilities

Current liabilities consist primarily of **accounts payable and accrued expenses**, including **payroll.** The current portion of long-term debt is generally examined as part of the audit of long-term debt. In obtaining evidence about current liabilities, the auditor will first evaluate whether there is reason to believe that current liabilities are misstated at the financial statement element or account balance level. Based on the auditor's knowledge of the entity's purchasing and payment policies, the auditor should be able to evaluate the relationship between accounts payable and inventories as well as a relationship between accrued expenses and the entity's regular monthly expenses that are generally paid in cash. If these items bear reasonable relationships, the auditor will not have a reason to believe that current liabilities are materially misstated.

Objectives
- Adequate I/C
- Rights and obligations (Payables are legitimate obligations of the entity)
- Allocation and valuation (Payables reported in appropriate amounts)
- Completeness (There are no unrecorded liabilities)
- Existence (Payables actually exist)

Applying the **RACE** approach (Account Balance):

Rights and Obligations
- Trace payables to transaction documentation

The entity received the goods or services creating the current liabilities making them the obligations of the entity. A misrepresentation in relation to rights and obligations might be the inclusion of a liability for goods or services that were provided to a member of management instead of the entity.

Allocation and Valuation
- Trace payables to transaction documentation
- Trace to subsequent payment

The amounts reported as current liabilities are accurately measured. A misrepresentation in relation to valuation and allocation might occur if the entity accrued expenses like rent or utilities in amounts that did not reflect a reasonable estimate of the actual amount.

Completeness

- Trace subsequent payments to payables
- Perform analytical procedures to determine reasonableness of payables

All current liabilities that are the obligations of the entity are included in the amounts reported on the balance sheet. A misrepresentation in relation to completeness might occur if the entity neglects to record a payable for the purchase of goods that have already been received by the entity.

Existence

- Trace to transaction documentation
- Trace subsequent payments

The amount reported as current liabilities are legitimate claims for payment for goods or services that were delivered. A misrepresentation in relation to existence might result from recording a liability for the purchase of merchandise that has not yet been transferred to the entity.

There are various *forms of evidence* the auditor may use in the audit of current liabilities. Some will be obtained from the client, some directly from outside sources, and some may result from the direct actions of the auditor. Evidence the auditor may use includes:

- Invoices from suppliers;
- Time cards, payroll summaries, payroll tax bills, and other internally generated schedules related to payroll; and
- Leases; agreements for regular services, such as janitorial or gardening; and bills from service providers, such as utility companies.

Applying the **PERCV** approach:

Presentation & Disclosure

- Review disclosures for compliance with GAAP
- Review purchase commitments

Existence or Occurrence

- Confirmation
- Inspect copies of notes and note agreements
- Vouch payables (examine purchase orders, receiving reports, invoices)

In seeking evidence that current liabilities exist, the auditor will determine if there are controls in place that would provide assurance that reported current liabilities represent actual claims for goods or services. These controls might include:

- Policies requiring that there much be matching purchase requisitions, purchase orders, receiving reports, before recording of a liability;
- Comparisons of vendor names to lists of approved payees; and
- Comparisons of accrued expenses to budgets.

Substantive procedures the auditor may perform in relation to existence may include:
- Confirmation – The auditor may obtain confirmations directly from suppliers verifying amounts payable;
- Inspection – The auditor may trace recorded amounts to supplier invoices, receiving reports, purchase orders, and materials requisitions;
- Analytical Procedure – The auditor may determine the length of time between the last date for which employees were paid and the end of the period to determine if accrued payroll liabilities seem legitimate;
- Analytical procedures – The auditor may compare a listing of items included in accrued expenses to budgets for monthly expenses and amounts incurred in previous periods; and
- Inspection – The auditor may review leases and service contracts involving regular payments, such as for janitorial or maintenance and bills from service providers.

Rights & Obligations

- Review cutoffs (purchases, purchase returns, disbursements)

In seeking evidence that the reported current liabilities are the obligations of the entity, the auditor will determine if there are controls in place that would provide assurance that the entity has not recorded liabilities when neither goods nor services were received that were for the benefit of the entity. These might include:
- Information processing controls that require that all recorded accounts payable be supported by properly authorized requisitions and purchase orders;
- Policies that require comparisons to budgeted amounts as a requirement for recognizing expenses; and
- Policies requiring authorizations for expenses not budgeted.

Substantive procedures the auditor may perform in relation to rights and obligations may include:
- Inspection – The auditor may trace recorded payables for both inventory, recorded in accounts payable, or expenses, recorded in accrued expenses, to supporting documentation; and
- Analytical Procedure – The auditor may compare expenses for the period to expectations developed by the auditor based on the auditor's knowledge of the client, the industry, and relevant aspects of the economy.

Completeness & Cutoff

- Perform analytical procedures
- Perform search for unrecorded payables (examine unrecorded invoices, receiving reports, purchase orders)
- Inquire of management as to completeness

In seeking evidence that the entity has reported all current liabilities, the auditor will determine if there are controls in place that would provide assurance that all current liabilities for purchases of merchandise or for expenses that were incurred during the period are reported. These might include:
- Policies requiring that expenses be compared to budgeted amounts with variances investigated;
- Timely reconciliation of statements received from vendors to amounts reported as liabilities; and
- Policies requiring that invoices received during a reasonable time after the end of the period be evaluated to determine if they should be included in the period-end accrual.

Substantive procedures the auditor may perform in relation to completeness may include:

- Analytical Procedure – The auditor may compare the relationship of accounts payable to inventories to expectations developed on the basis of the auditor's knowledge of the client and industry;
- Analytical Procedure – The auditor may compare the relationship between of accrued expenses and the entity's monthly payments for expenses to the auditor 's expectations;
- Inspection – The auditor may trace payments made during a reasonable time after the end of the period to supporting documents to identify those that were for goods or services received during the period and trace those amounts to recorded liabilities;
- Inspect – The auditor may review documents for purchased goods in transit to determine if those shipped under shipping contracts have been included in accounts payable;
- Analytical Procedure – The auditor may compare the amount accrued for payroll and payroll related expenses, such as payroll taxes, to the auditor's expectation for that amount based on the auditor's understanding of the entity's employees and knowledge of the number of work days that occurred between the last date for which they were paid and the end of the entity's fiscal period;
- Inspection – The auditor may inspect receiving reports that have not been matched to other documents to determine if amounts are included in accounts payable when appropriate;
- Inspection – The auditor may review leases and other arrangements, such as service agreements, calling for regular payments to determine if amounts accrued are appropriate;
- Analytical Procedure – The auditor may compare the amount reported as accrued expenses in the current period to amounts reported in prior periods, accounting for changes in the makeup or amount of various items; and
- Confirmation – The auditor may obtain confirmations directly from vendors and suppliers to verify that all amounts owed are properly reported.

Valuation, Allocation & Accuracy

- Foot subsidiary ledger
- Reconcile subsidiary ledger to general ledger
- Recalculate interest expense (if any)
- For payroll, review year-end accrual
- Recalculate other accrued liabilities

In seeking evidence that the entity has reported all current liabilities in appropriate amounts, the auditor will determine if there are controls in place that would provide assurance that all amounts are accurate. These might include:

- Policies requiring that expenses be compared to budgeted amounts with variances investigated; and
- Timely reconciliation of statements received from vendors to amounts reported as liabilities.

Substantive procedures the auditor may perform in relation to valuation and allocation may be the same as those performed to provide evidence to support completeness. These include:

- Analytical Procedure – The auditor may compare the relationship of accounts payable to inventories to expectations developed on the basis of the auditor's knowledge of the client and industry;
- Analytical Procedure – The auditor may compare the relationship between of accrued expenses and the entity's monthly payments for expenses to the auditor 's expectations;

- Inspection – The auditor may trace payments made during a reasonable time after the end of the period to supporting documents to identify those that were for goods or services received during the period and trace those amounts to recorded liabilities;
- Inspection – The auditor may review documents for purchased goods in transit to determine if those shipped under shipping contracts have been included in accounts payable;
- Analytical Procedure – The auditor may compare the amount accrued for payroll and payroll related expenses, such as payroll taxes, to the auditor's expectation for that amount based on the auditor's understanding of the entity's employees and knowledge of the number of work days that occurred between the last date for which they were paid and the end of the entity's fiscal period;
- Inspection – The auditor may inspect receiving reports that have not been matched to other documents to determine if amounts are included in accounts payable when appropriate;
- Inspection – The auditor may review leases and other arrangements, such as service agreements, calling for regular payments to determine if amounts accrued are appropriate;
- Analytical Procedure – The auditor may compare the amount reported as accrued expenses in the current period to amounts reported in prior periods, accounting for changes in the makeup or amount of various items; and
- Confirmation – The auditor may obtain confirmations directly from vendors and suppliers to verify that all amounts owed are properly reported.

When auditing accounts payable, the management assertion of **completeness** is often considered the most important, since the auditor's primary concern is **understatement** of liabilities rather than overstatement.

The procedure that is most effective in identifying *unrecorded liabilities* ("**Search for unrecorded liabilities**") is the examination of cash disbursements after the balance sheet date. In the case of accounts payable, these payments should be vouched to the related purchase orders and receiving reports to identify those payables that were owed as of the balance sheet date. Since most accounts payable are paid within 30 days of invoicing, subsequent payments provide very persuasive evidence as to the completeness of accounts payable.

Another method of determining completeness is to **trace receiving reports** to postings of purchases to ensure that all received items have been recorded. The auditor may also **vouch recorded liabilities** back to the supporting documents but, in this case, the emphasis is on the management assertions of **existence and valuation** rather than completeness.

The auditor may choose to **confirm** payables. Because of the emphasis on understatement, however, the bases for selection of payables to confirm will not be identical to those for receivables. In particular, the auditor will choose from the entire population of vendors with whom the client did business during the year, and may confirm with vendors showing low or zero balances owed at the balance sheet date.

When auditing payroll, the auditor is often able to place reliance on the internal control structure of the payroll cycle and assess risk of material misstatement at a low level, thereby permitting higher detection risk and limiting the necessary substantive testing.

Since payroll is generally more predictable than other costs, the auditor should perform **analytical procedures** involving the comparison of actual payroll costs with budgeted or standard costs to determine **completeness** of payroll records.

To support the assertion of **valuation**, the auditor should recalculate payroll accruals and compare calculations with source information, such as time cards to verify hours worked and personnel records to verify pay rates.

Contingent Liabilities (A gain or loss that may occur in the future as a result of an existing condition)

Contingencies represent gains or losses that may or may not occur in the future as a result of an event that has already occurred or an existing condition. Contingencies may result from asserted lawsuits as well as conditions that may result in a future lawsuit. If, for example, an entity is aware that it has sold a defective product, a condition exists that may result in future lawsuits and a future liability as purchasers become aware of the defects.

Contingnent gains may not be accrued and are not required to be disclosed. As a result, the auditor is only required to determine if those disclosures regarding gain contingencies that the entity has decided to include with its financial statements are appropriate. Contingent liabilities, on the other hand, are required to be accrued and disclosed when they are probable and estimable; disclosed without accrual if either they are probable but not subject to reasonable estimation or if they are reasonably possible; and neither accrued nor disclosed if remote.

In order to make certain that all such accruals and disclosures have been properly made, AU-C Section 501, ***Audit Evidence – Specific Considerations for Selected Items***, requires the auditor to perform audit procedures to determine if there are contingencies and, if so, if they are properly accounted for and disclosed. Procedures designed to identify contingent liabilities, including litigation, claims, and assessments, include:
- Making inquiries of management and others within the entity, such as in-house counsel;
- Obtaining from management a list of all litigation, claims, and assessments both existing at the date of the financial statements or during the period between the date of the financial statements and the date of the list, with a description and evaluation of each;
- Reviewing minutes of meetings of the board of directors and others;
- Reviewing documents regarding litigation, claims, and assessments received from management, including correspondencve between the entity and its legal counsel; and
- Reviewing legal expenses and invoices for legal services.

The auditor may detemine that no actual or potential litigation, claims, or assessments exist that require accrual or disclosure in the financial statements. Unless that is the case, however, the auditor is required to seek direct communication with the entity's legal counsel. The auditor will also obtain a letter from each attorney with which the client did business relevant to any litigation, claims, or assessments involving the client.

- Loss Contingencies
  - **Remote** – slight chance of occurring
    - Don't Disclose
    - Don't Accrue
  - **Reasonably Possible** – more than Remote, less than Probable.
    - Do Disclose – Full Disclosure
    - Don't Accrue – Fair presentation

- o **Probable** – Likely to occur
  - If not **Estimable**
    - Do Disclose
    - Don't Accrue
  - If **Estimable**
    - Do Disclose
    - Do Accrue
      - Conservatism / Matching

Loss Contingency

	Disclose	Accrue
Remote – Slight	No	No
Reasonably Possible	Yes	No
Probable & Estimable	Yes	**Yes**
Probable & Not Estimable	Yes	No

Estimated Loss (I/S)
Estimated Liability (B/S)

Lecture 4.12

Long-Term Debt (Notes Payable, Bonds Payable, Lease Liabilities)

Long-term debt consists of notes payable, bonds payable, and lease obligations. Transactions involving long-term debt tend to be well documented, including authorization from the board of directors or others who are charged with governance, formal agreements between the lender and the entity, and scheduled payments. When payments are made on a timely basis, all amounts, including interest expense, the ending balance of the long-term liability, and the current portion are all readily determinable.

Due to the nature of long-term debt, including the fact that transactions tend to be infrequent, material, and well documented, the auditor will frequently rely heavily on substantive testing.

Objectives

- Adequate I/C
- Rights and obligations (debt is obligation of entity)
- Allocation and valuation (debt is recorded in appropriate amount)
- Completeness (all debt recorded)
- Existence (debt actually exists)

Using the **RACE** approach (Balance Sheet):

Rights and Obligations

- Trace liabilities to loan documentation

The entity borrowed the money represented by long-term debt and is obligated on the liability. A misrepresentation in relation to rights and obligations might be the inclusion of a liability for money that was borrowed by a member of management instead of the entity.

Allocation and Valuation

- Trace liabilities to transaction documentation
- Trace to subsequent payment
- Confirm amounts with creditors

The amounts reported in long-term debt are accurately measured. A misrepresentation in relation to valuation and allocation might occur if the entity incorrectly allocated payments between principal and interest, overstating or understating the principal balance.

Completeness

- Evaluate subsequent
- To determine reasonableness of payables disbursements
- Obtain confirmations from creditors
- Review minutes for debt authorizations
- Obtain letter from attorney
- Perform analytical procedures

All long-term debt consists of liabilities that are the obligations of the entity and are included in the amounts reported on the balance sheet. A misrepresentation in relation to completeness might occur if the entity were to record proceeds from a borrowing transaction as revenue or as a capital contribution.

Existence

- Trace to loan documentation
- Trace subsequent payments

The amount reported as long-term debt represents legitimate obligations that resulted from borrowing transactions that actually occurred. A misrepresentation in relation to existence might result from recording a liability when cash is received for some reason, such as from revenues or a capital contribution that is recorded as long-term debt.

There are various *forms of evidence* the auditor may use in the audit of long-term debt. Some will be obtained from the client, some directly from outside sources, and some may result from the direct actions of the auditor. Evidence the auditor may use includes:

- Copies of notes and loans payable and long-term leases;
- Spreadsheets and other schedules prepared by the client to recognize principal and interest allocations, determine the current portion of long-term debt, and to keep track of long-term liabilities; and
- Confirmations from creditors.

Using the **PERCV** approach:

Presentation & Disclosure

- Review disclosures for compliance with GAAP
- Inquire about pledging of assets
- Review debt agreements for pledging and events causing default

Existence or Occurrence

- Confirmation
- Inspect copies of notes and note agreements
- Trace receipt of funds (and payment) to bank account and cash receipts journal

Substantive procedures the auditor may perform in relation to existence of long-term debt may include:

- Confirmation – The auditor may obtain confirmations directly from creditors verifying amounts payable and terms of the liabilities;
- Inspection – The auditor may inspect long-term leases, notes and loans payable, and other agreements documenting long-term debt arrangements;
- Inspection – The auditor may trace proceeds from borrowing transactions recorded in the cash receipts journal to supporting documents providing evidence of the existence of long-term liabilities; and
- Inspection – The auditor may review minutes from board of director meetings or meetings of those charged with governance to verify that borrowing transactions have been authorized.

Rights & Obligations

- Review cutoffs (examine transactions near year-end)
- Review minutes for proper authorization (and completeness)

Substantive procedures the auditor may perform in relation to rights and obligations may include:

- Inspection – The auditor may trace recorded liabilities to supporting documentation;
- Inspection – The auditor may verify that transactions in which long-term debt was recorded resulted in a deposit of cash for the proceeds; and
- Confirmation – The auditor may obtain direct confirmation from creditors indicating the indebtedness of the entity.

Completeness & Cutoff

- Perform analytical procedures
- Inquire of management as to completeness
- Review bank confirmations for unrecorded debt

Substantive procedures the auditor may perform in relation to completeness may include:

- Analytical Procedure – The auditor may compare the relationship between interest expense and the average balance in long-term debt to determine if the relationship is reasonable based on the auditor's knowledge of terms the entity would be subject to;
- Confirmation – The auditor may obtain confirmations directly from creditors, including a standard bank confirmation, requesting information about all liabilities owed by the entity to make certain that there are no exclusions; and
- Inspection – The auditor may review the cash receipts journal and trace significant deposits to source documents to determine if any represent liabilities that have not been recorded as such.

Valuation, Allocation & Accuracy

- Foot summary schedules
- Reconcile summary schedules to general ledger
- Vouch entries to account
- Recalculate interest expense and accrued interest payable

Substantive procedures the auditor may perform in relation to valuation and allocation may include:

- Analytical Procedure – The auditor may compare the ending balances reported for long-term debt to the auditor's expectations developed from reviewing loan documents and from repayment schedules;
- Confirmation – The auditor may obtain confirmation of ending balances directly from creditors;
- Recalculation – The auditor may recalculate the current portion of long-term debt to verify that the amount reported by the entity is accurate; and
- Recalculation – The auditor may recalculate allocations between principal and interest to determine that periodic payments have been properly reported.

The audit of long-term debt is normally quite limited since, by its nature, long-term debt is likely to involve few transactions during a typical year, except for interest payments. As a result, the verification of interest expense and accrued interest payable are the most common objectives, with analytical procedures comparing interest expense to the related debt being the most useful. Confirmation of long-term debt with payees, trustees and other appropriate third parties, may be used to verify any applicable sinking fund transactions. The auditor may also examine legal agreements in connection with such obligations.

Though there is little likelihood of notes and bonds payable going unrecorded, proper **classification** on the balance sheet is an important issue in connection with the assertion of **disclosure and presentation**. In particular, if a current note is renewed shortly after year-end, the auditor needs to ensure that the note is classified as a long-term debt rather than a current one.

Going Concern

Although not required in some special purpose financial reporting frameworks, when financial statements are prepared in accordance with GAAP, Topic ASC 205, Subtopic 40, requires management to evaluate whether the entity has the ability to continue as a going concern for a reasonable time. The ability to continue as a going concern implies that the entity will be able to meet its obligations as they come due. A reasonable period of time is considered one year from the date on which the financial statements are issued, or, when appropriate, one year from the date on which they are available to be issued.

Even when the applicable financial reporting framework does not require management to perform such an evaluation, if characteristics of the financial reporting framework according to which the financial statements are being prepared incorporates a going concern assumption, the preparation of the financial statements requires management to assess the entity's ability to continue as a going concern. The existence of receivables that are not written down to amounts received, payments for assets that are capitalized and amortized instead of being expensed when incurred, and other similar accounts that have long-term implications, indicate that the framework in use does incorporate such an assumption.

Unless financial statements are prepared in accordance with the cash basis or a comparable basis, they are likely being prepared in accordance with a going concern assumption. As a result, preparing the financial statements requires management to assess the entity's ability to continue as a going concern even when the applicable financial reporting framework does not explicitly require it.

During the performance of the risk assessment procedures applied by the auditor in obtaining an understanding of the entity and its environment, including its internal control, the auditor should determine if management has made a preliminary evaluation of whether events or conditions exist that raise doubts.

- If management has performed such an evaluation, the auditor should discuss it with management and, if management has identified events or conditions that raise substantial doubt, the auditor should understand management's plans to address them.
- If management has not performed such an evaluation, the auditor should inquire of management whether such events or conditions exist.

The auditor's evaluation should address management's evaluation, covering the same period of time, and should consider whether management has evaluated all events and conditions of which the auditor is aware.

When events or conditions have been identified, the auditor is required to obtain sufficient appropriate audit evidence as to whether they, when considered in the aggregate, raise a substantial doubt about the entity's ability to continue as a going concern for a reasonable period of time, as well as any mitigating factors. The auditor's procedures will include:

- Requesting management to make an evaluation if one has not already been made;
- Evaluating management's plans in relation to the events and conditions to determine if it is probable that they can be implemented effectively and would mitigate the events and conditions that raise the doubt;
- Evaluating a cash flow forecast and analysis, if one was prepared by management, including the reliability of the underlying data and determining if there is adequate support for assumptions made; and
- Considering whether additional facts or information has become available based on which management made its evaluaton.

If, before considering management's plans, the auditor believes that substantial doubt exists as to the entity's ability to continue as a going concern, the auditor should request written representations from management. They should:

- Describe management's plans intended to mitigate the adverse effects of events or conditions contributing to the substantial doubt, including the probability that they can be implemented effectively; and
- Indicate that all relevant matters of which management is aware have been disclosed, including significant conditions and events, and also including management's plans.

Based on the results of the audit procedures applied, the auditor will conclude that either management's plans do, or do not, alleviate the adverse effects of events and conditions causing the substantial doubt as to the entity's ability to continue as a going concern. Based on that conclusion, the auditor will determine if disclosure is adequate.

- If management's plans are expected to mitigate the adverse effects, indicating that there is no longer substantial doubt as to the entity's ability to continue as a going concern, the disclosure should describe the events and conditions that created the doubt, management's evaluation of their significance, and management's plans that mitigated the adverse effects.
- If management's plans are not expected to mitigate the adverse claims to the extent that they remove the doubt, the disclosure will be similar, except it will also indicate that there is substantial doubt. In addition, it will refer to management's plans that are intended to mitigate the effects, rather than indicate that the effects have been mitigated.

Stockholder's Equity

C/S, Pfd Stock, APIC, Treasury Stock, R/E, Comprehensive income, Dividends

Stockholders' equity consists of common and preferred stock, additional paid-in capital, retained earnings, and accumulated other comprehensive income. Transactions involving stockholders' equity are generally limited to issuances or reacquisitions of stock, which are relatively rare; paying dividends; and closing net income or loss and other comprehensive income or loss into retained earnings and accumulated other comprehensive income, respectively.

- Transactions involving issuance or reacquisition of stock or the payment of dividends tend to be well documented and require authorization by the board of directors or those others who are charged with governance.
- Since the auditor is applying auditing procedures to obtain evidence to support the components of, and amounts reported as, net income and other comprehensive income, the auditor will need to determine that the amounts have been appropriately recognized in retained earnings and accumulated other comprehensive income.

Due to the nature of stockholders' equity, including the fact that transactions tend to be infrequent, material, and well documented, the auditor will frequently rely heavily on substantive testing.

Objectives

- Adequacy of I/C over Stock transactions
- Transactions properly authorized and comply with regulations
- Transactions recorded in conformity with GAAP
- Adequately disclosed in financial statements

Stockholders' equity accounts are balance sheet accounts and, as a result, the assertions related to account balances (**RACE**) apply.

- **Rights and obligations** – Stockholders' equity represents ownership interests in the entity. A misrepresentation in relation to rights and obligations might be the inclusion a hybrid instrument that is more like debt than equity in the stockholders' equity section of the balance sheet.

- **Allocation and Valuation** – The amounts reported in stockholders' equity are accurately measured. A misrepresentation in relation to valuation and allocation might occur if the entity incorrectly allocated proceeds from the issuance of stock or amounts paid to reacquire stock between common stock or treasury stock and additional paid-in capital.

- **Completeness** – All equity interests in the entity are included in the stockholders' equity amounts reported on the balance sheet. A misrepresentation in relation to completeness might occur if the entity were to record proceeds from the issuance of stock as a borrowing transaction.

- **Existence** – The amount reported as stockholders' equity represents legitimate ownership claims to the entity. A misrepresentation in relation to existence might result from recording money borrowed as proceeds from the issuance of equity or unrecorded reacquisitions of shares.

There are various *forms of evidence* the auditor may use in the audit of stockholders' equity. Some will be obtained from the client, some directly from outside sources, and some may result from the direct actions of the auditor. Evidence the auditor may use includes:

- Copies of minutes of meetings of the board of directors or those charged with governance authorizing the issuance or reacquisition of equity shares or the payment of dividends;
- Confirmations from transfer agents or registrars indicating any transactions involving equity shares; and
- Stock certificate books for entities that do not use transfer agents.

Using the **PERCV** approach:

Presentation & Disclosure

- Review disclosures for compliance with GAAP
- Review information on stock options, dividend restrictions

Existence or Occurrence

- Confirmation with registrar and transfer agent (if applicable)
- Inspect stock certificate book (when no registrar or transfer agent)
- Vouch capital stock entries

Substantive procedures the auditor may perform in relation to existence of stockholders' equity include:

- Confirmation – The auditor may obtain confirmations directly from the entity's stock registrar or transfer agent, if applicable;
- Inspection – The auditor may inspect the stock certificate book in the custody of the entity if the entity does not use a transfer agent;
- Inspection – The auditor may trace entries made in the stockholders' equity accounts to underlying supporting documents; and
- Inspection – The auditor may review minutes from board of director meetings or meetings of those charged with governance to verify that transactions recognized in stockholders' equity accounts have been authorized.

Rights & Obligations

- Review minutes for proper authorization
- Inquire of legal counsel on legal issues
- Review Articles of Incorporation and bylaws for propriety of equity securities

Substantive procedures the auditor may perform in relation to rights and obligations include:

- Inspection – The auditor may review minutes from board of director meetings or meetings of those charged with governance to verify that transactions recognized in stockholders' equity accounts have been authorized;
- Inquiries – The auditor may make inquiries of the entity's attorneys to determine if there are any legal issues affecting equity interests; and
- Inspection – The auditor may inspect the articles of incorporation or other corporate documents to determine if there are restrictions on equity ownership and if all issuances of stock are authorized.

Completeness & Cutoff

- Perform analytical procedures
- Inspect treasury stock certificates

Substantive procedures the auditor may perform in relation to completeness include:

- Inspection – The auditor may review the cash receipts journal and trace significant deposits to source documents to determine if any represent issuances of equity securities that have not been recorded as such;
- Inspection – The auditor may review minutes from board of director meetings or meetings of those charged with governance to determine if there are any authorizations for the issuance of equity securities that did not result in increases in the amounts reported;
- Inquiries – The auditor may make inquiries of management and others as to whether there was an issuance of equity securities during the period;
- Inspection – The auditor may review the stock certificate book, if applicable, to make certain that all certificates have been accounted for; and
- Confirmation – The auditor obtains confirmations from transfer agents or registrars, if applicable, to determine if equity securities have been issued during the period that have not been recorded.

Valuation, Allocation & Accuracy

- Agree amounts to general ledger
- Vouch dividend payments
- Vouch all entries to retained earnings
- Recalculate treasury stock transactions

Substantive procedures the auditor may perform in relation to valuation and allocation include:

- Inspection – The auditor may trace dividend payments to supporting authorizations by those charged with governance and to entries to retained earnings to determine that they have properly been recognized as reductions to retained earnings in appropriate amounts;
- Inspection – The auditor may trace the closing of net income into retained earnings and other comprehensive income into accumulated other comprehensive income;
- Recalculate – The auditor may recalculate the adjustments that result from treasury stock transactions to verify the accuracy of their recording;
- Inspection – The auditor may trace entries to stockholders' equity accounts to the related cash receipts, for issuances, or disbursements, for reacquisitions, to determine that all have been properly reported; and
- Inspection – The auditor will trace all remaining transactions increasing or decreasing stockholders' equity accounts to supporting documentation to verify that they have been reported accurately.

There are generally very few transactions involving the stockholders' equity section, so audit procedures in this area are quite limited. With respect to capital stock and other securities, the auditor will verify that all issuances are approved by the board of directors and consistent with the articles of incorporation. A registrar is normally responsible for executing such transactions, so **confirmation** is an appropriate procedure along with **review of the minutes** of board meetings and inspection of corporate documents.

The primary concern with respect to Retained Earnings is that any **restrictions** on the use of it for the payment of dividends is disclosed on the face of the statement or in the notes to the financial statements.

The auditor should be familiar with 3 important dates related to the declaration and payment of dividends to make certain that they are reported in the appropriate periods.

- **Declaration date** – The date on which the board of directors commits to the dividend, determining the amount of the dividend to be distributed, at which time a liability has been incurred and is recorded.
- **Record date** – The date that is used to determine which shareholders will receive the dividend, which will be those who have legal rights to the shares on that date.
- **Payment date** – The date on which the distribution is made to the shareholders of record.

Dividends may be distributed in a variety of different forms:

- Cash dividends are the most common;
- Property dividends result when the entity distributes assets other than cash to shareholders, at which time a gain or loss is recognized as if the asset were sold for its fair market value, with that amount being reported as a liability;
- Scrip dividends are interest-bearing notes given to shareholders to be paid in the future, which are used when an entity wishes to declare a dividend when it does not have the cash to pay it;
- Liquidating dividends are distributions of the entity's cash and assets to shareholders during the process of liquidating the company, reported by shareholders as a return of their capital; and
- Stock dividends, in which the entity issues shares of stock instead of cash.

Stock dividends involve the distribution of additional shares to existing shareholders in lieu of a cash dividend. A stock dividend may be considered a *small* stock dividend, usually when the distribution is 20% or less of the outstanding stock, in which case retained earnings is reduced by the fair value of the shares issued and the stock is recorded as if issued for that amount. A stock dividend may be a *large* stock dividend, usually when the distribution is 25% or more of the outstanding stock, in which case retained earnings is decreased, and common stock is increased for the par or stated value of shares issued. Stock dividends that are for between 20 and 25 per cent of the shares outstanding may be considered large or small stock dividends, depending on the surrounding circumstances.

A *stock split* occurs when the entity issues additional shares to stockholders by decreasing the par or stated value per share and issuing a proportionate number of shares. A stock split does not generally require a journal entry as the amount reported in the common stock account will remain the same. A notation will be made for disclosure purposes, however, as the number of shares will increase and the par or stated value per share will decrease.

Types of Dividends

- Cash
- Property (FMV @ date of declaration)
- Scrip (interest bearing Note)
- Liquidating
- Stock - Small (FMV) / Large (Par)
- Stock split

Types of Dividends

Cash Dividend	Scrip – Give dividend but no money	Stock Dividend

RE   25
   Cash   25
	RE 25
	   Note Payable 25
		Small < 20 – 25% - FMV
		RE 25
		   CS 20
		   APIC 5

	Partial Liquidating Dividend
	RE 15
	APIC 10
	   Cash 25
		Large > 20 – 25% - Par
		RE 20
		   CS 20

Property (FMV)
RE   (25)
   Asset   20
   Gain   (5)
	Person receiving Liq Div
	Cash 25
	   Div income 15
	   Investment 10
		Stock Splits – Double shares, Half par
		CS (10(10)) 100
		   CS (20(5)) 100

Net effect on Stkhldrs equity = 20

Note: All dividends reduce Stockholders' Equity except for Stock dividends and Stock splits.

Revenue & Expenses

Revenue and expense transactions make up the core of the operations of many entities and, in many cases, the auditor will obtain the majority of evidence regarding revenues and expenses through the testing of controls applied to the operating systems. The auditor will first determine if there is reason to believe that revenues or expenses are materially misstated by applying analytical procedures. The auditor may compare recorded amounts to expectations developed independently by the auditor, to budgets prepared by the entity, or by comparison to prior periods.

Evidence supporting amounts reported as revenues and expenses is also obtained through the audit of other areas. The audit of accounts receivable provides evidence regarding revenues, and the audit of current liabilities provides evidence regarding many expenses. In addition, expenses like depreciation and amortization are generally audited at the same time as the related assets are examined.

A large portion of the amount reported as expenses results from cash disbursements made on a routine basis in the ordinary course of business. In performing tests of cash disbursements, including tests of controls, the auditor will generally verify that disbursements for expenses are properly reported. In addition, expenses may be put into *three broad categories*, each of which may be examined differently.
- Some expenses, such as depreciation and amortization, are determined on the basis of applying a formula. The auditor will often rely most heavily on *recalculation* or similar procedures to obtain satisfaction that they are not materially misstated.
- Some expenses, such as rent, interest expense, utilities, and other expenses incurred on a routine basis are subject to a high degree of predictability enabling the auditor to develop expectations as to the amounts that should be reported. Payroll-related expenses also often fall into this category. For those expenses for which expectations can be developed that are adequately precise and adequately reliable, the auditor will rely most heavily on *analytical procedures*.
- Many of the remaining expenses are incurred as circumstances create needs and are not subject to developing meaningful expectations. These expenses may be subjected to

various substantive procedures, including *tracing items* to underlying supporting documentation, as considered appropriate by the auditor.

Auditors will often rely more heavily on internal controls when obtaining evidence about revenues and expenses than when auditing balance sheet accounts. The auditor will determine, based on the required understanding, if the systems are designed to record revenues and expenses in appropriate amounts that are fairly presented. If the auditor concludes that the systems are potentially effective, the auditor will perform tests of controls to make certain that the systems were in place and operating effectively during the period under audit. Satisfactory results to the tests of controls will allow the auditor to limit the nature, timing, and extent of further audit procedures applied to revenue and expenses.

Many revenue and expense (I/S) accounts are verified when tests of controls are performed over the various functions, such as cash receipts and disbursements, purchases, and sales. In addition, they are verified in conjunction with the audit of related asset or liability (B/S) accounts.

B/S Account	I/S Account
Accounts receivable	Sales, bad debt expense
Inventories & Accounts payable	Purchases, Cost of goods sold, manufacturing payroll
Investments	Interest, dividends, gains & losses on sales
Property, Plant & Equipment	Rent, Gains & losses on sales, Depreciation, repairs & maintence expense
Notes Receivable	Interest
Accrued liabilities & prepaid expenses	Warranty expense, commissions, fees insurance expense, & various expenses

Revenues and expenses are *income statement accounts* and, as a result, the assertions related to **classes of transactions** (**CPA-CO**) apply.

- **Completeness** – All transactions giving rise to revenues or expenses that relate to the entity are recognized. A misrepresentation in relation to completeness might include capitalizing costs that should be recognized as expenses or neglecting to record a sale with the proceeds being misappropriated.

- **Period Cutoff** – All revenues and expenses are reported in the appropriate period. A misrepresentation in relation to cutoff may include recognizing a sale while goods shipped under a destination contract are still in transit or neglecting to accrue an expense that had been incurred as of the end of the year but had not yet been paid for.

- **Accuracy** (Amounts) – All revenues and expenses have been reported in appropriate amounts. A misrepresentation in relation to accuracy may involve a revenue transaction being reported at an amount lower than the actual sale, or an expense being reported at a higher amount, with the difference being misappropriated.

- **Classification** – All revenues and expenses are appropriately categorized on the financial statements. A misrepresentation in relation to classification may involve reporting the proceeds from the sale of an operating asset, such as a machine used in the manufacturing process, as revenues rather than reporting the difference between the proceeds and the carrying value as a gain or loss on sale.

- **Occurrence** – The transaction giving rise to the recorded revenue or expense did occur and pertains to the entity. A misrepresentation in relation to occurrence might result from recording a sale that no customer has approved or recognizing an expense that was incurred on behalf of a member of management but paid for by the entity.

There are various *forms of evidence* the auditor may use in the audit of revenues and expenses. Some will be obtained from the client, some directly from outside sources, and some may result from the direct actions of the auditor. Evidence the auditor may use includes:
- Copies of purchase orders received from customers, sales orders, vendor invoices, requisitions, receiving reports, and various other documents supporting specific transactions;
- Leases, service agreements, and other contracts related to the incurring of regular expenses;
- Spreadsheets and schedules calculating deprecation or amortization expense, interest expense, or other items requiring allocation or otherwise requiring analysis for proper reporting;
- Approvals from management or those charged with governance, as appropriate, for unusual and nonrecurring expenses; and
- Budgets and other analyses providing management's expectations as to revenues expected to be earned during the period and expenses expected to be incurred.

The detailed substantive audit procedures for Revenues and Expenses may include (CPA-CO):

Completeness

In seeking evidence that all revenue and expense transactions that occurred and pertained to the entity were recorded, the auditor will determine if there are controls in place that would prevent a revenue or expense that occurred and pertained to the entity from being recorded. These controls might include:
- The use of prenumbered sales invoices and the accounting for all numbers within a sequence; and
- Comparisons of expenses to budgeted amounts are made on a regular basis with any variances investigated on a timely basis.

Substantive procedures the auditor may perform in relation to the assertion as to the completeness of the recording of revenues and expenses may include:
- Analytical Procedure – The auditor may compare recorded revenues and various expenses to expectations developed by the auditor that the auditor considers adequately reliable and adequately precise to constitute meaningful evidence;
- Inspection – The auditor may select a sample of receiving reports and trace them to related transactions recognizing revenue; and
- Recalculation – In the examination of fixed assets, the auditor may analyze documents related to purchases to determine if costs that should have been recognized as an expense in the period were capitalized to the cost of the asset.

Period Cutoff

In seeking evidence that all revenue and expense transactions are recorded in the appropriate periods, the auditor will determine if there are controls in place that would prevent a revenue or expense from being recorded in the wrong period. These controls might include:
- Policies requiring that expenses be compared to budgeted amounts with variances investigated; and
- Policies requiring that invoices received during a reasonable time after the end of the period be evaluated to determine if they should be included in the period-end accrual.

Substantive procedures the auditor may perform in relation to cutoff may include:
- Analytical Procedure – The auditor may compare the relationship between accrued expenses and the entity's monthly payments for expenses to the auditor's expectations to make certain that expenses incurred near the end of the year are reported;
- Inspection – The auditor may trace payments made during a reasonable time after the end of the period to supporting documents to identify those that were for goods or services received during the period and verify that those amounts are recognized as expenses in the appropriate period;
- Analytical Procedure – The auditor may compare the amount accrued for payroll and payroll-related expenses, such as payroll taxes, to the auditor's expectation for that amount based on the auditor's understanding of the entity's employees and knowledge of the number of work days that occurred between the last date for which they were paid and the end of the entity's fiscal period; and
- Inspection – The auditor may review leases and other arrangements, such as service agreements, calling for regular payments to determine if all amounts related to the current period have been accounted for.

Accuracy (Amounts)

In seeking evidence that all revenue and expense transactions are recorded in appropriate amounts, the auditor will determine if there are controls in place that would prevent a revenue or expense from being recorded in an incorrect amount. These controls might include:
- Policies requiring that expenses be compared to budgeted amounts with variances investigated; and
- Timely reconciliation of statements received from vendors to amounts reported as expenses.

Substantive procedures the auditor may perform in relation to accuracy may include:
- Analytical Procedure – The auditor may compare recorded revenues and expenses to expectations developed by the auditor;
- Inspection – The auditor may select a sample of amounts recorded as expenses and trace them to supporting documentation to determine if expenses were recorded in correct amounts;
- Inspection – The auditor may select a sample of recorded sales transactions and trace them to supporting documentation to verify that they were recorded in correct amounts;
- Analytical Procedure – The auditor may compare amounts recorded for interest to estimates computed on the basis of average debt and the entity's borrowing rate;
- Analytical Procedure – The auditor may compare payroll and payroll-related expenses, such as employee benefits and payroll taxes, to auditor estimates based on the auditor's understanding of the number of employees retained by the entity and pay rates;
- Inspection – The auditor may review leases and other arrangements, such as service agreements, calling for regular payments to determine if amounts are appropriate; and

- Analytical Procedure – The auditor may compare the amounts reported as expenses in the current period to amounts reported in prior periods, accounting for changes in the makeup or amount of various items.

Classification

In seeking evidence that all revenue and expense transactions are classified into appropriate categories, the auditor will determine if there are controls in place that would prevent a revenue or expense from being categorized incorrectly. These controls might include:

- Maintenance of a list of regular vendors, such as utility companies, indicating the category that payments made to them should be classified as;
- A review of the coding of disbursements by the individual signing checks and cancelling the voucher package; and
- Policies requiring that all transactions recorded as revenues be supported by a customer purchase order, an appropriate prenumbered sales order form, a sales invoice, and a shipping report.

Substantive procedures the auditor may perform in classification may include:

- Inspection – The auditor may select a sample of transactions recorded as sales and trace them to supporting documentation to verify that they represent sales of goods or services in the ordinary course of business; and
- Inspection – The auditor may select a sample of transactions recorded in various expense categories and trace them to supporting documentation to verify that the expense category in which they were recorded is appropriate.

Occurrence

In seeking evidence that revenue and expense transactions actually occurred, the auditor will determine if there are controls in place that would prevent a revenue or expense from being recorded if the underlying transaction did not actually occur or did not pertain to the entity. These controls might include:

- Policies requiring that all regular expenses, such as rents, utilities, and various other expenses be compared to budget as part of the recording process with variances investigated on a timely basis;
- Policies requiring matching documentation including customer purchase orders, sales orders, shipping documents, and sales invoices for all revenue-related transactions before the recording of revenues;
- Policies requiring appropriate approvals for all unscheduled expenses; and
- Policies requiring comparisons of payees, including vendors and employees, to approved vendor lists and lists of active employees maintained by human resources.

Substantive procedures the auditor may perform in relation to the occurrence of recorded revenues and expenses may include:

- Inspection – The auditor may select a sample of recorded revenue transactions and trace them to supporting documentation, including a customer purchase order, a sales order, a shipping report, and an invoice;
- Inspection – The auditor may select a sample of recorded expense transactions and trace them to supporting documentation, which may include receiving reports, authorized requests, and vendor invoices; and
- Inspection – The auditor may review leases to determine if recorded rents are for the use of assets being used by the entity.

Payroll

When auditing payroll, the auditor is often able to place reliance on the internal control structure of the payroll cycle and assess risk of material misstatement at a low level, thereby permitting higher detection risk and limiting the necessary substantive testing.

Since payroll is generally more predictable than other costs, the auditor should perform **analytical procedures** involving the comparison of actual payroll costs with budgeted or standard costs to determine **completeness** of payroll accruals.

To support the assertion of **valuation**, the auditor should recalculate payroll accruals and compare calculations with source information, such as time cards to verify hours worked and personnel records to verify pay rates.

<u>Payroll</u>

- Objectives
    - I/C over payroll
    - Employees actually exist (existence)
    - Payroll computations correct (valuation)
    - Adequate disclosure

Lecture 4.13

CLASS QUESTIONS

Please see the Class Questions and Class Solutions for this Lecture at the end of this Section.

Lecture 4.14

DEVELOPING AN AUDIT PROGRAM/AUDIT PLAN

An audit program is a step-by-step list of audit procedures that emphasizes account balances, which is *required* for every GAAS audit. It is designed so that:
- The procedures will achieve specific audit objectives, which relate to management's assertions.
- Supports the auditor's conclusion

AU-C Section 330, Performing Audit Procedures in Response to Assessed Risks and Evaluating the Audit Evidence Obtained, indicates that an auditor is required to design and perform substantive procedures for all relevant assertions related to each material class of transaction, account balance, and disclosure.

This means that even when IR is very low (indicating a very low likelihood that a material misstatement will occur) and CR is very low (indicating a very low likelihood that, in that rare circumstance that a material misstatement does occur, there is a very low likelihood that the entity's internal control will not detect and correct it on a timely basis), resulting in an AR that is below the level that the auditor considers necessary, the auditor will still be required to design and perform substantive procedures in relation to that relevant assertion.

How to Draft an Audit Program/Audit Plan

Audit programs can be developed on an assertion-by-assertion basis using a process like the following:

1. *Identify a material class of transaction*, such as sales or salaries expense; account balance, such as cash or notes payable; or disclosure, such as the disclosure of the lease payments for the next five years for an operating lease.
   o The auditor develops audit programs using a cumulative top-down basis.
   o This is accomplished by beginning with the class of transaction, account balance, or disclosure that represents the highest risk of material misstatement.
   o Assume the auditor selects sales as a class of transaction or inventory as an account balance.

2. Based on whether the auditor is concerned about intentional overstatements or understatements, or misstatements due to error, which could be over or understatements, the auditor will *identify the relevant assertions*.
   o If the auditor believes that the client may intentionally overstate sales, for example, the assertion related to occurrence would clearly be relevant as the client may record sales that did not actually occur.
   o If the auditor believes that the client may intentionally overstate inventory, the assertion related to rights and obligations would clearly be relevant as the client may include on the balance sheet inventory that it may be holding on consignment or does not own for some other reason.

3. Using the understanding of internal control, *identify all control activities* that pertain to the relevant assertion and evaluate whether they appear to be sufficient to prevent or detect and correct a material misstatement.
   o The auditor will evaluate all of the control activities that were identified to prevent the recording of a sale that did not occur to determine if the identified controls would be sufficient to prevent a sale that did not actually occur from being recorded, or to detect such a misstatement and correct it on a timely basis, assuming the controls are in place and operating effectively.
   o If the auditor determines they are sufficient:
     ▪ The auditor may decide to perform tests of controls and modify the planned nature, timing, and extent of further audit procedures based on the results; or
     ▪ The auditor may decide to ignore controls, assess CR at maximum, and perform substantive procedures that will adequately reduce DR as if there are not internal controls to prevent the recording of a sale that did not occur.
   o If the auditor determines that they are not sufficient:
     ▪ The auditor will inquire of the client if there might be additional controls that were not identified at the time that the auditor was obtaining an understanding, in which case the auditor may determine that controls are sufficient.
     ▪ If there are not sufficient mitigating controls, the auditor will assess CR at maximum and design and perform substantive tests accordingly.

4. The auditor will decide on the procedure or procedures that will provide sufficient appropriate evidence to support the assertion being evaluated.
    o To determine if all sales that were recorded actually occurred, the auditor may select a sample of all recorded sales and trace them to supporting documentation, including customer purchase orders and shipping documents, to verify that the sale actually occurred.
    o To determine if the entity owns all of the inventory that it is reporting on its balance sheet, the auditor may select a sample of items that are included in inventory and trace them to purchase documents.

5. The auditor will evaluate whether the evidence obtained through the performance of the procedure also supports one or more other relevant assertions related to the same class of transactions, account balance, or disclosure, or related to a different one.
    o In addition to providing evidence that sales occurred, tracing sales to supporting documents may provide some evidence regarding the existence and the rights and obligations assertions related to accounts receivable.
    o In addition to providing evidence that inventory is owned by the entity, tracing items in inventory to purchase documents may provide evidence about the existence and valuation and allocation assertions related to accounts payable.

6. The audit programs for assertions that represent lower risks will then be prepared on an incremental basis, evaluating the additional procedures required to obtain sufficient appropriate audit evidence to support the assertion.
    o The auditor will determine what additional procedures, if any, are necessary to obtain evidence about the assertion related to the existence of accounts receivable, for example, if the auditor has traced a sample of sales to supporting documents and there were no significant exceptions.
    o The auditor will determine what additional procedures, if any, are necessary to obtain evidence to support the assertion related to the existence of accounts payable if a sample of items in inventory were traced to purchase documents and there were no significant exceptions.

In preparing a list of substantive tests to be performed, use the following approach:
- **Procedures** – Attempt to identify one procedure for each of the categories in the I-CORRIIA (observation may not be possible if the account is not a tangible asset).
- **Assertions** – Ensure that there is at least one test related to each of the financial statement assertions in U-PERCV (unless the problem explicitly is limited to one or two of the assertions).
- **Related accounts** – Include at least one procedure for each account that is related to the one being addressed in the essay (for example, when preparing a list for receivables, include tests of bad debt accounts).
- **Certain tests** are applicable to almost every account:
    o Read financial statements and notes.
    o Review minutes of board and shareholder meetings.
    o Representations from management should be obtained.
    o Reconcile the trial balance to supporting records.

Audit Program**/Audit Plan

1. Obtain schedule from client
   - Reperformance – (foot, tie to PY and GL)
2. I-CORRIIA
3. U-PERCV
4. Revenues & Expense/ Gains & Losses/ Contra Accounts
5. Generic tests
   a. Cut-Off Tests
   b. Board of Directors Minutes
   c. Perform Subsequent Events
   d. Read F/S and Footnotes

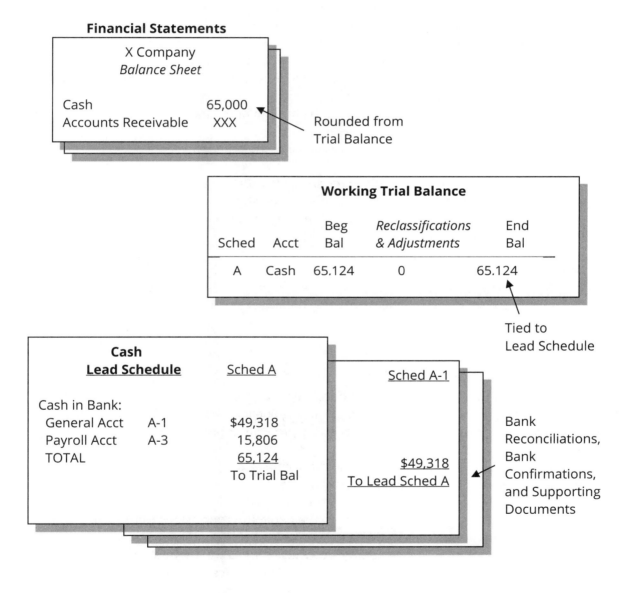

Financial Statements

X Company
Balance Sheet

Cash   65,000
Accounts Receivable   XXX

Rounded from
Trial Balance

Working Trial Balance

Sched	Acct	Beg Bal	*Reclassifications & Adjustments*	End Bal
A	Cash	65.124	0	65.124

Tied to
Lead Schedule

Cash
Lead Schedule   Sched A   Sched A-1

Cash in Bank:
  General Acct   A-1 $49,318
  Payroll Acct   A-3   15,806
  TOTAL   65,124 $49,318
                         To Trial Bal   To Lead Sched A

Bank
Reconciliations,
Bank
Confirmations,
and Supporting
Documents

AUDIT DOCUMENTATION (AU-C 230) & WORKPAPER DEFICIENCIES

The exam occasionally addresses **deficiencies** in audit workpapers. Look for the following possible deficiencies when a working paper is presented on the exam for analysis:

- In analyzing working paper for **weaknesses**, examine the following:
    - **C**omment on Exceptions – Comments in the body of the working paper or tickmark legend may refer to unusual circumstances or indications of a problem. Make sure each exceptional item has been resolved and that the resolution has been documented.
    - **C**onclusions – Closing comments at the bottom of the working paper should be reviewed to ensure they are consistent with the information in the audit documentation. They are usually wrong.
    - **H**eading – The name of the client, title of the working paper (such as the account being analyzed), and audit year should all be included.
    - **I**nitials – Each person who prepares or reviews a working paper should initial it.
    - **T**ickmarks (symbols) – Amounts on the working paper are often verified arithmetically or by comparison with other accounts, and symbols may be created as needed to place next to these amounts, referencing information about how they were verified in a legend placed at the bottom of the paper. Be sure each symbol is defined in the legend.
    - **F**oot – Check the mathematical accuracy of the schedule.

Working Trial Balance—A listing of ledger accounts with current year-end balances (as well as last year's ending balances), with columns for adjusting and reclassifying entries as well as for final balances for the current year. Typically, both balance sheet and income statement accounts are included.

Lead Schedules—Schedules that summarize like accounts, the total of which is typically transferred to the working trial balance. For example, a client's various cash accounts may be summarized on a lead schedule with only the total cash being transferred to the working trial balance.

Audit Documentation (Working Papers)

AU-C Section 230 has adopted the term **audit documentation** to refer to the working papers developed during the course of the audit. Under these guidelines, audit documentation should be sufficient to enable an experienced auditor, having no previous connection with the audit, to understand:

- The nature, timing, and extent of the audit procedures performed to comply with GAAS and applicable legal and regulatory requirements.
- The results of the audit procedures performed and the audit evidence obtained.
- Significant findings or issues arising during the audit, the conclusions reached thereon, and significant professional judgments made in reaching those conclusions.
    - Serves as a basis for the auditor's conclusion as to whether the objective of the audit, to obtain sufficient appropriate audit evidence to support the auditor's opinion, has been achieved; and
    - The auditor has planned and performed the engagement in accordance with GAAS and regulatory or other requirements, if applicable.

In addition, audit documentation should:

- Assist in the planning and performance of the engagement.

- Enable engagement team members with supervision and review responsibilities to understand the evidence obtained and the nature, timing, extent and results of auditing procedures performed.
- Indicate the engagement team members *who performed* and reviewed the work.
- While it is not necessary to document every matter considered during an audit, oral explanations alone (absent working paper documentation) are not sufficient to support the work of the auditor.
- Audit documentation must include a written audit program (or set of audit programs) for every audit.
- The documentation completion period is **60 days** following the report release date. That means that changes resulting from the process of assembling and completing the audit file may be made within 60 days following the date the audit report was released to the client. The fact that these changes have been made need not be documented. After the documentation completion date, the auditor should not delete or discard audit documentation.
- The retention period (how long audit documentation must be kept) should not be less than five years from the report release date (longer if legal and regulatory requirements so require).
- Audit documentation is the property of the auditor and is confidential.
- Document procedures performed, evidence examined, and conclusions reached.
- Provide a means of preserving information that may be relevant to future engagements.
- Enable the performance of quality control reviews and inspections, as well as external inspections or peer reviews.
- Assist successor auditors when they request to review the predecessor's working papers.
- Enhance an auditor's understanding of work performed in prior periods and its potential effect on the current period's engagement.

The accountant, not the client, owns the working papers and any other documentation that the accountant creates during an engagement. Nevertheless, the accountant must maintain **confidentiality**, and cannot provide the working papers or other information obtained during engagements to other parties without the permission of the client. Client confidentiality does not, however, preclude a CPA from providing access to other members of the auditor's firm. There are some **exceptions** to confidentiality, including:
- A **valid subpoena;**
- An **IRS administrative subpoena;**
- A **court order**, except in those few states that have a privilege statute; and
- A **quality control peer review**, providing access to other accountants and the PCAOB in connection with a valid program of peer review.

Common law does not recognize the concept of **privilege**, which would allow the accountant to refuse to honor a court subpoena. A small number of states have enacted privilege statutes, and the federal government now recognizes working papers developed in connection with the preparation of a tax return to be privileged in certain circumstances. Nevertheless, privilege may not be used if the accountant has already provided some of the information requested in a subpoena. The purpose of privilege is to protect the client, not the accountant, so the accountant may not assert privilege even where privilege statutes exist if the client waives the privilege.

When audit procedures include the inspection of significant contracts or agreements, copies or extracts of those documents should be included in the working papers. In addition, documentation should indicate discussions with management, those charged with governance, or others regarding significant findings or other issues and should include the nature of the items discussed and identification of who was involved in the discussions.

When an auditor has identified information that is inconsistent with the auditor's final conclusion in relation to the financial statements, documentation should include an indication as to how the issue was addressed.

In rare circumstances, an auditor may find it necessary to depart from a presumptively mandatory requirement and apply alternative procedures. When this is the case, the auditor must document the reason for the departure and an indication of how the alternative procedures performed achieved the objectives of the presumptively mandatory requirement.

Working papers will indicate the report release date and should be assembled on a timely basis, no later than **60 days** after that date. Once complete, the auditor may not delete or discard any documentation until the retention period expires. The retention period is established by the auditor's firm but must be at least equal to 5 years or the period required by law or regulation, whichever is longer. If the auditor determines it is necessary to modify existing documentation or add additional working papers, the auditor should document:
- The reasons for the changes; and
- Who made the changes, who reviewed them, when the changes were made, and when they were reviewed.

After the report's release date, the auditor may perform new or additional procedures or draw new conclusions. If so, the auditor will document:
- The circumstances causing the modification;
- The new or additional procedures performed, evidence obtained, and conclusions reached;
- The effect on the audit report; and
- Who made the changes, who they were reviewed by, when they were made, and when they were reviewed.

Six factors must be considered in determining the ***nature and extent*** of documentation for a particular audit area or procedure:
1. The risk of material misstatement associated with the assertion being examined;
2. The extent of judgment the auditor exercises in performing the work;
3. The nature of the auditing procedures performed;
4. The significance of the evidence obtained;
5. The nature and extent of exceptions identified, if any; and
6. The need to document a conclusion or basis for conclusion that is not evident from the other documentation.

Among the specific **types of audit documentation** that must be included are the following:
- Abstracts or copies of significant contracts or agreements.
- Identification of the items that were selected for tests of the operating effectiveness of controls and substantive tests of details that involve inspection or confirmation.
    - Identification should be specific enough so that another audit team member would be able to determine which documents and record items were actually tested.
    - An example of identification is a list of the invoice numbers selected in a sample.

The auditor is required to document significant **audit findings and issues** including:
- Matters involving the selection of accounting principles and related disclosures.
- Results of procedures that indicate the possibility of material misstatements and require modification of the auditing procedures.
- Circumstances that caused the auditor significant difficulty in applying audit procedures.
- Other findings that could result in modification of the auditor's report.

Retention of records after the completion of the audit is of extreme importance (as the Enron case demonstrates). In recognition of the importance of IT, audit documentation maintained in **electronic form** must enable the auditor to access the data throughout the retention period necessary to meet practice needs and legal and regulatory requirements. This may require file conversion and updated software in some cases after the completion of the engagement.

Some of the specific documentation requirements are:
- **Audit risk and materiality** – The auditor must document the nature and effect of aggregated misstatements and the auditor's conclusion as to whether the financial statements are materially misstated on a timely basis.
- **Analytical procedures** – The auditor must document (a) the factors considered in developing expected relationships, (b) the expected relationship, (c) the results of the comparisons made, and (d) any additional procedures performed in response to unexpected relationships.
- **Going concern doubts** – The auditor must document (a) the conditions or events that led to any significant doubts; (b) the work performed to evaluate management plans, (c) the conclusion as to whether doubt remains or has been alleviated by such plans, and (d) effect of the conclusion on the financial statements, disclosures, and audit report.*

Audit documentation is the principal support for the auditor's report. At a minimum, the audit documentation must **always** include:
- Reconciliation of the accounting records with the financial statements.
- An audit program that details the procedures to be performed during the engagement.
- Documentation of the auditor's understanding of the internal control structure.
- Documentation of the assessed level of control risk.
- Proof of sufficient evidence having been obtained to support the auditor's opinion on the financial statements.
- A client representation letter (obtained from management at the conclusion of fieldwork).

In addition, several factors will affect the **quantity, type, and content** of the audit documentation for a particular engagement. These factors include:
- The condition of the client's **accounting records** – Audit documentation may have to be prepared to complete the records in some cases.
- The risk of material misstatement.
- The **type of report** being issued by the auditor – A qualified or adverse opinion will require working paper discussion of the reasons.
- **Staff disagreements** – If a member of the audit team doesn't agree with a decision made that has an impact on the fieldwork or conclusions, the audit documentation should document the disagreement.

The audit documentation generated during an audit may go into either the **current** file (if they only relate to that year's engagement) or the **permanent** file (if they're related to more than one year).

Examples of items that will be included in the **current** file are:
- **Audit program** – Each audit is unique, so a program will only be relevant to documenting the work of that particular year.
- **Working trial balance** – This is a trial balance pulled from the client's records, which provides additional columns for reclassifications and adjustments. The final column is the adjusted balances of the accounts, which should agree with the financial statements that are issued that year.
- **Lead schedules** – These summarize all the major components that determine an amount appearing in the financial statements or notes, and serve as a form of table of contents referencing individual audit documentation that support the components listed. A separate lead schedule will normally be needed for each material account balance.
- **Responses to information requests** – These include confirmations, the attorney's letter, and the client representation letter.
- **Reconciliations and analyses by the auditor** – These refer to evidence directly obtained by the auditor to support amounts in the current financial statements or notes.

Examples of items that will be included in the **permanent** file are:
- **Organization documents** – These include the articles of incorporation and bylaws.
- **Minutes** – Board of director and shareholder meetings often discuss items of long-term significance.
- **Flowcharts of the internal control structure** – Though changes occur over the year, the general internal control structure will be similar enough that a flowchart will be useful for many years.
- **Debt agreements** – Contracts for long-term liabilities are, by their nature, relevant to many years. This category includes note, bond, lease, and pension agreements.
- **Analyses of equity accounts** – Capital stock and related accounts change rarely, so evidence is valid for many years.
- Depreciation schedules.

Audit documentation need not all be written documents: it may include computer printouts and itemized calculator tapes when appropriate.
- The audit documentation will be finalized and organized, usually by an audit manager, following the completion of fieldwork.
- The manager will review the audit documentation prepared by assistants to ensure that the results of their work are consistent with the audit report to be issued.
- They will also make sure that the audit documentation is understandable and reference each other as appropriate.

There will be a second review of the audit documentation, typically called the wrap-up review, which will normally be performed by a partner or equivalent. This review will focus on the fair presentation of the financial statements and the agreement of the working paper lead schedules to the statements and notes.

As mentioned before, if any member of the audit team disagrees with the conduct of the audit or the conclusions, this disagreement should also be documented in the audit documentation. The final decision is obviously the responsibility of the partner-in-charge (or equivalent), and it would be inappropriate to address these disagreements with the client.

Engagement Completion Document (PCAOB AS 1215)

For audits of public companies reporting to the SEC, the Public Company Accounting Oversight Board (PCAOB) has established standards for audit documentation. Most are identical to those required by GAAS (AU-C 230), but AS 1215 specifically added the requirement of the preparation of an **engagement completion document**, which will identify all significant findings and issues and be sufficiently specific for a reviewer to obtain a thorough understanding of them. It may include either:

- All information necessary to understand the significant findings and issues
- Cross-references, as appropriate, to other available supporting documentation

The documentation must demonstrate that the engagement complied with PCAOB standards, the documentation completion period is **45 days** (not 60 days) following the report release date, and the audit documentation must be retained for *7 years (rather than 5 years)* from the report release date, or the period required by law, if longer.

Evaluation of Misstatements Identified During the Audit (AU-C 450)

During the course of the engagement, AU-C Section 450, *Evaluation of Misstatements Identified During the Audit*, requires the auditor to accumulate misstatements, other than those that are clearly trivial for the purpose of determining the effect, if any, on the overall audit strategy and the audit plan. Misstatements are considered to be any difference between the manner in which an amount, classification, presentation, or disclosure is presented on or with the financial statements and how it should be presented on or with the financial statements in order to be fairly presented in accordance with the applicable financial reporting framework. Omissions of elements of financial reporting or required disclosures are also considered misstatements.

Revision to the overall audit strategy and audit plan will be called for if identified misstatements either:

- Indicate that other misstatements may occur, such as when errors are caused by a flaw in an aspect of the accounting system, the cumulative effect of which could be material when considered along with other misstatements identified during the engagement; or
- The aggregate effect of all misstatements identified during the audit approach the auditor's measurement of materiality.

In determining if misstatements are material, the auditor will consider both *quantitative and qualitative* factors. Some **qualitative factors** the auditor will consider will include whether:

- Misstatements affect trends of profitability;
- Misstatements change losses into income, or vice versa;
- Misstatements that affect segment information; and
- Misstatements that affect compliance with legal and contractual requirements.

The auditor will request that management correct those misstatements that have been identified by the auditor. Upon correction by the client, the auditor will apply procedures to obtain evidence as to whether or not the misstatements have been properly corrected. If the client does not correct the financial statements for identified misstatements, the auditor will:

- Obtain an understanding of the client's reasons for not correcting the misstatements; and
- Consider the effects when evaluating whether or not the financial statements taken as a whole are free of material misstatement.

Before determining if uncorrected misstatements result in material misstatement to the financial statements, the auditor will reevaluate materiality taking into account revisions to financial

statement amounts. The determination of whether or not financial statements are materially misstated will be based on the aggregate of all uncorrected misstatements. Consideration will be in relation to the financial statements taken as a whole as well as the particular account balances, classes of transactions, or disclosures affected. The auditor will consider:
- The size and nature of the uncorrected misstatements; and
- The effect of uncorrected misstatements in relation to prior periods.

Lecture 4.15

CLASS QUESTIONS

Please see the Class Questions and Class Solutions for this Lecture at the end of this Section.

Lecture 4.16

MANAGEMENT REPRESENTATION LETTER/CLIENT REP LETTER (REQUIRED) (AU-C 580)

The auditor is **required** to obtain a letter from the client's management reaffirming in writing some of the information that was provided to the auditor during the course of the audit and to confirm other matters, such as confirming that all appropriate information was made available to the auditor.
- U-PERCV is included in the letter
- Dated, no earlier than audit report date
- CEO/CFO/Governance
- Scope limitation if not received

The representations are made in the form of a letter written to the auditor. It should be signed by the chief executive officer and chief financial officer of the client, or, in some circumstances, those charged with governance. The letter of representations:
- Is dated as of the *audit report date*, which is the date on which the auditor has determined that sufficient appropriate audit evidence has been obtained, generally the final day of fieldwork; and
- Is required to cover all of the financial statements and periods referred to in the audit report.

Though the representations made in the letter are not audited further, requiring management to provide such a letter is a mandatory audit procedure, and the failure to receive such a letter is considered a **scope limitation** sufficient to preclude the expression of an unqualified opinion on the financial statements. In most circumstances, in fact, a disclaimer of opinion will have to be issued in the absence of such a letter.

An important purpose of this letter is to emphasize management's responsibility for the financial statements. Another is to provide the auditor with some assurance that management is not deliberately concealing any information that might have affected the auditor's opinion. Should the auditor have some evidence of intentional misbehavior by management, the auditor will, of course, place less reliance on the representations made by management in the letter.

The content of the letter will, to some extent, depend on what has taken place during the audit prior to that point. In addition, the management representation letter clearly cannot have an impact on the gathering of evidence by the auditor during the audit, since it is obtained after the planning and performance of all other tests. Certain representations, however, will be present in all such letters.

- Management is responsible for:
    - The preparation and fair presentation of the financial statements in accordance with the applicable financial reporting framework, and
    - The design, implementation, and maintenance (**DIM**) of internal control relevant to the preparation and fair presentation of financial statements that are free from material misstatement, whether due to fraud or error.
- An indication by management that:
    - Management is **unaware** of any **errors or fraud** that would have a **material effect** on the financial statements.
    - There have been **no acts of fraud or noncompliance** (illegal acts) of any kind (even immaterial ones) **by management** itself or other key employees responsible for the internal control structure.
    - **Minutes** of all board of director and shareholder meetings are **complete** and have been made available to the auditor.
    - **All financial records** that exist have been made available to the auditor.
    - There are **no pending legal matters** with a **material** impact on the financial statements that have not been disclosed to the auditor (such as legal restrictions on assets or pending lawsuits or government investigations).
    - Management believes all **estimates** are reasonable.
    - All related parties and **related-party transactions** have been identified to the auditor and properly accounted for and disclosed.
    - **Subsequent events** have been properly accounted for and disclosed.

Management **cannot** make a representation that there have been no errors or fraud committed by any employees. They only represent to be unaware of any and to have not committed any fraud themselves.

In some cases, the auditor will be expressing an opinion on *supplementary information* included with the financial statements. When this is the case, the auditor is also required to obtain **written representations** indicating:

- Management's acknowledgement of its responsibility for the preparation and fair presentation of the supplementary information in accordance with applicable criteria;
- Management's belief that the supplementary information is fairly presented in accordance with applicable criteria, including both its form and content;
- That measurement and presentation methods either have not changed from the prior period or, if they have, the reasons for the changes;
- Any significant assumptions or interpretations that affected the measurement or presentation of the supplementary information; and
- If the supplementary information is presented without the audited financial statements in the same document, that management will make the audited financial statements readily available to the users of the supplementary information.

Management (Client) Representation Letter

(Date of the Auditor's Report)

(To Independent Auditor)

This representation letter is provided in connection with your audit of the financial statements of ABC Company, which comprise the balance sheet as of December 31, 20XX, and the related statements of income, changes in stockholders' equity, and cash flows for the year then ended, and the related notes to the financial statements, for the purpose of expressing an opinion on whether the financial statements are presented fairly, in all material respects, in accordance with accounting principles generally accepted in the United States (US GAAP).

Certain representations in this letter are described as being limited to matters that are **material**. Items are considered material, regardless of size, if they involve an omission or misstatement of accounting information that, in the light of surrounding circumstances, makes it probable that the judgment of a reasonable person relying on the information would be changed or influenced by the omission or misstatement.

Except where otherwise stated below, immaterial matters less than $XXX collectively are not considered to be exceptions that require disclosure for the purpose of the following representations. This amount is not necessarily indicative of amounts that would require adjustment to or disclosure in the financial statements.

We confirm, to the best of our knowledge and belief, having made such inquiries as we considered necessary for the purpose of appropriately informing ourselves as of [*the date of the auditor's report*]:

Financial Statements

1. We have fulfilled our responsibilities, as set out in the terms of the engagement dated [insert date], for the *preparation and fair presentation of the financial statements in accordance with US GAAP.*
2. We acknowledge **our responsibility** for the design, implementation, and maintenance (DIM) of internal control relevant to the preparation and fair presentation of financial statements that are free from material misstatement, whether due to fraud or error.
3. We acknowledge our responsibility for the design, implementation, and maintenance of internal control *to prevent and detect fraud.*
4. Significant assumptions used by us in making accounting estimates, including those measured at fair value, are reasonable.
5. Related party relationships and transactions have been appropriately accounted for and disclosed in accordance with the requirements of US GAAP.
6. All events **subsequent to** the date of the financial statements and for which US GAAP requires adjustment or disclosure have been adjusted or disclosed.
7. The effects of uncorrected misstatements are immaterial, both individually and ·in the aggregate, to the financial statements as a whole. A list of the uncorrected misstatements is attached to the representation letter.
8. The effects of all known actual or possible litigation and claims have been accounted for and disclosed in accordance with US GAAP.

Information Provided

9. We have provided you with:
   a. Access to all information, of which we are aware that is relevant to the preparation and fair presentation of the financial statements such as records, documentation and other matters;
   b. Additional information that you have requested for the purpose of the audit; and
   c. Unrestricted access to persons within the entity from whom you determined it necessary to obtain audit evidence.
10. All transactions have been recorded in the accounting records and are reflected in the financial statements.
11. We have disclosed to you the results of our assessment of the risk that the financial statements may be materially misstated as a result of fraud.
12. We have [*no knowledge of any*] [*disclosed to you all information that we are aware of regarding*] fraud or suspected fraud that affects the entity and involves:
    a. Management;
    b. Employees who have significant roles in internal control; or
    c. Others when the fraud could have a material effect on the financial statements.
13. We have [*no knowledge of any*] [*disclosed to you all information that we are aware of regarding*] allegations of fraud, or suspected fraud, affecting the entity's financial statements communicated by employees, former employees, analysts, regulators or others.
14. We have disclosed to you all known instances of non-compliance with laws and regulations whose effects should be considered when preparing financial statements.
15. We [*have disclosed to you all known actual or possible*] [*are not aware of any pending or threatened*] litigation, claims, and assessments whose effects should be considered when preparing the financial statements.
16. We have disclosed to you the identity of the entity's related parties and all related party relationships and transactions of which we are aware.

[*Any other matters that the auditor may consider necessary*]

(Name of Chief Executive Officer and Title)   (Name of Chief Financial Officer and Title)

ATTORNEY'S LETTER (LETTER OF AUDIT INQUIRY) (AU-C 501)

The auditor will also obtain a letter from each attorney with which the client did business relevant to any litigation, claims, or assessments with which the client may have been involved.

- **Litigation, claims & assessments**
- **Corroborate info**
- If Attorneys letter is not received, it is considered a **Scope Limitation**.
- Management requests the inquiry, but the letter should be physically mailed by the auditor.

The primary source of evidence about litigation, claims, and assessments is the **management** of the client. Even though legal counsel will be involved, attorney-client privilege prevents the attorney from directly providing the auditor with information about legal matters.

Instead, the auditor will discuss with management the manner in which legal issues with a material effect on the financial statements can be identified. Management will meet with legal counsel and then report to the auditor those matters that should be communicated, eventually providing assurance in the **management representation letter,** that all litigation, claims, and assessments with a material effect on the financial statements have been disclosed to the auditor. Essentially, all information that the attorney has to provide will be communicated to the auditor directly by management.

The auditor will then prepare and arrange for management to sign a **letter of inquiry** to the attorney to obtain **corroborating evidence**. Management requests the inquiry, but the letter should be physically mailed by the auditor. The letter will identify those matters about which the auditor was informed by management, and request that the attorney corroborate information about the likelihood of losses and, where appropriate, estimates of the amount of losses. For losses with only a remote chance of occurring, no further information is needed. If the attorney's response indicates that a loss is reasonably possible or probable, clarification of the estimated loss may be needed to determine the appropriate disclosures and accruals, as appropriate.

If the attorney **refuses to respond** to the letter of inquiry, or if management refuses to give the auditor permission to communicate with the entity's external legal counsel, it is considered a **scope limitation** and may require a qualified opinion or disclaimer of opinion. If the attorney is uncertain about the possible resolution of certain issues, this **uncertainty** may result in an **emphasis-of-matter paragraph** in the auditor's report without requiring any modification of the opinion. If a client's lawyer resigns shortly after the receipt of an attorney's letter which indicated no significant disagreements with the client's assessment of contingent liabilities, the auditor should inquire as to the reason for the resignation, as this may indicate a problem.

ATTORNEY'S LETTER FOR FINANCIAL AUDITS
(Letter of Audit Inquiry)

(Entity Letterhead)
(Date)
(Legal Service Provider's Name and Address)

Dear (Name):

In connection with an audit of our financial statements as of (Balance Sheet date) and for the (period) then ended, management of (name of entity) has prepared, and furnished to auditors (name and address of auditors) a description and evaluation of certain contingencies, including those set forth below involving matters with respect to which you have been engaged and to which you have devoted substantive attention on behalf of (name of entity) in the form of legal consultation or representation. These contingencies are regarded by management as material for this purpose ($ amount). Your response should include all matters that existed at (balance sheet date) and during the period from that date to the date of your response.

[*Alternative wording will be used when management requests the lawyer to prepare the list that describes and evaluates pending or threatened litigation, claims, and assessments.*]

List of Pending or Threatened Litigation (excluding unasserted claims)
[Ordinarily, management's information would include (1) the nature of the litigation, (2) the progress of the case to date, (3) how management is responding or intends to respond to the litigation (for example, to contest the case vigorously or to seek an out-of-court settlement), (4) an evaluation of the likelihood of an unfavorable outcome, and (5) an estimate of the amount or range of potential loss.] This letter will serve as our consent for you to furnish to our auditor all the information requested herein. Accordingly, please furnish to our auditors such explanation, if any, that you consider necessary to supplement the foregoing information, including an explanation of those matter as to which your views may differ from those stated and an identification of the omission of any pending or threatened litigation, claims and assessments or a statement that the list of such matter is complete.

[*Alternative wording will be used when management requests the lawyer to prepare the list that describes and evaluates pending or threatened litigation, claims, and assessments.*]

List of Unasserted Claims and Assessments (Considered by management to be probable of assertion, and that, if asserted, would have at least a reasonable possibility of an unfavorable outcome)

 [Ordinarily, management's information would include (1) the nature of the matter, (2) how management intends to respond if the claim is asserted, (3) an evaluation of the likelihood of an unfavorable outcome, and (4) an estimate of the amount or range of potential loss.] Please furnish to the auditors such explanation, if any, that you consider necessary to supplement the foregoing information, including an explanation of those matters as to which your views may differ from those stated.

We understand that whenever, in the course of performing legal services for us with respect to a matter recognized to involve an unasserted possible claim or assessment that may call for financial statement disclosure, if you have formed a professional conclusion that we should disclose or consider disclosure concerning such possible claim or assessment, as a matter of professional responsibility to us, you will so advise us and will consult with us concerning the question of such disclosure and the applicable requirements of Financial Accounting Standards Board (FASB) *Accounting Standards Codification* (ASC) 450, *Contingencies*. Please specifically confirm to our auditors that our understanding is correct.

[*Alternative wording will be used when management requests the lawyer to prepare the list that describes and evaluates pending or threatened litigation, claims, and assessments.*]

Please specifically identify the nature of and reasons for any limitation on your response.

[*The auditor may request the client to inquire about additional matters, for example, unpaid or unbilled charges or specified information on certain contractually assumed obligations of the company, such as guarantees of indebtedness of others.*]

Please respond directly to the auditors at the above address by (date), with a specified effective date no earlier than (date).

Sincerely, (Signature and title of Management's Representative)

RELATED PARTIES (AU-C 550)

When a company has engaged in significant transactions with related parties, the auditor's primary concern is proper **disclosure and presentation**, so that users of the financial statements will be aware of them. The auditor will make inquiries of management as to the existence of related parties. Management, however, may have a desire to conceal related-party transactions from the auditor since related-party relationships may present a greater opportunity for collusion, concealment, or manipulation by management. In some circumstances, management may not be aware of certain related parties.

As a result, the auditor must remain alert when inspecting the accounting records and performing other audit procedures for transactions that **suggest involvement with related parties**, including:

- Loans at zero or unusually low interest rates.
- Sales at prices far above or below fair market value.
- Large, non-recurring transactions occurring very close to the balance sheet date.
- Loan guarantees.

Inquiries of management regarding related parties, made as part of the auditor's risk assessment procedures, will include:

- The identities of the entity's related parties, including changes from prior periods.
- The nature of the relationships between the entity and the related parties.
- Whether the entity entered into any transactions with the related parties during the period and, if so, the type and purpose of the transactions.

The auditor will also perform additional risk assessment procedures, which might include additional inquiries of management and others to obtain an understanding of management's controls for:

- Identifying, accounting for, and disclosing related-party relationships and transactions.
- Authorize and approve significant transactions and arrangements with related parties.
- Authorize and approve significant transactions and arrangements outside the normal course of business.

Once the auditor identifies such transactions, appropriate procedures might include:

- Determining the business purpose of the transactions.
- Verifying that such transactions are known to and have been approved by the board of directors.
- Reading the financial statements and notes to determine that related-party transactions are clearly identified.

There is no practical way to determine if all of these transactions would have taken place in the absence of the relationship, or if the terms would have been the same in an ***arm's-length transaction***. If management makes such claims in the notes to the financial statements, the auditor should obtain sufficient appropriate audit evidence about the assertion.

The auditor may identify related parties or related-party transactions that were not previously identified or disclosed to the auditor by management. When this occurs, the auditor should:

- Communicate relevant information to members of the engagement team.
- Request that management identify all transactions with the newly identified related parties.

- Inquire as to why the entity's controls over related parties failed to identify and disclose the related-party relationships or transactions.
- Perform appropriate substantive audit procedures related to the newly identified related-party relationships or transactions.
- Reconsider the risk that other related-party relationships or transactions may exist that management has not previously identified and disclosed to the auditor.
- Evaluate the implications on the audit if the nondisclosure by management appears intentional.

SPECIALISTS (AU-C 620)

Circumstances sometimes arise in an audit when the work of a **specialist** is needed. In an audit of a jewelry store, the auditor will likely require the services of an expert gemologist to verify the **valuation** of items during the inventory count. A land surveyor might be needed to help gauge the **quantity** of property owned by the client. An actuary may be needed to provide **interpretation** of a pension agreement and determine the client's liability. An internal auditor is not considered to be a specialist. When using a specialist, the auditor should keep in mind that the audit opinion is solely the responsibility of the auditor and the findings of a specialist constitute audit evidence to be evaluated by the auditor.

AU-C Section 620, ***Using the Work of an Auditor's Specialist***, establishes the auditor's responsibilities when using the work of a specialist. Although the specialist will often be performing tasks that the auditor is not personally capable of performing, the **auditor must understand the methods and assumptions** underlying the specialist's work, and must be able to **evaluate** the results of that work.

The **specialist**, in turn, **must understand** the manner in which the auditor will be utilizing the specialist's work to provide **corroborative evidence** to support the auditor's opinion. These understandings should be documented.

In evaluating the timing, nature, and extent of audit procedures that will be applied to the work of a specialist, the auditor will consider:
- The nature of the subject matter the specialist will address.
- The risk of material misstatement associated with the subject matter.
- The significance of the specialist's work in the context of the audit.
- The auditor's knowledge of, and previous experience with, the work of the specialist.
- Whether the specialist is subject to the auditor's firm's quality control policies and procedures.

The auditor should carefully consider the specialist's **Competence and Objectivity.** Competence may be demonstrated by licenses, reputation, and the quality of written reports. Objectivity depends on the specialist not having any relationship with the client that would impair the specialist's independence. An auditor may still utilize the work of a specialist who lacks objectivity, but must consider the situation in gauging the level of persuasiveness of the evidence received from the specialist.

The auditor will evaluate the adequacy of the work of the specialist, including:
- The relevance and reasonableness of the findings and conclusions and their consistency with the audit evidence.
- If the work of the specialist involved the use of significant assumptions and methods, which the auditor should understand and evaluate.

- If the work of the specialist involved the use of source data, in which case the auditor will evaluate its relevance, accuracy, and completeness.

The auditor must be cautious about references to the work of the specialist in the audit report. Since it is not appropriate to divide responsibility for the opinion with someone who is not also an auditor, the auditor must **not refer** to the specialist in the audit report if it contains an **unmodified** opinion.

The auditor may make reference to the work of a specialist if it is relevant to the understanding of a modification to the auditor's opinion. When referring to the work of a specialist, the auditor should indicate in the report that the reference does not reduce the auditor's responsibility for the opinion.

USING THE WORK OF INTERNAL AUDITORS (AU-C 610)

When an audit client has an internal audit function, the external auditor may have the opportunity to modify the nature or timing of, or reduce the extent of, further audit procedures. AU-C Section 610, *Using the Work of Internal Auditors*, requires the auditor to obtain an understanding of the role of the internal audit function while obtaining an understanding of the entity and its environment, including its internal control. Based on that understanding, the auditor may conclude that the work of the internal audit function may provide audit evidence. In addition, the auditor may determine that members of the internal audit function may be used to directly assist the external auditor in performing audit procedures.

- The external auditor will evaluate the **objectivity and competence** of internal auditors and the internal audit function in determining whether or not internal auditors can provide direct assistance to the auditor in performing audit procedures.
- The external auditor will evaluate whether or not the internal audit function applies a *systematic and disciplined approach* that includes quality control in the performance of its responsibilities.

Use of internal auditors, or the internal audit function, in an audit of an entity's financial statements does not relieve the external auditor of the ultimate responsibility for supporting any opinion expressed. As a result, the external auditor's involvement in the audit is evaluated throughout all stages of the engagement to determine whether or not it is sufficient.

Prior to deciding to modify the nature, timing, or extent of audit procedures as a result of using the work of the internal audit function or the assistance of internal auditors, the external auditor is required to be satisfied as to the internal auditors' objectivity and competence and that the internal auditors are applying a systematic and disciplined approach that is subject to quality control considerations.

- The evaluation will be applied to the internal audit function when the external auditor intends to use the work of the internal audit function to obtain audit evidence.
- The evaluation will be applied to individual internal auditors when the external auditor intends to obtain the direct assistance of members of the internal audit function to perform audit procedures under the direction, supervision, and review of the external auditor.

Internal Audit *Objectivity*

In evaluating the objectivity of internal auditors, the external auditor will determine whether internal auditors are *free of bias or conflicts of interests, and whether they are subject to the undue influence of others such that the professional judgment of internal auditors may be overridden or otherwise affected.* When performing an evaluation of the objectivity of the internal audit function and of individual internal auditors, the external auditor should keep in mind that neither the internal audit function nor the internal auditors can be independent in relation to the entity.

There are several **factors that affect the Objectivity of internal auditors** and the internal audit function.
- The level of authority within the organization to which internal auditors report will significantly affect objectivity.
  - Objectivity is enhanced when internal auditors **report to** those charged with governance or an officer with appropriate authority.
  - Objectivity, on the other hand, is impaired when internal auditors report to management, although this can be mitigated if the internal auditors have access to those charged with governance.
- Other responsibilities of internal auditors, such as participation in management or operations, may impair objectivity as internal auditors may end up responsible for drawing conclusions about their own performance.
- Constraints or restrictions on internal auditors, such as restrictions on communications with the external auditors, impairs objectivity.
- The level at which employment and remuneration decisions related to internal auditors is made also affects objectivity. Conclusions based on internal audit procedures applied to those responsible for such decisions may be affected.
- Objectivity is enhanced when internal auditors participate in professional associations that impose professional standards related to objectivity on their members or when the entity's internal policies are designed to achieve comparable objectives.

Internal Auditor *Competence*

The external auditor will *evaluate the knowledge and skills of the internal audit function and, when appropriate, individual internal auditors, to determine if they are sufficient to enable internal auditors to perform diligently with the appropriate level of quality.* There are several **factors that affect the Competency** of internal auditors.
- The resources available to the internal audit function, relative to the size of the entity and the nature of its operations, will directly affect the competency of the internal audit function.
- Policies related to the hiring, training, and assignment of internal auditors to engagements enhance competency.
- Technical training and experience providing proficiency as an auditor enhance the competence of internal auditors, which may be further enhanced when internal auditors obtain professional designations that establish standards related to competence as a means of achievement.
- Knowledge of the entity's applicable financial reporting framework and knowledge specific to the industry and the entity's financial reporting are components of internal auditor competence.
- Membership in professional associations establishing relevant professional standards and requirements for the continuing education of its members also enhance competency.

The external auditor will consider the objectivity and competency of internal auditors in relation to one another. A deficiency in objectivity cannot be compensated for by strength in competency, nor can a deficiency in competence be compensated for by strength in objectivity. Entity policies and procedures, along with the status of internal audit within the organization, which support objectivity, combined with a high level of competence, increase the degree to which the external auditor may modify the nature, timing, or extent of audit procedures as a result of reliance on the work or the direct assistance of internal auditors.

When considering using the work of the internal audit function in obtaining audit evidence, it is essential that the work is performed applying a systematic and disciplined approach that includes an element of quality control. When such an approach is not applied, neither a high level of competence nor the strong support of the internal audit function's objectivity can compensate.

To judge **both competence and objectivity**, the outside auditor may also consider:
- Audit documentation documenting the internal auditor's work.
- Discussions with management.
- The external auditor's previous dealings with the internal auditor.
- The Internal auditor's compliance with professional internal auditing standards.

The internal auditor can assist the external auditor in a variety of areas which include:
- Gaining an **understanding of the internal control** structure – The internal auditor will be a useful source of information about the structure.
- **Testing controls** – The internal auditor can obtain evidence for review by the outside auditor.
- **Substantive testing** – The internal auditor can pull appropriate documents and assist the outside auditor in locating assets to prove their **existence**.

Applying a Systematic and Disciplined Approach

The external auditor needs to determine if the internal audit function *applies a systematic and disciplined approach to the performance of its activities*. Activities that do not apply a systematic and disciplined approach to their planning, performance, supervision, review and evaluation, and documentation are considered to be the monitoring of control activities, a component of the entity's internal control. When a systematic and disciplined approach is applied, however, the auditor may consider the work of the internal audit function in relation to obtaining audit evidence.

Various factors will be considered when the external auditor is determining whether a systematic and disciplined approach is being applied.
- Documentation of internal audit procedures or guidance covering areas such as risk assessment, audit procedures and programs, documentation, and reporting enhance the external auditor's perception that a systematic and disciplined approach is being applied.
- The existence of quality control procedures, such as those related to leadership, human resources, and engagement performance, including quality control requirements established by professional associations that are applied to the internal audit function further enhance the perception that a systematic and disciplined approach is being applied.

Regardless of the level of objectivity and competence of the internal audit function and the internal auditors, and regardless of whether or not the internal audit function applies a systematic and disciplined approach, the external auditor will not rely on the internal audit function or internal

auditors in relation to any matters that require the application of the ***auditor's judgment***. This includes significant judgments, such as:
- Assessing the risk of material misstatement.
- Evaluating the sufficiency of tests performed.
- Evaluating management's assumptions as to substantial doubt as to whether or not the entity is a going concern. Note: SAS 132 makes it clear that management **must** assess the ability to continue as a going concern even if no such explicit requirement exists in the applicable financial reporting framework.
- Evaluating significant estimates.
- Evaluating the adequacy of disclosures or any other issues that may affect the external auditor's report on the financial statements.

If the external auditor plans to either use the work of the internal audit function to obtain audit evidence, or to obtain direct assistance form internal auditors in the performance of audit procedures, the external auditor will include this information in the communication with those charged with governance in providing an understanding of the proposed audit approach.

The auditor will **document** the results of the evaluation of:
- The objectivity of the internal audit function and the internal auditors, including its status within the organization and entity policies and procedures that support objectivity;
- The competence of the internal audit function and the internal auditors; and
- If using the work of the internal audit function to obtain audit evidence, the application of a systematic and disciplined approach by the internal audit function, including quality control.

Using the Work of the Internal Audit Function to Obtain Audit Evidence

Once the external auditor has determined that the internal audit function maintains appropriate levels of objectivity and competence, and that it applies a systematic and disciplined approach to the performance of its activities, the auditor will determine if the work of the internal audit function is relevant to the audit strategy and audit plan that has been established for the engagement.
- Based on the auditor's assessed risk of material misstatement at the assertion level, the external auditor determines the nature, timing, and extent of further audit procedures that are responsive to that assessment.
- Further audit procedures may include some combination of tests of controls and substantive audit procedures, some of which may be similar to, or the same as, procedures performed by the internal audit function.
- When this is the case, the external auditor may decide to modify the nature or timing of, or reduce the extent of, further audit procedures that will be performed directly by the external auditor.

The external auditor may use the work of the internal audit function in relation to either tests of controls or substantive tests.

The work of the internal audit function may include **tests of controls** that are designed to determine if appropriate controls have been put into place and are operating effectively. The external auditor may be able to use the results of those tests of controls to modify the nature or timing of, or to reduce the extent of, tests of controls that the auditor had planned to perform.

The work of the internal audit function may include **substantive tests** that are designed to support one or more assertions related to the reporting of events or circumstances or an account balance. The external auditor may be able to use the results of those substantive tests to modify the nature or timing, or to reduce the extent, of substantive tests that the auditor had planned to perform in obtaining audit evidence relevant to that assertion.

The work of the internal audit function may be applied to a **component of a group** for which the external auditor is the group auditor. The external auditor may be able to use the results of those procedures, for example, to reduce the number of components to which audit procedures are applied.

The work of the internal audit function can also be used by the external auditor in obtaining evidence regarding the tracing of transactions through the accounting and information system to determine if information is being properly and accurately captured and summarized for reporting purposes and regarding compliance with regulatory requirements.

The degree to which the work of the internal audit function may affect the nature or timing, or reduce the extent, of further audit procedures to be performed by the external auditor will be enhanced by effective communication and coordination between the external auditor and the internal audit function.

Matters to be communicated will include:
- The timing of the work of the internal audit function
- The nature of the work performed or to be performed
- The extent of audit coverage that is anticipated
- Performance materiality and materiality at the financial statement level and, as applicable, for particular classes of transactions, account balances, or disclosures
- Methods for determining sample sizes and selecting items for testing
- Procedures related to the review and reporting of the results of the procedures

Coordination is likely to be most effective when communication occurs at various intervals throughout the process. External auditors should inform the internal audit function of significant matters affecting it. In addition, the internal audit function should keep the external auditor informed as to matters that affect the audit of the financial statements and should provide information about, and access to, reports of the internal audit function.

Before relying on the work of the internal audit function, the external auditor will perform certain procedures to determine that the work was properly planned, performed, supervised, reviewed, and documented; that sufficient appropriate evidence was obtained to support any conclusions drawn; and that conclusions that were reached were appropriate under the circumstances. The external auditor will evaluate the overall quality of the work and the objectivity with which the work was performed through:
- Making inquiries
- Observing procedures
- Reviewing work programs and documentation

In addition, the external auditor will reperform some of the procedures included in the body of work of the internal audit function. **Reperformance**, which provides more persuasive evidence than other procedures that might be applied, is not required of every area of work that is being used but is required on the body of work of the internal audit function as a whole. In many cases, the external audit will focus on reperformance in those areas requiring a greater degree of judgment.

When using the work of the internal audit function to obtain audit evidence, the external auditor will document the nature and extent of the work used and the basis for the decision to use it. It will indicate the period covered by the work performed by the internal audit function and the results of the work. The external auditor will also document the procedures performed to evaluate the adequacy of the work of the internal audit function, including procedures applied in reperforming some of the work.

Using Internal Auditors to Provide Direct Assistance in the Performance of Audit Procedures

When the auditor decides to use internal auditors to provide direct assistance in the performance of audit procedures, it will be under the *direction, supervision, and review of the external auditor*. Before making such a decision, however, the external auditor evaluates threats to the objectivity and level of competence of the internal auditors providing the assistance, and internal auditors should not be used to the extent that they either lack the necessary objectivity or the necessary competence to perform the work anticipated.

Prior to using internal auditors to provide direct assistance in the performance of audit procedures, the external auditor will *obtain* **written representation** *from management* or those charged with governance *indicating* that:
- The internal auditors will be allowed to follow the instructions of the external auditor; and
- The entity will not intervene in the work performed for the external auditor by the internal auditors.

The amount of direction, supervision, and review will be based on the external auditor's evaluation of the objectivity and competence of the internal auditors. Review procedures will include, however, testing by the external auditor of some of the work performed by the internal auditor. In addition, the external auditor will instruct internal auditors to bring identified accounting and auditing issues to the attention of the external auditor and will remain alert to any indications that evaluations of the internal auditor's objectivity or competence are no longer appropriate.

When using internal auditors to provide direct assistance to the external auditor in performing audit procedures, **documentation** will include:
- Threats to the objectivity of the internal auditors and safeguards that eliminated the threats or reduced them to an acceptable level;
- The level of competence of the internal auditors providing direct assistance;
- The basis for deciding on the nature and extent of work to be performed by internal auditors;
- The nature and extent of the review performed by the external auditor in relation to work performed by internal auditors; and
- Working papers prepared by internal auditors providing direct assistance to the external audit in the performance of audit procedures.

If an external auditor either uses the work of the internal audit function to obtain audit evidence or obtains the direct assistance from internal auditors in the performance of audit procedures, the external auditor will also document the basis for concluding that the external auditor was adequately involved in the engagement.

AUDITING ACCOUNTING ESTIMATES, INCLUDING FAIR VALUE

With respect to estimates that are used in the financial statements (such as the allowance for bad debts and estimated warranty liability accounts), the auditor's main concern is to determine the **reasonableness** of the estimates made by management. In evaluating the reasonableness of estimates, auditors normally concentrate on assumptions that are subjective and therefore susceptible to bias. An accounting estimate is an approximation of a financial statement element, item or account.

Many items that are required to be reported or disclosed in the financial statements may not be susceptible to precise measurement as of the date of the financial statements and, as a result, require the use of accounting estimate. AU-C Section 540, *Auditing Accounting Estimates, Including Fair Value Accounting Estimates, and Related Disclosures*, provides guidance and requirements relative to the auditor's responsibility for accounting estimates.

When auditing estimates, a combination of four approaches is often used: (**1**) review and test management's process, including the method of measurement, assumptions made, and the data used; (**2**) independently develop an estimate; (**3**) review subsequent events up to the date of the auditor's report; or (**4**) test the effectiveness of internal controls related to accounting estimates.

The auditor's initial step is to **understand the process used by management** to prepare significant estimates. The auditor may then develop an independent expectation of the estimates or examine events in the subsequent period prior to the completion of the audit to determine if the estimates are reasonable.

Although all accounting estimates are subject to a degree of estimation uncertainty, which results in a risk of material misstatement, some estimates involve a *relatively low risk*. These may include:
- Accounting estimates related to transactions and activities that are not complex;
- Estimates related to routine transactions made and updated on a regular basis;
- Estimates that are based on data that is reliable and readily available, such as published interest rates or market values; and
- Estimates of fair value using simple and easily applied measurement approaches, or measured under models that are generally accepted and uses observable inputs or assumptions.

Some accounting estimates involve a high degree of estimation uncertainty, resulting in a relatively *high risk* of material misstatement. These may include:
- Estimates involving the outcome of litigation;
- Estimates of fair value for derivatives or other securities that are not publicly traded; or
- Fair value estimates that are formulated using a complex or sophisticated model or involving assumptions or inputs that are not observable.

Examples of financial statement estimates that *do not involve fair value* include:
- Bad debts;
- Inventory obsolescence;
- Warranty obligations;
- Depreciation methods, salvage values, and useful lives;
- Allowances recognizing the uncertainty of recoverability of certain investments;
- The results of long-term contracts; and
- The financial effects of litigation settlements or judgments.

Financial statement estimates involving *fair value* may include:

- The values of complex financial instruments that are not actively traded;
- Share-based payments;
- Assets held for disposal;
- Assets or liabilities acquired in a business combination, including identifiable intangibles and goodwill; and
- Nonmonetary exchanges.

The auditor will consider estimates when performing risk assessment procedures by obtaining an understanding of:

- Requirements of the applicable financial reporting framework regarding estimates;
- How management determines when estimates are necessary for the recognition or disclosure of items in the financial statements; and
- How management develops accounting estimates and the data upon which they are based.

Based on the understanding, the auditor will evaluate the risk of material misstatement of estimates and will undertake one or more of the following, taking into account the nature of the accounting estimate:

- Determine whether events up to the date of the auditor's report provide evidence regarding the estimate;
- Test the methods and assumptions used by management and the data on which they are based;
- Test the operating effectiveness of controls over the development of accounting estimates; and
- Develop an expectation in the form of a point or range of estimates to use as a basis for evaluating management's estimate.

In addition, when estimates represent significant risks of material misstatement to the financial statements, the auditor will apply additional procedures:

- Address the effects of **estimation uncertainty,** including whether management has considered alternative assumptions and whether management's assumptions are reasonable;
- Evaluate management's decision to recognize or not recognize accounting estimates and the basis used for measurement;
- Evaluate the reasonableness of the accounting estimates;
- Determine if disclosures are in compliance with the applicable financial reporting framework; and
- Review decisions and estimates to evaluate for potential management bias.

The auditor will also document the basis for the auditor's conclusions about the reasonableness of estimates giving rise to significant risks and indicators of possible management bias.

Generally accepted accounting principles require companies to use **fair value** for measuring, presenting, and disclosing various accounts, including investments in marketable equity securities; assets and liabilities acquired in a business combination; assets and liabilities exchanged in nonmonetary transactions; derivatives; impaired assets; and financial assets or liabilities for which the entity has elected the fair value option. Fair value is generally considered to be the amount at which an asset could be sold in a current transaction between willing parties or the amount that would have to be paid to transfer a liability.

AU-C 540 includes guidelines for auditing ***fair value estimates***. Fair value estimates are not given any special consideration other than the fact that the auditor needs to be aware that fair value estimates may be particularly susceptible to misstatement, depending on the availability of reliable information to measure fair value. Comparable to other estimates:

- Management is responsible for making the fair value measurements and disclosures included in the financial statements as well as identifying the significant assumptions underlying fair value measurements and disclosures.
- The auditor evaluates whether fair value measurements and disclosures, as determined by management, including the allocation of the acquisition cost relating to a business combination, are in conformity with the guidance in accounting technical literature.
- The auditor should gain an understanding of:
    - How management develops its fair value measurements and disclosures, including:
        - The experience of the personnel involved in the measurements.
        - The significant assumptions used to develop the estimates.
        - The relevant market information used to develop these assumptions (for example, stock price quotations and official commodity price indexes).
        - The procedures used to monitor changes in the assumptions and estimates.
        - The extent to which management used outside specialists to develop the estimates.
    - Procedures for estimating fair values in accordance with GAAP, including:
        - The market approach, using observable market price data.
        - The revenue or cash flow approach, using discounted cash flow methods.
        - The cost approach, using the replacement cost of the asset.
    - Risks associated with the use of estimates that could result in misstatement, based on the number, significance, and subjectivity of assumptions used to make the estimates.

SUBSEQUENT EVENTS AND SUBSEQUENTLY DISCOVERED FACTS
(AU-C 560)

An audit cannot be completed until after the balance sheet date, and often is not completed until several weeks or more after year-end. Subsequent events, those occurring during the time interval between the balance sheet date but before the report is issued, may have an impact in one of **two ways:**

- **Type 1** – Some events provide evidence of **conditions existing** at the balance sheet date that are **recognized** and require **adjustment**. The filing of bankruptcy by a customer early in the period subsequent to year-end may indicate that a receivable from that customer was not collectible as of the end of the period and should be written off. Another example might be the settlement of litigation for an amount different than the amount that had been accrued.

- **Type 2** – Some events do not affect the balance sheet, as the **condition did NOT exist** at the balance sheet date, but still represent important information that should not be recognized by adjusting the financial statements but should be **disclosed** to assist users of the financial statements. A fire that destroys the company's main warehouse shortly after the end of the period does not affect either the inventory balance or the amount reported as property, plant, and equipment at year-end, but would affect the significance of those assets and may suggest possible future difficulties. Other examples include: sale of bonds or issuance of stock, a purchase of a business, or a loss due to flood.

Subsequent events must be evaluated by nonpublic entities (nonissuers) through either the *date of issuance of the financial statements* or the *date that the financial statements are available to be issued*. In the case of issuers, however, subsequent events are evaluated through the date of issuance of the financial statements. The date on which financial statements are available to be issued is the date the auditor signs the audit report. The client may issue their financial statements on that date or at some later date, but the responsibility for subsequent events does not extend beyond that date.

The auditor's responsibility is to make certain that management has properly identified, evaluated, and recognized or disclosed, as appropriate, subsequent events up through the date of the auditor's report. There are several audit procedures occurring **after the balance sheet date** that may reveal evidence of subsequent events:

- Read minutes of meetings of the board of directors and other appropriate committees occurring after year-end to determine if there is discussion of major events occurring in the subsequent period;
- Make inquiries of the client's legal counsel to determine if there is litigation, or if there are claims or assessments arising or being settled after the balance sheet date;
- Read interim reports prepared by management in the subsequent period to determine if they show unusual transactions occurring after year-end;
- Make inquiries of the client and obtain a management representation letter to determine if there were unusual transactions or major events occurring in the subsequent period; and
- Evaluate changes in long-term debt after year-end to determine if there were major financial transactions occurring after the balance sheet date that affect the classification of liabilities and require adjustment of the balance sheet or may need to be disclosed to users.

The search for subsequent events does **not** refer to **all audit procedures** applied after the balance sheet date, **only** those that are designed to identify **events occurring after the balance sheet date**. Confirmations of receivables reported by the client at the balance sheet date are sent to customers after year-end and responses are received after year-end. This is **not**, however, a part of the search for subsequent events since it is verification of transactions and activities occurring on or before the balance sheet date. The examination of write-offs of customer receivables after year-end, on the other hand, is used to determine either the need to adjust the balance sheet or make disclosures for a subsequent event, since the write-offs were events occurring after year-end.

Once the audit report has been issued, the auditor normally has no ongoing responsibility to update the report for events occurring after that, including the resolution of lawsuits that were properly disclosed. The subsequent event's period refers only to the period between the balance sheet date and the date of the auditor's report, so the auditor's responsibility for subsequent events does not indicate a responsibility for events occurring after the report date.

A problem arises, however, if the auditor **discovers after the report** has been issued that there was a transaction or **event occurring before the report date**. This would **not** be limited to the subsequent events period between the balance sheet and report dates, but could include events that occurred during the year under audit which were not identified by the auditor before the report was issued. Such discovery may affect the ability of the auditor to support the opinion expressed in the report, but only if it represented information that should have been available at the report date.

Assume for example, that the audit of a client's calendar-year 20X0 financial statements is completed and a report dated March 5, 20X1 is issued, expressing an unqualified opinion on the 20X0 statements. On May 28, 20X1, the auditor discovers that the client had recently suffered major losses due to the destruction by fire of a public warehouse which was holding in storage major assets of the client. This information was previously unknown to the auditor.

- If the fire occurred on December 15, 20X0, then the financial statements for the year ended December 31, 20X0 require **adjustment.**
- If the fire occurred on February 15, 20X1, then the 20X0 financial statements should have included a **disclosure** of this subsequent event.
- If the fire occurred on April 15, 20X1, then the auditor has **no responsibility** for the new information, since it did not represent information existing at the March 5, 20X1 report date.

In the first two cases, the auditor should determine if there are parties relying on the March 5, 20X1 report who would find this information important. If so, the auditor must take steps to ensure that those parties are notified that the auditor's report can no longer be relied on.

Omitted procedures (or subsequent discovery of facts)

Occasionally, the auditor will discover after the report is issued that they **omitted procedures (AU-C 585) (or subsequent discovery of facts – AU-C 560)** which were believed to be necessary at the time of the audit. This could result from a miscommunication among the audit staff or the failure to note an item in the audit program.

- Assess importance of omitted procedure
- Anything to compensate for the omitted procedure (e.g., Subsequent receipts test for A/R).
- Perform procedure
- Minimize reliance on the Financial Statements
  - Notify the client, regulatory agencies and anyone relying on the statements

Notice that this discovery does not automatically indicate that the audit was deficient or that there were misstatements in the financial statements or notes. The auditor should first consider the actual importance of the omitted procedure to the auditor's opinion. The auditor may decide that the omitted procedure wasn't significant enough to impair their ability to support their opinion or that other tests applied during the engagement provided sufficient competent evidential matter to support the opinion, so that no further action is necessary.

If the auditor decides that the omitted procedure is needed to support the opinion, then the client should be contacted and the procedure performed. Once completed, there is no need to notify parties relying on the report, since the auditor will once again feel they can support their opinion. Only if the client refuses to permit the auditor to perform the omitted procedure will it be necessary to withdraw the report and notify parties that they may not rely on it.

If the procedure leads to information affecting the statements and/or notes, this will be treated as a subsequent discovery of facts and handled in the manner discussed earlier in this section.

Lecture 4.18

CLASS QUESTIONS

Please see the Class Questions and Class Solutions for this Lecture at the end of this Section.

Lecture 4.19

CLASS QUESTIONS

Please see the Class Questions and Class Solutions for this Lecture at the end of this Section.

CLASS QUESTIONS

Work through the below Class Questions while following along with the respective lectures. Once this is complete, you can begin independently practicing what you've learned by quizzing yourself on this course section in your Interactive Practice Questions (IPQ), which can be found in your online Student Dashboard. Your IPQ simulates the computer-based testing experience, and will also help you understand how concepts are applied to the exam. Each question includes answer explanations from expert CPAs that will help you determine why you answered a question correctly or incorrectly. This is key to your success on the CPA Exam.

Lecture 4.06

1.   Which of the following types of audit evidence is the most persuasive?

    a.   Prenumbered client purchase order forms.
    b.   Client work sheets supporting cost allocations.
    c.   Bank statements obtained from the client.
    d.   Client representation letter.

2.   Which of the following presumptions is correct about the reliability/validity of audit evidence?

    a.   Information obtained indirectly from outside sources is the most reliable audit evidence.
    b.   To be reliable, audit evidence should be convincing rather than persuasive.
    c.   Reliability of audit evidence refers to the amount of corroborative evidence obtained.
    d.   Effective internal control provides more assurance about the reliability of audit evidence.

3.   Which of the following statements relating to the appropriateness of audit evidence is always true?

    a.   Audit evidence gathered by an auditor from outside an enterprise is reliable.
    b.   Accounting data developed under satisfactory conditions of internal control are more relevant than data developed under unsatisfactory internal control conditions.
    c.   Oral representations made by management are **not** valid evidence.
    d.   Evidence gathered by auditors must be both reliable and relevant to be considered appropriate.

4.   In determining whether transactions have been recorded, the direction of the audit testing should be from the

    a.   General ledger balances.
    b.   Adjusted trial balance.
    c.   Original source documents.
    d.   General journal entries.

5.   Which of the following comparisons would an auditor most likely make in evaluating an entity's costs and expenses?

    a.   The current year's accounts receivable with the prior year's accounts receivable.
    b.   The current year's payroll expense with the prior year's payroll expense.
    c.   The budgeted current year's sales with the prior year's sales.
    d.   The budgeted current year's warranty expense with the current year's contingent liabilities.

6. To be effective, analytical procedures in the overall review stage of an audit engagement should be performed by

    a. The staff accountant who performed the substantive auditing procedures.
    b. The managing partner who has responsibility for all audit engagements at that practice office.
    c. A manager or partner who has a comprehensive knowledge of the client's business and industry.
    d. The CPA firm's quality control manager or partner who has responsibility for the firm's peer review program.

7. An auditor most likely would analyze inventory turnover rates to obtain evidence concerning management's assertions about

    a. Existence.
    b. Rights.
    c. Presentation.
    d. Valuation.

Lecture 4.13

8. The primary purpose of sending a standard confirmation request to financial institutions with which the client has done business during the year is to

    a. Detect kiting activities that may otherwise not be discovered.
    b. Corroborate information regarding deposit and loan balances.
    c. Provide the data necessary to prepare a proof of cash.
    d. Request information about contingent liabilities and secured transactions.

9. When an auditor does not receive replies to positive requests for year-end accounts receivable confirmations, the auditor most likely would

    a. Inspect the allowance account to verify whether the accounts were subsequently written off.
    b. Increase the assessed level of detection risk for the valuation and completeness assertions.
    c. Ask the client to contact the customers to request that the confirmations be returned.
    d. Increase the assessed level of inherent risk for the revenue cycle.

10. In auditing accounts receivable, the negative form of confirmation request most likely would be used when

    a. The total recorded amount of accounts receivable is immaterial to the financial statements taken as a whole.
    b. Response rates in prior years to properly designed positive confirmation requests were inadequate.
    c. Recipients are likely to return positive confirmation requests without verifying the accuracy of the information.
    d. The combined assessed level of inherent risk and control risk relative to accounts receivable is low.

11. An auditor most likely would make inquiries of production and sales personnel concerning possible obsolete or slow-moving inventory to support management's financial statement assertion of

    a. Valuation.
    b. Rights.
    c. Existence.
    d. Presentation.

Lecture 4.18

12. The refusal of a client's attorney to provide information requested in an inquiry letter generally is considered

    a. Grounds for an adverse opinion.
    b. A limitation on the scope of the audit.
    c. Reason to withdraw from the engagement.
    d. Equivalent to a significant deficiency.

13. An auditor most likely would modify an unmodified opinion if the entity's financial statements include a footnote on related-party transactions

    a. Disclosing loans to related parties at interest rates significantly below prevailing market rates.
    b. Describing an exchange of real estate for similar property in a nonmonetary related-party transaction.
    c. Stating that a particular related-party transaction occurred on terms equivalent to those that would have prevailed in an arm's-length transaction.
    d. Presenting the dollar volume of related-party transactions and the effects of any change in the method of establishing terms from prior periods.

14. Which of the following procedures would an auditor ordinarily perform first in evaluating management's accounting estimates for reasonableness?

    a. Develop independent expectations of management's estimates.
    b. Consider the appropriateness of the key factors or assumptions used in preparing the estimates.
    c. Test the calculations used by management in developing the estimates.
    d. Obtain an understanding of how management developed its estimates.

15. "We have disclosed to you all known instances of non-compliance with laws and regulations whose effects should be considered when preparing financial statements". The foregoing passage is most likely from a

    a. Report on internal control.
    b. Special report.
    c. Management representation letter.
    d. Letter for underwriters.

16. An entity's income statements were misstated due to the recording of journal entries that involved debits and credits to an unusual combination of expense and revenue accounts. The auditor most likely could have detected this irregularity by

    a. Tracing a sample of journal entries to the general ledger.
    b. Evaluating the effectiveness of the internal control structure policies and procedures.
    c. Investigating the reconciliations between controlling accounts and subsidiary records.
    d. Performing analytical procedures designed to disclose differences from expectations.

17. In designing written audit programs, an auditor should establish specific audit objectives that relate primarily to the

    a. Timing of audit procedures
    b. Cost-benefit of gathering evidence
    c. Selected audit techniques
    d. Financial statement assertions

CLASS SOLUTIONS

1. (**c**) Evidence provided by the entity is less reliable than evidence provided by independent sources, and evidence generated internally is less reliable than evidence generated by sources outside the entity. Prenumbered client purchase order forms (a), client work sheets supporting cost allocations (b), and the client representation letter (d), are all generated by the entity. The bank statement is more reliable since it was generated by an external party, the bank.

2. (**d**) Information obtained directly by the auditor is more reliable than evidence obtained from outside sources (a). By its nature, audit evidence is convincing, rather than persuasive, but persuasive evidence would be more reliable than evidence that is convincing (b). Reliability of audit evidence refers to the quality of the evidence, while sufficiency refers to the quantity (c). When evidence is internally generated, it is more reliable when developed under an effective system of internal control than one that is not.

3. (**d**) Evidence obtained from outside the entity is more reliable than evidence obtained from the entity, but it is not necessarily reliable in all circumstances (a). Accounting data developed under satisfactory conditions of internal control are more reliable than data developed under unsatisfactory conditions, but whether or not the data is relevant is dependent on the nature of the data, rather than the source (b). Oral representations by management are less reliable than evidence obtained in writing, but that does not make oral representations invalid (c). Evidence gathered by auditors must be valid to be reliable and must be relevant to be appropriate to the test being performed.

4. (**c**) When auditing from the general ledger balances (a), the adjusted trial balance (b), or general journal entries (d), the auditor is only evaluating transactions that have been recorded, which will not assist the auditor in determining if all transactions have been recorded. To do so, the auditor will audit from the transaction, which will be evidenced by the original source documents, and trace them to the accounting records, thereby making certain that the transactions have been recorded.

5. (**b**) Comparing the current to prior year's accounts receivable will provide evidence about sales and collections, but will not provide evidence about costs and expenses (a). Likewise, comparing the current year's sales to those of the prior year will provide information about sales but not about costs and expenses (c). Comparing the current year's warranty expense with the current year's contingent liability will provide evidence about the portion of the contingent liability that is made up of warranty costs, but will not provide much meaningful evidence about costs and expenses in general (d). Comparing the current year's payroll expense to the prior year's amount will provide evidence as to whether expenses, and in particular payroll expense, has changed by a reasonable amount from the previous period, providing evidence about costs and expenses.

6. (**c**) Analytical procedures performed in the overall review stage are designed to allow the auditor to evaluate, at the completion of the audit, if the financial statements fairly reflect the auditor's understanding of the entity, its financial position and results of operations. This should be performed by someone at the manager or partner level with a comprehensive understanding of the entity. A staff accountant would not likely have the knowledge or experience to perform an overall review (a). The managing partner may have the general knowledge and experience to perform an overall review but would not necessarily have the direct knowledge of the client necessary to be effective (b). The same would be true of the

CPA firm's quality control manager or a partner with responsibility for the firm's peer review program (d).

7. (**d**) Inventory turnover is calculated by dividing cost of goods sold by average inventory. If the result is not consistent with the auditor's expectations, it may alert the auditor to a possible misstatement involving the valuation of cost of sales or inventory. The auditor would test existence through observation (a), rights by tracing to inventory purchase documents (b), and presentation by reading the financial statements (c).

8. (**b**) The primary purpose of the standard bank confirmation is to verify that the amount reported as cash (deposits) and loans are fairly stated on the financial statements. A proof of cash is a more effective way to detect kiting (a), the data for which comes from a combination of the client's accounting records and the client's bank statements, but does not come from the confirmation (c). Although the bank confirmation may provide information about contingent liabilities and secured transactions (d), that is not its primary purpose.

9. (**c**) The fact that a debtor does not return a confirmation does not necessarily indicate that the receivable is not collectible and the auditor would not necessarily try to determine if the account had been written off (a). Since confirmations are sent to customers that have been recorded in the records, they do not provide evidence of completeness (b). Inherent risk is a function of the nature of the entity's transactions and receivables and is not affected by audit procedures (d). When confirmations are not returned, the auditor will want to encourage the debtor to return it, which may require contact from the client.

10. (**d**) Negative confirmations do not require the debtor to return them unless there is a discrepancy and would only be appropriate when the auditor believes that risk is low as there are likely to be few discrepancies and that debtors would be likely to respond. Confirmations would not be used at all if accounts receivable was immaterial to the financial statements as a whole (a). Negative confirmations would not be used if responses are not expected, such as when returns have been inadequate in prior periods, as the auditor will not be able to determine if a non-reply is due to a lack of discrepancy or some other reason (b). Likewise, negative confirmations would not be appropriate if recipients would return positive confirmations without verifying the information as these would be least likely to respond to negative confirmations in the case of a discrepancy (c).

11. (**a**) Slow-moving and obsolete inventory would require inventory amounts to be reduced, affecting the valuation assertion. The fact that an item is slow-moving or obsolete has no bearing on whether or not the entity owns it, the rights assertion (b); whether or not it exists (c), or whether or not it inventory is properly presented and disclosed in the financial statements (d).

12. (**b**) If a client's attorney refuses to provide information requested, it represents a scope limitation and the auditor will have to determine if sufficient appropriate audit evidence can be obtained by other means. It does not necessarily mean that the financial statements are not fairly presented, requiring an adverse opinion (a). The auditor would likely only consider withdrawal if the client refused to request the information from the attorney, not if the attorney refused to respond (c). The attorney's refusal is not within the control of the entity and would not represent a control deficiency, significant or otherwise (d).

13.   (**c**) It would be appropriate for an entity to disclose a related party loan at below-market interest rates (a), and an exchange of real estate in a nonmonetary transaction (b), or the dollar volume of related-party transactions (d). Since it is not possible for the auditor to determine if a related party transaction occurred on terms equivalent to an arm's-length transaction, if the footnotes so indicated, the auditor would likely modify the report.

14.   (**d**) The first step in evaluating estimates is to obtain an understanding of how estimates are developed by management, which is done when the auditor performs risk assessment procedures in obtaining an understanding of the entity and its environment. If the auditor believes the approach is sound and will result in reasonable estimates, the auditor will consider the factors used in preparing the estimates (b) and test management's calculations (c). If the auditor does not believe management's approach is reliable, the auditor may, as an alternative procedure, develop independent estimates and compare them to management's estimates (a).

15.   (**c**) A report on internal control (I/C) generally is issued by an auditor (or independent accounting firm) and an auditor (or firm) generally does not make such disclosures (a). A special report is used when an auditor is performing an engagement other than an audit of a complete set of financial statements prepared in accordance with US GAAP and would not refer to communications from regulatory agencies (b). A letter for underwriters is a report on a nonissuer's financial statements that is included in a registration statement filed with the SEC (d). A statement indicating that we have disclosed to you all known instances of non-compliance with laws and regulations whose effects should be considered when preparing financial statements, would be an assurance provided by the client to the auditor in a letter of representations.

16.   (**d**) Analytical procedures are required to be used in both planning and as an overall review at the end of the audit to look for unusual differences that were not expected. This is based on the expectation or anticipation theory. One would not normally expect significant changes from year to year in revenue and expense accounts, so if they did exist, they may be found when performing analytical procedures.

17.   (**d**) Audit programs should be designed so the auditor who follows the program will achieve the audit objectives that relate to the financial statement assertions of interest. Remember the assertions are PERCV and we can accomplish our objectives by performing audit procedures.

TASK-BASED SIMULATIONS

Task-Based Simulation 1

R The Uniform CPA Examination

Unsplit   Split Horiz   Split Vertical   Authoritative Literature   Spreadsheet   Calculator   Submit Testlet

| Work Tab | Resources | Help |

Required:

Items 1 through 15 represent a series of unrelated statements, questions, excerpts, and comments taken from various parts of an auditor's working paper file. Below the items is a list of the likely sources of the statements, questions, excerpts, and comments. Select, as the best answer for each item, the most likely source. Select only one source for each item. A source may be selected once, more than once, or not at all.

> **A** Partner's engagement review program.
> **B** Communication with predecessor auditor.
> **C** Auditor's engagement letter.
> **D** Management representation letter.
> **E** Standard financial institution confirmation request.
> **F** Auditor's communication with the audit committee.
> **G** Auditor's report.
> **H** Letter for underwriters.
> **I** Audit inquiry letter to legal counsel.
> **J** Accounts receivable confirmation

Items to be answered:

1. All transactions have been recorded in the accounting records and are reflected in the financial statements.

2. In connection with an audit of our financial statements, management has prepared, and furnished to our auditors, a description and evaluation of certain contingencies.

3. Provision has been made for any material loss to be sustained in the fulfillment of, or from the inability to fulfill, any sales commitments.

4. Fees for our services are based on our regular per diem rates, plus travel and other out-of-pocket expenses.

5. The objective of our audit is to express an unmodified opinion on the financial statements, although it is possible that facts or circumstances encountered may preclude us from expressing an unqualified opinion.

6. We are not aware of any instances of non-compliance with laws and regulations that have not been fully disclosed.

7. Are you aware of any facts or circumstances that may indicate a lack of integrity by any member of senior management?

8. If a difference of opinion on a practice problem existed between engagement personnel and a specialist or other consultant, was the difference resolved in accordance with firm policy and appropriately documented?

9. Although we have not conducted a comprehensive, detailed search of our records, no other deposit or loan accounts have come to our attention except as noted below.

10. At the conclusion of our audit, we will request certain written representations from you about the financial statements and related matters.

11. Significant assumptions used by us in making accounting estimates, including those measured at fair value, are reasonable.

12. As discussed in Note 14 to the financial statements, the Company has had numerous dealings with businesses controlled by, and people who are related to, the officers of the Company.

13. There were unreasonable delays by management in permitting the commencement of the audit and in providing needed information.

14. If this statement is not correct, please write promptly, using the enclosed envelope, and give details of any differences directly to our auditors.

15. The Company has suffered recurring losses from operations and has a net capital deficiency that raises substantial doubt about its ability to continue as a going concern.

Task-Based Simulation 2

The Uniform
CPA Examination

Unsplit | Split Horiz | Split Vertical | Authoritative Literature | Spreadsheet | Calculator | Submit Testlet

Work Tab | **Resources** | **Help**

Required:

Items 1 through 10 represent audit objectives for the investments, accounts receivable, and property and equipment accounts. To the right of each set of audit objectives is a listing of possible audit procedures for that account. For each audit objective, select the audit procedure that would primarily respond to the objective. Select only one procedure for each audit objective. A procedure may be selected only once, or not at all.

Items to be answered:

Audit Objectives for Investments	*Audit Procedures for Investments*
1. Investments are properly described and classified in the financial statements. 2. Recorded investments represent investments actually owned at the balance sheet date. 3. Investments are properly valued at market at the balance sheet date.	A. Trace opening balances in the subsidiary ledger to prior year's audit working papers. B. Determine that employees who are authorized to sell investments do not have access to cash. C. Examine supporting documents for a sample of investment transactions to verify that pre-numbered documents are used. D. Determine that any impairments in the price of investments have been properly recorded. E. Verify that transfers from the trading to the available-for-sale investment portfolio have been properly recorded. F. Obtain positive confirmations as of the balance sheet date of investments held by independent custodians. G. Trace investment transactions to minutes of the Board of Directors meetings to determine that transactions were properly authorized.

Audit Objectives for Accounts Receivable	**_Audit Procedures for Accounts Receivable_**
4. Accounts receivable represent all amounts owed to the entity at the balance sheet date. 5. The entity has legal right to all accounts receivable at the balance sheet date. 6. Accounts receivable are stated at net realizable value. 7. Accounts receivable are properly described and presented in the financial statements.	A. Analyze the relationship of accounts receivable and sales and compare it with relationships for preceding periods. B. Perform sales cut-off tests to obtain assurance that sales transactions and corresponding entries for inventories and cost of goods sold are recorded in the same and proper period. C. Review the aged trial balance for significant past due accounts. D. Obtain an understanding of the business purpose of transactions that resulted in accounts receivable balances. E. Review loan agreements for indications of whether accounts receivable have been factored or pledged. F. Review the accounts receivable trial balance for amounts due from officers and employees. G. Analyze unusual relationships between monthly accounts receivable balances and monthly accounts payable balance

Audit Objectives for Property & Equipment	**_Audit Procedures for Property & Equipment_**
8. The entity has legal right to property and equipment acquired during the year. 9. Recorded property and equipment represent assets that actually exist at the balance sheet date. 10. Net property and equipment are properly valued at the balance sheet date.	A. Trace opening balances in the summary schedules to the prior year's audit working papers. B. Review the provision for depreciation expense and determine that depreciable lives and methods used in the current year is consistent with those used in the prior year. C. Determine that the responsibility for maintaining the property and equipment records is segregated from the responsibility for custody of property and equipment. D. Examine deeds and title insurance certificates. E. Perform cut-off tests to verify that property and equipment additions are recorded in the proper period. F. Determine that property and equipment is adequately insured. G. Physically examine all major property and equipment additions.

Task-Based Simulation 3

Required:

Items 1 through 12 represent possible errors and fraud that an auditor suspects are present. The accompanying *List of Auditing Procedures* represents procedures that the auditor would consider performing to gather evidence concerning possible errors and fraud. For each item, select one or two procedures, as indicated, that the auditor most likely would perform to gather evidence in support of that item. The procedures on the list may be selected once, more than once, or not at all.

Possible misstatements due to errors and fraud

1. The auditor suspects that a kiting scheme exists because an accounting department employee who can issue and record checks seems to be leading an unusually luxurious lifestyle. (**Select only 1 procedure**)

2. An auditor suspects that the controller wrote several checks and recorded the cash disbursements just before year-end but did not mail the checks until after the first week of the subsequent year. (**Select only 1 procedure**)

3. The entity borrowed funds from a financial institution. Although the transaction was properly recorded, the auditor suspects that the loan created a lien on the entity's real estate that is not disclosed in its financial statements. (**Select only 1 procedure**)

4. The auditor discovered an unusually large receivable from one of the entity's new customers. The auditor suspects that the receivable may be fictitious because the auditor has never heard of the customer and because the auditor's initial attempt to confirm the receivable has been ignored by the customer. (**Select only 2 procedures**)

5. The auditor suspects that fictitious employees have been placed on the payroll by the entity's payroll supervisor, who has access to payroll records and to the paychecks. (**Select only 1 procedure**)

6. The auditor suspects that selected employees of the entity received unauthorized raises from the entity's payroll supervisor, who has access to payroll records. (**Select only 1 procedure**)

7. The entity's cash receipts of the first few days of the subsequent year were properly deposited in its general operating account after the year-end. However, the auditor suspects that the entity recorded the cash receipts in its books during the last week of the year under audit. (**Select only 1 procedure**)

8. The auditor suspects that vouchers were prepared and processed by an accounting department employee for merchandise that was neither ordered nor received by the entity. (**Select only 1 procedure**)

9.   The details of invoices for equipment repairs were not clearly identified or explained to the accounting department employees. The auditor suspects that the bookkeeper incorrectly recorded the repairs as fixed assets. (**Select only 1 procedure**)

10. The auditor suspects that a lapping scheme exists because an accounting department employee who has access to cash receipts also maintains the accounts receivable ledger and refuses to take any vacation or sick days. (**Select only 2 procedures**)

11. The auditor suspects that the entity is inappropriately increasing the cash reported on its balance sheet by drawing a check on one account and not recording it as an outstanding check on that account and simultaneously recording it as a deposit in a second account. (**Select only 1 procedure**)

12. The auditor suspects that the entity's controller has overstated sales and accounts receivable by recording fictitious sales to regular customers in the entity's books. (**Select only 2 procedures**)

Items to be answered:

List of Auditing Procedures

A. Compare the details of the cash receipts journal entries with the details of the corresponding daily deposit slips.

B. Scan the debits to the fixed asset accounts and vouch selected amounts to vendors' invoices and management's authorization.

C. Perform analytical procedures that compare documented authorized pay rates to the entity's budget and forecast.

D. Obtain the cutoff bank statement and compare the cleared checks to the year-end bank reconciliation.

E. Prepare a bank transfer schedule.

F. Inspect the entity's deeds to its real estate.

G. Make inquiries of the entity's attorney concerning the details of real estate transactions.

H. Confirm the terms of borrowing arrangements with the lender.

I. Examine selected equipment repair orders and supporting documentation to determine the propriety of the charges.

J. Send requests to confirm the entity's accounts receivable on a surprise basis at an interim date.

K. Send a second request for confirmation of the receivable to the customer and make inquiries of a reputable credit agency concerning the customer's creditworthiness.

L. Examine the entity's shipping documents to verify that the merchandise that produced the receivable was actually sent to the customer.

M. Inspect the entity's correspondence files for indications of customer disputes for evidence that certain shipments were on consignment.

N. Perform edit checks of data on the payroll transaction tapes.

O. Inspect payroll check endorsements for similar handwriting.

P. Observe payroll check distribution on a surprise basis.

Q. Vouch data in the payroll register to documented authorized pay rates in the human resources department's files.

R. Reconcile the payroll checking account and determine if there were unusual time lags between the issuance and payment of payroll checks.

S. Inspect the file of prenumbered vouchers for consecutive numbering and proper approval by an appropriate employee.

T. Determine that the details of selected prenumbered vouchers match the related vendors' invoices.

U. Examine the supporting purchase orders and receiving reports for selected paid vouchers.

Task-Based Simulation 4

The Uniform
CPA Examination

| Unsplit | Split Horiz | Split Vertical | Authoritative Literature | Spreadsheet | Calculator | Submit Testlet |

Work Tab | **Resources** | **Help**

Required:

Question Number 4 consists of 15 items pertaining to analytical procedures. Select the best answer for each item.

Analytical procedures are evaluations of financial information made by a study of plausible relationships among financial and nonfinancial data. Understanding and evaluating such relationships are essential to the audit process.

The following financial statements were prepared by Holiday Manufacturing Co. for the year ended December 31, 20X5. Also presented are various financial statement ratios for Holiday as calculated from the prior year's financial statements. Sales represent net credit sales. The total assets and the receivables and inventory balances at December 31, 20X5, were the same as at December 31, 20X4.

Holiday Manufacturing Co.
Balance Sheet
December 31, 20X5

Assets		Liabilities and Capital	
Cash	$240,000	Accounts payable	$160,000
Receivables	$400,000	Notes payable	$100,000
Inventory	$600,000	Other current liabilities	$140,000
Total current assets	$1,240,000	Total current liabilities	$400,000
Plant and equipment – net	$760,000	Long-term debt	$350,000
		Common stock	$750,000
Total assets	**$2,000,000**	Retained earnings	$500,000
		Total liabilities and capital	**$2,000,000**

Holiday Manufacturing Co.
Income Statement
Year Ended December 31, 20X5

Sales			$3,000,000
Cost of goods sold			
	Material	$800,000	
	Labor	$700,000	
	Overhead	$300,000	$1,800,000
Gross margin			$1,200,000
	Selling expenses	$240,000	
	General and administrative expenses	$300,000	$540,000
Operating income			$660,000
Less interest expense			$40,000
Income before taxes			$620,000
Less federal income taxes			$220,000
Net income			**$400,000**

Items to be answered:

a.   **Items 1 through 9** below represent financial ratios that the auditor calculated during the prior year's audit. For each ratio, calculate the current year's ratio from the financial statements presented on the previous page, select the answer from List A. Calculations should be rounded, if necessary, to the same number of places as the prior year's ratios. Answers on the list may be selected once, more than once, or not at all.

Ratio	Holiday Mfg. Co. 12/31/X5	Holiday Mfg. Co. 12/31/X4	List A Ratio calculations
1. Current ratio		2.5	A 0.6
2. Quick ratio		1.3	B 0.7
3. Accounts receivable turnover		5.5	C 1.0
4. Inventory turnover		2.5	D 1.5
5. Total asset turnover		1.2	E 1.6
6. Gross margin percentage		35%	F 2.0
7. Net Operating margin percentage		25%	G 3.0
8. Times interest earned		10.3	H 3.1
9. Total debt to equity percentage		50%	I 4.5
			J 5.0
			K 7.5
			L 10.0
			M 15.5
			N 16.5
			O 13%
			P 22%
			Q 28%
			R 33%
			S 38%
			T 40%
			U 60%
			V 67%

Required:

b. **Items 10 through 15** represent an auditor's observed changes in certain financial statement ratios or amounts from the prior year's ratios or amounts. For each observed change, select the most likely explanation or explanations from List B. Select only the number of explanations as indicated. **The observed changes are not related to the calculations in requirement a, above, and are independent of each other.** Answers on the list may be selected once, more than once, or not at all.

Items to be answered:

Auditor's observed changes (not related to Items 1-9 and independent of each other).

10. Inventory turnover increased substantially from the prior year. (Select 3 explanations)

11. Accounts receivable turnover decreased substantially from the prior year. (Select 3 explanations)

12. Allowance for doubtful account increased from the prior year, but allowance for doubtful accounts as a percentage of accounts receivable decreased from the prior year. (Select 3 explanations)

13. Long-term debt increased from the prior year, but interest expense increased a larger-than-proportionate amount than long-term debt. (Select 1 explanation)

14. Operating income increased from the prior year although the entity was less profitable than in the prior year. (Select 2 explanations)

15. Gross margin percentage was unchanged from the prior year although gross margin increased from the prior year. (Select 1 explanation)

List B
Explanations
A. Items shipped on consignment during the last month of the year were recorded as sales.
B. A significant number of credit memos for returned merchandise that were issued during the last month of the year were not recorded.
C. Year-end purchases of inventory were overstated by incorrectly including items received in the first month of the subsequent year.
D. Year-end purchases of inventory were understated by incorrectly excluding items received before the year-end.
E. A larger percentage of sales occurred during the last month of the year, as compared to the prior year.
F. A smaller percentage of sales occurred during the last month of the year, as compared to the prior year.
G. The same percentage of sales occurred during the last month of the year, as compared to the prior year.
H. Sales increased at the same percentage as cost of goods sold, as compared to the prior year.
I. Sales increased at a greater percentage than cost of goods sold increased, as compared to the prior year.
J. Sales increased at a lower percentage than cost of goods sold increased, as compared to the prior year.
K. Interest expense decreased, as compared to the prior year.
L. The effective income tax rate increased, as compared to the prior year.
M. The effective income tax rate decreased, as compared to the prior year.
N. Short-term borrowing was refinanced on a long-term basis at the same interest rate.
O. Short-term borrowing was refinanced on a long-term basis at lower interest rates.
P. Short-term borrowing was refinanced on a long-term basis at higher interest rates.

Lecture 4.15

Task-Based Simulation 5

The Uniform
CPA Examination

Unsplit | Split Horiz | Split Vertical | Authoritative Literature | Spreadsheet | Calculator | Submit Testlet

Work Tab | **Resources** | **Help**

Required:

This Question consists of 2 parts. Part **A**. consists of 10 items and Part **B** consists of 8 items. Select the **best** answer for each item.

A. **Items 1 through 10** represent tickmarks (symbols) that indicate procedures performed or comments documented in auditing the **Long-term debt** account of American Manufacturers, Inc. Select, from the list of procedures/comments below, the procedure/comment that the auditor most likely performed/documented at each point of the audit where a tickmark was made on the working papers. Select only one procedure/comment for each item. A procedure/comment may be selected once or not at all. Assume that the working papers foot and crossfoot.

American Manufacturers, Inc.
Long-Term Debt
October 31, 20x7

Lender	Interest rate	Payment terms	Collateral	Balance 10/31/x6	Current year borrowings	Current year reductions	Balance 10/31/x7	Interest paid to	Accrued interest payable 10/31/x7	Comments
♦ First National Bank	10%	Interest only on last day of each quarter; principal due in full on 9/30/x9	Manufacturing equipment	500,000 v	200,000 • 3/31/x7	(100,000) ♣ 6/30/x7	600,000 ▽	9/30/x7	5,000 ♥	First National confirms that interest payments are current and agrees with account balance.
♦ Second State Bank	9%	$10,000 principal plus interest due on the 1st of each month; due in full on 1/1/00	First mortgage on production facilities	380,000 v	0	(110,000) ♠	270,000 ▽*	9/30/x7	2,025 ♥	Monthly payment for $12,025 was mailed on 11/3/x7; Second State agrees with account balance.
♦ Third Savings & Loan	12%	$5,000 principal plus interest due on the 15th of each month; due in full on 10/15/x9	Second mortgage on production facilities	180,000 v	0	(60,000)	120,000 ◊*	10/15/x7	600	Third Savings & Loan claims 10/15/x7 payment wasn't received as of 11/5/x7; adjusting entry proposed to increase balance $5,000 and increase accrued interest payable
♦ A. Clark majority stock-holder	0%	Due in full 10/31/x9	Unsecured	700,000 v	0	(200,000) 10/28/x7	500,000		0	Borrowed additional $200,000 from Clark on 11/5/x7; need to investigate reborrowing just after year-end and consider imputed interest on 0% stockholder loan.
				1,760,000	200,000	(470,000)	1,490,000#		7,625#	

Items to be answered:

List of procedures / comments — Long-Term Debt	
A. Confirmed, without exception. **B**. Confirmed, with exception. **C**. Traced amount to prior year's working papers. **D**. Traced amount to current year's trial balance and general ledger. **E**. Does not recompute correctly. **F**. Tested reasonableness of calculations.	**G**. Agreed to canceled checks and lender's monthly statements. **H**. Agreed to canceled check and board of directors' authorization. **I**. Agreed interest rate, terms, and collateral to note & loan agreement. **J**. Agreed to loan agreement, validated bank deposit ticket, and board of directors' authorization. **K**. Reclassification entry proposed for current portion of long-term debt.

1. ♦	**6.** ▽
2. v	**7.** ∗
3. ●	**8.** ◊
4. ♣	**9.** #
5. ♠	**10.** ♥

Required:

B. **Items 11 through 18** represent tick marks (symbols) that indicate procedures performed or comments documented in auditing the **Property, plant, and equipment** and **Accumulated depreciation** accounts of American Manufacturers, Inc. During the year under audit, American Manufacturers purchased new computers directly from wholesalers and constructed an addition to one of its buildings. The company's employees also refurbished the fixtures of several older buildings. Select, from the list of procedures/comments below, the procedure/comment that the auditor most likely performed/documented at each point of the audit where a tick mark was made on the working papers. Select only one procedure/comment for each item. A procedure/comment may be selected once or not at all. Assume that the working papers foot and crossfoot.

American Manufacturers, Inc.
Property, Plant, and Equipment and Accumulated Depreciation
October 31, 20x7

| Account | Property, Plant, and Equipment | | | | | Depreciation | | Accumulated Depreciation | | | |
	Balance 10/31/x6	Additions	Disposals	Other	Balance 10/31/x7	Rate	Method	Balance 10/31/x6	Provision	Disposal	Balance 10/31/x7
Land	650,000 ↗	70,000 ◄	0	0	720,000 ⊃						
Buildings	3,270,000 ↗	230,000 ✓	0	(30,000) ✚	3,470,000 ⊃	5%	S/L	1,144,500 ↗	168,500 ✳	0	1,313,000 ⊃
Equipment	1,750,000 ↗	90,000 ☐	(12,000) ⊙	0	1,828,000 ⊃	10%	S/L	700,000 ↗	179,500 ✳	(12,000)	867,500 ⊃
Fixtures	850,000 ↗	200,000 ✓	0	30,000 ✚	1,080,000 ⊃	15%	S/L	510,000 ↗	144,750 ✳	0	654,750 ⊃
	6,520,000	590,000	(12,000)	0	7,098,000			2,354,500	492,750	(12,000)	2,835,250

Items to be answered:

> 11. ↗
> 12. ◁
> 13. ✓
> 14. ❑
> 15. ⊙
> 16. ✦
> 17. ➲
> 18. ✳

List of procedures/comments — Property, Plant, and Equipment and Accumulated Depreciation

A. Does not recompute correctly.
B. Tested reasonableness of calculation.
C. Traced amount to current year's trial balance and general ledger.
D. Reclassification entry for fixtures erroneously recorded as buildings.
E. Reclassification entry for buildings erroneously recorded as fixtures.
F. Traced amount to prior year's working papers.
G. Sold six fully-depreciated computers to employees; no audit procedures necessary.
H. Confirmed, with exception.
I. Confirmed, without exception.
J. Examined supporting vendors' invoices, canceled checks, asset subsidiary ledger and board of directors' minutes of meetings authorizing transactions.
K. Examined supporting work orders and engineers' reports, canceled checks, asset subsidiary ledger, and board of directors' minutes of meetings authorizing transactions.
L. Examined supporting deed and purchase contract, canceled checks, asset subsidiary ledger, and board of directors' minutes of meetings authorizing transactions.

Task-Based Simulation 6

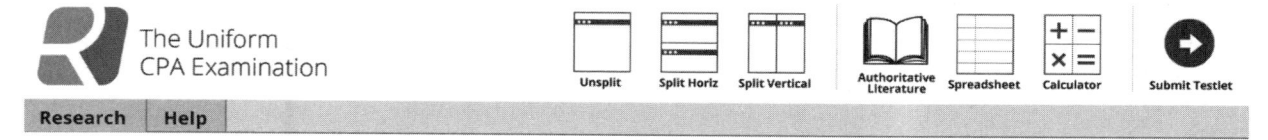

Kerrington, CPA, is trying to determine if the engagement time has obtained sufficient appropriate audit evidence to support an opinion on the financial statements. One concern is the reliability of the evidence obtained and Kerrington is trying to determine if some forms of evidence are considered more reliable than others.

1. Which title of Professional Standards addresses this issue & will be helpful in understanding whether certain forms of audit evidence are more reliable than others?

2. Enter the exact section and paragraph with helpful information.

Task-Based Simulation 7

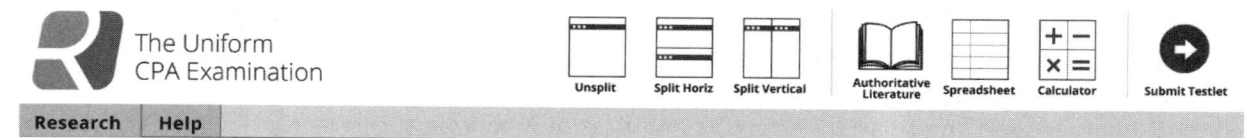

Corbin, CPA, is performing analytical procedures as substantive tests because there are some very predictable relationships among items on the financial statements and reliable expectations can be developed. Corbin is trying to determine the extent to which the analytical procedures should be documented.

1. Which title of Professional Standards addresses this issue & will be helpful in understanding the auditor's responsibilities for documenting analytical procedures?

2. Enter the exact section and paragraph with helpful information.

Task-Based Simulation 8

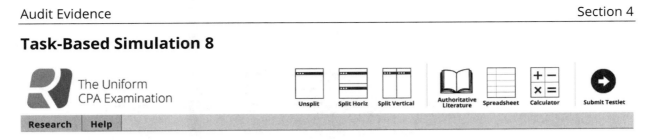

Janis & Stone, CPAs, are developing a plan for sending confirmations to some of their client's customers as a procedure to obtain evidence relative to accounts receivable. They are thinking of using negative confirmations for a large volume of small balances and are trying to decide if that is an appropriate use of negative confirmations.

1. Which title of Professional Standards addresses this issue & will be helpful in understanding the appropriate use of negative confirmations?

2. Enter the exact section and paragraph with helpful information.

Task-Based Simulation 9

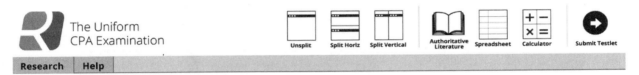

In obtaining evidence about the valuation of an audit client's investment in derivatives, the auditor receives estimates of fair value from broker-dealers and wishes to make certain that appropriate audit procedures are applied.

1. Which title of Professional Standards addresses this issue & will be helpful in understanding what audit procedures should be applied to estimates of fair value received from broker-dealers?

2. Enter the exact section and paragraph with helpful information.

Task-Based Simulation 10

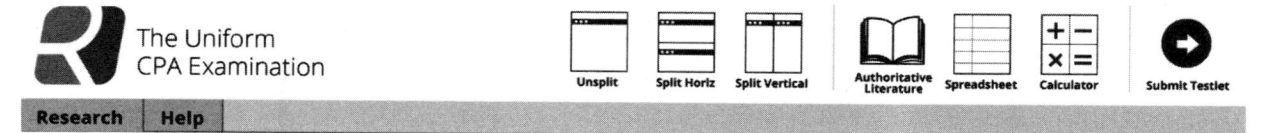

Singh & Patel, CPAs, are performing risk assessment procedures to, among other things, identify and assess the risk of material misstatement related to accounting estimates. They are trying to determine what risk assessment procedures will be most helpful in accomplishing that objective.

1. Which title of Professional Standards addresses this issue & will be helpful in understanding the risk assessment procedures most helpful in identifying and assessing risk of material misstatement associated with accounting estimates?

2. Enter the exact section and paragraph with helpful information.

TASK-BASED SIMULATION SOLUTIONS

Task-Based Simulation Solution 1

1.   D   The auditor would want management to provide assurance that all transactions have been recorded in the accounting records and are reflected in the financial statements. This relates to the completeness assertion.

2.   I   In order for the auditor to obtain information about contingencies from the entity's legal counsel, management will prepare a list of contingencies for the auditor and prepare a letter of inquiry.

3.   D   Management, in its letter of representation to the auditor, will give the auditor assurance that any contingent losses resulting from the inability to fulfill sales commitments have been accrued.

4.   C   To avoid a misunderstanding with the client, the auditor will prepare an engagement letter which will include information about how fees for services are determined.

5.   C   To avoid a misunderstanding with the client, the auditor will prepare an engagement letter which will include a statement as to the objective of the engagement, the expression of an opinion on the financial statements, and the fact that circumstances could preclude the expression of an opinion.

6.   D   Management, in its letter of representation to the auditor, will give the auditor assurance that they are not aware of any instances of non-compliance with laws and regulations that have not been fully disclosed.

7.   B   The auditor will want to be aware of any circumstances that may indicate that members of senior management lack integrity. This information can be learned from a predecessor auditor.

8.   A   When reviewing the engagement prior to the issuance of an opinion, a partner will want to make certain that all differences of opinion that may affect information on the financial statements have been resolved.

9.   E   Among the issues that an auditor will want to learn from a financial institution will be whether the entity has loans or other accounts about which the auditor is not aware. A request for this information is included on a standard bank confirmation.

10.   C   To avoid a misunderstanding with the client, the auditor will prepare an engagement letter which will include an indication that the auditor will be expecting a letter of representations from the client.

11.   D   In its letter of representation, management will assure the auditor that the significant assumptions used in making accounting estimates, including those measured at fair value, are reasonable.

12.   G   The auditor may wish to emphasize a matter, such as the existence of related party transactions, by adding an emphasis-of-matter paragraph to the auditor's report.

13.   F   When management does not cooperate with the auditors, such as through unreasonable delays in permitting audit procedures, the auditor will communicate the problem to the board of through communication with the audit committee.

14.   J   In an accounts receivable confirmation, a customer will be asked to review the balance owing as of a particular date and respond directly to the auditor as to agreement or disagreement.

15.   G   The auditor will generally emphasize going concern doubts by including an emphasis-of-matter paragraph in the audit report.

Task-Based Simulation Solution 2

1. E To obtain evidence that investments are properly described and classified in the financial statements (presentation & disclosure), the auditor should be seeking evidence about the nature of the investments to determine if they are properly classified and tracing the information to the financial statements. By verifying that transfers from trading to available for sale have been properly recorded, the auditor is obtaining evidence about the classification of the investments.

2. F To obtain evidence that investments are actually owned at the balance sheet date (rights & obligations), the auditor should be seeking evidence about ownership. This will generally include the inspection of investment certificates that are in the possession of the entity and confirmation of those held by brokers or other independent custodians.

3. D To obtain evidence that investments are properly valued at market at the balance sheet date (valuation & allocation), the auditor should be seeking evidence about market value as of the balance sheet date and trace the information to the financial statements. By determining that impairments in value have been properly recorded, the auditor is obtaining evidence about value.

4. B To obtain evidence that all amounts owed to the entity are included in accounts receivable at the balance sheet date (completeness), the auditor should be seeking evidence to verify that all sales transactions that occurred during the period were recorded in the period. By performing sales cut-off tests, the auditor is making certain that sales occurring just before or after year-end are recorded in the proper period.

5. E To obtain evidence that the entity has legal right to all accounts receivable at the balance sheet date (rights & obligations), the auditor should be seeking evidence to determine if the entity has surrendered legal right to any accounts receivable. By reviewing loan agreements for indications of factoring or pledging accounts receivable, the auditor is obtaining evidence as to whether the legal right to accounts receivable has been given up by either selling the receivables or using them as collateral for a loan.

6. C To obtain evidence that accounts receivable are stated at net realizable value (valuation & allocation), the auditor should be seeking evidence that supports the client's allowance for uncollectible accounts. By reviewing the aged analysis for significant past due accounts, the auditor is obtaining evidence as to whether accounts should be written down or off as part of the measurement of the allowance for uncollectible accounts.

7. F To obtain evidence that accounts receivable are properly described and presented in the financial statements (presentation & disclosure), the auditor should be seeking evidence that indicates whether all amounts included in accounts receivable result for sales in the ordinary course of business and tract the information to the financial statements. By reviewing the accounts receivable trial balance for amounts due from officers and employees, the auditor is obtaining evidence as to whether receivables other than trade accounts receivable are included in the balance.

8.   D   To obtain evidence that the entity has legal right to property and equipment acquired during the year (rights & obligations), the auditor should be seeking evidence that verifies that the entity has obtained proper title for items purchased. By examining deeds, the auditor is obtaining evidence as to ownership and by examining title insurance certificates; the auditor is obtaining evidence as to whether others might have claims to the property.

9.   G   To obtain evidence that property and equipment actually exists at the balance sheet date (existence or occurrence); the auditor can physically examine the assets.

10.   B   To obtain evidence that net property and equipment are properly valued at the balance sheet date (valuation & allocation), the auditor should be seeking evidence that supports the amount at which the assets have been recorded and the amount reported as accumulated depreciation. By reviewing the provision for depreciation expense and determining if lives and methods have been used consistently, the auditor is obtaining evidence to support the amount reported as accumulated depreciation.

Task-Based Simulation Solution 3

1. **E** Kiting occurs when a deposit resulting from a transfer between two cash accounts within the same entity is recorded in an earlier period than the disbursement from the other account, resulting in an overstatement of cash. By preparing a bank transfer schedule, the auditor can make certain that all transfers deposited are recorded in the same period as the disbursements.

2. **D** When checks are written and held, it will take a greater period of time for them to clear the bank than when they are mailed on a timely basis. By reviewing the bank cutoff statement, the auditor can determine if there are any unreasonable delays in the time it takes for checks written near the end of the period to clear the bank.

3. **H** If the auditor suspects that a loan created a lien on the entity's property, it can best be verified by obtaining a written confirmation from the lender. This can be accomplished by using a standard bank confirmation to the lending institution.

4. **K, L** When an auditor's suspicions of a fictitious receivable are supported by an unsuccessful attempt to confirm the account receivable, the auditor can try to confirm it a second time and make inquiries among credit agencies about the customer (k). In addition, the auditor can examine supporting shipping documents and purchase orders to make certain that the sale creating the receivable did actually occur (L).

5. **P** By observing the distribution of payroll checks, the auditor can determine if there are unclaimed checks which may be an indication of fictitious employees. Observing the distribution on a surprise basis prevents the person distributing the checks from concealing the activity from the auditor by not preparing such checks when the auditor is observing.

6. **Q** When the auditor suspects that employees received unauthorized pay raises, the auditor may select items from the payroll to identify individuals who have received pay raises. By tracing the raises to approved pay rates, the auditor can determine if the raises are legitimate.

7. **A** When the auditor suspects that cash receipts were recorded in the period prior to when they were received and deposited, the auditor may trace the amounts recorded near the end of the period of the year to the deposits slips to determine if they were recorded in the same in which they were deposited.

8. **U** If the auditor suspects that vouchers were prepared for merchandise that was neither ordered nor received, the auditor should select a sample from the vouchers and trace them to the supporting purchase orders and receiving reports. This will provide the auditor with evidence that vouchers are only for merchandise that was ordered and received.

9. **B** If the auditor believes that items that should have been recognized as expense were incorrectly capitalized in a fixed asset account, the auditor can analyze increases in the fixed asset accounts, tracing them to vendor invoices. By reviewing the invoices, the auditor can determine if capitalization was appropriate.

10. A, J Lapping occurs when an employee misappropriates cash received and uses subsequent amounts received from other customers to reduce the balances of the misappropriated accounts. As a result, reductions to accounts involved in the lapping scheme will be reduced later than the payment is actually made by the customer. By sending confirmations to customers on a surprise basis, customers may notify the auditor of balances that do not reflect payments that were made.

11. E If the auditor suspects that the company is writing a check from an account and not listing it as an outstanding check, artificially increasing the balance, while recording it as a deposit to another account, which is a kiting scheme, a bank transfer schedule will show transfers in that exceed transfers out.

12. J, L If the auditor suspects that fictitious sales have been recorded, increasing sales and accounts receivable, the auditor can use accounts receivable confirmations to detect overstated accounts receivable. In addition, tracing recorded sales to the company's shipping documents will reveal sales that are not supported by shipping documents indicating that goods were not actually shipped.

Task-Based Simulation Solution 4

1. H The current ratio is current assets of $1,240,000 divided by current liabilities of $400,000 or 3.1.

2. E The quick ratio is liquid assets, consisting of cash and accounts receivable for a total of $640,000 (240,000 + 400,000), divided by current liabilities of $400,000 or 1.6.

3. K Accounts receivable turnover is sales of $3,000,000 divided by average accounts receivable. Since the beginning and ending accounts receivable are the same at $400,000 that is also the average. As a result, accounts receivable turnover is 7.5 times.

4. G Inventory turnover is cost of sales of $1,800,000 divided by average inventory. Since the beginning and ending inventories are the same at $600,000 that is also the average. As a result, inventory turnover is 3 times.

5. D Total asset turnover is sales of $3,000,000 divided by average total assets. Since the beginning and ending total assets are the same at $2,000,000 that is also the average. As a result, total assets turnover is 1.5 times.

6. T The gross margin percentage is the gross margin of $1,200,000 divided by sales of $3,000,000 or 40%.

7. P The net operating margin percentage is the operating income of $660,000 divided by sales of $3,000,000 or 22%.

8. N Times interest earned is net income before interest and taxes, which is $660,000 divided by interest of $40,000 resulting in a ratio of 16.5 times.

9. U The total debt to equity percentage is total liabilities, including current liabilities and long-term debt with a total of $750,000 (400,000 + 350,000), divided by total stockholders' equity, consisting of common stock and retained earnings for a total of $1,250,000 (750,000 + 500,000), resulting in a ratio of 60%.

10. ABD Inventory turnover is cost of goods sold divided by average inventory. It will increase if cost of goods sold increases or if average inventory decreases. If items shipped on consignment were recorded as sales (A), cost of sales would be overstated and inventory would be understated increasing inventory turnover. If credit memos for merchandise returned were not recorded (B), inventory would also be understated and cost of goods would be overstated. If year-end purchase of inventory were understated (D), year-end inventory would be understated resulting in a reduction in average inventory and an increase in the ratio.

11. ABE Accounts receivable turnover is sales divided by average accounts receivable. It will decrease if there is a decrease in sales or an increase in average accounts receivable. If items shipped on consignment were recorded as sales (A), both sales and accounts receivable would be overstated and the increase to accounts receivable would be proportionately higher resulting in a decrease to accounts receivable turnover. If credit memos for merchandise returned were not recorded (B), again both sales and accounts receivable would be overstated with the increase to accounts receivable proportionately higher resulting in a decrease to accounts receivable turnover. If a larger percentage of sales occurred at the end of the current year compared to the previous year (E), the ending accounts receivable balance would be higher, increasing average accounts receivable and decreasing accounts receivable turnover.

12.   ABE   When the ratio of the allowance for doubtful accounts to accounts receivable decreases, either the allowance must decrease or accounts receivable must increase. Since the allowance increased, accounts receivable must have increased by a proportionately greater amount. Recording items shipped on consignment as sales (A) would overstate accounts receivable as would failure to record credit memos for merchandise returned (B). If a larger percentage of sales occur at the end of the current year compared to the previous year (E), the ending accounts receivable balance would be higher, also decreasing the ratio.

13.   P   When interest expense increases by a proportionately higher amount than the increase in long-term debt, it will generally indicate that the interest rate on the newer long-term debt is higher than the rate paid on the previous debt. This would be the case if short-term borrowings were refinanced on a long-term basis at higher interest rates (P).

14.   LP   If operating income increases and net income decreases, there must have been an increase in either nonoperating items like interest expense, or income taxes. This would be the case if there is an increase in the tax rate (L), or if short-term debt is refinanced on a long-term basis at a higher interest rate (P).

15.   H   If the gross margin percentage remained the same while the amount of the gross margin increased, both sales and cost of sales must have increased proportionately during the period (H).

Task-Based Simulation Solution 5

1.   I   Since this symbol appears to the left of each of the listed lenders, in a section of the spreadsheet that shows the lender, the interest rate, the payment terms, and the collateral, combined with the fact that there are no additional comments, makes it likely that this symbol indicates that the auditor confirmed the interest rates, payment terms, and collateral for these loans.

2.   C   Since this symbol appears next to each of the beginning loan balances, it is likely that it is intended to indicate that the auditor is satisfied that the balance was brought forward correctly, which would be determined by tracing the balance to the prior year's working papers.

3.   J   Since this symbol only appears next to an amount in the column for current year borrowings, it is likely intended to indicate that the auditor has verified that the current year's borrowings were properly recorded. This might involve tracing the amount to the loan agreement, tracing it to a deposit, and checking for authorization by the board of directors.

4.   H   Since this symbol appears next to the current year reduction in the First National Bank Loan. It most likely is intended to indicate that the auditor has determined that it was properly reported. The loan is not due until 9/30/X9, but was paid early. As a result, the auditor would both trace the payment to a cancelled check and verify that the early payment was authorized by the board of directors.

5.   G   This symbol appears next to the reduction to the Second State Bank loan, which the agreement indicates is paid in monthly payments of $10,000 in principal plus interest. It is likely intended to indicate that the auditor has determined that the reductions were properly recorded. This would probably involve tracing the reductions to cancelled checks and monthly statements received from the lender.

6.   A   Since this symbol appears next to the ending balances of the two loans for which the confirmations indicate that the lender agrees with the current balance. As a result, it is likely intended to indicate that the balance was confirmed without exception.

7.   K   This symbol appears only next to the ending loan balances that are paid in monthly payments, which are also the only loans that have a current portion. It is likely an indication that the auditor has proposed an entry to reclassify the current portion of these debts to current liabilities.

8.   B   Since this symbol appears next to the ending balance for the loan from Third Savings & Loan, and the Comments column indicates a disagreement regarding the receipt of a payment, it is likely that this symbol indicates an exception in a confirmation.

9.   D   Since this symbol appears next to the ending balances of both loans payable and interest payable, it is likely that the auditor made certain that these balances are the same as those in the general ledger and the trial balance.

10.   F   Since this symbol appears next to the year-end interest accruals, it is likely that it is intended to indicate that the auditor has verified the calculation such as be testing whether or not the amount is reasonable.

11.   F   Since this symbol appears next to the beginning balances for each of the items, it is likely intended to indicate that the auditor has checked to see if they agree with the balances in the previous year's amounts. This would be accomplished by tracing the amounts to the prior year's working papers.

12.   L   Since this symbol appears next to the increase in land, it is likely intended to indicate that the auditor has determined that the acquisition occurred and that it was recorded properly. This will involve tracing the amount to purchase agreements, a deed, and cancelled checks. The auditor will also determine that the transaction was authorized by tracing it to minutes of meetings of the board of directors.

13.   K   Since this symbol appears next to the increases buildings, which the company constructed an addition to, and fixtures, which the entity refurbished during the period, it is likely intended to indicate that the auditor verified that the amounts include appropriately capitalized costs. This might involve examining supporting work orders and engineers' reports, canceled checks, asset subsidiary ledger, and minutes of board of directors' meetings.

14.   J   Since this symbol appears next to the increase in equipment, which resulted from the purchase of new computers, it is likely intended to indicate that the auditor verified that the purchase was properly reported. This may involve tracing the purchase to board authorization as well as purchase documents such as vendors' invoices and canceled checks.

15.   G   Since this symbol appears next to the reduction to equipment, it apparently relates to a sale or disposal or a reclassification. None of the choices indicate a reclassification out of equipment. The only reasonable possibility is that it represents the sale of computers to employees, which would result in a decrease in equipment.

16.   D   This symbol appears next to a decrease in buildings and an increase in fixtures. It is therefore likely to indicate a reclassification adjustment for fixtures that were improperly reported as buildings.

17.   C   Since this symbol appears next to each of the ending balances for the various property, plant, and equipment accounts, it is likely intended to indicate that the amounts are correct and have been traced to the trial balance and to the general ledger.

18.   B   Since this symbol appears next to the current year's provision for depreciation expense for each of the depreciable assets, it is likely intended to indicate that the auditor has verified that the amount is correct by testing the reasonableness of the calculation.

Task-Based Simulation Solution 6

AU-C	500	.A32

Task-Based Simulation Solution 7

AU-C	520	.08

Task-Based Simulation Solution 8

AU-C	505	.15

Task-Based Simulation Solution 9

AU-C	501	.07

Task-Based Simulation Solution 10

AU-C	540	.08

Lecture 4.19

DOCUMENT REVIEW SIMULATION

Document Review Simulation 1

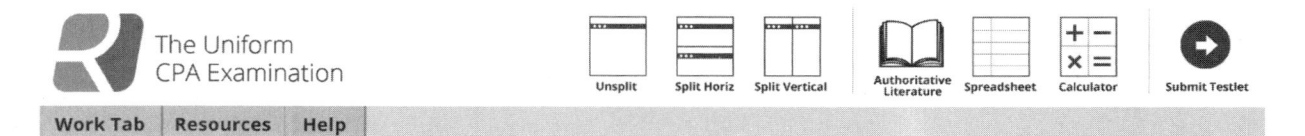

Scroll down to complete all parts of this task.

Client Company Profile

The Finer Things Company is a small chain of retail stores, specializing in gifts, such as unique jewelry, handbags, and other accessories, as well as candles, greeting cards, and wrapping paper. The Finer Things opened its first two stores twelve years ago, and experienced such positive results that it opened its third store during 20X3. These three stores are all located in upper middle class towns, within a fifteen-mile radius of the company's headquarters. Looking to further continue its growth, The Finer Things sought to purchase a small building for a "good" price in order to open another store. It found its ideal building in a small, industrial town nearly fifty miles from the company's headquarters. The Finer Things closed on the Centre Building on January 2, 20X6, for a price of $577,000, utilizing a nine-year note, which requires equal payments due each January 1. The company successfully opened its fourth store during 20X6. The company's long-term goal is to continue to grow so that it can launch an initial public offering within eight to ten years.

Marketing

Although the retail industry is highly competitive and can be difficult to enter, The Finer Things found its niche with its unique gift offerings. At the company's inception, its unique offerings were difficult for customers to procure from other places. However, due to the near exponential growth of online shopping, customers are now able to purchase many of The Finer Things' items directly from their manufacturers. In order to combat this challenge, The Finer Things has opened an "internet store," where it has had reasonable success attracting customers with its "Never Pay for Shipping" policy.

Management

The company is a partnership formed by Janice Neighbors and Olivia Park, two college roommates. The original vision had been for each partner to run one of the two stores, almost as if each was an independent entity. As time progressed and the business grew, the women changed their business model and hired several friends as part of the management team. Ms. Neighbors assumed the role of CEO, while Ms. Park became CFO. They formed a five-person Board of Directors, with each partner choosing two trusted individuals from her family, and the two partners together chose a business associate as the fifth member. As there is not a separate audit committee, the Board of Directors fulfills this function. As an incentive to join the Board of Directors, each member received a small stake in the company.

Engagement

You are a manager with Providence LLC ("Providence"), a mid-sized national auditing firm. You are in the process of completing the Financial Statement audit of The Finer Things Company ("The Finer Things"), a non-issuer, for the year ended 20X6. You have participated in the audit of The Finer Things for all five years that they have been one of Providence's clients.

Providence is a growing firm, known especially for its expertise in the retail and manufacturing industries. Providence has been fortunate to have gained several large, new clients during 20X6. The firm assigned a newly promoted senior associate to the audit staff after the interim planning and fieldwork phase had been completed. The former senior associate on the engagement, John Swanson, has been shifted to one of Providence's new clients, which is also one of your clients. You have worked with John on multiple engagements and have complete faith in his work. At Providence, The Finer Things account has the reputation of being "easy and straightforward, perfect for a new senior associate."

Due to the increased number of audit clients for Providence, the partners have requested that engagement staff evaluate the timing of their audit procedures, and shift as much audit work as possible from the year-end fieldwork phase to the interim planning and fieldwork phase in order to free up auditor time to take on additional clients during the busiest time of the year. This is possible as Providence's interim testing of The Finer Things' internal controls has been favorable. The partners have also assigned earlier deadlines for finishing audit work on existing clients. You are experiencing a lot of pressure to complete work on The Finer Things so that you may focus your attention on some new, more complex clients.

The Finer Things has provided you with its December 31, 20X6 and 20X5, balance sheets, its December 31, 20X6 and 20X5, income statements, its Unadjusted Pre-closing 20X6 Trial Balance, and its 20X6 Budget. You are completing your review of your staff's workpapers, including analytical procedures performed, in order to prepare for a final meeting with the engagement partner. The partner has requested that the meeting occur in the next few days, prior to his two weeks of travel to work on a new west coast client.

Task

Review the Balance Sheet Fluctuation Analysis (for items 1 through 10) and the Budget to Actual Comparison (for the last item), focusing especially on the conclusions formed. These documents will form the crux of the discussion areas with the partner and you will utilize these documents in your meeting. Based on the review of the comparative balance sheets, income statements, trial balance, and budget, review the senior associate's analytics and conclusion. Revise the comments and conclusion as needed, correcting any errors, and adding any necessary comments. You also may wish to delete an entire comment, and separately instruct the senior associate to perform additional procedures. Ensure that the workpaper's results are appropriate, given the information provided.

To revise the workpaper review comments, click on each segment of underlined text below and select the needed correction, if any, from the list provided. If the text already is correct in the context of the document, select [Original text] from the list. If removal of the text is the best revision to the workpapers, select [Delete text] from the list.

Balance Sheet Fluctuation Analysis

The Finer Things Company
Balance Sheets Fluctuation Analysis
December 31, 20X6 and 20X5

	20X6	20X5	$ Change	% Change
Cash & Cash Equivalents	1,553,805	1,723,915	(170,110)	-9.9%
Accounts Receivable	292,370	297,500	(5,130)	-1.7%
Less: allowance for doubtful accounts	-	-	-	
Prepaid Expenses	44,690	41,940	2,750	6.6%
Inventory - Goods Held for Sale	788,650	363,530	425,120	116.9%
Notes Receivable	460,000	540,000	(80,000)	-14.8%
Total Current Assets	3,139,515	2,966,885		
Buildings, at cost	577,000	-	577,000	100.0%
Furniture & Fixtures	760,000	760,000	-	0.0%
Less: accumulated depreciation	(600,000)	(570,000)	(30,000)	5.3%
Other Fixed Assets	65,000	65,000	-	0.0%
Less: accumulated depreciation	(39,000)	(26,000)	(13,000)	50.0%
Total Long-term Assets	763,000	229,000		
Total Assets	3,902,515	3,195,885		
Current Liabilities:				
Accounts Payable	347,800	218,400	129,400	59.2%
Taxes Payable	124,640	123,950	690	0.6%
Accrued Expenses	47,850	53,910	(6,060)	-11.2%
Total Current Liabilities	520,290	396,260		
Notes Payable	577,000	-	577,000	100.0%
Total Liabilities	1,097,290	396,260		
Common Stock	2,250,000	2,250,000	-	0.0%
Retained Earnings	555,225	549,625	5,600	1.0%
Total Equity	2,805,225	2,799,625		
Total Liabilities and Equity	3,902,515	3,195,885		

Comments:

1. Decrease in Cash & Cash Equivalents is reasonable because net income also decreased.

2. Increase in Inventory is reasonable due to addition of fourth store.

3. Notes Receivable decrease is consistent with decrease in Cash & Cash Equivalents.

4. Increase in Buildings, at cost is reasonable due to Centre building purchase.

5. Compared Accumulated Depreciation as a % of Furniture & Fixtures. Increased slightly from 75% to 79%. Change is too immaterial to investigate.

6. Increase in Accounts Payable is reasonable due to addition of another store and due to its inverse relationship to Accrued Expenses.

7. Minimal increase in Taxes Payable; too immaterial to investigate.

8. Decrease in Accrued Expenses is reasonable due to its inverse relationship to Accounts Payable.

9. Notes Payable balance of $577,000 is reasonable due to purchase of Centre Building. As there was no Note Payable at December 31, 20X5, the 20X5 balance is appropriately shown as $0.

10. Conclusion: Based on end-of-audit analytics performed, Balance Sheet is reasonably stated and is free of material misstatement.

Budget to Actual Comparison

The Finer Things Company
Budget to Actual Comparison
20X6 Budget compared to 20X5 Actual

	Budget 20X6	Actual 20X5	$ Change F/(U)	% Change F/(U)	
Sales, net of returns & allowances	4,900,000	4,184,650	715,350	17.1%	[1]
Less: cost of goods sold	(2,136,400)	(1,824,300)	(312,100)	17.1%	[1]
Net sales	2,763,600	2,360,350	403,250	17.1%	[1]
Other Income	11,000	11,000	-	0.0%	
Net revenue	2,774,600	2,371,350	403,250	17.0%	
Compensation expense	1,152,733	1,130,130	22,603	2.0%	[2]
Legal and professional expense	120,000	116,700	3,300	2.8%	[3]
Facilities expense	712,000	680,000	32,000	4.7%	[3]
Depreciation expense	43,000	43,000	-	0.0%	[4]
Other expense	395,000	294,660	100,340	34.1%	[5]
Total expense	2,422,733	2,264,490	158,243	7.0%	
Net operating revenue	351,867	106,860	245,007	229.3%	[1]
Income taxes	110,563	94,860	15,703	16.6%	[6]
Net revenue	241,304	12,000	229,304	1910.9%	[7]

F/(U) = favorable/(unfavorable)

[1]   Increase appears reasonable due to opening new store.
[2]   Expected higher increase due to opening new store. However, per client discussion, staff was moved to different locations in lieu of making additional hires. More hiring to come in 20X7.
[3]   Increase consistent with prior year increases.
[4]   Appears reasonable as no new Furniture & Fixtures additions.
[5]   Based on discussion with client, appears reasonable due to costs associated with opening new store.
[6]   Increase is consistent with increase in net revenue.
[7]   The Finer Things has accomplished its goal of increasing revenue while holding expenses to less of an increase.

Comments:

11. <u>Conclusion: Per discussions with client and audit work performed, year-end results for December 31, 20X6 and 20X5, appear reasonable. Overall results are consistent with our understanding of The Finer Things Company.</u>

Items for Analysis

Decrease in Cash & Cash Equivalents is reasonable because net income also decreased.

1. Choose an option below:

   - [Original text] Decrease in Cash & Cash Equivalents is reasonable because net income also decreased.

   - [Delete text]

   - Decrease in Cash & Cash Equivalents is not reasonable because net income also decreased.

   - Decrease in Cash & Cash Equivalents is reasonable because net income increased.

   - Decrease in Cash & Cash Equivalents is not reasonable because net income increased.

Increase in Inventory is reasonable due to addition of fourth store.

2. Choose an option below:

   - [Original text] Increase in Inventory is reasonable due to addition of fourth store.

   - [Delete text]

   - Decrease in Inventory is reasonable due to addition of fourth store.

   - Increase in Inventory is not reasonable due to addition of fourth store.

   - Decrease in Inventory is not reasonable due to addition of fourth store.

Notes Receivable decrease is consistent with decrease in Cash & Cash Equivalents.

3. Choose an option below:

   - [Original text] Notes Receivable decrease is consistent with decrease in Cash & Cash Equivalents.

   - [Delete text]

   - Notes Receivable decrease is inconsistent with decrease in Cash & Cash Equivalents.

   - Notes Receivable decrease is proportional with decrease in Cash & Cash Equivalents.

   - Notes Receivable decrease is unrelated to decrease in Cash & Cash Equivalents.

Increase in Buildings, at cost is reasonable due to Centre Building purchase.

4. Choose an option below:

   - [Original text] Increase in Buildings, at cost is reasonable due to Centre Building purchase.

   - [Delete text]

   - Increase in Buildings, at cost is unreasonable due to Centre Building purchase.

   - Increase in Buildings, at cost is reasonable due to Centre Building capital lease and leasehold improvements.

   - Increase in Buildings, at cost is unreasonable due to Centre Building capital lease and leasehold improvements.

   - Increase in Buildings, at cost is reasonable due to Centre Building purchase and the resulting leasehold improvements.

- Increase in Buildings, at cost is unreasonable due to Centre Building purchase and the resulting leasehold improvements.

Compared Accumulated Depreciation as a % of Furniture and Fixtures. The percentage increased slightly from 75% in 20X5 to 78% in 20X6. Change is too immaterial to investigate.

5. Choose an option below:

   - [Original text] Compared Accumulated Depreciation as a % of Furniture and Fixtures. The percentage increased slightly from 75% in 20X5 to 78% in 20X6. Change is too immaterial to investigate.

   - [Delete text]

   - Compared Accumulated Depreciation as a % of Furniture and Fixtures. The percentage decreased slightly from 78% in 20X5 to 75% in 20X6. Change is too immaterial to investigate.

   - Compared Accumulated Depreciation to Depreciation Expense. Accumulated Depreciation for Furniture & Fixtures is reasonable as it is equal to Depreciation Expense for the year.

   - Compared Accumulated Depreciation to Depreciation Expense. Accumulated Depreciation for Furniture & Fixtures is reasonable as its change from 20X5 is equal to Depreciation Expense for the year for 20X6.

Increase in Accounts Payable is reasonable due to addition of another store and due to its inverse relationship with Accrued Expenses.

6. Choose an option below:

   - [Original text] Increase in Accounts Payable is reasonable due to addition of another store and due to its inverse relationship with Accrued Expenses.

   - [Delete text]

   - Increase in Accounts Payable is reasonable due to its inverse relationship with Accrued Expenses.

   - Increase in Accounts Payable is reasonable due to its proportional relationship with Accrued Expenses.

   - Increase in Accounts Payable is reasonable due to the addition of another store.

Minimal increase in Taxes Payable; too immaterial to investigate.

7. Choose an option below:

   - [Original text] Minimal increase in Taxes Payable; too immaterial to investigate.

   - [Delete text]

   - Minimal increase in Taxes Payable; amount appears reasonable.

   - Minimal increase in Taxes Payable; too material to investigate.

   - Minimal increase in Taxes Payable; further investigation required.

Decrease in Accrued Expenses is reasonable due to its inverse relationship to Accounts Payable.

8. Choose an option below:

    - [Original text] Decrease in Accrued Expenses is reasonable due to its inverse relationship to Accounts Payable.

    - [Delete text]

    - Decrease in Accrued Expenses is not reasonable due to its inverse relationship to Accounts Payable.

    - Decrease in Accrued Expenses is reasonable due to its direct relationship to Accounts Payable.

    - Decrease in Accrued Expenses is not reasonable due to its direct relationship to Accounts Payable.

Notes Payable balance of $577,000 is reasonable due to purchase of Centre Building. As there was no Note Payable at December 31, 20X5, the 20X5 balance is appropriately shown as $0.

9. Choose an option below:

    - [Original text] Notes Payable balance of $577,000 is reasonable due to purchase of Centre Building. As there was no Note Payable at December 31, 20X5, the 20X5 balance is appropriately shown as $0.

    - [Delete text]

    - Notes Payable balance of $577,000 due to purchase of Centre Building is incorrect. Since the Centre Building is appropriately classified as an asset, this liability should be removed from the Balance Sheet.

    - Notes Payable balance of $577,000 due to purchase of Centre Building is incorrect, as the dollar amount is incorrect. As there was no Note Payable at December 31, 20X5, the 20X5 balance is appropriately shown as $0.

    - Notes Payable balance of $577,000 is reasonable due to purchase of Centre Building. However, the Notes Payable balance at December 31, 20X5, is incorrect. Since The Finer Things knew that the Centre Building transaction was scheduled to close on January 2, 20X6, the Note Payable qualifies as a subsequent event, and should be reflected on the December 31, 20X5, Balance Sheet as well.

Conclusion: Based on end-of-audit analytics performed, Balance Sheet is reasonably stated and is free of material misstatement.

10. Choose an option below:

- [Original text] Conclusion: Based on end-of-audit analytics performed, Balance Sheet is reasonably stated and is free of material misstatement.

- [Delete text]

- Conclusion: Balance Sheet is reasonably stated.

- Conclusion: Based on end-of-audit analytics performed, Balance Sheet is not reasonably stated and is not free of material misstatement.

- Conclusion: Balance Sheet is not reasonably stated.

Conclusion: Per discussions with client and audit work performed, year-end results for December 31, 20X6 and 20X5, appear reasonable. Overall results are consistent with our understanding of The Finer Things Company.

11. Choose an option below:

- [Original text] Conclusion: Per discussions with client and audit work performed, year-end results for December 31, 20X6 and 20X5, appear reasonable. Overall results are consistent with our understanding of The Finer Things Company.

- [Delete text]

- Conclusion: Per discussions with client, audit work, and analytical procedures performed, year-end results for December 31, 20X6 and 20X5, appear reasonable. Overall results are consistent with our understanding of The Finer Things Company.

- Conclusion: Per discussions with client and analytical procedures performed, year-end results for December 31, 20X6 and 20X5, appear reasonable. Overall results are consistent with our understanding of The Finer Things Company.

- Conclusion: Per analytical procedures and audit work performed, year-end results for December 31, 20X6 and 20X5, appear reasonable. Overall results are consistent with our understanding of The Finer Things Company.

Resources/Exhibits

Comparative Draft Financial Statements

The Finer Things Company
Balance Sheets - Draft for Discussion Purposes Only
December 31, 20X6 and 20X5

	20X6	20X5
Cash & Cash Equivalents	1,553,805	1,723,915
Accounts Receivable	292,370	297,500
Less: allowance for doubtful accounts	-	-
Prepaid Expenses	44,690	41,940
Inventory - Goods Held for Sale	788,650	363,530
Notes Receivable	460,000	540,000
Total Current Assets	3,139,515	2,966,885
Buildings, at cost	577,000	-
Furniture & Fixtures	760,000	760,000
Less: accumulated depreciation	(600,000)	(570,000)
Other Fixed Assets	65,000	65,000
Less: accumulated depreciation	(39,000)	(26,000)
Total Long-term Assets	763,000	229,000
Total Assets	3,902,515	3,195,885

	20X6	20X5
Current Liabilities:		
Accounts Payable	347,800	218,400
Taxes Payable	124,640	123,950
Accrued Expenses	47,850	53,910
Total Current Liabilities	520,290	396,260
Long-term Liabilities:		
Notes Payable	577,000	-
Total Liabilities	1,097,290	396,260
Common Stock	2,250,000	2,250,000
Retained Earnings	555,225	549,625
Total Equity	2,805,225	2,799,625
Total Liabilities and Equity	3,902,515	3,195,885

The Finer Things Company
Income Statements - Draft for Discussion Purposes Only
For the years ended December 31, 20X6 and 20X5

	20X6	20X5
Sales, net of returns & allowances	4,534,030	4,184,650
Less: cost of goods sold	(1,925,965)	(1,824,300)
Net sales	2,608,065	2,360,350
Other Income	12,000	11,000
Net revenue	2,620,065	2,371,350
Compensation expense	1,213,220	1,130,130
Legal and professional expense	164,200	116,700
Facilities expense	742,340	680,000
Depreciation expense	43,000	43,000
Other expense	403,405	294,660
Total expense	2,566,165	2,264,490
Net operating revenue	53,900	106,860
Income taxes	48,300	94,860
Net revenue	5,600	12,000

Analytical Procedures Computations

The Finer Things Company
Analytical Procedures Computations
December 31, 20X6 and 20X5

Ratio (Formula)	20X6 Result	20X5 Result
Working Capital (Current Assets - Current Liabilities)	2,619,225	2,927,259
Current Ratio (Current Assets / Current Liabilities)	6.03	7.49
Quick Ratio ((Cash + Net Receivables) / Current Liabilities)	4.43	6.46
Inventory Turnover (Cost of Goods Sold / Average Inventory)	3.34	4.68
Days Supply in Average Inventory (360 / Inventory Turnover)	107.78	76.92
Debt to Equity Ratio (Total Debt / Total Equity)	0.39	0.14
Debt to Total Assets (Total Debt / Total Assets)	0.28	0.12

Trial Balances

The Finer Things Company
Year Ended December 31, 20X6
Preclosing, Unadjusted Trial Balance

Account No.	Account Description		Year 20X6 Debit	Year 20X6 Credit	Year 20X5 Debit	Year 20X5 Credit
1101	Cash - checking account 1234567		610,205		841,785	
1102	Cash - payroll account 1234568		93,250		81,780	
1103	Cash - CD		850,000		800,000	
1110	Petty Cash		350		350	
1201	Account Receivable - credit card companies		292,370		297,500	
1202	Allowance for Doubtful accounts		-		-	
1301	Prepaid Insurance		43,400		41,000	
1302	Other Prepaid Expenses		1,290		940	
1401	Inventory - Goods held for sale		788,650		363,530	
1501	Notes Receivable		460,000		540,000	
1601	Furniture and Fixtures		760,000		760,000	
1602	Accumulated Depreciation, Furniture & Fixtures			600,000		570,000
1603	Vehicle - Park		65,000		65,000	
1604	Accumulated Depreciation, Vehicle			39,000		26,000
1605	Centre Building		577,000		-	
2101	Accounts Payable			347,800		218,400
2201	Sales Tax Payable			27,860		46,450
2202	Payroll Tax Payable			81,400		67,500
2203	Income Taxes Payable			15,380		10,000
2301	Accrued Expenses			47,850		53,910
2601	Notes Payable			577,000		-
3101	Common Stock			2,250,000		2,250,000
3201	Retained Earnings			549,625		537,625
3301	Dividends Paid					
4101	Sales Revenue - Store 1			2,500,000		2,340,000
4102	Sales Revenue - Store 2			990,000		1,060,000
4103	Sales Revenue - Store 3			699,700		847,000
4104	Sales Revenue - Internet Store			450,000		175,000
4105	Sales Revenue - Store 4			127,400		-
4150	Sales Returns, Allowances, Discounts		233,070		237,350	
4200	Bank Interest Income			12,000		11,000
6101	Sales Expense - Cost of Goods Sold		1,882,965		1,808,800	
6102	Sales Expense - Shipping Expense		43,000		15,500	
6201	Payroll Expense - Partners	c	330,000		300,000	
6202	Payroll Expense - Employees	c	447,020		461,770	
6203	Benefits Expense - Partners	c	92,500		87,600	
6204	Benefits Expense - Employees	c	164,100		142,560	
6301	Legal Fees	LP	89,200		46,700	
6302	Accounting and Auditing Fees	LP	75,000		70,000	

Account No.	Account Description		Year 20X6		Year 20X5	
			Debit	**Credit**	**Debit**	**Credit**
6401	Rent Expense	f	398,000		380,000	
6402	Repairs and Maintenance Expense	f	37,600		35,400	
6403	Store Supplies Expense	f	23,200		22,700	
7101	Utilities Expense	f	283,540		241,900	
7102	Office Supplies Expense	o	2,870		2,760	
7301	Miscellaneous Expense	o	329,375		266,900	
7302	Dividend Expense	o	25,000		25,000	
7501	Depreciation Expense, Furniture & Fixtures		43,000		43,000	
7901	Interest Expense	o	46,160			
8101	Payroll Tax Expense	c	179,600		138,200	
8102	Income Taxes Expense		48,300		94,860	
			9,315,015	9,315,015	8,212,885	8,212,885
	Variance		-		-	
	5,600		4,773,500	4,779,100		
	Note: net income not yet closed into retained earnings			5,600		12,000

Document Review Simulation Solution 1

Comments

(Worksheet portion omitted for brevity.)

1. [Delete text]

2. [Delete text]

3. [Delete text]

4. [Original text] Increase in Buildings, at cost is reasonable due to Centre building purchase.

5. Compared Accumulated Depreciation to Depreciation Expense. Accumulated Depreciation for Furniture & Fixtures is reasonable as its change from 20X5 is equal to Depreciation Expense for the year for 20X6.

6. [Delete text]

7. [Original text] Minimal increase in Taxes Payable; to immaterial to investigate.

8. [Delete text]

9. Notes Payable balance of $577,000 due to purchase of Centre Building is incorrect, as the dollar amount is incorrect. As there was no Note Payable at December 31, 20X5, the 20X5 balance is appropriately shown as $0.

10. [Delete text]

(Worksheet portion omitted for brevity.)

11. [Delete text]

Explanations

1. [Delete text]

    The change in Cash & Cash Equivalents is unrelated to the change in Net Income. You should instruct the senior associate to (1) meet with the client to discuss the reasons for the $170,110 decrease in Cash & Cash Equivalents and obtain appropriate documentation to support the client's statements, (2) review the audit workpapers once again, and (3) review the Statement of Cash Flows. After the senior associate has finished these steps, he should update the Balance Sheet Fluctuation Analysis with a better explanation of the decrease in Cash & Cash Equivalents.

2. [Delete text]

    While the addition of a fourth store may have contributed to a portion of the Inventory increase, it does not make sense that increasing the number of stores by 33.3% would cause Inventory to increase by 116.9%. You should instruct the senior associate to (1) meet with the client to discuss the reasons for the $425,120 increase in Inventory and to obtain appropriate documentation to support the client's statements, (2) review the audit workpapers once again, and (3) compute the Inventory Turnover Ratio (Cost of Goods Sold divided by Average Inventory). A very low Inventory Ratio may identify obsolete or slow-moving inventory that needs to be written down or written off in the valuation of Ending Inventory. A write down may have a material effect on the financial statements. After the senior associate has completed these procedures, he should update the Balance Sheet Fluctuation Analysis with a better explanation for the increase in Inventory.

3. [Delete text]

    A decrease in Notes Receivable would either generate an increase in Cash & Cash Equivalents (if payment is received) or an increase in Miscellaneous Expense (if an amount is written off as a bad debt expense). Since Cash & Cash Equivalents decreased year over year, its change is not related to the change in the Notes Receivable line item. You should instruct the senior associate to (1) meet with the client to discuss the reasons for the $80,000 decrease in Notes Receivable and to obtain appropriate documentation to support the client's statements, and (2) review the audit workpapers once again. After the senior associate has completed these procedures, he should update the Balance Sheet Fluctuation Analysis with a better explanation of the decrease in Notes Receivable. The answer is not "Notes Receivable decrease is inconsistent with decrease in Cash & Cash Equivalents" as the comments ideally indicate that the accounts are materially accurate, indicate what change is necessary to make them so, or refer the reader to other workpapers that do.

4. [Original text] Increase in Buildings, at cost is reasonable due to Centre Building purchase.

    The background information states that The Finer Things closed on its purchase of Centre Building on January 2, 20X6, for a price of $577,000. Since The Finer Things owns the Centre Building, there are no leasehold improvements resulting from this purchase.

5. Compared Accumulated Depreciation to Depreciation Expense. Accumulated Depreciation for Furniture & Fixtures is reasonable as its change from 20X5 is equal to Depreciation Expense for the year for 20X6.

    There is not necessarily any relationship between Furniture & Fixtures and Accumulated Depreciation, other than the fact that Accumulated Depreciation should never exceed the total of Furniture & Fixtures—making any variance meaningless. However, there is a relationship between Furniture & Fixtures and Depreciation Expense on Furniture & Fixtures that reflects the average useful life of the assets, which is the basis for the calculation of the annual expense. Unless a company disposes of an item, the change in Accumulated Depreciation should equal Depreciation Expense for the year. The Furniture & Fixtures balance is the same as the previous year, indicating no disposals.

6. [Delete text]

There is no relationship between Accounts Payable and Accrued Expenses. While the addition of a fourth store may have contributed to a portion of the Accounts Payable increase, it does not necessarily make sense that increasing the number of stores by 33.3% would cause Accounts Payable to increase by 59.2%. You should instruct the senior associate to (1) meet with the client to discuss the reasons for the $129,400 increase in Accounts Payable and to obtain appropriate documentation to support the client's statements and (2) review the audit workpapers once again. After the senior associate has followed these procedures, he should update the Balance Sheet Fluctuation Analysis to provide a better explanation of the increase in Accounts Payable.

7. [Original text] Minimal increase in Taxes Payable; too immaterial to investigate.

The auditor can rely on the combination of testing of the Payables system that was performed during the interim planning and testing phase and any substantive tests performed during the year-end fieldwork phase to ensure that the balance is reasonable. As a result of this assurance, there is no need to investigate a 0.6% change.

8. [Delete text]

There is no relationship between Accounts Payable and Accrued Expenses. You should instruct the senior associate to (1) meet with the client to discuss the reasons for the $6,060 decrease in Accrued Expenses and to obtain appropriate documentation to support the client's statements and (2) review the audit workpapers once again. After the senior associate has followed these procedures, he should update the Balance Sheet Fluctuation Analysis to provide a better explanation of the decrease in Accrued Expenses.

9. Notes Payable balance of $577,000 due to purchase of Centre Building is incorrect, as the dollar amount is incorrect. As there was no Note Payable at December 31, 20X5, the 20X5 balance is appropriately shown as $0.

The background information states that The Finer Things closed on the Centre Building on January 2, 20X6, utilizing a nine-year note, which requires equal payments due each January 1. However, the Balance Sheet amount is incorrect. There is a payment due on January 1, 20X7, which should be shown in a Current Liability line item of "Short term Portion of Long term Debt." The December 31, 20X6, Notes Payable amount should be $577,000 less the amount of the short-term portion of the long-term debt. The December 31, 20X5, balance is appropriately shown to be $0. Since the purchase was not completed and the note payable was not signed until January 2, 20X6, there is no subsequent event affecting the financial statement amounts at December 31, 20X5, although The Finer Things should have disclosed the transaction in the Notes to the December 31, 20X5, Financial Statements.

10. [Delete text]

At this time, the auditor cannot determine whether the Balance Sheet is reasonably stated for several reasons, including: (1) The auditor needs to obtain more information about the changes in Cash & Cash Equivalents, Inventory, Notes Receivable, Accounts Payable, and

Accrued Expenses. (2) The auditor also did not comment upon the changes in Accounts Receivable or Prepaid Expenses, which may indicate that the work in that area is incomplete. (3) The Balance Sheet does not break out the current portion of long-term debt. (4) Additionally, there is no Accumulated Depreciation line item for Buildings, at cost (nor is there any Depreciation Expense present in the Trial Balance for Buildings), which indicates another potential problem with the financial statements. (5) There is no explanation as to why there is no increase to Furniture & Fixtures, despite the opening of a new store. There is still quite a bit of work to be done on this engagement in order to form a proper opinion on the financial statements.

11. [Delete text]

While the comparisons and client explanations appear reasonable, there is a fundamental flaw in this workpaper. When performing analytical procedures, the data being compared must include at least one amount from the actual results of the period under audit, which is year ended December 31, 20X6. The December 31, 20X5, Income Statement already was audited and reported upon in the prior year audit. Budgeted amounts are neither audited nor reported upon. The manager needs to instruct the senior associate to delete the entire workpaper, and to complete a new analysis of 20X6 Budget amounts compared to 20X6 Actual amounts. This workpaper underscores the importance of properly supervising the work of staff.

Section 5 – Audit Sampling

Corresponding Lectures

Watch the following course lectures with this section:

Lecture 5.01 – Audit Sampling
Lecture 5.02 – Attribute Sampling
Lecture 5.03 – Variables Sampling
Lecture 5.04 – Audit Sampling – Class Questions
Lecture 5.05 – Probability Proportional to Size Sampling
Lecture 5.06 – Probability Proportional to Size Sampling – Class Questions

EXAM NOTE: *Please refer to the AICPA AUD Blueprint in the Introduction of this book to find a listing of the representative tasks (and their associated skill levels—i.e., Remembering and Understanding, Application, Analysis, and Evaluation) that the candidate should be able to perform based on the knowledge obtained in this section.*

Audit Sampling

AUDIT SAMPLING

AU-C Section 530, Audit Sampling refers to the examination of **less than 100%** of a population and using the results as a basis for drawing a **general conclusion** on the entire population. Since there is far more data available than an auditor will have time to examine during an audit, the use of sampling is an essential technique.

Audit Risk

- Risk of Material Misstatement (RMM)
  - *Inherent Risk* (IR)
  - *Control Risk* (CR)
- Detection Risk (DR)
  - *Test of Details Risk* (TD)
  - *Substantive Analytical Procedures Risk* (AP)
  - **Nonsampling Risk** (Human error, misinterpreting audit test results, not recognizing misstatements in documents audited)
    - The risk that test results will be misinterpreted due to human error, such as not recognizing a misstatement in items being audited. Nonsampling error is reduced by using qualified staff and through adequate supervision and review.

  - **Sampling Risk** (Bad Sample, Sample is not representative of population) – Risk of drawing wrong conclusion.
    - The risk that a sample will not be representative of the population, causing the auditor to draw an invalid conclusion on the basis of the test results.

    - **Type I – Efficiency Error** (Alpha risk)
      - Population is okay but based on the sample, don't rely.
        - **Under-rely** on internal control = assess **RMM ↑**
        - **Incorrectly reject** an account balance for substantive testing purposes (less efficient audit).
        - A type I risk, or alpha risk, is the risk that the sample will have disproportionately more errors than the population. This may cause the auditor to perform additional procedures to obtain sufficient appropriate evidence that the assertion is not misrepresented, or may cause the auditor to reject the assertion, potentially affecting the auditor's report.

    - **Type II – Less Effective** (Beta risk)
      - Population is bad but based on the sample, the auditor believes everything is correct.
        - **Over-rely** on internal control = assess **RMM↓**
        - **Incorrectly accept** an account balance for substantive testing purposes (less effective audit).

- A type II risk, or beta risk, is the risk that the sample will have disproportionately fewer errors than the population. This may cause the auditor to accept a control as effective even though it is not or accept an assertion that is actually misrepresented. The result may be an ineffective engagement with the issuance of an unmodified report despite a material misstatement to the financial statements.

Sampling is used both in the tests of controls and in substantive testing:

1. During the **internal control phase** of the audit, the auditor will perform **tests of controls** on a sample basis to determine the operating effectiveness of controls they plan to rely on.

2. During the **substantive testing phase** of the audit, the auditor will perform **tests of details** of transactions, accounts, and disclosures on a sample basis to obtain sufficient appropriate audit evidence to support management assertions.

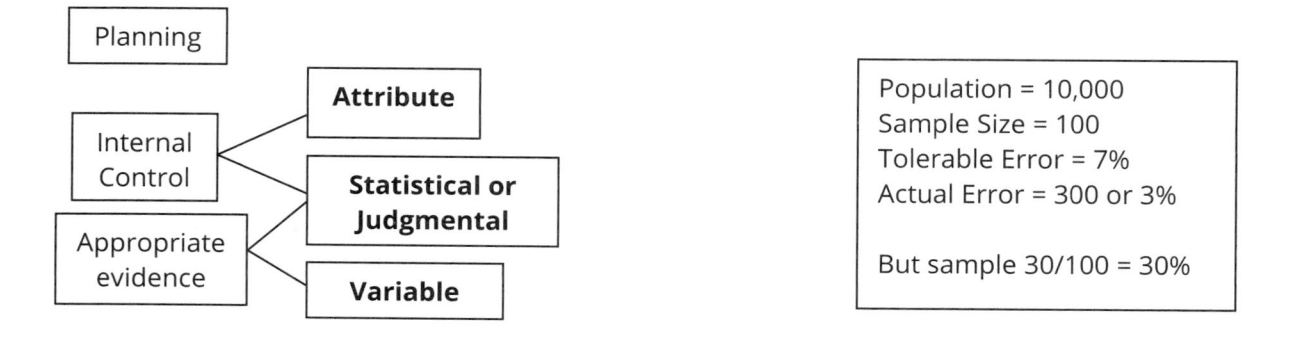

Sampling is **not** practical for all parts of the audit. In **gaining an understanding of the internal control structure** and **documenting the understanding**, the auditor cannot simply look at a part of the structure and use that as a basis for claiming understanding of the entirety. During substantive testing, the application of **analytical procedures** to some accounts cannot be considered evidence applicable to all of the accounts.

The primary risk in sampling is that you may draw a conclusion from the sample that is different from the conclusion you would have drawn if you had examined the entire population (Risk of drawing the incorrect conclusion).

In the case of **tests of controls**, the auditor will be examining the implementation of a control activity in order to ensure that the client doesn't deviate from the control more often than the auditor considers tolerable. The auditor will apply judgment in establishing a **tolerable deviation rate**, which is the percentage of times a control not being applied that would not cause the auditor to consider the control ineffective. This will be compared to the actual percentage of items examined in the sample to which the control was not being properly applied, the **true deviation rate**.

- If the **true deviation rate** of the population is **lower** than the **tolerable deviation rate**, then the auditor will want to rely on the control, **reducing the assessed RMM** and increasing the acceptable level of DR. This will result in the auditor not performing as many substantive tests in drawing an audit conclusion in relation to the control's effectiveness.

- If the **true deviation rate** is **higher** than the **tolerable deviation rate**, then the auditor will not want to rely on the control, **increasing the assessed RMM** and reducing the acceptable level of DR. This will result in the auditor performing a greater amount of substantive testing before drawing an audit conclusion as to the effectiveness of the control.

The sampling technique normally applied to tests of controls is called **attribute sampling**. There are **two** different sampling risks associated with attribute sampling:

- The auditor may conclude from the sample that the deviation rate is lower than the tolerable rate, but the overall population has a true deviation rate that is higher than the tolerable rate. Based on the sample, the auditor will improperly rely on the control. This is known as the risk of **assessing the Risk of Material Misstatements too low**. The consequence of this risk is that the auditor will not do a sufficient amount of substantive testing, and may fail to uncover material misstatements in the financial statements under audit. This means the audit will be **ineffective** and not achieve its goals.

- The auditor may conclude from the sample that the deviation rate is higher than the tolerable rate, but the overall population has a true deviation rate that is lower than the tolerable rate. Based on the sample, the auditor will improperly choose not to rely on the control. This is known as the risk of **assessing the Risk of Material Misstatements too high**. The consequence of this risk is that the auditor will do more substantive testing than was necessary for the audit conclusions. The audit will be effective, but the unnecessary additional substantive means the audit will be **inefficient**.

		Actual Population	
		Good	**Bad**
Sample Results	**Good**	Appropriately Rely	Over-rely
	Bad	Under-rely	Appropriately Don't rely

During substantive **tests of details** of transactions and accounts, the auditor is attempting to determine if an account balance is materially correct. The form of sampling normally used is called **variable estimation sampling.** The two sampling risks are:

- Based on the sample, the auditor may estimate an amount that is close enough to the recorded amount for the auditor to conclude that the number is materially correct, when the amount is actually materially misstated. This is known as the risk of **incorrect acceptance**. The result will be that the auditor draws an inappropriate conclusion, so that the audit is **ineffective**.

- Based on the sample, the auditor may estimate an amount that is different enough from the recorded amount for the auditor to decide that the number is materially misstated, when the amount is actually materially correct. This is known as the risk of **incorrect rejection**. The result will be that the auditor performs a large amount of additional substantive tests on the amount, finally determining that the recorded amount was, in fact, correct. The result will be that the auditor's conclusion is correct, but an unnecessary amount of additional substantive testing takes place, so that the audit is **inefficient.**

The technique known as **statistical sampling** refers to the use of quantitative measures of the risks the auditor is taking in the use of sampling. Formulas are used to determine the sample size necessary to achieve a specified level of risk of the sample results not being consistent with the entire population. The auditor will still have to **use judgment** to determine what level of risk is acceptable.

An auditor using **non-statistical sampling** (Judgmental sampling) will determine the appropriate sample size by deciding what makes them comfortable that their conclusions are correct. In practice, the lack of mathematical certainty as to the appropriate sample size causes auditors using non-statistical sampling to overestimate the needed sample size in order to feel comfortable with the conclusions. This means the audit will still be effective, but not as efficient as it might have been using statistical techniques to determine a sufficient sample size.

In both approaches, however, the same sampling risks exist. To summarize these risks:

	Internal Control **(Tests of Controls)** **Attribute Sampling**	**Substantive Testing** **(Tests of Details)** **Variable Estimation Sampling**
Consequences to Audit:		
Ineffective	**Assessing RMM Too Low**	**Incorrect Acceptance**
Inefficient	**Assessing RMM Too High**	**Incorrect Rejection**

Naturally, an auditor is more concerned about an audit being ineffective than inefficient. In particular, when the cost of additional testing is low, the auditor will often allow higher risks of assessing control risk too high and incorrect rejection.

Lecture 5.02

ATTRIBUTE SAMPLING

The risks associated with attribute sampling are the risk of assessing RMM too high, which will result in an *inefficient* engagement, and the risk of assessing RMM too low, which will result in an *ineffective* engagement. The risk of an ineffective engagement is greater since that means that users will rely on financial statements that should not be relied upon. As a result, the auditor will seek to reduce the risk of assessing RMM too low by making certain that the sample size is appropriate.

Factors affecting sample size in an attribute sample include:
- The **tolerable rate of error**, which has an **inverse** relationship to sample size. When a control is not significant and, as a result, the auditor is not as concerned about whether or not it is being followed properly, the auditor will use a smaller sample size, which is less likely to be representative of the population.
- The **expected rate of error**, which has a **direct** relationship to sample size. When the auditor expects that a control is not operating as intended, the auditor will seek a sample size that is adequately large to make certain that there are likely to be a representative number of exceptions in the sample to reflect the error rate in the population.
- The **acceptable risk** of assessing RMM too low, which has an **inverse** relationship to sample size. When a high assessment of RMM is acceptable, the auditor is not concerned about errors that will result from the control not being applied properly and is less likely to be concerned about an accurate measure of the degree to which it is not being complied with.

- To summarize:
    - Internal control – tests of controls

- Two risks
  - Assessing **Risk of Material Misstatement too low** – audit ineffective
  - Assessing **Risk of Material Misstatement too high** – audit inefficient
- Factors affecting **sample size**
  - Tolerable rate – Inverse effect
  - Expected rate – Direct effect
  - Acceptable risk – Inverse effect
- Evaluation of sample results
  - Sample rate plus allowance for sampling risk
  - Must not exceed tolerable rate or else auditor must modify planned reliance

There are various types of attribute sampling. These include:
- **Attribute sampling,** or fixed sample-size attribute sampling, used to estimate the rate of deviations in the population.
- **Stop-or-go sampling (Sequential sampling)** is a special type of attribute sampling which allows the auditor to stop when sufficient data is gathered. It is appropriate when the expected deviation rate is low and may provide the auditor with the most efficient sample size in an attribute sampling plan. The sample is selected in several steps and each step relies on the results of the previous step. By selecting sequential samples, the auditor may stop sampling if no deviations are found.
- **Discovery sampling** is also a special type of attribute sampling and is used when the expected deviation rate is very low, near zero. The sample size in this method is usually large enough to find at least one deviation if it exists. Discovery sample sizes and discovery sampling tables are designed to measure the probability of at least one error occurring in a sample if the error rate in the population exceeds the tolerable rate.

When performing tests of controls, the form of sampling that is typically used is **attribute sampling,** which refers to examining a sample of items from a population to determine what percentage of them contain a specific attribute. Notice that attribute sampling cannot be used to verify a quantity or dollar amount, since it only provides information on the presence or absence of something, not its size.

Sampling applies to tests of controls when the auditor needs to decide whether a rate of deviation is equal to or less than a tolerable rate. However, sampling does not apply to risk assessment procedures performed to obtain an understanding of internal control. Furthermore, sampling concepts may not apply to some tests of controls, such as the following: (1) tests of automated application; (2) analyses of controls for determining appropriate segregation of duties or other analyses that do not examine documentary evidence of performance; (3) tests of certain documented controls or analyses of the effectiveness of security and access controls; or (4) tests directed toward obtaining audit evidence about the operation of the control environment or accounting system.

The "**attribute**" or **characteristic** that the auditor is looking to find is a deviation from the proper application of the internal control activity being tested. For example, the auditor, while gaining an understanding of the internal control structure, might have identified a control activity requiring the authorization by an officer of all purchase requisitions. If the auditor considers this a potential strength and wants to rely on the control, it must be tested to determine its operating effectiveness. The auditor will pull a sample from the population of purchase requisitions, and see how many in the sample did not include proper authorization. Failure to authorize is the attribute or **deviation**, being sought.

A few items should be considered **when performing attribute sampling:**

- It is considered a deviation when the client cannot provide the document the auditor wishes to examine, as well as when the document fails to demonstrate the application of the control being tested.
- For each deviation that is identified, the auditor should consider the **qualitative** issues as well as quantitative. If a deviation gives evidence of **fraud** committed by an employee, the auditor must consider the **broader implications** of that employee's impact on company operations and financial information as a whole, not limited to the specific control being tested.
- When a deviation from control is identified, this doesn't mean there is a misstatement in the financial statements as a result. For example, the failure of a purchase to be properly authorized does not mean it wasn't correctly processed and accounted for in the financial records. **Deviation** at a particular **rate** will usually result in actual **misstatements** at a much **lower rate**.

Attribute sampling is appropriate for tests involving **reperformance** or **inspection**, where there is an identifiable population of documents or records from which the auditor can select a sample, but is **not** normally appropriate for tests involving **inquiry** or **observation,** since each inquiry usually is made only once, and sample observations can rarely be performed randomly through the year so as to be representative of the entire year.

In order to determine the appropriate **sample size**, the auditor using attribute sampling will consider three different key factors (**TEA**):

1. **Tolerable deviation rate** – This refers to the percentage of time a control can be violated but still lead the auditor to believe it is operating effectively. It is rarely a problem if a control is not followed on occasion, and since the auditor treats the inability to locate a document as a deviation (which might not be a true violation of the control but simply a problem with the ability of the client personnel to locate the evidence for the auditor), some deviations are normally considered acceptable. The auditor's decision as to the tolerable rate is based on the importance of the control being tested and the impact that each deviation could have on the accuracy of the financial statement assertions.
   - **Tolerable deviation rate has an inverse effect on sample size**.
   - If the auditor is willing to tolerate a large number of deviations, a smaller sample will be able to satisfy the auditor that the true deviation rate is within these high acceptable limits.

2. **Expected deviation rate** – This refers to the percentage of time the auditor expects the control to have been violated. Clearly, the true deviation rate must be lower than the tolerable rate in order for the auditor to rely on a control. If the deviation rate in a sample is only **slightly** lower than the tolerable rate, though, the auditor will have a problem due to the lack of precision of results.
   - If, for example, in a sample size of 10 items, there is 1 deviation, the deviation rate in the sample is 10%.
   - Based on such a small sample size, the auditor might conclude that the deviation rate in the population is approximately 10%, but could not conclude that the deviation rate in the population is approximately 10%.
     - If the tolerable rate is close to 10%, such as 11%, the auditor may conclude that the potential deviation rate in the population is too high and will decide not to rely on the control.
     - If the tolerable rate is considerably higher than 10%, such as 15%, the auditor may conclude that it is likely, based on that sample, that the actual deviation

rate in the population is likely to be below that rate and the auditor may decide to rely on the control.

- o The **expected deviation rate has a direct effect on sample size**. The closer the expected rate gets to the tolerable limit, the larger the sample size the auditor will need to provide results that are precise enough.

3. **Allowable risk of assessing risk of material misstatement (RMM) too low** – This refers to the risk the auditor is taking that the sample will cause them to rely on the control when the true deviation rate of the population was high enough that they should not have relied. There is always a possibility that the sample results are so unrepresentative of the population that a sample which appears to suggest few deviations was drawn from a population in which there were many.

- o **The Allowable risk of assessing the risk of material misstatement too low has an inverse effect on sample size**.
- o if the auditor is willing to accept a large risk of drawing the wrong conclusion, they can reduce the size of the sample.

The first letters of the three factors spell out **TEA**, which is a mnemonic to remind you that if statistical sampling is your cup of tea, you'll need to know what factors to put into the calculation of sample size.

In determining sample size, the auditor does **not** need to know the size of the population. Although an increase in the population size would seem to suggest the need for a larger sample, the effect is actually minimal, and the auditor can simplify the calculations by simply assuming a population of infinite size. In political polling, people are often surprised that the results of polling only a few hundred people can often produce estimates about the sentiment of voters throughout the nation that prove extremely accurate. Similarly, if you flipped a coin 1,000 times and it came up heads around 500 times, you'd probably feel comfortable that it was an honest coin, and not think that flipping it 1,000,000 times would make the slightest difference.

Many populations of items, such as invoices, that the auditor is sampling from may number in the thousands. This is sufficiently large such that the appropriate sample size for that population will be about the same as the sample size needed out for a population of many times as many transactions, even if they number in the billions or more. As a result, there is no need to know the population size to determine an adequate sample size in the audit.

Once a sample is taken, the evaluation of the results must be performed carefully. Even if the deviation rate in the sample is lower than the tolerable deviation rate, the results of a sample are not likely to be identical to the true deviation rate of the entire population. If a sample of 50 invoices resulted in 5 deviations (a sample deviation rate of 10%), it would not be unusual for another sample of 50 invoices from the same population to result in 6 or 4 deviations.

The fact that the results of a sample are not precise requires the addition of an **allowance for sampling risk** to the results of the sample, to be more certain that the true deviation rate of the population does not exceed the tolerable rate. The allowance for sampling risk is the amount that is both added to and subtracted from the rate in the sample to determine the actual anticipated range of error in the population. This is similar to the "plus-or-minus" that is mentioned in polling results. Since the auditor is primarily concerned about relying on a control that is not effective, the focus is on the upper end of the range, which is the maximum expected rate in the population, and which is compared to the tolerable rate.

To evaluate the results of a sample, the auditor will:
1. Calculate the sample deviation rate (number of deviations found divided by sample size).
2. Determine the allowance for sampling risk (always provided in CPA exam problems), which is based solely on the sample size.
3. Add the two figures together to obtain the **maximum deviation rate**.
4. Compare the maximum deviation rate to the tolerable deviation rate.
5. If the maximum rate is higher than the tolerable rate, the auditor will modify their original intention to rely on the control, because it does not appear to be operating effectively. This will increase the assessed level of control risk.
6. If the maximum rate is lower than the tolerable rate, the auditor will accept the results as a valid basis for relying on the control. This will allow them to maintain the lower assessed level of control risk from their preliminary determination based on the controls that were placed into operation.

For example, if an auditor's sample of 50 invoices found 5 deviations, the tolerable deviation rate was 11%, and the allowance for sampling risk was 2%, the auditor will calculate a sample deviation rate of 5 / 50 = 10% with a maximum deviation rate of 10% + 2% = 12%. Since this is higher than the tolerable rate of 11%, the auditor must modify their original plan to rely on the control.

Effect on Sample Size

Tolerable Rate ↓	Sample Size ↑
Confidence Level (Reliability) ↑	Sample Size ↑
Deviation Rate ↑	Sample Size ↑
Population size ↑	Sample Size ↑
Allowance (Precision) (More Accurate) ↓	Sample Size ↑

To **develop an Attribute Sampling Plan**, the following steps should be followed:

Step 1 – Determine the audit objective, the control that is being tested. (What testing for?)

Step 2 – Determine the **tolerable rate,** also referred to as the *tolerable deviation rate* or *tolerable rate of deviation*. This represents the greatest error rate the auditor is willing to tolerate and still conclude that the control is operating effectively (accept the population).

Step 3 – Determine **reliability** or the *level of confidence* which represents the degree of sampling risk the auditor is willing to accept. A 98% reliability indicates that the auditor is willing to accept the risk that there is a 2% risk of drawing an incorrect conclusion based on the sample.

Step 4 – Determine the **expected population deviation rate,** also referred to as the *expected rate of deviation used in planning the sample*, the *population expected error rate*, or the *expected deviation rate*. The auditor may use prior experience and knowledge to determine the deviation rate expected in the population.

Step 5 – Determine the method for selecting the sample *(random, systematic, block or cluster sampling)*.

Step 6 – Calculate the sample size. The auditor determines the sample size based on the tolerable rate, the allowable risk of assessing control risk too low, and the expected deviation rate.

Step 7 – Select and test the sample.

Step 8 – Calculate the sample deviation rate as:

> Number of deviations
>   Sample size

Using the number of deviations and the acceptable risk of assessing control risk too low (risk of overreliance), the auditor calculates the **upper precision limit**. The upper precision limit is a statistical measure of the maximum rate of deviations that exist within a population. The upper precision limit can be calculated as follows:

> Sample Deviation rate + Allowance for Sampling Risk = Upper Precision Limit

Step 9 – Compare the upper precision limit to the tolerable rate to reach conclusions and document the results.

Sampling Methodologies

A sample, by definition, should be representative of the population under consideration. For a sampling method to be valid, all items in the population should have an equal opportunity to be selected. Such methods include:
- **Random-Number Sampling**: Numbered documents or transactions are selected through the use of random number tables or computer software.
- **Systemic Sampling**: Every "nth" item is selected from a randomly-distributed population from a randomly-selected starting point.
- **Haphazard Sampling**: A sample consisting of units selected without any conscious bias—again assuming the random distribution of the population.
- **Block Sampling** (or Cluster sampling): A sample consisting of contiguous units; for example, a selection of three blocks of ten vouchers each. While this method eases sample selection, its major disadvantage is that the samples selected may not be representative, and thus is regarded as the least desirable method.

All of these methods are forms of random sampling. When all items are randomly selected for the sample, as in random number sampling, it is considered simple random sampling. Systematic sampling with a random starting point, haphazard sampling without known bias, and block sampling with blocks randomly selected are all forms of random sampling, referred to as systematic random sampling.

Lecture 5.03

VARIABLES SAMPLING
Classical Variables Sampling

The risks associated with variables sampling are concluding that an item contains a misstatement when it does not—the risk of incorrect rejection—which will result in an inefficient engagement, and the risk of concluding that an item does not contain a misstatement despite the fact that it does—the risk of incorrect acceptance—which will result in an ineffective engagement. The risk of an ineffective engagement is greater since that means that users will rely on financial statements that should not be relied upon. As a result, the auditor will seek to reduce the risk of incorrect acceptance by making certain that the sample size is appropriate.
- Substantive testing – tests of details
- Two risks
  - **Incorrect acceptance – audit ineffective**

     o   **Incorrect rejection – audit inefficient**

Factors affecting **sample size** in an attribute sample include:
- Tolerable misstatement, which has an *inverse* relationship;
- Acceptable risk, which has an *inverse* relationship;
- Population size, which has a *direct* relationship;
- Expected misstatement, which has a *direct* relationship;
- Standard deviation, which has a *direct* relationship; and
- Risk of Material Misstatement (RMM), which has a *direct* relationship.

Tolerable misstatement should usually be set for a particular audit procedure at less than financial statement materiality so that when the results of all audit procedures are aggregated, the required overall assurance will be attained.

Classical Variables Sampling Approaches

Variable sampling is used to estimate an amount, or the amount of a misstatement. It is used to estimate an amount, using an approach referred to as **mean-per-unit estimation**, by measuring the value of items in a sample to determine an average value and applying that average to the number of items in the population. It can be used to estimate the amount of a misstatement, using an approach referred to as **difference estimation**, by comparing the recorded amounts to the actual amounts for a sample of items, estimating an average error per item, and projecting that error to the population. **Ratio estimation**, where the relationship between items in a sample is projected to the population, may be used to estimate an amount or the amount of a misstatement.

When items within a population vary widely, the auditor may increase the efficiency and the effectiveness of sampling by using **stratified sampling**. Under this approach:
- The population is divided into groups or strata, with all items within each group having similar characteristics.
- The groups may be based on quantitative factors, such as putting expensive items in one group and inexpensive items in another, or some other characteristic, such as the profit margin.
- The groups may also be based on other factors such as putting transactions with a higher likelihood of error in one group and those with a lower likelihood in another group.
- A sample is drawn from each group, resulting in a smaller total sample size.

During the substantive testing phase, the auditor will be testing the details of transactions and accounts in order to determine if the individual account balances are materially correct. To do so, they must use sampling to estimate the numerical value of the account balance, and this is known as **variable estimation sampling** or **sampling for variables**.

Of course, the estimate resulting from sampling for variables is not going to exactly equal the account balance, so the estimate will be expressed with an amount to be added and subtracted to determine the range of amounts within which the value of the population is likely to fall. This is known as the **precision** of the results or the precision range. As long as the account balance is within the acceptable precision range, the auditor will consider the sample to support the account balance.

- If the auditor accepts an account balance that turns out to be materially misstated, the result is **incorrect acceptance** and results in an **ineffective** audit.

- If the auditor rejects an account balance that turns out not to be materially misstated, the result is **incorrect rejection** and results in an **inefficient** audit.

The normal sampling unit for a population of documents is each individual document. When the dollar values on the various documents are widely different from each other, the auditor may **stratify** the sample by dividing the documents into different groups based on approximate values, using larger sample sizes for the more important large documents and smaller sample sizes for the documents with smaller dollar amounts, since they are less significant in determining whether the account being audited is materially correct. Another method of dealing with widely-varying document values is to abandon classical sampling for variables and use **Probability in Proportion to Size Sampling,** or **PPS sampling**, which treats each dollar as a sampling unit.

Four factors enter into the determination of **sample size**: three of them parallel factors used in attribute sampling, and the fourth is specific to sampling for variables. The factors are:
1. **Tolerable misstatement –** This refers to the amount by which an account can differ from the recorded value without being considered materially misstated. It is based on the auditor's determination of the materiality level. The larger the tolerable misstatement, the smaller the sample size.
    a. Tolerable misstatement combined for all audit tests should not exceed financial statement materiality.
    b. Tolerable misstatement for any specific audit procedure will generally be less than financial statement materiality.

2. **Expected misstatement –** This is the amount by which the auditor expects the account to be misstated. It is based on previous audits as well as information gathered while obtaining an understanding of internal control structure. The larger the expected misstatement, the larger the sample size.

3. **Allowable risk of incorrect acceptance –** This refers to the risk the auditor is willing to take of accepting the account value as materially correct and have it be materially misstated. It is based on the auditor's overall willingness to accept audit risk as well as the assessed level of risk of material misstatement, since the auditor may be willing to accept greater detection risk when RMM is low. The larger the allowable risk of incorrect acceptance, the smaller the sample size.

4. **Standard deviation –** This is the variability of the dollar values of the individual items in the population. It is usually based on previous audits or a tiny sample of the items in the current population. The larger the standard deviation, the larger the sample size (as discussed earlier, when standard deviation is extremely high, it may be appropriate to stratify the sample or use PPS sampling instead).

Since we used TEA as the mnemonic for attribute sampling, using TEAS for variable estimation sampling makes sense: since substantive testing is the second phase of fieldwork, TEAS can be considered tea for two.

Types of Classical Variables Sampling

Evaluating a sample for variables is normally a matter of determining the average value of the items in the sample and then multiplying this average by the number of items in the population to estimate the total numerical value of the population. This is known as **mean-per-unit estimation**.

Occasionally, other methods are used to evaluate a sample. If there is a consistent bias in the book amounts, the auditor may use difference estimation or ratio estimation:
- **Difference estimation –** The auditor determines the average dollar amount by which the audited amounts exceed the book amounts in the sample (or vice versa), and assumes this

average difference applies to the entire population, so that the difference per item is multiplied by the number of items in the population, and the result is added to (or subtracted from) the total book amount.

- **Ratio estimation** – The auditor determines the ratio of the audited amounts to the book amounts in the sample (audited amount divided by book amount), and then multiplies the total book amount by this ratio.

For example, assume that 3 invoices are pulled from a population of 100 invoices (with a total account balance of $3,000 on the books). The 3 invoices have recorded amounts of $40, $20, and $27, respectively, but when the auditor examines the support, they find the correct values are $42, $24, and $27, respectively. The evaluation under the 3 methods would be as follows:
- **Mean-per-unit estimation** – $42 + $24 + $27 = $93 / 3 = $31. With a mean-per-unit of $31, the population of 100 invoices is estimated at $31 × 100 = $3,100.
- **Difference estimation** – $2 + $4 + $0 = $6 / 3 = $2. With an average excess of audited over book amount of $2, the population of 100 invoices should be increased by $2 × 100 = $200, estimating the population at $3,000 + $200 = $3,200.
- **Ratio estimation** – 1.05 + 1.20 + 1.00 = 3.25 / 3 = 1.08 (rounded). With an average ratio of audited amount to book amount of 1.08, the population is estimated to have a value of $3,000 × 1.08 = $3,240

MISSTATEMENTS

The AICPA has created a specific definition of **misstatements** and discussed the need to identify likely misstatements as well as known misstatements (the primary points being that misstatements in a sample create the likelihood of greater misstatements in the total population, and that the use of estimates increases likely misstatements). The *definition of a misstatement* is:
- A difference between the amount, classification, or presentation of a reported financial statement element, account, or item and the amount, classification or presentation that would have been reported under GAAP.
- The omission of a financial statement element, account, or item.
- A financial statement disclosure that is not presented in accordance with GAAP.
- The omission of information required to be disclosed in accordance with GAAP.

In addition, misstatements should be evaluated *qualitatively*, such as:
- Misstatements that affect trends of profitability.
- Misstatements that change losses into income.
- Misstatements that affect segment information.
- Misstatements that affect compliance with legal and contractual requirements.

Lecture 5.04

CLASS QUESTIONS

Please see the Class Questions and Class Solutions for this Lecture at the end of this Section.

PROBABILITY PROPORTIONAL TO SIZE SAMPLING (PPS)

PPS sampling is a form of sampling for variables in which the sampling unit is each dollar in a population. For this reason, it is also known as **dollar-unit sampling (DUS) or cumulative monetary amount (CMA) sampling**. Under PPS sampling, a **sampling interval** is determined and used to pick out the documents to be examined.

The method for determining the interval amount is complicated, but is based on tolerable misstatement, expected number of misstatements, and allowable risk of incorrect acceptance. The sample size is approximately equal to the dollar value of the population divided by the sampling interval. Beginning with the first item in the population, the dollar amount is counted until the interval is reached and the item containing that amount becomes part of the sample. When items are so large that they include more than one interval, the sample size will be smaller.

- **Probability-Proportional-to-Size** (PPS) or Dollar-unit sampling (DUS)
  - Substantive testing – tests of details
  - **Advantages** over classical variables sampling:
    - Standard deviation not needed
    - Stratifies sample automatically
    - Smaller sample usually results if few errors expected
    - Start sampling without having entire population available
  - **Disadvantages:**
    - Large sample results if many errors expected
    - Zero and negative balances require special handling
    - Not useful to detect understatement
  - **Calculations needed:**
    - **Sampling interval** (SI) = Tolerable misstatement / Reliability factor (from table) or Population amount / sample size
    - **Sample size** = Population amount / SI
    - To determine **projected misstatement:**
      - Misstatement = Book amount – Audited amount
      - Tainting factor (TF) = Misstatement / Book amount
      - Projected misstatement:
        - If SI > book amount then
          - PM = TF * SI
        - If SI <= book amount then
        - PM = Misstatement from step

For example, assume the auditor is examining an account with a total recorded amount of $100,000, and that the auditor has determined the sampling interval ought to be $10,000. A random number between $1 and $10,000 is selected: let's say the number chosen is $3,112. If the account is represented by 63 invoices, the auditor might obtain a ledger that lists each invoice and then reports the running total of the invoices, such as:

Invoice #	Amount	Cumulative
1	$2,000	$2,000
2	6,500	8,500
3	4,000	12,500
4	1,000	13,500
5	11,000	24,500
....	....	....
63	2,700	100,000

The auditor will examine the invoices that brought the cumulative amount to $3,112 (#2), $13,112 (#4), $23,112 (#5), $33,112, $43,112, $53,112, $63,112, $73,112, $83,112, and $93,112. The total number of invoices selected to examine should be $100,000 / $10,000 = 10, unless an invoice exceeding $10,000 individually was large enough to cross over 2 or more thresholds.

Once the documents have been examined, any misstatements that are found are applied to the entire interval by the calculation of **projected misstatement** (or projected error). This is determined by calculating the misstatement in a document as a percentage of the recorded amount, then applying this percentage to the interval. However, if the document selected is larger than the interval, the actual misstatement in the document is also the projected misstatement.

For example, assume that 2 of the documents in the example contain errors, as follows:

Invoice #	Recorded Amount	Audited Amount
4	$1,000	$800
5	11,000	10,300

In the example, the sampling interval was $10,000 so that the misstatement in invoice #4 will have to be projected to the entire interval, while the misstatement in invoice #5 will be accepted without adjustment, as follows:

Invoice #	Recorded	Audited	Misstatement	Tainting %	Sampling Interval	Projected Misstatement
4	$1,000	$800	$200	20%	$10,000	$2,000
5	11,000	10,300	700	----	--------	$700

The total projected misstatement is $2,700, and this will be compared with the tolerable misstatement to determine whether to accept the account balance as being materially correct.

Some of the **advantages of PPS** sampling over classical variable estimation sampling are:
- Larger accounts automatically have a greater chance of being selected, and individual accounts exceeding the sampling interval are always selected, so the method **automatically stratifies** the population.
- The method accommodates populations with items that vary widely in value **without** any need to compute **standard deviation**.

- A sample can be designed more easily and sample selection can begin before the final and full population is available.

Some of the **disadvantages** of the method are:
- The method is **not useful** in detecting **understated** accounts, since smaller accounts have a proportionately smaller chance of being selected.
- Special methods must be used in order to deal with **zero or negative accounts**, since they will ordinarily never be selected under this approach.
- Identified understatements require special consideration and large understatements may lead to invalid projections or conclusions.
- Larger anticipated misstatements require larger sample sizes, often making classical variable sampling more efficient.

PPS sampling is more conservative than classical variables sampling, and is more likely to reject an account balance. This is particularly the case for a population that contains several misstatements. As a result, this method is best for populations that are not believed to contain a large number of misstatements.

This type of sampling is particularly useful for:
- Confirming accounts receivable or loans receivable
- Tests of pricing of investments securities or inventory
- Tests of fixed-asset additions where existence is the primary risk

This type of sampling is generally NOT appropriate for:
- Confirming accounts receivable when there are a large number of unapplied credits
- Inventory test counts and price tests when the auditor anticipates a significant number of misstatements that could be overstatements or understatements
- Converting inventory from FIFO to LIFO
- Populations without individual recorded amounts
- Any application in which the primary objective is to estimate an amount

Lecture 5.06

CLASS QUESTIONS

Please see the Class Questions and Class Solutions for this Lecture at the end of this Section.

CLASS QUESTIONS

Work through the below Class Questions while following along with the respective lectures. Once this is complete, you can begin independently practicing what you've learned by quizzing yourself on this course section in your Interactive Practice Questions (IPQ), which can be found in your online Student Dashboard. Your IPQ simulates the computer-based testing experience, and will also help you understand how concepts are applied to the exam. Each question includes answer explanations from expert CPAs that will help you determine why you answered a question correctly or incorrectly. This is key to your success on the CPA Exam.

Lecture 5.04

1.   The risk of incorrect acceptance and the likelihood of assessing risk of material misstatement too low relate to the

     a.   Allowable risk of tolerable misstatement.
     b.   Preliminary estimates of materiality levels.
     c.   Efficiency of the audit.
     d.   Effectiveness of the audit.

Items 2 and 3 are based on the following information:
The diagram below depicts the auditor's estimated deviation rate compared with the tolerable rate, and also depicts the true population deviation rate compared with the tolerable rate.

	True State of Population	
	Deviation rate exceeds tolerable rate	**Deviation rate is less than tolerable rate**
Auditor's estimate based on <u>*sample results*</u> **Deviation rate exceeds tolerable rate**	I.	II.
Deviation rate is less than tolerable rate	III.	IV.

2.   In which of the situations would the auditor have properly concluded that risk of material misstatement is at or below the planned assessed level?

     a.   I.
     b.   II.
     c.   III.
     d.   IV.

3. As a result of tests of controls, the auditor assesses risk of material misstatement too high and thereby increases substantive testing. This is illustrated by situation

    a. I.
    b. II.
    c. III.
    d. IV.

4. Which of the following sampling methods would be used to estimate a numerical measurement of a population, such as a dollar value?

    a. Attribute sampling.
    b. Stop-or-go sampling.
    c. Variables sampling.
    d. Random-number sampling.

5. What is an auditor's evaluation of a statistical sample for attributes when a test of fifty documents results in three deviations if tolerable rate is 7%, the expected population deviation rate is 5%, and the allowance for sampling risk is 2%?

    a. Modify the planned assessed level of control risk because the tolerable rate plus the allowance for sampling risk exceeds the expected population deviation rate.
    b. Accept the sample results as support for the planned assessed level of control risk because the sample deviation rate plus the allowance for sampling risk exceeds the tolerable rate.
    c. Accept the sample results as support for the planned assessed level of control risk because the tolerable rate less the allowance for sampling risk equals the expected population deviation rate.
    d. Modify the planned assessed level of control risk because the sample deviation rate plus the allowance for sampling risk exceeds the tolerable rate.

Lecture 5.06

6.   Hill has decided to use probability-proportional-to-size (PPS) sampling, sometimes called dollar-unit sampling, in the audit of a client's accounts receivable balances. Hill plans to use the following PPS sampling table:

TABLE
Reliability Factors for Overstatements

Number of over-		Risk of incorrect acceptance			
statements	1%	5%	10%	15%	20%
0	4.61	3.00	2.31	1.90	1.61
1	6.64	4.75	3.89	3.38	3.00
2	8.41	6.30	5.33	4.72	4.28
3	10.05	7.76	6.69	6.02	5.52
4	11.61	9.16	8.00	7.27	6.73

Additional information

Tolerable misstatements (net of effect of expected misstatements)	$ 24,000
Risk of incorrect acceptance	20%
Number of misstatements	1
Recorded amount of accounts receivable	$240,000
Number of accounts	360

What sample size should Hill use?

a. 120
b. 108
c. 60
d. 30

7.   In a probability-proportional-to-size sample with a sampling interval of $5,000, an auditor discovered that a selected account receivable with a recorded amount of $10,000 had an audit amount of $8,000. If this were the only error discovered by the auditor, the projected error of this sample would be

a. $1,000
b. $2,000
c. $4,000
d. $5,000

CLASS SOLUTIONS

1. (**d**) The risk of incorrect acceptance is the risk that an item will be accepted despite the fact that it is materially misstated. The risk of assessing RMM too low is the risk that the auditor will rely on controls that are not effective, affecting the nature, timing, and extent of further audit procedures, as a result of which a material misstatement may not be detected. In either case, the auditor risks issuing an unmodified report when a modification would be required, making the audit ineffective. The allowable risk of tolerable misstatement (a) is the benchmark against which the auditor compares the exception rate or the estimated misstatement error in a sample to determine whether or not to reject the population. Preliminary estimates of materiality level (b) are used to estimate the tolerable misstatement. The efficiency of an audit relates to the risk of incorrect rejection, not incorrect acceptance, or the risk of assessing RMM too high, not too low (c).

2. (**d**) Section I is when the sample results indicate an intolerable error rate, which is consistent with the error rate in the population (a). This will cause the auditor to properly reject the population, affecting the nature, timing, and extent of further audit procedures. Section II is when the sample results indicate an intolerable error rate even though the error rate of the population is actually acceptable (b). This will cause the auditor to incorrectly reject the population resulting in an inefficient audit due to the effect on the nature, timing, and extent of further audit procedures. Section III is when the sample results indicate a tolerable error rate even though the error rate in the population is actually too high (c). This will cause the auditor to incorrectly accept the population. If this is a test of controls, it will result in an inappropriate reliance on internal control increasing the risk that auditor may not detect a material misstatement. If this is a substantive test, it indicates that the auditor did not detect a material misstatement that is likely to be material. In either case, the auditor risks issuing an inappropriate unmodified opinion, making the audit ineffective. Section IV is when the sample results indicate a tolerable error rate, which is consistent with the error rate in the population (d). This will cause the auditor to correctly accept the population.

3. (**b**) Section I is when the sample results indicate an intolerable error rate, which is consistent with the error rate in the population (a). This will cause the auditor to properly reject the population, affecting the nature, timing, and extent of further audit procedures. Section II is when the sample results indicate an intolerable error rate even though the error rate of the population is actually acceptable (b). This will cause the auditor to incorrectly reject the population resulting in an inefficient audit due to the effect on the nature, timing, and extent of further audit procedures. Section III is when the sample results indicate a tolerable error rate even though the error rate in the population is actually too high (c). This will cause the auditor to incorrectly accept the population. If this is a test of control, it will result in an inappropriate reliance on internal control increasing the risk that auditor may not detect a material misstatement. If this is a substantive test, it indicates that the auditor did not detect a material misstatement that is likely to be material. In either case, the auditor risks issuing an inappropriate unmodified opinion, making the audit ineffective. Section IV is when the sample results indicate a tolerable error rate, which is consistent with the error rate in the population (d). This will cause the auditor to correctly accept the population.

4.   (**c**) Variables sampling is the method used to estimate an amount, such as the value of a population, on the basis of the value of the sample. Attribute sampling (a) is used to determine if a population has an attribute, such as a particular type of error, and whether the frequency is at a tolerable rate. Stop-or-go sampling (b) is a technique of attribute sampling that is used when the error rate is expected to be low. It allows the auditor to conclude a test and draw conclusions before all items in the sample have been tested if the error rate in items tested is at an acceptably low level. Random-number sampling (d) is a method for selecting items to be included in a sample.

5.   (**d**) With three deviations in a sample size of 50, the sample deviation rate is 6%. Taking into account the 2% allowance for sampling risk, the auditor would conclude that the actual error rate in the population will be somewhere between 4% and 8% (6% ± 2%). Since the maximum error rate exceeds the tolerable rate of 7%, the auditor will conclude that the control is not effective and will reduce the planned assessed level of control risk. If the tolerable rate had exceeded the maximum amount (a), the auditor would have concluded that the control could be relied upon, affecting the nature, timing, and extent of further audit procedures. The auditor would accept sample results as support for the planned level of control risk if the maximum error was below the tolerable rate, not when it exceeds it (c), but the error rate was above, not below or equal to the tolerable rate (c).

6.   (**d**) A risk of incorrect acceptance of 20% with 1 expected misstatement results in a factor of 3.0, which is divided into the tolerable misstatement of $24,000, resulting in an interval of $8,000. This is divided into the total value of the population to give a sample size equal to $240,000/$8,000 or 30.

7.   (**b**) Under PPS, the projected error for a sample is a function of the errors detected and the relationship of the size of the item containing the error to the sampling interval. In this case, the item contained an overstatement of $2,000. If the item were smaller in amount than the sampling interval, the ratio of the error to the recorded amount would be multiplied by the sampling interval to determine the projected error. When the item containing the sample is equal to or larger than the sampling interval, the projected error is the amount of the detected error.

TASK-BASED SIMULATIONS

Task-Based Simulation 1

The Uniform
CPA Examination

Unsplit | Split Horiz | Split Vertical | Authoritative Literature | Spreadsheet | Calculator | Submit Testlet

Work Tab | Resources | Help

An auditor had decided to use probability-proportional-to-size (PPS) sampling, also called dollar-unit or cumulative monetary unit (CMU) sampling, in the audit of the client's accounts receivable balance. The auditor discovered 3 misstatements while doing their testing. Complete the spreadsheet below and calculate the total projected misstatement.

	Recorded amount	Audit amount	Sampling interval	Difference	Tainting %	Projected misstatement
1st misstatement	$ 400	$ 320	$1,000			
2nd misstatement	500	0	1,000			
3rd misstatement	3,000	2,500	1,000			

Task-Based Simulation 2

The Uniform
CPA Examination

Unsplit | Split Horiz | Split Vertical | Authoritative Literature | Spreadsheet | Calculator | Submit Testlet

Research | Help

Kapil & Assoc. has decided that sampling is appropriate for testing a characteristic in a fairly large population of transactions and is seeking guidance on how to select items from the population for the sample.

1. Which title of Professional Standards addresses this issue & will be helpful in understanding how to select items from a population for a sample?

2. Enter the exact section and paragraph with helpful information.

Task-Based Simulation 3

The Uniform
CPA Examination

Unsplit   Split Horiz   Split Vertical   Authoritative Literature   Spreadsheet   Calculator   Submit Testlet

Research   Help

Walden, CPA, is performing a test of controls on a sample of transactions. One of the transactions selected in the sample was void and Walden could not apply the appropriate audit procedure to it. Walden is trying to determine how to handle a circumstance when an audit procedure is not applicable to a selected item.

1.   Which title of Professional Standards addresses this issue & will be helpful in understanding what to do when an audit procedure is not applicable to an item selected in a sample?

2.   Enter the exact section and paragraph with helpful information.

TASK-BASED SIMULATION SOLUTIONS

Task-Based Simulation Solution 1

To solve this problem, first calculate the differences from each misstatement found. Then divide the difference by the recorded amount to get the tainting percentage (for example, 400-320 = 80/400=20%). Then multiply the tainting percentage by the sampling interval. That will give you the projected misstatement for that misstatement applied to the entire sampling interval. So, 20% x 1,000 = $200. Remember that if the recorded amount is LARGER than the interval, then no tainting percentage is used, the difference calculate for that misstatement is the actual projected misstatement for that misstatement (3,000 is larger than $1,000, so the difference of $500, is the actual projected misstatement for the 3rd misstatement). We then sum the total of the 3 projected misstatements to calculate our total projected misstatement of $1,700.

	Recorded amount	Audit amount	Sampling interval	Difference	Tainting %	Projected Misstatement (interval x tainting %)
1st misstatement	$ 400	$ 320	$1,000	$80	20% (80/400)	$ 200
2nd misstatement	500	0	1,000	500	100% (500/500)	1,000
3rd misstatement	3,000	2,500	1,000	500	N/A (since 3,000 is larger than 1,000)	500
						$ 1,700

Task-Based Simulation Solution 2

AU-C	530	.08

Task-Based Simulation Solution 3

AU-C	530	.10

Section 6 – Audit Reports
Corresponding Lectures

Watch the following course lectures with this section:

Lecture 6.01 – Unmodified Audit Report Opinion
Lecture 6.02 – PCAOB Audit Report
Lecture 6.03 – Chart for Audit Reports
Lecture 6.04 – Emphasis-of-Matter and Other-Matter Paragraph
Lecture 6.05 – Framework for Reporting
Lecture 6.06 – Group Financial Audit, Uncertainty, Scope Limitation
Lecture 6.07 – Adverse, Disclaimer, Comparative Financial Statements
Lecture 6.08 – Summary of Non-Standard Reports and Overview
Lecture 6.09 – Audit Reports – Class Questions

EXAM NOTE: Please refer to the AICPA AUD Blueprint in the Introduction of this book to find a listing of the representative tasks (and their associated skill levels—i.e., Remembering and Understanding, Application, Analysis, and Evaluation) that the candidate should be able to perform based on the knowledge obtained in this section.

Audit Reports

UNMODIFIED AUDIT REPORT OPINION

The Auditors **objective** as it relates to reporting is to form an opinion on the financial statements based on an evaluation of the audit evidence obtained, and express clearly that opinion on the financial statements through a written report that also describes the "basis" for that opinion.

AU-C Section 700, ***Forming an Opinion and Reporting on Financial Statements***, requires the auditor to form an opinion as to whether the financial statements are ***presented fairly***, in all material respects, in accordance with the applicable financial reporting framework. To support such an opinion, the auditor draws a conclusion as to whether the financial statements, taken as a whole, are free of material misstatement, which may be caused by error or fraud.

The auditor will evaluate whether sufficient appropriate audit evidence has been obtained, considering the results of the risk assessment that was performed to identify areas representing potentially greater risks of material misstatement and the results of procedures that were performed in response to those risks. The auditor will also evaluate conclusions reached as to whether uncorrected misstatements are material, either individually or in the aggregate.

The auditor will also make a determination as to whether the financial statements have been prepared, in all material respects, in accordance with the applicable financial reporting framework.

Fair presentation also relates to the overall presentation, structure, and content of the financial statements; and whether the financial statements, including the related notes, represent underlying events and transactions and adequately refer to or describe the applicable financial reporting framework.

When the auditor concludes that the financial statements are fairly presented, in all material respects, in accordance with the applicable financial reporting framework, the auditor will express an **unmodified opinion**. A **modified opinion** will be expressed if either:
- The auditor concludes that the financial statements are materially misstated; or
- The auditor has not been able to obtain sufficient appropriate audit evidence to conclude that the financial statements as a whole are free from material misstatement.

In deciding whether or not to modify the opinion, the auditor should discuss with management the auditor's conclusion that the objective of fair presentation was not achieved.

There are *5 basic types* of Opinions **(AU-C 700)**:
- Unmodified opinion, which is a Standard "clean" Report
- Unmodified opinion with an emphasis-of-matter or other-matter paragraph added to the report
- Types of modified opinions include:
    - Qualified opinion – "except for"
    - Adverse opinion – "do not present fairly"
    - Disclaimer of opinion – "we do not express an opinion"
        - Note that the AICPA and International standards use the term "Unmodified," while the PCAOB standards uses the term "Unqualified."

The Steps in an Audit

Prepare for → Obtain Understanding → Assess Risks of Material → Perform Tests → Perform → Formulate → Issue
The audit   of Client, its Environment,   Misstatement and Determine   of Controls   Substantive   an Opinion   Audit
                 including Internal Control   Nature, Timing & Extent   Procedures   Report
                                               of Further Procedures

Standard Unmodified Opinion (Nonpublic Companies - Nonissuer)

INDEPENDENT AUDITOR'S REPORT (Nonissuer Company)

To: The Board of Directors of X Company (Those charged with Governance)

Report on the Financial Statements (Introductory)

We have audited the accompanying financial statements of X Company, which comprise the balance sheet as of December 31, 20X1, and the related statements of income, changes in stockholders' equity, and cash flows for the year then ended, and the related notes to the financial statements.

Management's Responsibility for the Financial Statements

Management is responsible for the preparation and fair presentation of these financial statements in accordance with accounting principles generally accepted in the United States of America; this includes the design, implementation, and maintenance (DIM) of internal control relevant to the preparation and fair presentation of financial statements that are free from material misstatement, whether due to fraud or error.

Auditor's Responsibility

Our responsibility is to express an opinion on these financial statements based on our audit. We conducted our audit in accordance with auditing standards generally accepted in the United States of America. Those standards require that we plan and perform the audit to obtain reasonable assurance about whether the financial statements are free of material misstatement.

An audit involves performing procedures to obtain audit evidence about the amounts and disclosures in the financial statements. The procedures selected depend on the auditor's judgment, including the assessment of risks of material misstatement of the financial statements, whether due to fraud or error. In making those risk assessments, the auditor considers internal control relevant to the entity's preparation and fair presentation of the financial statements in order to design audit procedures that are appropriate in the circumstances, but not for the purpose of expressing an opinion on the effectiveness of the entity's internal control. Accordingly, we express no such opinion. An audit also includes evaluating the appropriateness of accounting policies used and the reasonableness of significant accounting estimates made by management, as well as evaluating the overall presentation of the financial statements.

We believe that the audit evidence we have obtained is sufficient and appropriate to provide a basis for our audit opinion.

Opinion

In our opinion, the financial statements referred to above present fairly, in all material respects, the financial position of X Company as of December 31, 20X1, and the results of its operations and its cash flows for the year then ended in accordance with accounting principles generally accepted in the United States of America.

[*Auditor's signature*] (Manual or printed signature)

[*Auditor's city and state*]

[*Date of the auditor's report*] – (Sufficient Appropriate Audit Evidence Obtained/ Dual Date)

AUDIT REPORTS

An audit report is required to be in writing and include certain components.

The report is required to have a **title** that includes the word ***independent***. The identification of the page as *"independent auditor's report"* is made in order to emphasize that the other pages of the annual report were prepared by the client, not the auditor.

The report indicates the **addressee as** "to the Board of Directors of X Company" when the audit committee of the board of directors hired the auditor, which is likely to be the case in audits of publicly held companies but, depending on the size and structure of the entity, may be to owners or others. The addressee will be the party to which the auditor is reporting.

It is acceptable to address the report directly to the company, or its shareholders, or to a third party that hired the auditor to examine the statements of X Company. It is **not** acceptable to address the report to members of the management team, since management is the party the auditor is reporting **on**; the auditor's independence requires that management **not** be the party the auditor is reporting **to**. The report may also be addressed to those charged with Governance.

The body of an **unmodified report** will consist of four paragraphs, each of which is required to include an appropriate title. They are:
- An **Introductory Paragraph**;
- **Management's Responsibility for the Financial Statements**;
- **Auditor's Responsibility**; and
- **Auditor's Opinion**.

The opening paragraph of the report, often called the **introductory** paragraph or **The Report on the Financial Statements**, includes four components:
1. Identify the **entity** whose financial statements have been audited
2. State that the financial statements **have been audited**
3. Identify the **title of each statement** that the financial statements are comprised of
4. Specify the **date or period covered** by each financial statement

The second paragraph, with the subheading **Management's Responsibility for the Financial Statements**, describes management's responsibility for the preparation and fair presentation of the financial statements. This includes responsibility for the **D**esign, **I**mplementation, and **M**aintenance (**DIM**) of internal control that is relevant to reliable financial reporting.

The third paragraph is entitled **Auditor's Responsibility** and states that the auditor's responsibility is to express an opinion on the financial statements based on the audit. It states that the audit was conducted in accordance with standards generally accepted in the USA (U.S. GAAS), which require the audit to plan and perform the audit to obtain reasonable assurance that the financial statements are free of material misstatement.

It describes **an audit**, stating:
- It involves performing procedures to obtain audit evidence about the amounts and disclosures reported in the financial statements;
- That procedures depend on the auditor's judgment, including the auditor's assessment of the risk of material misstatement, and the auditor's consideration of the entity's internal controls relevant to the preparation and fair presentation of the financial statements; and
- That an audit considers the appropriateness of accounting policies, reasonableness of significant accounting estimates, and the overall presentation of the financial statements.

The fourth paragraph, entitled **Auditor's Opinion**, should state, when expressing an unmodified opinion, that the financial statements present fairly, in all material respects, the financial position, results of operations, and cash flows in accordance with the **applicable financial reporting framework (AFRF)**:

- The financial position of the entity as of the balance sheet date
- The results of its operations and its cash flows for the period then ended

The applicable financial reporting framework refers to the system of accounting under which the financial statements have been prepared, and determines the form and content of the financial statements. 2 examples of applicable financial reporting frameworks include a general-purpose framework or a special-purpose framework.

- ***A general-purpose framework*** is designed to meet the common financial information objectives of a wide range of users. Accounting principles generally accepted in the United States of America (GAAP) is considered a *general-purpose framework*. General-purpose frameworks include:
  - GAAP, issued by the Financial Accounting Standards Board (FASB)
  - International Financial Reporting Standards (IFRS), issued by the International Accounting Standards Board (IASB)
  - Statements of Federal Financial Accounting Standards issued by the Federal Accounting Standards Advisory Board for U.S. federal governmental entities
  - Statements of Governmental Accounting Standards issued by the Governmental Accounting Standards Board (GASB) for U.S. state and local governmental entities

- ***A special-purpose framework*** (OCBOA) is a framework other than GAAP that could include the cash basis, tax basis, regulatory agency basis, contractual basis or an "other basis of accounting."

Evaluations related to consistency and the adequacy of disclosures do **not** result in **explicit** statements in an unmodified report. These matters only require comment when there is a lack of consistency from one period to the next, such as when **new** principles are adopted, or when disclosure is **inadequate**.

The opinion paragraph does not refer to the financial statements by name, but indicates that the financial statements fairly present:

- Financial position as depicted on the Balance sheet;
- Results of operations, as represented in the statements of income and changes in stockholders' equity; and
- Cash flows, as represented in the statement of cash flows.

The body of the report will be followed by the auditor's **signature**, which is that of the in-charge auditor. The report is also required to indicate the *city and state* (or city and country if outside the U.S.) in which the auditor practices.

The date is not the date on which the report is signed, but the auditor's report should be ***dated on or after the date on which sufficient appropriate audit evidence to support the opinion has been obtained***. Sufficient appropriate audit evidence includes evidence that the audit documentation has been reviewed; that the entity's financial statements, including disclosures and related notes, have been prepared; and that management has asserted that it has taken responsibility for them. This could result in a report date that is close to the report release date.

This is the last day on which any evidence about the client is obtained, so the auditor's responsibilities cannot include awareness of information arising after they have stopped seeking evidence. Even if an auditor is asked to reissue an earlier report on a client or former client, it will contain the date of the original report.

Occasionally, an auditor will discover information after the date that sufficient appropriate audit evidence is obtained, but prior to releasing the report. If such information requires the preparation of a **footnote referring to a date after the audit report date**, it may result in some confusion on the part of a user who sees an earlier date on the audit report than the date in the footnote. To eliminate the confusion, the auditor **dual dates** the report, providing the date on which the footnote information was obtained to supplement the basic date. For example, if the auditor has obtained sufficient appropriate audit evidence as of March 1 but discovers on March 8 that a fire destroyed the company's warehouse the night before, and a footnote is drafted that day referring to the details of the March 7 fire, the report date is as follows:

March 1, 20X1, except for Note T, as to which the date is March 8, 20X1

A dual date must always be later than the basic date, since it is used to extend the auditor's responsibility on a single note to the financial statements. The auditor is already responsible for everything else in the financial statements and notes up to the completion of fieldwork. No change is necessary to the body of the audit report unless the auditor decides to draw attention to the matter by adding an emphasis-of-matter paragraph.

Lecture 6.02

PCAOB AUDITING STANDARD 3101 (ISSUERS – PUBLIC COMPANIES) (UNQUALIFIED)

The audit report must be prepared differently for a company that reports to the SEC and is, therefore, subject to the requirements of the Public Company Accounting Oversight Board (PCAOB). A "clean," unmodified report under the PCAOB standards is called an "unqualified" opinion. The following adjustments to the report are required:

1. The title of the page is "Report of Independent Registered Public Accounting Firm."
2. The scope paragraph must **not** refer to generally accepted auditing standards, and instead refer to "the standards of the Public Company Accounting Oversight Board (United States)."

These changes apply to all audit reports of public companies as well as reviews of interim financial information performed under PCAOB standards.

Standard Unqualified Opinion (Public Companies – Issuer)

REPORT OF INDEPENDENT REGISTERED PUBLIC ACCOUNTING FIRM

TO:

(Introductory)

We have audited the accompanying balance sheets of X Company as of December 31, 20X3 and 20X2, and the related statements of operations, stockholders' equity, and cash flows for each of the three years in the period ended December 31, 20X3. These financial statements are the responsibility of the Company's management. Our responsibility is to express an opinion on these financial statements based on our audits.

(Scope)

We conducted our audits in accordance with the standards of the **Public Company Accounting Oversight Board (United States)**. Those standards require that we plan and perform the audit to obtain reasonable assurance about whether the financial statements are free of material misstatement. An audit includes examining, on a test basis, evidence supporting the amounts and disclosures in the financial statements. An audit also includes assessing the accounting principles used and significant estimates made by management, as well as evaluating the overall financial statement presentation. We believe that our audits provide a reasonable basis for our opinion.

(Opinion)

In our opinion, the financial statements referred to above present fairly, in all material respects, the financial position of the Company as of [at] December 31, 20X3 and 20X2, and the results of its operations and its cash flows for each of the three years in the period ended December 31, 20X3, in conformity with U.S. Generally Accepted Accounting Principles.

(Reference to auditor's report on internal control – explanatory paragraph)

We also have audited, in accordance with the standards of the Public Company Accounting Oversight Board (United States), X company's internal control over financial reporting as of December 31, 20X3, based on criteria established in Internal Control—Integrated Framework issued by the Committee of Sponsoring Organizations of the Treadway Commission and our report dated February 24, 20X4, expressed an unqualified opinion thereon.

[Signature]
[City and State or Country]
[Date]

Audits Performed in Accordance with GAAS as well as a Different Set of Standards

An auditor may be engaged to perform an audit in accordance with some set of standards, other than PCAOB standards, but in addition to auditing standards generally accepted in the United States of America (GAAS). The auditor may accept such an engagement, but would be required to perform the engagement in accordance with GAAS as well as the other set of standards.

- If the audit was conducted applying both sets of standards in their entirety, the audit report would indicate that the audit was conducted in accordance with GAAS and the other set of standards, naming the source of the standards.
- If, on the other hand, the second set of standards was not applied in its entirety, the report will indicate compliance with GAAS, excluding any mention of the other standards.

If the second set of standards is PCAOB standards, the content of the report will depend on whether the audit was within the jurisdiction of the PCAOB. If the audit is not within the jurisdiction of the PCAOB, the report will refer to the PCAOB standards in addition to GAAS. The report will follow the guidelines of one prepared in accordance with the PCAOB standards and indicate that it was also performed in accordance with GAAS.

CHART FOR AUDIT REPORTS

	Immaterial	Material (Not Pervasive)	Very Material (Pervasive)
Disagreement -Not GAAP (Not Applicable Financial Reporting Framework) -Inconsistency (improperly handled) -Inadequate Disclosures	Unmodified opinion	Modified (Misstatements are material, but not pervasive) "Except for" (Basis for Qualified)	Modified (Misstatements are both material & pervasive) Adverse (Basis for Adverse)
Scope Limit → Restriction on ability to obtain "Sufficient Appropriate audit evidence"		Modified (unable to obtain suffic approp audit evidence, material but not pervasive) "Except for" (Basis for Qualified)	Modified (unable to obtain suffic approp audit evidence, both material & pervasive) Disclaimer (Basis for Disclaimer)
Emphasis-of-Matter or Other-Matter (Uncertainty) - Contingent Liability - Going Concern Doubt - Audit C/y-Review P/y (Extreme Going Concern Doubt – **Disclaimer**)		Unmodified with Emphasis-of-Matter/Other-Matter (After Opinion) "Emphasis-of-matter" or "Other-matter" (Properly presented and disclosed) (Not req'd to be presented or disclosed) (After Opinion) (After Emphasis and Opinion)	

("Basis For" Before Opinion" appears as a box between the Material and Very Material columns in the Disagreement row)

GAAP (AICPA) **Audit** (nonissuer)

- **3 types of modified opinions**
  - ○ **Qualified, adverse and disclaimer**

Pervasive means that, in the auditor's judgment, the effects are (1) not confined to a specific element, account, or item of the F/S; (2) could represent a substantial portion of the F/S; or (3) relate to disclosures that are fundamental to the users' understanding of the F/S. This relates to the "scope" of the effect on the F/S.

PARAGRAPHS TO FOLLOW THE OPINION PARAGRAPH WITHOUT MODIFYING THE OPINION

Emphasis of Matter (AU-C 706)

An auditor has broad discretion to add an additional paragraph to the end of a report whenever the auditor wants to emphasize a matter. Sometimes the client has *properly accounted for and disclosed* an item of extreme importance, but the auditor is concerned that a careless reader of the financial statements might not examine the notes to the financial statements and, thus, not notice the information provided by the client. These include matters that are *of such importance that they are **fundamental** to the users' understanding of the financial statements.*

Circumstances that may lead the auditor to add an **optional** emphasis-of-matter paragraph **following the opinion** include:
- Significant related party transactions.
- Material uncertainties (unresolved lawsuit).
- Important subsequent events.
- Lack of consistency in the application of accounting principles.

When the auditor decides to include an emphasis-of-matter paragraph, the auditor should include it immediately **after** the opinion paragraph in the report. In addition, it should:
- Have an appropriate heading, such as Emphasis of Matter
- Include a clear reference to the matter being emphasized and where the matter is addressed in the financial statements
- Indicate that the auditor's opinion is not modified with respect to the matter

Since the client has properly accounted for and disclosed the matter, the opinion will be unmodified. An example of an emphasis-of-matter paragraph that might result from uncertainty related to a significant pending litigation matter follows:

Unmodified Opinion – Emphasis of a Matter (After Opinion)

INDEPENDENT AUDITOR'S REPORT

Addressee

Report on the Financial Statements (Intro)
Standard introductory paragraph

Management's Responsibility for the Financial Statements
Standard paragraph

Auditor's Responsibility
Standard paragraph

Opinion
Standard paragraph

Emphasis of Matter
As discussed in *Note X* to the financial statements, the Company is a defendant in a lawsuit [briefly describe the nature of the litigation consistent with the Company's description in the notes to the financial statements]. *Our opinion is not modified with respect to this matter.*

In addition to the circumstances just discussed, in which the inclusion of an **emphasis-of-matter** paragraph is optional, there are some circumstances in which the inclusion of such a paragraph is **mandatory.** Examples are:

- The auditor's opinion on revised financial statements differs from the opinion previously expressed, although an other-matter paragraph may be used.
- Substantial doubt as to the ability of the client to continue as a going concern, requiring the inclusion of the wording "substantial doubt" and "going concern" in the paragraph.
- A justified change in accounting principles affecting consistency, including:
  - A change in reporting entity.
  - A change in accounting principle by an investee accounted for using the equity method by the reporting entity.
  - Adjustments to correct a misstatement in previously issued financial statements.
- Financial statements prepared in accordance with a special-purpose framework (i.e., a financial reporting framework other than GAAP).
- Financial statements prepared in accordance with a regulatory basis that are intended for general use.

For Public companies (PCAOB), an additional paragraph appears *after the opinion* referring to the auditor's report on internal control. Note: This reference is only required when the reports on the financial statements and internal control are separate. See below.

> We also have audited, in accordance with the standards of the Public Company Accounting Oversight Board (United States), X company's internal control over financial reporting as of December 31, 20X3, based on criteria established in Internal Control—Integrated Framework issued by the Committee of Sponsoring Organizations of the Treadway Commission and our report dated February 24, 20X4, expressed an unqualified opinion thereon.

Other Matter (AU-C 706)

An auditor will use an **other-matter** paragraph to communicate matters that are appropriately reported or disclosed in the financial statements but, in the auditor's judgment, *enhances a user's ability to understand the audit*, the auditor's responsibilities, or the auditor's report. An other-matter paragraph will have a heading that states Other Matter and will **follow any emphasis-of-matter paragraphs and Opinion**.

Certain circumstances require the auditor to include an ***other-matter paragraph***. These include:

- The auditor's opinion on revised financial statements differs from the opinion previously expressed, although an emphasis-of-matter paragraph may be used.
- The report of another auditor who reported on prior period financial statements is not presented with comparative financial statements.
- When prior periods presented in comparative financial statements were reviewed or compiled, or when they have not been audited, reviewed, or compiled.
- When *other information* accompanying audited financial statements contains a material inconsistency, which management refuses to revise, unless the auditor decides to withhold the auditor's report or withdraw from the engagement.
- When the entity presents supplementary information with the financial statements, unless the auditor issues a separate report on the supplementary information.
- When the financial statements are accompanied by required supplementary information (RSI).
- Financial statements prepared in accordance with a special-purpose framework (i.e., a financial reporting framework other than GAAP) that are restricted to internal use.

Unmodified Opinion – Other-Matter (After Opinion)

> **INDEPENDENT AUDITOR'S REPORT**
>
> *Addressee*
>
> ***Report on the Financial Statements (Intro)***
> Standard introductory paragraph
>
> ***Management's Responsibility for the Financial Statements***
> Standard paragraph
>
> ***Auditor's Responsibility***
> Standard paragraph
>
> ***Opinion***
> Standard paragraph
>
> ***Other-Matter***
> **In our report dated March 1, 20X1, we expressed an opinion that the 20X0 financial statements did not fairly present the financial position, results of operations, and cash flows of ABC Company in accordance with accounting principles generally accepted in the United States of America because of two departures from such principles: (1) ABC Company carried its property, plant, and equipment at appraisal values, and provided for depreciation on the basis of such values, and (2) ABC Company did not provide for deferred income taxes with respect to differences between income for financial reporting purposes and taxable income. As described in Note X, the Company has changed its method of accounting for these items and restated its 20X0 financial statements to conform with accounting principles generally accepted in the United States of America. Accordingly, our present opinion on the restated 20X0 financial statements, as presented herein, is different from that expressed in our previous report.**

Compliance with Contractual Agreements or Regulatory Requirements (Other-Matter)

An auditor, in conjunction with the audit of financial statements, may be responsible for reporting on an entity's compliance with aspects of contractual agreements or with regulatory requirements. As discussed in a later section, this is often done in the form of a special report. In some circumstances, however, the report on compliance may be included in the auditor's report on the financial statements.

When a report on compliance is included in the auditor's report on the financial statements, the auditor will include an **other-matter** paragraph. It will include a reference to the specific covenants or paragraphs of the contractual agreement or regulatory requirements, to the extent they relate to accounting matters.

The **other-matter** paragraph should include:
- When appropriate, a statement that nothing came to the auditor's attention that caused the auditor to believe that the entity failed to comply with specified aspects of the contractual agreements or regulatory requirements, insofar as they relate to accounting matters.
- When appropriate, a description of identified instances of noncompliance.
- A statement indicating that the communication is being provided in connection with the audit of the financial statements.
- A statement that the audit was not directed primarily toward obtaining knowledge regarding compliance and, accordingly, had the auditor performed additional procedures, additional matters may have come to the auditor's attention regarding noncompliance with requirements, insofar as they relate to accounting matters.

- If appropriate, a paragraph that includes a description and the source of significant interpretations made by management relating to provisions of the contractual agreement or regulatory requirements.
- A paragraph that includes an appropriate alert restricting the use of the auditor's communication.

While, with the exception of the addition of the other-matter paragraph, the auditor's report will remain unchanged, there are some modifications that may be required:

- If the auditor is responsible for expressing an opinion on the effectiveness of internal control in conjunction with the audit of financial statements, the 2nd paragraph of the section of the report indicating the auditor's responsibility will be modified.
  - The reference to procedures not being applied for the purpose of expressing an opinion on the effectiveness of internal control is deleted.
  - The sentence indicating that, accordingly, no such opinion is expressed is also deleted.

Auditor's Responsibility

Our responsibility is to express an opinion on these financial statements based on our audit. We conducted our audit in accordance with auditing standards generally accepted in the United States of America. Those standards require that we plan and perform the audit to obtain reasonable assurance about whether the financial statements are free of material misstatement.

An audit involves performing procedures to obtain audit evidence about the amounts and disclosures in the financial statements. The procedures selected depend on the auditor's judgment, including the assessment of risks of material misstatement of the financial statements, whether due to fraud or error. In making those risk assessments, the auditor considers internal control relevant to the entity's preparation and fair presentation of the financial statements in order to design audit procedures that are appropriate in the circumstances. **(but not for the purpose of expressing an opinion on the effectiveness of the entity's internal control. Accordingly, we express no such opinion - DELETED).** An audit of financial statements also includes evaluating the appropriateness of accounting policies used and the reasonableness of significant accounting estimates made by management, as well as evaluating the overall presentation of the financial statements.

We believe that the audit evidence we have obtained is sufficient and appropriate to provide a basis for our audit opinion.

The opinion paragraph will be followed by an **other-matter paragraph** as follows:

Other Matter
In connection with our audit, nothing came to our attention that caused us to believe that X Company failed to comply with the terms, covenants, provisions, or conditions of sections XX to &&, inclusive of the Indenture dated July 21, 20XX with ABC Bank, insofar as they relate to accounting matters. However, our audit was not directed primarily toward obtaining knowledge of such noncompliance. Accordingly, had we performed additional procedures, other matters may have come to our attention regarding the Company's noncompliance with the above-referenced terms, covenants, provisions, or conditions of the Indenture, insofar as they relate to accounting matters.

After the Other-Matter paragraph, the audit report will include an alert that *restricts the use of the report*. In general, it will read:

> **Restricted Use Relating to the Other Matter**
> The communication related to compliance with the aforementioned Indenture described in the Other Matter paragraph is intended solely for the information and use of the boards of directors and management of X Company and ABC Bank and is *not intended to be and should not be used* by anyone other than those specified parties.

If the engagement is performed in accordance with Government Auditing Standards, the restricted use alert may read:

> **Restricted Use Relating to the Other Matter**
> The purpose of the communication related to compliance with the aforementioned [compliance requirements] described in the Other Matter paragraph is solely to describe the scope of our testing of compliance and the results of that testing. This communication is an integral part of an audit performed in accordance with Government Auditing Standards in considering X Company's compliance. *Accordingly, this communication is not suitable for any other purpose.*

Lecture 6.05

REPORTING REQUIREMENTS

Framework for Reporting – Explicit

In a **standard report**, the opinion paragraph **explicitly states** that the financial statements are in conformity with GAAP. For nonissuers, the FASB Accounting Standards Codification (ASC) is the only authoritative source of GAAP. Issuers must also take into account requirements imposed by the SEC in addition to the requirements of the FASB.

In unusual circumstances, a new type of transaction or new legislation may arise that causes existing authoritative principles to be inapplicable. In such a case, it actually might be **misleading** to apply these principles, and GAAP would require presentation of the transaction in a reasonable manner that would be generally accepted as more appropriate. In such a **justified departure** from a promulgated accounting principle, an unmodified opinion will still be issued, but an emphasis-of-matter paragraph will be included after the opinion, mentioning the departure and explaining that unusual circumstances make it appropriate.

When the client's management is not preparing the financial statements in conformity with GAAP, the auditor should, of course, first suggest that the statements be corrected. If management refuses, then the auditor will normally issue a **qualified** opinion (also known as an "except for" opinion). In such an opinion, the auditor indicates that the financial statements are fairly presented, except for the specific departure from GAAP. In rare cases, a departure from GAAP will be so extreme so as to make the financial statements as a whole misleading, and in such cases the auditor will issue an **adverse** opinion, stating the financial statements are not fairly presented.

When a modified opinion is issued, the auditor will explain the reasons for the opinion, and a paragraph that explains the Basis for the qualification will appear immediately **before** the opinion paragraph in order to forewarn the reader that the opinion is different from the normal situation. The paragraph will be headed "**Basis for Qualified Opinion.**"

Qualified Opinion – Unjustifiable Departure from GAAP (Before)

INDEPENDENT AUDITOR'S REPORT

Addressee

Report on the Financial Statements (Intro)
- Standard Introductory Paragraph

Management's Responsibility for the Financial Statements
- Standard paragraph

Auditor's Responsibility
- Standard paragraph

Basis for Qualified Opinion (new paragraph before)
The Company has stated inventories at cost in the accompanying balance sheets. Accounting principles generally accepted in the United States of America require inventories to be stated at the lower of cost or net realizable value. If the Company stated inventories at the lower of cost or net realizable value, a write down of $XXX would have been required at December 31, 20X1. Accordingly, cost of sales would have been increased by $XXXX, and net income, income taxes, and stockholders' equity would have been reduced by $XXXX, $XXXX, and $XXXX as of and for the year ended December 31, 20X1.

Qualified Opinion (new title)
In our opinion, ***except for* the effects of the matter described in the Basis for Qualified Opinion paragraph,** the financial statements referred to above present fairly, in all material respects, the financial position of X Company as of December 31, 20XX, and the results of its operations and its cash flows for the year then ended in accordance with accounting principles generally accepted in the United States of America.

Consistency – Implicit

The auditor is required to evaluate the consistency of financial statements for the periods presented and communicate in the auditor's report when the comparability of financial statements from one period to the next is affected. When accounting principles have been applied consistently, there is no mention of consistency in the audit report. Consistency is, instead, **implicit** in that it is only mentioned if accounting principles have not been consistently applied from period to period.

Consistency is evaluated for all periods presented in relation to each other as well as to the period prior to the earliest period presented. When comparative financial statements are presented, the auditor evaluates consistency for all periods presented as well as the consistency with which accounting principles were applied in the earliest period presented in relation to the immediately preceding period. When financial statements are presented for a single period, the auditor evaluates the consistency of the current period financial statements to those for the immediately preceding period.

The inconsistency may be due to:
- A change in accounting principle.
- An adjustment to correct a material misstatement in previously issued financial statements.

When there is a change in accounting principle, the auditor determines whether:
- The new principle is in accordance with the applicable financial reporting framework.
- The accounting for the change in principles conforms to the requirements of the framework (i.e., the change is proper).
- Disclosures are appropriate and adequate.
- There is justification that the change is preferable.

When the auditor is satisfied that all conditions have been met, the auditor will issue an unmodified opinion but will modify the report by including an emphasis-of-matter paragraph. This paragraph is included in future reports until the new accounting principle has applied in all periods presented as well as the period immediately preceding the first period presented. When the auditor is unable to determine that all conditions have been met, the auditor should evaluate if the change constitutes a departure from the applicable financial reporting framework, which would require a **qualified or adverse** opinion.

Changes that would result in an **unmodified opinion and an emphasis-of-matter** paragraph would include:
- A change from one acceptable principle to another preferable acceptable accounting principle.
- A change in accounting estimate that is inseparable from a change in accounting principle (e.g., change in depreciation method or useful life).
- A change in reporting entity resulting from including or excluding entities from consolidated financial statements that is not accompanied by a change in ownership.
- A significant change in accounting principle by an investee that is accounted for under the equity method of accounting.
- An adjustment to correct a material misstatement in previously issued financial statements.

A change in classification of an item on the financial statements, if material, may represent a change in accounting principle or a correction of an error (e.g., reclassifying cash flows from operating activities to investing activities due to a mistake in previous years' F/S), in which case, it will also result in an emphasis-of-matter paragraph.

AS 3101 in **PCAOB** standards indicates that a change from an unacceptable principle to an acceptable one is a correction of a misstatement in a previously issued financial statement and is not a change in accounting principle.

Notwithstanding the above, a change will not require identification if it doesn't have a **material** impact on the **comparability of the current and preceding years**.

An inconsistency is **not** necessarily a departure from GAAP. As long as the auditor **concurs** with the change and it is accounted for and disclosed properly, the audit opinion will continue to be **unmodified**. The report will include, however, an emphasis-of-matter paragraph, which may appear as follows:

Change in Principle – Concur – Unmodified (After Opinion)

Emphasis of Matter

As discussed in **Note X** to the consolidated financial statements, the company changed its method of accounting for Goodwill and changed its method of accounting for Derivative instruments and hedging activities in 20XX. **Our opinion is not modified with respect to this matter.**

The essential item to include in the explanatory paragraph is a reference to the footnote in which the client discusses the change. Notice that the auditor does **not** explicitly state that they concur with the change and that it is accounted for and disclosed properly. This is assumed because of the unmodified opinion. A sentence mentioning that the opinion is not modified is also added.

AS 3101 also addresses adjustments to correct misstatements (errors) in previously issued financial statements. This standard broadens the Second Standard of Reporting by including errors not involving an accounting principle. AS 3101 indicates that If a material misstatement in previously issued financial statements is corrected, an *explanatory paragraph* should be added to the auditor's report describing this situation.

Correction of a Material Misstatement (After)

Standard introductory paragraph

Standard scope paragraph

Standard opinion paragraph
> **"As discussed in Note X to the financial statements, the 20X1 financial statements have been restated to correct a misstatement."**

There are certain circumstances that will cause an inconsistency to be a **GAAP departure** requiring either a **qualified or adverse** opinion. In such cases, as indicated above, the audit report includes a paragraph entitled **Basis for Qualification**, which appears **before** the opinion, since it is affecting it. Examples include:
- A change to an unacceptable principle.
- A change that is not accounted for in the proper manner.
- A change that is not properly disclosed.
- A change that is made without sufficient justification.

A report resulting from an unjustified change in principle might appear as follows:

Change in Principle – Do not concur – Qualified (Before)

Basis for Qualification
As discussed in Note B to the financial statements, the Company changed its method of inventory pricing during 20X1 from the last-in, first-out method to the first-in, first-out method. Although the use of the first-in, first-out method is in conformity with U.S. generally accepted accounting principles, in our opinion, the Company has not provided reasonable justification for making the change as required by U.S. generally accepted accounting principles.

Qualified Opinion
In our opinion, *except for* **the change in accounting principle discussed in the preceding paragraph,** the financial statements referred to above present fairly, in all material respects, the financial position of X Company as of December 31, 20X1, and the results of its operations and its cash flows for the year then ended in conformity with U.S. generally accepted accounting principles.

Subsequent years: If the year in which the change occurred is presented, the explanatory paragraph is required in the subsequent year's reports. If the change was treated as a retroactive restatement, the explanatory paragraph is not needed in subsequent years.

If it is a **First Year Audit** and the auditor is satisfied as to the consistency of the accounting principles, no reference to consistency is made.

Omitted Disclosures (Inadequate Disclosure) – Implicit

The audit report does not make any mention of disclosures, other than in the introductory paragraph, which indicates that they are among the financial information that is being audited, unless disclosures are considered incorrect, incomplete, or otherwise unsatisfactory. In an unmodified opinion, the auditor **implicitly** indicates that disclosures are adequate by not indicating otherwise in the report.

Omitted Disclosures – Qualified Opinion (Before)

> *__Basis for Qualification__*
> *The Company's statements do not disclose (describe the nature of the omitted disclosures). In our opinion, disclosure of this information is required by U.S. Generally Accepted Accounting Principles.*
>
> *__Qualified Opinion__*
> In our opinion, *except for* the omission of the information discussed in the preceding paragraph, the financial statements referred to above present fairly, in all material respects, the financial position of X Company as of December 31, 20XX, and the results of its operations and its cash flows for the year then ended in accordance with U.S. Generally Accepted Accounting Principles.

One special violation is the failure to include a **statement of cash flows** in a set of financial statements. GAAP requires the inclusion of such a statement whenever a company is presenting results of operations, i.e., an income statement. The failure to include the statement of cash flows results in a qualified opinion, but also requires modification to the introductory and opinion paragraphs to delete reference to it:

- **No cash flows** (Qualified Opinion, not a Scope Limit – **Inadequate disclosure)**
  - Omit "Cash flows" in Intro paragraph
  - Basis for qualification paragraph is added before the opinion, explaining that the company declined to present the statement as required by GAAP.
  - Opinion paragraph mentions, "except that omission of Cash Flows results in an incomplete presentation."

No Statement of Cash Flows – Qualified Opinion (Before)

INDEPENDENT AUDITOR'S REPORT
(Nonissuer Company)

+

To: The Board of Directors of X Company (Those charged with Governance)

Report on the Financial Statements (Intro)
We have audited the accompanying financial statements of X Company, which comprise the balance sheet as of December 31, 20X1, and the related statements of income and changes in stockholders' equity **(Cash flows omitted)** for the year then ended, and the related notes to the financial statements.

Management's Responsibility for the Financial Statements
-Standard

Auditor's Responsibility
-Standard

Basis for Qualification
The Company declined to present a statement of cash flows for the year ended December 31, 20X1. Presentation of such a statement summarizing the Company's operating, investing, and financing activities is required by U.S. generally accepted accounting principles.

Qualified Opinion
In our opinion, ***except that*** the omission of a statement of cash flows results in an incomplete presentation as explained in the preceding paragraph, the financial statements referred to above present fairly, in all material respects, the financial position of X Company as of December 31, 20X1, and the results of its operations for the year then ended in accordance with accounting principles generally accepted in the United States of America.

Comprehensive income may be reported in one of 2 ways, this would affect only the introductory paragraph (no change in opinion paragraph).
- A separate mentioned statement – "statement of comprehensive income"
- Included with the income statement – "statement of income and comprehensive income"

Sometimes, a client will include the name of the CPA firm in a report on financial statements that were not audited or reviewed by the CPA. By naming the CPA, the client has now associated them with the financial statements, and it is critical for the CPA to demand that the client **either**:
- Remove the CPA's name from the client's report, or
- Mark each page of the financial statements "Unaudited. No opinion expressed on them."

A CPA must at least do the level of work equivalent to a compilation in order to attach any report to such statements. Compilations and reviews are discussed in another section.

Lecture 6.06

GROUP FINANCIAL AUDITS (AU-C 600)

Making Reference to the Work of a Component Auditor – Shared Responsibility Opinion – Division of Responsibility – Explicit

Sometimes, there are other auditors involved in the engagement (we are not referring to predecessor auditors who are not an issue if the client is presenting single-period financial statements only). If the client owns a subsidiary or has a major investment in another company requiring the use of the equity method of accounting, the financial statements of the client may be materially impacted by the investee's results. If the accountant happened to be the auditor of both the investor and investee companies, no responsibility issue arises. Often, however, the financial statements of the investor company are audited by one accounting firm while the statements of the investee are audited by another.

In such cases, a determination must be made as to who is the **group engagement partner**, which refers to the accounting firm that has examined the company having the largest impact on the overall report. Most examples on the CPA exam involve a group engagement partner who is the auditor of a parent corporation that needs to rely on the work of **component auditors** who audited one or more subsidiaries. Assuming the results of the subsidiary have a material impact on the consolidated statements of the parent, the group engagement partner must evaluate component auditors, taking into consideration:

- The component auditor's understanding and willingness to comply with ethical requirements, including independence.
- The component auditor's competence.
- The extent to which the group engagement team will be involved in the work of the component auditor.
- Whether the group engagement team will be able to obtain necessary consolidating information from the component auditor.
- Whether the component auditor operates in an environment with appropriate oversight.

When the component auditor does not meet independence requirements, or when the group engagement auditor has reservations about other matters, the group engagement team should obtain sufficient appropriate audit evidence in regard to the component without using any of the work of the component auditor in forming an opinion on the financial statements.

In preparing the audit report, the group engagement auditor determines whether or not to make reference to the component auditor as a means of indicating a division of responsibility. No reference should be made unless:

- Component financial statements were prepared according to the same framework as the group financial statements;
- The component auditor has complied with GAAS; and
- The component auditor's report is not restricted.

When the financial statements of a component, audited by a component auditor, were prepared in accordance with a financial reporting framework that is different than the financial reporting framework applicable to the group financial statements, reference to the report of the component auditor should not be made unless:

- The measurement, recognition, presentation, and disclosure criterial incorporated into the framework used for the component are similar to those applicable to the framework applied to the group financial statements; and
- The group auditor has obtained evidence indicating that adjustments made to convert the information of the component to the financial reporting framework used in the group financial statements are appropriate.

When the group engagement auditor decides to make reference to the component auditor in the audit report, the report should indicate clearly that the component was not audited by the group engagement auditor but the component auditor. The indication should include the magnitude of the portion of the financial statements audited by the component auditor.

If the group engagement auditor decides to name the component auditor, the group auditor should:
- Obtain the component auditor's express permission.
- Present the component auditor's report together with the report on the group financial statements.

The group engagement auditor should also consider whether modifications to the component auditor's report may necessitate modifications to the group auditor's report.

The group auditor may decide to **assume responsibility** for the work of a component auditor. When that is the case, the report will make **no reference** to the component auditor.

An illustration of an audit report in which the group auditor decides to make reference to the component auditor follows:

Group Financial Audit (Shared Responsibility Opinion)

INDEPENDENT AUDITOR'S REPORT

[*Appropriate Addressee*]

Report on the Consolidated Financial Statements (Intro)

We have audited the accompanying **consolidated** financial statements of X Company and its subsidiaries, which comprise the consolidated balance sheet as of December 31, 20X1, and the related **consolidated** statements of income, changes in stockholders' equity, and cash flows for the year then ended, and the related notes to the financial statements.

Management's Responsibility for the Financial Statements

-Standard paragraph

Auditor's Responsibility

Our responsibility is to express an opinion on these consolidated financial statements based on our audit. *We did not audit the financial statements of B Company, a wholly-owned subsidiary, which statements reflect total assets constituting 20 percent of consolidated total assets at December 31, 20X1, and total revenues constituting 18 percent of consolidated total revenues for the year then ended. Those statements were audited by other auditors, whose report has been furnished to us, and our opinion, insofar as it relates to the amounts included for B Company, is based solely on the report of the other auditors.* We conducted our audit in accordance with auditing standards generally accepted in the United States of America. Those standards require that we plan and perform the audit to obtain reasonable assurance about whether the consolidated financial statements are free from material misstatement.

-Standard 2 other paragraphs in Auditor's Responsibility

Opinion

In our opinion, **based on our audit and the report of the other auditors,** the **consolidated** financial statements referred to above present fairly, in all material respects, the financial position of X Company and its subsidiaries as of December 31, 20X1, and the results of its operations and its cash flows for the year then ended in accordance with accounting principles generally accepted in the United States of America.

Note the reference in the auditor's responsibility paragraph to assets and revenues, the largest individual numbers on the balance sheet and income statement, respectively. If the principal auditor prefers, these amounts may be stated as **percentages** of the consolidated total or as **dollar** amounts.

UNCERTAINTY (UNMODIFIED OR DISCLAIMER) (AU-C 706)

Occasionally, an auditor will be unable to determine the effects of an item on the financial statements, not because of any limitation on the scope of the engagement, but because the condition itself is one with an uncertain resolution. The most common example is an unresolved lawsuit.

So long as the client has properly **disclosed** the **uncertainty**, and **accrued** any potential losses that are **probable** and **estimable**, the financial statements are in conformity with generally accepted accounting principles (i.e., there is no GAAP departure). So long as the auditor has been able to obtain all available information about the matter, the audit is in accordance with generally accepted auditing standards (i.e., there is no scope limitation).

In such a circumstance, the auditor may issue a standard report expressing an unmodified opinion. If, however, the auditor is concerned that a user might not pay close enough attention to the financial statement and notes to notice the information provided by the client, the auditor has the **option** of adding an **emphasis-of-matter** paragraph to the audit report. This paragraph must appear **after** the opinion, in order to not detract from it, since it merely represents the auditor's desire to call the reader's attention to important information that the client has provided. The auditor will normally consider the likelihood of the loss and its materiality, but the decision on whether to add this paragraph is based on the auditor's judgment. An example of such a modification follows:

Uncertainty – Contingent Liability (After)

> ***Emphasis of Matter***
> **As discussed in *note Q* to the financial statements, the Company is a defendant in a lawsuit alleging patent infringement. The ultimate *outcome* of the litigation cannot presently be determined. Accordingly, *no provision* for any liability that may result upon adjudication has been made in the accompanying financial statements. *Our opinion is not modified with respect to this matter.***

One of the circumstances involving an uncertainty where the auditor is **required** to add an emphasis-of-matter paragraph to the end of the report is when there is **substantial doubt** as to the ability of the client to continue as a **going concern**. Since any company can be considered at risk of going out of business in the indefinite future (for example, in the next 10,000 years), the AICPA has established a limit of **one year after the balance sheet date** for concerns about the client's status to require the additional paragraph.

When considering the risk of a client going out of existence, the primary issues to be considered relate to **cash flow**, since a company is most likely to fail if it is unable to pay its debts as they come due. Factors that may produce substantial doubt as to the going concern status of the client include:
- Several years of operating losses.
- Negative working capital.
- Defaults or restructuring of debts.
- Losses of key customers.
- Denial or losses of licenses or patents.

There are, however, certain **mitigating factors** that may reduce the risk of going out of business by improving cash flow, such as plans to:
- Increase ownership equity through stock issuances for cash.
- Dispose of marketable assets that are not needed in the operations of the business.
- Delay or reduce optional expenditures, such as research and development.

In performing the engagement, the auditor will apply certain tests that are likely to identify conditions and events that could lead to substantial doubt as to the client's going concern status, including:
- Review of debt agreements and third-party commitments of financial support.
- Reading of minutes of board of directors' meetings.
- Inquiries of the client's legal counsel.
- Analytical procedures.

When the auditor concludes that there **is** substantial doubt as to the ability of the client to continue as a going concern for a reasonable period of time, the auditor must determine the adequacy of the client's disclosure of these matters. If the client has made proper disclosure of going concern doubts in a footnote, the audit report will contain an **unmodified opinion** and must contain an *emphasis-of-matter* paragraph containing language referring specifically to **substantial doubt** and **going concern**, such as the following:

Uncertainty – Going Concern Doubt (After)

> **Emphasis of Matter**
> **The accompanying financial statements have been prepared assuming that the Company will continue as a going concern. As discussed in <u>Note C</u> to the financial statements, the Company has suffered recurring losses from operations and has a net capital deficiency that raises <u>substantial doubts</u> about its ability to continue as a <u>going concern</u>. Management's plans in regard to these matters are also described in Note C. The financial statements do not include any adjustments that might result from the outcome of this uncertainty. *Our opinion is not modified with respect to this matter.***

Events or conditions may indicate that there could be substantial doubt as to whether the entity has the ability to continue as a going concern. If this is the case, the auditor will make inquiries of management and gather reliable audit evidence to support one of several possible conclusions: The auditor will address whether events and conditions actually indicate a going concern issue. If so, the auditor will address whether management's plans to mitigate the adverse effects of the events and conditions are likely to be adequate to alleviate the issue.
- If the auditor resolved that the events and conditions are not severe enough to warrant a going concern modification, the auditor will document the findings, but the audit report is not affected.
- If the auditor concludes that there is a going concern issue, it is required to be disclosed in the footnotes to the financial statements, with one set of disclosures if management's plans are expected to be adequate and another set of disclosures if they are not.
  - If disclosure is adequate, the auditor will issue a report with an unmodified opinion and the report will have an emphasis-of-matter paragraph drawing attention to the matter after the opinion in the auditor's report.
  - If disclosure is not adequate, it represents a departure from the applicable financial reporting framework.

If the client has not properly disclosed a going concern doubt or other material uncertainty, this will be considered inadequate disclosure, a form of GAAP departure, and will require a **qualified** opinion and **basis for** qualification paragraph **before** the opinion instead of after, discussing the uncertainty as well as noting that the absence of disclosure is a departure from GAAP.

The auditor is required to communicate going concern issues to those charged with governance.

In rare cases, the going concern uncertainty may be considered extreme or there are multiple uncertainties where it is not possible to form an opinion on the statements taken as a whole, requiring a *Disclaimer of opinion*.

SCOPE LIMITATION (QUALIFIED OR DISCLAIMER) (AU-C 705)

Inability to obtain **Sufficient Appropriate Audit Evidence** may occur.

Sometimes the problem isn't GAAP, but GAAS. Instead of the auditor drawing the conclusion that the statements depart from generally accepted accounting principles, the auditor is prevented from performing an audit in accordance with generally accepted auditing standards and is unable to draw any conclusion. When the auditor is unable to obtain sufficient appropriate audit evidence, it may not be possible to express an opinion on certain accounts or disclosures, or it may not even be possible to express an opinion on the financial statements as a whole at all.

When circumstances prevent an auditor from performing a particular procedure the auditor intended to perform, the auditor's initial response will be to determine if there are alternative procedures that can provide satisfactory evidence. If so, these alternative procedures will be performed and there is no injury to the audit; a standard report with an unmodified opinion can be issued and there is no need to mention the use of alternative tests from those originally contemplated.
- If the procedures that the auditor was unable to perform are considered unconditional requirements, there are no acceptable alternative procedures.
- If the procedures that the auditor was unable to perform are presumptively mandatory requirements, the auditor must document how alternative procedures were able to accomplish the objectives that the replaced procedures were intended to accomplish.

If, however, certain procedures that cannot be performed were deemed essential and acceptable alternative procedures cannot be performed, the auditor faces a **scope limitation** (scope restriction). A scope limitation may result from:
- Circumstances beyond the control of the auditor and the client.
- Circumstances related to the nature or timing of the auditor's procedures.
- Management-imposed limitations.

In general, scope limitations will result in a **qualified opinion** when the auditor is unable to obtain sufficient appropriate audit evidence on which to base an opinion but, although potentially material, an undetected misstatement would not be pervasive.
- The report would include a paragraph entitled Basis for Qualification before the opinion paragraph describing the reason for the qualification.
- The opinion paragraph will include the phrase "except for the possible effects of the matter(s)…"

If, on the other hand, the possible effects of an undetected misstatement could be material and pervasive, the auditor will issue a **disclaimer of opinion**.

- A scope limitation imposed by management requires special consideration.
- If undetected misstatements are potentially material and pervasive, the auditor may issue a disclaimer of opinion or withdraw from the engagement.
  - **Pervasive** means that, in the auditor's judgment, the effects are (1) not confined to a specific element, account, or item of the F/S; (2) could represent a substantial portion of the F/S; or (3) relate to disclosures that are fundamental to the users' understanding of the F/S. This relates to the "scope" of the effect on the F/S.

A disclaimer of opinion will include a paragraph entitled *Basis for Disclaimer* **before** the opinion paragraph with a description of the substantive scope limitations. The opinion paragraph will indicate:

- Because of the significance of the matters described in the basis for disclaimer paragraph, the auditor was unable to obtain sufficient appropriate audit evidence as a basis for an opinion.
- The auditor does not express an opinion.

In circumstances where a scope limitation prevents an auditor from obtaining sufficient appropriate audit evidence regarding an item that does not affect the ending balance of a balance sheet account, the auditor may issue an unmodified opinion in regard to financial position and disclaim an opinion in regard to the results of operations and cash flows.

Scope Limitation
(Restriction on ability to obtain "Sufficient Appropriate Audit Evidence")
- **Circumstances**
  - Cannot confirm A/R.
  - Auditor did not observe ending inventory.
  - Circumstances beyond the control of the entity.

- **Client imposed** (may be Disclaimer or withdraw)
  - Client's records are inadequate.
  - Client refuses permission to contact Attorney.
  - Management will not sign Management Representation letter.

If an auditor is unable to attend the year-end inventory count due to a minor automobile accident occurring on the drive to the client's offices on the evening of the count, a scope limitation requiring a qualified opinion will normally be the result (assuming the auditor cannot satisfactorily obtain evidence using alternative procedures). The report might appear as follows:

Scope Limitation – Qualified Opinion (Material but not Pervasive - Before)

INDEPENDENT AUDITOR'S REPORT

[*Appropriate Addressee*]

Report on the Financial Statements (Intro)

We have audited the accompanying financial statements of X Company, which comprise the balance sheet as of December 31, 20X1, and the related statements of income and changes in stockholders' equity for the year then ended, and the related notes to the financial statements.

Management's Responsibility for the Financial Statements

Management is responsible for the preparation and fair presentation of these financial statements in accordance with accounting principles generally accepted in the United States of America; this includes the design, implementation, and maintenance of internal control relevant to the preparation and fair presentation of financial statements that are free from material misstatement, whether due to fraud or error.

Auditor's Responsibility

Our responsibility is to express an opinion on these financial statements based on our audit. We conducted our audit in accordance with auditing standards generally accepted in the United States of America. Those standards require that we plan and perform the audit to obtain reasonable assurance about whether the financial statements are free of material misstatement.

An audit involves performing procedures to obtain audit evidence about the amounts and disclosures in the financial statements. The procedures selected depend on the auditor's judgment, including the assessment of risks of material misstatement of the financial statements, whether due to fraud or error. In making those risk assessments, the auditor considers internal control relevant to the entity's preparation and fair presentation of the financial statements in order to design audit procedures that are appropriate in the circumstances, but not for the purpose of expressing an opinion on the effectiveness of the entity's internal control. Accordingly, we express no such opinion. An audit also includes evaluating the appropriateness of accounting policies used and the reasonableness of significant accounting estimates made by management, as well as evaluating the overall presentation of the financial statements.

We believe that the audit evidence we have obtained is sufficient and appropriate to provide a basis for our **Qualified** audit opinion.

Basis for Qualified Opinion

We could not observe the taking of the physical inventory as of December 31, 20X1 due to circumstances unrelated to the client, and we were unable to satisfy ourselves regarding inventory quantities by means of other auditing procedures. Inventory amounts as of December 31, 20X1 also enter into the determination of net income and cash flows for the year ended December 31, 20X1.

Qualified Opinion

In our opinion, **except for the possible effects of the matter described in the Basis for Qualified Opinion paragraph,** the financial statements referred to above *present fairly*, in all material respects, the financial position of X Company as of December 31, 20X1, and the results of its operations and its cash flows for the year then ended in conformity with U.S. generally accepted accounting principles.

Notice that the qualification in the opinion paragraph is based on the possible effects on the financial statements and does not refer to the omitted procedures themselves. Also note that, as in all qualified opinions, a Basis for Qualified Opinion paragraph must appear **before** the opinion to explain the reasons for the alteration of the opinion.

Limited Reporting Engagements – Client asks auditor to report on only one financial statement and not the others. This is acceptable and is not considered a scope limit.

On occasion, a client will not require a complete set of financial statements to be audited, but will only be presenting a balance sheet. So long as the auditor is permitted to examine any evidence that the auditor chooses, this does not constitute any type of scope limitation. Also, the omission of the statement of cash flows in this circumstance is not a departure from GAAP, since the client is not presenting an income statement and, thus, is not purporting to present the results of operations. Finally, it is not considered a piecemeal opinion, since it covers an entire financial statement and not merely an individual account.

This type of engagement is known as a **limited reporting engagement**, and so long as the auditor completes an audit and is satisfied with the fair presentation of the balance sheet, an **unmodified** opinion will be issued.

Limited Reporting Engagement – Opinion on Balance Sheet Only

INDEPENDENT AUDITOR'S REPORT

[*Appropriate Addressee*]

Report on the Financial Statement (Intro)

We have audited the accompanying **balance sheet** of X Company as of December 31, 20X1, and the related notes to the balance sheet.

Management's Responsibility for the Financial Statements

Management is responsible for the preparation and fair presentation
of **this financial statement** in accordance with accounting principles generally accepted in the United States of America; this includes the design, implementation, and maintenance of internal control relevant to the preparation and fair presentation of the financial statement that is free from material misstatement, whether due to fraud or error.

Auditor's Responsibility

Our responsibility is to express an opinion **on the financial statement** based on our audit. We conducted our audit in accordance with auditing standards generally accepted in the United States of America. Those standards require that we plan and perform the audit to obtain reasonable assurance about whether the financial statements are free of material misstatement.

(Other 2 Auditor Responsibility paragraphs are standard)

Opinion

In our opinion, the **financial statement** referred to above presents fairly, in all material respects, the financial position of X Company as of December 31, 20X1, in accordance with accounting principles generally accepted in the United States of America.

Lecture 6.07

ADVERSE OPINION (BEFORE)

An adverse opinion is rare and would result from a departure from GAAP that is both material and pervasive. It may be in the form of an application of accounting principles with which the auditor does not agree, inadequate disclosure, or an unreasonable accounting estimate. **A *Basis for an Adverse Opinion*** paragraph would be included **before** the opinion paragraph, which would be entitled *Adverse Opinion*. Anytime the auditor feels the statements are false, fraudulent, deceptive, or misleading, the auditor always has the option of withdrawing from the engagement.

Adverse Opinion (Material and Pervasive Misstatements - Before)

INDEPENDENT AUDITOR'S REPORT

Addressee

Report on the Financial Statements (Intro)

-Standard Introductory Paragraph

Management's Responsibility for the Financial Statements

-Standard Paragraph

Auditor's Responsibility

-Standard Paragraph except the last paragraph will be modified to read:

*We believe that the audit evidence we have obtained is sufficient and appropriate to provide a basis for our **adverse** audit opinion.*

Basis for Adverse Opinion

As discussed in Note X to the financial statements, the Company carries its property, plant, and equipment accounts at appraisal values, and provides depreciation on the basis of such values. Further, the Company does not provide for income taxes with respect to differences between financial statement income and taxable income arising because of the use, for income tax purposes, of the installment method of reporting gross profit from certain types of sales. U.S. Generally Accepted Accounting Principles require that property, plant, and equipment be stated at an amount not in excess of cost, reduced by depreciation based on such amount and that deferred income taxes be provided.

Adverse Opinion

In our opinion**, because of the significance of the matter discussed in the Basis for Adverse Opinion paragraph,** the financial statements referred to above ***do not present fairly*** the financial position of X Company as of December 31, 20X1, or the results of their operations or their cash flows for the year then ended.

DISCLAIMER OF OPINION (BEFORE)

If the auditor is unable to observe inventory, for example, because the client refused to allow the auditor to do so, this may constitute an interference that is so serious as to make the work performed not constitute a valid audit and, thus, require a disclaimer of opinion. A Disclaimer may result from a very material and pervasive Scope limitation or a very material and pervasive Uncertainty. The report might appear as follows:

Disclaimer of Opinion (Material and Pervasive - Before)

INDEPENDENT AUDITORS REPORT

[*Appropriate Addressee*]

Report on the Financial Statements (Intro)

We **were engaged to audit** the accompanying financial statements of X Company, which comprise the balance sheet as of December 31, 20X1, and the related statements of income, changes in stockholders' equity, and cash flows for the year then ended, and the related notes to the financial statements.

Management's Responsibility for the Financial Statements

Management is responsible for the preparation and fair presentation of these financial statements in accordance with accounting principles generally accepted in the United States of America; this includes the design, implementation, and maintenance of internal control relevant to the preparation and fair presentation of financial statements that are free from material misstatement, whether due to fraud or error.

<u>*Auditor's Responsibility*</u>

Our responsibility is to express an opinion on these financial statements **based on conducting the audit in accordance with auditing standards generally accepted in the United States of America. Because of the matter described in the Basis for Disclaimer of Opinion paragraph, however, we were not able to obtain sufficient appropriate audit evidence to provide a basis for an audit opinion.**

(Omit next 2 paragraphs – definition of Audit and "we believe...")

<u>*Basis for Disclaimer of Opinion*</u>

We could not observe the taking of the physical inventory as of December 31, 20X1, due to the refusal of the client to permit our presence, and we were unable to satisfy ourselves regarding inventory quantities by means of other auditing procedures.

<u>*Disclaimer of Opinion (Opinion)*</u>

Because of the significance of the matter described in the Basis for Disclaimer paragraph, we have not been able to obtain sufficient audit evidence to provide a basis for an audit opinion. Accordingly, *we do not express* an opinion on these financial statements.

A disclaimer may cover only some of the financial statements, with an opinion expressed on others. For example, if the auditor was unable to obtain evidence regarding **beginning** inventory, but was able to verify ending inventory, an unmodified opinion might be issued on the balance sheet as of the ending date, with a disclaimer on the other statements that cover the entire year.

When an auditor has decided to disclaim an opinion on a financial statement, the disclaimer applies to **all** of the individual accounts on **that** statement. The auditor may **not** express an opinion on any of the individual accounts, because this would tend to overshadow the disclaimer. (It is also not acceptable to express an opinion on an individual account when issuing an adverse opinion on the statement as a result of an extreme GAAP departure.) Such a violation is known as a **piecemeal opinion**.

Lack of Independence

If the auditor lacks independence – 1 paragraph (**Do not** include reasons.)
- No intro or other paragraphs; no basis paragraph.
- Disclaimer – "we do not express an opinion"
- Do not give reasons for lack of independence.

COMPARATIVE FINANCIAL STATEMENTS

When the financial statements of the previous year are shown alongside those of the current year, the reporting requirements vary depending on the circumstances. If the auditor of the current year also audited the previous year, then the report will simply be updated so that both years are included in the audit report. The standard report on comparative statements is virtually identical to that of single period statements, except for the minor changes needed to refer to both years. The report date should be the completion of fieldwork.

Comparative – Standard Unmodified

INDEPENDENT AUDITOR'S REPORT

[*Appropriate Addressee*]

Report on the Financial Statements (Introductory)

We have audited the accompanying **consolidated** financial statements of ABC Company and its subsidiaries, which comprise the consolidated balance sheets as of December 31, **20X1 and 20X0**, and the related consolidated statements of income, changes in stockholders' equity, and cash flows for the **years then ended**, and the related notes to the financial statements.

Management's Responsibility for the Financial Statements

-Standard Paragraph

Auditor's Responsibility

-Standard Paragraph

Opinion

In our opinion, the **consolidated** financial statements referred to above present fairly, in all material respects, the financial position of ABC Company and its subsidiaries as of December 31, **20X1 and 20X0**, and the results of their operations and their cash flows for the **years then ended** in accordance with accounting principles generally accepted in the United States of America.

When reporting on comparative financial statements, the auditor is required to perform procedures in addition to those required when reporting on financial statements for a single period. The auditor will make a determination as to whether the comparative financial statements are presented in accordance with the requirements of the applicable financial reporting framework. The auditor will also determine if:
- The comparative financial statements and disclosures agree with those reported in the prior period or they have been restated to correct a departure in the prior period or they have been retroactively adjusted for a change in accounting principle; and
- The accounting principles and policies applied in the comparative financial statements and disclosures are consistent with those applied in the current period or that there has been a change in accounting principles that has been properly accounted for and disclosed.

During the current period's engagement, the auditor may become aware of a material misstatement in the comparative financial statements. Upon performing procedures to determine if, in fact, such a misstatement does exist, and the comparative financial statements are restated, the auditor should determine that the comparative financial statements agree with the restated financial statements.

When reporting on comparative financial statements, the auditor will obtain management representations for all periods referred to in the report.

Prior Period Examined by us (Qualified X2, Unmodified X1)

INDEPENDENT AUDITOR'S REPORT

[*Appropriate Addressee*]

Report on the Financial Statements (Intro)

We have audited the accompanying financial statements of ABC Company, which comprise the balance sheets as of December 31, 20X1 and 20X0, and the related statements of income, changes in stockholders' equity, and cash flows for the years then ended, and the related notes to the financial statements.

Management's Responsibility for the Financial Statements

-Standard Paragraph

Auditor's Responsibility

-Standard Paragraph

Basis for Qualified Opinion

The Company has excluded, from property and debt in the accompanying 20X1 balance sheet, certain lease obligations that were entered into in 20X1 which, in our opinion, should be capitalized in accordance with accounting principles generally accepted in the United States of America. If these lease obligations were capitalized, property would be increased by $XXX, long-term debt by $XXX, and retained earnings by $XXX as of December 31, 20X1, and net income and earnings per share would be increased (decreased) by $XXX and $XXX, respectively, for the year then ended.

Qualified Opinion

In our opinion, **except for the effects on the 20X1 financial statements of not capitalizing certain lease obligations as described in the Basis for Qualified Opinion paragraph**, the financial statements referred to above present fairly, in all material respects, the financial position of ABC Company as of December 31, 20X1 and 20X0, and the results of its operations and its cash flows for the years then ended in accordance with accounting principles generally accepted in the United States of America.

In some cases, the auditor's opinion on the previous year will be different than the opinion expressed on those statements in the earlier report. One example might be if the previous opinion was qualified due to inadequate disclosure of a lawsuit, and the lawsuit was settled during the current year (or the client agrees to disclose the suit in the notes to the current comparative financial statements).

When the auditor's opinion has changed, the opinion will reflect the current situation but an other-matter paragraph will refer to the earlier report indicating:
- The date of the previous report;
- The type of opinion previously expressed;
- Substantive reasons for the different opinion; and
- An indication that the auditor's opinion on the amended financial statements differs from the previous opinion.

Prior Period NOT Examined by us (Predecessor Auditor)

When a predecessor auditor examined the financial statements of the earlier year, the successor's comparative report of the current year can only express an opinion on the current year since that is the only year the successor audited. There are two ways of handling the earlier year:

1. The predecessor's report can be reissued and included along with the successor's audit report, or
2. The successor can reference the predecessor's earlier report in an "other-matter paragraph."

If the first alternative is chosen, the predecessor must:

- **Compare the financial statements** that they reported on with their presentation in the current comparative form.
- Obtain a **representation letter** from the **successor auditor.**

As long as the successor has not informed the predecessor of any reason for revision of the original report, the predecessor will simply reissue the original report with the original report date. If the successor is aware of any such reason, they should arrange for a three-way meeting (including the client) to discuss the appropriateness of the predecessor applying certain procedures to verify the need for changes. Any revisions would result in the predecessor's report being dual-dated to refer to any new information obtained.

If the second alternative is chosen, the successor will issue a standard unmodified report and add an **other-matter paragraph** after the opinion paragraph with reference to the predecessor's previous report date, opinion, and reasons for any qualification of the opinion or inclusion of an explanatory paragraph by the predecessor in that report. If the predecessor has issued a different opinion on amended financial statements, the other-matter paragraph should indicate so. The predecessor's name must **not** be included in the successor's report when the predecessor's report is not being reissued.

If predecessor auditor **reissues report**:
- Read F/S.
- Obtain Representation letter from successor auditor and client.
- If no adjustment to P/Y F/S, use original report date.
- If restate P/Y F/S, dual-date report.

If predecessor auditor **Does NOT agree to reissue** report:
- "Other-matter paragraph"
  - Prior period audited by other auditors
  - Date of predecessor's report
  - Type of opinion
  - If modified opinion, the reasons why modified

A comparative report in which a predecessor examined the preceding year and has *ceased operations* (e.g., Arthur Anderson) must state that the predecessor has ceased operations.

If no audit, review, or compilation was performed in relation to prior-period financial statements that are presented on a comparative basis with the current period's audited financial statements, those financial statements should clearly indicate their status. The report will include an other-matter paragraph that will indicate that the auditor did not audit, review, or compile those financial statements and that the auditor does not assume any responsibility for them.

Comparative F/S – Prior Period NOT Examined by us (Predecessor Auditor)

> ### *Other Matter (After)*
> The financial statements of ABC Company for the year ended December 31, 20X1, were audited by another auditor who expressed an unmodified opinion on those statements on March 16, 20X2.

Different Levels of Service

In some cases, an auditor will audit the current period's financial statements while the prior period's statements were reviewed or compiled. When that is the case, if the report on the prior period's financial statements is not reissued, the auditor will provide an **other-matter** paragraph in the current period's audit report. It will indicate:
- The service performed in the prior period.
- The date of the report on that service.
- A description of any material modifications noted in the report.

Current Year Audited, Prior Year Reviewed (Other-Matter paragraph – After)

> ### *Other Matter*
> The 20X1 financial statements were reviewed by us (other accountants) and our (their) report thereon, dated March 1, 20X2, stated we (they) were not aware of any material modifications that should be made to those statements for them to be in conformity with U.S. Generally Accepted Accounting Principles. A review is substantially less in scope than an audit and does not provide a basis for the expression of an opinion on the financial statements taken as a whole.

Current Year Unaudited, Prior Year Audited (Other-Matter Paragraph – After)

> ### *Other Matter*
> The financial statements for the year ended December 31, 20X1, were audited by us (other accountants) and we (they) expressed an unmodified opinion on them in our (their) report dated March 1, 20X2, but we (they) have not performed any auditing procedures since that date.

Lecture 6.08

SUMMARY OF NON-STANDARD REPORTS

Summary of Non-Standard Reports					
Situation	Introductory (Report on the F/S)	Management's Responsibility for F/S	Auditor's Responsibility	Opinion	Additional Paragraph
Material Departure	Standard	Standard	Adeq basis for qualified or adverse opinion	Qualified or Adverse	Basis for qualification - before Basis for adverse opinion - before
Justified Departure	Standard	Standard	Standard	Standard	Emphasis of matter - after
Inconsistent - Properly rep & justifiable (concur)	Standard	Standard	Standard	Standard	Emphasis of matter - after
Inconsistent - Not properly rep or not justifiable	Standard	Standard	Standard	Qualified or Adverse	Basis for qualification - before Basis for adverse opinion - before
Inadequate Disclosure (Omitted Disclosure)	Standard	Standard	Standard	Qualified or Adverse	Basis for qualification - before Basis for adverse opinion - before
No statement of cash flows	Delete reference	Standard	Standard	Qualified	Basis for qualification - before
Group Financial Audit (Division of responsibility)	Standard	Standard	Ref to % or $ audited by other	Unmodified with ref to report of other	Not required
Contingent liability	Standard	Standard	Standard	Standard	Emphasis of matter - after Not Required
Going concern doubts	Standard	Standard	Standard	Standard	Emphasis of matter - after
Scope limit - Mat & Not pervasive	Standard	Standard	Standard	Qualified	Basis for qualification - before
Scope limit - Mat & pervasive	Standard	Standard	Inability to obtain evid	Disclaimer	Basis for disclaimer - before
Scope limit - imposed by mgmt	Withdraw or only state eng to aud	Standard	Inability to obtain evid	Disclaimer	Basis for disclaimer - before
Balance sheet only	Refer only to b/s	Refer to financial statement instead of financial statements			

Lecture 6.09

CLASS QUESTIONS

Please see the Class Questions and Class Solutions for this Lecture at the end of this Section.

CLASS QUESTIONS

Work through the below Class Questions while following along with the respective lectures. Once this is complete, you can begin independently practicing what you've learned by quizzing yourself on this course section in your Interactive Practice Questions (IPQ), which can be found in your online Student Dashboard. Your IPQ simulates the computer-based testing experience, and will also help you understand how concepts are applied to the exam. Each question includes answer explanations from expert CPAs that will help you determine why you answered a question correctly or incorrectly. This is key to your success on the CPA Exam.

Lecture 6.09

1. Which of the following statements is a basic element of the auditor's standard report?

    a. The disclosures provide reasonable assurance that the financial statements are free of material misstatement.
    b. The auditor tested the overall internal control.
    c. An audit includes evaluating the reasonableness of significant estimates made by management.
    d. The financial statements are consistent with those of the prior period.

2. Which paragraphs of an auditor's standard report on financial statements of a nonissuer should refer to auditing standards generally accepted in the U.S. and Principles generally accepted in the U.S.?

	Auditing standards generally accepted in the U.S.	**Principles generally accepted in the U.S.**
a.	Intro (report on F/S)	Managements Responsibility
b.	Management's Responsibility	Auditor's Responsibility
c.	Auditor's Responsibility	Opinion
d.	Intro	Opinion

3. In which paragraph of a standard unmodified report is a disclaimer on internal control mentioned?

    a. Report on the Financial Statements (Intro)
    b. Management's Responsibility for the Financial Statements
    c. Auditor's Responsibility
    d. Opinion

4.   Green, CPA, concludes that there is substantial doubt about JKL Co.'s ability to continue as a going concern. If JKL's financial statements adequately disclose its financial difficulties, Green's auditor's report should

	Include an emphasis of a matter paragraph following the opinion paragraph	Specifically use the words "going concern"	Specifically use the words "substantial doubt"
a.	Yes	Yes	Yes
b.	Yes	Yes	No
c.	Yes	No	Yes
d.	No	Yes	Yes

5.   For which of the following events would an auditor issue a report that omits any reference to consistency?

   a.   A change in the method of accounting for inventories.
   b.   A change from an accounting principle that is **not** generally accepted to one that is generally accepted.
   c.   A change in the useful life used to calculate the provision for depreciation expense.
   d.   Management's lack of reasonable justification for a change in accounting principle.

6.   Under which of the following circumstances would a disclaimer of opinion not be appropriate?

   a.   The auditor is unable to determine the amounts associated with an employee fraud scheme.
   b.   Management does **not** provide reasonable justification for a change in accounting principles.
   c.   The client refuses to permit the auditor to confirm certain accounts receivable or apply alternative procedures to verify their balances.
   d.   The chief executive officer is unwilling to sign the management representation letter.

7.   An auditor concludes that a client's illegal act, which has a material effect on the financial statements, has not been properly accounted for or disclosed. Depending on the materiality of the effect on the financial statements, the auditor should express either a(n)

   a.   Adverse opinion or a disclaimer of opinion.
   b.   Qualified opinion or an adverse opinion.
   c.   Disclaimer of opinion or an unmodified opinion with a separate explanatory paragraph.
   d.   Unmodified opinion with a separate explanatory paragraph or a qualified opinion.

8. When an auditor qualifies an opinion in an audit of an issuer under PCAOB because of inadequate disclosure, the auditor should describe the nature of the omission in a separate explanatory paragraph and modify the

	Introductory paragraph	Scope paragraph	Opinion paragraph
a.	Yes	No	No
b.	Yes	Yes	No
c.	No	Yes	Yes
d.	No	No	Yes

9. Park, CPA, was engaged to audit the financial statements of Tech Co., a new client, for the year ended December 31, 20X1. Park obtained sufficient audit evidence for all of Tech's financial statement items except Tech's opening inventory. Due to inadequate financial records, Park could not verify Tech's January 1, 20X1 inventory balances. Park's opinion on Tech's 20X1 financial statements most likely will be

	Balance sheet	Income statement
a.	Disclaimer	Disclaimer
b.	Unmodified	Disclaimer
c.	Disclaimer	Adverse
d.	Unmodified	Adverse

10. When auditing group financial statements and the auditor decides to prepare a "shared responsibility opinion" report with the component auditor, which of the following paragraphs are adjusted?

	Auditor responsibility paragraph	Opinion paragraph
a.	No	Yes
b.	Yes	Yes
c.	No	No
d.	Yes	No

11. A scope limitation sufficient to preclude an unmodified opinion always will result when management

 a. Prevents the auditor from reviewing the working papers of the predecessor auditor.
 b. Engages the auditor after the year-end physical inventory is completed.
 c. Requests that certain material accounts receivable **not** be confirmed.
 d. Refuses to acknowledge its responsibility for the fair presentation of the financial statements in conformity with GAAP.

12. An auditor should disclose the reasons for expressing an adverse opinion in a "Basis for Adverse Opinion" paragraph which is located where in the audit report?

 a. Preceding the auditor's responsibility paragraph.
 b. Preceding the opinion paragraph.
 c. Following the opinion paragraph.
 d. Within the notes to the financial statements.

CLASS SOLUTIONS

1. **(c)** In the Auditor's Responsibility paragraph, it mentions that an auditor evaluates the appropriateness of accounting policies used and the reasonableness of significant accounting estimates made by management. The report does not specifically mention the disclosures, nor do they provide assurance (a). The auditor does not test overall control, but only those controls that the auditor intends to rely upon (b). The report only mentions consistency when there is a lack of it. Consistency is implied, rather than being explicitly stated in the report (d).

2. **(c)** The auditor is required to perform the engagement in accordance with generally accepted auditing standards, which is stated in the auditor's responsibilities paragraph. The audit enables the auditor to express an opinion as to whether the financial statements were prepared in accordance with the applicable financial reporting framework, commonly accounting principles generally accepted in the United States of America. This is indicated in the opinion paragraph.

3. **(c)** The auditor's responsibility paragraph states that the auditor considers internal control relevant to the entity's preparation and fair presentation of the financial statements in order to design audit procedures that are appropriate in the circumstances. It also states that it is not for the purpose of expressing an opinion, and accordingly, no such opinion is expressed.

4. **(a)** When an uncertainty exists raising substantial doubt as to an entity's ability to continue as a going concern, as long as it is properly disclosed, the auditor will not qualify the opinion but will draw attention to the issue by including an emphasis-of-matter paragraph following the opinion paragraph, indicating the footnote in which the uncertainty is disclosed. To make certain that there is no misunderstanding, the paragraph is required to use the words "going concern" and "substantial doubt".

5. **(c)** Consistency is implicit in the auditor's report, which, makes no mention of it when the financial statements have been prepared in a consistent manner. The financial statements would not have been consistently prepared whenever there is a change in accounting principles, including a change in the method of accounting for inventories (a), a change from an unacceptable principle to an acceptable one (b), or a change that management cannot reasonably justify (d). A change in the useful life of a depreciable asset is a change in accounting estimate, which does not affect consistency.

6. **(b)** The inability of an auditor to determine the amounts associated with employee fraud (a), the client refusing to permit the auditor to confirm certain accounts receivable or apply alternative procedures (c), and the unwillingness of the chief executive officer to sign a management representation letter (d) all represent scope limitations. Depending on the materiality, a qualified opinion or a disclaimer of opinion may be issued. If management does not provide reasonable justification for a change in accounting principles, it represents a departure from GAAP, which, depending on materiality would require the auditor to issue a qualified opinion or an adverse opinion, but not a disclaimer.

7. **(b)** Improperly accounting for a material illegal act and not disclosing it, represents departures from GAAP. As a result, depending on materiality, the auditor's will either issue a qualified opinion or an adverse opinion. A disclaimer of opinion is only issued as a result of a significant scope limitation, not a departure from GAAP.

8.   **(d)** Inadequate disclosure represents a departure from GAAP, which would require the auditor to modify the opinion paragraph and issue a qualified opinion. It does not have any impact on the information in the introductory paragraph, which primarily indicates that the auditor was engaged to perform an audit and identifies the financial statements being audited. Likewise, it has no effect on the scope of the work that the auditor is required to perform nor on any of the auditor's responsibilities and, as a result, has no effect on the scope paragraph.

9.   **(b)** If Park is unable to obtain satisfaction as to the opening balances of inventory, the value of cost of goods sold cannot be verified and would result in a qualified opinion or a disclaimer of opinion on the income statement. The beginning inventory does not affect the amount reported as ending inventory. As a result, Park would be able to express an unmodified opinion on the ending balance sheet.

10. **(b)** When an auditor is auditing group financial statements, having component auditors responsible for portions of the audit, the group auditor may indicate the shared responsibility in the auditor's report. If the group auditor decides to do so, the paragraph indicating the auditor's responsibility will mention the division of responsibility, including the dollar amount or percent audited by the component auditor. The opinion paragraph would also be modified to indicate that the opinion is based on the group auditor's audit as well as the audit of the other auditors.

11. **(d)** Preventing the auditor from reviewing the working papers of the predecessor auditor (a), engaging the auditor after completion of the year-end physical inventory (b), and requesting that material accounts receivable not be confirmed (c) are all scope limitations that may preclude an unmodified opinion, unless the auditor is able to obtain sufficient appropriate audit evidence in relation to those matters by applying alternative procedures. Management's refusal to acknowledge responsibility for fair presentation of the financial statements in conformity with GAAP is a limitation for which there are no alternate procedures and would always preclude issuance of an unmodified opinion.

12. **(b)** Whenever a qualified, adverse, or disclaimer of opinion is expressed, the reasons for the report modification are included in a paragraph, immediately preceding the opinion paragraph., indicating the basis for the modification.

Lecture 6.09

TASK-BASED SIMULATIONS

Task-Based Simulation 1

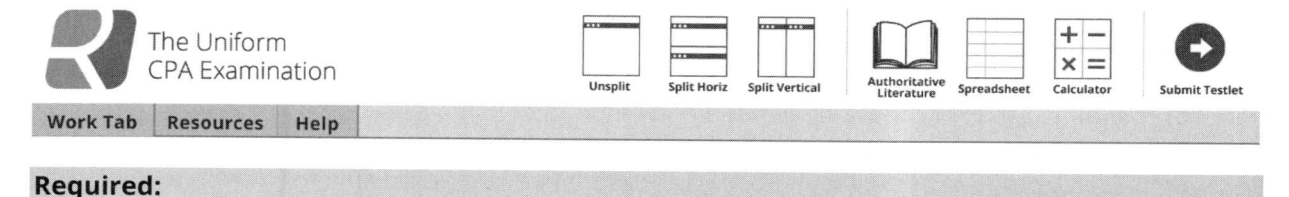

Work Tab   **Resources**   **Help**

Required:

Items 1 through 7 present various independent factual situations an auditor might encounter in conducting an audit. List A represents the types of opinions the auditor ordinarily would issue and List B represents the report modifications (if any) that would be necessary. For each situation, select one response from List A and one from List B. Select as the best answer for each item, the action the auditor normally would take. The types of opinions in List A and the report modifications in List B may be selected once, more than once, or not at all.

Assume:
- The auditor is independent.
- The auditor previously expressed an unmodified opinion on the prior year's financial statements.
- Only single-year (not comparative) statements are presented for the current year.
- The conditions for an unmodified opinion exist unless contradicted in the factual situations.
- The conditions stated in the factual situations are material.
- No report modifications are to be made except in response to the factual situation.

Items to be answered:

1. In auditing the long-term investments account, an auditor is unable to obtain audited financial statements for an investee located in a foreign country. The auditor concludes that sufficient appropriate audit evidence regarding this investment cannot be obtained.

2. Due to recurring operating losses and working capital deficiencies, an auditor has substantial doubt about an entity's ability to continue as a going concern for a reasonable period of time. However, the financial statement disclosures concerning these matters are adequate.

3. A principal auditor decides to take responsibility for the work of another CPA who audited a wholly-owned subsidiary of the entity and issued an unmodified opinion. The total assets and revenues of the subsidiary represent 17% and 18%, respectively, of the total assets and revenues of the entity being audited.

4. An entity issues financial statements that present financial position and results of operations but omits the related statement of cash flows. Management discloses in the notes to the financial statements that it does not believe the statement of cash flows to be a useful financial statement.

5. An entity changes its inventory valuation method from FIFO to LIFO. The auditor concurs with the change although it has a material effect on the comparability of the entity's financial statements.

6. An entity is a defendant in a lawsuit alleging infringement of certain patent rights. However, the ultimate outcome of the litigation cannot be reasonably estimated by management. The auditor believes there is a reasonable possibility of a significantly material loss, but the lawsuit is adequately disclosed in the notes to the financial statements.

7. An entity discloses in the notes to the financial statements certain lease obligations. The auditor believes that the failure to capitalize these leases is a departure from generally accepted accounting principles.

List A	List B
Types of Opinions	**Report Modifications**
A An "except for" qualified opinion	H Describe the circumstances in an explanatory paragraph preceding the opinion paragraph without modifying the opinion paragraph.
B An unmodified opinion	I Describe the circumstances in an emphasis-of-matter paragraph following the opinion paragraph without modifying the other paragraphs.
C An adverse opinion	
D A disclaimer of opinion	
E Either an "except for" qualified opinion or an adverse opinion	J Describe the circumstances in an other-matter paragraph following the opinion paragraph without modifying the other paragraphs.
F Either a disclaimer of opinion or an "except for" qualified opinion	K Describe the circumstances in a basis-for-modification paragraph preceding the opinion paragraph and modify the opinion paragraph.
G Either an adverse opinion or a disclaimer of opinion	L Describe the circumstances in an emphasis-of-matter paragraph following the opinion paragraph and modify the opinion paragraph.
	M Describe the circumstances in a basis-for-modification paragraph preceding the opinion paragraph and modify the introductory and opinion paragraphs.
	N Describe the circumstances in an emphasis-of-matter paragraph following the opinion paragraph and modify the introductory and opinion paragraphs.
	O Describe the circumstances within the introductory paragraph without adding any additional paragraphs.
	P Describe the circumstances within the opinion paragraph without adding any additional paragraphs.
	Q Describe the circumstances within the introductory and opinion paragraphs without adding any additional paragraphs.
	R Issue the standard auditor's report without modification.

Task-Based Simulation 2

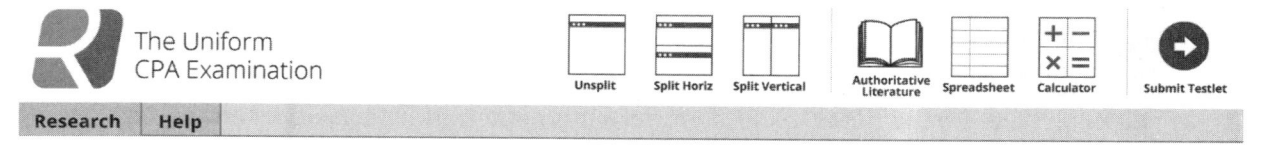

Arnold Co. changed its method of accounting for inventories from FIFO to the weighted average method. Billups, CPA, concurs with the change and has noted that it has been properly accounted for and is adequately disclosed in the financial statements. Billups is curious as to whether or not the report on the audited financial statements should be modified.

1. Which title of Professional Standards addresses this issue & will be helpful in understanding whether or not the auditor's report should be modified under the circumstances?

2. Enter the exact section and paragraph with helpful information.

Task-Based Simulation 3

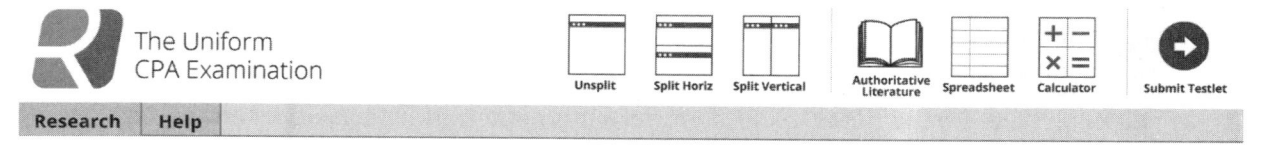

Richard Fellows, CPA, is preparing a report on current period financial statements that are being presented in comparative form with the prior year's financial statements. The prior year's statements were audited by another CPA. The predecessor's report, which is not being reissued, included a qualified opinion. Richard is trying to determine how, if at all, the report on the current period's financial statements should be modified.

1. Which title of Professional Standards addresses this issue & will be helpful in understanding the auditor's reporting responsibilities in these circumstances?

2. Enter the exact section and paragraph with helpful information.

Task-Based Simulation 4

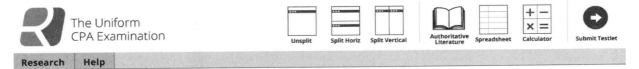

Standard Report Elements

Due to a significant transaction with related parties, Jeffries, CPA, has decided to include an emphasis-of-matter paragraph in the auditor's report, but is not certain as to what is required to be included in such a paragraph.

1.   Which title of Professional Standards addresses this issue & will be helpful in understanding what must be included in an emphasis-of-matter paragraph?

2.   Enter the exact section and paragraph with helpful information.

Task-Based Simulation 5

In the current year, AB Corp, a publicly-held company, realized that it had incorrectly accounted for certain derivative instruments in the preceding period. As a result, they made an adjusting entry to correct the prior period's financial statements, presented on a comparative basis with the current period's financial statements. The correction was properly accounted for and adequately disclosed. The auditor, Wald, CPA, wishes to determine if, and how, the audit report should be modified as a result.

1.   Which title of Professional Standards addresses this issue & will be helpful in understanding whether or not the report should be modified and, if so, how it should be modified?

2.   Enter the exact section and paragraph with helpful information.

Task-Based Simulation 6

The Uniform
CPA Examination

Unsplit   Split Horiz   Split Vertical   Authoritative Literature   Spreadsheet   Calculator   Submit Testlet

Research   Help

Bigg, CPA, is auditing the consolidated financial statements of Pretty Large Corp and has enlisted the assistance of Somm, Watts, Maul, CPAs (SWM) to audit one of the subsidiaries. Bigg would prefer not to take responsibility for SWM's work and is trying to determine under what circumstances it is acceptable to refer to SWM in the audit report to indicate a division of responsibilities (component auditor).

1.   Which title of Professional Standards addresses this issue & will be helpful in understanding when Bigg may refer to SWM in the report?

2.   Enter the exact section and paragraph with helpful information.

TASK-BASED SIMULATION SOLUTIONS

Task-Based Simulation Solution 1

1.   FK   The inability to obtain sufficient appropriate audit evidence is a scope limitation. We know that the long-term investment is material. We do not, however, know if it is so material that a material misstatement would also result in a material misstatement to the financial statements taken as a whole. At a minimum, we will issue a qualified opinion since we cannot express an opinion about an item that is material to the financial statements. If it is pervasive, however, we would not be able to express an opinion on the financial statements taken as a whole and would issue a disclaimer. Either of these represents a modification of the opinion paragraph, which would be preceded by a paragraph entitled either "Basis for Qualification" or "Basis for Disclaimer of Opinion," as appropriate.

2.   BI   As long as an entity properly discloses a substantial doubt about its ability to continue as a going concern, the auditor will issue a report with an unmodified opinion. Due to the significance of a going concern doubt, however, the auditor is required to draw attention to it. This will be done by including an emphasis-of-matter paragraph, which always immediately follows the opinion paragraph.

3.   BR   When an auditor decides to take responsibility for the work of another auditor, there should be no indication in the audit report that any portion of the financial statements was audited by another auditor. Neither the opinion nor any of the other paragraphs are modified since the auditor was able to obtain sufficient appropriate audit evidence and there were apparently no material misstatements.

4.   AM   The omission of the statement of cash flows is a violation of GAAP and would result in a qualified opinion. It's omission does not, however, cause the remaining financial statements to be materially misstated and, as a result, an adverse opinion would not be appropriate. Since the introductory paragraph names the financial statements that are being audited, it will have to be modified to omit mention of the statement of cash flows. A basis for modification paragraph is required for any modified opinion, which would be before the opinion paragraph. In addition, the opinion paragraph is modified to indicate the qualification and to eliminate the reference to cash flows.

5.   BI   A user assumes financial statements were prepared in a manner consistent with the previous year unless the auditor's report indicates otherwise. Since the auditor concurs with the change in accounting principles and since there is no indication that it was not accounted for and disclosed properly, there is no basis for a modified opinion. The auditor will alert users to the inconsistency with an emphasis-of-matter paragraph, which always immediately follows the opinion paragraph.

6.   BI   When the entity has a loss contingency that is reasonably possible, it is required to be disclosed but not accrued. If it is adequately disclosed, there is no basis for modifying the auditor's opinion and an unmodified opinion will be issued. Since it is material, however, the auditor will likely wish to bring it to the attention of users of the financial statements, which will be done by adding an emphasis-of-matter paragraph immediately following the opinion paragraph.

7.   EK   If the auditor believes there is a violation of GAAP that the client refuses to correct, the auditor will issue a qualified opinion if the matter is material to the financial statements but is not so material as to cause the financial statements taken as a whole to be materially misstated. If it is so material as to affect the fairness of the financial statements taken as a whole, an adverse opinion would be required. In either case, the opinion paragraph would be modified and a basis-for-modification paragraph will be added immediately before the opinion paragraph.

Task-Based Simulation Solution 2

AU-C	708	.08

Task-Based Simulation Solution 3

AU-C	700	.55

Task-Based Simulation Solution 4

AU-C	706	.07

Task-Based Simulation Solution 5

PCAOB	AS 3101	Par .18A

Task-Based Simulation Solution 6

AU-C	600	.25

Section 7 –Statements on Standards for Accounting and Review Services
(SSARS)

Corresponding Lectures

Watch the following course lectures with this section:

Lecture 7.01 – Association with Financial Statements & SSARS Engagements

Lecture 7.02 – Preparation of Financial Statements Engagement

Lecture 7.03 – Preparation of Financial Statements Engagement - Class Questions

Lecture 7.04 – Comparison of Prep Eng, Compilation & Review

Lecture 7.05 – Compilation Engagements

Lecture 7.06 – Compilations Engagements – Class Questions

Lecture 7.07 – Review Engagements

Lecture 7.08 – Comparison of Engagements, Interim Review (10Q) and Codified SSARS AR

Lecture 7.09 – Compilations and Reviews – Class Questions

EXAM NOTE: *Please refer to the AICPA AUD Blueprint in the Introduction of this book to find a listing of the representative tasks (and their associated skill levels—i.e., Remembering and Understanding, Application, Analysis, and Evaluation) that the candidate should be able to perform based on the knowledge obtained in this section.*

Statements on Standards for Accounting and Review Services (SSARS) (AR-C 60 – AR-C 120)

ASSOCIATION WITH FINANCIAL STATEMENTS

When a CPA is associated with a client's financial statements, there are numerous types of engagements that may be entered into. The nature of the engagement will determine which standards the CPA must be in compliance with. When associated with the financial statements of a **publicly-held entity**, the accountant will follow the requirements of the Public Company Accounting Oversight Board (PCAOB).

When the CPA is associated with the financial statements of a **nonpublic, nongovernmental entity**:
- The accountant may be engaged to **audit** financial statements, in which case the accountant will follow Generally Accepted Auditing Standards (GAAS) in the form of the clarified Statements on Auditing Standards (clarified SAS) issued by the Auditing Standards Board (ASB) of the AICPA.
- The accountant may be engaged to **review** the financial statements, in which case the accountant will follow Statements on Standards for Accounting and Review Services (SSARS) issued by the Accounting and Review Services Committee (ARSC) of the AICPA.
- The accountant may be engaged to **compile** the financial statements, in which case the accountant will also follow SSARS.
- The accountant may be engaged to **prepare** financial statements, in which case the accountant will also follow SSARS.
    - The accountant may be engaged to perform bookkeeping for a client, as a result of which financial statements may be prepared. The preparation of financial statements, under those circumstances, is part of the bookkeeping engagement, not a SSARS engagement.
    - In order for a financial statement preparation engagement to fall under SSARS, the client would specifically request that the accountant prepare the financial statements.

In a SSARS engagement to prepare financial statements, the client selects the applicable financial reporting framework but the accountant takes responsibility for the preparation and fair presentation of the financial statements, not the client.

Audits and reviews are considered **attest engagements**. An attest engagement is an engagement that requires independence as defined by the AICPA professional standards. Although not an attest engagement, a compilation also requires the accountant to be independent. As discussed below, however, it is not considered an attest engagement because SSARS allows the CPA to perform a compilation when not independent provided certain requirements are met.

Audits and reviews are also considered **assurance engagements**. An assurance engagement is an engagement in which the accountant is required to evaluate the *accuracy or completeness* of the information provided by management or otherwise gather evidence that will serve as a basis for a report in which the accountant expresses an opinion, in an audit, or a conclusion, in a review, on the information. Although a compilation is not an assurance engagement, a report is issued. It does not contain, however, the expression of an opinion or conclusion, nor does it express any assurance.

Preparation engagements are nonattest engagements as well as nonassurance engagements. Since it is a nonattest engagement, the accountant is not required to be independent to perform a preparation engagement. In addition, since it is a nonassurance engagement, the accountant is not required to verify the accuracy or completeness of the information nor does the accountant prepare a report.

SSARS ENGAGEMENTS

The AICPA authorized the issuance of **Statements on Standards for Accounting & Review Services (SSARS)**, to apply to the work of accountants in connection with the financial statements of **Nonissuer (nonpublic)** clients (including individuals). Nonissuers are defined as all entities except for those defined in Section 3 of the Securities Exchange Act of 1934, the securities of which are registered under Section 12 of that Act, or that are required to file reports under Section 15(d), or that file or have filed a registration statement that has not yet become effective under the Securities Act of 1933, and that has not been withdrawn.

All SSARS engagements are required to be performed in accordance with *General Principles for Engagements Performed in Accordance With Statements on Standards for Accounting and Review Services* (**AR-C 60**). These general principles are described in the following five categories:
- Financial Statements
- Ethical Requirements
- Professional Judgment
- Conduct of the Engagement in Accordance With SSARS
- Engagement Level Quality Control

Financial Statements

The financial statements, or other historical or prospective financial information that is the subject of the SSARS engagement, are those of the entity, not the CPA performing the engagement (management's statements). Although the CPA is subject to the requirements of SSARS, SSARS do not impose any responsibilities on management. Nor do SSARS override any of the laws or regulations that govern management's responsibilities.

Financial statements may be prepared in accordance with a general purpose framework, such as GAAP or IFRS, designed to meet the needs of a wide range of users. They may also be prepared in accordance with a special purpose framework, also often referred to as an OCBOA (Other Comprehensive Basis of Accounting), such as the tax basis, cash basis, a contractual or regulatory basis, or some other framework like FRF for SMEs (Financial Reporting Framework for Small to Medium Sized Enterprises). Regardless, it is *management's responsibility* to make certain that the financial statements are prepared and fairly presented in accordance with the applicable financial reporting framework.

The preparation and fair presentation of financial information requires management to exercise reasonable judgment when making accounting estimates or when selecting and applying accounting policies within the context of the applicable financial reporting framework. In addition, management is **required to**:
- Identify the applicable financial reporting framework;

- Prepare and fairly present the financial statements in accordance with that framework; and
- Adequately describe the framework in the financial statements.

Ethical Requirements

The accountant is required to comply with all relevant ethical requirements, including those included in the AICPA Code of Professional Conduct as well as those imposed by state boards of accountancy or other applicable regulatory agencies. This entails compliance with the fundamental principles of professional ethics established by the Code. These include:
- Responsibilities
- The public interest
- Integrity
- Objectivity and independence
- Due care
- Scope and nature of services

Professional Judgment

Decisions are required to be made throughout a SSARS engagement and an informed decision can only be made by applying the accountant's knowledge and experience to the facts and circumstances. Informed decisions may also require consultation with others and should lead to judgments that reflect applications of SSARS and accounting principles that are both *competent and appropriate* under the circumstances.

Conduct of the Engagement in Accordance With SSARS

Conducting an engagement in accordance with SSARS requires the accountant to be familiar with, and apply, all relevant AR-C sections. This includes not only the text of each relevant section but also the information provided in the section of the standards related to application and other explanatory material.

In some cases, the accountant may be required to comply with requirements in addition to those of SSARS. This would be the case, for example, if laws or regulations imposed other requirements.
- These requirements would be fulfilled in addition to any requirements included in relevant sections of SSARS.
- An engagement that complies only with the requirements of laws and regulations may not be in conformity with SSARS.

The accountant may be engaged to compile or review financial statements in accordance with SSARS and some other set of standards, such as International Standards on Related Services 4410 (Revised), *Compilation Engagements*; International Standards on Review Engagements 2400 (Revised), *Engagements to Review Historical Financial Statements*; or other compilation or review standards imposed by a particular jurisdiction.

It would be inappropriate to indicate, such as in a report, that an engagement was performed in accordance with SSARS unless all relevant sections of SSARS are complied with. Relevant sections include requirements that must be performed in every engagement and requirements that are only applicable if a certain condition exists. For example,

- A certain circumstance may require an accountant to withdraw from a SSARS engagement, if possible, due to some condition, such as a discovery that the accountant is not independent.
- This would not be a relevant requirement if laws or regulations prohibited the accountant from withdrawing from the engagement since withdrawal, under the circumstances, would not be possible.

As is the case in auditing standards, SSARS impose *two types of requirements*.
- An **unconditional requirement**, associated with the word **"must"** or the phrase **"is required to"** is one for which there is no alternative. When it is relevant to an engagement, the accountant will have performed in conformity with standards only if the requirement is complied with.
- A **presumptively mandatory requirement**, associated with the word **"should,"** is also required to be complied with when relevant. In rare circumstances, however, the accountant may find it necessary to perform alternative procedures, such as when performance of the procedure presumptively required would likely be ineffective. In such cases, the accountant must document the reason for the departure and an indication of how the alternative procedures performed achieved the objectives of the presumptively mandatory requirement.
    - In addition to the specific relevant requirements of SSARS, the accountant should consider interpretive publications.
    - The fact that the accountant *should consider* interpretive publications establishes a presumptively mandatory requirement to consider the guidance in the publications, but does not to establish a requirement to apply it.
    - The accountant is, of course, not required to comply with guidelines in interpretive publications. They are nonauthoritative and, if the accountant intends to comply with their guidelines, the accountant should make certain that they do not contradict or reduce the effectiveness of actions taken to follow authoritative literature.

Engagement Level Quality Control

The engagement partner in a SSARS engagement is responsible for the overall quality of the engagement; its direction, planning, supervision, and performance; the appropriateness of the report, if any; and compliance with the firm's quality control policies and procedures, including those related to:
- Client and engagement acceptance or continuance;
- Ascertaining that the engagement team has the qualifications to perform the engagement competently; and
- Engagement documentation.

The engagement partner is also responsible for:
- Identifying and communicating circumstances that may affect the client or engagement acceptance or continuance decision; and
- Being aware of potential noncompliance with ethical requirements.

Before accepting or continuing an engagement or a relationship with a client, the accountant should ascertain that:
- All ethical requirements will be satisfied;
- Reliable information needed to complete the engagement will be available;
- There is no reason to doubt the client's integrity;

- The financial reporting framework selected by management is acceptable; and
- Management has acknowledged responsibility for:
  - Selecting the financial reporting framework;
  - The design, implementation, and maintenance (DIM) of internal control relevant to financial reporting, although this would not be the case if the accountant decides to accept such responsibility, which could only occur if no assurance is being provided because accepting those responsibilities would be an example of an accountant assuming management responsibilities, which would impair the accountant's independence;
  - Preventing and detecting fraud;
  - Compliance with applicable laws and regulations;
  - The accuracy and completeness of information provided by management; and
  - Providing the accountant with access to all relevant information and to persons within the entity, as considered appropriate by the accountant.

Lecture 7.02

PREPARATION OF FINANCIAL STATEMENTS (AR-C 70)

An engagement to prepare financial statements is a nonattest/nonassurance engagement in which the accountant prepares financial statements in accordance with an applicable financial reporting framework on the basis of information provided by management. The accountant is *not required* to verify the accuracy or completeness of the information provided by management. In addition, since a preparation is a nonattest engagement, the accountant is not required to evaluate independence.

These standards also apply when the accountant is engaged to prepare historical financial information other than financial statements. In such cases, the requirements are adapted, as appropriate.

When a CPA is engaged to compile, review, or audit a client's financial statements or prospective financial statements, but the client has not prepared the financial statements and expects the CPA to do so, the CPA is actually involved in two related engagements:

- There is a nonattest engagement, which is a form of **bookkeeping** engagement, to prepare the financial statements.
  - This engagement **is not subject to SSARS**.
  - While, on separate occasions, the accountant may be asked to perform two separate engagements in relation to the same financial statements, such as reviewed financial statements prepared for the client's banker, and audited financial statements requested later as a result of a contract being entered into, the accountant would not have two SSARS engagements in relation to a single set of financial statements performed simultaneously.
  - The accountant is required to determine if independence is impaired under the AICPA Code of Professional Conduct.
- There is a compilation or review engagement, which are also engagements subject to the requirements of SSARS.
  - If independence is not impaired, the accountant may perform either a review or a compilation.
  - If independence is impaired, the accountant may not perform a review and may only perform a compilation if certain requirements are adhered to.

When a CPA is engaged to prepare financial statements that will **not** be compiled, reviewed, or audited, or, if they will be but that engagement will be performed by another CPA, the preparation engagement is a nonattest engagement that *is subject to SSARS*.
- Since the engagement is not an attest engagement, nor will the accountant be performing an attest engagement, there is no requirement to evaluate independence.
- If, however, the accountant expects to perform services for the client that will require independence, such as when the CPA prepares quarterly financial statements but reviews or audits the annual statement, the accountant will wish to make certain that the independence related requirements of the Code are complied with.

In certain circumstances, an accountant may be engaged to prepare historical financial statements, other historical financial information, or prospective financial information in an engagement that is not required to be performed in accordance with SSARS. These other nonattest engagements include:
- Information that is solely for submission to a taxing authority;
- Information to be included in a written personal financial plan prepared by the accountant;
- Information to be used in conjunction with litigation services that involve pending or potential legal or regulatory proceedings; or
- Information prepared in conjunction with business valuation services.

Requirements in a Preparation Engagement

As is true of all SSARS engagements, an accountant engaged to prepare financial statements for a client is required to adhere to the *General Principles for Engagements Performed in Accordance With SSARS* (AR-C 60). In addition, there are specific requirements that apply to a preparation engagement.

The accountant is required to reach an agreement with the client on the terms of the engagement, which should be documented in an **engagement letter** that is signed by *both* the client and the accountant's firm. The agreement should include:
- That the objective of the engagement is for the accountant to prepare the financial statements in accordance with the applicable financial reporting framework;
- Management's responsibilities, as indicated in AR-C 60;
- The accountant's responsibilities, which are to comply with the requirements of SSARS;
- Limitations of an engagement to prepare financial statements
- Identification of the applicable financial reporting framework; and
- Whether certain conditions are expected to exist, such as:
  ○ A known departure from the applicable financial reporting framework; or
  ○ The omission of substantially all disclosures required by the applicable financial reporting framework.
- An agreement by management that *each page* of the financial statements will include a statement indicating that *no assurance is provided*;

The accountant is not precluded from preparing a client's financial statements when the client cannot, or will not, agree to include a statement that *no assurance is provided* on each page of the financial statements. As an alternative, the accountant will:
- Issue a disclaimer, indicating the lack of assurance, that will accompany the financial statements; or
- With the client's permission, compile the financial statements and issue a compilation report, or
- Withdraw from the engagement.

As indicated, the accountant is responsible for complying with all of the requirements of SSARS. The other specific performance requirements associated with a preparation engagement require the accountant to:

- Have or obtain an understanding of the financial reporting framework that will be used in the preparation of the financial statements, including an understanding of any of the client's significant accounting policies.
- Prepare the financial statements in accordance with the applicable financial reporting framework from the information provided by management.
- Make certain that either *every page* of the financial statements has an indication that no assurance is being provided; or provide a disclaimer indicating the lack of assurance to accompany the financial statements; or compile the financial statements.
- If the financial statements are being prepared in accordance with a special purpose framework, include a description of the applicable financial reporting framework, which may simply be a line in the title to the financial statements, such as "Statement of Assets and Liabilities – Tax Basis."
- Discuss with management the implications of significant judgments affecting the financial statements that the accountant assisted in making such that the client can take responsibility for them.
- Bring to the attention of management any indication that information provided for the preparation of the financial statements is incomplete, inaccurate, or otherwise unsatisfactory, requesting additional or corrected information.
- Disclose any known material misstatements.

The accountant may prepare financial statements that **omit substantially all disclosures** required by the applicable financial reporting framework, provided the omission was not for the purpose of misleading users. The omission should, however, be disclosed in the financial statements.

As indicated, the accountant is not required to verify the accuracy or the completeness of the information from which the financial statements are prepared and, as a result, is neither expected to, nor responsible for the detection of material misstatements, whether due to error or fraud. The accountant may not, however, ignore information about which the accountant is aware. If, due to knowledge obtained by the accountant in another engagement for the same client, in an engagement for another client in the same industry, the accountant's knowledge of the industry, or some other source, the accountant becomes aware of a potential material misstatement to the financial statements, the accountant should take some action. An accountant should never knowingly be associated with materially misstated financial statements unless the accountant is satisfied that the misstatement has been adequately disclosed to the financial statement users.

In such circumstances, the accountant should request that the client:

- Can demonstrate why the information is correct and should be accepted by the accountant;
- Corrects the information; or
- Finds an effective way to communicate the misstatement to users of the financial statements so that they will not be lead to inappropriate conclusions.

Documentation in a Preparation Engagement

The accountant's documentation for a preparation engagement is required to include:
- The engagement letter; and
- A copy of the financial statements.

Preparing Prospective Financial Information

The preparation of prospective financial information requires management to make various significant assumptions about what will occur in the future, including the state of the economy, the industry in which the entity operates, the regulatory environment, and numerous other items. Because an understanding of these assumptions is essential to a user's understanding of the prospective financial information, the accountant should not prepare prospective financial information that does not include a *summary of significant assumptions*.

A financial projection is a unique type of prospective financial information in that it illustrates what management believes will result from the occurrence or nonoccurrence of a future transaction or event. As a result, the accountant should not accept an engagement to prepare a financial *projection* that does not include both:
- Identification of the hypothetical assumptions upon which the projection is based; and
- A description of the limitations on the usefulness of the presentation.

Lecture 7.03

CLASS QUESTIONS

Please see the Class Questions and Class Solutions for this Lecture at the end of this Section.

Lecture 7.04

3 SSARS ENGAGEMENTS (Nonissuer/Nonpublic) (all must adhere to *General Principles* for Engagements Performed in Accordance with SSARS **AR-C 60**)

Preparation of F/S (AR-C 70)	Compilation (AR-C 80)	Review (ICORRI**A**) (AR-C 90)
-Signed Engagement Letter Both Client & Acct	-Signed Engagement Letter	-Signed Engagement Letter - Mgt rep letter - Required
OBJ: - *Prepare F/S* in accord w applicable Fin Reporting Framework (F/W)	- Apply accounting and financial reporting expertise to assist management in the presentation of financial statements and report in accordance with AR-C 80 w/o giving any assurance / no mat modif made to be accord w applic fin rept F/W.	- **Obtain limited assurance** as a basis for reporting whether the accountant is aware of any material modifications that should be made to the financial statements for them to be in accordance with the applicable financial reporting framework, primarily through the performance of ***inquiry and analytical procedures***."
- **Understanding** of financial reporting framework and signif acct policies.	- Understanding of financial reporting framework and signif acct policies. - ***Read*** the F/S - free of obvious material misstatements and appropriate in form?	- Understanding of financial reporting framework and signif acct policies - Industry and entity knowledge - *Analytical Procedures & Inquiries*
- Not required to evaluate independence	- Not independent, add sentence (if title used, do not include word: Independent)	- MUST be independent
NonAttest engagement	NonAttest engagement	Attest engagement
- NO assurance	- NO assurance	- Obtain Limited Assurance
- Express NO opinion or conclusion	- Express NO opinion or conclusion	- Express a conclusion providing limited assurance but express NO opinion

- Listed in Engagement letter:
    - Objective of eng
    - Mgt Resp:
    - Acct's Resp - comply w SARS
    - Limitations of eng.
    - I.D. applicable fin rept framework
    - *indicate and explain non-GAAP or Inadeq disclosure*
    - *Mgt agrees, each page "no assurance is provided"*
	- Listed in Engagement letter:
	    - Objective of eng
	    - Mgt Resp: - prep & fair presentation of F/S (AR-C 60)
	    - Acct's Resp - comply w SSARS
	    - Limitations of eng.
	    - I.D. applicable fin rept framework
	    - *expected form & content of compilation report*
		- Listed in Engagement letter:
		    - Objective of eng
		    - Mgt Resp: - prep & fair presentation of F/S (AR-C 60)
		    - Acct's Resp - comply w SSARS
		    - Limitations of eng.
		    - I.D. applicable fin rept framework
		    - *expected form & content of review report*

- SSARS, by ARSC of AICPA	- SSARS, by ARSC of AICPA	- SSARS, by ARSC of AICPA
- *No report*, each page of F/S, *"No Assurance is Provided"*	*Report Required:*- 1 ¶ - Mgt Resp, SSARS, did NOT audit/Rev, no procedures performed to verify accuracy or completeness but no opinion, conclusion or assurance	*Report Required:*- 4 ¶s → 4th ¶ is limited assurance: - *Intro* – reviewed F/S, Analy & Inq, less in scope - *Mgt Resp* - prep and fair present of F/S design, implement, maintain (dim) I/C - *Acct's Resp* – SSARS, ARSC of AICPA - perform proc to provide Lim assur, mat modif.... Reas basis for conclusion - *Acct's conclusion* – Lim Assur

Preparation of F/S (AR-C 70)	Compilation (AR-C 80)	Review (ICORRIIA) (AR-C 90)

If client refuses 'no assurance is provided' within F/S
• Issue disclaimer,
• Upgrade to compilation (client must agree); or
• Withdraw from the engagement.
	If need to modify, add **Additional Explanatory** Paragraph:
	• Comparative Reports (PY Reviewed, this year compiled)
	• Special Purpose Framework (OCBOA) (lim use if regulatory or contractual basis)
	• Lack of Independence (may include reasons)
	• *Inadequate Disclosure
	    *A Limited Use ¶ = "Not designed for those who are not informed about such matters"
	• Departures from applicable fin rept framework (Non-GAAP)
	• Supplementary info included in rept
	• Additional **Explanatory** Paragraph – (Going Concern doubt, material subsequent event, change in principle/estimate)
		Add a 5th ¶ if modify with **Emphasis or Other Matter** Paragraph:
		• Comparative Reports (PY Reviewed, this year compiled)
		• Special Purpose Framework (OCBOA) (lim use if regulatory or contractual basis)
		• *Inadequate Disclosure
		    *A Limited Use ¶ = "Not designed for those who are not informed about such matters"
		• Departures from applicable fin rept framework (Non-GAAP)
		• Supplementary info included in rept
		• Emphasize a matter – (Going Concern doubt, material subsequent event, change in principle/estimate)

Lecture 7.05

COMPILATION ENGAGEMENTS (AR-C 80)

AR-C section 80 indicates that "the objective of the accountant in a compilation engagement is to apply accounting and financial reporting expertise to assist management in the presentation of financial statements and report in accordance with this section without undertaking to obtain or provide any assurance that there are *no material modifications that should be made* to the financial statements in order for them to be in accordance with the applicable financial reporting framework."

A CPA may also be engaged to compile *other historical financial information, pro forma financial information (AR-C 120), or prospective financial information*. **Pro forma** financial information is historical financial information adjusted to reflect what management believes would have happened in that period if an event or circumstance had or had not occurred. It may, for example, show what management believes its prior period's results would have been if they had purchased a particular machine or if they had not lost a major customer to a competitor.

A CPA may also compile *prospective financial information* (AR-C 80). One basic type of prospective financial information is the financial **forecast**, which reports what management believes (*expects*) its future results of operations and financial position will be based on management's assumptions as to the conditions under which the entity will be operating in the future. These assumptions may relate to the economy, the industry in which the entity operates, the availability of human and physical resources, and a variety of other factors.

The other basic type of prospective financial information is a financial **projection,** which incorporates the same assumptions as applicable to a financial forecast but also considers a hypothetical assumption related to the occurrence or nonoccurrence of some significant event or transaction.

- All prospective financial statements should include a summary of significant assumptions. In addition, financial projections should include an indication of the *hypothetical assumption* upon which it is based and an indication of the limitations on the usefulness of such a presentation.

Requirements in a Compilation Engagement

As is true of all SSARS engagements, an accountant engaged to compile financial statements for a client is required to adhere to the *General Principles for Engagements Performed in Accordance With SSARS* (AR-C 60). In addition, there are specific requirements that apply to a compilation engagement.

The accountant must make a determination as to whether the accountant is independent in relation to the entity. In addition, prior to accepting the engagement, the accountant should obtain the client's agreement that it understands and accepts its responsibility:
- For the preparation and fair presentation of the financial statements; and
- To include the compilation report in any document containing the compiled financial statements.

Taking responsibility for the preparation and fair presentation of the financial statements includes providing all informative disclosures required by the framework, whether GAAP or a special purpose framework; and:
- If the financial statements are prepared in conformity with a special purpose framework, providing a description of the framework, including significant differences from GAAP.
- If the special purpose framework is a contractual basis of accounting, describing significant interpretations of the contract that affect the special purpose framework.
- In either case, providing any additional disclosures required for fair presentation under the special purpose framework.

The accountant is required to reach an agreement with the client on the terms of the engagement, which should be documented in an **engagement letter** that is signed both by the client and the accountant's firm. The agreement should include:
- The objective of the compilation engagement;
- Management's responsibilities, as indicated in AR-C 60;
- The accountant's responsibilities, which are to comply with the requirements of SSARS;
- Limitations of an engagement to compile financial statements;
- Identification of the applicable financial reporting framework; and
- The expected form and content of the compilation report.

The engagement letter should also indicate circumstances under which the report may differ in form or content from that which is expected. For example, the engagement letter would indicate if the report will disclose a lack of independence.

As indicated, the accountant is responsible for complying with all requirements of SSARS. The other specific performance requirements associated with a compilation engagement require the accountant to:
- Have or obtain an **understanding** of the financial reporting framework that will be used in the preparation of the financial statements, including an understanding of any of the client's significant accounting policies.
- **Read** the financial statements

- o The accountant's knowledge of the client, the financial reporting framework, and management's significant accounting policies is taken into account.
- o The accountant considers if the financial statements appear to be free of obvious material misstatements and appropriate in form.

In performing the compilation engagement, the accountant may become aware of actual or suspected deficiencies in the financial statements.
- An awareness that information provided by management is *incomplete, inaccurate, or otherwise unsatisfactory* will require the accountant to inform management and request additional or corrected information.
- The accountant should *propose revisions* when the accountant becomes aware that:
  - o The applicable financial reporting framework is not adequately described;
  - o The financial statements require revision in order to be in accordance with the applicable financial reporting framework; or
  - o The financial statements are misleading.

Under certain circumstances, the accountant is required to **withdraw** from the engagement, informing management of the reasons. This will be the case if:
- Management is unable or unwilling to *provide information* the accountant considers necessary in order to satisfactorily complete the engagement; or
- The financial statements contain *departures* from the applicable financial reporting framework and management will not make proposed changes or disclose the departures, although the accountant would not be required to withdraw if disclosure of the departures in the compilation report would sufficiently inform users.

Compilation Reports

Whenever an accountant compiles financial statements, those financial statements must be accompanied by the accountant's compilation report. When the financial statements are prepared in conformity with GAAP and nothing makes it appear to the accountant that the financial statements are not appropriate in form or are inaccurate, incomplete, or otherwise unsatisfactory, the accountant will issue an unmodified compilation report.

Unmodified Compilation Report

The accountant's standard written compilation report will **include certain elements**:
- An indication that management is responsible for the financial statements;
- Identification of the financial statements that were compiled, the entity for which they were compiled, and the date or period covered by the financial statements;
- An indication that the compilation was performed in accordance with SSARS, promulgated by the ARSC of the AICPA;
- An indication that the accountant:
  - o Did not audit or review the financial statements;
  - o Was not required to perform any procedures to verify the accuracy or completeness of the information provided by management; and
  - o Does not express an opinion, a conclusion, nor provide any assurance on the financial statements.
- The accountant's signature or that of the accountant's firm;
- An indication of the city and state in which the accountant practices; and
- The date of the report.

The report is dated as of the date on which the accountant completes all requirements under AR-C section 80.

The standard report for a compilation should be studied closely since there is extensive testing of each sentence that appears in it. It may have a title indicating it is the accountants' compilation report, which should only include the word independent when the accountant is independent. A sample report might appear as follows:

INDEPENDENT ACCOUNTANT'S COMPILATION REPORT

Board of Directors and Stockholders
X Company

Management is responsible for the accompanying financial statements of X Company, which comprise the balance sheet as of December 31, 20X2, and the related statements of income, changes in stockholders' equity, and cash flows for the year then ended, and the related notes to the financial statements in accordance with accounting principles generally accepted in the United States of America. We have performed a compilation engagement in *accordance with* Statements on Standards for Accounting and Review Services (SSARS) promulgated by the Accounting and Review Services Committee (ARSC) of the AICPA. We did not audit or review the financial statements nor were we required to perform any procedures to verify the accuracy or the completeness of the information provided by management. Accordingly, *we do not express* an opinion, a conclusion, nor provide any form of assurance on these financial statements.

Signature of Accountant or Firm
Accountant's city and state
Date: Completion of the compilation

Notice that there are four elements in the report (**CARD**):
- **Compiled -** The compiled statements are identified.
- **AICPA standards -** The reference to SSARS distinguishes the accountant's work from similar work that might be performed by a non-CPA. This wasn't needed in an audit (since non-CPAs are legally prohibited from performing audits), but non-CPAs are capable of simply presenting statements, so the distinction of work conforming to AICPA standards (which require that a CPA perform the engagement) is added to enhance the perceived value.
- **Responsibility of management -** We emphasize that these are the financial statements of management, they are not the accountant's.
- **Do not express an opinion or provide assurance -** We explicitly state that we didn't audit or review and do not express an opinion or provide assurance, so that the user of the statements will not misunderstand our involvement.

The mnemonic CARD reminds us that the compilation report is small enough to fit on a small card.

The accountant may request that each page of the financial statements state *"See Accountant's Compilation Report."* Notice that the CPA is referred to as an accountant and **not** as an auditor, since no audit was performed.

A CPA may be engaged to compile comparative financial statements. The standard compilation report on comparative financial statements is only different from the standard report on a single year's statement in that both dates are indicated and items are referred to in the plural, such as financial statements and compilations.

The standard report for a compilation of comparative financial statement will appear as follows:

INDEPENDENT ACCOUNTANT'S COMPILATION REPORT
(Comparative F/S)

Board of Directors and Stockholders
X Company

Management is responsible for the accompanying financial statements of X Company, which comprise the balance shee**ts** as of December 31, 20X2 ***and 20X1***, and the related statements of income, changes in stockholders' equity, and cash flows for the **years** then ended, and the related notes to the financial statements in accordance with accounting principles generally accepted in the United States of America. We have performed compilation engagement**s** in accordance with Statements on Standards for Accounting and Review Services promulgated by the Accounting and Review Services Committee of the AICPA. We did not audit or review the financial statements nor were we required to perform any procedures to verify the accuracy or the completeness of the information provided by management. Accordingly, we do not express an opinion, a conclusion, nor provide any form of assurance on these financial statements.

Signature of Accountant or Firm
Accountant's city and state
Date

When comparative financial statements include statements from one or more prior periods that had been reviewed or audited, the report will include the same language as an unmodified compilation report on comparative financial statements. An **explanatory paragraph** will be added, however, indicating:
- The prior financial statements had been audited or reviewed;
- The date and type of report originally issued on the prior period financial statements, and the reasons for a modification to the prior period report, if applicable.

ACCOUNTANT'S COMPILATION REPORT
(Comparative F/S, P/Y Reviewed)

Standard 1st paragraph:

The accompanying 20X1 financial statements were previously *Reviewed* by us (another accountant) and we (they) stated that we (they) were not aware of any material modifications that should be made to those financial statements in order for them to be in conformity with accounting principles generally accepted in the United States of America in our (their) report dated March 31, 20X2, but we (they) have not performed any procedures in connection with that review engagement since that date.

Modified Reports

There are several reasons that an accountant may issue a modified compilation report. These include:

- Financial statements prepared in accordance with a *special purpose* financial reporting framework
- A lack of independence
- Omission of substantially all disclosures required by the applicable financial reporting framework
- Known departures from the applicable financial reporting framework
- Supplementary information accompanying the financial statements
- Required supplementary information

The accountant may be engaged to compile financial statements that are prepared in accordance with a financial reporting framework other than GAAP. They may be prepared in accordance with a *general purpose framework*, one that is widely recognized and about which it is reasonable to expect that users will be knowledgeable. GAAP and IFRS are general purpose frameworks.

The financial statements may also be prepared in accordance with a *special purpose framework*, also referred to as an OCBOA (Other Comprehensive Basis of Accounting). Special purpose frameworks include the cash or modified cash basis, tax basis, contractual or regulatory basis, IFRS for SMEs (small to medium sized enterprises), or FRF (financial reporting framework) for SMEs promulgated by the AICPA.

When financial statements are prepared in accordance with a **special purpose financial reporting framework**, the accountant's compilation report will be modified as follows:

- If the special purpose framework is a result of management's election, the report will refer to management's responsibility for determining that the special purpose framework is appropriate under the circumstances,
- If the special purpose framework is a contractual or regulatory financial reporting framework, the report will either describe the purpose for which the financial statements are prepared or refer to a note in the financial statements that does so.

INDEPENDENT ACCOUNTANT'S COMPILATION REPORT
(Cash Basis)

Board of Directors and Stockholders
X Company

Management is responsible for the accompanying financial statements of X Company, which comprise the *statement of assets, liabilities, and equity – **cash basis*** as of December 31, 20X2 and the related *statements of revenue and expenses – cash basis and changes in equity – cash basis* for the year then ended, and the related notes to the financial statements in accordance with the *cash basis of accounting*, and for determining that the *cash basis* of accounting is an acceptable financial reporting framework. We have performed a compilation engagement in accordance with Statements on Standards for Accounting and Review Services promulgated by the Accounting and Review Services Committee of the AICPA. We did not audit or review the financial statements nor were we required to perform any procedures to verify the accuracy or the completeness of the information provided by management. Accordingly, we do not express an opinion, a conclusion, nor provide any form of assurance on these financial statements.

We draw attention to Note 7 of the financial statements, which describes the basis of accounting. The financial statements are prepared in accordance with the *cash basis* of accounting, which is a basis of accounting other than accounting principles generally accepted in the United States of America.

Accountant's signature
Accountant's city and state
Date

INDEPENDENT ACCOUNTANT'S COMPILATION REPORT
(AICPA SME Basis)

Board of Directors and Stockholders
X Company

Management is responsible for the accompanying financial statements of XYZ Company, which comprise the statements of financial position as of December 31, 20X2 and 20X1 and the related statements of operations and cash flows for the years then ended, and the related notes to the financial statements in accordance with the AICPA's Financial Reporting Framework for Small- and Medium-Sized Entities, and for determining that the AICPA's Financial Reporting Framework for Small- and Medium-Sized Entities is an acceptable financial reporting framework. I (We) have performed compilation engagements in accordance with Statements on Standards for Accounting and Review Services promulgated by the Accounting and Review Services Committee of the AICPA. I (We) did not audit or review the financial statements nor was (were) I (we) required to perform any procedures to verify the accuracy or completeness of the information provided by management. Accordingly, I (we) do not express an opinion, a conclusion, nor provide any form of assurance on these financial statements.

I (We) draw attention to Note X of the financial statements, which describes the basis of accounting. The financial statements are prepared in accordance with the AICPA's Financial Reporting Framework for Small- and Medium-Sized Entities (SME), which is a basis of accounting other than accounting principles generally accepted in the United States of America.

Accountant's signature
Accountant's city and state
Date

Additional modifications to the accountant's compilation report may be necessary when certain circumstances apply:

- Unless disclosures are omitted, the report will be modified if the financial statements do not describe the special purpose framework, a summary of significant accounting policies; a description of differences between the framework and GAAP, and informative disclosures comparable to those required by GAAP.
- If the financial statements are prepared in accordance with a contractual basis, the report will be modified if significant interpretations of the contract affecting the framework are not adequately described.

INDEPENDENT ACCOUNTANT'S COMPILATION REPORT
(Omitted Disclosures)

Board of Directors and Stockholders
X Company

Management is responsible for the accompanying financial statements of XYZ Partnership, which comprise the statements of assets, liabilities, and partners' capital—**tax-basis** as of December 31, 20X2 and 20X1 and the related statements of revenue and expenses—tax-basis, and changes in partners' capital—tax-basis for the years then ended in accordance with the tax-basis of accounting, and for determining that the tax-basis of accounting is an acceptable financial reporting framework. I (We) have performed compilation engagements in accordance with Statements on Standards for Accounting and Review Services promulgated by the Accounting and Review Services Committee of the AICPA. I (We) did not audit or review the financial statements nor was (were) I (we) required to perform any procedures to verify the accuracy or completeness of the information provided by management. Accordingly, I (we) do not express an opinion, a conclusion, nor provide any form of assurance on these financial statements.

The financial statements are prepared in accordance with the tax-basis of accounting, which is a basis of accounting other than accounting principles generally accepted in the United States of America.

Management has elected to omit substantially all the disclosures ordinarily included in financial statements prepared in accordance with the tax-basis of accounting. If the omitted disclosures were included in the financial statements, they might influence the user's conclusions about the company's assets, liabilities, equity, revenue, and expenses. *Accordingly, the financial statements are not designed for those who are not informed about such matters.*

Accountant's signature
Accountant's city and state
Date

The accountant may compile financial statements that **omit substantially all disclosures** required by the applicable financial reporting framework. The accountant's compilation report will be modified by adding a separate paragraph indicating that:
- Management has elected to omit substantially all disclosures required by the applicable financial reporting framework.
- The information, had it not been omitted, may influence conclusions about the entity's performance or financial position.
- The financial statements are designed exclusively for those knowledgeable about such matters.

The accountant may not report on statements that omit disclosures if the omissions were intended to mislead the user. This might be the case, for example, if the client is trying to conceal a large potential loss due to a pending lawsuit from a potential lender.

When the accountant is **not independent** of the entity, the report will be modified to indicate the lack of independence.
- The indication will be in a separate final paragraph of the report.
- The accountant may, but is not required to, disclose the reasons for the lack of independence.
  - The description may be as brief or extensive as the accountant feels appropriate under the circumstances.
  - If disclosure is made, all *reasons* impairing independence must be disclosed.

If the accountant uses a title on the compilation report, it should not include the word independent.

ACCOUNTANT'S COMPILATION REPORT
(Lack of Independence – Reasons *Not Disclosed*)

Standard 1st paragraph:

We are not independent with respect to X Company.

ACCOUNTANT'S COMPILATION REPORT
(Lack of Independence – Reasons *Disclosed*)

Standard 1st paragraph:

We are not independent with respect to X Company as during the year ended December 31, 20X2, a member of the engagement team had a material indirect financial interest in X Company.

The modification, in the form of a separate paragraph, will:
- Disclose the departure; and
- Either indicate the effect on the financial statements, if determined by management; or indicate that the effect has not been determined by management.

INDEPENDENT ACCOUNTANT'S COMPILATION REPORT
(Departure from the Applicable Financial Reporting Framework)

Standard 1st paragraph:

Accounting principles generally accepted in the United States of America require that investments in marketable securities classified as available for sale be stated at market value with unrealized gains and losses recognized in other comprehensive income, a component of stockholders' equity. Management has informed us that X Company has stated its investments in available for sale securities at cost and that if accounting principles generally accepted in the United States of America had been followed, the investment account and stockholders' equity account would have been decreased by $150,000.

The accountant's compilation report may not be modified to indicate that the financial statements are not in conformity with the applicable financial reporting framework. If the accountant does not believe that disclosure adequately describes the deficiencies in financial reporting, the accountant should *withdraw* from the engagement and provide no further services in relation to those financial statements.

The accountant may be engaged to **compile comparative financial statements** in which the prior period financial statements had a GAAP departure that was subsequently remedied. When this is the case, the compilation report on the comparative financial statements will be the same as an unmodified report on comparative statements with the following other-matter paragraph added to the end:

INDEPENDENT ACCOUNTANT'S COMPILATION REPORT
(Changing Reference from Prior Year)

Standard 1st paragraph:

In our report dated March 1, 20X2 with respect to the 20X1 financial statements, we referred to a departure from accounting principles generally accepted in the United States of America because the company carried its land at appraised values. As described in Note X, the Company has *changed* its method of accounting for land and *restated* its 20X1 financial statements to conform with accounting principles generally accepted in the United States of America.

When **supplementary information accompanies compiled financial statements**, the accountant will indicate that either the supplementary information was or was not compiled and if the accountant is reporting on the supplementary information.

When the applicable financial reporting framework under which the financial statements were prepared requires supplementary information, the accountant's report will be modified to indicate:
- Whether the **required supplementary information** is included, partially included, or omitted
- Whether or not the required supplementary information that is included was compiled by the accountant and is being reported upon.

Although not covered under SSARS, the unaudited financial statements of a public company often involve work comparable to a compilation. Nonetheless, the report on unaudited financial statements of a public company must not say they were compiled, but merely state in a one-sentence report:

> **The accompanying balance sheet of X Company as of December 31, 20X1, and the related statements of income and comprehensive income, retained earnings, and cash flows for the year then ended were *not audited by us* and, accordingly, we do not express an opinion on them.**

When reporting on prospective financial information, in addition to the requirements associated with a compilation report, the report will include:
- A statement that the forecasted or projected results may not be achieved; and
- A statement that the accountant assumes no responsibility to update the report for events and circumstances occurring after the date of the report.

Documentation in a Compilation Engagement

The accountant's documentation for a compilation engagement is required to include:
- The engagement letter;
- A copy of the financial statements and
- A copy of the accountant's compilation report.

Lecture 7.06

CLASS QUESTIONS

Please see the Class Questions and Class Solutions for this Lecture at the end of this Section.

Lecture 7.07

REVIEW ENGAGEMENTS (AR-C 90)

Section AR-C 90 of SSARS indicates that "the objective of the accountant when performing a review of financial statements is to **obtain** limited assurance as a basis for reporting whether the accountant is aware of any material modifications that should be made to the financial statements for them to be in accordance with the applicable financial reporting framework, primarily through the performance of *inquiry and analytical procedures*."

In addition to historical financial statements, reviews may be performed in accordance with SSARS in relation to other historical financial information, but may not be performed in relation to pro forma financial information. Reviews of pro forma financial information are performed in accordance with Statements on Standards for Attestation Engagements (SSAE).

Note that the objective is to obtain limited assurance, not to provide limited assurance that the financial statements are not in need of material modification in order to be in accordance with the applicable financial reporting framework. The accountant's review report is designed to provide the users with limited assurance regarding those financial statements. The accountant performs the review to obtain review evidence, providing comfort to the accountant who, in turn, provides limited assurance.

Materiality is not addressed in SSARS. Since, however, a review report refers to the potential need for material modifications it is important to have an understanding of what is meant by the term. Some financial reporting frameworks will define materiality but for those that do not, the accountant should keep in mind that materiality takes into account *three concepts*:

- Misstatements are material if they, individually or in the aggregate, could reasonably be expected to influence the economic decisions of users taken on the basis of the financial statements.
- Judgments about materiality are made in light of surrounding circumstances and are affected by the size or nature of a misstatement or a combination of both.
- Judgments about matters that are material to users of the financial statements are based on a consideration of the common financial information needs of users as a group. The possible effect of misstatements on specific individual users, whose needs may vary widely, is not considered.

Requirements in a Review Engagement

As is true of all SSARS engagements, an accountant engaged to review financial statements for a client is required to adhere to the *General Principles for Engagements Performed in Accordance With SSARS* (AR-C 60). In addition, there are specific requirements that apply to a review engagement.

The accountant is *required to be independent* of the entity and may not perform a review if independence is impaired. The accountant should withdraw from a review engagement upon learning after the commencement of the engagement that independence is impaired.

The accountant should not accept a review engagement when there is the belief there will be a limitation on the accountant's ability to apply adequate review procedures due to a scope limitation imposed by the client.

In addition, prior to accepting the engagement, the accountant should obtain the client's agreement that it understands and accepts its responsibility:

- For the preparation and fair presentation of the financial statements;
- To provide the accountant with a letter of representations at the conclusion of the engagement (**Management Representation Letter**); and
- To include the review report in any document containing the reviewed financial statements.

As in a compilation, taking responsibility for the preparation and fair presentation of the financial statements includes providing all informative disclosures required by the framework, whether GAAP or a special purpose framework; and:

- If the financial statements are prepared in conformity with a special purpose framework, providing a description of the framework, including significant differences from GAAP.
- If the special purpose framework is a contractual basis of accounting, describing significant interpretations of the contract that affect the special purpose framework.
- In either case, providing any additional disclosures required for fair presentation under the special purpose framework.

The accountant is required to reach an agreement with the client on the terms of the engagement, which should be documented in an **engagement letter** that is signed both by the client and the accountant's firm. The agreement should include:

- The objective of the review engagement;
- Management's responsibilities, as indicated in AR-C 60;

- The accountant's responsibilities, which are to comply with the requirements of SSARS;
- Limitations of an engagement to review financial statements
- Identification of the applicable financial reporting framework; and
- The expected form and content of the review report.

The engagement letter should also indicate circumstances under which the report may differ in form or content from that which is expected.

Unmodified Review Report

The accountant's standard written review report will include certain elements:
- A title with the word independent;
- An appropriate addressee;
- An ***Introductory Paragraph*** that:
  - Identifies the financial statements that were reviewed, the entity for which they were reviewed, and the date or period covered by the financial statements;
  - States that the financial statements were reviewed;
  - Indicates that a review consists primarily of applying analytical procedures to information provided by management and making inquiries of management; and
  - States that a review is less in scope than an audit, which contemplates expressing an opinion on the financial statements taken as a whole, and, as a result, no such opinion is expressed.
- A section headed ***"Management's Responsibilities"*** that indicates that:
  - Management is responsible for the preparation and fair presentation of the financial statements in accordance with the applicable financial reporting framework; and
  - For the design, implementation, and maintenance (DIM) of internal control relevant to reliable financial reporting;
- A section with the heading ***"Accountant's Responsibility"*** that indicates that the accountant:
  - Is responsible for conducting the engagement in accordance with SSARS, promulgated by the ARSC;
  - Is required by SSARS to perform procedures to obtain limited assurance for reporting if the accountant is aware of the need for material modification to be made to the financial statements in order for them to be in accordance with the applicable financial reporting framework; and
  - Believes that review evidence obtained is sufficient to support the accountant's conclusion.
- A section with an appropriate heading that contains the ***"Accountant's Conclusion"*** as to whether the accountant is aware of any material modification that should be made to the accompanying financial statements in order for them to be in accordance with the applicable financial reporting framework, identifying the country of origin of that framework, if applicable.
- The accountant's signature or that of the accountant's firm;
- An indication of the city and state in which the accountant practices; and
- The date of the report.

The report is dated as of the date on which the accountant completes all requirements under AR-C section 90. An **unmodified report** will appear as follows:

INDEPENDENT ACCOUNTANT'S REVIEW REPORT

Board of Directors and Stockholders
X Company

Introductory

We have **reviewed** the accompanying financial statements of X Company, which comprise the balance sheet as of December 31, 20X2, and the related statements of income, changes in stockholders' equity, and cash flows for the year then ended, and the related notes to the financial statements. A review includes primarily applying *analytical procedures* to management's financial data and making *inquiries* of company management. A review is substantially less in scope than an audit, the objective of which is the expression of an opinion regarding the financial statements as a whole. Accordingly, we do not express such an opinion.

Management's Responsibility for the Financial Statements

Management is responsible for the preparation and fair presentation of these financial statements in accordance with accounting principles generally accepted in the United States of America; this includes the design, implementation, and maintenance (**DIM**) of *internal control* relevant to the preparation and fair presentation of financial statements that are free from material misstatement, whether due to fraud or error.

Accountant's Responsibility

Our responsibility is to conduct the review engagement in accordance with Statements on Standards for Accounting and Review Services (SSARS) promulgated by the Accounting and Review Services Committee (ARSC) of the AICPA. Those standards require us to perform procedures to obtain limited assurance as a basis for reporting whether we are aware of any material modifications that should be made to the financial statements for them to be in accordance with accounting principles generally accepted in the United States of America. We believe that the results of our procedures provide a reasonable basis for our conclusion.

Accountant's Conclusion (Limited Assurance ¶)

Based on our review, we are not aware of any material modifications that should be made to the accompanying financial statements in order for them to be in accordance with accounting principles generally accepted in the United States of America.

Signature of accountant or firm
Accountant's city and state
Date

There are eight key elements in the report: (**FAMILIAR**)

- **Financial statements being reviewed -** The statements are identified first.
- **AICPA standards (SSARS) -** In many jurisdictions, non-CPAs are permitted to review statements, so the reference to SSARS is made in order to distinguish the work of a CPA from others.
- **Management representation -** Since the accountant will be providing limited assurance, it is critical to emphasize that the statements are presented by management, not the accountant.

- **Inquiry and analytical procedures -** We provide a brief description of the nature of a review.
- **Less in scope than audit -** Since a layperson might not understand that reviewing statements means something different from auditing them, we explicitly distinguish the two and emphasize the lesser scope of the review.
- **Incapable of opinion -** Since we didn't do an audit, we cannot express an opinion, and explicitly disclaim one.
- **Assurance provided -** We express limited assurance on the statements.
- **Refer to U.S. Principles -** We identify Accounting Principles Generally Accepted in the United States of America, as the standard for the statements to which we don't believe modification is needed.

The **mnemonic FAMILIAR** reminds us that an accountant dealing with non-public clients must be familiar with the unique review report available for such clients.

The accountant may request that each page of the financial statements state *"See Accountant's Review Report*.

As indicated, the accountant is responsible for complying with all requirements of SSARS. The other **specific performance requirements** associated with a review engagement address:
- Communication with the client
- Understanding the client's industry
- Client knowledge
- Review procedures
- Analytical procedures
- Inquiries
- Reading the financial statements
- Work of other accountants
- Relationship of the financial statements to the underlying accounting records
- Review evidence
- Written representations (Management Representation Letter)
- Review reports

Communication with the Client

If, during the course of the engagement, matters come to the accountant's attention that, in the accountant's professional judgment, are significant enough to merit the client's attention, the accountant has the obligation to communicate this information to an appropriate representative of the client on a timely basis.

Industry Understanding

Knowledge of a client's industry, including accounting principles and practices associated with that industry, enable the accountant to make a determination as to whether any review evidence obtained indicates that the financial statements are not appropriate for an entity operating in that industry.

Knowledge of the industry, which may be obtained from a variety of sources including AICPA guides, industry publications, textbooks, and other sources, may be obtained prior to accepting the engagement or after acceptance provided the accountant has obtained a sufficient understanding to be able to perform the engagement.

Client Knowledge

In order to effectively perform a review, the accountant is required to understand the client's business and its accounting policies and practices. Among other purposes, this understanding enables the accountant to identify any policies or practices that may be unusual, perhaps when compared to those generally used in the client's industry. Overall, it enables the accountant to understand the nature of the financial statement elements that should appear on the financial statements and to evaluate those aspects of the financial statements that represent the highest risks.

Review Procedures

Since the accountant's report is providing financial statements users with limited assurance that the financial statements are not in need of material modification in order to be in accordance with the applicable financial reporting framework, the accountant obtains review evidence to support such a conclusion through the performance of review procedures. In determining what procedures are likely to be most effective, the accountant will consider the accountant's:
- Understanding of the industry; and
- Knowledge of the client.

In the design and performance of review procedures, the accountant should remain aware that the financial statements may be materially misstated and there is the risk that the accountant will not become aware of the misstatement and will, unknowingly, fail to modify the review report. To minimize this risk, the accountant will focus review procedures, consisting predominantly of analytical procedures and inquiries, on those areas that represent the greatest risk of material misstatement of the financial statements.

Analytical Procedures

Analytical procedures generally provide the primary form of review evidence obtained by the accountant. Analytical procedures consist of the performance of *three essential steps*:
- The accountant uses an understanding of the industry, client knowledge, and general knowledge about business, accounting and the economy to develop expectations as to information that might appear on the financial statements.
  - Expectations may be in the form of an amount, such as a range of amounts that the accountant believes the client's revenue will be within.
  - They may be in the form of ratios or relationships, such as an expected relationship between accounts receivable and recent sales that is based on the accountant's knowledge of the client's credit and collection policies.
- The accountant will compare the client's data to expectations to determine if variances are within a reasonable range based on the precision and reliability of the expectation.
- Any differences that exceed what the accountant considers to be reasonable are to be investigated further to determine if they are indications of the need for a material adjustment to the financial statements.

Specific analytical procedures that the accountant is required to perform include:
- Comparing current period data to that of the prior period;
- Considering plausible relationships, which may be among different components of financial data or may be between financial and nonfinancial data, such as using the number of employees as a basis for estimating a certain payroll related cost

- Comparing amounts reported by in the financial statements, or ratios or amounts that are derived from those amounts, to expectations; and
- Make comparisons using disaggregated revenue data, when applicable.

When determining the types of analytical procedures to be performed and designing the specific procedures, the accountant will:
- Consider which analytical procedures are suitable for the circumstances;
- Evaluate the reliability of the information from which expectations are developed;
- Evaluate the precision of expectations to determine the degree to which a difference between the expectation and the client's recorded data is an indication of a potential material misstatement to the financial statements.
  - If a company presumably enforces a strict markup policy such that gross profit should always equal 25% of sales, a gross profit percentage that is even slightly higher or lower may indicate a misstatement to the financial statements.
  - If a company has a wide range of products having significantly varying gross profit percentages, even a gross profit percentage that is significantly higher or lower than a percentage used to develop expectations may not be indicative of a material misstatement to the financial statements.
- Based on the reliability and precision of expectations, determine if differences from expectations are acceptable without further investigation.

When fluctuations or differences from expected amounts exceed what the accountant considers acceptable, the accountant will investigate the differences further by making inquiries of management or by performing other analytical procedures.

Inquiries

Making inquiries of management and of others with knowledge of, or responsibility for, the financial statements or other accounting matters is another significant means by which the accountant obtains review evidence. Certain inquiries should be made in every review engagement, including inquiries regarding:
- The preparation and fair presentation of the financial statements in accordance with the applicable financial reporting framework;
- Any unusual or complex transactions or other circumstances that may impact the financial statements;
- Significant transactions, especially those occurring near the end of the period;
- Uncorrected errors identified in prior period engagements;
- Results of analytical procedures requiring further clarification or support;
- Subsequent events;
- Any knowledge or suspicion of fraud, or any allegations of fraud made by employees or others;
- Management's disclosure to the accountant of known circumstances involving noncompliance with applicable laws or regulations that may have a potential material effect on the financial statements;
- Significant journal entries or adjustments;
- Applicable communication from regulators;
- Related parties and related party transactions;
- Litigation, claims, and assessments;
- The reasonableness of management's estimates;
- Actions taken at meetings of the board, stockholders, or other relevant groups; and
- Other matters considered necessary by the accountant under the circumstances.

Reading the Financial Statements

Upon completing other review procedures, taking into account all review evidence obtained, the accountant is then required to *read* the financial statements to evaluate whether anything has come to the accountant's attention to indicate that the financial statements are not in conformity with the applicable financial reporting framework.

Work of Other Accountants

Other accountants may have issued reports on the financial statements related to significant components of the financial statements being reviewed by the accountant. Another accountant, for example, may have performed a compilation, review, or audit of a subsidiary of the entity or a company in which the entity has a significant investment. When that is the case, the accountant should read the other accountants' reports and evaluate the effect, if any, on the reviewed financial statements.

Relationship of the Financial Statements to the Underlying Accounting Records

The accountant is required to obtain evidence that the financial statements were derived from the accounting records. This may be accomplished by reconciling the financial statements to:
- The underlying accounting records;
- A consolidating schedule derived from the accounting records; or
- Other data in the entity's records that supports the financial statements.

Review Evidence

In obtaining review evidence, the accountant will become aware of misstatements, which may be in the form of inadequate disclosure. The accountant will:
- Accumulate these misstatements;
- Evaluate the misstatements, both individually and in the aggregate; and
- Determine if material modifications should be made to the financial statements in order for them to be in accordance with the applicable financial reporting framework.

The accountant may become aware that information provided by the entity is incorrect, incomplete, or otherwise unsatisfactory. The accountant should:
- Request that management consider the implications in relation to the financial statements, communicating the results of that consideration to the accountant; and
- Consider if management's response indicates that the financial statements may be materially misstated.

Upon concluding that the financial statements may be materially misstated, the accountant will perform whatever procedures the accountant considers necessary to obtain limited assurance that the financial statements are not in need of material modification in order for the financial statements to be in accordance with the applicable financial reporting framework.
- This will generally be in the form of additional analytical procedures or inquiries.
- The accountant may, however, apply procedures that might ordinarily be associated with another level of service, such as an audit procedure, if it is determined that the procedure is necessary to obtain sufficient review evidence to support the accountant's conclusion.

Even after performing additional or other procedures, the accountant may not have obtained sufficient review evidence to support a conclusion as to whether or not the financial statements are in need of material adjustment in order to be in accordance with the applicable financial reporting framework. When this occurs, the accountant may not be able to complete the engagement.

Written Representations (Management Representation Letter)

The accountant is *required* to obtain written representations, in the form of a representation letter to the accountant, from those members of management who are responsible for the financial statements and are knowledgeable about relevant matters. This is called a management representation letter.

- Putting representations in writing may cause management to more carefully consider responses to inquiries and other information supplied to the accountant.
- Management's refusal to provide written responses alerts the accountant to the possibility of significant issues affecting the financial statements.

Representations are dated as of the date of the review report, which is the date on which the accountant has determined that sufficient review evidence has been obtained to support the accountant's conclusion. Standards require the accountant to obtain specific representations, including that management (**Management Representation Letter**):

- Has fulfilled its responsibility to prepare the financial statements such that they are fairly presented in accordance with the applicable financial reporting framework;
- Is responsible for the design, implementation, and maintenance (DIM) of internal control relevant to reliable financial reporting;
- Has given the accountant all relevant information and access to all information and parties considered relevant by the accountant;
- Has been complete and truthful in its responses to inquiries;
- Has disclosed any knowledge or suspicions of fraud, including allegations by others;
- Has disclosed known or suspected circumstances involving noncompliance with applicable laws or regulations that may affect the financial statements;
- Believes that uncorrected misstatements are not material to the financial statements, whether considered individually or in the aggregate;
- Has disclosed known or threatened litigation and claims that may affect the financial statements;
- Believes that significant assumptions used in preparing the financial statements are reasonable;
- Has disclosed all related parties and related party transactions; and
- Has adjusted for or disclosed subsequent events requiring recognition or disclosure.

Management also represents that all transactions have been recorded and are reflected in the financial statements (completeness).

In addition, the accountant may require management to provide written representations regarding any matters that, in the accountant's professional judgment, are significant and relevant.

COMMUNICATION WITH THOSE CHARGED WITH GOVERNANCE IN ENGAGEMENTS CONDUCTED IN ACCORDANCE WITH SSARS

The only area of SSARS in which requirements are established for communication with management and those charged with governance is in AR-C section 90, Review of Financial Statements. It requires timely communication of all matters concerning the engagement that, in the auditor's professional judgment, are considered of significant importance, sufficient to merit the attention of management or those charged with governance.

Matters to be communicated may include:

- The accountant's responsibilities in the engagement, as documented in the engagement letter or its equivalent;

- Significant findings from the engagement, such as:
    o Views regarding the qualitative aspects of the entity's accounting policies, practices, estimates, and disclosures;
    o Circumstances where the accountant decided to apply additional procedures or were otherwise influenced by the results of review procedures;
    o Matters that may require the modification of the accountant's report; or
    o Significant difficulties encountered during the engagement.

The accountant may not report to those charged with governance on behalf of management and the accountant's communication with those charged with governance does not relieve management of its responsibility to do so.

In addition to the accountant's responsibility for communicating certain matters to those charged with governance, the accountant has responsibilities to communicate with an appropriate level of management or, in some circumstances those charged with governance, in relation to matters involving fraud and noncompliance with laws and regulations. During the course of a review engagement, the accountant may become aware or suspicious of fraud. Such knowledge or suspicion should be communicated to the client at an appropriate level above that at which the fraud is purported to have occurred.

In addition, if the accountant becomes aware or suspicious of noncompliance with applicable laws or regulations, that information should also be communicated to the client unless it is clearly inconsequential.

When the accountant becomes aware or suspicious of incidents involving fraud or noncompliance with laws and regulations, the accountant should obtain sufficient information to support a conclusion that the financial statements are not materially misstated due to fraud and that the entity is in compliance with applicable laws and regulations. If the accountant is not satisfied, the accountant should:
- Seek legal advice; and
- Consider *withdrawal* from the engagement.

Review Reports

Whenever an accountant reviews financial statements, those financial statements must be accompanied by the accountant's review report. When the accountant reviews GAAP financial statements and nothing comes to the accountant's attention indicating that the financial statements are in need of material modification in order to be in conformity with GAAP, the accountant will issue an *unmodified* review report.

Modified Review Reports

There are several reasons an accountant may issue a modified review report. Factors may include:
- Comparative financial statements;
- Emphasis-of-matter and other-matter paragraphs;
- Known departures from the applicable financial reporting framework;
- Restrictions on the use of the accountant's review report;
- Financial statements prepared in accordance with a special purpose framework;
- Going concern considerations;
- Subsequent events;
- Work of other accountants;
- Supplementary information accompanying reviewed financial statements; and
- Required supplementary information.

Comparative Financial Statements

When reporting on comparative financial statements when all periods have been reviewed and for which there were no departures from the applicable financial reporting framework nor any other circumstances requiring modification of the report, other than the fact that the report related to comparative financial statements instead of those for a single year, the only change to the report will be reference to all periods included and the use of plurals when referring to the reviews performed and the statements reviewed.

INDEPENDENT ACCOUNTANT'S REVIEW REPORT
(Comparative F/S)

Board of Directors and Stockholders
X Company

Introductory

We have reviewed the accompanying financial statements of X Company, which comprise the balance sheet**s** as of December 31, 20X2 **and 20X1**, and the related statements of income, changes in stockholders' equity, and cash flows for the year**s** then ended, and the related notes to the financial statements. A review includes primarily applying *analytical procedures* to management's financial data and making *inquiries* of company management. A review is substantially less in scope than an audit, the objective of which is the expression of an opinion regarding the financial statements as a whole. Accordingly, we do not express such an opinion.

Management's Responsibility for the Financial Statements

Management is responsible for the preparation and fair presentation of these financial statements in accordance with accounting principles generally accepted in the United States of America; this includes the design, implementation, and maintenance (DIM) of internal control relevant to the preparation and fair presentation of financial statements that are free from material misstatement whether due to fraud or error.

Accountant's Responsibility

Our responsibility is to conduct the review engagement**s** in accordance with Statements on Standards for Accounting and Review Services promulgated by the Accounting and Review Services Committee of the AICPA. Those standards require us to perform procedures to obtain limited assurance as a basis for reporting whether we are aware of any material modifications that should be made to the financial statements for them to be in accordance with accounting principles generally accepted in the United States of America. We believe that the results of our procedures provide a reasonable basis for our conclusion.

Accountant's Conclusion

Based on our review, we are not aware of any material modifications that should be made to the accompanying financial statements in order for them to be in accordance with accounting principles generally accepted in the United States of America.

Signature of accountant or firm
Accountant's city and state
Date

The accountant may be engaged to report on comparative financial statements in which the prior year's financial statements had been audited but the audit report on the prior period's financial statements is not being reissued. The accountant's review report will be the same as an unmodified report for comparative financial statements with the addition of an **other-matter paragraph** that indicates:

- The prior period's financial statements had been audited;
- The date and type of opinion issued on the prior periods financial statements, including substantive reasons for any modification; and
- That no audit procedures have been applied since the date of the previous report.

If Current Year is Reviewed and the Previous Year was Audited

INDEPENDENT ACCOUNTANT'S REVIEW REPORT
(Comparative F/S, P/Y Audited, C/Y Reviewed)

Standard 1st, 2nd, 3rd and 4th paragraphs:

(Other-Matter Paragraph)
The 20X1 financial statements were audited by us (other accountants) and we (they) expressed an unmodified opinion on them in our (their) report dated March 1, 20X2, but we (they) have not performed any auditing procedures since that date.

Emphasis-of-Matter and Other-Matter Paragraphs

An emphasis-of-matter paragraph is used whenever an accountant wishes to draw attention to a matter that has been properly accounted for and disclosed in the financial statements but, in the accountant's judgment, merits special attention in the report. An emphasis-of-matter paragraph will:

- Immediately follow the accountant's conclusion;
- Have a heading specifying "Emphasis of a Matter" or another suitable heading;
- Include a clear reference to where the matter is described in the financial statements; and
- Specify that the accountant's conclusion is not modified with respect to the matter being emphasized.

An other-matter paragraph is appropriate when the accountant considers it necessary to communicate a matter that is not, nor is it required to be, presented or disclosed in the financial statements but which the accountant believes to be relevant in enabling users to better understand:

- The review;
- The accountant's responsibilities; or
- The review report.

An other-matter paragraph will be presented immediately after the accountant's conclusion and any emphasis-of-matter paragraphs.

An **emphasis-of-matter** or **other-matter paragraph** is required in any of the following situations:

- Financial statements prepared in accordance with a special purpose framework;
- A change in a reference to a departure from the applicable financial reporting framework on prior period financial statements presented on a comparative basis;
- When prior period financial statements being presented on a comparative basis were audited;

- A material departure from the applicable financial reporting framework known to the accountant;
- A modification to prior period financial statements presented on a comparative basis resulting from facts discovered subsequent to the release of the accountant's report and affecting the prior period's report;
- Supplementary information accompanies the reviewed financial statements; and
- The applicable financial reporting framework provides for required supplementary information.

When the accountant intends to include an emphasis-of-matter or other-matter paragraph in the review report, management should be informed of the expectation and the proposed wording.

Known Departure from the Applicable Financial Reporting Framework

When the CPA is aware of a **departure from the applicable financial reporting framework**, which may be in the form of inadequate disclosure, the accountant's review report will be modified.

The departure will be disclosed in a separate paragraph, immediately following the accountant's conclusion, that will be headed "Known Departure From Accounting Principles Generally Accepted in the United States of America [*or describe an alternative applicable financial reporting framework*]".
- The effects of the departure will be disclosed if they have been determined by management;
- If the effects have not been determined, the paragraph will so indicate.

INDEPENDENT ACCOUNTANT'S REVIEW REPORT
(Departure from the Applicable Financial Reporting Framework)

Standard 1st, 2nd, and 3rd paragraphs:

Accountant's Conclusion
Based on our review, **except for the issue noted in the Known Departure from Accounting Principles Generally Accepted in the United States of America paragraph**, we are not aware of any material modifications that should be made to the accompanying financial statements in order for them to be in accordance with accounting principles generally accepted in the United States of America.

Known Departure from Accounting Principles Generally Accepted in the United States of America
Accounting principles generally accepted in the United States of America require that investments in marketable securities classified as available for sale be stated at market value with unrealized gains and losses recognized in other comprehensive income, a component of stockholders' equity. Management has informed us that X Company has stated its investments in available for sale securities at cost and that if accounting principles generally accepted in the United States of America had been followed, the investment account and stockholders' equity account would have been decreased by $150,000.

The accountant's review report may not be modified to indicate that the financial statements are not in conformity with the applicable financial reporting framework. If the accountant does not believe that disclosure adequately describes the deficiencies in financial reporting, the accountant should **withdraw** from the engagement and provide no further services in relation to those financial statements.

The accountant may be engaged to review comparative financial statements in which the prior period financial statements had a GAAP departure that was subsequently remedied. When this is the case, the review report on the comparative financial statements will be the same as an unmodified report on comparative statements with the following **other-matter paragraph** added to the end:

INDEPENDENT ACCOUNTANT'S REVIEW REPORT
(Changing Reference from Prior Year)

Standard 1st, 2nd, 3rd, and 4th paragraphs:

In our report dated March 1, 20X2 with respect to the 20X1 financial statements, we referred to a departure from accounting principles generally accepted in the United States of America because the company carried its land at appraised values. As described in Note X, the Company has changed its method of accounting for land and restated its 20X1 financial statements to conform with accounting principles generally accepted in the United States of America. Accordingly, our present statement on the 20X1 financial statements, as presented herein, that we are not aware of any material modification that should be made to the accompanying financial statements is different from that expressed in the previous report.

Restricting the Use of the Accountant's Review Report

In some circumstances, the accountant is engaged to review financial statements that have been prepared in accordance with a special purpose framework. In some cases, where the framework is not widely known, only a limited number of potential users may be aware of the measurement or disclosure criteria applied in the framework.

In other circumstances, the accountant may be engaged to review financial statements that have been prepared in accordance with a special purpose framework, such as a contractual basis of accounting, that have measurement and disclosure criteria that are only available to limited individuals, such as the parties to the contract.

In either of these cases, or under similar circumstances, the accountant will wish to restrict distribution of the review report to those parties who have an adequate understanding of the criteria to be able to understand the financial statements and not misinterpret them. The accountant restricts the report with an alert in the form of a separate paragraph, stating:
- The review report is intended solely for the information and use of specified parties, who are specified in the paragraph; and
- The report in not intended for use, and should not be used, by parties other than those specified.

Financial Statements Prepared in Accordance with a Special Purpose Framework

When financial statements are prepared in accordance with a **special purpose financial reporting framework**, the disclosures are required to include:
- A description of the special purpose framework, including how it differs from GAAP;
- A summary of significant accounting policies; and
- Disclosures that are comparable to those that would be required under GAAP.

Failure to include any of this information represents a departure from the applicable financial reporting framework with a report modified accordingly. Assuming the appropriate disclosures are made, the accountant's review report will be modified as follows:
- If the special purpose framework is a result of management's election, the report will refer to management's responsibility for determining that the special purpose framework is appropriate under the circumstances,
- If the special purpose framework is a contractual or regulatory financial reporting framework, the report will either describe the purpose for which the financial statements are prepared or refer to a note in the financial statements that does so.

The review report will also include an **emphasis-of-matter** paragraph with an appropriate heading. The paragraph will:
- Inform users that the financial statements are prepared in accordance with the applicable special purpose framework;
- Identify the note to the financial statements that describes the framework; and
- State that the applicable framework is a basis of accounting other than GAAP.

In certain circumstances, an **other-matter** paragraph with an appropriate heading will be added to the review report, following the emphasis-of-matter paragraph, restricting the use of the report to specified parties. This will be the case when:
- The framework is a contractual or regulatory basis of accounting;
- The basis of accounting requires an adequate understanding of measurement and disclosure criteria, which is held, in the accountant's judgment, by a limited number of users; or
- The measurement and disclosure criteria for the applicable framework are only available to a limited number of users.

INDEPENDENT ACCOUNTANT'S REVIEW REPORT
(Special Purpose Financial Reporting Framework – Contractual Basis)

Board of Directors and Stockholders
X Company

We have reviewed the accompanying special purpose financial statements of X Company, which comprise the special purpose statement of assets and liabilities as of December 31, 20X2, and the related special purpose statements of revenues and expenses and of cash flows for the year then ended, and the related notes to the special purpose financial statements. A review includes primarily applying analytical procedures to management's financial data and making inquiries of company management. A review is substantially less in scope than an audit, the objective of which is the expression of an opinion regarding the financial statements as a whole. Accordingly, we do not express such an opinion.

Management's Responsibility for the Financial Statements
Management is responsible for the preparation and fair presentation of the special purpose financial statements in accordance with the basis of accounting pursuant to Section 3 of a loan agreement between First Bank and X Company; this includes determining that the basis of accounting used is an acceptable basis for the preparation of the special purpose financial statements in the circumstances. Management is also responsible for the design, implementation, and maintenance of internal control relevant to the preparation and fair presentation of the special purpose financial statements that are free from material misstatement, whether due to fraud or error.

Accountant's Responsibility
Our responsibility is to conduct the review engagement in accordance with Statements on Standards for Accounting and Review Services promulgated by the Accounting and Review Services Committee of the AICPA. Those standards require us to perform procedures to obtain limited assurance as a basis for reporting whether we are aware of any material modifications that should be made to the special purpose financial statements for them to be in accordance with the basis of accounting pursuant to Section 3 of a loan agreement between First Bank and X Company. We believe that the results of our procedures provide a reasonable basis for our conclusion.

Accountant's Conclusion
Based on our review, we are not aware of any material modifications that should be made to the accompanying special purpose financial statements in order for them to be in accordance with the basis of accounting pursuant to Section 3 of a loan agreement between First Bank and X Company.

Basis of Accounting
We draw attention to Note G of the special purpose financial statements, which describes the basis of accounting. The accompanying special purpose financial statements are prepared for the purpose of complying with Section 3 of a loan agreement between First Bank and X Company and the basis of accounting discussed in Note G, which is a basis of accounting other than accounting principles generally accepted in the United States of America. Our conclusion is not modified with respect to this matter.

Restriction on Use of Report
This report is intended solely for the information and use of the boards of directors and managements of X Company and First Bank and is *not intended to be, and should not be, used by anyone other than those specified parties.*

Signature of accountant or firm
Accountant's city and state
Date

Going Concern Considerations

Evidence obtained during the course of the review engagement may indicate uncertainty as to the entity's ability to continue as a going concern for a reasonable period of time, typically one year from the date of the financial statements or the date on which the financial statements are available to be issued, which is the date of the accountant's report. When this is the case:

- If the accountant is satisfied that management has adequately disclosed the going concern issue, the conclusion will not be modified and the only modification of the report may be in the form of an emphasis-of-matter paragraph drawing attention to management's disclosure of the issue, at the discretion of the accountant.
- If the accountant is not satisfied that management has adequately disclosed the going concern issue, the accountant will treat it as a departure from the applicable financial reporting framework and handle it accordingly.

Subsequent Events

Upon becoming aware of subsequent events that may require reporting or disclosure in the financial statements, the accountant will evaluate how the event is reflected in the financial statements.

- If the subsequent event is appropriately accounted for or disclosed, as required, the accountant may decide to include an emphasis-of-matter paragraph in the report to draw attention to the matter.
- If the subsequent is not appropriately accounted for or disclosed, the accountant will treat it as a departure from the applicable financial reporting framework and modify the report or take other action, as appropriate.

The date on which the accountant has obtained sufficient review evidence to support the accountant's conclusion is the date of the report and is also the date on which the financial statements are available to be issued. The client may not necessarily issue them immediately, however, and there may be a period of time between the date on which they are available to be issued and their actual release date.

Although the accountant is not required to perform any procedures during that period, the accountant may still become aware of information that may have affected the financial statements or the accountant's review report if the **subsequently discovered facts** had been known to the accountant prior to signing the report. When this occurs, the accountant should:

- Discuss the matter with the client;
- Determine if the financial statements need revision in terms of adjustment or additional disclosure; and
- Determine how management intends to address the matter in the financial statements.
- If management appropriately revises the financial statements, the accountant will:
  - Apply review procedures to the revision; and
    Either:
    - Date the accountant's review report as of the later date on which the additional procedures are completed; or
    - Dual date the report by retaining the original date as to the financial statements taken as a whole with the later date referenced exclusively to the revision, indicating that subsequent review procedures were also limited to that matter.

If the accountant becomes aware of such information after the report has been released, the accountant will follow the same procedures by discussing it with the client and evaluating the client's intended means of addressing the matter.

If management's response is to appropriately revise the financial statements, the accountant will:
- Either apply the later date to the report or dual date it; and
- Determine if management is taking the appropriate steps to make certain that those who received the previously issued financial statements are appropriately informed about the matter and instructed not to use the reviewed financial statements.

If the financial statements are revised as a result of these subsequently discovered facts, the accountant's conclusion may differ from that in the original report. When that is the case, the revised report will include an emphasis-of-matter paragraph that will disclose:
- The date of the previous report;
- A description of the revisions; and
- Substantive reasons for the revision.

If the client does not make appropriate revisions to the financial statements, which have not yet been issued to third parties, the accountant should notify the client that the reviewed financial statements should not be made available to third parties.

Under certain circumstances, the accountant may be **required to take additional action**. This would be the case when:
- Regardless of whether or not the financial statements are revised, management may not take appropriate steps to prevent use of the previously released reviewed financial statements; or
- The financial statements are not revised and management makes them available to third parties despite the accountant's notification that the reviewed financial statements should not be made available.

In these cases, the accountant should notify the client that the accountant will attempt to prevent future reliance on the accountant's review report. If management persists in not taking appropriate action, the accountant should seek legal advice and may decide to do any or all of the following:
- Notify management and governance that the review report is not to be used;
- Notify relevant regulatory agencies that the accountant's review report is not to be relied upon and request that the regulatory agency take appropriate steps to make the necessary disclosure; and
- Notify known users of the financial statements that the accountant's review report should not be used.

Work of Other Accountants

The accountant may rely upon the work of other accountants who may have performed reviews or audits on significant components of the reviewed financial statements, such as consolidated or unconsolidated subsidiaries or significant investees. When that is the case, the accountant should communicate with the other accountant to make certain that:
- The other accountant is aware that reviewed financial statements will include that component;
- The audit or review report on the component will be relied upon;

- When applicable, the review report will refer to the audit or review report of the component;
- The other accountant is familiar with the applicable financial reporting standards and relevant professional standards to enable performance of the audit or review in conformity with them; and
- Review procedures will be applied to the elimination of intercompany activity and the uniformity of accounting policies and practices of the component in relation to those of the reviewed entity.

If the accountant decides not to take responsibility for the work of the accountant performing the audit or review of the component, the accountant will make reference to the audit or review of the other accountant in the review report. The reference should clearly indicate:
- That the accountant used the work of other accountants; and
- The magnitude of the portion of the financial statements attested to by the other accountants.

Supplementary Information Accompanying Reviewed Financial Statements

When supplementary information accompanies reviewed financial statements, the accountant will indicate the degree of responsibility the accountant is taking in relation to the supplementary information. This may be done in either an other-matter paragraph in the accountant's review report or a separate report on the supplementary information. The other-matter paragraph or separate report will state:
- The supplementary information is the representation of management and is derived from, and relates directly to, the underlying accounting and other records used to prepare the financial statements;
- That it is not a required part of the financial statements, but rather is provided for further analysis; and
- If the accountant has reviewed the supplementary information, that:
  - It has been reviewed, applying the review procedures applied in the accountant's review of the basic financial statements;
  - Whether the accountant is aware of any material modifications required in order for it to be in accordance with the applicable financial reporting framework; and
  - It has not been audited and, accordingly, no opinion is expressed.
- If the accountant has not reviewed the supplementary information that:
  - It has not been audited or reviewed; and
  - The accountant does not express an opinion, a conclusion, nor provide any assurance in relation to the supplementary information.

Required Supplementary Information

When the applicable financial reporting framework under which the financial statements were prepared requires supplementary information, the accountant's report will be modified to include an emphasis of matter paragraph that will indicate whichever of the following are applicable:
- The required supplementary information is included and:
  - The accountant performed a compilation engagement upon it;
  - The accountant reviewed it; or
  - The accountant did not compile, review, or audit it.
- The required supplementary information is omitted.

- Some required supplementary information is presented in accordance with prescribed guidelines and some is missing.
- There are departures from the prescribed guidelines.
- There are unresolved doubts as to whether or not the required supplementary information is presented in accordance with the prescribed guidelines.

When some or all of the required supplementary information is presented that was not compiled or reviewed by the accountant, certain items will be included in the other-matter paragraph:

- The required supplementary information is required to be presented to supplement the basic financial statements by the applicable financial reporting framework, which considers the required supplementary information essential to a proper understanding of the financial statements.
- The required supplementary information presented was not subjected to compilation, review, or audit and, as a result, no opinion is expressed nor is any assurance provided.
- A description of any required supplementary information that has been omitted along with an indication that, although not part of the basic financial statements, the applicable financial reporting framework requires it to be an essential part of financial reporting.
- Any material departures from prescribed guidelines for reporting on or presenting the required supplementary information.
- Any doubts the accountant may have about whether material modification to the required supplementary information is required in order for it to be in accordance with the guidelines prescribed by the applicable financial reporting framework.

'When required supplementary information is omitted in its entirety, the other-matter paragraph will indicate that:

- Information required by the applicable financial reporting framework to accompany the financial statements has been omitted by management; and
- Although not a part of the basic financial statements, the omitted information is considered by the standard setter responsible for the applicable financial reporting framework to be essential.

There are certain circumstances that require the accountant to **withdraw from the engagement** without issuing a report, including:

- A **limitation by the client on the scope** of the accountant's inquiries and/or analytical procedures.
- **Departures from GAAP** that are so numerous or **extreme** as to make a modification of the report inadequate to deal with them.
- Client refuses to provide a **representation letter** for a Review.

A client occasionally requests that the accountant perform a compilation or review of the balance sheet only, and not the other financial statements. So long as there is no limitation placed on the scope of the inquiries and analytical procedures, the accountant may accept such an engagement and report on the balance sheet (*limited reporting engagement*).

Documentation in a Review Engagement

The accountant's documentation for a review engagement is required to include:

- The engagement letter
- Communication with management regarding fraud or noncompliance with applicable laws and regulations

- Communication with management if the accountant expects the report to include an emphasis-of-matter or other-matter paragraph
- Communication with other accountants that have audited or reviewed significant components of the financial statements
- Representation letter
- Reviewed financial statements
- Review report

Lecture 7.08

COMPARISON OF THE DIFFERENT TYPES OF ENGAGEMENTS

It may be useful to restate the differences between the **four types of engagements** available for non-public entities as a hierarchy. Although the following list is not exhaustive, it covers nearly all of the differences addressed on previous CPA exams.

For **preparation of F/S, compilations, reviews, and audits**, the accountant must:
- Obtain an *Engagement letter*, signed by both the client and the accountant's firm; and
- **Understand** the applicable accounting framework and significant accounting policies of the client.

For **compilations, reviews, and audits**, the accountant must:
- *Read* the financial statements and notes to ensure free of obvious material error and in appropriate form; and
- Communicate any illegal acts in the form of *noncompliance* with applicable laws or regulations that are not clearly inconsequential and any fraud, regardless of materiality, to the appropriate level of management and to the accountant's legal counsel.

In addition, the accountant:
- May add additional paragraph to emphasize a matter such as a going concern doubt, a material subsequent event or a change in accounting principle or estimate.
- May be required to indicate a lack of independence if performing a compilation when not independent.

For **reviews and audits**, the accountant must:
- Have or obtain knowledge of the client's industry and its accounting practices.
- Be independent of the client;
- Obtain a management representation letter;
- Make inquiries of company personnel; and
- Apply analytical procedures to the financial data.

For **audits**, the accountant must:
- Obtain and document an understanding of internal control;
- Assess Risk of Material Misstatement;
- Perform tests involving inspection, observation, and confirmation;
- Evaluate the client's assessment as to whether there is substantial doubt about the ability of the client to continue as a going concern for a reasonable period of time;
- Perform inquiries of the client's attorney; and
- Apply analytical procedures to the detailed financial records and corroborative evidence.

Summary Comparison Chart

TASK	Required for **Preparation Engagement**	Required for **Compilation**	Required for **Review**	Required for **Audit**
Obtain signed **engagement letter**	Yes	Yes	Yes	Yes
Understanding of the applicable financial reporting framework and significant accounting policies	Yes	Yes	Yes	Yes
Read the financial statements and notes to ensure free of material error and in appropriate form.	No	Yes	Yes	Yes
Obtain **knowledge** of the accounting principles and practices of the entity's industry.	No	No	Yes	Yes
Have a general **understanding** of the client's business transactions and accounting records.	No	No	Yes	Yes
Make **inquiries** concerning actions taken at board of directors' meetings.	No	No	Yes	Yes
Communicate with the predecessor accountant to obtain access to the predecessor's audit documentation.	No	No	No	Yes
Obtain an understanding of the entity's internal controls.	No	No	No	Yes
Perform **analytical procedures** designed to identify relationships that appear to be unusual.	No	No	Yes	Yes
Make an assessment of risk of material misstatement (RMM).	No	No	No	Yes
Send a letter of inquiry to the entity's attorney to corroborate the information furnished by management concerning litigation.	No	No	No	Yes
Obtain a management representation letter.	No	No	Yes	Yes
Study the relationship of the financial statement elements that would be expected to conform to a predictable pattern.	No	No	Yes	Yes
Make reference in the report about events subsequent to the date of the financial statements that would have a material effect on the financial statements.	No	Yes	Yes	Yes
Modify the accountant's report with an emphasis-of-matter paragraph if there is a change in accounting principles that is adequately disclosed.	No	Yes	Yes	Yes
Make reference in the report in an emphasis-of-matter paragraph if there is substantial doubt about the entity's ability to continue as a going concern.	No	Yes	Yes	Yes
Maintain **independence** with respect to the entity.	No	No, may disclose reasons	Yes	Yes

Downgrading an Engagement

Occasionally, an accountant will be in the midst of an audit of a non-public entity, and the client will request that the engagement be downgraded to a review or compilation. Similarly, an accountant performing a review may be asked to downgrade to a compilation. In such circumstances, the accountant should carefully consider:

- The **reasons** offered by the client for the downgraded engagement (Change in circumstances or a misunderstanding of the nature of an audit, review or compilation).
- The **additional Effort** and **additional Cost** needed to complete the original engagement.

If the request of the client is reasonable, the accountant will switch to the downgraded engagement. It is important that the report resulting from such an engagement make **no reference** to the original engagement or the reasons for the downgrade, as it would only serve to confuse the reader as to the nature of the work performed by the accountant. If the reasons are not justifiable, the auditor should consider withdrawing from the engagement.

REVIEW OF INTERIM FINANCIAL STATEMENTS (10Q) (PCAOB AS 4105, GAAS AU-C 930, AND AR-C 90)

While the annual financial statements of a public (issuer) client may be audited, the quarterly (interim) information typically is not. Instead, the auditor of the annual financial statements will normally perform a **review of interim financial information**. The auditor is required to establish an understanding with his client regarding the services to be performed in an engagement to review interim financial information.

Like all reviews, this engagement consists principally of inquiries of company personnel (including reading minutes of board and shareholder meetings) and analytical procedures applied to financial data, and results in the expression of **limited assurance (negative assurance)** by the accountant. The difference is that a review of interim information may be performed for a public company according to clarified SAS (AU-C Audit Standards), while compilations and reviews of annual financial statements under SSARS are specifically restricted to non-public entities.

These interim reviews are performed under the clarified SAS (as opposed to SSARS) when:
- The entity's latest annual financial statements have been audited;
  Either:
    - The accountant has been engaged to audit the entity's current year financial statements, or
    - The accountant audited the entity's latest annual financial statements and expects to be engaged to audit the current year financial statements; and
- The same financial reporting framework used to prepare the annual financial statements is used for the interim financial information.

If all of these conditions are not met, a review of interim financial information is ***required*** to be performed in accordance with SSARS.

The report will indicate that the accountant is unaware of any material modifications that should be made to the interim information in order for it to conform to GAAP. This report may be utilized by an underwriter in connection with a public offering of securities under the Securities Act of 1933, but the report itself is not a part of the registration statement.

Where the review is of a *public company* under the **jurisdiction of the PCAOB**, the report must be changed in a few ways:
1. The title of the page is "Report of Independent Registered Public Accounting Firm."
2. The second paragraph must **not** refer to Statements on Standards for Accounting and Review Services of the American Institute of Certified Public Accountants, and instead refer to "the standards of the Public Company Accounting Oversight Board (United States)."
3. Below the signature of the CPA-in-charge must be listed the city and state (or city and country for non-US-auditors) of the office where the accountant is based.

Some of the required procedures that an accountant must perform in an *interim review* engagement include:
- Comparing disaggregated revenue data, for example comparing revenue by month and by product line or business segment for the current interim period with that of comparable prior periods.
- Obtaining evidence that the interim financial information agrees or reconciles with the accounting records.
- Inquiring of management who have responsibility for financial and accounting matters about their knowledge of any fraud or suspected fraud affecting the entity.
- Having (or obtaining during the engagement) **knowledge** of the accounting principles and practices of the client's industry.
- Having a general **understanding** of the client's business transactions and accounting records.
- **Reading** the financial statements and notes to ensure that they are free of material error and appropriate in form.

May *Modify* Interim Review report for:
- Comparative interim financial information
- Division of responsibility (Group audit engagement)
- Departures from GAAP
- Inadequate Disclosure
- Going Concern Doubts
- Lack of Consistency
- Emphasis of a matter

INDEPENDENT REGISTERED PUBLIC ACCOUNTING FIRM

We have reviewed the accompanying [*describe the interim financial information or statements reviewed*] of ABC Company and consolidated subsidiaries as of September 30, 20X1, and for the three-month and nine-month periods then ended. This interim financial information is [*These interim financial statements are*] the responsibility of the company's management.

We conducted our review in accordance with standards of the **Public Company Accounting Oversight Board (United States)**. A review of interim financial information consists principally of applying analytical procedures and making inquiries of persons responsible for financial and accounting matters. It is substantially less in scope than an audit conducted in accordance with the standards of the Public Company Accounting Oversight Board, the objective of which is the expression of an opinion regarding the financial statements taken as a whole. Accordingly, we do not express such an opinion.

Based on our review, we are not aware of any material modifications that should be made to the accompanying interim financial information [*statements*] for it [*them*] to be in conformity with US generally accepted accounting principles.

[Signature]

[City and State or Country]

[Date – completion of the review procedures]

OTHER SSARS ISSUES

Compilation of *Pro Forma* Financial Information – AR-C Section 120

When SSARS 21 was issued, it replaced all of the existing standards for compilation and review engagements by re-writing them in the clarity format, with the exception of AR Section 120, Compilation of Pro Forma Financial Information. It was re-written applying clarity protocol with the issuance of SSARS 22, which was issued in September 2016 and became effective May 1, 2017, creating AR-C Section 120.

Pro forma financial information consists of historical financial information that is derived from historical financial statements of an entity, but modified to reflect what management believes the financial statements would have looked like if certain decisions had or had not been made, affecting the period being presented. These decisions may relate to a specific transaction or event such as a business combination, disposal of a business segment, making a significant capital expenditure, or a change in the form of business organization.

An accountant may assist a client in presenting pro forma financial information without issuing a compilation report. Such an engagement is a nonattest engagement and the accountant is subject to the applicable sections of the code of professional conduct, but there are currently no professional standards to be followed in its conduct. When an accountant is engaged to report on pro forma information, the accountant is required to comply with the applicable standards. As a result, when engaged to report on pro forma financial information, the accountant would perform a compilation in accordance with SSARS.

AR-C Section 120 specifies that the objective of the accountant in a compilation of pro forma financial information is to apply accounting and financial reporting expertise to assist management in the presentation of pro forma financial information and report in accordance with this section

(AR-C Section 120) without undertaking to obtain or provide any assurance on the pro forma financial information.

As is true of other SSARS engagements, the accountant is required to apply AR-C Section 60, the General Principles for Engagements Performed in Accordance with SSARS. In addition, as is true for any compilation engagement, the accountant is required to determine whether independence has been impaired. If it has been, the accountant may still accept the engagement but the compilation report will be required to indicate the lack of independence.

Acceptance and Continuance of the Engagement and the Client Relationship

As a prerequisite to acceptance, management is required to acknowledge and accept its responsibilities, which include responsibility for the preparation and fair presentation of the pro forma financial information in accordance with the applicable financial reporting framework. Even if the accountant prepares the pro forma financial information, which would be done in a nonattest bookkeeping engagement, the client is required to take responsibility for the preparation and fair presentation of the information.

Due to the unique nature of pro forma financial information, the client is required to agree that, in any document containing the compiled pro forma financial information, the following will be included:

- The complete financial statements for the entity for the immediately preceding period.
    - In some cases, the financial statements for the most recent period may not have yet been prepared. When that is the case, the financial statements for the period preceding that are to be included.
- If the pro forma financial information is for an interim period, the historical financial information for that period is to be included.
    - It may be in condensed form.
    - If the financial statements for that interim period are not available, those for the most recent period available should be included.
- If the pro forma financial information is related to a business combination, the financial information for all significant constituent entities should be included.
    - The financial statements that are included, either those of the entity or those of all constituent entities in the case of a business combination, are to have been subjected to a compilation, review, or audit engagement.
- The accountant's audit, review, or compilation report on the included financial statements should also be included.
    - Making the report available is sufficient.

Pro forma financial information is to be accompanied by a summary of significant assumptions so that users will understand not only the framework but also management's plans that are being considered or events that are being planned for.

The client is expected to agree to obtain the accountant's permission to include the compilation report in any document containing the pro forma financial information when it indicates that the information has been compiled. The permission should be obtained prior to the inclusion of the information.

If any of the conditions are not met to the accountant's satisfaction, the matters should be discussed with the client's management so that the accountant can make an appropriate decision regarding whether to accept the engagement.

Agreement on Engagement Terms

In an engagement letter, continuing the signatures of both the accountant, or the accountant's firm, and the appropriate representative from the client, either management or those responsible for governance, the terms of the engagement should be agreed upon and documented. The engagement letter should include:

- The objectives of the engagement;
- Management's responsibilities;
- The accountant's responsibilities;
- The limitations of the compilation engagement;
- Identification of the applicable financial reporting framework, according to which the pro forma financial information has been prepared; and
- The expected form and content of the accountant's compilation report with an indication that circumstances may require a report that may differ in form or content.

As is the case in all compilations, the accountant is required to have or obtain an understanding of the financial reporting framework in accordance with which the pro forma financial information is being prepared. This will include the client's significant accounting policies and, if a business combination is involved, those of the constituent entities.

Compilation Procedures

The same procedures as those required for any compilation are required, however, they may need some modification to adapt to the fact that the information is pro forma, as opposed to historical, financial information. In addition, the accountant should:

- Obtain an understanding of the event or transaction underlying the pro forma financial information;
- Ascertain that management has fulfilled its responsibilities to include the historical financial information indicated above, that the information has been subjected to a compilation, review, or audit engagement, and that the report has been included in the document or made readily available.

The Accountant's Compilation Report

The accountant's compilation report is required to be in writing and to comply with all of the requirements delineated in AR-C Section 80, as discussed above. In addition, the report should include a reference to the historical financial statements from which the information was derived, indicating whether the information had been subjected to an audit, a review, or a compilation. Any modifications of the report on the historical information should be referenced and the nature and limitations of pro forma financial information should be described.

ACCOUNTANT'S COMPILATION REPORT
(Pro Forma)

ACCOUNTANT'S COMPILATION REPORT
(Pro Forma)

Management is responsible for the accompanying ***pro forma*** condensed balance sheet of X Company as of December 31, 20X1, and the related pro forma condensed statement of income for the year then ended (pro forma financial information), based on the criteria in Note 1. The historical condensed financial statements are derived from the financial statements of X Company, on which we performed a compilation engagement, and of A Company, on which other accountants performed a compilation engagement. The pro forma adjustments are based on management's assumptions described in Note 1. We have performed a compilation engagement in accordance with Statements on Standards for Accounting and Review Services promulgated by the Accounting and Review Services Committee of the AICPA. We did not examine or review the pro forma financial information nor were we required to perform any procedures to verify the accuracy or completeness of the information provided by management. Accordingly, we do not express an opinion, a conclusion, nor provide any form of assurance on the pro forma financial information.

The objective of this pro forma financial information is to show what the significant effects on the historical financial information might have been had the underlying transaction (or event) occurred at an earlier date. However, the pro forma condensed financial statements are not necessarily indicative of the results of operations or related effects on financial position that would have been attained had the above-mentioned transaction (or event) actually occurred at such earlier date.

An additional paragraph may be added to emphasize certain matters relating to the compilation engagement or the subject matter. If it refers to information that is properly accounted for and disclosed, an emphasis-of-matter paragraph will be used. If it is to provide information about the engagement or the subject matter that is not required to be disclosed but, in the accountant's judgment, will be useful to the users of the information, it will be in an other-matter paragraph.

The report will also include the accountant's city and state, the date of the report, and the accountant's signature or that of the firm.

Documentation Required for a Compilation of Pro Forma Financial Information

As is true for all professional engagements, documentation should be sufficient to provide a clear understanding of the work performed. It should include, as a minimum:
- The engagement letter or other documentation of the understanding;
- The results of procedures performed;
- A copy of the pro forma financial information; and
- A copy of the compilation report.

Compilation Reports on Financial Statements Included in Certain *Prescribed Forms*

An accountant may be engaged to report on financial statements that are included in a prescribed form, which is any standard preprinted form designed or adopted by the body to which it is to be submitted. This may be a bank or other financial institution, a governmental or regulatory agency, trade association, or some other body whose primary concern is not the sale and trading of securities.

If the accountant is aware of a departure from the requirements of the prescribed form or some other circumstance that would require the issuance of a modified compilation report, the same modifications would be made to the report on financial statements included in a prescribed form.

Assuming the accountant has no reason to modify the report, it will be very similar to an unmodified compilation report with the following exceptions
1. The report will refer to the prescribed form.
2. It will include an explanatory paragraph describing that the financial statements are not intended to conform to GAAP.
3. It will include a paragraph *restricting the use* of the financial statements and the report.

ACCOUNTANT'S COMPILATION REPORT
(Prescribed Form)

Management is responsible for the accompanying financial statements of X Company included in the accompanying prescribed form, which comprise the balance sheet as of December 31, 20X2 and the related statements of income, changes in stockholders' equity, and cash flows for the year then ended, and the related notes to the financial statements in accordance with accounting principles generally accepted in the Unites States of America. We have performed a compilation engagement in accordance with Statements on Standards for Accounting and Review Services promulgated by the Accounting and Review Services Committee of the AICPA. We did not audit or review the financial statements included in the accompanying prescribed form nor were we required to perform any procedures to verify the accuracy or the completeness of the information provided by management. Accordingly, we do not express an opinion, a conclusion, nor provide any form of assurance on these financial statements.

The financial statements presented in the accompanying prescribed form are presented in accordance with the requirements of [*name of body*], and are not intended to be a presentation in accordance with accounting principles generally accepted in the United States of America.

This report is intended solely for the information and use of [*the specified parties*] and is not intended to be and should not be used by anyone other than these specified parties.

Communications between Predecessor and Successor Accountants

- Not required, but if chose to do, would follow the guidance provided for "communication prior to accepting an audit engagement" discussed in a previous section. The goal is to obtain info that is useful in deciding whether to accept the engagement. Including (**RID**):
    - **R**easons for the change
    - **I**ntegrity of management

- o **D**isagreements with management about accounting principles
  - Must obtain permission from client to obtain access to predecessor's workpapers.

Reporting on Personal Financial Statements Included in Written Personal Financial Plans

- Financial statements in personal financial plans need not be compiled, reviewed, or audited (per SSARS) if the statements are to be used to assist the client in developing financial goals and objectives, and will **not** be used to obtain **credit**.
- The accountant's report should state that the financial statements:
  - o Are for the financial plan
  - o May be incomplete or contain GAAP departures and should not be used for other purposes, and
  - o Have not been audited, reviewed, or compiled.

Passage from a Personal Financial Statement Report

The accompanying Statement of Financial Condition of ABC Co, as of December 31, 20X1, was prepared solely to help you develop your personal financial plan. Accordingly, it may be incomplete or contain other departures from GAAP and should **not be used to obtain credit** or for any purposes other than developing your financial plan. We have not audited, reviewed or compiled the statement.

Lecture 7.09

CLASS QUESTIONS

Please see the Class Questions and Class Solutions for this Lecture at the end of this Section.

CLASS QUESTIONS

Work through the below Class Questions while following along with the respective lectures. Once this is complete, you can begin independently practicing what you've learned by quizzing yourself on this course section in your Interactive Practice Questions (IPQ), which can be found in your online Student Dashboard. Your IPQ simulates the computer-based testing experience, and will also help you understand how concepts are applied to the exam. Each question includes answer explanations from expert CPAs that will help you determine why you answered a question correctly or incorrectly. This is key to your success on the CPA Exam.

Lecture 7.03

1. Which of the following is an attest engagement?

   I.   A review.
   II. An engagement to prepare financial statements.
   III. A compilation.

    a. I only
    b. I and III only
    c. I, II and III
    d. II and III only

2. Statements on Standards for Accounting and Review Services (SSARS) would govern the conduct of which of the following?

   I.   Beck, CPA, prepares financial statements as a necessary step prior to Beck's engagement to compile the financial statements.
   II. Preparation of financial statements that will not be compiled, reviewed or audited.
   III. Gumpert, CPA, prepares financial statements that will be compiled by Martinez, CPA.

    a. II only
    b. II and III only
    c. I and II only
    d. I, II and III

3. Which of the following would **not** be found in an engagement letter for a financial statement preparation engagement to be performed in accordance with SSARS?

    a. An agreement by management that each page of the financial statements will include a statement indicating that no assurance is provided, if management agrees to this measure.
    b. A statement regarding the expected omission of substantially all disclosures required by the applicable accounting framework, if such an omission is expected.
    c. A statement indicating that the report will specify that the accountant is not independent, when that is the case.
    d. The accountant's responsibilities, which are to comply with the requirements of SSARS.

4. In a financial statement preparation engagement, a client refuses to include a 'no assurance provided' statement on each page of the financial statements. There are no other issues with the engagement. As a result, which of the following actions is most likely?

   a. The accountant will withdraw from the engagement and file a complaint with the state board of accountancy.
   b. The accountant will, without consulting the client, compile the financial statements and issue a compilation report.
   c. The accountant will automatically withdraw from the engagement but file no complaint.
   d. The accountant will issue a disclaimer that indicates that no assurance is provided to accompany the financial statements.

Lecture 7.06

5. Which of the following procedures is ordinarily performed by an accountant in a compilation engagement of a nonissuer (nonpublic entity)?

   a. Reading the financial statements to consider whether they are free of obvious mistakes in the application of accounting principles.
   b. Obtaining written representations from management indicating that the compiled financial statements will **not** be used to obtain credit.
   c. Making inquiries of management concerning actions taken at meetings of the stockholders and the board of directors.
   d. Applying analytical procedures designed to corroborate management's assertions that are embodied in the financial statement components.

6. How does an accountant make the following representations when issuing the standard report for the compilation of a nonissuer's (nonpublic entity's) financial statements?

	The financial statements have NOT been audited	The accountant has compiled the financial statements
a.	Implicitly	Implicitly
b.	Explicitly	Explicitly
c.	Implicitly	Explicitly
d.	Explicitly	Implicitly

7. An accountant compiled the financial statements of a nonissuer in accordance with *Statements on Standards for Accounting and Review Services* (SSARS). If the accountant has an ownership interest in the entity, which of the following statements is correct?

   a. The accountant should refuse the compilation engagement.
   b. A report need **not** be issued for a compilation of a nonissuer.
   c. The accountant should include the disclaimer "I am an owner of the entity" in the report.
   d. The accountant should include the statement "I am **not** independent with respect to the entity" in the compilation report.

8. According to Statements on Standards for Accounting and Review Engagements, in which of the following situations would the accountant be required to issue a report?

    I.   A compilation engagement where the accountant is independent of the client.
    II. A review engagement from which the accountant withdrew after completing substantially all of the required work.
    III. An engagement to prepare financial statements.

    a. I only
    b. II only
    c. I and II only
    d. I, II and III

Lecture 7.09

9. Which of the following procedures would an accountant least likely perform during an engagement to review the financial statements of a nonissuer (nonpublic entity)?

    a. Observing the safeguards over access to and use of assets and records.
    b. Comparing the financial statements with anticipated results in budgets and forecasts.
    c. Inquiring of management about actions taken at the board of directors' meetings.
    d. Studying the relationships of financial statement elements expected to conform to predictable patterns.

10. Which of the following procedures should an accountant perform during an engagement to review the financial statements of a nonissuer (nonpublic entity)?

    a. Communicating significant deficiencies discovered during the assessment of the risk of material misstatement.
    b. Obtaining a client representation letter from members of management.
    c. Sending bank confirmation letters to the entity's financial institutions.
    d. Examining cash disbursements in the subsequent period for unrecorded liabilities.

11. Baker, CPA, was engaged to review the financial statements of Hall Co., a nonissuer (nonpublic) entity. During the engagement Baker uncovered a complex scheme involving client noncompliance (illegal acts) that materially affect Hall's financial statements. If Baker believes that modification of the standard review report is not adequate to indicate the deficiencies in the financial statements, Baker should

    a. Disclaim an opinion.
    b. Issue an adverse opinion.
    c. Withdraw from the engagement.
    d. Issue a qualified opinion.

12. An accountant's standard report on a review of the financial statements of a nonissuer (nonpublic entity) should state that the accountant

    a. Does **not** express an opinion or any form of limited assurance on the financial statements.

    b. Is **not** aware of any material modifications that should be made to the financial statements for them to conform with GAAP.

    c. Obtained reasonable assurance about whether the financial statements are free of material misstatement.

    d. Examined evidence, on a test basis, supporting the amounts and disclosures in the financial statements.

13. The objective of a review of interim financial information of an issuer (public entity) is to provide an accountant with a basis for reporting whether

    a. Material modifications should be made to conform to generally accepted accounting principles.

    b. A reasonable basis exists for expressing an updated opinion regarding the financial statements that were previously audited.

    c. Condensed financial statements or pro forma financial information should be included in a registration statement.

    d. The financial statements are presented fairly in accordance with generally accepted accounting principles.

14. Kell engaged March, CPA, to submit to Kell a written personal financial plan containing unaudited personal financial statements. March anticipates omitting certain disclosures required by GAAP because the engagement's sole purpose is to assist Kell in developing a personal financial plan. For March to be exempt from complying with the requirements of Statements on Standards for Accounting and Review Services, Kell is required to agree that the

    a. Financial statements will **not** be presented in comparative form with those of the prior period.

    b. Omitted disclosures required by GAAP are **not** material.

    c. Financial statements will **not** be disclosed to a non-CPA financial planner.

    d. Financial statements will **not** be used to obtain credit.

CLASS SOLUTIONS

1. (**a**) Reviews are considered attest engagements. A review is also an assurance engagement. Compilation and preparation engagements are neither attest engagements nor assurance engagements.

2. (**b**) When the preparation of financial statements is the highest level of service an accountant will be performing, the preparation engagement is a nonattest engagement that is subject to the requirements of SSARS. This will still be the case if the financial statements are compiled, reviewed, or audited, as long as that engagement is performed by another accountant. When the accountant prepares financial statements in anticipation of compiling, auditing, or reviewing them, the engagement is a nonattest engagement that is not subject to the requirements of SSARS. For the subsequent engagement to compile, review or audit the statements, however, the accountant will need to determine if independence is impaired.

3. (**c**) The agreement between the accountant and a client, as documented in an engagement letter, will include either management's agreement to indicate on every page that no assurance is provided or to allow the accountant to attach a disclaimer so indicating. When substantially all disclosures are omitted, the financial statements are required to indicate that the disclosures are not provided and the engagement letter will indicate management's agreement to do so. It will also specify the accountant's responsibility to perform the engagement in accordance with SSARS. An accountant is not required to be independent to perform a preparation engagement. In addition, a preparation engagement will not be accompanied by a report.

4. (**d**) When management either will not, or for some reason cannot, agree to include a statement on every page of the financial statements indicating that no assurance is provided on them, the accountant will be required to issue a disclaimer that makes clear that no assurance is provided. If there are no other issues about which the accountant is concerned, there is no reason to withdraw from the engagement or to upgrade it to a compilation.

5. (**a**) The accountant performing a compilation is required to have or obtain an understanding of the financial reporting framework that will be applied in the preparation of the financial statements and is required to read the financial statements. Written representation letters (b), inquiries of management (c), and the application of analytical procedures (d) are requirements for the performance of an audit or a review, but not for a compilation.

6. (**b**) The compilation report is required to indicate management's responsibility for the financial statements, the statements being compiled, making the representation explicit, and that the accountant has performed a compilation (explicit). The accountant also explicitly indicates that the financial statements were neither audited nor reviewed.

7. (**d**) When an accountant is not independent of a client, the accountant may perform a compilation (a) and will issue a report (b). The report will indicate that the accountant is not independent with respect to the entity and may, but is not required to, indicate the reason for the lack of independence (c).

8. (a) A report is required in a compilation engagement, regardless of whether or not the accountant is independent. Although a review report is required when the accountant reviews a client's financial statements, no report is issued when an accountant withdraws from an engagement. A preparation engagement does not require the issuance of a report.

9. (a) When performing a review, in addition to having or obtaining an understanding of the client and its business, the accountant is required to make inquiries of management (c) and perform analytical procedures, which involve developing expectations based on relationships among financial statement elements that have predictable patterns (d) and comparing actual results to expectations, which may also include those indicated in budgets and forecasts (b). The accountant is not required to obtain an understanding of internal control in a review engagement and, as a result, would probably not observe controls such as safeguards over access to and use of assets.

10. (b) When performing a review, the accountant is required to have or obtain an understanding of the client and its business, perform inquiries and analytical procedures, and obtain a letter of representation from the client. The accountant is not required to obtain an understanding of internal control and would therefore not be responsible for communicating significant deficiencies (a). Substantive tests, including sending bank confirmation letters (c) and examining cash disbursements (d) are performed in an audit but not in a review.

11. (c) Upon uncovering an act of noncompliance, or illegal act, that has a material effect on the financial statements, the Accountant will determine if issuing as modified report will be sufficient to meet the needs of financial statement users. If so, a modified review report would be issued. If not, the accountant should withdraw from the engagement. Since a review engagement does not result in the expression of an opinion by the accountant, it would not be appropriate to issue a report with a disclaimer of opinion (a), an adverse opinion (b), or a qualified opinion (d).

12. (b) The unmodified review report indicates that the accountant is not aware of any material modifications that should be made to the financial statements in order for them to be in conformity with GAAP. This is a form of limited assurance and, although the accountant does not express an opinion in a review report, limited assurance is provided (a). The accountant obtains reasonable assurance about the absence of material misstatements (c) in an audit but not in a review. Likewise, evidence supporting amounts and disclosures in the financial statements (d) is examined in an audit but a review involves obtaining knowledge of the client, performing inquiries and analytical procedures, and obtaining a letter of representation without the requirement to examine evidence supporting amounts and disclosures.

13. (a) A review, whether performed in relation to interim information of an issuer, or the interim or annual financial statements of a nonissuer, is designed to provide the accountant with limited assurance that the financial statements are not in need of material modifications to be in conformity with GAAP. Expressing an updated opinion regarding previously audited financial statements (b) would require the application of audit procedures. A review does not provide information that is helpful in determining that condensed financial statements or pro forma financial information should be included in a registration statement (c). An audit, not a review, would provide an accountant with a basis for indicating that the financial statements are presented fairly in accordance with GAAP (d).

14. (d) An accountant is not required to issue a compilation report with unaudited personal financial statements that are included in a written personal financial plan as long as they will not be used to obtain credit. There is no restriction on presenting personal financial statements in comparative form (a). It is common for disclosures to be omitted in such circumstances and it is not determined on the basis of their materiality (b) but rather because they are largely not relevant to a personal financial plan. A written personal financial plan is often written by a non-CPA financial planner (c) and there is no restriction preventing an accountant from assisting a client in preparing unaudited personal financial statements that will be disclosed to a non-CPA financial planner.

Lecture 7.09

TASK-BASED SIMULATION 1

Task-Based Simulation 1

The Uniform CPA Examination

| Unsplit | Split Horiz | Split Vertical | Authoritative Literature | Spreadsheet | Calculator | Submit Testlet |

Work Tab | **Resources** | **Help**

Required:

Items 1 through 14 consists of items pertaining to possible deficiencies in an accountant's review report. Select the best answer for each item.

Jordan & Stone, CPAs, audited the financial statements of Tech Co., a nonpublic entity, for the year ended December 31, 20X1, and expressed an unmodified opinion. For the year ended December 31, 20X2, Tech issued comparative financial statements. Jordan & Stone reviewed Tech's 20X2 financial statements and Kent, an assistant on the engagement, drafted the accountants' review report below. Land, the engagement supervisor, decided not to reissue the prior year's auditors' report, but instructed Kent to include a separate paragraph in the current year's review report describing the responsibility assumed for the prior year's audited financial statements. This is an appropriate reporting procedure.

Land reviewed Kent's draft and indicated in the *Supervisor's Review Notes* below that there were several deficiencies in Kent's draft.

INDEPENDENT ACCOUNTANT'S REVIEW REPORT

We have reviewed and audited the accompanying balance sheet of Tech Co. as of December 31, 20X2 and 20X1, and the related statements of income, changes in stockholders' equity, and cash flows for the years then ended in accordance with Statements of Standards for Accounting and Review Services and Statements on Auditing Standards issued by the American Institute of Certified Public Accountants.

All information included in these financial statements is the representation of the management of Tech Co.

Review standards require us to perform procedures to obtain limited assurance that there are no material modifications that should be made to the financial statements. A review consists principally of inquiries of company personnel and analytical procedures applied to financial data. It is substantially less in scope than an audit in accordance with generally accepted auditing standards, the objective of which is the expression of an opinion regarding the financial statements taken as a whole.

Based on our review, we are not aware of any material modifications that should be made to the 20X2 financial statements. Because of the inherent limitations of a review engagement, this report is intended for the information of management and should not be used for any other purpose.

The 20X1 financial statements were audited by us and our report was dated March 2, 20X2. We have no responsibility for updating that report for events or circumstances occurring after that date.

Jordan and Stone, CPAs

March 1, 20X3

Required:

Items 1 through 14 represent deficiencies noted by Land. For each deficiency, indicate whether Land is correct **C** or incorrect **I** in the criticism of Kent's draft.

Items to be Answered:

Supervisor's Review Notes

1. There should be no reference to the prior year's audited financial statements in the first (introductory) paragraph.

2. All the current-year basic financial statements are not properly identified in the first (introductory) paragraph.

3. There should be no reference to the American Institute of Certified Public Accountants in the first (introductory) paragraph.

4. The accountant's review and audit responsibilities should be referenced in a paragraph that follows management's responsibilities.

5. The second paragraph (management responsibility) does not adequately describe management's responsibilities.

6. There should be no comparison of the scope of a review to an audit in the third (auditor responsibility) paragraph.

7. Limited assurance should be expressed on the current year's reviewed financial statements in the third (management responsibility) paragraph.

8. There should be a statement that no opinion is expressed on the current year's financial statements in the first (introductory) paragraph.

9. There should be a reference to "conformity with accounting principles generally accepted in the United States" in the fourth paragraph.

10. There should be no restriction on the distribution of the accountant's review report in the third paragraph.

11. There should be no reference to "material modifications" in the fourth paragraph.

12. There should be an indication of the type of opinion expressed on the prior year's audited financial statements in the fifth (separate) paragraph.

13. There should be an indication that no auditing procedures were performed after the date of the report on the prior year's financial statements in the fifth (separate) paragraph.

14. There should be no reference to "updating the prior year's auditor's report for events and circumstances occurring after that date" in the fifth (separate) paragraph.

Task-Based Simulation 2

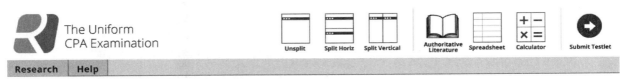

Davidson has compiled the financial statements of Xavier's X-ray Service and is reviewing the compilation file to make certain that documentation is complete and adequate. Davidson wants to determine what the documentation should include.

1. Which title of Professional Standards addresses this issue & will be helpful in understanding the documentation requirements for a compilation engagement?

2. Enter the exact section and paragraph with helpful information.

Task-Based Simulation 3

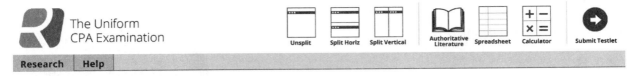

Stevenson's client has asked Stevenson to prepare financial statements that the client intends to distribute to the entity's lender and a few other interested parties. The client has indicated an inability to include a legend on each page indicating that "no assurance is provided" on the financial statements and Stevenson is considering what alternatives are available.

1. Which title of the Professional Standards addresses this issue and will be helpful in understanding the alternatives available when the accountant is unable to include a statement on each page of the financial statements indicating that no assurance is provided on them?

2. Enter the exact section and paragraph with helpful information.

Task-Based Simulation 4

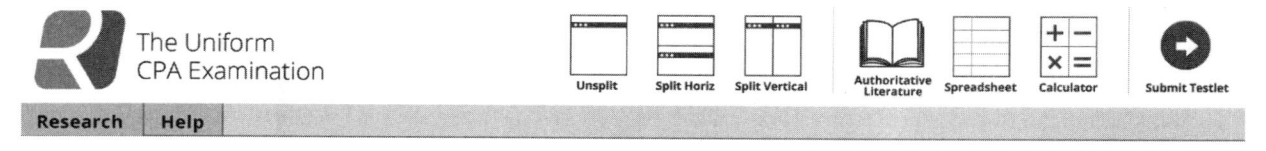

Rivers & Streams, CPAs, has compiled the financial statements of a client that omit substantially all disclosures required by the financial reporting framework that were applied in preparing the financial statements. Rivers & Streams is not certain if the compilation report should be modified and, if so, how it should be modified.

1   Which title of Professional Standards addresses this issue & will be helpful in understanding whether the compilation report should be modified and, if so, how it should be modified?

2.   Enter the exact section and paragraph with helpful information.

Task-Based Simulation 5

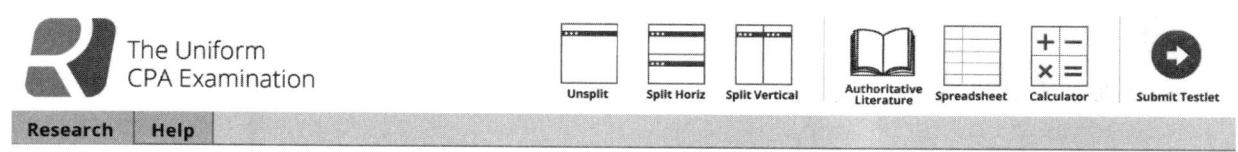

During the course of a review engagement, Hardy, CPA, became aware of information that appeared to be incorrect. Hardy is trying to determine the best way to respond to the situation.

1.   Which title of Professional Standards addresses this issue & will be helpful in understanding the accountant's alternatives when becoming aware of information that appears to be incorrect?

2.   Enter the exact section and paragraph with helpful information.

Task-Based Simulation 6

Nelson had been engaged to audit the financial statements of Aviation, Inc. but, prior to the completion of the engagement, was asked to change the engagement to a review. Before Nelson agrees to change the engagement, there are certain things that should be considered.

1. Which title of Professional Standards addresses this issue & will be helpful in understanding the factors to consider when deciding to accept a change in an engagement from an audit to a review?

2. Enter the exact section and paragraph with helpful information.

TASK-BASED SIMULATION SOLUTIONS

Task-Based Simulation Solution 1

1.   C   When reviewed financial statements are issued on a comparative basis with audited financial statements for a prior period, a review report should be issued along with either the reissuance of the prior period's report or a separate paragraph describing the responsibility being assumed for the prior period's financial statements. Reference to the prior period's audited financial statements in the body of the review report, other than in a separate paragraph, is not appropriate.

2.   I   All of the financial statements are identified by the reference to the balance sheet and the related statements of income, changes in stockholders' equity, and cash flows.

3.   C   Reference to the AICPA is made in the third paragraph, which indicates the accountants' responsibilities, which include performing the engagement in accordance with SSARS promulgated by the ARSC of the AICPA.

4.   I   Although the accountant's responsibilities in relation to the review are indicated in the third paragraph, following the paragraph containing management's responsibilities, it includes only the accountant's responsibilities in relation to the review, not the audit.

5.   C   The second paragraph (management responsibility) should indicate management's responsibility for the preparation and fair presentation of the financial statements as well as for the design, implementation, and maintenance (DIM) of internal control relevant to financial reporting.

6.   C   The scope of a review is compared to the scope of an audit so that users will understand that a review does not provide as much assurance as an audit. It is, however, included in the first (introductory) paragraph, not the third (auditor responsibility) paragraph.

7.   I   Limited assurance should be expressed in the fourth paragraph (Accountant's Conclusion), following the accountant's responsibility paragraph, not in the accountant's responsibility paragraph itself.

8.   C   A review report should contain an indication in the introductory paragraph that, since a review is less in scope than an audit, no opinion is expressed.

9.   C   The fourth paragraph gives limited assurance that no modifications are necessary in order for the financial statements to conform to accounting principles generally accepted in the United States of America.

10.   C   Unless the engagement was to report on financial statements that are restricted to internal use, it is not appropriate to indicate a restriction on the distribution of the report.

11.   I   The fourth paragraph appropriately provides limited assurance by indicating that the accountant is not aware of any material modifications that need be made to the financial statements.

12.   C   Since the previous period's report is not being reissued, a separate paragraph should include an indication of the type of report issued on the previous period's financial statements, the date of the report and that no audit procedures have been performed since that date.

13.   C   The separate paragraph should include an indication that no audit procedures were performed after the date of the report on the prior year's financial statements.

14.   C   It is sufficient to indicate that no procedures were performed since the date of the report on the prior period's financial statements. There is no need for a reference to the fact that the report has not been updated for events and circumstances occurring after that date.

Task-Based Simulation Solution 2

AR-C	80	.40

Task-Based Simulation Solution 3

AR-C	70	.14

Task-Based Simulation Solution 4

AR-C	80	.27

Task-Based Simulation Solution 5

AR-C	90	.29

Task-Based Simulation Solution 6

AR-C	90	.86

Section 8 – Other Services and Reports

Corresponding Lectures

Watch the following course lectures with this section:

Lecture 8.01 – Supplemental Information
Lecture 8.02 – Special Reports
Lecture 8.03 – Attestation Engagements
Lecture 8.04 – Specific Types of Subject Matter
Lecture 8.05 – Supplemental Info, Special Reports, and Attestation
              Engagements – Class Questions
Lecture 8.06 – Government Reporting
Lecture 8.07 – Government Reporting – Class Questions

EXAM NOTE: *Please refer to the AICPA AUD Blueprint in the Introduction of this book to find a listing of the representative tasks (and their associated skill levels—i.e., Remembering and Understanding, Application, Analysis, and Evaluation) that the candidate should be able to perform based on the knowledge obtained in this section.*

Other Services and Reports

Lecture 8.01

SUPPLEMENTAL INFORMATION (SI)

There are 6 different standards that apply to supplemental information (i.e., information that is *not* part of the *basic financial statements*, whether required to be presented or not): 3 of them apply to audits of nonpublic entities (i.e., nonissuers) issued by the ASB and the other 3 apply to publicly traded entities (i.e., issuers) under the PCAOB auditing standards. Each standard setter has provided standards in relation to 3 categories of supplemental information (**SI**). While there are slight differences in how they define these categories, they basically boil down to the following:

- **O**ther **I**nformation (OI)—*un*audited SI *voluntarily* provided
  - E.g., financial summaries or highlights, financial ratios, etc.
- **S**upplemental **I**nformation (SI)—*audited* SI, *voluntary or required*
  - E.g., additional details on items in or related to basic F/S, consolidating info, historical summaries, statistical data.
- **R**equired **S**upplemental **I**nformation (RSI)—*un*audited SI *required*
  - E.g., certain disclosures required by FASB, GASB, or FASAB outside the basic F/S.

We will focus our discussion on the 3 standards issued by the ASB and highlight the differences found in the PCAOB's parallel standards. The following diagram has been provided to show how all this information is related and can overlap.

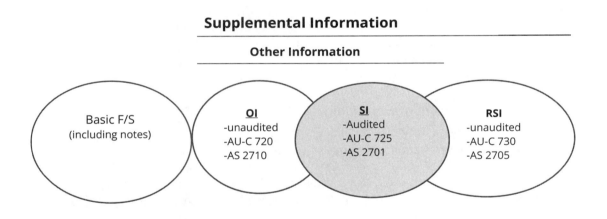

Other Information (OI) in Documents Containing Audited F/S (AU-C 720)

A document containing audited financial statements (F/S), such as the annual report, may also contain other information (AU-C 720) that is *not part of the basic F/S*. This may include supplementary information, but would not include required supplementary information (AU-C 730). Examples may include financial summaries or highlights, financial ratios, etc.

Unless the auditor is engaged to perform procedures in relation to other information (OI), the auditor's report generally does not cover it. A difference between the other information and the information in the audited F/S, however, could undermine the credibility of the F/S; therefore, the auditor should ***read the other information*** to determine if there are any **material inconsistencies**. If there are, the auditor should determine if the F/S or the other information needs correction.

- If it is determined that the F/S need correction, *discovered prior to the date of the audit report*, the client should revise the F/S and their refusal to do so will require a modification of the report.
- If it is determined that the F/S need correction, *discovered after the date of the audit report but prior to its release*, the auditor should follow the guidelines in AU-C 560, Subsequent Events and Subsequently Discovered Facts.
- If it is determined that the other information needs correction, *discovered prior to the release of the audit report*, and the client refuses to do so, the auditor should communicate the matter to those charged with governance and modify the report with an other-matter paragraph describing the inconsistency, withhold the report, or withdraw from the engagement.

When material inconsistencies are *discovered after the release of the report* that require modification of the F/S, the auditor should follow the guidance in AU-C 560, Subsequent Events and Subsequently Discovered Facts. When material inconsistencies are discovered after the release of the report that require modification of the other information:

- If management agrees to make the changes, the auditor should perform appropriate procedures, such as determining if management is making appropriate provisions to notify financial statement users.
- If management refuses to make the changes, the auditor should inform those charged with governance and take any further action deemed necessary, such as consulting with an attorney.

Upon reading the other information, the auditor may become aware of a **material misstatement of fact**, which should be discussed with management. If, after such discussions, the auditor continues to believe that there is a material misstatement of fact, the auditor should request that management consult with an appropriate qualified third party to determine if the other information does, in fact, contain a material misstatement of fact. If it is determined that there is such a material misstatement of fact, the auditor should discuss the matter with those charged with governance and take other actions as appropriate.

Other Information in Documents Containing Audited F/S (PCAOB AS 2710)

While an auditor of a public entity is technically required to follow PCAOB AS 2710 rather than AU-C 720, there are no fundamental differences to note between the two.

Supplementary Information (SI) in Relation to F/S as a Whole (AU-C 725)

The auditor may be engaged to report on whether supplementary information (SI) is fairly stated, in all material respects, in relation to the F/S as a whole. The auditor may only accept such an engagement if the following **conditions** are met:

- The SI and the F/S were derived from the same records.
- They relate to the same period.
- The F/S were audited and a report was issued that was neither adverse nor contained a disclaimer of opinion.
- Either the SI will accompany the F/S or the F/S will be readily available.

In addition to the procedures performed during the audit, in order to express an opinion regarding the SI, the auditor should perform **additional procedures** that include:

- Making inquiries of management regarding the *purpose* of the SI, *how it was prepared*, and *significant assumptions*.

- Evaluating whether form and content *comply with applicable criteria*, whether the criteria have been *consistently applied*, and whether the SI is *appropriate* and *complete*.
- Comparing and reconciling the SI to the underlying accounting records.
- Obtaining written representations from management regarding:
  - Its *responsibility* for the SI
  - Its belief that it is *fairly presented* in accordance with applicable criteria
  - Its *consistency*
  - Its *significant assumptions*
  - The availability of the audited F/S if they do not accompany the SI

If the SI is presented with the F/S, the auditor should report on the SI in either an **other-matter paragraph** or in a **separate report**. If the F/S are not presented with the SI, the auditor should report on the SI in a separate report, which should include a reference to the report on the F/S, the date of that report, the nature of the opinion, and any report modifications.

Remember that the accuracy or inaccuracy of SI does **not** affect the auditor's opinion on the basic F/S, since *such information is outside those statements*. However, if the auditor expresses an adverse or disclaimer of opinion on the basic F/S, the auditors are *precluded from expressing an opinion* on the SI.

If the SI is determined to be materially misstated, the auditor should discuss the matter with management and propose a revision. If management refuses to revise the SI, the auditor should modify the opinion on the SI and describe the misstatement in the report, or withhold the report on the SI if a separate report is to be issued.

Auditing Supplemental Information Accompanying Audited F/S (PCAOB AS 2701)

An auditor of a public entity is required to follow PCAOB AS 2701, which is very similar to AU-C 725, but there are some *additional requirements*.

- The required procedures set forth for SI are basically the same as under AU-C 725; however, the PCAOB requires the auditor to perform "audit procedures necessary to obtain sufficient appropriate audit evidence" to support the auditor's opinion on the SI. The nature, timing, and extent of these procedures are dependent upon the risk of material misstatement of the SI, materiality considerations, audit evidence supporting the F/S, and the type of opinion expressed on the F/S.
- In addition to the written representations required from management under AU-C 725, AS 2701 specifically requires the auditor to obtain a statement from management that
  - identifies any applicable regulatory requirements for the form and content of the SI and
  - provides that the SI complies, in all material respects, with such requirements.
- With regard to the evaluation of audit results on SI, AS 2701 provides that the auditor should:
  - Evaluate whether the SI, including its form and content, is *fairly stated* in relation to the F/S as a whole, and is presented in conformity with relevant regulatory requirements or other applicable criteria.
  - Accumulate misstatements identified regarding the SI and communicate them to management to give them an opportunity to make corrections.
  - Evaluate whether uncorrected misstatements are material, taking into account relevant quantitative and qualitative factors.
  - Evaluate the effect of uncorrected misstatements related to the SI in evaluating the results of the financial statement audit.

- o Evaluate the effect of any modifications to the audit report on the F/S when forming an opinion on the SI.
    - ▪ If a qualified opinion is expressed on the F/S and the basis for the qualification also applies to the SI, the auditor should describe the effects of the qualification on the SI and express a qualified opinion on the SI as well.
    - ▪ If an adverse opinion is expressed on the F/S or an opinion is disclaimed, the auditor should also express an adverse opinion, or disclaim an opinion, on the SI, as appropriate.
- If it is determined that the SI is materially misstated in relation to the F/S as a whole, the auditor should describe the material misstatement in the auditor's report on the SI and express a qualified or adverse opinion on the SI.
- If the auditor is unable to obtain sufficient appropriate audit evidence to support an opinion on the SI, the auditor should disclaim an opinion on the SI. In those situations, the auditor's report on the SI should describe the reason for the disclaimer and state that the auditor is unable to and does not express an opinion on the SI.
- The auditor may express an opinion on some SI but disclaim an opinion on other SI. For example, if the SI consists of more than one schedule, and the auditor is able to support an opinion on one schedule but not the other, the auditor may express an opinion on the schedule for which sufficient appropriate evidence was obtained and disclaim an opinion on the other schedule.

Required Supplementary Information (RSI) (AU-C 730)

In some cases, supplementary information is required by the applicable financial reporting framework (AFRF). This is, for example, often the case when the framework is established by a regulatory agency, such as FASB, GASB, or FASAB. With regard to **Required Supplementary Information** (**RSI**), the auditor must apply **limited procedures** to see if the required info has been provided and whether or not it appears to be correct. Examples of this information as it relates to GASB include management's discussion and analysis, budgetary comparison schedules, and schedules of funding progress and employer contributions for other post-employment benefits and pensions.

The required procedures include:
- Inquiring of management about its methods of preparing the information:
    - o Are the methods of measurement or presentation in accordance with prescribed guidelines?
    - o Are such methods consistent with prior periods and, if not, why?
    - o Were there any significant assumptions or interpretations underlying the measurement or presentation of the information?
- Comparing information for consistency
- Obtaining written representations from management regarding their responsibility for the RSI and the methods of preparation

The procedures do not constitute an audit of the RSI; thus, no opinion on the RSI is required and the opinion on the F/S will not be affected. However, the auditor should include an **other-matter paragraph** explaining the following circumstances, as applicable:
- The RSI is included and the auditor applied the appropriate procedures.
- The RSI is omitted.
- Some RSI is missing.
- The information is not in compliance with applicable requirements.
- The auditor is not able to complete required procedures.

- There is substantial doubt about the conformity of the RSI.

Required Supplementary Information (PCAOB AS 2705)

With respect to supplemental information required by FASB, GASB, and FASAB, an auditor of a public entity is required to follow PCAOB AS 2705, which is very similar to AU-C 730, but there are some *differences*.

- If an entity voluntarily provides SI that is RSI to other entities, the auditor is required to either apply the procedures under AS 2705 or provide a disclaimer on the information in an explanatory paragraph, unless the entity itself specifies that the information was not subjected to such procedures.
- In addition to the limited procedures required by AU-C 730, PCAOB AS 2705 requires the auditor to:
    o Consider whether representations on RSI should be included in specific written representations obtained from management under AS 2805, Management Representations;
    o Apply additional procedures, if any, that other statements or interpretations prescribe for specific types of RSI; and
    o Make additional inquiries if the auditor believes that the information may not be measured or presented within applicable guidelines.
- While under AU-C 730 the auditor is required to include **an other-matter paragraph** even if no issues are found with the RSI, AS 2705 requires an explanatory paragraph only in the following circumstances:
    o The RSI is omitted.
    o There is a material departure from prescribed guidelines.
    o The auditor is not able to complete required procedures.
    o There is substantial doubt about the conformity of the RSI.

Note: AS 2701 (Auditing SI Accompanying Audited F/S) applies instead of AS 2705 if the auditor is engaged to audit the RSI.

Segment Information (>10%)—Notes to the F/S

Annual financial statements of public entities are required to contain segment information (FASB ASC 280) about a company's operations in different industries, foreign operations and export sales and major customers. This is part of the basic F/S. If it is omitted or contains a material misstatement (disagreement), the auditor will either qualify or give an adverse opinion on the financial statements taken as a whole.

Summary

To summarize the approach to other information (OI), supplementary information (SI), and required supplementary information (RSI):

Situation	Effect on Fieldwork	Effect on Report
-Voluntary by client (**OI**)	Read for consistency	-Report inconsistencies in Other-matter para., withhold report, or withdraw
-Engaged to Audit (**SI**)	Audit Procedures	-Other-matter par. Or Separate report
-Required by FASB/GASB (**RSI**)	Limited procedures	-Other-matter para. (ASB) -Explanatory para. only for exceptions (PCAOB)

SPECIAL REPORTS

An accountant may be asked to prepare a **special report** in certain engagements, including:

1. Reporting on F/S that are prepared in conformity with some special purpose framework, often referred to as an other comprehensive basis of accounting (**OCBOA**) other than GAAP.
2. Reporting on a **single F/S**, or on **specified elements**, **accounts, or items** on a financial statement.
3. Completing **prescribed report forms** of a government agency on behalf of the client.
4. Reporting on the client's **compliance** with aspects of **contracts or regulatory requirements** in connection with an **audit.**

1. Audits of F/S Prepared in Accordance With Special Purpose Frameworks (OCBOA) (AU-C 800)

A special purpose framework is a financial reporting framework other than GAAP, often referred to as an OCBOA. Examples are the income tax basis, the cash basis, a contractual basis, a basis used by a regulatory agency (restricted use), or an "other basis of accounting." To be considered a special purpose framework, there must be a definite set of criteria that would enable the auditor to determine conformity with the approach.

- An entity may prepare its F/S using a framework based on GAAP with certain differences.
  - This is **not** considered a special report.
  - The auditor will consider differences to be departures from GAAP and would issue a qualified or adverse opinion, as appropriate.

Prescribed forms of government agencies often require special handling, because they may include specific representations that the accountant is expected to make.

Third parties dealing with the client may request reports on compliance with agreements related to the F/S. For example, a creditor may wish the auditor to provide a report on whether the client's working capital ratio has been maintained through the year at the level required in connection with a loan agreement.

Forming an Opinion and Reporting

When an auditor accepts an engagement to examine F/S that are intended to conform to a comprehensive basis of accounting other than GAAP, the audit will still conform to generally accepted auditing standards (GAAS), and the opinion may still be unmodified, qualified, or adverse, depending on whether the statements conform to the OCBOA.

When forming an opinion and reporting on F/S prepared in accordance with a special purpose framework, the auditor should evaluate the following considerations.

- Whether the F/S adequately refer to or describe the AFRF, including:
  - Whether the F/S are *suitably titled* (e.g., "Statement of Income—Regulatory Basis" instead of "Statement of Income").
  - Whether the F/S include a summary of *significant accounting policies*.
  - Whether the F/S adequately describe the *material differences* in how the special purpose framework differs from GAAP.
  - If the F/S are prepared in accordance with a contractual basis of accounting, whether the F/S adequately describe any *significant interpretations of the contract* on which the F/S are based.

- Whether the F/S are fairly presented:
  - When the special purpose F/S contain items that are similar to those in F/S prepared in accordance with GAAP, whether the F/S include informative disclosures similar to those required by GAAP.
  - Whether additional disclosures are necessary to achieve fair presentation (e.g., disclosures regarding related-party transactions, restrictions on assets/owners' equity, subsequent events, and significant uncertainties).
- Whether the auditor's report requires:
  - A description of the purpose for which the F/S were prepared or a reference to a note in the F/S with this information (generally for *regulatory or contractual basis* of accounting).
  - An emphasis-of-matter paragraph that alerts users regarding the basis of accounting other than GAAP used to prepare the F/S (applies in most cases).
  - An other-matter paragraph that restricts the use of the report to certain parties to avoid misunderstandings (generally when the F/S are prepared under a *regulatory or contractual basis* of accounting).
  - An opinion as to whether the F/S are presented fairly in accordance with GAAP in addition to the opinion regarding the special purpose framework, instead of the other-matter and emphasis-of-matter paragraphs described above (only applicable for *Regulatory Basis F/S for General Use*).

A sample report following an audit of F/S designed to conform to the cash receipts and disbursements method follows:

Special Purpose Framework Report (OCBOA)

INDEPENDENT AUDITOR'S REPORT
(OCBOA)

To the Board of Directors of X Company:

Report on the Financial Statements (Introductory)

We have **Audited** the accompanying financial statements of X Co, which comprise the **statement of assets and liabilities arising from cash transactions** as of December 31, 20X1, and the related **statement of revenue collected and expenses paid** for the year then ended, and the related notes to the financial statements.

Management's Responsibility for the Financial Statements

Management is responsible for the preparation and fair presentation of these financial statements in accordance with the **cash basis of accounting described in Note X; this includes determining that the cash basis of accounting is an acceptable basis for the preparation of the financial statements in the circumstances.** Management is also responsible for the design, implementation, and maintenance of internal control relevant to the preparation and fair presentation of financial statements that are free from material misstatement, whether due to fraud or error.

Auditor's Responsibility

Our responsibility is to express an opinion on these financial statements based on our audit. We conducted our audit in accordance with auditing standards generally accepted in the United States of America. Those standards require that we plan and perform the audit to obtain reasonable assurance about whether the financial statements are free from material misstatement.

An audit involves performing procedures to obtain evidence about the amounts and disclosures in the financial statements. The procedures selected depend on the auditor's judgment, including the assessment of the risks of material misstatement of the financial statements, whether due to fraud or error. In making those risk assessments, the auditor considers internal control relevant to the entity's preparation and fair presentation of the financial statements in order to design audit procedures that are appropriate in the circumstances, but not for the purpose of expressing an opinion on the effectiveness of the entity's internal control. Accordingly, we express no such opinion. An audit also includes evaluating the appropriateness of accounting policies used and the reasonableness of significant accounting estimates made by management, as well as evaluating the overall presentation of the financial statements.

We believe that the audit evidence we have obtained is sufficient and appropriate to provide a basis for our audit opinion.

Opinion

In our opinion, the financial statements referred to above present fairly, in all material respects, the **assets and liabilities arising from cash transactions** of X Company as of December 31, 20X1, and its **revenue collected and expenses paid** for the year then ended, **in accordance with the cash basis of accounting described in Note X.**

Basis of Accounting (emphasis-of-matter)

We draw attention to Note X of the financial statements, which describes the basis of accounting. The financial statements are prepared on the cash basis of accounting, which is a basis of accounting other than accounting principles generally accepted in the United States of America. Our opinion is not modified with respect to this matter.

L.F. Rosenthal, CPA

Auditor's city & state

March 1, 20X2

When an accountant is asked to follow an audit report form, layout or wording prescribed by law or a regulatory agency, and the prescribed form is unacceptable, the auditor should:
- Reword the prescribed form, or
- Attach a separate, appropriately worded audit report.

Note: An accountant may be asked to **compile or review** OCBOA statements of a nonpublic entity. In that case, the accountant will apply **SSARS** to such an engagement, as discussed earlier.

2. Audits of Single F/S and Specified Elements, Accounts, or Items of a F/S (AU-C 805)

An auditor may accept an engagement to examine a single F/S or specified elements, accounts, or items of a F/S as long as the client imposes no restriction on the scope of the auditor's procedures. This may be either a separate engagement or one performed in conjunction with an audit of the F/S of the client.

Audits of a single F/S, specified elements, accounts, or items are sometimes needed to satisfy a creditor, landlord, or employee about the calculations related to certain agreements. A landlord might want an opinion on the calculation of rent expense under a percentage agreement, or an officer might want verification of a profit-sharing calculation related to net income. Also, a CPA is sometimes asked for an opinion on the application of GAAP to a specific transaction when the client of another CPA firm disagrees with that firm about the appropriate treatment.

Forming an Opinion and Reporting

The opinion on the single F/S or specified element may be expressed in a **separate report** that accompanies the report on the complete set of F/S, as long as the **opinion is either unmodified or qualified**. Such separate report and presentation of the single F/S should be sufficiently differentiated from the report on the complete F/S.

If the auditor has issued either an **adverse** opinion or a **disclaimer** of opinion on the complete F/S, the auditor cannot issue an unmodified opinion on the single F/S or specified element in a report that accompanies the report on the complete F/S; to do so would be confusing to the reader of the reports and would be considered essentially equivalent to a **"piecemeal opinion."** If an unmodified opinion on a **specified element** is still appropriate despite the adverse opinion or disclaimer on the complete F/S, the auditor can express such opinion only if:
- The opinion is expressed in a report that is *neither published with nor accompanies the auditor's report* containing the adverse opinion or disclaimer of opinion, and
- The specific element is neither considered to be a *major portion* of the complete F/S nor based on stockholders' equity or net income or equivalent.

Note: A single F/S is considered to be a major portion of the complete F/S, so an unmodified opinion cannot be expressed on a single F/S when an adverse/disclaimer of opinion has been expressed on the complete F/S, regardless of how or where it is published.

If an accountant is asked to give an opinion on the application of GAAP to a specific transaction by a client of another CPA firm, the accountant must consult with the other CPA firm on the transaction in question. If the accountant is being asked for this opinion as part of a proposal to become the new auditor of the client, the report must specifically indicate that the conclusion might change if there is a change in facts, circumstances, or assumptions behind the report. This is needed to prevent a client from being able to "shop around" for accounting principles.

Note: SSARS apply when the CPA is engaged to prepare, compile, or review F/S elements, accounts, or items.

3. Completing a Prescribed Audit Report Form of a Government Agency on Behalf of the Client (AU-C 800)

When an accountant is asked to follow an audit report form, layout or wording prescribed by law or a regulatory agency, the report should only refer to GAAS if the report includes all of the following:
- Title
- Addressee
- Introductory paragraph identifying the special purpose financial statements audited
- Description of management's responsibility
  - For the preparation and fair presentation of the special purpose statements
  - For determining that the applicable financial reporting framework is acceptable under the circumstances
- When prepared in accordance with a regulatory or contractual basis, a description of the purpose for which the financial statements are prepared
- Description of the auditor's responsibility to express an opinion, including:
  - Reference to GAAS and, if appropriate, the law or regulation
  - Description of an audit in accordance with the standards
- Opinion paragraph
- Emphasis-of-matter paragraph
- Other-matter paragraph restricting the use of the report
- Auditor's signature and city and state
- Date of report

If the report is intended for general distribution, the auditor will not include the emphasis-of-matter or other-matter paragraph and will, instead, express an opinion as to whether or not the financial statements are in conformity with GAAP.

If the prescribed form of the report differs significantly from GAAS, and the auditor is worried that users might misunderstand the audit report, the auditor may:
- Reword the prescribed form and sign it, or
- Attach a separate audit report to the form, or
- The auditor should NOT accept the audit engagement (unless required by law or regulation).

4. Reporting on Compliance with Aspects of Contracts or Regulatory Requirements in Connection with Audited F/S (AU-C 806)

When the auditor is asked to *verify compliance* with contractual agreements (such as a loan agreement) or regulatory requirements related to the F/S, the resulting report is generally referred to as a "by-product report." Such report should include:
- The accountant's findings in an **other-matter paragraph** or a **separate report.**
  - The auditor should state that nothing came to the auditor's attention to suggest the client had not complied with all requirements if (1) the auditor found *no instances of noncompliance*, (2) an *unmodified or qualified opinion* has been expressed on the related F/S, and (3) the *applicable requirements relate to accounting matters* subjected to audit procedures during the audit of the F/S.

- - o   Otherwise, each instance of noncompliance should be described.
  - o   If an *adverse opinion or disclaimer of opinion* has been expressed on the F/S, a compliance report should NOT be issued unless there are instances of noncompliance.
- A statement indicating that the audit was not directed primarily toward obtaining knowledge regarding compliance, and thus, had additional procedures been performed, other matters may have come to the auditor's attention regarding noncompliance.
- A description and the source of *significant interpretations* made by management relating to the provisions of the contractual or regulatory requirement.
- An alert that restricts the use of the report.

CPA candidates could be asked to prepare this type of compliance report on the exam starting with a report example, such as those that follow.

Paragraphs Added for Combined Report When NO Instances of Noncompliance

---

Independent Auditor's Report

To: *Appropriate addressee*

***

Other Matter

In connection with our audit, nothing came to our attention that caused us to believe that ABC Company failed to comply with the terms, covenants, provisions, or conditions of sections XX to YY, inclusive, of the Indenture dated July 21, 20XX with XYZ Bank, insofar as they relate to accounting matters. However, our audit was not directed primarily toward obtaining knowledge of such noncompliance. Accordingly, had we performed additional procedures, other matters may have come to our attention regarding the Company's noncompliance with the above-referenced terms, covenants, provisions, or conditions of the Indenture, insofar as they relate to accounting matters.

Restricted Use Relating to the Other Matter

The communication related to compliance with the aforementioned Indenture described in the Other Matter paragraph is intended solely for the information and use of the boards of directors and management of ABC Company and XYZ Bank and is not intended to be and should not be used by anyone other than these specified parties.

Armin Lindegger, CPA
Santa Ana, CA
March 1, 20XX

A Separate Report on Compliance with NO Instances of Noncompliance

---

Independent Auditor's Report

To: *Appropriate addressee*

We have **audited**, in accordance with auditing standards generally accepted in the United States of America, the financial statements of XYZ Company, which comprise the balance sheet as of December 31, 20XX, and the related statements of income, changes in stockholders' equity, and cash flows for the year then ended, and the related notes to the financial statements, and have issued our report thereon dated February 16, 20XX. In connection with our audit, nothing came to our attention that caused us to believe that XYZ Company failed to comply with the terms, covenants, provisions, or conditions of sections XX to YY, inclusive, of the Indenture dated July 21, 20XX, with ABC Bank, insofar as they relate to accounting matters. However, our audit was not directed primarily toward obtaining knowledge of such noncompliance.

Accordingly, had we performed additional procedures, other matters may have come to our attention regarding the Company's noncompliance with the above-referenced terms, covenants, provisions, or conditions of the Indenture, insofar as they relate to accounting matters.

This report is intended solely for the information and use of the board of directors and management of XYZ Company and ABC Bank and is not intended to be and should not be used by anyone other than these specified parties.

Patrick Aaron, CPA
Santa Ana, CA
March 1, 20XX

A Separate Report on Compliance WITH Instances of Noncompliance

---

Independent Auditor's Report

To: *Appropriate addressee*

We have **audited**, in accordance with auditing standards generally accepted in the United States of America, the financial statements of XYZ Company, which comprise the balance sheet as of December 31, 20XX, and the related statements of income, changes in stockholders' equity, and cash flows for the year then ended, and the related notes to the financial statements, and have issued our report thereon dated March 5, 20XX.

In connection with our audit, we noted that XYZ Company failed to comply with the "Working Capital" provision of section XX of the Loan Agreement dated March 1, 20XX, with ABC Bank. Our audit was not directed primarily toward obtaining knowledge as to whether XYZ Company failed to comply with the terms, covenants, provisions, or conditions of sections XX to YY, inclusive, of the Loan Agreement, insofar as they relate to accounting matters. Accordingly, had we performed additional procedures, other matters may have come to our attention regarding noncompliance with the above-referenced terms, covenants, provisions, or conditions of the Loan Agreement, insofar as they relate to accounting matters.

This report is intended solely for the information and use of the board of directors and management of XYZ Company and ABC Bank and is not intended to be and should not be used by anyone other than these specified parties.

Noah P. Benedict, CPA
Santa Ana, CA
March 1, 20XX

Note: AU-C 935, *Compliance Audits*, applies if the auditor is engaged, or required by law, to perform a compliance audit in accordance with GAAS, GAGAS, or some other governmental audit requirement that requires the expression of an opinion on compliance. AT-C 315, *Compliance Attestation*, applies if the auditor is engaged to perform a separate attestation engagement on an entity's compliance with certain requirements or the effectiveness of the entity's internal control over compliance with certain requirements. These engagements are discussed later in this section.

Lecture 8.03

ATTESTATION ENGAGEMENTS (SSAE)

Ever since the first accounting firm was asked to count the ballots at the Academy Awards, CPA firms have been expanding into areas beyond historical financial statements. These now include engagements to verify the accuracy and security of Web sites (WebTrust), the truth of advertising claims, the completeness of personal disclosures by political candidates, internal control opinions, prospective information and compliance with contracts or laws and regulations. Compilation engagements provide no assurance and are not attest engagements. They are not addressed in the attestation standards.

- AT-C 200 – Level of Service (**ERA**)
  - AT-C 205 – Examination Engagements
  - AT-C 210 – Review Engagements
  - AT-C 215 – Agreed-Upon Procedures Engagements

- AT-C 300 – Subject Matter
  - AT-C 305 – Prospective Financial Statements
  - AT-C 310 – Reporting on Pro Forma Financial Information
  - AT-C 315 – Compliance Attestation
  - AT-C 320 – Reporting on an Examination of Internal Controls at a Service Organization Relevant to User Entities' Internal Control Over Financial Reporting (see Section 3)
  - AT-C 395 – Management's Discussion and Analysis (MD&A)

Note: The attestation standards were clarified and recodified in SSAE No. 18, effective for reports dated as of May 1, 2017.

Common Concepts (AT-C 105)

The AICPA uses the term **attestation** to refer to any engagement in which the accountant expresses a **written conclusion about** the reliability of a **written assertion** by another party. There are three categories of attest engagements (**ERA**):

- **Examination** – An engagement in which the end result is the expression of an **opinion** (*reasonable assurance*) by the accountant about the subject matter or assertion of another party. The work performed will involve a level of service comparable to audits of historical F/S.
- **Review** – An engagement in which the end result is the expression of a **conclusion** with *limited assurance* (i.e., *negative assurance*) on the subject matter or assertion. Procedures such as inquiry of the other party as to the methods used and analytical procedures applied to numerical information related to the assertion will be performed.
- **Agreed-upon procedures** – An engagement in which the end result is a report of the accountant's **findings** (*no opinion or conclusion*) regarding agreed-upon procedures applied to subject matter for the use of specified parties. The procedures will depend on the agreement made among the parties to the engagement. The distribution of the report is **restricted** to specific users knowledgeable about the agreement. In all such engagements, the accountant will disclaim any responsibility for the sufficiency of the procedures.

The mnemonic **ERAS** reminds us that attestation standards are part of a new era in which accountants are performing engagements that go beyond reports on historical F/S.

Note: The following attestation standards do not apply to (1) audits under the SASs, (2) compilations and reviews of F/S under the SSARS, or (3) tax services under the SSTSs.

Preconditions for Acceptance

- All attestation engagements require that the accountant be **independent** of the party whose assertion is being evaluated, unless the accountant is required by law or regulation to accept the engagement.
- The responsible party (e.g., senior management; not the accountant) assumes responsibility for the subject matter.
- The subject matter is appropriate; i.e., can it be identified and measured or evaluated against specific criteria?
- The criteria to be applied is appropriate and will be available to the users.
- The accountant expects to be able to obtain sufficient evidence to provide an opinion, conclusion, or findings. This means the accountant will have access to all relevant information as well as individuals who may provide such evidence.

- The accountant's opinion, conclusion, or findings will be contained in a written report, as appropriate.

Prescribed Forms
When an accountant is required to use a specified report form, layout or wording prescribed by law or a regulatory agency, and the *prescribed form is unacceptable*, the auditor should:
- Reword the prescribed form, or
- Attach a separate, appropriately worded report.

Change of Engagement
If the client decides to *change the terms of the engagement* after acceptance, the accountant should only agree to such a change when there is *reasonable justification* for doing so. If the change is made during the engagement, evidence obtained prior to the change cannot be disregarded. However, so long as the accountant complies with the standards for the new level of service, the accountant should issue the appropriate report and should NOT make reference to:
- The original engagement,
- Any procedures performed, or
- Any scope limitations that resulted in the changed engagement.

Using the Work of Another
When the accountant uses the *work of another accountant*, the accountant should:
- Determine whether the other accountant is independent and understands the applicable ethical requirements.
- Determine whether the other accountant is professionally competent.
- Communicate the scope and timing of the other accountant's work.
- Evaluate whether the other accountant's work is adequate.
- Determine whether the report should reference the work of the other practitioner.

Engagement Documentation Requirements
With regard to engagement documentation, the accountant should:
- Prepare it on a timely basis (i.e., as the work is performed or shortly after).
- Assemble the final engagement file within 60 days of the accountant's report release date.
- Retain all documentation after the documentation completion date for the appropriate retention period. If it is necessary to add or discard any documentation after such time, the specific reasons for the changes, who made the changes, and the date of such changes should be documented.
- Adopt reasonable procedures to keep the documentation confidential and prevent unauthorized access.
- Include written justification for departing from any presumptively mandatory requirements (i.e., requirements specified with "should" rather than "must") and how alternative procedures achieved the intent of the requirement.

Examination Engagements (AT-C 205)

In addition to the concepts just covered that are applicable to *all attestation engagements*, all *examination engagements* (including, for example, the examination of prospective financial information, which is also covered under AT-C 305, discussed later) are subject to yet another set of requirements specific to examinations. An examination, you might remember, is a level of service comparable to audits of historical F/S, involving the expression of an **opinion** (*reasonable assurance*) about the subject matter or written assertion of another party. With this type of engagement, the accountant should:

- Specify the agreed-upon terms of the engagement in an **engagement letter** or other written agreement, including the objective and scope of the engagement; responsibilities of the practitioner; a statement that the engagement will be conducted in accordance with attestation standards established by the AICPA; responsibilities of the responsible/engaging party; inherent limitations of the engagement; the criteria for measuring, evaluating, or disclosing the subject matter; and an agreement by the engaging party (e.g., those charged with governance) to provide a representation letter at the conclusion of the engagement.

- Request a **written assertion from the responsible party** regarding measurement/evaluation of the subject matter. If the responsible party is *not* the engaging party and refuses to comply, the accountant must disclose the refusal in the report and restrict the report to the engaging party. If the responsible party *is* also the engaging party and they refuse to comply, the accountant must withdraw from the engagement, or disclaim an opinion if law/regulation prevents withdrawal.

- Establish an **overall engagement strategy**, which sets the scope, timing and direction of the engagement and assists in the development of the engagement plan.

- Develop an **engagement plan** that includes the nature, timing and extent of procedures to be performed, including risk assessment procedures.

- Obtain an understanding of the subject matter and relevant circumstances (including internal controls over the preparation of the subject matter) to be able to (1) identify and **assess the risks of material misstatement** and (2) design procedures to respond to such risks and obtain reasonable assurance to support the opinion.

- Consider **materiality** for the subject matter when establishing the overall engagement strategy, and reconsider materiality if new information brings it into question.

- Obtain **sufficient appropriate evidence** to reduce attestation risk to an acceptably low level.

- Design and perform **tests of controls** if (1) the accountant intends to rely on the operating effectiveness of controls in determining the nature, timing, and extent of other procedures; (2) if other procedures will not provide sufficient appropriate evidence alone; or (3) if the subject matter itself is internal control.

- Design and perform **tests of details** or **analytical procedures** (unless the subject matter is internal control).

- Consider and inquire as to whether there are any indications of **fraud or noncompliance** with laws/regulations.

- Consider and inquire about **subsequent events** (i.e., events occurring after the period covered by the engagement up to the report date) and subsequently discovered facts (i.e., facts discovered after the report date).

- Request **written representations** (in the form of a letter to the accountant as of the date of the report) from (1) the responsible party regarding the assertion, relevant matters, their responsibilities, subsequent events, immaterial uncorrected misstatements, etc.; and (2) the engaging party (if a separate party) regarding the responsible party's responsibilities, their lack of knowledge of any material misstatements, subsequent events, etc.

- **Read other information** in the document that will contain the accountant's report to identify any material inconsistencies.

- **Evaluate the results** of the procedures, **form an opinion,** and **prepare a written report** on a written assertion or on the subject matter directly. See following examples.
    - If the accountant was unable to obtain sufficient appropriate evidence or the subject matter is not in accordance with the specified criteria, in all material respects, and the effect of any such insufficiencies are material, the opinion should

be modified and a separate paragraph describing such matters should be included in the report.

- Effects are *material, but not pervasive*—Qualified opinion
- Misstatements are *material and pervasive*—Adverse opinion
- Unable to obtain sufficient appropriate evidence (i.e., scope limitation) and effects *could be material and pervasive*—Disclaimer of opinion

o When the opinion is modified, external specialists can be referenced in the report if it is relevant to the opinion; however, they should not be referenced when the opinion is unmodified.

o The report should include a separate paragraph that restricts the use of the report (1) if the criteria used are appropriate for, or available to, only specified parties, or (2) if the responsible party is *not* the engaging party and refuses to comply with the request for written representations, but does provide oral responses, the report should be restricted to the engaging party.

Examination Report on Subject Matter—Unmodified Opinion

Independent Accountant's Report

To: *Appropriate addressee*

We have **examined** [*identify the subject matter, for example, the accompanying schedule of investment returns of XYZ Company for the year ended December 31, 20XX*]. XYZ Company's management is responsible for [*identify the subject matter, for example, presenting the schedule of investment returns*] in accordance with (or based on) [*identify the criteria, for example, the ABC criteria set forth in Note 1*]. Our responsibility is to express an opinion on [*identify the subject matter, for example, the schedule of investment returns*] based on our examination.

Our examination was conducted in accordance with attestation standards established by the American Institute of Certified Public Accountants. Those standards require that we plan and perform the examination to obtain reasonable assurance about whether [*identify the subject matter, for example, the schedule of investment returns*] is in accordance with (or based on) the criteria, in all material respects. An examination involves performing procedures to obtain evidence about [identify the subject matter, for example, the schedule of investment returns]. The nature, timing, and extent of the procedures selected depend on our judgment, including an assessment of the risks of material misstatement of [identify the subject matter, for example, the schedule of investment returns], whether due to fraud or error. We believe that the evidence we obtained is sufficient and appropriate to provide a reasonable basis for our opinion.

[*Include a description of significant inherent limitations, if any, associated with the measurement or evaluation of the subject matter against the criteria.*]

[*Additional paragraph(s) may be added to emphasize certain matters relating to the attestation engagement or the subject matter.*]

In our opinion, [*identify the subject matter, for example, the schedule of investment returns of XYZ Company for the year ended December 31, 20XX or the schedule of investment returns referred to above*], is presented in accordance with (or based on) [*identify the criteria, for example, the ABC criteria set forth in Note 1*], in all material respects.

Asher P. Levy, CPA
Santa Ana, CA
March 1, 20XX

Examination Report on Subject Matter—Qualified Opinion

Independent Accountant's Report

To: *Appropriate addressee*

***

Our examination disclosed [*describe condition(s) that, individually or in the aggregate, resulted in a material misstatement or deviation from the criteria*].

In our opinion, except for the material misstatement [*or deviation from the criteria*] described in the preceding paragraph, [*identify the subject matter, for example, the accompanying schedule of investment returns of XYZ Company for the year ended December 31, 20XX, or the schedule of investment returns referred to above*], is presented in accordance with (or based on) [*identify the criteria, for example, the ABC criteria set forth in Note 1*], in all material respects.

Alexes B. Ruiz, CPA
Santa Ana, CA
March 1, 20XX

Examination—Disclaimer of Opinion

Independent Accountant's Report

To: *Appropriate addressee*

We were engaged to examine [*identify the subject matter, for example, the accompanying schedule of investment returns of XYZ Company for the year ended December 31, 20XX*], in accordance with (or based on) [*identify the criteria, for example, the ABC criteria set forth in Note 1*]. XYZ Company's management is responsible for [*identify the subject matter, for example, presenting the schedule of investment returns*]. Our responsibility is to express an opinion on [*identify the subject matter, for example, the schedule of investment returns*] based on conducting the examination in accordance with attestation standards established by the American Institute of Certified Public Accountants.

[*Include a paragraph to describe scope limitations*.]

Because of the limitation on the scope of our examination discussed in the preceding paragraph, the scope of our work was not sufficient to enable us to express, and we do not express, an opinion on whether [*identify the subject matter, for example, the accompanying schedule of investment returns of XYZ Company for the year ended December 31, 20XX, or the schedule of investment returns referred to above*] is in accordance with (or based on) [*identify the criteria, for example, the ABC criteria set forth in Note 1*], in all material respects.

Darren Chris, CPA
Santa Ana, CA
March 1, 20XX

Review Engagements (AT-C 210)

As previously discussed, a review engagement under the attestation standards is one in which the end result is the expression of a **conclusion** with **limited assurance** (i.e., negative assurance) about whether the **subject matter or assertion** of another party is fairly stated. Such engagements are generally limited to *inquiries and analytical procedures*. Since we have already covered reviews of F/S under SSARS (in another Section), the concepts common to all attestation engagements, as well as examination engagements under the attestation standards (i.e., SSAEs) in great detail, we will only discuss the differences in the reporting requirements under the SSAEs here.

In a review engagement, the accountant will evaluate the results of the procedures and **form a conclusion** as to whether there are any material modifications that need to be made to (1) the subject matter in order for it to be in accordance with the criteria, or (2) the responsible party's assertion in order for it to be fairly stated. In forming this conclusion, the accountant should evaluate whether sufficient appropriate evidence was obtained and whether any uncorrected misstatements are material, individually or collectively.

- If the accountant is aware of an uncorrected misstatement in the subject matter, the accountant should consider whether **qualification of the conclusion** is sufficient to disclose the matter (if not, withdraw).
  - Effects are *material, but not pervasive*—Qualified conclusion
    - Include a separate paragraph in the report providing a description of the misstatement.
    - Report directly on the subject matter rather than the assertion (even if it acknowledges the misstatement).
  - Misstatements are *material and pervasive* or unable to obtain sufficient appropriate evidence (i.e., scope limitation)—Withdraw from the engagement, if possible
    - Generally includes being unable to obtain written representations. In some cases, oral representations may be accepted.

CPA candidates could be asked to prepare this type of report on the exam starting with a report example, such as one of those that follow.

Please note that reviews are generally *prohibited* for the following:
- Prospective financial information
- Internal control
- Compliance with laws, rules, regulations, contracts, and grants

Review Report on Subject Matter—Unmodified Conclusion

Independent Accountant's Review Report

To: *Appropriate addressee*

We have **reviewed** [*identify the subject matter, for example, the accompanying schedule of investment returns of XYZ Company for the year ended December 31, 20XX*]. XYZ Company's management is responsible for [*identify the subject matter, for example, presenting the schedule of investment returns*] in accordance with (or based on) [*identify the criteria, for example, the ABC criteria set forth in Note 1*]. Our responsibility is to express **a conclusion** on [*identify the subject matter, for example, the schedule of investment returns*] based on our **review**.

Our **review** was conducted in accordance with attestation standards established by the American Institute of Certified Public Accountants. Those standards require that we plan and perform the **review** to obtain **limited assurance** about whether **any material modifications should be made to** [*identify the subject matter, for example, the schedule of investment returns*] **in** order for it to be **in accordance with** (or based on) the **criteria. A review is substantially less in scope than an examination, the objective of which is to obtain reasonable assurance about whether** [*identify the subject matter, for example, the schedule of investment returns*] **is in accordance with (or based on) the criteria, in all material respects, in order to express an opinion. Accordingly, we do not express such an opinion. We believe that our review provides a reasonable basis for our conclusion.**

[*Include a description of significant inherent limitations, if any, associated with the measurement or evaluation of the subject matter against the criteria.*]

[*Additional paragraph(s) may be added to emphasize certain matters relating to the attestation engagement or the subject matter.*]

Based on our review, we are not aware of any material modifications that should be made to [*identify the subject matter, for example, the accompanying schedule of investment returns of XYZ Company for the year ended December 31, 20XX*]**, in order for it be in accordance with (or based on)** [*identify the criteria, for example, the ABC criteria set forth in Note 1*]**.**

Kristin Charberts, CPA
Santa Ana, CA
March 1, 20XX

Review Report on Subject Matter—Qualified Conclusion

Independent Accountant's Review Report

To: *Appropriate addressee*

***

Our **review** disclosed [*describe condition(s) that, individually or in the aggregate, resulted in a material misstatement or deviation from the criteria*].

Based on our review, except for the matter(s) described in the preceding paragraph, we are not aware of any material modifications that should be made to [*identify the subject matter, for example, the accompanying schedule of investment returns of XYZ Company for the year ended December 31, 20XX*], **in order for it to be in accordance with (or based on)** [*identify the criteria, for example, the ABC criteria set forth in Note 1*].

Wendy Robson, CPA
Santa Ana, CA
March 1, 20XX

Agreed-Upon Procedures Engagements (AT-C 215)

AT-C 215 provides requirements applicable to agreed-upon procedures engagements in addition to the requirements applicable to all attestation engagements under AT-C 105, discussed earlier. Many of the requirements of AT-C 215 are similar to those for examinations (AT-C 205) and reviews (ATC-210), which we've already covered, so we will cover some of the more important requirements specific to agreed-upon procedures engagements and then summarize and compare the three different types of attestation engagements.

As previously discussed, an agreed-upon procedures engagement is one in which the end result is a report of the accountant's **findings** (*no opinion or conclusion*) with regard to agreed-upon procedures applied to subject matter for use by specified parties. The procedures will depend on the agreement made among the parties to the engagement, and distribution of the report is **restricted** to the specific users knowledgeable about the agreement. In all such engagements, the specified users are responsible for the sufficiency of the procedures for their purposes, and the accountant will disclaim any responsibility for the sufficiency of the procedures. With regard to this type of engagement, the accountant should:

- NOT agree to perform procedures that are described by terms that are too generic or open to interpretation (e.g., general review, limited review, check, or test).
    - Other examples of inappropriate procedures:
        - Reading of the work performed by others to describe their findings
        - Evaluating the competency and/or objectivity of another party
        - Obtaining an understanding of a particular subject
        - Interpreting documents outside the scope of the accountant's expertise
    - Examples of appropriate procedures:
        - Inspection of specified documents evidencing certain types of transactions
        - Confirmation of specific information with third parties

- - - Comparison of documents, schedules, or analyses with certain specified attributes
    - Performance of mathematical computations
- Report all findings from applying the agreed-upon procedures, avoiding any vague or ambiguous language.
- Describe any agreed-upon materiality limits in the report.
- Disclose the responsible party's refusal to provide a written assertion in the report, if applicable.
- Describe in the report any circumstances imposing restrictions on the performance of procedures when an agreement cannot be obtained to modify the procedures. Alternatively, the accountant could withdraw from the engagement.
- Include in the report knowledge of matters brought to the accountant's attention outside of the agreed-upon procedures if they significantly contradict the subject matter or assertion (e.g., a material weakness in internal control).

CPA candidates could be asked to prepare this type of report on the exam starting with a report example, like the one that follows.

Agreed-Upon Procedures Report Example

**Independent Accountant's Report on Applying
Agreed-Upon Procedures**

To: *Appropriate addressee*

We have performed the procedures enumerated below, which were agreed to by [*identify the specified party(ies), for example, the audit committees and managements of ABC Inc. and XYZ Fund*], on [*identify the subject matter, for example, the accompanying Statement of Investment Performance Statistics of XYZ Fund for the year ended December 31, 20X1*]. XYZ Fund's management is responsible for [*identify the subject matter, for example, the Statement of Investment Performance Statistics for the year ended December 31, 20X1*]. The sufficiency of these procedures is solely the responsibility of the parties specified in this report. Consequently, we make no representation regarding the sufficiency of the procedures enumerated below either for the purpose for which this report has been requested or for any other purpose.

[*Include paragraphs to enumerate procedures and findings.*]

This agreed-upon procedures engagement was conducted in accordance with attestation standards established by the American Institute of Certified Public Accountants. We were not engaged to and did not conduct an examination or review, the objective of which would be the expression of an opinion or conclusion, respectively, on [*identify the subject matter, for example, the accompanying Statement of Investment Performance Statistics of XYZ Fund for the year ended December 31, 20X1*]. Accordingly, we do not express such an opinion or conclusion. Had we performed additional procedures, other matters might have come to our attention that would have been reported to you.

[*Additional paragraph(s) may be added to describe other matters.*]

This report is intended solely for the information and use of [*identify the specified party(ies), for example, the audit committees and managements of ABC Inc. and XYZ Fund*], and is not intended to be, and should not be, used by anyone other than the specified parties.

Jae Evers, CPA
Santa Ana, CA
March 1, 20XX

SSAE Summary Comparison Chart (ERA)

Requirements	Examination	Review	Agreed-Upon Procedures
Maintain **independence**	Yes	Yes	Yes
Obtain signed **engagement letter**	Yes	Yes	Yes
Request **written assertion** regarding measurement/ evaluation of subject matter	Yes	Yes	Yes
Obtain understanding of subject matter and relevant circumstances	Sufficient to assess RMM	Sufficient to achieve objectives of engagement	No
Consider **materiality**	Yes	Yes	No, unless materiality limits are agreed-upon
Obtain **sufficient appropriate evidence**	Yes	Yes	No
Design/perform **tests of controls**	If relying on controls	No	No
Testing of subject matter	Tests of details / analytical procedures	Generally only inquiries / analytical procedures	Agreed-upon procedures
Inquire about **fraud or noncompliance**	Yes	Yes	No
Inquire about **subsequent events**	Yes	Yes	No
Request **written representations** from responsible/engaging parties	Yes	Yes	Yes
Read other information for material inconsistencies	Yes	Yes	No
Written Report	Opinion	Conclusion	Findings
Level of Assurance	Reasonable	Limited	None
Restriction on Use	If necessary	If necessary	Yes

Lecture 8.04

SPECIFIC TYPES OF SUBJECT MATTER

Prospective Financial Statements (AT-C 305)

Prospective financial statements present expected or hypothetical future results of an entity. There are two different types of prospective statements:

- **Forecast** – This presents what management **expects to occur** in the future based on expected conditions and expected courses of action.
- **Projection** – This presents what management believes will occur given certain **hypothetical assumptions** based on a "what if" scenario.

For example, a drug manufacturer might be expecting to receive government approval for a new drug, and will prepare a financial forecast based on expected results over the next few years given approval of the drug. The manufacturer may also prepare a financial projection on expected results over the next few years in the event the new drug does not receive approval.

Although a financial **forecast** is based on certain *significant assumptions* made by management about the future, the assumptions are general in nature, regarding factors that will affect the entity's performance. These may include the economy; competition; the availability of resources, capital, and employees; demand; and comparable factors. As a result, a forecast is appropriate for either **general or limited use.**

A financial **projection**, is based on *hypothetical propositions*, which are assumptions about events or transactions that may not actually be expected to occur. As a result, a projection is only appropriate for **limited use** by parties with whom the entity is negotiating directly and who are aware of the use of the assumptions.

When third-party users seek some level of assurance regarding prospective F/S, an accountant may perform an attestation engagement to provide that assurance. There are two different types of engagements that an accountant may undertake in connection with prospective F/S:
- **Examination –** The accountant expresses an opinion on the prospective statements.
- **Agreed-Upon Procedures –** The accountant applies tests that are the result of an agreement between the CPA, the client, and a third party with whom the client is negotiating. Such an engagement can only result in a report for **limited use**, even when it involves a forecast.
  - Note: As previously mentioned, a review of prospective F/S is not allowed.

As is true for all attestation engagements, the accountant is required to comply with the requirements of the section of the attestation standards that is applicable to the specific engagement, as well as with AT-C Section 105, Concepts Common to All Attestation Engagements, discussed above.

Examinations of Prospective Financial Statements

The objective of an examination of prospective financial is for the accountant to obtain, and to convey in a written report, reasonable assurance that the presentation of prospective information conforms, in all material respects, to the guidelines established by the AICPA for the presentation of prospective information and that the assumptions underlying the forecast, or the assumptions underlying the projection, are suitably supported and provide a reasonable basis for the responsible party's forecast, or the responsible party's projection given the hypothetical assumptions.

Before an accountant agrees to be associated with a projection, the accountant should determine that the projection will only be distributed to parties that are negotiating directly with the responsible party since a projection is not appropriate for general use.

An accountant should NOT agree to:
- Examine a forecast if the responsible party does not agree to disclose significant assumptions.
- Examine a projection if the responsible party either does not agree to disclose significant assumptions or does not identify the hypothetical assumptions or describe the limitations of the presentation.
- Examine a partial presentation that does not describe the limitations on the usefulness of the presentation.

As preconditions for an examination engagement, the accountant should understand the guidelines for preparation and presentation in the AICPA guide and have or obtain knowledge of the industry in which the entity operates and the accounting principles and practices appropriate for it.

The accountant should obtain a written assertion from the client and develop an overall strategy for the engagement that sets the scope, timing, and direction of the engagement. The procedures applied in the examination engagement should take into account the nature and materiality of the information; knowledge obtained in the current and previous engagements; the competence of the responsible party; the extent to which the prospective financial information is affected by the responsible party's judgment; and the available support for the responsible party's assumptions.

The accountant will perform those procedures the accountant considers necessary to report on whether the assumptions are suitably supported and provide a reasonable basis for the forecast, or provide a reasonable basis for the projection taking into account the hypothetical assumption. The accountant will evaluate the preparation and presentation of the prospective financial information to obtain reasonable assurance as to whether the presentation reflects the identified assumptions; computations are mathematically accurate; assumptions are internally consistent; accounting principles applied are appropriate; the prospective financial information is presented in accordance with AICPA guidelines; and that the assumptions are adequately disclosed.

The report following an **examination** must include the following:
- A title that includes the word independent.
- An appropriate addressee.
- Identification of the prospective financial information being reported on and the time period it relates to.
- An indication that the prospective financial information was evaluated against guidelines established by the AICPA.
- A statement identifying the responsible party, indicating their responsibility for the preparation and presentation of the prospective financial information in accordance with the AICPA guidelines.
- The accountant's responsibility for expressing an opinion on the prospective financial information.
- A statement that the examination was performed in accordance with the AICPA attestation standards, which require the accountant to plan and perform the engagement to obtain reasonable assurance that the AICPA guidelines were followed and that the accountant believes that the examination provided a reasonable basis for the opinion.
- A description of the nature of an examination.
- An **opinion** as to whether the statements conform to AICPA presentation guidelines and the underlying assumptions provide a reasonable basis for the presentation.
- A warning (Caveat) that the prospective **results may not be achieved.**
- A statement that the accountant has **no responsibility to update** the report for events occurring after the report date.
- The manual or printed signature of the accountant or the accountant's firm.
- The accountant's city and state.
- The date of the report.
- For **projections**, a separate paragraph with an indication of the **limitations on the usefulness** of the presentation.
  - "The accompanying projection and this report are intended solely for the information and use of [*identify specified parties, for example, XYZ Company and DEF*

National Bank], and are not intended to be and should not be used by anyone other than these specified parties."

Examination Report of a Financial Forecast

Independent Accountant's Report

To: *Appropriate addressee*

We have **examined** the accompanying forecast of XYZ Company, which comprises the forecasted balance sheet as of December 31, 20XX, and the related forecasted statements of income, retained earnings, and cash flows for the year then ended, based on the guidelines for the presentation of a forecast established by the American Institute of Certified Public Accountants. XYZ Company's management is responsible for preparing and presenting the forecast in accordance with the guidelines for the presentation of a forecast established by the American Institute of Certified Public Accountants. Our responsibility is to express an opinion on the forecast based on our examination.

Our examination was conducted in accordance with **attestation standards established by the American Institute of Certified Public Accountants.** Those standards require that we plan and perform the examination to obtain reasonable assurance about whether the forecast is presented in accordance with the guidelines for the presentation of a forecast established by the American Institute of Certified Public Accountants, in all material respects. An examination involves performing procedures to obtain evidence about the forecast. The nature, timing, and extent of the procedures selected depend on our judgment, including an assessment of the risks of material misstatement of the forecast, whether due to fraud or error. We believe that the evidence we obtained is sufficient and appropriate to provide a reasonable basis for our opinion.

In our opinion, the accompanying forecast is presented, in all material respects, in accordance with the guidelines for presentation of a forecast established by the American Institute of Certified Public Accountants, and the underlying assumptions are reasonably supported and provide a reasonable basis for management's forecast.

There will usually be **differences** between the forecasted and actual results, because events and circumstances frequently do not occur as expected, and those differences may be material. We have **no responsibility to update** this report for events and circumstances occurring after the date of this report.

Jessica Daubson, CPA
Santa Ana, CA
March 1, 20XX

For **agreed-upon procedures**, the report must include the following:
- The **findings** of the accountant resulting from the procedures.
- A statement that the procedures applied **may not be sufficient**, and that the specified users accept responsibility for this fact.
- A warning (Caveat) that the prospective **results may not be achieved.**
- A statement that the accountant has **no responsibility to update** the report for events occurring after the report date.
- A separate paragraph with an indication of the **limitations on the usefulness** of the presentation (remember that all agreed-upon procedures engagements result in limited use reports).

- A summary of **significant assumptions** is also required.

PROSPECTIVE FINANCIAL STATEMENTS

- **Forecast** (General Use) → Expects to occur
- **Projection** (Limited Use ⇒ Add a Middle ¶) → "Hypothetical" – May or may not occur; Can only give it to people directly negotiating with you
  1. **Examination** → Giving an Opinion
     a. Met AICPA minimum presentation guidelines
     b. F/S reasonable given assumptions   } Opinion
        - If not, called partial presentation (limited use)
  2. **Agreed-Upon Procedures**
     a. Only going to do procedures you told us to do   Independent
     b. Distribution & Use is Limited ───────────→   Findings
                                                                Disclaimer

- Included in both reports
  1. Results may NOT be achieved
  2. NO responsibility to update

Compliance Attestation (AT-C 315)

AT-C 315 provides the aspects an accountant should consider with respect to attestation engagements related to an entity's compliance with specified laws, regulations, rules, contracts or grants, including reports on the effectiveness of internal controls over compliance with those requirements. There are two different types of engagements that are covered under AT-C 315:

- **Examination –** The accountant obtains reasonable assurance and expresses an opinion on (1) the entity's compliance with specified requirements of laws, regulations, rules, contracts, or grants; or (2) an assertion about compliance with such requirements.
  - Note that AT-C 315 does NOT apply to *examination engagements* with respect to internal control over compliance with specified requirements; such engagements are covered only under AT-C 105 and 205. AU-C 940, *An Audit of an Entity's Internal Control Over Financial Reporting That Is Integrated With an Audit of Its Financial Statements,* can also be used for guidance.
- **Agreed-Upon Procedures –** The accountant applies tests that are the result of an agreement between the CPA, the client, and a third party with whom the client is negotiating. Such an engagement can only result in a report for **limited use** in which the accountant describes the procedures applied and the accountant's findings. The agreed-upon procedures may relate to (1) compliance with specified requirements as described above or (2) internal control over compliance with such requirements.

As previously mentioned, a review is not allowed for testing compliance with laws, rules, regulations, contracts, or grants. AT-C also does not apply to situations covered under AU-C 806, *Reporting on Compliance With Aspects of Contractual Agreements or Regulatory Requirements in Connection With Audited Financial Statements*, as previously discussed; and AU-C 935, *Compliance Audits,* discussed later.

Among the **requirements specific to an examination** of compliance with specified requirements, the accountant should:

- Determine that management (1) accepts responsibility for such compliance with specified requirements, including its internal control over compliance; and (2) evaluates the entity's compliance, which may include documentation, written policies, accounting manuals, etc.
- Request a **written assertion** from management. If management refuses, the accountant should withdraw from the engagement, if possible.
- Design the engagement to detect **material noncompliance**, whether intentional or not.
- Consider **materiality** with establishing the overall engagement strategy.
- *Obtain an understanding of specified requirements.* This should include obtaining an understanding of the applicable laws, rules, regulations, etc. as well as relevant knowledge obtained in previous engagements, and discussing such matters with appropriate personnel (e.g., internal auditors).
- Evaluate the following factors when the client has **multiple components** (e.g., locations, branches, etc.):
  - How the compliance requirements apply at each level of the organization
  - Materiality
  - Centralization of records
  - The control environment, including management's direct control over delegation of authority and its ability to supervise the various components
  - Nature and extent of operations at the various components
  - The similarities of operations over compliance for the various components
- *Obtain an understanding of relevant I/C over compliance* sufficient to plan the engagement and *assess control risk* for compliance with specified requirements.
- *Review any relevant reports and communications with regulatory agencies* and inquire of the regulatory agencies as to any current or ongoing examinations.
- Obtain **written representations** that (1) acknowledge management's responsibility for establishing and maintaining effective I/C over compliance, (2) provide that management has evaluated the entity's compliance with specified requirements, and (3) provide management's understanding of any compliance requirements subject to interpretation. Note that these are in addition to the representations required for examination engagements in general under AT-C 205, as previously discussed, and refusal to provide any written representation constitutes a scope limitation sufficient to preclude an unmodified opinion or cause the accountant to withdraw, if possible.
- Form an **opinion** based on the accountant's evaluation of (1) the nature and frequency of any noncompliance instances found and (2) whether such noncompliance is material in relation to the nature of the compliance requirements.
  - If there is material noncompliance, it should be described and the opinion should be modified.

With respect to an **agreed-upon procedures engagement** related to compliance with specified requirements or I/C over compliance, the accountant should:

- Determine that management (1) accepts responsibility for such compliance with specified requirements, including its internal control over compliance; and (2) evaluates the entity's compliance with specified requirements or I/C over compliance.
- *Obtain an understanding of specified requirements.* Same considerations as for an examination (see above).
- Obtain written representations that (1) acknowledge management's responsibility for establishing and maintaining effective I/C over compliance, (2) provide that management has evaluated the entity's compliance with specified requirements or I/C over compliance, as appropriate, (3) provide management's understanding of any compliance requirements

subject to interpretation, and (4) provide that management has disclosed any known noncompliance occurring after the period covered by the accountant's report. Note that these are in addition to the representations required for agreed-upon procedures engagements in general under AT-C 215, as previously discussed.

Candidates could be asked to prepare this type of report on the CPA exam, starting with a report example, such as any of the three that follow.

Examination Report on Compliance—Unmodified Opinion

Independent Accountant's Report

To: *Appropriate addressee*

We have **examined** XYZ Company's compliance with [*identify the specified requirements, for example, the requirements listed in Attachment 1*] during the period January 1, 20X1, to December 31, 20X1. Management of XYZ Company is responsible for XYZ Company's compliance with the specified requirements. Our responsibility is to express an opinion on XYZ Company's compliance with the specified requirements based on our examination.

Our examination was conducted in accordance with attestation standards established by the American Institute of Certified Public Accountants. Those standards require that we plan and perform the examination to obtain reasonable assurance about whether XYZ Company complied, in all material respects, with the specified requirements referenced above. An examination involves performing procedures to obtain evidence about whether XYZ Company complied with the specified requirements. The nature, timing, and extent of the procedures selected depend on our judgment, including an assessment of the risks of material noncompliance, whether due to fraud or error. We believe that the evidence we obtained is sufficient and appropriate to provide a reasonable basis for our opinion.

Our examination does not provide a legal determination on XYZ Company's compliance with specified requirements.

In our opinion, XYZ Company complied, in all material respects, with [*identify the specified requirements, for example, the requirements listed in Attachment 1*] during the period January 1, 20X1 to December 31, 20X1.

Peter Wilson, CPA
Santa Ana, CA
March 1, 20XX

Agreed-Upon Procedures Report on Compliance

**Independent Accountant's Report on Applying
Agreed-Upon Procedures**

To: *Appropriate addressee*

We have performed the procedures enumerated below, which were agreed to by [*identify the specified parties, for example, the management and board of directors of XYZ Company*], related to XYZ Company's compliance with [*identify the specified requirements, for example, the requirements listed in Attachment 1*] during the period January 1, 20X1 to December 31, 20X1. XYZ Company's management is responsible for its compliance with those requirements. The sufficiency of these procedures is solely the responsibility of those parties specified in this report. Consequently, we make no representations regarding the sufficiency of the procedures enumerated below either for the purpose for which this report has been requested or for any other purpose.

[*Include paragraphs to enumerate procedures and findings*.]

This agreed-upon procedures engagement was conducted in accordance with attestation standards established by the American Institute of Certified Public Accountants. We were not engaged to and did not conduct an examination or review, the objective of which would be the expression of an opinion or conclusion, respectively, on compliance with specified requirements. Accordingly, we do not express such an opinion or conclusion. Had we performed additional procedures, other matters might have come to our attention that would have been reported to you.

This report is intended solely for the information and use of [*identify the specified parties, for example, the management and board of directors of XYZ Company*] and is not intended to be, and should not be, used by anyone other than the specified parties.

Ruiza Guillermo, CPA
Santa Ana, CA
March 1, 20XX

Agreed-Upon Procedures Report on I/C Over Compliance

**Independent Accountant's Report on Applying
Agreed-Upon Procedures**

To: *Appropriate addressee*

We have performed the procedures enumerated below, which were agreed to by [*identify the specified parties, for example, the management and board of directors of XYZ Company*], related to XYZ Company's internal control over compliance with [*identify the specified requirements for example, the requirements listed in Attachment 1*], as of December 31, 20X1. XYZ Company's management is responsible for its internal control over compliance with those requirements. The sufficiency of these procedures is solely the responsibility of the parties specified in this report. Consequently, we make no representations regarding the sufficiency of the procedures enumerated below either for the purpose for which this report has been requested or for any other purpose.

[*Include paragraphs to enumerate procedures and findings.*]

This agreed-upon procedures engagement was conducted in accordance with attestation standards established by the American Institute of Certified Public Accountants. We were not engaged to and did not conduct an examination or review, the objective of which would be the expression of an opinion or conclusion, respectively, on internal control over compliance with specified requirements. Accordingly, we do not express such an opinion or conclusion. Had we performed additional procedures, other matters might have come to our attention that would have been reported to you.

This report is intended solely for the information and use of [*identify the specified parties, for example, the management and board of directors of XYZ Company*] and is not intended to be, and should not be, used by anyone other than the specified parties.

Zachary Armins, CPA
Santa Ana, CA
March 1, 20XX

Management's Discussion and Analysis (MD&A) (AT-C 395)

Publicly held entities are required to provide a set of disclosures referred to as Management Discussion and Analysis (MD&A) in accordance with certain rules prescribed by the SEC. In addition, some nonpublic entities prepare MD&A and management asserts that it is presented in accordance with SEC requirements. A CPA may be engaged to perform either an examination or a review of MD&A for either type of entity.

- An *examination* would ordinarily be performed in conjunction with an audit of the F/S.
- A *review* may be performed for an annual period, an interim period, or a combination of an annual and an interim period.

Such an engagement may only be accepted if the most recent period covered by the MD&A was audited by the CPA and all other periods covered by the MD&A were audited by either the CPA or a predecessor.

As a result of the engagement, the CPA will issue either an examination report or a review report, as appropriate. Both reports address the same issues:

- Does the MD&A include all of the required elements?

- o An examination report will indicate that the presentation *includes all required elements*.
        - o A review report will indicate that *nothing came to the accountant's attention* to indicate that all required elements were not included.
    - Was the historical financial information included in MD&A accurately derived from the F/S?
        - o An examination report will indicate that the historical financial information *was accurately derived* from the F/S.
        - o A review report will indicate that *nothing came to the accountant's attention* to indicate that the historical financial information was not derived from the F/S.
    - Do the underlying information, determinations, estimates, and assumptions provide a reasonable basis for the disclosures included in MD&A?
        - o An examination report will indicate that the information, determinations, estimates, and assumptions *provide a reasonable basis for the disclosures*.
        - o A review report will indicate that *nothing came to the accountant's attention* that the information, determinations, estimates, and assumptions did not provide a reasonable basis for the disclosures.

VARIOUS ENGAGEMENTS

There are various other types of engagements that an accountant may perform that are each lightly tested on the exam.

1. A client may wish to present **condensed financial statements** or **selected data** in an advertisement, brochure, or other presentation which doesn't include the basic F/S and notes. The accountant may issue a report on such information as long as they audited the basic F/S from which the condensed data is derived. The report on the condensed F/S must:
    - o Refer to the audit, providing the report date and type of opinion expressed.
    - o State whether the condensed data is fairly stated in all material respects in relation to the complete F/S.

2. An accountant may be asked to report on **pro forma financial statements (AT-C 310)** that are derived from historical F/S. This refers to a presentation in which information is restated for an event that actually hadn't occurred. For example, a client that is considering a change in accounting principle might want to see how the F/S of the preceding year would have appeared had the change been made earlier. As long as the F/S from which the pro forma statements were derived were audited an examination engagement of this type is permitted. Similarly, as long as the F/S from which the pro forma statements were derived were *audited or reviewed*, a review engagement of this type may be performed.

    Note: AT-C 310 covers examination and reviews of the information. Note: Agreed-upon procedures engagements are also allowed, but they are subject only to the applicable rules for agreed-upon procedures engagements under AT-C 215 as well as the common concepts under AT-C 105, not AT-C 310. Compilations of pro forma financial information are covered by SSARS, not SSAE; specifically, AR-C 120.

The examination (or review) report must:
- o   Refer to the audit (or review), providing the report date and type of opinion (or conclusion) expressed.
- o   Provide **reasonable assurance** (or limited if a review) as to the assumptions and presentation of the pro forma data being reasonable. Should also obtain a management representation letter.

SSARS 22 expands the applicability of the SSARS to apply when the CPA is engaged to compile or issue a **compilation report** on *pro forma* financial information. The CPA's compilation or review report, or the auditor's report on the historical F/S, should be included (or incorporated by reference) in the document containing the *pro forma* financial information. No management representation letter is required.

Examination Report on Pro Forma Financial Information—Unmodified Opinion

---

Independent Accountant's Report

We have **examined** the pro forma adjustments giving effect to the underlying transaction (or event) described in Note 1 and the application of those adjustments to the historical amounts in the accompanying pro forma condensed balance sheet of X Company as of December 31, 20X1, and the related pro forma condensed statement of income for the year then ended (pro forma financial information), based on the criteria in Note 1. The historical condensed financial statements are derived from the historical financial statements of X Company, which were **audited by us**, and of Y Company, which were audited by other accountants, appearing elsewhere herein [or "and are readily available"]. The pro forma adjustments are based on **management's assumptions** described in Note 1. X Company's management is responsible for the pro forma financial information. Our responsibility is to express an opinion on the pro forma financial information based on our examination.

Our examination was conducted in accordance with attestation standards established by the American Institute of Certified Public Accountants. Those standards require that we plan and perform the examination to obtain reasonable assurance about whether, based on the criteria in Note 1, management's assumptions provide a reasonable basis for presenting the significant effects directly attributable to the underlying transaction (or event), and, in all material respects, the related pro forma adjustments give appropriate effect to those assumptions, and the pro forma amounts reflect the proper application of those adjustments to the historical financial statement amounts. An examination involves performing procedures to obtain evidence about management's assumptions, the related pro forma adjustments, and the pro forma amounts in the pro forma condensed balance sheet of X Company as of December 31, 20X1, and the related pro forma condensed statement of income for the year then ended. The nature, timing, and extent of the procedures selected depend on our judgment, including an assessment of the risks of material misstatement of the pro forma financial information, whether due to fraud or error. We believe that the evidence we obtained is sufficient and appropriate to provide a reasonable basis for our opinion.

The objective of this pro forma financial information is to show what the significant effects on the historical financial information might have been had the underlying transaction (or event) occurred at an earlier date. However, the pro forma condensed financial statements are not necessarily indicative of the results of operations or related effects on financial position that would have been attained had the above-mentioned transaction (or event) actually occurred at such earlier date.

In our opinion, based on the criteria in Note 1, management's assumptions provide a **reasonable basis** for presenting the significant effects directly attributable to the above-mentioned transaction (or event) described in Note 1, and, in all material respects, the related pro forma adjustments give appropriate effect to those assumptions, and the pro forma amounts reflect the proper application of those adjustments to the historical financial statement amounts in the pro forma condensed balance sheet of X Company as of December 31, 20X1, and the related pro forma condensed statement of income for the year then ended.

***

---

3. An accountant may be auditing a U.S. entity which requires F/S that are in conformity with the accounting principles of **another country** and are intended for use **outside the U.S.** This might be as part of an attempt to raise capital in the other country or because the U.S. entity is a subsidiary to be consolidated with a parent of the other country. SAS 124 (AU-C 910) requires the auditor to obtain an understanding of the purpose of the F/S, whether the reporting framework applied provides fair presentation of the F/S, the intended users of the F/S, and the steps taken by management to determine whether the reporting framework is acceptable. The audit will still conform to GAAS, but the report must indicate conformity with the principles of the other country and be presented in either of the following ways.

   o A U.S.-style report modified to express an opinion on conformity with the principles of the other country (essentially comparable to a special report on OCBOA statements) with an explanatory paragraph "emphasizing a matter."

   o A report in which the form and content is consistent with that of the other country if such a report would be issued by auditors in the other country in similar circumstances; the auditor understands and has obtained sufficient appropriate audit evidence to support the report; and the auditor has complied with the other country's reporting standards and identifies the other country in the report. Issuing such a report may require the auditor to:

      ▪ Report on statutory compliance or otherwise understand the local laws and regulations.

      ▪ Obtain an understanding of applicable legal responsibilities, in addition to the auditing standards and the financial reporting framework generally accepted in the other country.

In instances where a report that is to be *used in the United States* was prepared in accordance with a financial reporting framework generally accepted in another country, the auditor is **required** to include an ***emphasis-of-matter* paragraph** to highlight the foreign financial reporting framework, but permits the auditor to express an unqualified opinion. This paragraph would follow the opinion paragraph.

4. An **underwriter** preparing a prospectus in connection with a public offering of securities under the Securities Act of 1933 will often ask the auditor for a letter that provides various levels of assurance on the information the underwriter must provide to the SEC. These letters are known as **letter to underwriters** or **comfort letters (AU-C 920).**

In this letter, the accountant may express an **opinion** on whether **audited** F/S conform to all of the SEC requirements for these statements. Since the filing information is derived from audited F/S, this type of engagement is similar to the reporting on condensed data or pro forma information.

However, the underwriter must include in the SEC filing certain **capsule financial information** about the company for the period **after** the balance sheet date of the last audit. Since the accountant has not audited this information, no opinion can be expressed on it. Instead, the accountant and underwriter will determine **agreed-upon procedures** for the CPA to perform, and the accountant will then provide **negative assurance**, stating that "nothing came to our attention" indicating a need to change the unaudited information. Notice that the wording of negative assurance is different from every other engagement discussed in this course, and is not permitted for other examinations, reviews, or agreed-upon procedure engagements in the absence of specific authority in auditing pronouncements. The auditor is also required to inform the party requesting the comfort letter that the auditor cannot provide any assurance that the agreed-upon procedures are sufficient for that party's purposes.

The accountant must, of course, be **independent** (since both audits and agreed-upon procedures engagements result in written conclusions by the CPA), and will state so in the comfort letter.

When the auditor is a group auditor, the auditor is required to read the comfort letters of all component auditors whose reports are included in the securities offering. This applies to all component auditors and is not limited to those auditors of significant components.

An accountant is not required by standards to accept an engagement to issue a comfort letter. In addition, if such an engagement is accepted, the accountant is not required to provide assurance relative to all matters for which assurance is requested.

The letter to the underwriter is provided by the accountant to the underwriter (or dealer, broker or client), and this report is **not** considered to be a part of the registration statement filed by the underwriter with the SEC. If the underwriter makes any reference to the accountant's report, it is important that the CPA not be referred to as an "auditor" except in connection with information that was audited. A term such as "expert in accounting and auditing" might be a reasonable alternative.

When audited F/S of a nonissuer are included in a registration statement, AU-C 925 provides that it is the predecessor auditor's responsibility when the F/S they have audited are being included in an SEC registration statement filing to:
- o   Read pertinent portions of the document.
- o   Perform subsequent events procedures.
- o   Obtain a letter of representation from the successor auditor.

Lecture 8.05

CLASS QUESTIONS

Please see the Class Questions and Class Solutions for this Lecture at the end of this Section.

Lecture 8.06

GOVERNMENT REPORTING ("YELLOW BOOK" – GAGAS)

When performing audits of government entities or audits of entities receiving governmental financial assistance, the auditor must consider Government Auditing Standards (GAS), referred to as the "**yellow book.**" This is a book of standards issued by the Comptroller General of the U.S. For those entities receiving major federal financial assistance (i.e., more than $750,000 within a single fiscal year), Title 2 of the Code of Federal Regulations (CFR) must also be considered (previously referred to as the Single Audit Act – SAA).

We will break Governmental compliance audits down into 3 different types. All of these audits include testing compliance with Laws and Regulations: **(1)** Audits conducted in accordance with GAAS, **(2)** GAS audits in accordance with GAGAS and **(3)** GAS audits of non-Federal entities receiving federal financial assistance (CFR). These are normally in conjunction with financial statement audits (previously referred to as the Single Audit Act – SAA).

1. Audits Conducted in Accordance with GAAS

Audits conducted in accordance with GAAS apply when a nongovernmental entity has received Governmental federal financial assistance, or for a governmental entity that is not required by law to adhere to GAS (Government Auditing Standards) or the CFR (Single Audit Act).

AU-C 935 requires the focus of the audit to be on violations of laws and regulations that have a direct and material effect on the amounts in the organization's F/S.

The GAO "yellow book" suggests that the scope of the governmental audit should also include the F/S and consideration of program results, compliance with laws and regulations and economy and efficiency.

If significant deficiencies in internal control are identified, then the auditor is required to report upon the scope of the auditor's testing of internal control and the scope of tests of compliance with laws and regulations. The reporting of noteworthy accomplishments of the program or recommendations for actions to improve operations is not required.

A standard audit report is normally issued; however, if material noncompliance is detected, it is disclosed and treated as a departure from GAAP, resulting in a qualified or adverse opinion (disagreement). No compliance report is issued and an internal control report is only issued when significant deficiencies have been identified.

2. GAS Audits in Accordance with GAGAS

GAS audits in accordance with GAGAS (generally accepted government auditing standards) are required for certain organizations that receive federal financial assistance, depending upon the requirements of the program. All the GAAS requirements in (1) above still apply, plus more. The audit report on the F/S is still required, plus a written Internal Control report and a report on compliance with Laws and Regulations are also required.

I/C deficiencies, material noncompliance with laws and regulations and falsification of accounting records should be communicated to legislative and regulatory bodies as well as a federal inspector general if the auditee fails to communicate them. A qualified or adverse opinion on compliance would also be issued.

Government Auditing Standards (GAS) include designing the audit to provide reasonable assurance of detecting material misstatements resulting from noncompliance with contract provisions or grant agreements that have a direct and material effect on the F/S. For financial audits, GAS prescribes fieldwork and reporting standards beyond those required by GAAS.

GAGAS (i.e., Yellow-book) include, in the general standards, requirements as to the qualifications of the staff, independence, due professional care, and quality control.

To provide assurance that an auditor is **independent** both in mind and in appearance, GAGAS incorporates an independence conceptual framework that can be applied in making a determination as to whether or not independence has been impaired. An auditor evaluates independence, applying the framework, whenever facts or circumstances create threats to independence. The approach is very similar to that incorporated into the independence requirements for nongovernmental auditors.

The framework is applied by first identifying facts and circumstances that create **threats to independence**. There are 7 categories of threats to independence:

- A *self-interest* threat occurs when the auditor has a financial or other interest in the entity that might affect the auditor's judgment.
- A *self-review* threat occurs when the extent of nonattest services performed by the auditor for the client raise a question as to whether the auditor will be reviewing judgments and estimates that they participated in the development of.
- A *bias* threat occurs when the auditor is not objective about the client. This may result from the relationship between the auditor and the client. It may also be a result of the beliefs of the auditor, which may be political, religious, or philosophical; such beliefs may or may not conform to the objectives, mission, or operations of the client.
- A *familiarity* threat occurs as a result of the duration and closeness of the relationship between the auditor and the client. This includes the threat that the client may anticipate what may be emphasized by the auditor and may be able to effectively deceive the auditor as a result.
- An *undue influence* threat occurs when factors or parties separate from the client might create influence or pressure that may affect the auditor's judgments with regard to the client.
- A *management participation* threat occurs when the auditor takes on the role of management or performs management functions for the client.
- A *structural* threat occurs when the audit entity is connected to the government entity in such a way that may impair the auditor's ability to remain objective in the performance of the engagement or reporting of the results.

If the threat to independence results from the performance on nonattest services, the auditor will first determine if the service was prohibited. If so, independence is impaired and the auditor will not be able to perform the engagement. If the threat does not result from the performance of nonattest services, or if the nonattest services were not prohibited, the auditor will consider the magnitude of threats.

Prohibited nonattest services include:

- Performing *management responsibilities*, such as strategic planning, directing employees, custody of assets, reporting to governance, accepting responsibility for internal controls, and voting in the management committee or board of directors.
- Performing certain *accounting functions without obtaining management approval*, such as determining or changing journal entries, authorizing or approving transactions, preparing or altering source documents, and accepting responsibility for the preparation or fair presentation of the F/S.
- Providing *internal audit assistance* in the form of setting policies, strategic direction, or scope for the internal audit function or performing internal control procedures.
- *Accepting responsibility* for the design, implementation, or maintenance (DIM) of internal control, or its monitoring.
- Participation in *information technology services*, including the design, development, or alteration of IT systems that manage aspects of the operations that will be audited, or operating or supervising the operation of such a system.
- Providing *valuation services* that impact information included in the F/S.
- Performing specific *additional services* related to non-tax disbursements, benefit plan administration, investment advisory or management, corporate finance, executive or employee personnel, and business risk consulting.

The auditor will consider threats individually and in the aggregate to determine if they are at an acceptable level, which would not impair the auditor's ability to perform and report on the engagement objectively. If threats are not at an acceptable level, the auditor will consider **safeguards** against those threats. Safeguards are policies and procedures instituted by the auditor to address threats to independence. Safeguards may include:

- Consulting with other auditors, regulators, or other independent third parties.
- Disclosing the nature and extent of services that could potentially impair independence to governance and discussing independence issues with governance.
- Using an outside auditor to participate in the audit by performing or reperforming parts of it or reviewing the work performed.

The client can also initiate policies and procedures designed to create safeguards. These may include:

- Requiring appointment of the auditor to be approved by parties who are not part of management.
- Establishing procedures for selecting providers of nonaudit services designed to enhance objectivity.
- Oversight of the auditor's services by those charged with governance.

If safeguards are sufficient to reduce threats to an acceptable level, the auditor will document the analysis and may perform the audit engagement. If safeguards are not sufficient, the auditor's independence is impaired and the auditor may not perform the engagement.

The **quality control** standard requires an auditor to participate in an external quality review program such as those provided by the AICPA, PCAOB or other agencies. Such a review would be performed periodically and will result in a report, which must be provided to the party contracting for the audit and may be distributed.

When GAS applies, an audit must still conform to U.S. Generally Accepted Auditing Standards (GAAS). In addition, GAS requires:

- A report on internal control.
- A report on compliance with laws and regulations.

GAS does not impose any additional fieldwork standards. To prove that general standards have been satisfied prior to the acceptance of the engagement, the auditor must provide the client with a quality control review report on the CPA firm's audit practice, which establishes its competence to perform an audit under GAAS and GAS.

The GAO standards of reporting for governmental financial audits require auditors to include in their report either (1) a description of the scope of the auditors' testing of internal control over financial reporting and compliance with laws, regulations, and provisions of contracts or grant agreements and the results of those tests or, if sufficient work was performed, an opinion; or (2) a reference to the separate report(s) containing that information. In some circumstances, auditors must report noncompliance (illegal acts) directly to parties external to the audited entity.

3. Audits of non-Federal Entities Receiving Federal Financial Assistance Performed under Title 2 of the Code of Federal Regulations (CFR) (formally the Single Audit Act – SAA)

Audits of non-Federal entities receiving federal financial assistance performed under Title 2 of the Code of Federal Regulations (CFR) (formally the Single Audit Act – SAA) are *more extensive* than audits conducted in accordance with GAAS and GAS audits in accordance with GAGAS. The Code requires certain state and local governments receiving federal financial assistance, who spend $750,000 or more during the entity's fiscal year, to engage an auditor to perform a single coordinated audit of the applicable federal financial assistance program requirements. It requires an auditor to report on the F/S, compliance with laws and regulations, compliance with program requirements and on internal controls. Additionally, the auditor is required to:

- Report on compliance with general requirements that apply to federal financial assistance programs
- Report on compliance with specific requirements of major federal programs
- Report on compliance with specific requirements of nonmajor federal programs tested

When performing an audit in accordance with these requirements, the auditor must conform to GAAS and GAS. In addition, the auditor is required to **test both** *internal control* and *compliance with laws and regulations related to **major federal financial assistance**.* In these tests, the materiality level is set at the level of each major program rather than the overall F/S of the entity, so this will involve a greater audit fieldwork effort than a GAAS audit. In addition to the other reports, the Code requires:

- An **opinion on internal control** related to each major program.
- An opinion on compliance with laws and regulations applicable to each major program.
- An opinion on the schedule of expenditures of federal awards.

The report on internal control under GAS is similar to the management letter that is often issued by an auditor in a non-government financial audit. It should indicate that the auditor obtained an understanding of internal control and assessed control risk as part of the audit of the F/S. It should identify any **significant deficiencies** that were discovered during the engagement, and indicate if any are **material weaknesses**. Deficiencies are normally communicated to the appropriate legislative or regulatory bodies overseeing the entity.

The report on compliance under GAS describes the scope of tests applied by the auditor to identify laws and regulations with a direct and material effect on the F/S as well as the auditor's findings. **Noncompliance** that results in **material misstatement** of the F/S must be identified, as well as any noncompliance (illegal acts) that may result in **criminal prosecution**. Once again, communication may be necessary to appropriate legislative or regulatory bodies.

The auditor will obtain the assistance of management of the entity to identify laws and regulations that have a direct and material effect on the F/S, and the **management representation letter** must include an assertion by management that it has identified all such laws and regulations. The auditor's report will indicate that compliance with laws and regulations is the responsibility of management.

An auditor's audit documentation must provide sufficient support for these additional required reports as well as for the opinion on the F/S.

When the Code applies, the auditor is required to perform additional tests and issue audit opinions on internal control, compliance with laws and regulations, and the schedule of expenditures of federal awards. When there are material weaknesses, noncompliance, or misstatements in the schedule, respectively, these opinions may be **qualified or adverse**, just as in the case of the opinion on the F/S.

Occasionally, an auditor may engage in a **performance audit** that is primarily designed to determine the economy, efficiency, and effectiveness of the organization in achieving its goals. Such audits also include consideration of management controls and compliance with laws and regulations related to achieving these goals. The auditor's report will include the auditor's findings, identification of potential noncompliance (illegal acts), and the views of relevant officials on the auditor's findings. The report should include the scope of work on I/C and any deficiencies in I/C that are significant. If fraud or abuse has occurred, this should also be reported as a finding.

All reports issued in connection with audits under GAS and CFR are directed to specific agencies, but are available for public inspection.

A low-risk auditee is eligible for reduced audit coverage under a compliance audit. To be considered low risk, an entity will have had:
- An unmodified opinion on the schedule of expenditures of federal awards
- No material weaknesses
- No going concern modification
- No federal program audit findings in preceding two audits of Type A programs that were classified as material weaknesses or modifications to the compliance opinion

Reporting Internal Control Deficiencies, Fraud, Noncompliance, Violations and Abuse

For all financial audit and attestation engagements, auditors must report, as applicable to the engagement objectives, all instances of noncompliance (illegal acts), unless clearly inconsequential and all instances of fraud; violations of provisions of contracts or grant agreements; and abuse that could have a material effect on the F/S or the subject matter of the engagement. When auditors detect violations of provisions of contracts or grant agreements or abuse that has an effect on the F/S or the subject matter that is less than material but more than inconsequential, they should communicate those findings in writing to entity officials. Also, auditors should report the following deficiencies in internal control: (a) significant deficiencies and (b) material weaknesses.

Governmental Audit (Laws & Regulations)

- A regular GAAS audit plus more.

1. GAAS Audit – Opinion on F/S

  - No compliance report is issued.
  - No I/C report unless significant deficiencies are I.D.

+ 2. GAS Audit
  1. Opinion on F/S
  2. Report on Internal Control (Written Report)
  3. Report on Compliance with Laws & Regulations (direct & material effect).
     -Must include description of material instances of noncompliance.
       a. GAAS
       b. GAGAS (Quality Control)

+ 3. Entities Receiving Federal Financial Assistance (CFR) (formally SAA)
  1. Opinion on F/S
  2. Report on Internal Control (written report)
  3. Report on Compliance with Laws & Regulations
       a. GAAS
       b. GAGAS (Quality Control)
  4. Report on scope of audit testing on I/C
       a. Compliance with Major programs – opinion
       b. I/C report of Major programs

  5. Report on Schedule of expenditures of federal awards
       - Non-Major → Limited Assurance

The following is an example of a Combined Report on Compliance with Applicable Requirements and Internal Control over Compliance (AU-C 935):

Independent Auditor's Report

[*Addressee*]

Compliance

We have audited Example Entity's compliance with the [*identify the applicable compliance requirements or refer to the document that describes the applicable compliance requirements*] applicable to Example Entity's [*identify the government program(s) audited or refer to a separate schedule that identifies the program(s)*] for the year ended June 30, 20X1.

Management's Responsibility

Compliance with the requirements referred to above is the responsibility of Example Entity's management.

Auditor's Responsibility

Our responsibility is to express an opinion on Example Entity's compliance based on our audit.

We conducted our audit of compliance in accordance with auditing standards generally accepted in the United States of America; the standards applicable to financial audits contained in Government Auditing Standards issued by the Comptroller General of the United States; and [*insert the name of the governmental audit requirement or program-specific audit guide*]. Those standards and [*insert the name of the governmental audit requirement or program-specific audit guide*] require that we plan and perform the audit to obtain **reasonable assurance about whether noncompliance** with the compliance requirements referred to above that could have a material effect on [*identify the government program(s) audited or refer to a separate schedule that identifies the program(s)*] occurred. An audit includes examining, on a test basis, evidence about Example Entity's compliance with those requirements and performing such other procedures as we considered necessary in the circumstances. We believe that our audit provides a reasonable basis for our opinion. Our audit does not provide a legal determination of Example Entity's compliance with those requirements.

Opinion

In our opinion, Example Entity **complied**, in all material respects, with the compliance requirements referred to above that are applicable to [*identify the government program(s) audited*] for the year ended June 30, 20X1.

Internal Control over Compliance

Management of Example Entity is responsible for establishing and maintaining effective internal control over compliance with the compliance requirements referred to above. In planning and performing our audit, we considered Example Entity's internal control over compliance to determine the auditing procedures for the purpose of expressing our opinion on compliance, but not for the purpose of expressing an opinion on the effectiveness of internal control over compliance. Accordingly, we do not express an opinion on the effectiveness of Example Entity's internal control over compliance.

A *deficiency in internal control over compliance* exists when the design or operation of a control does not allow management or employees, in the normal course of performing their assigned functions, to prevent, or detect and correct, noncompliance on a timely basis. A *material weakness* in internal control over compliance is a deficiency, or combination of deficiencies in internal control over compliance, such that there is a reasonable possibility that material noncompliance with a compliance requirement will not be prevented, or detected and corrected, on a timely basis.

Our consideration of internal control over compliance was for the limited purpose described in the first paragraph of this section and was not designed to identify all deficiencies in internal control that might be deficiencies, significant deficiencies, or material weaknesses in internal control over compliance. We did not identify any deficiencies in internal control over compliance that we consider to be material weaknesses, as defined above.

The purpose of this report on internal control over compliance is solely to describe the scope of our testing of internal control over compliance and the results of that testing based on the [*insert the name of the governmental audit requirement or program-specific audit guide*]. Accordingly, this report is not suitable for any other purpose.

[*Signature*]
Sara Alicia Edwards
[*Date*]

Lecture 8.07

CLASS QUESTIONS

Please see the Class Questions and Class Solutions for this Lecture at the end of this Section.

CLASS QUESTIONS

Work through the below Class Questions while following along with the respective lectures. Once this is complete, you can begin independently practicing what you've learned by quizzing yourself on this course section in your Interactive Practice Questions (IPQ), which can be found in your online Student Dashboard. Your IPQ simulates the computer-based testing experience, and will also help you understand how concepts are applied to the exam. Each question includes answer explanations from expert CPAs that will help you determine why you answered a question correctly or incorrectly. This is key to your success on the CPA Exam.

Lecture 8.05

1. When an auditor reports on financial statements prepared on an entity's income tax basis, the auditor's report should

    a. Disclaim an opinion on whether the statements were examined in accordance with generally accepted auditing standards.
    b. Not express an opinion on whether the statements are presented in conformity with the comprehensive basis of accounting used.
    c. Include an explanation of how the results of operations differ from the cash receipts and disbursements basis of accounting.
    d. State that the basis of accounting is described in a footnote in the Financial Statements.

2. Helpful Co., a nonprofit entity, prepared its financial statements on an accounting basis prescribed by a regulatory agency solely for filing with that agency. Green audited the financial statements in accordance with generally accepted auditing standards and concluded that the financial statements were fairly presented on the prescribed basis. Green should issue a

    a. Qualified opinion.
    b. Standard three-paragraph report with reference to footnote disclosure.
    c. Disclaimer of opinion.
    d. Special purpose report.

3. The client's financial reporting includes supplementary financial information outside the basic financial statements but required by the Financial Accounting Standards Board (FASB). Which of the following statements is correct regarding the auditor's responsibility for this supplementary financial information?

    a. The auditor should perform limited procedures.
    b. The auditor should apply tests of details of transactions.
    c. The auditor is not required to report omissions.
    d. The auditor should read the supplementary financial information.

4. When an accountant issues to an underwriter a comfort letter containing comments on data that have **not** been audited, the underwriter most likely will receive

    a. Negative assurance on capsule information.
    b. Positive assurance on supplementary disclosures.
    c. A limited opinion on pro forma financial statements.
    d. A disclaimer on prospective financial statements.

5. A practitioner has examined a client's compliance with debt covenants associated with a bank loan and is ready to issue a report. Which of the following standards apply to the report?

    a. Internal control standards.
    b. Compliance attestation standards.
    c. Agreed-upon procedures standards.
    d. Auditing standards of field work.

6. Accepting an engagement to examine an entity's financial projection most likely would be appropriate if the projection were to be distributed to

    a. All employees who work for the entity.
    b. Potential stockholders who request a prospectus or a registration statement.
    c. A bank with which the entity is negotiating for a loan.
    d. All stockholders of record as of the report date.

7. Which of the following is a prospective financial statement for general use upon which an accountant may appropriately report?

    a. Financial projection.
    b. Partial presentation.
    c. Pro forma financial statement.
    d. Financial forecast.

8. In which of the following engagements would a practitioner provide limited assurance about the possible significant effects on the historical financial statements if a change in capitalization had occurred at an earlier date?

    a. A compilation of a financial projection.
    b. A review of pro forma financial information.
    c. An examination of management's discussion and analysis.
    d. An audit of condensed interim financial information.

Lecture 8.07

9. Hill, CPA, is auditing the financial statements of Helping Hand, a not-for-profit organization that receives financial assistance from governmental agencies. To detect misstatements in Helping Hand's financial statements resulting from violations of laws and regulations, Hill should focus on violations that

    a. Could result in criminal prosecution against the organization.
    b. Involve significant deficiencies to be communicated to the organization's trustees and the funding agencies.
    c. Have a direct and material effect on the amounts in the organization's financial statements.
    d. Demonstrate the existence of material weaknesses.

10. When auditing an entity's financial statements in accordance with Government Auditing Standards (the "yellow book"), an auditor is required to report on

    I.   Noteworthy accomplishments of the program.
    II.   The scope of the auditor's testing of internal controls.

      a.   I only.
      b.   II only.
      c.   Both I and II.
      d.   Neither I nor II.

11. When auditing an entity's financial statements in accordance with Government Auditing Standards (the "yellow book"), an auditor is required to report on

    I.   Recommendations for actions to improve operations.
    II.   The scope of the auditor's tests of compliance with laws and regulations.

      a.   I only.
      b.   II only.
      c.   Both I and II.
      d.   Neither I nor II.

12. In performing a financial statement audit in accordance with Government Auditing Standards, an auditor is required to report on the entity's compliance with laws and regulations. This report should

      a.   State that compliance with laws and regulations is the responsibility of the entity's management.
      b.   Describe the laws and regulations that the entity must comply with.
      c.   Provide an opinion on overall compliance with laws and regulations.
      d.   Indicate that the auditor does **not** possess legal skills and **cannot** make legal judgments.

13. In reporting under Government Auditing Standards, an auditor most likely would be required to communicate management's misappropriation of assets directly to a federal inspector general when the fraudulent activities are

      a.   Concealed by management by circumventing specific internal controls designed to safeguard those assets.
      b.   Reported to the entity's governing body and the governing body fails to make a required report to the federal inspector general.
      c.   Accompanied by fraudulent financial reporting that results in material misstatements of asset balances.
      d.   Perpetrated by several levels of management in a scheme that is likely to continue in future years.

14. Wolf is auditing an entity's compliance with requirements governing a major federal financial assistance program in accordance with Government Auditing Standards. Wolf detected noncompliance with requirements that have a material effect on the program. Wolf's report on compliance should express

    a. No assurance on the compliance tests.
    b. Reasonable assurance on the compliance tests.
    c. A qualified or adverse opinion.
    d. An adverse or disclaimer of opinion.

CLASS SOLUTIONS

1. **(d)** An auditor may accept an engagement to express an opinion on financial statements prepared in conformity with a comprehensive basis of accounting other than GAAP, referred to as a special purpose framework. If there are no scope limitations, the auditor will express an opinion and a disclaimer is not required (a). The opinion will indicate whether the financial statements were presented fairly in conformity with the comprehensive basis of accounting under which they were prepared (b). The entity will provide an explanation of how the comprehensive basis of accounting differs from GAAP, not the auditor, although the auditor will generally refer to the entity's footnote in an emphasis-of-a-matter paragraph (c). The auditor will state that the basis of accounting is described in a footnote to the financial statements.

2. **(d)** A regulatory basis of accounting is considered a special purpose framework. An auditor may accept an engagement to report on financial statements prepared in accordance with a special purpose framework, and will issue a disclaimer if there is a scope limitation preventing the auditor from obtaining sufficient appropriate audit evidence (c), or a qualified opinion if there is either a departure from the framework or an uncertainty that the auditor was unable to resolve (a). The auditor may not use the standard report (b) but will instead issue a special report that is appropriate for the circumstances.

3. **(a)** An auditor's opinion on financial statements does not apply to required supplementary information. Since it is required, however, omission would constitute a departure from the applicable financial reporting framework, which is required to be addressed in the auditor's report. As a result, the auditor will apply limited procedures to required supplementary information, consisting of making inquiries of management; comparing the information to management's responses to the inquiries, the financial statements, and other knowledge obtained by the auditor, which would generally require the reading of the required supplementary information. These procedures are designed to enable the auditor to meet the requirement to describe in the auditor's report whether the required supplementary information is presented and to communicate when some or all of it has not been presented, when it is not presented in accordance with guidelines, or if it requires material modification. The auditor is not required to perform tests of details of the transaction. Although the auditor will most likely need to read the required supplementary information to achieve the reporting objectives, there is no specific requirement to do so other than performing a comparison. Note, however, the auditor's responsibility with respect to other information (i.e., unaudited, voluntary information included in the document with audited F/S) is generally limited to reading the information for material inconsistencies.

4. **(a)** Accountants may be asked to issue letters to underwriters, also referred to as comfort letters. The subjects that may be covered in a comfort letter include: the independence of the accountant, an opinion as to whether the audited financial statements and schedules included in the registration statement comply with the requirements of the 1933 act, negative assurance on unaudited interim financial and capsule information, and negative assurance as to whether certain non-financial statement information included in the registration statement complies as to form in all material respects with Regulation S-K. When financial information has not been subjected to audit procedures, the auditor may not provide either positive assurance (b) or a limited opinion (c). An accountant's association with prospective financial statements (d) is not a component of a comfort letter.

5. (**b**) Attestation standards apply to examinations, other than audits, which are subject to Statements on Auditing Standards; reviews, other than reviews of financial statements and other historical financial information, which are subject to Statements on Standards for Accounting and Review Services; and agreed-upon procedures engagements. An examination to determine if a client is in compliance with debt covenants is not an examination of financial statements subject to SAS and is, therefore, subject to the attestation standards. Internal control standards, to the extent that they exist, are directed toward the development of internal controls, not an examination of the client's compliance with debt covenants. Agreed-upon procedures standards are part of the attestation standards and apply only to engagements in which the practitioner is only applying those procedures the specified parties agree to have the auditor perform. Auditing standards apply to audits of financial statements, not examinations of compliance with debt covenants.

6. (**c**) Financial projections are based on hypothetical assumptions, creating the danger that someone who is not familiar with those assumptions may draw invalid conclusions as to the meaning and reliability of the projections. As a result, reports on projected financial information are limited to individuals who are familiar with the matters and the hypothetical assumptions, such as a bank involved in negotiations with the entity. General groups, including employee groups (a), potential stockholders (b), or existing stockholders (d) who do not have certain qualifications would not be likely recipients.

7. (**d**) A financial forecast is a prospective financial statement that is based on the past performance of the entity and is appropriate for general use. A financial projection, on the other hand, involves certain assumptions, projecting the possible outcome of certain future transactions or events. As a result, a report on a projection should be limited to those with an understanding of the transactions or events (b). Similarly, a pro forma financial statement represents a restatement of historical information, showing the possible effects that might have occurred if a transaction or event that may or may not have actually occurred had occurred earlier. Users should also be limited to those with an understanding (c). A partial presentation, by its nature, does not provide all of the information that is considered necessary under GAAP and should be limited to those who understand the deficiencies (b).

8. (**b**) Limited assurance is only provided in a review. No assurance is provided in a compilation and an opinion is expressed in an examination or an audit. Pro forma financial statements are historical financial statements that are adjusted to reflect management's estimate of the effects that would have been incurred if an event or transaction had occurred during or before the fiscal period being reported on.

9. (**c**) To detect misstatements in the financial statements, the auditor will look for violations that have a financial statement implication. An auditor is not an attorney and will not necessarily know what violations would result in criminal prosecution (a). An auditor does not perform procedures to seek deficiencies that are required to be communicated (b) or material weaknesses (d), but communicates those that are detected during the course of the engagement.

10. (**b**) While an entity's management may wish to boast of noteworthy accomplishments, the auditor reports on those matters that are the subject of the audit, including the scope of the auditor's testing of internal control.

11. (**b**) An auditor may or may not find areas where the auditor can make recommendations to improve operations, which is beyond the scope of what an audit addresses anyway. An auditor does test compliance with laws and regulations, particularly those that have the potential of materially affecting information in the financial statements.

12. (**a**) Compliance with laws and regulations is the responsibility of management and the auditor's report so indicates. The auditor will not necessarily be familiar with all laws and regulations the entity must comply with and such a description will not be included in the report (b). The auditor only addresses those laws and regulations that have a potential material effect on the financial statements and cannot express an opinion on overall compliance (c). Since becoming an auditor does not require an in-depth knowledge of the law, there is no need to indicate that the auditor does not possess such knowledge and skills (d).

13. (**b**) In general, an auditor will limit communication about fraud to those within the entity at a level of management or governance that is above that at which the fraud was committed. The fact that the fraud was concealed by circumventing controls (a), involved fraudulent financial reporting (c), or involved several levels of management (d) would not change the auditor's reporting responsibilities. If the governing body, however, fails to meet its obligations to report the matter to the federal inspector general, the auditor will be required to do so.

14. (**c**) When engaged to audit an entity's compliance with requirements governing a major federal financial assistance program, identification of incidents of noncompliance are comparable to identification of departures from GAAP in an audit of an entity's compliance with GAAP. Depending on the severity of the noncompliance, the auditor will issue either a qualified opinion, if material but not necessarily pervasive, or an adverse opinion if pervasive as well. An auditor cannot avoid disclosure by providing no assurance (a), and reasonable assurance (b) would only be appropriate if there were no significant incidents of noncompliance. A disclaimer of opinion (d) would only be appropriate if the auditor was unable to obtain sufficient appropriate audit evidence to develop an opinion.

TASK-BASED SIMULATIONS

Task-Based Simulation 1

The Uniform CPA Examination

Unsplit | Split Horiz | Split Vertical | Authoritative Literature | Spreadsheet | Calculator | Submit Testlet

Research | Help

The financial statements that Davenport audited are included in a document that contains other information that is not supplementary information required by GAAP. Davenport does not intend to express an opinion on the other information and is uncertain as to whether or not there are audit procedures that are required to be applied to it.

1. Which title of Professional Standards addresses this issue & will be helpful in understanding what procedures, if any, should be applied to other information, other than required supplementary information, included in a document with audited financial statements?

2. Enter the exact section and paragraph with helpful information.

Task-Based Simulation 2

The Uniform CPA Examination

Unsplit | Split Horiz | Split Vertical | Authoritative Literature | Spreadsheet | Calculator | Submit Testlet

Research | Help

Gervin, CPA, has been engaged to report on supplementary information in relation to the client's financial statements as a whole. In addition to the procedures performed during the audit, Gervin is trying to determine what other procedures should be performed in order to express an opinion on the supplementary information.

1. Which title of Professional Standards addresses this issue & will be helpful in understanding what procedures should be performed, in addition to procedures performed during the audit, for an auditor to express an opinion on supplementary information?

2. Enter the exact section and paragraph with helpful information.

Task-Based Simulation 3

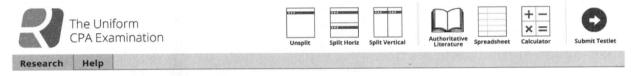

In preparing its financial statements, Xavier's Helmet Factory has omitted all required supplementary information. Parker, CPA, is including an other-matter paragraph and is uncertain as to what should be included.

1. Which title of Professional Standards addresses this issue & will be helpful in understanding what should be included in an other-matter paragraph when required supplementary information has been omitted?

2. Enter the exact section and paragraph with helpful information.

Task-Based Simulation 4

Matthews & Matthews, CPAs, is issuing a report on whether or not the client's financial information complies with aspects of a contractual agreement. They are anticipating including a statement in the report indicating that nothing came to their attention to make them believe that the entity failed to comply with the contractual agreement as they relate to accounting matters and wants to make certain that all conditions necessary to include such a statement exist.

1. Which title of Professional Standards addresses this issue & will be helpful in understanding whether it is appropriate to indicate that nothing came to the auditors' attention to make them believe the entity failed to comply?

2. Enter the exact section and paragraph with helpful information.

TASK-BASED SIMULATION SOLUTIONS

Task-Based Simulation Solution 1

AU-C	720	.06

Task-Based Simulation Solution 2

AU-C	725	.07

Task-Based Simulation Solution 3

AU-C	730	.09

Task-Based Simulation Solution 4

AU-C	806	.07

Section 9 – Information Technology

Corresponding Lectures

Watch the following course lectures with this section:

Lecture 9.01 – Environment & General Controls
Lecture 9.02 – Application Controls & XBRL
Lecture 9.03 – Controls – Class Questions
Lecture 9.04 – Auditing Issues
Lecture 9.05 – Auditing Issues – Class Questions

EXAM NOTE: *Please refer to the AICPA AUD Blueprint in the Introduction of this book to find a listing of the representative tasks (and their associated skill levels—i.e., Remembering and Understanding, Application, Analysis, and Evaluation) that the candidate should be able to perform based on the knowledge obtained in this section.*

Information Technology (IT)

ENVIRONMENT & GENERAL CONTROLS

Characteristics of an IT Environment

Although the existence of an electronic system does not change the basic objectives of an audit engagement, it has a major impact on the approach used to achieve those objectives.

The responsibility for determining the acceptable level of audit risk and assessing the component risks remains with the auditor. Computer software cannot replace the judgment of the auditor. The auditor cannot give an opinion on the effectiveness of Internal Control if the "auditing around the computer" approach is used.

The use of IT affects the initiation, authorization, recording, processing, and reporting of transactions, and may affect any of the five components of internal control (CRIME). Virtually every accounting system has, by now, incorporated computers to a great extent, and the area of **Information Technology (IT)** has, in response, become a more important subject on the CPA exam. With IT also tested in the BEC exam section, AUD exam section questions tend to focus on the CPA's examination and use of the client's IT system.

- **Benefits of IT**
    - Consistency – Computers process data the same way every time.
    - Timeliness – Electronic processing and updating is normally more efficient.
    - Analysis – Data can be accessed for analytical procedures more conveniently (with proper software).
    - Monitoring – Electronic controls can be monitored by the computer system itself.
    - Circumvention – Controls are difficult to circumvent when programmed properly, and exceptions are unlikely to be permitted.
    - Segregation of Duties – Enhanced segregation of duties through effective implementation of security controls.
- **Risks of IT**
    - Overreliance – Without clear output, IT systems are often assumed to be working when they are not.
    - Access – Destruction, and alteration of large amounts of data without detection are possible if unauthorized access occurs—aside from the potential unauthorized use of confidential information.
    - Changes in programs – Severe consequences without detection are possible if unauthorized program changes occur.
    - Failure to change – Programs are sometimes not updated for new laws, rules, or activities.
    - Manual intervention – Knowledgeable individuals can sometimes alter files by bypassing the appropriate programs.
    - Loss of data – Catastrophic data loss is possible if appropriate controls aren't in place.

The auditor should obtain audit evidence about the accuracy and completeness of information produced by the entity's information system when that information is used in performing audit procedures. The primary **advantage** of IT as it relates to an audit is that a computer is not as subject to **random errors** as a human. As a result, an auditor who is able to **verify** that a computer

program is working properly will **not** have to **test individual transactions** to be sure the computer is following directions consistently because it will always follow its program. An audit of a computerized system can, therefore, rely more heavily on internal control structure and reduce the need for substantive testing, making the audit potentially more efficient.

There are **two risks** of major concern to the auditor:
- **Unauthorized access** to a computer system can cause more damage to the accounting system as a whole than in a manual system where it is difficult for one person to access, change, or destroy all the different records of the system.
- The **audit trail** is an electronically visible trail of evidence enabling one to trace information contained in statements or reports back to the original input source. An audit trail is also important to the client for the proper functioning of the system during the year, since such a trail allows monitoring of activities, providing a deterrent to fraud and making it possible to answer queries by examining the source data. This would require the auditor to establish the reliability and extent of the audit trail.

The **processing of transactions** can take place in one of two general ways:
- Online Transaction Processing (OLTP)
- Batch processing

OLTP means that the database is updated as soon as a transaction is received (**Immediately**). Transaction processing keeps business records up-to-date the moment transactions are keyed or transmitted into a system. This produces records that are as current as possible, but poses a problem of requiring that computers be continually running and accessible at all points-of-transaction.

Batch processing involves gathering information and then entering transactions in a group to the computer periodically. This allows for greater control over the input process, including more possibility for verifying data entry with control totals and authorization before input. The major difficulty is associated with the **delay** between the transactions and the input, which can result in accounting records not accurately reflecting the current situation.

As an example of the choice between the two approaches, a bank is going to use OLRT for the processing of cash withdrawals, since it is critical that these be immediately reflected in the customer's balance, and errors can be easily reversed later with little harm to the bank. On the other hand, it probably will use batch processing for payroll, enabling it to be processed efficiently. Since, in most business environments, employees are paid on designated dates, either all on the same date or in groups, it is more efficient to report all the payroll transactions occurring on the same date with a single entry summarizing all the payments.

Different computers will often communicate with each other, and a link of different computers is known as a **network**. The sharing of data within a company among its various computers is known as an **intranet** due to the fact that only computers **within** the same company can communicate with each other in such a system. The linking of computers may be done in different ways using different **Network configurations:**
- **Local area networks (LANs) -** Communication network that serves several users within a specified geographical area. A personal computer LAN functions as distributed processing system in which each computer in the network does its own processing and manages some of the data. Shared data are stored in a file server that acts as a remote disk drive for all users in the network.
- **Value-added network (VAN)** – Links different companies' computer files together.

- **Wide area networks (WANs)** - A computer network connecting different remote locations that may range from short distances, such as a floor or building, to extremely long transmissions that encompass a large region or several countries.

The need for solid physical transmission media in local area networks (LANs) has been overcome through the development of **wireless local area networks (WLANs).** Short-range radio transmission allows different computers to communicate with each other and share printers, Internet connections, and other devices. The two prominent standards for WLANs are **Wi-Fi** (also known as 802.11) and **Bluetooth**. Any devices that are in the same vicinity that follow the same standard can communicate. In addition to computers, cell phones and personal digital assistants (PDAs) are often equipped to use one or both standards. Clearly, unauthorized access is a major danger with WLANs, and both encryption of data and passwords to connect to the system are critical security needs to prevent others with wireless devices from accessing the system. On the other side, many businesses, such as hotels and restaurants, have Wi-Fi connections for the benefit of guests and patrons to allow them high-speed Internet access (sometimes requiring logging into a network at a fee and sometimes at no charge to encourage visitors). Employees using these networks (while traveling, for instance) could put their employers at additional risk of unauthorized access.

Electronic commerce

Electronic commerce (e-commerce) is one of the most popular electronic business (e-business) implementations. It is the buying and selling of goods online, usually via the internet. Typically, a website will advertise goods and services, and the buyer will fill in a form on the website to select the items to be purchased and provide delivery and payment details or banking services such as transfers and payment orders. The website may gather details about customers and offer other items that may be of interest. The cost of a brick-and-mortar (physical store location) is avoided and the savings are often a benefit to the customers, sometimes leading to spectacular growth. The term e-business includes buying and selling online as well as other aspects of online business such as customer support relationships between businesses.

E-commerce, as a general model, uses technology to enhance the processes of commercial transactions among a company, its customers and business partners. The used technology can include the Internet, multimedia, web browsers, proprietary networks, ATMs, and home banking, and the traditional approach to Electronic Data Interchange (EDI). However, the primary area of growth in e-commerce is through the use of the Internet as an enabling technology.

Some communication of company computers with outside computers belonging to suppliers, customers, and other correspondents (trading partners) requires the use of **Electronic Data Interchange (EDI).** The worldwide linking that currently allows almost any computer in the world to participate is known as the **Internet**, but more restricted systems can be created that will be strictly limited to the company and known outsiders such as customers. These are known as **extranets**. An EDI system requires communications software, translation software and access to standards. Communications software moves data from one point to another, flags the start and end of an EDI transmission, and determines how acknowledgments are transmitted and reconciled. Translation software helps build a map and shows how the data fields from the application correspond to elements of an EDI standard. Later, it uses this map to convert data back and forth between the application and EDI formats. There are several **special considerations related to EDI:**

- **Strict standards** are needed for the form of data so that it will be understood by the computers at both ends. An example is the use of the ASCII format for text data.
- **Translation software** is needed by each computer so that it can convert data between the standard used for EDI and the form needed for processing internally. An example is the use of browser programs to access websites.

- **Unauthorized access** to company computers and interception of transmissions are much greater dangers, requiring the use of **encryption** (application control) programs that make stolen data unreadable to someone without knowledge of the coding method and **firewall** programs that prevent access to the network without the explicit permission originating from the company computer.

A **virus** is a program with the ability to reproduce by modifying other programs to include a copy of itself. A virus may contain destructive code that can move into multiple programs, data files or devices on a system and spread through multiple systems in a network. A **Trojan horse** is purposefully hidden malicious or damaging code within an authorized computer program. Unlike viruses, they do not replicate themselves, but they can be just as destructive to a single computer. A **worm** is a program that duplicates itself over a network so as to infect many computers with viruses. A **hoax virus** is a widely distributed e-mail message warning of a virus that doesn't exist. A **killer application** simply refers to a program that is extremely useful, and is not dangerous. **Phishing** (brand spoofing or carding) is the act of sending an e-mail to a user falsely claiming to be an established legitimate enterprise in an attempt to scam the user into surrendering private information that will be used for identity theft. Various types of software have been developed to protect computers against these types of invasive problems. **Antivirus software**, for example, is used to protect software against viruses that may destroy or erase it.

A tool for establishing security is a **firewall**, which prevents unauthorized users from accessing data. A firewall can be in the form of a computer program (software) or a physical device that blocks the transmission media being used (hardware). A **network firewall** is designed to prevent unauthorized access to the company computers, while **application firewalls** protect individual programs. Network firewalls are easier and cheaper to implement, but if penetrated, leave the computers at severe risk. Application firewalls need to be installed for each individual program the company wishes to protect, but allow additional user authentication procedures to protect the program and data and make access more difficult.

GENERAL CONTROLS

Since the auditor will usually want to rely heavily on the internal control structure of a computer-based accounting system, gaining an understanding of the internal control structure is crucial. Initially, the focus of the auditor will be on understanding the **general controls** that relate to the overall integrity of the system. Later, the auditor may examine **application controls** that relate to the performance of individual computer programs. If the general controls are poor, it is unlikely that the application controls will be effective, no matter how strong they are.

General Controls – Overall Environment	**Application Controls** – Program Controls)
Overall Computer Environment	Specific Program Controls
1) **Personnel Policies**	1) **Input**
<ul><li>***Systems* = Development & Maintenance** (analysts, application programmer, database administrator)</li><li>***Operations* = Input** (data entry → make sure computer operator is screened and receives ethics training) = **Output** (control clerk or librarian)</li></ul>	<ul><li>Check Digit → Input correctly</li><li>Validity Check (Valid SS#)</li><li>Edit Test → #s in SS not letters</li><li>Limit Test → SSs not greater than 9 characters</li><li>Financial total</li><li>Record counts</li><li>Hash = A meaningless total</li><li>Non-financial totals</li><li>Digital signature (authorization)</li></ul>
2) **File Security**	2) **Processing**
<ul><li>Back Up – Grandfather/father/son retention system</li><li>Lock Out</li><li>Read-Only</li></ul>	<ul><li>System & software documentation</li><li>Error-checking compiler</li><li>Test data</li><li>System testing</li></ul>
3) **Business Continuity Planning** – Business Interruption – identify the business processes of strategic importance – Disaster Recovery (hot/cold site)	3) **Output** – Accurate
<ul><li>Hot Site (Computer's are ready to go)</li><li>Cold Site (No computer waiting)</li></ul>	<ul><li>Distribution lists</li><li>Shredders</li><li>System testing</li></ul>
4) **Computer Facilities** – Fire/Insurance	
5) **Access Controls**	

Just as in a manual system, one of the **general controls** in an IT environment involves segregation of the incompatible duties of authorization, recording, and custody:

- **Authorization** – The development of new programs and changes to existing programs should be performed by **systems analysts** and **programmers**. These personnel should not be involved in the supervision of computer operations or the control and review of output.
- **Recording** – **Data input clerks** and **computer operators** have the role of entering information into the computer and running the programs. These personnel should not have access to program code that would enable them to modify programs nor should they control the output.

- **Custody** – **Control clerks** and **librarians** obtain and review the output from computers to review exception reports indicating inappropriate functioning of the computer, send printouts and other output to the appropriate destinations, and maintain disks, tapes, or other storage units of data. These personnel should not have the ability to create or alter programs or to operate the computers that generate the information.

Clearly, general controls over **access** to computers and files are of great significance in evaluating internal control in an IT environment. This is particularly important in networks, since the data is distributed widely in such cases. Access to programs and data should require the entry of **passwords** or identification numbers, and different levels of password authority should apply so that employees only gain access to the programs and files that are compatible with their assigned responsibilities. An auditor can test these procedures by entering invalid passwords to see that they are rejected and verifying that valid passwords only provide compatible access.

- Passwords should be changed regularly to make unauthorized access more difficult.
- Protocols for passwords should encourage the use of random letters, numbers, and symbols, making it more difficult for someone to break through a firewall.

Business Continuity Planning

The purpose of business continuity/disaster recovery is to enable a business to continue offering critical services in the event of a disruption and to survive a disastrous interruption to activities. This includes:

- **Identify the business processes of strategic importance** – Those key processes that are responsible for both the permanent growth of the business and for the fulfillment of the business goals. Based on the key processes, the risk management process should begin with a risk assessment. The risk is directly proportional to the impact on the organization and the probability of occurrence of the perceived threat.
- **Backup controls** – Copies of files and programs should be maintained to allow reconstruction of destroyed or altered files. This may include copies on the same computer, backups to removable storage media, such as disks, and off-premises backups to computers and locations outside the company. Copies may be identical or the client may use the **grandfather-father-son** retention system in which periodic saving of data versions allows the reconstruction of records by starting with an older file and reentering lost data since that time (the name comes from the general idea of saving at least two generations of older data so that, if the immediate version before the lost file is also lost, reconstruction can start two versions back with reentry of all data processed since that point).
- **Planned downtime controls** – Since some downtime is inevitable, planned downtime allows maintenance so that unplanned downtime doesn't interrupt system operations.
- **Checkpoint** – Similar to grandfather-father-son, but at certain points, "checkpoints," the system makes a copy of the database and this "checkpoint" file is stored on a separate disk or tape. If a problem occurs, the system is restarted at the last checkpoint.
- **Disaster recovery** – The Company should have plans in place that will allow operations to be restored and continued in the event of physical destruction or disabling of the site of computer operations. This can be done by maintaining an alternate **hot site,** which has available computers and data ready to begin operations immediately in the event of the disaster, or a **cold site,** which has available space for operations but will require setup of computers and loading of data before operations can begin at that site.

Documentation of new programs and alterations to existing programs ensures that IT personnel are aware of the availability and proper use of programs and that changes in programming personnel during projects does not interfere with the ability of other employees to understand what has been done previously. This also may assist the auditor in learning about the system.

Hardware controls are built into computers by the manufacturer. Since computers do not actually think and visualize, but are simply electronic machines, the storage of data is in the form of switches. The term **binary** refers to the fact that the switches have only two possible positions. Binary computers can only think in terms of **bits** (binary digits) of information that are *on or off ("1"* *or "0")*. A series of 8 consecutive bits will produce a **byte** of information that represents a unit of human thought such as a letter, number, or other character. The manner in which data is described includes the following terms:

- *Character* – A letter, number, punctuation mark, or special character
- *Alphanumeric* – A character that is either a letter or number
- *Field* – an individual data element in a computer record. (such as a phone number or a city name)
- *Record* – A collection of related information treated as a unit. Separate fields within the record are used for processing the information. (Such as the name, address, and telephone of one employee).
- *File* – A group of logically related records (such as the contact info for all the employees)
- *Database* – A stored collection of related data needed by organizations and individuals to meet their information processing and retrieval requirements. (such as a payroll database that might have a file for contact info, a file with rate and withholding information, a file indicating hours worked, etc.).

Hardware controls may include:

- **Parity check** – In the storage of bytes, one bit will be a "dummy" bit that doesn't represent any actual information, but is turned on automatically when necessary so that the total number of bits in the on position is an odd number (in an odd-parity computer). When the computer is reading bytes of data from a chip or disk drive, a byte with an even number of bits turned on will be known to be functioning improperly.
- **Echo check** – When data is being transmitted from one computer to another, especially over telephone lines, distortions caused by static or other causes can cause information to be transmitted improperly. An echo check involves the data sent from one computer to another being transmitted back to the original one, which will verify that it has received what it sent. If the echoed data doesn't agree with the transmission, the packet of data is resent.
- **Virus protection software** – McAfee antivirus software, for example.

Lecture 9.02

APPLICATION CONTROLS

The policies, procedures and activities designed to provide reasonable assurance that objectives relevant to a given automated solution (application) are achieved. They are designed to ensure that an individual computer application program performs properly, accepting authorized input, processing it correctly, and generating appropriate output. Many of the controls discussed on the exam involve verifying data that has been input to ensure the program doesn't accept inappropriate information. These include:

- **Field checks** – Data is validated as to the correct length and format. For example, an entry of a license plate might be verified for type (alphanumeric, so that only letters and numbers are acceptable) and length (not longer than 7).
- **Validity checks** – Data is compared with a list of acceptable entries to be sure it matches one of them. For example, a field to accept the two-letter state abbreviation will be checked against a file that lists all the acceptable choices, so that an entry of OG for the state will be rejected as invalid.

- **Limit tests** – Numbers are compared to limits that have been set for acceptability. For example, the entry of a pay rate may be compared to the current minimum wage on the lower side and $50 per hour on the upper side to be sure the number entered makes sense. This is sometimes called a reasonableness test, and is the closest computer equivalent to human judgment in reviewing information.
- **Check digits** – Numbers with no obvious meaning, such as identification numbers, are often designed so that one of the digits is determined by a formula applied to the rest of the number. The computer applies the formula when a number is entered to determine if it is an acceptable one. This control makes it difficult for someone to invent a fake number if they don't know the formula, since the program will recognize a number that isn't designed so that the check digit is correct. The check digit can actually be either a number or letter, and can be placed in any position in any consistent position in the overall identification. For example, many states have driver licenses that start with a letter which is derived from a formula applied to the numbers which follow it, and a person trying to create a fictional license will only have a 1 in 26 chance of correctly guessing the letter that should be in the first position based on the numbers.

When using batch processing of data, the data input clerk will often prepare manual **control totals** to be compared with computer-generated totals of entered information in order to ensure accuracy of inputs. These totals include:

- **Record count** – The total number of records entered into the program at that time.
- **Financial total** – The total dollar amount of entries that are financial in nature.
- **Hash total -** The total of values which cannot be meaningfully added together, but which serve as a way to verify the correct entry of these values.
- **Other quantitative total** – The total of some column of numbers, such as check numbers or invoice numbers that can be used to determine that all transactions have been entered as well as that a sequence has not been broken.

For example, assume that the checks written during a particular day are being entered into a checkbook program, and that the data input clerk is working from the following sheet to make the entries:

Check Number	Payee	Amount	Account Code
1001	Philipp Corporation	$500.00	307
1002	Rog Enterprises	$3,000.00	602
1003	Ruiz Company	$600.00	302
3006		$4,100.00	1211

After the data input clerk enters each of the checks, the computer will then indicate:

Checks Entered = 3 (record count)
Check Number total = 3006 (quantitative total)
Amount total = $4,100.00 (financial total)
Account Code total = 1211 (hash total)

The data input clerk would have also determined these numbers by computing them from the input sheet, and the agreement of the clerk's totals with those of the program will indicate all lines must have been entered correctly.

A program may also perform **edit checks** on batch-processed data to verify that each individual entry is appropriate, and generate a list of rejected transactions for review by the control clerk.

EXTENSIBLE BUSINESS REPORTING LANGUAGE (XBRL)

XBRL is a specification for publishing financial information in the XML format. It is designed to provide a standard set of XML tags for exchanging accounting information and financial statements between companies and analysts. Instead of treating financial information as a block of text (e.g., standard internet page or Word document), it provides a computer-readable identifying tag for each individual item of data. For example, "net income" has its own unique tag and a computer can immediately generate a comparison of net income for multiple companies or periods. XBRL eliminates the costly process of manual data comparison as computers can select, analyze, store, and exchange data in XBRL documents. Another benefit to XBRL is that it reduces the chance of error when generating reports.

- XBRL can handle data in different languages and accounting standards.
- Built upon the XML (eXtensible Mark-up Language) – promulgated through the World Wide Web Consortium, XML is a web-based application development technique that allows designers to create their own customized tags, thus enabling the definition, transmission, validation and interpretation of data between applications and organizations.
- The SEC **mandates** all public companies file financial statements in XBRL. The SEC uses these XBRL filings to facilitate financial statement review.

Lecture 9.03

CLASS QUESTIONS

Please see the Class Questions and Class Solutions for this Lecture at the end of this Section.

Lecture 9.04

AUDITING ISSUES

When examining a company in an IT environment, the auditor will use a **generalized audit software** package. This refers to a series of programs that are useful in the auditing process, enabling the auditor to use **computer assisted auditing techniques (CAATs)**. These might include:

- Programs to **access client files** for purposes of testing. For example, the auditor's program may access computerized inventory files to determine the location of inventory, perform analytical procedures (such as calculating inventory turnover), or review dates of last purchase and sale in order to identify obsolete or slow-moving inventory.
- **Source code comparison** programs that can detect unauthorized changes made by the client in programs that the auditor is testing. For example, after the auditor has verified the proper functioning of a copy of the payroll program provided to them by the client for testing, this program would compare the tested program with the one being used by the client to process an actual payroll period to be sure the files are identical.
- Programs that duplicate common functions of client software that can be used to perform **parallel simulation**, in which the auditor inputs client data in to the auditor's program (created by the auditor) to see if it produces the same results as the client's program. For example, the auditor might obtain the raw data for an actual payroll period and run it through a payroll program included in the generalized audit software package to see if the checks and payroll records produced are identical to the checks and records generated by the client's program.
- Programs to produce **spreadsheets** for working trial balances and similar audit needs as well as analyzing data and recalculating balances.

When the client has a program that the auditor wishes to verify and for which there is no appropriate equivalent program available to the auditor, techniques involving the direct use of the client program are required. One approach is known as the **test data** approach, in which the auditor will develop simulated data to enter into the client's program. Characteristics of this approach include:

- The auditor can include both valid and invalid data to verify that the program processes appropriate data correctly and rejects inappropriate data.
- The auditor only needs to design simulated data for those **valid and invalid conditions** that interest the auditor.
- Only **one example** of each valid and invalid condition needs to be included (since computer programs are consistent in the way they handle items), making this an efficient method of testing.

One danger is that the client may provide the auditor with a program to verify which isn't the actual program used by the client. To avoid this, the auditor will often include the test data in an **integrated test facility**, including the simulated data (fictitious transactions) along with actual data during a program run. For example, the auditor may add simulated payroll data to the actual data for a pay period, so that the testing occurs at the same time the actual employee information is being processed (of course, the simulated data is specially coded so as not to be permanently mixed with the real data).

Another use of an integrated test facility approach involves the use of **embedded audit modules**. These are programs that are implanted in the client's processing system and can perform audit procedures on a real-time basis. For conditions that can be appropriately defined, embedded audit modules can identify exceptions as they occur.

An auditor can walk through a specific transaction to evaluate the logic of the process.

If it isn't practical to use an integrated test facility, the auditor may use an approach known as **controlled reprocessing,** in which the auditor supervises the entry of actual client data into the client program to reproduce the results of a previous run of the program by the client. After verifying that the results are identical to the previous run, the auditor knows that the program is the actual one used, and can enter the test data into it at a separate time.

To summarize the techniques available:

	Actual Client Data	Simulated Data
Actual Client Program	Controlled Reprocessing	Test Data (Integrated Test Facility)
Program Purchased Separately by Auditor	Parallel Simulation	No Relevance to Audit of Client

	Data	Program
Test Data (Phony Data) – theoretically only have to check one above and one below credit limit.	Auditor's	Client's
Controlled reprocessing	Client's	Client's (but Auditor's computer)
Integrated Test Facility (ITF) (Dummy Division or file & Fictitious transactions)	Auditor & Client's	Client's
Transaction Tagging	Client's information with a Tag	Client's
Parallel Simulation	Client's	Auditor's (Going around their system)

Trust Services are governed by SSAE (Statements on Standards for Attestation engagements) and represent attest engagements in which a CPA assesses a client's commercial internet site and reports on whether the system meets one or more of the following **principles** (security, availability for operation, processing integrity, online privacy, confidentiality). For each Principle reported, the auditor considers each of the following 4 **criteria** (Policies, communications, procedures, monitoring).

Both WebTrust and SysTrust are designed to incorporate a seal management process by which a seal (logo) may be included on a client's website as an electronic representation of the practitioner's unqualified WebTrust report. If the client wishes to use the seal (logo), the engagement must be updated at least annually. Also, the initial reporting period must include at least two months. Any of the 5 types of opinions may be issued as discussed in the audit report section.

- **WebTrust** – This engagement provides reasonable assurance that a client's **website** complies with certain principles and criteria for electronic commerce and assurance about the ability of these systems to adhere to online privacy, consumer protection, certificate authorities along with one or more combinations of the Trust Services Principles and Criteria areas. The CPA performs an examination to determine if the client complied with the trust services criteria and if effective controls were maintained over the system using trust services criteria. Examine the website for:
    - Adequacy of disclosure, Transaction Integrity, Information integrity
- **SysTrust** – This engagement provides reasonable assurance that a client's information system complies with certain principles and criteria for electronic commerce. The "SysTrust" category by itself is a designation given from an engagement by a CPA firm that actually includes one or more combinations of the Trust Services Principles and Criteria areas. The CPA's examination is exclusively designed to determine if a client maintained effective controls over the system based on the trust services criteria. The auditor examines the Information systems for:
    - Availability for operation, Security against unauthorized access, Integrity of system process, Maintainability of system resources

Lecture 9.05

CLASS QUESTIONS

Please see the Class Questions and Class Solutions for this Lecture at the end of this Section.

CLASS QUESTIONS

Work through the below Class Questions while following along with the respective lectures. Once this is complete, you can begin independently practicing what you've learned by quizzing yourself on this course section in your Interactive Practice Questions (IPQ), which can be found in your online Student Dashboard. Your IPQ simulates the computer-based testing experience, and will also help you understand how concepts are applied to the exam. Each question includes answer explanations from expert CPAs that will help you determine why you answered a question correctly or incorrectly. This is key to your success on the CPA Exam.

Lecture 9.03

1. Which of the following is **not** a major reason for maintaining an audit trail for a computer system?

    a. Deterrent to fraud.
    b. Monitoring purposes.
    c. Analytical procedures.
    d. Query answering.

Questions 2 and 3 are based on the following information. An entity has the following invoices in a batch:

Invoice #	Product	Quantity	Unit price
201	F10	150	$ 5.00
202	G15	200	$10.00
203	H20	250	$25.00
204	K35	300	$30.00

2. Which of the following numbers represents the record count?

    a. 1
    b. 4
    c. 810
    d. 900

3. Which of the following most likely represents a hash total?

    a. FGHK80
    b. 4
    c. 204
    d. 810

4. Which of the following types of control best describes procedures to ensure appropriate systems software acquisition?

    a. Application.
    b. Physical.
    c. General.
    d. Monitoring.

Lecture 9.05

5. When an auditor tests a computerized accounting system, which of the following is true of the test data approach?

    a. Several transactions of each type must be tested.
    b. Test data are processed by the client's computer programs under the auditor's control.
    c. Test data must consist of all possible valid and invalid conditions.
    d. The program tested is different from the program used throughout the year by the client.

6. Which of the following statements is **not** true of the test data approach when testing a computerized accounting system?

    a. The test need consist of only those valid and invalid conditions which interest the auditor.
    b. Only one transaction of each type need be tested.
    c. The test data must consist of all possible valid and invalid conditions.
    d. Test data are processed by the client's computer programs under the auditor's control.

7. After the preliminary phase of the review of a client's computer controls, an auditor may decide not to perform tests of controls (compliance tests) related to the controls within the computer portion of the client's internal control. Which of the following would not be a valid reason for choosing to omit such tests?

    a. The controls duplicate operative controls existing elsewhere in the structure.
    b. There appear to be major weaknesses that would preclude reliance on the stated procedure.
    c. The time and dollar costs of testing exceed the time and dollar savings in substantive testing if the tests of controls show the controls to be operative.
    d. The controls appear adequate.

8. Which of the following computer-assisted auditing techniques allows fictitious and real transactions to be processed together without client operating personnel being aware of the testing process?

    a. Integrated test facility.
    b. Input controls matrix.
    c. Parallel simulation.
    d. Data entry monitor.

9. Which of the following tasks can be achieved using generalized audit software?

    a. Determining acceptable risk levels for substantive testing of account balances.
    b. Filtering data based on accounts receivable data recording.
    c. Detecting transactions that may be suspicious due to alteration of data input.
    d. Assessing likelihood of fraud based on fraud input factors.

10. An auditor will most likely use computer-assisted audit techniques, rather than manual techniques, when it is necessary to

    a. Examine all data in an accounts payable file.
    b. Review approval of dividends.
    c. Verify unrecorded legal liabilities.
    d. Assess compliance with policies and procedures related to information security.

CLASS SOLUTIONS

1. (**c**) An audit trail can be a deterrent to fraud (a) as it gives an auditor a means of tracing a transaction from beginning to end increasing the possibility of detection. It assists in monitoring (b) as it allows an auditor to look back at transactions to determine if they have been processed correctly. An audit trail also facilitates query answering (d) as it allows someone to trace a transaction from beginning to end to respond to a query regarding some aspect of the transaction. Analytical procedures involve comparing auditor expectations to client data, regardless of its source, to evaluate the reasonableness of the client's data. Since the source of the client data is not significant, an audit trail is not a significant factor.

2. (**b**) The record count is the number of items in a batch. This batch includes invoice numbers 201, 202, 203, and 204—a total of 4 records.

3. (**d**) A hash total is the total of a column of values that have no meaning other than as an identifier. This might include, for example, a total of part or invoice numbers, which does not represent a meaningful quantity. If it matches the check figure, however, it may indicate that all line items on an invoice have been entered. The number 810 is the total of the invoice numbers, not a meaningful value, so this represents an example of a hash total. Answer (a) is incorrect because it appears to be an accumulation of all letters, plus a sum of the numbers. The total number of records (or record count) is 4 (b), which is a meaningful total. The number 204 is simply an invoice number of the last invoice in the batch, not a total (c).

4. (**c**) General controls typically encompass all controls except application controls; generally, this includes the change controls. Application controls (a) typically apply to application software, not systems software. Physical (or mechanical) controls (b) are general controls that typically involve such things as locks on doors and identification badges to allow only appropriate personnel into sensitive areas; acquisition of appropriate software is a qualitative judgment. Monitoring (d) typically occurs after a system is installed and operating; it is too late to ensure appropriate software acquisition at that point.

5. (**b**) The test data approach involves running data compiled by the auditor through the client's IT system. The data will include certain errors, and be used to determine if the client's IT system will deal with them appropriately. The test data will only include errors or conditions that the auditor wishes to test, not all possible conditions (c) and need only include one example of each condition the auditor wishes to test (a). The data is processed through the same program used by the client throughout the period (d) to determine if it was working properly.

6. (**c**) The test data approach involves running data compiled by the auditor through the client's IT system, under the auditor's control (d). The data will include certain errors, and be used to determine if the client's IT system will deal with them appropriately. The test data will only include errors or conditions that the auditor wishes to test (a), **not** all possible conditions (c) and need only include one example of each condition the auditor wishes to test (b).

7. (**d**) After obtaining an understanding of the client's internal controls, the auditor will test those controls that the auditor believes to be adequate for preventing or detecting and correcting material misstatements on a timely basis. The auditor would not test controls that do not appear reliable (b). Nor would the auditor test controls when the cost of testing exceeds the likely savings in the performance of additional audit procedures that would result from relying on the control (c). The auditor would also decide not to test controls that accomplish the same benefits of other controls within the system (a).

8. (**a**) Using the integrated test facility approach, the auditor will run fictitious transactions through the client's system along with the client's data, to make certain that it is receiving the same treatment and enabling the auditor to compare results to expected results. Parallel simulation (c) involves running the client's data through an auditor developed software package. The auditor can compare the results to the client's results to see if the client's system processed the data similarly. An input controls matrix (b) and monitoring of data entry (d) are both input controls and do not provide evidence about the processing of data.

9. (**b**) Generalized audit software (GAS) typically performs many of the tasks auditors formerly did manually, particularly the more mechanical processes, such as filtering data. Artificial intelligence has not progressed to the point where GAS is able to apply judgment, such as (a) determining acceptable risk levels, (c) determining suspicious transactions, or (d) assessing the likelihood of fraud.

10. (**a**) Computer-assisted audit techniques (CAAT) are efficient and effective at handling large amounts of data in machine-readable form when the task involves a repetitive process and the identification or accumulation of objective information. They can be used, for example, to obtain statistical data, such as the number of times, or the frequency with which, an error occurred., or accumulate amounts. They cannot be used to apply judgment in interpreting data or drawing subjective conclusions. As a practical matter—due to the volume of data, to examine all data in an accounts payable file generally would require CAAT. CAAT can readily determine whether each account in the file contained all of the appropriate information. Reviewing approval of dividends (b) generally involves reviewing the minutes of board of director meetings; while these may be in a machine-readable form, this task involves interpreting the minutes, a skill involving subjectivity that is generally beyond the scope of CAAT. Verifying unrecorded legal liabilities (c) involves applying judgment to interpret the likelihood that the liability will be incurred, for example, or determining the amount of the liability, a skill requiring subjectivity and generally beyond the scope of CAAT. Depending on the environment, assessing CAAT can quantify compliance with policies and procedures related to information security by determining the frequency with which noncompliance occurs, including separating each type of noncompliance. It cannot, however, assess compliance (d) as that requires judgment to determine which actions or omissions resulting in noncompliance are significant to information security, such as lax protection of passwords, and which are not, such as instances in which information is being retained briefly longer than the entity's retention policies mandate.

Section 10 – AUD Final Review

Corresponding Lecture

Watch the following course lecture with this section:

Lecture 10.01 – AUD Final Review
Lecture 10.02 – AUD Exam Overview

YOU FINISHED YOUR AUD COURSE...NOW WHAT?
A quick guide to the final days leading up to, and following, the CPA exam

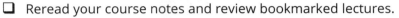

FINAL REVIEW

Now is the time to make connections and solidify your understanding of the topics you found most challenging, and to review the most heavily tested topics on the exam.

- ❑ Reread your course notes and review bookmarked lectures.

- ❑ Go back and look at your Score History in the Interactive Practice Questions (IPQ) software. Review past quizzes on which you had low scores, paying particular attention to bookmarked questions, as well as those that are most highly tested.

- ❑ A great way gear up for the upcoming exam is by adding a Roger CPA Review Cram Courses to your studies. The Cram Course works very well as a final review, as it is designed to reinforce your understanding of the most heavily tested CPA Exam topics.

- ❑ Take an AICPA Sample Test at www.cpa-exam.org to familiarize yourself with the exam format and welcome (instruction) screens.

DAY OF THE EXAM

- ❑ Get a good night's rest before heading into your exam.

- ❑ Arrive to the Prometric testing center at least 60 minutes before your appointment so you have time to park, check-in, and use the restroom before your exam begins.

- ❑ Bring your Notice to Schedule (NTS) and two forms of acceptable identification (see Intro for more details).

- ❑ Proceed through check-in: store belongings, get fingerprinted, have photo taken, sign log book, get seated, write your Launch Code (from your NTS) on your noteboard.

- ❑ Don't stress. You've prepared for this; now, just breathe and power through!

DURING THE EXAM

- ❑ Remember your AUD Exam time strategy, and jot down the times at which you want to be at your benchmarks:
    - o Use 75 seconds per multiple choice question as a benchmark
    - o Allocate 15-25 minutes per task-based simulation, depending on complexity
    - o Plan to use no more than 10 minutes per research question
    - o Take the standard 15-minute break after the 3rd testlet – it does not count against your time
    - o (Remember that any other break will count against your time)

AUD: 4 Hour Exam						
Testlet 1	**Testlet 2**	**Testlet 3**	Break	**Testlet 4**	**Testlet 5**
36 MCQs	**36 MCQs**	**2 TBSs**		**3 TBSs**	**3 TBSs**
45 min	**45 min**	**30 min**		**60 min**	**60 min**

❑ You will be given 10 minutes to review the welcome screens and exam instructions. You should already be familiar with these screens after taking the AICPA Sample Test, and can bypass them during your exam.

❑ Once you begin testing, make sure to read each question carefully, paying close attention to the keywords that dictate the question's intention (e.g. *except, is greater than, always, never*).

❑ Take note if your questions are getting more difficult. That's a good sign! A progressively harder exam indicates that you are performing well.

AFTER THE EXAM

❑ Remember, it is normal to not feel great after you're done with your exam. It's a tough exam and designed to challenge your confidence and competencies.

❑ Relax and celebrate! You've earned it.

❑ Your scores will be released within a couple of weeks (see Intro for table).

❑ GOOD LUCK!!!

Section 11 – Document Review Simulations (DRS) Appendix

Corresponding Lectures

Watch the following course lectures with this section:

Lecture 11.01 – DRS Introduction – Part 1
Lecture 11.02 – DRS Introduction – Part 2

Document Review Simulations (DRS) Appendix

Lecture 11.01

Lecture 11.02

DOCUMENT REVIEW SIMULATIONS OVERVIEW

In 2016, the CPA Exam introduced a new type of Task-based simulation known as Document Review Simulations (DRS). These problems were added to the AUD, FAR and REG exams in 2016, and were added to the BEC exam in conjunction with the CPA Exam changes effective April 1, 2017.

What is a DRS?

DRS are designed to simulate tasks that the candidate will be required to perform as a newly licensed CPA (based on up to two years' experience as a CPA). Each DRS presents a document that has a series of highlighted phrases or sentences that the candidate will need to determine are correct or incorrect. To help make these conclusions, numerous supporting documents, or resources, such as legal letters, phone transcripts, financial statements, trial balances and authoritative literature will be included. The candidate will need to sort through these documents to determine what is, and what is not important to solving the problem.

A DRS is one of many formats of Task-based simulation available to the examiners. There is no guarantee that the exam of any one candidate will have a DRS or any other particular format.

Why is this happening?

The AICPA conducted a Practice Analysis from 2014-2015 in which one main finding was clear: firms are expecting newly licensed CPAs on their staff to perform at a higher level—and they aren't. So the AICPA is raising the bar with a revamped CPA Exam that more authentically tests candidates on the tasks and skill level that will be required of them as newly licensed CPAs. The introduction of DRS in July of 2016 was the first step in this larger initiative, with the overarching changes soon to follow in 2017.

What will DRS be testing?

Up until recently, the CPA Exam has only tested candidates on the skill levels *Remembering & Understanding* and *Application* (skill levels based on Bloom's Taxonomy of Educational Objectives). To meet industry demands for the CPA Exam to test at a higher skill level, the CPA Exam is pivoting to test the higher order skills *Analysis* and *Evaluation* (Evaluation in AUD only). As a direct correlation to this exam evolution, DRS problems are designed to test these higher order skills by requiring candidates to actually analyze and evaluate documents they would see in the work force.

HOW A DRS WORKS

As shown below, the DRS will present several tabs:

- **Document Review**: The main document for the candidate to review
- **Authoritative Literature**: Which is available on all Task-based simulations
- **Exhibits/Resources/Financial Statements**: A series of supporting documents which may, or may not help candidates complete the problem
- **Help**: Explanation of how to answer the problem

Notice the highlighted items within the main document. These represent the specific sentences or phrases that the candidate is required to analyze.

The Uniform CPA Examination

Unsplit | Split Horiz | Split Vertical | Authoritative Literature | Spreadsheet | Calculator | Submit Testlet

Work Tab | **Resources** | **Help**

Scroll down to complete all parts of this task.

A CPA firm is preparing for the year 6 audit of Hiver Co., a calendar-year-end nonissuer. An audit staff member used the year 5 audit request list for Hiver as the basis for drafting the year 6 request list. Additional client information was obtained during the audit planning meeting with the client.

As the audit senior for this engagement, it is your responsibility to review and revise the year 6 request list for Hiver, as needed. Use the additional client information in the Resources tab to revise the draft request list, correcting any errors and removing any inappropriate or unnecessary items, given the overall context and purpose of the list. Ensure that the year 6 list is appropriate, given the information provided.

The materiality for the year 6 audit has been set at $55,000.

To revise the Audit Request List, click on each segment of underlined text below and select the needed correction, if any, from the list provided. If the underlined text is already correct in the context of the document, select [Original text] from the list. If removal of the entire underlined text is the best revision to the document as a whole, select [Delete] from the list.

Hiver Co.
Year ended December 31, year 6
Audit Request List (DRAFT)

Please have the materials listed below ready when we arrive on site. Unless a different date is specifically stated, these documents should be as of and for the year ended December 31, year 6.

- Final trial balance

- Bank reconciliations for March, September and December, year 6.

- Bank statements for December, year 6 and January, year 7

- Property, plant and equipment roll-forward

- Edgewater industrial estate sale contract

- Furniture and fixtures purchase documentation

- New motor vehicle purchase agreement

- Accounts receivable aging analysis

- Documentation supporting the 2% general allowance calculation for doubtful accounts

- Accounts payable aging analysis

To address each item within the problem, click on the highlighted phrase to see answer options. Each item will include the option to leave original text, delete text, or edit the text using the provided edit choices.

Once an item has been answered, a checkmark icon will appear next to the item in the document.

Approaching an AUD DRS

Step 1 – Get the lay of the land. YOU are the CPA – what is being asked of you? Skim over all the content in the Document Review tab to find out. You could be asked to do any of the following:

- Review the work of others – use your professional judgment, professional skepticism, and technical expertise to identify issues or correct errors. ← very likely for AUD!
- Plan the work of others. ← very likely for AUD!
- Analyze and choose the best course of action from various alternatives presented.
- Address a client's technical questions and requests.
- Draw on knowledge that is more extensively tested in a different exam section – detailed FAR knowledge may be expected for an AUD DRS, for instance.

Step 2 – Mentally note the gist of the DRS. "OK, this problem is about me, the audit senior, reviewing the work of a staff member. Specifically, I must review the year 6 Audit Request List an audit staff member has prepared, review the accompanying documentation, and make changes to the list as necessary. NOTE: Materiality threshold is $55,000."

Step 3 – Note the DRS subquestions. Briefly note down each DRS subquestion on your scratch whiteboard – you bought a handheld whiteboard just for CPA Exam study, right? Use your own shorthand. For instance, you might write:

1. Edgewater
2. F&F (for furniture and fixtures)
3. Vehicle
4. Doubtful accounts
5. Securities val.
6. Shares
7. Loan stuff
8. Account 6900

Step 4 (Optional) – Choose an order of attack. Consider customizing the order in which you approach questions. It won't always be possible to tell, but if a few subquestions appear to be more time-consuming than others, consider moving them to the back of the queue. We don't know for sure, but we suspect each DRS subquestion is worth exactly as much as all the others – there are no bonus points for getting the most time-consuming ones right. Therefore, do the easiest ones first.

Step 5 – Attack each subquestion one at a time. In either the default or custom order, work on each subquestion one at a time in order to be as efficient as possible to avoid getting overwhelmed. Remember that the necessary information for any one subquestion will almost certainly be contained across multiple documents. You may also need to research in the Authoritative Literature.

Try to focus strictly on one subquestion at a time, but if you find yourself spending too much time on any one subquestion, make a tactical decision to skip it and move on to the next one. You may even decide to leave that subquestion undone and only return to it after completing other TBSs in your TBS testlet.

Check off each subquestion on your list as you complete it.

Step 6 – Go through a process of elimination for each subquestion.

Each DRS subquestion is similar to a multiple-choice question. The process of elimination, therefore, is a great tactic to employ. You can first eliminate **documents** and then **answer choices**.

Read the subquestion and all its answer choices first. For instance, the subquestion with default text 'Edgewater industrial estate sale contract' appears to be about a real estate transaction. In the Exhibits/Resources tab, briefly skim over each document. Note any documents that clearly have no information about a real estate transaction, and **ignore them**. Then hone in on the documents that do appear relevant.

One of these will usually be the 'home base' document – most DRSs have one, an information-dense accounting information document with numbers. In our example, that document is the year 5 and year 6 Comparative Trial Balance. Important information must be gleaned from this 'home base' document for all or nearly all DRS subquestions.

Next, as you focus on the relevant documents, eliminate answer choices one by one. The Email from CFO document makes clear that the Edgewater deal was a purchase, not a sale or lease, though the purchase ended the existing lease. The Buildings account in the Comparative Trial Balance supports the fact that a building was purchased. Therefore, the default text answer is wrong because it concerns a sale, and the lease agreement answer is wrong unless some unusual situation with the lease is mentioned. Delete Text is clearly wrong, because a material Edgewater transaction did occur. That just leaves three out of the original six choices.

- ~~Original text] Edgewater industrial estate sale contract~~
- ~~[Delete Text]~~
- ~~Edgewater industrial estate lease agreement~~
- Edgewater industrial estate property tax expense analysis
- Edgewater industrial estate purchase contract
- Proof of Edgewater industrial estate property insurance

The clear winner from the three remaining is 'Edgewater industrial sale purchase contract' because nothing in the documents suggests we need to see a property tax expense analysis or proof of property insurance **more** than we need to see the purchase contract. Purchase contract, then, is clearly the **best** answer.

Follow this process of elimination for each subquestion, first eliminating documents, then answer choices. Even in cases where you're not sure there is a clear 'winner' answer choice, you will at least have eliminated some clear losers and given yourself a fighting chance.

SAMPLE AUD DRS

Document Review

R| The Uniform CPA Examination

Unsplit | Split Horiz | Split Vertical | Authoritative Literature | Spreadsheet | Calculator | Submit Testlet

| Work Tab | Resources | Help |

Scroll down to complete all parts of this task.

A CPA firm is preparing for the year 6 audit of Hiver Co., a calendar-year-end nonissuer. An audit staff member used the year 5 audit request list for Hiver as the basis for drafting the year 6 request list. Additional client information was obtained during the audit planning meeting with the client.

As the audit senior for this engagement, it is your responsibility to review and revise the year 6 request list for Hiver, as needed. Use the additional client information in the Resources tab to revise the draft request list, correcting any errors and removing any inappropriate or unnecessary items, given the overall context and purpose of the list. Ensure that the year 6 list is appropriate, given the information provided.

The materiality for the year 6 audit has been set at $55,000.

To revise the Audit Request List, click on each segment of underlined text below and select the needed correction, if any, from the list provided. If the underlined text is already correct in the context of the document, select [Original text] from the list. If removal of the entire underlined text is the best revision to the document as a whole, select [Delete] from the list.

Hiver Co.
Year ended December 31, year 6
Audit Request List (DRAFT)

Please have the materials listed below ready when we arrive on site. Unless a different date is specifically stated, these documents should be as of and for the year ended December 31, year 6.

- Final trial balance
- Bank reconciliations for March, September and December, year 6.
- Bank statements for December, year 6 and January, year 7
- Property, plant and equipment roll-forward
    1) **Edgewater industrial estate sale contract**
    2) **Furniture and fixtures purchase documentation**
    3) **New motor vehicle purchase agreement**
- Accounts receivable aging analysis
    4) **Documentation supporting the 2% general allowance calculation for doubtful accounts**
- Accounts payable aging analysis
- Finished inventory detail
- WIP inventory detail
- Raw material inventory detail
    5) **Trading securities valuation at year end**
    6) **Documentation supporting issuance of 50,000 shares at $0.30 per share**
- Quarterly board of directors meeting minutes
    7.) **Management's review of third party loan interest rates**

- Prepaid expenses analysis
- Accrued expenses analysis
- Sales register
- Documentation supporting dividends paid
  ### 8) **Account 6900 Expense analysis**
- Payroll reconciliation

Resources/Exhibits

Comparative Trial Balance:

Hiver Co
Year Ended December 31, year 6
Unadjusted Trial Balance

		Year 6		Year 5	
Account Number	**Account Description**	**Debit**	**Credit**	**Debit**	**Credit**
1010	Bank Account No. 001039673	5,136,000		5,735,000	
1012	Bank Account No. 001035821	25,400		31,250	
1014	Bank account - deposit	1,200,000		2,100,000	
1050	Bank account - payroll	12,635		21,760	
1200	Accounts Receivable	3,264,500		2,975,800	
1205	Allowance for doubtful accounts		(458,250)		(82,000)
1300	Prepaid expenses	7,200		8,100	
1401	Finished goods inventory	780,500		725,300	
1405	WIP inventory	72,850		82,450	
1408	Raw materials inventory	203,640		197,350	
1600	Office equipment	175,000		175,000	
1601	Accumulated depreciation - office equipment		(62,500)		(36,500)
1650	Furniture & fixtures	201,500		201,500	
1651	Accumulated depreciation - furniture & fixtures		(153,150)		(112,000)
1700	Vehicles	0		36,500	
1701	Accumulated depreciation - vehicles		0		(27,425)
1750	Buildings	2,287,525		0	
1751	Accumulated depreciation - buildings		(23,800)		0
1800	Investments in securities	325,000		400,000	
2200	Accounts payable		(961,500)		(864,200)
2300	Accrued expenses		(11,300)		(10,800)
2400	Income taxes payable		(6,200)		(6,450)

Comparative Trial Balance (continued):

Hiver Co
Year Ended December 31, year 6
Unadjusted Trial Balance

Account Number	Account Description	Year 6 Debit	Year 6 Credit	Year 5 Debit	Year 5 Credit
2600	Bank loan		(1,026,000)		(1,142,000)
2620	Loan to shareholders	250,000		25,000	
3000	Common stock (par $.10 per share)		(15,000)		(10,000)
3100	Additional Paid in capital		(110,000)		(100,000)
3400	Other Comprehensive Income	75,000		0	
3500	Retained earnings		(10,323,325)		(2,257,600)
3550	Dividends paid	7,200,000		0	
4000	Revenue		(22,665,275)		(19,452,500)
4010	Freight revenue		(63,200)		(58,470)
4110	Sales discount	143,800		152,400	
4111	Sales return	72,400		78,350	
4200	Bank interest income		(77,500)		(97,200)
4300	Gain on sale of motor vehicles		(8,925)		(4,200)
5050	Raw materials	9,058,140		8,090,720	
5060	Payroll - manufacturing	1,436,000		1,413,700	
5090	Freight expenses	42,300		37,650	
6500	Insurance expenses	23,110		23,000	
6800	Payroll - management	861,500		790,600	
6805	Payroll- administrative	498,205		462,400	
6806	Payroll processor fees	2,400		2,400	
6900	Sundry expense	890		940	
7105	Legal fees	23,000		21,500	
7016	Auditing and accounting fees	32,500		29,800	
7100	Meals and entertainment	5,200		5,130	
7105	Travel expense	12,700		13,950	
7115	Postage expenses	670		590	
7201	Utilities	18,560		16,350	
7210	Operating lease expense	64,300		84,300	
7500	Repairs and maintenance	62,000		14,500	
7600	Depreciation expenses	77,950		75,400	
7700	Bad debt expense	374,250		12,750	
7800	Bank interest expense	35,910		38,460	
8000	Income tax expense	1,903,390		181,445	
		35,965,925	**(35,965,925)**	**24,261,345**	**(24,261,345)**

From: cfo@hiver.com
Sent: June 6, year 6 2:13 PM
To: 'controller@hiverco.com'
Subject: Edgewater Industrial Estate

Controller,

We have agreed on the terms for the purchase of our office in Edgewater Industrial Estate with a closing date of August 31, year 6. We are purchasing the property from our current lessor and therefore this will end our leasing agreement, reducing our rent expense by $5,000 each month effective the date of purchase. The agreed purchase price of the property is $2,287,525.

I also wanted to inform you that the year 5 investment valuation is complete and no impairment has been identified. Management does not plan on selling this investment or buying any additional investments during year 6.

Thank you,

CFO
P: +1.234.657.8910
cfo@hiverco.com

Hiver Co.
Accounts Receivable Memorandum – Year Ended December 31, year 6

At December 31, year 6, the Company had an allowance for doubtful accounts balance of $458,250, compared to $82,000 at December 31, year 5.

The Company has a standard policy in place that a full allowance is taken against any balances exceeding 180 days at year end. At December 31, year 6, there were no amounts outstanding for longer than 180 days and therefore the general allowance was $0 (year 5: $0).

In October, year 6, the Company received $2,000 from a former customer. This amount was previously written off during year 5, as it was considered to be uncollectible.

At December 31, year 6, there are concerns about the ability of Fibern Co. to pay their outstanding balance of $52,000. The concerns arose as a result of a press release issued on December 18, year 6, which discussed the credit issues that the Company in experiencing. Management had discussed their concerns with the owners of Fibern Co. and they do not consider the issues at Fibern Co. to be sufficient to require the need for any allowances in the year end financial statements.

In November, year 6, Janer, Inc. ("Janer") declared bankruptcy. Hiver had a balance outstanding of $374,250 from Janer at the time of bankruptcy and has not received any payment subsequent to this date. Management does not expect to recover any of the balance due and has therefore made a full allowance against the accounts receivable balance at the year end.

Hiver Co.
Minutes of Special Meeting of August 28, year 6

Members Present: A. Jaunes
                           L. Hiver
                           M. Hannen

Not Present: D. Chen

Agenda Item: **Loans to Shareholders**

This special meeting of the board of directors has been called for the purpose of approving a new loan to a shareholder.

Management routinely provided loans to shareholders when requested in prior periods. There is a current loan balance outstanding relating to a loan to M. Moore. The outstanding balance at December 31, year 6 will be $25,000. The loan will be repaid in full by July 31, year 7.

J. Hiver has made a request to management for a loan of $225,000. The monthly loan repayments will commence on January 1, year 8 over a period of 20 months. Repayments will be equal installments of $12,500. The loan will be interest free.

MOTION: That the loan to J. Hiver be approved as circulated and distributed September 1, year 6.

ACTION: APPROVED by quorum

Items for Analysis

Edgewater industrial estate sale contract

1. Choose an option below:

   - [Original text] Edgewater industrial estate sale contract

   - [Delete Text]

   - Edgewater industrial estate lease agreement

   - Edgewater industrial estate property tax expense analysis

   - Edgewater industrial estate purchase contract

   - Proof of Edgewater industrial estate property insurance

Furniture and fixtures purchase documentation

2. Choose an option below:

   - [Original text] Furniture and fixtures purchase documentation

   - [Delete Text]

   - Furniture and fixtures sale documentation

   - Office equipment purchase documentation

   - Office equipment sale documentation

New motor vehicle purchase agreement

3. Choose an option below:

   - [Original text] New motor vehicle purchase agreement

   - [Delete Text]

   - Documentation supporting the sale of the motor vehicle asset

   - Documentation supporting the scrapping of the motor vehicle asset

   - New motor vehicle lease agreement

Documentation supporting the 2% general allowance calculation for doubtful accounts

4. Choose an option below:

   - [Original text] Documentation supporting the 2% general allowance calculation for doubtful accounts

   - [Delete Text]

   - Documentation supporting the allowance against the accounts receivable balance due from Janer, Inc.

   - Documentation supporting the recovery of previously written off accounts receivable balances

   - Documentation supporting the 100% general allowance made against all balances exceeding 180 days overdue

- Documentation supporting the allowance against the accounts receivable balance due from Fibern Co.

Trading securities valuation at year end

5. Choose an option below:

    - [Original text] Trading securities valuation at year end

    - [Delete Text]

    - Available for sale securities valuation at year end

    - Equity method investment valuation at year end

    - Joint venture valuation at year end

    - Subsidiary company valuation at year end

Documentation supporting issuance of 50,000 shares at $0.30 per share

6. Choose an option below:

    - [Original text] Documentation supporting issuance of 50,000 shares at $0.30 per share

    - [Delete Text]

    - Documentation supporting issuance of 150,000 shares at $0.10 per share

    - Documentation supporting issuance of 150,000 shares at $0.20 per share

    - Documentation supporting issuance of 150,000 shares at $0.30 per share

    - Documentation supporting issuance of 50,000 shares at $0.10 per share

    - Documentation supporting issuance of 50,000 shares at $0.20 per share

Management's review of third party loan interest rates

7. Choose an option below:

    - [Original text] Management's review of third party loan interest rates

    - [Delete Text]

    - Copy of the loan agreement with J. Hiver

    - Copy of the loan agreement with M. Moore

    - Evidence of approval by D. Chen for the loan to J. Hiver

    - Management's due diligence work related to providing the loans

Account 6900 Expense analysis

8. Choose an option below:

    - [Original text] Account 6900 Expense analysis

    - [Delete Text]

    - Account 6806 expense analysis

    - Account 7115 expense analysis

    - Account 7500 expense analysis

Solution to AUD DRS

This question is asking the candidate to determine what documents to request for the current period's audit, using the document list for the previous period as a base. Items on the list that are not underlined are presumed to be required in the current year, similarly to the prior year, because of their ongoing relevance. For example, a final trial balance would be necessary for every period. As a result, it is not underlined and the candidate need not address it.

1. To approach this type of problem, the candidate will generally find it most appropriate to deal with each issue in the order in which it is presented. The first underlined item indicates "Edgewater industrial estate sale contract" and, when clicked upon, the following choices appear:

    *   *[Original text]* Edgewater industrial estate sale contract –This will be selected if we determine that a sale of the Edgewater industrial estate occurred.

    *   *[Delete Text]* – This will be selected if there is no transaction related to the Edgewater industrial estate during the period.

    *   Edgewater industrial estate lease agreement – This will be selected if the company entered into a lease of the Edgewater industrial estate during the period.

    *   Edgewater industrial estate property tax expense analysis – if own property and want to review property tax amounts.

    *   Edgewater industrial estate purchase contract – This will be selected if the company purchased the Edgewater industrial estate during the period.

    *   Proof of Edgewater industrial estate property insurance – This may be selected if the auditor was concerned about a potential liability related to the property and wanted to verify insurance coverage.

To determine what transactions, if any related to the Edgewater industrial estate, the candidate will have to review the available documentation.
*   The first document is a trial balance. Scanning down the trial balance does not reveal anything with a title indicating it relates to the Edgewater industrial estate.
*   The next document is an email from the CFO to the controller discussing the purchase of an office in Edgewater Industrial Estate.

Apparently, Hiver purchased an office at Edgewater industrial estate and the auditor will wish to review the purchase agreement. You can also see this on the trial balance as a new building and accumulated depreciation (Accounts 1750, 1751).

The item to be selected will be:

*   ***Edgewater industrial estate purchase contract***

2. The next underlined item indicates "Furniture and fixtures purchase documentation". The choices are:

- *[Original text]* Furniture and fixtures purchase documentation – This will be selected if there were acquisitions of furniture and fixtures.

- *[Delete Text]* – This will be selected if there were neither purchases nor disposals of furniture and fixtures.

- Furniture and fixtures sales documentation – This will be selected if there were sales of furniture and fixtures.

- Office equipment purchase document – This will be selected if there were purchases of office equipment.

- Office equipment sale documentation – This will be selected if there were sales of office equipment.

Looking at the trial balance, furniture and fixtures (Account 1650) remained unchanged at $201,500, and office equipment (Account 1600) remained unchanged at $175,000. Apparently there were neither sales nor purchases of either furniture and fixtures or office equipment and no documentation would be necessary.

The item to be selected will be:
- **[Delete Text]**

3. The next underlined item indicates "New motor vehicle purchase agreement". The choices are:

- *[Original text]* New motor vehicle purchase agreement – This will be selected if there was a new motor vehicle purchased during the period.

- *[Delete Text]* – This will be selected if there were neither purchases nor disposals of motor vehicles during the period.

- Documentation supporting the sale of the motor vehicle asset – This will be selected if a motor vehicle was sold during the period.

- Documentation supporting the scrapping of the motor vehicle asset – This will be selected if a motor vehicle was salvaged during the period.

- New motor vehicle lease agreement – This will be selected if a motor vehicle was leased during the period.

There is nothing in the remaining documents regarding motor vehicles except what can be derived from the trial balance. The balance in Vehicles (Account 1700) went from $36,500 to $0, indicating that the asset was either sold or otherwise disposed of. The balance in accumulated depreciation – vehicles (Account 1701) also decreased from $27,425 to $0. Looking further down the trial balance, there is a gain on the sale of a motor vehicle (account 4300/$8,925) indicating that a vehicle was sold.

As a result, the item to be selected will be:
- **Documentation supporting the sale of the motor vehicle asset**

4. The next underlined item indicates "Documentation supporting the 2% general allowance calculation for doubtful accounts". The choices are:

- *[Original text]* Documentation supporting the 2% general allowance calculation for doubtful accounts – This will be selected if the auditor wishes to review the analysis to verify the appropriateness of the allowance.

- *[Delete Text]* – This will be selected if the auditor dose not seek any documentation supporting the allowance for doubtful accounts.

- Documentation supporting the allowance against accounts receivable balance due from Janer, Inc. – This will be selected if there is an indication that a special allowance was established for an account due from Janer, Inc.

- Documentation supporting the recovery of previously written off accounts receivable balances – This will be selected if the auditor believes verification of recoveries is necessary.

- Documentation supporting the 100% general allowance made against all balances exceeding 180 days overdue – This will be selected if there were significant accounts that were more than 180 days overdue.

- Documentation supporting the allowance against the accounts receivable balance due from Fibern Co. - This will be selected if there is an indication that a special allowance was established for an account due from Fibern Co.

The items that will be helpful in solving this line item will be the trial balance and an Accounts Receivable Memorandum. On the trial balance it can be noted that accounts receivable has a balance of approximately $3.25 million. An allowance of 2% would be approximately $65,000, yet the actual allowance is $458,250, indicating that there had been one or more adjustments to the allowance for specific doubtful accounts.

The memo indicates that no amounts were outstanding for more than 180 days, eliminating the 5th alternative. In addition, it refers to a $2,000 recovery, which would be a Dr. to Cash for 2,000 and a Cr. to Allowance, which would increase the allowance account. It is unlikely that the auditor will request documentary support, eliminating the 4th alternative.

In the next paragraph, the memo indicates that the concern over Fibern Co. is not sufficient to justify an allowance against the receivable, eliminating the 6th alternative. If indicates in the next paragraph, however, that an allowance is being established in the amount of $374,250, the balance of a receivable from Janer, Inc., due to that entity's bankruptcy. The journal entry to record this is Dr. Bad Debt expense for $374,250 and Cr. Allowance for $374,250. It is likely that the auditor will request documentation regarding the Janer account, making the 3rd alternative the best choice. Notice the change in the allowance account which starts with $82,000, an increase of $2,000 (above) and an additional increase of $374,250 equals the ending balance of $458,250. Also notice Bad debt expense (account 7700) for the year is $374,250, which also appears to tie to the Journal Entry above.

Finally, the 1st alternative can be eliminated since the auditor will obtain satisfaction about the 2% general allowance by reviewing the entity's policies and history to make certain that the auditor considers 2% reasonable. In addition, the auditor will likely recalculate the expense to make certain that it was accurately reported. It is not likely, however, that documentation supporting the 2% will be necessary.

The item to be selected will be:

- ***Documentation supporting the allowance against accounts receivable balance due from Janer, Inc.***

5. The next underlined item indicates "Trading securities valuation at year end", with the following alternatives:

- *[Original text]* Trading securities valuation at year end – This will be selected if there is a significant investment in trading securities as of the end of the period.

- *[Delete Text]* – this will be selected if the auditor does not seek any documentary evidence to support investments.

- Available for sale securities valuation at year end – This will be selected if there is a significant investment in available for sale securities as of the end of the period.

- Equity method investment valuation at year end – This will be selected if there are significant equity method investments as of the end of the period.

- Joint venture valuation at year end – This will be selected if there is one or more significant joint venture in which the company is participating.

- Subsidiary company valuation at year end – This will be selected if the company has one or more subsidiaries.

There is only one related item on the trial balance, Investments in securities, with a balance of $325,000 as of the end of the period. Note that there is also a $75,000 adjustment to Other Comprehensive Income (OCI) (account 3400). The journal entry recorded must have been Dr. OCI $75,000 and Cr. Investments in securities (AVS). The fact that the loss went to OCI (B/S) and not the Income Statement tells us it is an AVS (Available For Sale Security) as opposed to a Trading Security. Had it been Trading, there would also need to be a loss on the income statement, but there isn't one. In the 2nd paragraph of the email from the CFO to the controller regarding Edgewater Industrial Estate, there is an indication that the investment valuation is complete and that management does not have plans to sell the investment or buying additional investments in the short term.

There is apparently no investment in an equity method investment, a joint venture, or a subsidiary, eliminating the last 3 alternatives. Since the securities will not be sold in the near future, they are securities available for sale, not trading securities.
As a result, the alternative to be selected will be:

- ***Available for sale securities valuation at year end***

6. The next underlined item indicates "Documentation supporting issuance of 50,000 shares at $0.30 per share". The alternatives are:

- *[Original text]* Documentation supporting issuance of 50,000 shares at $0.30 per share – This will be selected if the auditor determines that 50,000 shares were issued during the period at $0.30 per share.

- *[Delete Text]* – This will be selected if no shares were issued or retired during the period.

- Documentation supporting issuance of 150,000 shares at $0.10 per share – This will be selected if the auditor determines that 150,000 shares were issued during the period at $0.10 per share.

- Documentation supporting issuance of 150,000 shares at $0.20 per share – This will be selected if the auditor determines that 150,000 shares were issued during the period at $0.20 per share.

- Documentation supporting issuance of 150,000 shares at $0.30 per share – This will be selected if the auditor determines that 150,000 shares were issued during the period at $0.30 per share.

- Documentation supporting issuance of 50,000 shares at $0.10 per share – This will be selected if the auditor determines that 50,000 shares were issued during the period at $0.10 per share.

- Documentation supporting issuance of 50,000 shares at $0.20 per share – This will be selected if the auditor determines that 50,000 shares were issued during the period at $0.20 per share.

From the trial balance it can be determined that common stock (account 3000) increased from $10,000 to $15,000, an increase of $5,000. At a par value of $0.10 per share, this indicates that $5,000/$0.10 or 50,000 shares were issued. In addition to the $5,000 increase in common stock, there is a $10,000 increase in Additional Paid-In Capital (Account 3100) from $100,000 to $110,000, indicating that the total proceeds were $15,000 or $15,000/50,000 = $0.30 per share. As a result, the alternative to be selected will be:

- *[Original text]* **Documentation supporting issuance of 50,000 shares at $0.30 per share**

7. The next underlined item is "Management's review of third party loan interest rates" with the following alternatives:

- *[Original text]* Management's review of third party loan interest rates – This will be selected if there are significant loans to third parties to determine if the interest rate is accurately disclosed and to verify calculations.

- *[Delete Text]* – This will be selected if there are not significant loans receivable outstanding.

- Copy of loan agreement with J. Hiver – This will be selected if there was a new loan to J. Hiver during the period.

- Copy of loan agreement with M. Moore – This will be selected if there was a new loan to M. Moore during the period.

- Evidence of approval by D. Chen for the loan to J. Hiver – This will be selected if there was a loan to J Hiver and the auditor was not certain as to whether or not it was properly authorized.

- Management's due diligence work related to providing the loans – This would be selected if the auditor were performing a test of control to determine if management's policies for research and documentation of new loans are being followed.

The only loan receivable on the trial balance is a Loan to shareholder (Account 2620) in the amount of $250,000, an increase of $225,000 during the period. This indicates that a loan was made to a shareholder during the period. There were no loans to third parties making a review of third party loan interest rates irrelevant.

The last document made available reflects the Minutes of a special meeting in which a loan to J. Hiver was approved. It references the outstanding $25,000 balance of a loan to M. Moore, which is apparently not a new loan and would not require documentation. There is no need for evidence of D. Chen's approval since the minutes indicate that the transaction was approved by quorum.

As a result, the alternative to be selected will be:

- ***Copy of loan agreement with J. Hiver***

8. The last item underlined indicates "Account 6900 Expense analysis" with the following alternatives:

- [Original text] Account 6900 Expense analysis – This will be selected if the auditor desires support for items included in this category.

- [Delete Text} – This will be selected if the auditor is not seeking support for any of the expense items on the trial balance.

- Account 6806 Expense analysis – This will be selected if the auditor desires support for items included in this category.

- Account 7115 Expense analysis – This will be selected if the auditor desires support for items included in this category.

- Account 7500 Expense analysis – This will be selected if the auditor desires support for items included in this category.

Upon review of the trial balance, the amounts reported for Accounts 6900, 6806, and 7115 are $890, $2,400, and $670, respectively. None of these amounts are material and the auditor is not likely to request documentation to support any of them. The balance for Account 7500, however, is $62,000, which exceeds the $55,000 materiality threshold. The auditor will likely seek documentary support for this amount.

As a result, the alternative to be selected will be:

- ***Account 7500 Expense analysis***